ITALY
1530–1630

LONGMAN HISTORY OF ITALY

General editor: Denys Hay

Italy in the Early Middle Ages 600–1216
T. S. Brown

* Italy in the Age of Dante and Petrarch 1216–1380
John Larner

Italy in the Age of the Renaissance 1380–1530
Denys Hay and John Law

* Italy 1530–1630
Eric Cochrane (edited by Julius Kirshner)

Italy in the Seventeenth Century 1598–1713
Domenico Sella

* Italy in the Age of Reason 1685–1789
Dino Carpanetto and Giuseppe Ricuperati

* Italy in the Age of the Risorgimento 1790–1870
Harry Hearder

* Modern Italy: 1871–1982
Martin Clark

* already published

LONGMAN HISTORY OF ITALY

ITALY
1530–1630

ERIC COCHRANE

Edited by
Julius Kirshner

LONGMAN
London and New York

Longman Group UK Limited,
Longman House, Burnt Mill, Harlow,
Essex CM20 2JE, England
and Associated Companies throughout the world

Published in the United States of America
by Longman Inc., New York

© Longman Group UK Limited 1988

First published 1988
Second impression 1993

British Library Cataloguing in Publication Data

Cochrane, Eric
Italy, 1530–1630. – (Longman history of
Italy).
1. Italy – History – 16th century
2. Italy – History – 17th century
I. Title   II. Kirshner, Julius
945′.06   DG540

ISBN 0-582-48364-6 CSD
ISBN 0-582-49144-4 PPR

Library of Congress Cataloging-in-Publication Data

Cochrane, Eric W.
Italy 1530–1630.

(Longman history of Italy)
1. Italy – History 16th century. 2 Italy –
History – 17th century. I. Kirshner, Julius.
II. Title.   III. Series: Longman history of Italy
(Unnumbered)
DG540.C62   1988   945′.07   87-36655
ISBN 0-582-48364-6
ISBN 0-582-49144-4 (pbk.)

Set in 11/12 pt Linotron 202 Garamond

Produced by Longman Singapore Publishers (Pte) Ltd.
Printed in Singapore

Contents

List of Tables		vi
Editorial Note		vii
Abbreviations		x
List of Plates		xi
Map		xii

Chapter One	Introduction	1
Chapter Two	Prologue: The Sack of Rome	7
Chapter Three	Monuments of the High Renaissance	19
Chapter Four	A New Political Order	33
	The Imperial Alliance	33
	The Italian States	42
Chapter Five	Institutions of Culture	55
Chapter Six	Mannerism	69
	The survival of the models	69
	Variations upon the models	74
	The dramatists and the novella writers	79
	The faithful rebels	82
	From imitation to innovation	86
	From palaces to cities	91
	Toward a national culture	93
Chapter Seven	Tridentine Reform	106
	The religious revival	106
	Religious orders and confraternities	111
	The contribution of the humanists	118
	The new ecclesiastical institutions	123
	Orthodoxy and heterodoxy	134
	The Inquisition and the Index	141
	The Council of Trent	145
Chapter Eight	Consolidation	165
	Peace	165
	Prosperity	171

	The religious establishment	184
	The aesthetic establishment	202
	The philosophic establishment	209
	Salvaging the systems	216
Chapter Nine	Destabilization	242
	Consolidation complete	242
	The nation defined	250
	The crises	259

Appendix: Tables of Succession 291
Index 295

List of Tables

1. Popes 291
2. Emperors 291
3. Ferrara, the Este 291
4. Florence, the Medici 292
5. Genoa (Doges) 292
6. Mantua (Marquises and Dukes) 293
7. Parma (Dukes) 293
8. Savoy (Dukes) 293
9. Urbino (Dukes) 293
10. Venice (Doges) 293

Editorial Note

At the time of his tragic death in November 1985, Eric Cochrane was on the verge of completing a full draft of his long-awaited book on early modern Italy that would have brought to fruition a lifetime of research and reflection. As his friend and colleague, I became intimately acquainted with the gestation of the project. Besides reading drafts of chapters, I had taught a course with him on early modern Italy, and we had innumerable conversations concerning the historiographical issues in which he was engaged. On several occasions during this period, when he and I were commiserating about how far behind we lagged in our various projects, he admonished me that should death prevent him from completing the book, it would be my responsibility to do what was necessary for its publication. This was said in jest, but he was also expressing a mutual intellectual commitment and trust. Since he was in excellent health and a formidable athlete, his admonition provoked neither alarm nor even a reply from me. The last time we saw each other was at a joyous farewell party just before his departure for Florence, where he expected to complete the manuscript on which he had been working for almost a decade.

In the aftermath of his sudden death, I learned that he had left me all his papers and manuscripts to do with as I saw fit. Although the oblique language of the bequest masked his own wishes, I knew he was depending on me to oversee works in press, and above all the publication of his manuscript on Baroque Italy. With the unstinting help of Lydia Cochrane, the author's wife, I was able to determine which of the successive drafts, all lacking dates, was the most recent. Lingering doubts about the proper sequence of the eight extant chapters were dispelled by a memo he drafted in April 1985, furnishing a general outline of the book. The projected final chapter, 'Age of the Baroque (1630–1690)', and postscript, 'Toward Arcadia', alas, were never written. Having established the manuscript, the next step was toward publication. After consulting with Denys Hay, General Editor of the series in which this volume appears, and Andrew MacLennan of Longman, it was agreed that I should undertake editorial revisions and prepare the manuscript for publication. We also agreed that the distinctiveness of the author's style, methods, and conceptualization of the period made it unwise for me to attempt to reconstruct the concluding section from his notes or to commission another scholar to write a final chapter. At any rate, the absence of the final chapter and postscript, I believed, was less damaging than it might have been: the coverage of the period, beginning with the Sack of Rome and terminating with the trial and condemnation of Galileo, is thematically complete and makes a comprehensive and coherent whole.

When I began editing the manuscript, my original goal was to correct blatant errors, to complete truncated references, and to keep other changes to a minimum. This proved unfeasible. Although the volume was meant to be self-sufficient and complete in itself, the manuscript as it stood was not consistent with the other volumes in the series. There was a bulky apparatus of notes, replete with references in modern Greek, Latin, and the various dialects of sixteenth-century Italy, which was inappropriate for a series primarily aimed at a readership of non-experts. There were, as well, excesses and omissions, threatening the intelligibility of the text. It abounded in redundancies, material extraneous to the principal themes, quotations left in the original language, of which some were untranslatable as well as untranslated, and polemical asides that, while a trademark of the author, were often irrelevant and disruptive. The omission of proper identification for the hundreds of minor characters parading through the volume, whose collective exploits constitute its subject, would leave all but erudite readers to fend for themselves. Had he lived, the author would have certainly undertaken the necessary revisions and produced a lucid and highly polished text. Hints of what he might have done are contained in a 1985 memo, where he stated that he planned to pare down the size of the prologue by one third and the first four chapters by one half. In an earlier memo, dated April 1984, he indicated that he had decided to save the full text for a subsequent volume on the culture of the late Renaissance, 'probably to be entitled *The Harvest of Renaissance Italy*'.

With these considerations in mind, I have revised the manuscript in the following ways. First, I have reduced both the number and length of notes. At the same time I have retained all references to the sources for quotations and translations found in the body of the text and references to scholarly works which are germane to Cochrane's theses or which may serve as a guide to further inquiry. As an aid to the reader I have added to the notes references to English translations of primary sources and to titles of major books and significant articles which he did not cite or which appeared after his death. Second, I have pruned repetitious as well as extraneous passages, and have preserved polemical remarks in instances when, in my opinion, they were fundamental to the comprehension of a particular argument. Third, for the sake of clarity, I have made minor changes in wording throughout the text and have slimmed some paragraphs weighed down with rhetorical flourishes. Fourth, wherever possible, I have added information that situates persons mentioned in the volume with respect to time, place, and profession. Similarly, I have supplied the dates of publication for written works, for the performances of theatrical productions, and the relevant dates and current locations for paintings, sculptures, and architectural monuments. Fifth, I have checked as many as possible of Cochrane's splendid translations and have made slight alterations when warranted by an examination of the original source. Except where the meaning is obvious, I have translated all words, phrases, and quotations in foreign languages which were left untranslated. Quotations in dialect that proved untranslatable were eliminated. Throughout the process of editing, I have tried to resist the temptation of modifying views that differed with my own and of smuggling into the text interpretations that I preferred. Though in number the changes have been considerable, in substance they remain minor. The overall design, the provocative theses and massive scholarship on which they rest, the luminous observations, the irony laced with moralism, and the Guicciardinian embellishments – all belong to Eric Cochrane.

Upon completing a draft of a chapter, it was Cochrane's custom to have the manuscript vetted by his seminar students as well as colleagues. Several drafts have turned up with criticisms, suggested emendations, and glosses written in different hands, which, in most instances, I have been able to identify. Although he welcomed the correction of factual errors and references to books and articles that he had inadvertently overlooked, Cochrane was reluctant to make changes, at the insistence of others, having a bearing on his finely woven interpretations. In the end, there is no way of knowing how he might have responded to these critiques. Still, I found many criticisms and suggestions concerning facts and issues of clarity well taken and, where appropriate, I have incorporated them into the text. Had Eric Cochrane had the opportunity, he would have gratefully acknowledged the stimulation and assistance of his seminar students, who read portions of the manuscript and listened to his dilemmas. Likewise, he would have thanked Charles Cohen, who read the chapter on Mannerism, for his critical advice; and John Tedeschi, who read the chapter on Tridentine reform, for his emendations. Finally, he would have expressed his gratitude for the support for research he received from the American Council of Learned Societies and the Social Science Division of the University of Chicago.

For my part, I gratefully acknowledge the assistance of David Reis, who spent many hours patiently checking notes. I am indebted to Domenico Sella, whose critical reading of the entire manuscript was of inestimable value in the early stages of editing; and to Brendan Dooley for his advice and for sharing with me his knowledge of the *Sei-Settecento*. I have also benefited from the generosity and advice of colleagues for whom Eric had great admiration and with whom he had shared his enthusiasms and ideas: Constantin Fasolt, Anne Jacobson Schutte, Carolyn Valone, and especially Massimo Firpo and Elissa Weaver, who read the penultimate draft of the manuscript. Above all, I want to express my thanks to Eric Cochrane's former students, friends and colleagues, in Italy as well as the United States, whose eagerness for the publication of his work was a potent source of encouragement to its editor and remains a tribute to its remarkable author.

Julius Kirshner

Abbreviations

Annuario ISIEMC	*Annuario dell'Istituto Storico Italiano per l'età moderna e contemporanea*
ASI	*Archivio storico italiano*
CS	*Critica storica*
DBI	*Dizionario biografico degli italiani*, Rome, 1960–
Einaudi Storia d'Italia	*Storia d'Italia*, 6 vols, Turin 1972–77
Mél EFR	*Mélanges de l'Ecole Française de Rome*
Mitt Kunst F	*Mitteilungen des Kunsthistorischen Instituts von Florenz*
MSDM	*Memorie storiche della diocesi di Milano*
QS	*Quaderni storici*
Riv SLR	*Rivista di storia e letteratura religiosa*
RSCI	*Rivista di storia della chiesa in Italia*
RSI	*Rivista storica italiana*
SS	*Studi storici*
Storia cult ven	*Storia della cultura veneta*, Vol. 3: *Dal primo Quattrocento al Concilio di Trento*, eds Girolamo Arnaldi and Manlio Pastore Stocchi, Vicenza 1980–81.
SV	*Studi Veneziani*

List of Plates

(between pp. 82 and 83)

1. Zuccari, *The Armistice between Francis I and Charles V.*
2. Titian, *Pope Paul III and his Nephews.*
3. Titian, *Venus and the Organ Player.*
4. Pontormo, *Deposition.*
5. Rosso Fiorentino, *The Deposition from the Cross.*
6. Bronzino, *Venus, Cupid, Folly and Time.*
7. Parmigianino, *Madonna dal Collo Lungo.*
8. The *Studiolo* of Francesco I.
9. 'Goldsmiths' from the *Studiolo* of Francesco I.
10. Caravaggio, *The Calling of St Matthew.*
11. Carracci, *Butcher's Shop.*
12. The title page for Galileo's *Dialogo.*

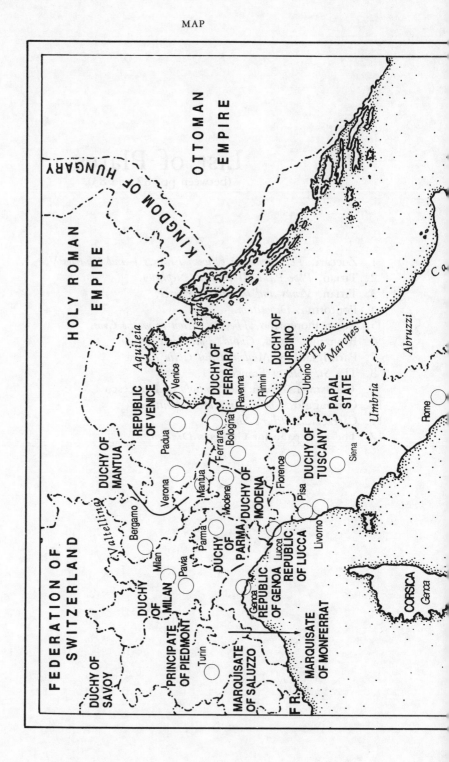

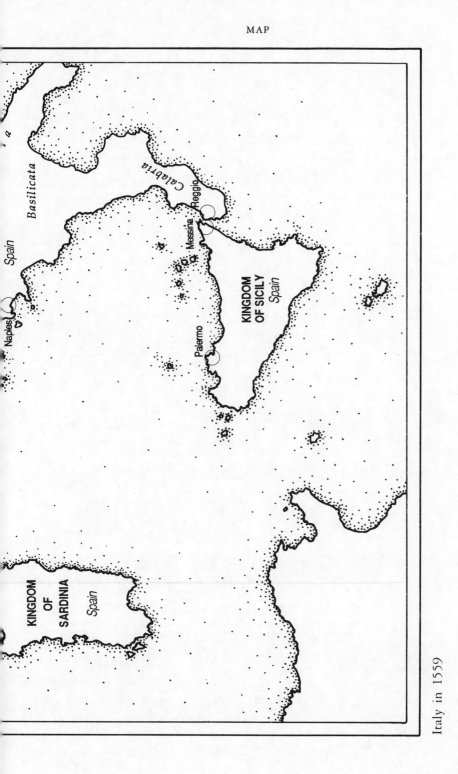

Italy in 1559

CHAPTER ONE

Introduction

Of all the periods covered in the Longman series, the years 1530–1630 have long been one of the least known in Italian history among English and American historians. They have preferred to study the Middle Ages, a turbulent yet formative period; or the Renaissance, an age when Italy became the epicentre of cultural and artistic creativity. They have favoured the *Risorgimento* of the nineteenth century, which witnessed the florescence of the Liberal State; or the twentieth century, which saw the rise and fall of Fascism and the establishment of the Communist party as a major force in Italian politics. Decadence, the falling away or declining from a prior state of excellence in art and literature, is a term often applied to the period after the Renaissance. It comes as no surprise that the *Oxford English Dictionary* gives as an example of 'decadence' 'the period subsequent to Raphael and Michelangelo'. 'Baroque', referring to queerness, grotesqueness, over-ornateness, is another denigrating label routinely applied to the period. No wonder, then, that Anglophone historians have been chary of investing their time and energy in the period between the Renaissance and Enlightenment, whose chief attributes are considered to be political absolutism, re-feudalization of the countryside, economic crisis, religious repression, and cultural decline.

Intent on finding a scapegoat for the assorted ills that delayed Italy's transition into modernity, nationalist historians of the *Risorgimento* attributed decadence to foreign invasions and Spanish domination. What began as an explanation quickly solidified into a preconception, one that was buttressed by the authority of the great literary historian and critic Francesco De Sanctis (1817–1883) and of the philosopher and historian Benedetto Croce (1866–1952), who produced the first major edition of De Sanctis' writings. For De Sanctis, culture could only flourish within the confines of an independent and democratic national state, and so when Italy succumbed to Spanish domination in the early sixteenth century its vibrant cultural and moral life fell into decay. He characterized the Baroque as nothing more than a degeneration of the Renaissance.[1] Cochrane observed, 'the enormous prestige enjoyed by De Sanctis' work during the half-century after national unification and its canonization in the Gentile educational reform of the 1920s as the

1

official textbook of Italian literature in the schools of Italy assured for the "decadence" thesis a prosperous future'.[2] From the mid-sixteenth to the end of the seventeenth century, Croce accordingly pronounced, Italy 'was bereft of all political life and national sentiment, freedom of thought was extinguished, culture impoverished, literature became mannered and ponderous, the figurative arts and architecture became extravagant and grotesque [*imbarocchirono*]'.[3] In his masterful *History of the Age of the Baroque in Italy*, he also indicted the Counter-Reformation Church, to which the Italian spirit meekly submitted, for the loss of artistic and intellectual leadership and the moral and spiritual torpor of the age.[4] If, on empirical grounds, the works of De Sanctis and Croce are now outdated, their influence on the framing of questions has continued to thrive: it can be detected both in studies that dismiss the sixteenth and seventeenth centuries as a dreary interlude in Italian history[5] and in revisionist works like Cochrane's, which treat the period as an age of authentic cultural creativity and religious renewal, an age demanding our respect.

A militant revisionist, Eric Cochrane spent his scholarly career combating the 'decadence thesis', which he believed was at variance with what he had discovered about the period. In his first book, *Tradition and Enlightenment in the Tuscan Academies*, published in 1962, he revealed the role these learned institutions played in the transformation of Tuscany from a hodgepodge of medieval city-states into a unified regional state and suggested that, despite the importance of French models, the intellectual vitality of eighteenth-century Tuscany was crucially indebted to the legacy of the Renaissance and to the labours of native academicians. A number of the themes advanced in this path-breaking work were enlarged in *Florence in the Forgotten Centuries, 1527–1800*, published in 1973. Styled by the author as a journey for readers seeking pleasure as well as provocation, his picaresque recreation of Florence under the Grand Duchy was also deadly serious. It was aimed at destroying the universal assumption that, with Florence's fall from republican grace in 1530 and the passing of the generation of Leonardo da Vinci, Niccolò Machiavelli and Francesco Guicciardini, the well of creativity that had sustained Florentine culture in the Renaissance suddenly dried up. It was equally aimed at demonstrating that, even after the city's fall from cultural preeminence, Florentines continued to make original contributions to the fields of music and natural sciences and to the science of civil administration under the benign tutelage of the grand dukes. The essential validity of his bold hypotheses has now been stunningly confirmed by R. Burr Litchfield's *Emergence of a Bureaucracy. The Florentine Patricians 1530–1790*, published in 1986.

In singling out Cochrane's contributions, we must not ignore those of other scholars, which have both challenged rigid preconceptions and stimulated debate. Cochrane's debt to Hubert Jedin, Giuseppe Alberigo, Paolo Prodi, Alberto Vecchi, H. Outram Evennett and Jean Delumeau, for insisting that the Counter-Reformation was a multi-dimensional event – in character, time, place, and goals – and also for showing that it unleashed intense activity in administrative and social reconstruction, is enormous. His debt to S. J. Freedberg, John Sherman, Eugenio Battisti, Georg Weise, Riccardo Scrivano and other scholars, for providing working definitions of Mannerism as an artistic and literary style, is obvious. His debt to Paola Barocci, Bernard Weinberg, Cesare Vasoli and Eugenio Garin, for illuminating the paths taken by Renaissance humanism in the sixteenth century; to musicologists like Edward Lowinsky and Howard Mayer Brown, for documenting the bold innovations of Italian musicians and composers of the sixteenth and seventeenth centuries; and to economic historians like Ruggiero Romano, for pointing to the economic crisis of the 1620s, and Domenico Sella, for deflating the myth of the re-feudalization of Spanish Lombardy, are amply recognized in the notes of this volume.

Thoroughly acquainted with recent scholarship and steeped in the literary and visual sources of the period, Cochrane set forth to produce a work covering a wide diversity of specialized disciplines and geographical areas, but also a narrative structured by distinguishable phases. As a self-avowed historicist, he firmly believed, along with Croce, that without careful attendance to the problem of periodization 'history inevitably degenerates either into an "undifferentiated continuum" or into metahistory or else into chronicle'.[6] *Italy 1530–1630* begins with the ruin perpetrated by the foreign invasions and the Sack of Rome in 1527. Yet, these calamities coincided with the completion of High Renaissance masterpieces: Michelangelo's *Moses* (*c.* 1515) and his Medici Chapel (1519–33), Raphael's Vatican fresco cycle (1509–14), Lodovico Ariosto's epic romance *Orlando furioso* (1532) and Baldassare Castiglione's dialogue *The Courtier* (1528). Mannerism, a stylistic term that continues to provoke controversy, refers to the audacious experiments in painting, sculpture, architecture, poetry and prose of the next two generations. These experiments, Cochrane insists, must be understood as a further evolution, not a rejection, of High Renaissance models. The first half of the sixteenth century was, moreover, a period of profound religious piety, manifested in the mystic flights of Caterina Fieschi of Genoa, the pastoral activities of the Veronese bishop, Gian Matteo Giberti, and the pastoral activities, preaching, missions and retreats of the Society of Jesus founded by Ignatius Loyola (1540).

The pan-Italian or Imperial alliance forged by the Emperor Charles V ushered in a period of peace and stability, reaching a climax in the half-century after the Treaty of Cateau-Cambrésis of 1559. Here was the beginning, not of the Counter-Reformation, but of a period of consolidation. Besides political reconstruction and national unity, the 'age of consolidation' experienced population increase and industrial and commercial recovery. Ecclesiastical reform, which penetrated parishes up and down the peninsula, was achieved through the successful implementation of the disciplinary decrees of the Council of Trent (1545–62) and the heroic leadership of bishops like Carlo Borromeo of Milan. Religious devotion was reinforced by a revised catechism and standard editions of the Roman Missal, the Breviary, the Vulgate Bible and the writings of the Church Fathers. The result was a well-instructed and devout laity. By the end of this phase, however, experimentation in the realms of visual arts, architecture and literature was becoming an end in itself.

Destabilization was brought about by a series of shocks that struck Italy in the early seventeenth century. The War of Monferrato (1613–17) brought to a halt half a century of peaceful coexistence among the northern Italian states, while the collision between Pope Paul v and Venice over the Church's prerogatives squandered the renewed power and prestige of the papacy. Competition from Dutch and English merchants and the European recession of the 1620s combined with the epidemics that struck in 1630–33 and again in 1656–57 to produce social dislocations and economic stagnation that would last for another hundred years. Mannerism was assaulted by Caravaggio's dramatic naturalism, the Petrarchan universe by Alessandro Tassoni's and Giambattista Marino's iconoclasm and overweening conceits, and the Aristotelian–Ptolemaic system by Galileo Galilei's astronomical discoveries.

Cochrane's views on 'the Baroque' are contained in a published summary of what was to be the final section of this volume.[7] This final phase, he wrote, commenced after 1630 and was marked by the downward trajectory of the economy and a failure of nerve. Politics became a stage set where decorum-conscious elites employed technical virtuosity and thematic originality to divert attention from social and economic ills defying traditional remedies. Mannerist refinement and artifice gave way to the robust naturalism of Baroque art, which subverted the High Renaissance models on which it claimed to be grounded. Parochialism narrowed the imaginative horizons of historians, whose works began to resemble news bulletins (*avvisi*). Meanwhile, the trial and condemnation of Galileo – who was compelled to abjure the Copernican system in 1633 – cast a pall over the work of his disciples, who feared to examine the theoretical consequences of their scientific experiments. The practical piety of the Tridentine reformers withered in a fetishistic economy of miracles, hagiolatry, indulgence-counting, rosary recitals and processions. Eventually, the Baroque would spark the neo-Petrarchan, rationalist reaction first represented by neo-cultist jurists in Tuscany and the literary critics and poets who founded the Roman academy Arcadia in 1690.

In his summary of the Baroque Cochrane scrupulously avoids use of the term 'decadence'. Still, the years between 1630 and 1690, as seen through his eyes, were a period of palpable decay. His esteem for Renaissance moral values and humanism and Tridentine religiosity may have prevented him from extending to Baroque culture his refined, yet capacious, historical empathy. It certainly prevented him from fully appreciating the monumental accomplishments of Francesco Borromini (1599–1667), Pietro da Cortona (1596–1669), and Gian Lorenzo Bernini (1598–1680). Had he been able to complete the book, recent research as well as his own investigations of post-Galilean science, post-Tridentine theology, non-Florentine poetry and art, and Neapolitan metaphysics might have led him to modify the unsympathetic picture of the Baroque presented in 1983. Galileo's intellectual heirs, for instance, continued to build upon their master's discoveries at the universities

4

of Pisa, Bologna, Padua and the Jesuit Collegio Romano in Rome. They revised and updated their ideas as news reached them of the advances of Descartes and Newton.[8] Baroque aesthetic theory, it now appears, represented yet another development in the humanist and Aristotelian ideas of literary criticism.[9] Traditional urban crafts and industries, admittedly, declined in the face of transalpine competition and protectionism. In contrast, agriculture exhibited resilience in northern Italy, while new industries and technologies were introduced in provincial areas.[10] Current work on the links connecting these developments to the reforms of the eighteenth century should provide fresh perspectives on the native origins of the Italian Enlightenment and serve to demolish the equation between decadence and the Baroque.

The history of Italy in the age of the Baroque is like a giant puzzle. Finding all the pieces, let alone making them fit together into a coherent pattern, seems, even in the age of the computer, a quixotic goal. More than anyone else, Cochrane, who had never before attempted a work of synthesis, was acutely aware of the provisional nature of his theses and the criticisms they would surely invite from specialists. This is not meant as a disclaimer. Cochrane's intent was to stir debate about a recalcitrant past that defied cheap description and trivialization, to shake the reader's confidence in the inevitability of the present by demonstrating the contingent nature of ideas and institutions, and, finally, to draw attention to the interdependence of past and present, a knowledge of which, he always insisted, was essential in order to bring about constructive change in the future.

Julius Kirshner

NOTES AND REFERENCES

1. Francisco De Sanctis, *Storia della letteratura italiana*, ed. Benedetto Croce, Bari 1939, 2, p. 143. For an astute appraisal of De Sanctis' method, see Gennaro Savarese, 'De Sanctis e i problemi dell'umanesimo', in Carlo Muscetta (ed.), *Francesco De Sanctis nella storia e nella cultura*, Rome and Bari 1984, pp. 279–300.
2. Eric Cochrane, 'The Renaissance academies in their Italian and European setting', in *The Fairest Flower: The Emergence of Linguistic National Consciousness in Renaissance Europe*, Florence 1985, p. 22.
3. Benedetto Croce, *La Spagna nella vita italiana durante la rinascenza* (4th edn), Bari 1949, p. 257.
4. Benedetto Croce, *Storia della età barocca in Italia*, Bari 1929, pp. 10, 16, 471 ff. For the intellectual background of this work, see Federico Chabod, 'Croce historien', in his *De Machiavel à Benedetto Croce*, Geneva 1970, pp. 179–230.
5. For example, Guido Quazza, *La decadenza italiana nella storia europea. Saggi sul Sei-Settecento*, Milan 1971; Maurice Aymard, 'La transizione dal feudalesimo al capitalismo', in *Storia d'Italia, Annali 1: Dal feudalesimo al capitalismo*, Turin 1978, pp. 1131–92, an English translation of which is provided in *Review*, 6, 1982, pp. 131–208; Stuart Woolf, *A History of Italy 1700–1860*, London 1979, pp. 19–26; Gino Benzoni, *Gli affanni della cultura: Intellettuali e potere nell'Italia*

della Controriforma e Barocca, Milan 1978; Michele Cuaz, *Intellettuali, potere e circolazione delle idee nell'Italia moderna (1500–1700)*, Torino 1982; Romeo De Maio, *Pittura e Controriforma a Napoli*, Bari 1983. See also the historiographical essays of James Grubb, 'When myths lose power: Four decades of Venetian historiography', and Eric Cochrane, 'Southern Italy in the age of the Spanish viceroys: Some recent titles', *Journal of Modern History*, 58, 1986. The sweeping indictment of the corruption and inefficiency of Spanish administration in southern Italy has been convincingly challenged by Roberto Mantelli, *Il pubblico impiego nell'economia del Regno di Napoli: Retribuzioni, reclutamento e ricambio sociale nell'epoca spagnuola (secc. XVI–XVII)*, Naples 1986.

6. Eric Cochrane, *Western Civilization at the University of Chicago. An Introduction for Teachers*, ed. John W. Boyer and Julius Kirshner, Chicago and London 1986, p. 9.

7. See his contribution to John Julius Norwich (ed.), *The Italians. History, Art, and the Genius of a People*, London and New York 1983, pp. 182–6.

8. Ugo Baldini, 'La Chiesa e le scienze. La scienza gesuitica', *Storia d'Italia, Annali 3: Scienza e tecnica*, Turin 1980. For the opposing view, see Vincenzo Ferrone, 'La rivoluzione scientifica', in *La storia. L'età moderna*, 2: *La vita religiosa e la cultura*, Turin 1986.

9. Maria Luisa Doglio's introduction to her edition of Emmanuele Tesauro, *Idea delle perfette imprese*, Florence 1975, pp. 5–27; Mario Zanardi, 'Sulla genesi del Cannocchiale aristotelico di E. Tesauro', *Studi seicenteschi*, 23, 1982; Paul B. Diffley, 'Paolo Beni's Commentary on the "Poetics" and its relationship to the Commentaries of Robortelli, Maggi, Vettori and Castelvetro', *Studi seicenteschi*, 25, 1984, pp. 53–99.

10. Domenico Sella, *Crisis and Continuity in the Economy of Spanish Lombardy in the Seventeenth Century*, Cambridge, Mass. 1979, reviewed by Aldo De Maddalena, 'Vespri e mattutino in una società preindustriale', *Rivista storica italiana*, 93, 1982; Enrico Stumpo, *Finanza e stato moderno nel Piemonte del Seicento*, Rome 1979; Salvatore Ciriacono, 'Protoindustria, lavoro a domicilio e sviluppo economico nelle campagne venete in epoca moderna', *QS*, 18, 1983; Raffaello Vergani, 'Technology and organization of labour in the Venetian copper industry (16th–18th centuries)', *Journal of European Economic History*, 14, 1985.

CHAPTER TWO

Prologue: The Sack of Rome

After four hours of intense fighting that had begun before dawn on 6 May 1527, the polyglot mob of mercenaries that made up the army of the Emperor Charles V finally managed, under the cover of a thick morning fog, to break through a weak point in the walls of Rome just east of the Vatican. Those of the hastily assembled defenders who noticed them in time raced in disorder across the Tiber, in the vain hope of finding protection among the winding, cluttered streets of the medieval city. Those who failed to notice them in time were butchered on the spot. The pope, with the resident cardinals and their retinue, fled through the covered causeway recently constructed for just such emergencies to Castel Sant'Angelo, which had fortunately been rendered impregnable by the construction of a bastion and a moat around the rebuilt ruins of the second-century AD tomb of the Emperor Hadrian. By the end of the day, all Rome had been occupied except the Castello, which no longer served any offensive purpose other than that of firing off an occasional cannon ball. The victorious army, now leaderless after the unexpected death of its commander and reinforced three days later by the private army of the Colonna family, set forth systematically to plunder churches, despoil monasteries and burn palaces, to torture or hold in chains whoever was suspected of knowing the location of a hidden treasure, to violate the bodies as well as the possessions of whoever might become the object of long-frustrated passions, distinguishing neither between the sacred and the profane, men and women, nuns and matrons, young and old, prelates and plebeians, former enemies and professed allies. In the words of one eye-witness,

Naught could be seen on the streets but vile ruffians carrying bundles of rich vestments and ecclesiastical ornaments and large sacks full of gold and silver vessels, bands of prisoners of all classes wailing and screaming, dead bodies cut into pieces covered with mud and their own blood. . . . Many persons were suspended by their arms for hours on end; others were tied up by their genitals or hung high over the street by their feet or half-buried in cellars or boxes or lacerated all over their bodies with hot irons.[1]

The army – or, rather, the soldiers, since every attempt to restore some measure of discipline proved to be equally ineffective – then settled down to consume what it seized or extorted; and for ten long months, according to another witness,

no bells were rung in the chief city of Christendom, no churches were visited, no masses were said. The rich shops of the merchants became like horse stables. The great edifices lost their luster. Many houses were demolished. Men and animals shared the same burial ground. Churches were inhabited by packs of dogs.[2]

The Sack of Rome did not take the Romans wholly by surprise. Just seven months earlier they had suffered another such invasion, albeit led by one of their own baronial families and directed not against them, but against their ruler, Pope Clement VII. They were well aware that papal finances had been disastrously compromised by the efforts of Clement's uncle and predecessor, Leo X, who attempted to carve out a permanent temporal state for the lay head of his family, the Medici, and by the precipitous drop in revenues provoked by the preaching of Martin Luther in Germany and by the collapse of the tourist business, their chief source of income as the innkeepers to pilgrims from all over Christendom. They were constantly called upon to refill the constantly empty papal treasury by paying even more taxes on the necessities of life and by buying shares in the *Monte della Fede*, the funded state debt that Pope Clement had reluctantly inaugurated in imitation of similar institutions set up on much sounder economic bases in most northern Italian states.

The Romans also knew that Clement's chief source of political as well as financial power was rapidly slipping through his fingers – namely, the Republic of Florence, which his family, and for some years he personally, dominated through the well-tried system of controlling elections. His appointment of the cardinal of Cortona, so called after the city of his birth, as representative of his authority in Florence during the minority of his two nephews had offended all the Florentine patricians, who resented being made subjects of a citizen hailing from their own subject city. The cardinal's fiscal exactions – all on behalf of interests that even the pro-Medici patricians could no longer identify as their own – had wiped out what small financial advantage they reaped from Clement's rather halting concession to the traditional papal policy of distributing benefices and privileges to the pope's fellow citizens. By April 1527, 'the hatred of this regime' and 'the discontent over [its] discouragingly inept manner of government' had become so great, according to the pope's own commissioner,[3] that an anti-Medici rebellion was thwarted only by frightening the rebels with the prospect of having the Imperial army visit them too on its way to Rome. The moment the cardinal heard that the pope had been shut up in the Castello, he took the nephews and slipped out of the city, carelessly sacrificing in an hour the hegemonic position that Clement's forefathers had worked so hard to build for a century.

Finally, the Romans had known since January, when their renegade French commander used up every cent he had managed to squeeze from the unfortunate citizens of Milan and beg from the bankers of Ferrara to pay off his chronically unpaid German soldiers, that the army would no longer obey orders. They had known since February, when the Imperial commander managed to put down a mutiny of his Spanish soldiers only with promises of more plunder, that the Imperial army was moving inexorably toward Rome. They also knew that Clement had thrown away what little money might have been left for strengthening the long neglected defences of the city in the form of a vain peace offering to his erstwhile enemy, the Imperial viceroy of Naples, and that he had then dismissed his own mercenaries in the appallingly naive expectation that the viceroy would, or could, halt the approaching army. But when the pope was finally reduced to asking them to do themselves what he had taxed them so heavily to do for them, the citizens responded with impassive incredulity. Besides, what could have been done in three short days to turn subjects long accustomed to prohibitions against bearing arms into anything like a match for some of the best trained professional warriors of all Christendom?

The Sack of Rome was neither unexpected nor unprecedented. Similar misfortunes had befallen other Italian cities ever since their emergence as autonomous political entities four centuries earlier; and many of their citizens still remembered what a Florentine army had done in Volterra in 1472, what a Neapolitan army had done in the towns of the Valdelsa in 1478 and what the Turkish armies had done in the towns of Friuli and Puglia in 1472, 1477, 1480 and 1499. Such misfortunes had increased in intensity after October 1494, when the soldiers of King Charles VIII of France set a new example of barbarity in the Florentine outpost of Fivizzano; and they had increased in frequency after 1499, when the second major French invasion of the peninsula turned it into the battleground of not just Italians, but of all the powers of Europe. In 1509 the Venetians destroyed one of their own towns on the Adda in reprisal for its having prematurely admitted the French. In 1512 alone Ravenna was almost wholly consumed by iron, flames and death, some 5,666 residents of Prato were put to death and Brescia was reduced to desolation: 'In the streets no one was to be seen except women . . . looking for the bodies of their fathers, brothers or husbands' – or being violated by the sackers on top of the bodies they identified. In 1519 Fabiano was torn to pieces. In 1521 Como was 'miserably put to the sack', in spite of the solemn promise of the Neapolitan commander of the besieging Spanish troops not to do so. In 1522 'all the property of the city [of Genoa] was seized by the victors', despite their pledge to respect the terms of surrender. In 1525 'the French continuously committed the greatest cruelties and burned many buildings' during the eight days they occupied the city of Pavia.[4]

Friendly armies behaved almost as badly as officially hostile armies. The French representatives of King Francis I in his quality of duke burned all the suburbs of Milan in 1521. The Spanish representatives of the legal overlord of the Sforza duke 'kept not only men and women but also children tied up' in the Milanese houses in which they were billeted in 1526 'and used the other members of the families as their slaves'. The Milanese captain of the French troops who occupied Cremona in the name of a French duke in 1515 'forced many of the citizens to work digging and enlarging the trenches around the walls and held many others for ransom' until they finished paying the huge imposition of 30,000 lire. The Imperial captain of the Spanish troops who occupied the same city in the name of a Milanese duke in 1521 'made the citizens pay the soldiers', since he could not pay them himself; and all those he suspected of collaborating with Venetians, the former masters of the city, were placed naked on a cart, tortured at length with red hot pincers and finally quartered alive.[5]

Thus the significance of the Sack of Rome lay not in its singularity, nor in its intensity – although the sackers were indeed more numerous and the booty more abundant than in other similar cases – nor even in its duration. Its significance lay first of all in its destruction of a myth: that the city which happened also to be the spiritual capital of Latin Christendom was somehow exempt from the common experience of all other Italian cities. Its significance also lay in its being viewed as a symbol of the many calamities that had struck one part of the peninsula after another during the preceding half-century; that is, ever since the most recent attempt to block them – the formation of the 'Italic League' in 1454 – had begun to show signs of congenital weaknesses.[6]

The Italic League had tried to render permanent the third of the attempted solutions to the problem of internal political organization created by the collapse of Imperial authority in the mid-thirteenth century. It had tacitly rejected the division of the peninsula – or at least the northern half of it – into a myriad of independent communes. It had recognized the failure of the various projects to reduce all the communes to the status of dependents of a single hegemonic power, be it the Angevins of Naples, the Scaligeri of Verona or, the most nearly successful of all, the Visconti of Milan. Instead, it gave legal (or at least diplomatic) recognition to the five major and several minor regional political organizations that had emerged during the fifty years since the Venetians and the Florentines had embarked upon a policy of concerted territorial expansion and during the thirty years since the re-establishment of the Papal State in Rome.

For the next four decades, the League succeeded in realizing one of its goals: that of maintaining a monopoly of political power in the hands of the signatories. But it did so largely because their traditional extra-peninsular rivals – the French, the Hungarians, the Catalans and the Germans – were too occupied with problems at home to give them much trouble. One final attempt to revive the Angevin claims to the throne of Naples, which had been conquered in the 1440s by the Aragonese, was quickly put down. The final attempt to overthrow the current Sforza dominion in Genoa foundered on the reluctance of the current king of France to abandon his efforts to overcome the opposition of his own nobles to his policy of internal reconstruction.

The League did not succeed in avoiding the breakdown of the original five-member alliance into a succession of mutually hostile two- or three-member alliances. Pope Sixtus IV and Alfonso d'Aragona were prevented from overthrowing the Medici regime in Florence, but not from destroying much of the Florentine territorial domain. The Venetians were prevented from gobbling up the whole of the Este dominion in Ferrara, but not from annexing the cities of Rovigo and Ravenna. The League was thus unable to give its single members sufficient respite from the task of watching each other with unabated suspicion so that they could turn their attention to consolidating their domestic power bases; and they accomplished little more than wiping out the more obvious manifestations of internal dissent, like the Pazzi faction in Florence and the pro-Angevin barons in the Kingdom of Naples. Rebellions on the part of any consistent group of their subjects were rare, it is true, for terror proved for the moment to be an adequate substitute for consent. But plots and conspiracies abounded; and occasionally, as in the case of the assassination of Duke Giangaleazzo Sforza of Milan, they achieved their goal.

All that was needed to upset this uneasy equilibrium, and to eliminate the first as well as the second of the goals of the League, was to add one more to the five major contending powers. That is what happened in 1494. Freed at last of domestic concerns and spurred on by the hope of realising the two-century-old dreams of his ancestors of a pan-Mediterranean empire, King Charles VIII led an army almost without resistance from the Alps to Naples. He thus demonstrated how easy it was, with the active cooperation of one Italian power (the regent and then duke of Milan, Ludovico 'Il Moro' Sforza), and with the passive or active consent of two others (the Venetian Senate and Pope Alexander VI), to overthrow the established regime in a fourth power and to provoke the overthrow of the regime in the fifth. The Neapolitans welcomed Charles as the legitimate successor to King Alfonso II d'Aragona, who fled to Sicily; and the disgruntled Florentine patricians banished Piero de' Medici and established a broad oligarchy under the inspiration of the prophet-preacher Girolamo Savonarola.

The reconstitution of the League in 1495 for the purpose of getting King Charles out of Italy foundered almost immediately on the reluctance of the Venetians to destroy the French army for the possible benefit of the duke of Milan. It foundered also upon the reluctance of the Florentines to risk the loss of their substantial capital investment in France. It collapsed altogether in 1499, when the Venetians invited Charles' successor, King Louis XII, to divide the duchy of Milan with them, thus eliminating the principal obstacle to their ambitions for territorial expansion in the west. In 1508 Pope Julius II invited King Louis and the German Emperor Maximilian I to join him and the duke of Ferrara in carving up the *terraferma* dominions of the Venetians. In 1511 he then invited King Ferdinand of Aragon and Castille, who had since partitioned and then conquered the Neapolitan kingdom of his distant cousin Ferdinando d'Aragona, to join him and the Venetians in driving out King Louis. As a result, the oligarchical regime in Florence collapsed under a pro-Medici *coup d'état* backed by the Spanish army; and the vacuum created in Lombardy was filled by the armies of the Swiss cantons which, once having been mercenaries in the French service, began to assume the character of a cohesive political force, albeit still in the guise of a military force in the service of the restored Sforza government.

By 1515, when Louis' successor King Francis I once again conquered Milan, four new powers had been added to the equilibrium: the French in

Lombardy and Genoa, the Spanish in Sicily and Naples, the Germans under the emperor in the Veneto and the Swiss in the permanent remnant of their former conquests on behalf of others, the future Canton Ticino. Three of the former major powers had been eliminated – two of them (Milan and Naples) permanently, the other (the Venetians) temporarily. One other, Florence, had for practical purposes become a subject of the papacy through the election of its *de facto* ruler as Pope Leo x in 1513.

Only one of the former powers had benefited – and continued to benefit – from this radical realignment: the Papal State. Under Julius II it had absorbed the cities in the Romagna and the Marche formerly conquered by the son of Julius' predecessor, Cesare Borgia, as well as those once owned by the Venetians. Under Leo x it absorbed the former Este and Sforza cities in Emilia – Modena, Reggio, Parma and Piacenza. This remarkable accomplishment was made possible largely by the skill of the papal diplomats in playing off one major power against the other and in occasionally supplementing the authority they derived from their temporal possessions in Italy with what still remained of their authority in the church elsewhere in Europe. They thus dispersed the anti-papal church council that King Louis had called in reprisal for their switch of alliances in 1512 by conjuring up memories of the chaotic Council of Basel a half-century earlier – and by inviting them to attend instead the equally inconclusive Fifth Lateran Council that met in Rome a few months later. On the morrow of the Battle of Marignano, which suddenly reversed the balance of power in favour of the French in 1515, Pope Leo managed to turn the victor, King Francis I, from foe into friend almost overnight. He sacrificed his erstwhile ally Duke Massimiliano Sforza of Milan and gave up all effective control over appointments in the Gallican Church; and Francis obliged him by burying forever the Pragmatic Sanction of Bourges (1438) and leaving the pope to settle the affairs of Emilia and Umbria as he saw fit.

After 1519 this game became much more difficult to play, for two of the non-Italian centres of power, Spain and the German Empire, were suddenly united under the same ruler. It became still more difficult to play after 1521, when the Swiss dropped out of foreign politics in order to quarrel about much more pressing religious questions at home. It became wholly impossible after 1525, when the French army was destroyed and when King Francis himself was taken prisoner at the Battle of Pavia. Pope Clement and his gallophile political advisors refused to recognize the battle for what it was: a major turning point in the history of Italy. Instead, they tried to reverse its by now irreversible consequences by gathering together the reluctant Florentines, the suspicious Venetians, the impotent duke of Milan and the chastened, if at last freed, king of France into a shadowy 'League of Cognac'. The result was the Sack of Rome, which destroyed in a moment what had been the most, if not the only, successful effort of state-building in Italy in the previous three decades. As the general who was supposed to be rescuing the pope from Castel Sant'Angelo went off instead to Perugia to substitute his own for the pope's representatives in the communal government, the Papal State dissolved into its component parts. The Sack also offered the first major demonstration that the equilibrium among several powers had given way to the hegemony of a single power; and that hegemony was at last sealed the following summer when the Genoese admiral Andrea Doria suddenly transferred his powerful private navy from French to Imperial service. Those who in the next few years repeated Pope Clement's folly also suffered Pope Clement's reward. The nostalgic Neapolitans who rallied to the call of the last French general to lead an army into the kingdom in 1528 were shorn of their property, if not of their heads. The latter-day Savonarolans who terrorized the Florentines into waiting patiently for God or the king of France to come save them suffered a ten-month siege. And many of them, after surrendering half-starved in August 1530, then suffered as well the same penalty of exile, confinement and confiscation that had traditionally been meted out to losing parties in all previous Florentine civil wars.

Meanwhile, the price exacted for this realignment of power proved to be much higher than any paid since the Lombard invasion of the sixth century AD. Most of what had been painfully accomplished during the fifteenth century toward transforming the defunct medieval communes into cohesive, extensive and permanent political organisms was wiped out. Milan was shorn of a third of its territorial state between 1499 and 1515; another quarter was given away thereafter in the form of autonomous feudal domains to domestic or foreign servants of the victorious emperor. The Venetian territorial state was reduced to the single city of Vicenza on the morrow of the Battle of Agnadello in 1509; and only after ten years of exhaustive diplomatic and military effort was it restored to something approaching its former size. The Florentines lost Pisa in 1494 and the Val di Chiana in 1502. In 1529, after failing to assure their subjects' loyalty by threats of reprisals – like the one visited on Volterra in July 1530 – they abandoned them to their fate, once again demonstrating that in virtuous republics the dominant city (*dominante*) owed nothing to the territorial state it dominated (*dominio*) as soon as the expense of holding onto it began to exceed the profit derived from it.

Political regimes were no more permanent than the shape of the states they governed. Reggio and Modena were continuously passed back and forth between Este and papal governors. The duchy of Urbino passed from a Montefeltro duke to a Borgia duke, then from a Della Rovere duke to a Medici duke and back to a Della Rovere duke. The Kingdom of Naples passed from an Italianized Aragonese king to a totally foreign French king and back to the successor of the Aragonese king within a year; it was then partitioned between a Spanish king and another French king, conquered and reunified by the Spanish king and then almost reconquered by still another French king. Genoa was ruled first by a Sforza governor, then by a French governor, then by a popularly elected native 'plebeian', then in turn by a pro-French doge, by a pro-Imperial doge who was nevertheless willing to negotiate with the emperor's enemies, and by a Milanese governor in the name of the king of France. The infamous local tyrannies in the Romagna were united into a single state in 1500 and then annexed to the Papal State when the new state dissolved two years later. Another new state in the Roman Campania was throttled at the moment of its birth only because its probable capital, Velletri, was encouraged to proclaim itself a 'free city'.[7]

Indeed, the very notion of a system of states soon vanished before the reality of a system of more or less powerful families, each bent upon 'seizing' any 'occasion' that 'Fortune' might present (to use the contemporary terminology accurately reflected in the works of Machiavelli) in order to 'get' and then 'hold' a state. Just where such a state might eventually be located, no one much cared. As the Aragonese had settled in Naples, where they hardly understood the language, in the 1440s, and as the Sforza had moved without a moment's hesitation from Abruzzo, where they had previously lived, to Milan in the 1450s, so in 1515–16 the Medici debated between Parma and Urbino as a possible temporal seat, even though they had roots in neither, and in the 1530s the Farnese proclaimed themselves willing to yield Castro or Camerino, which were far closer to their base in Rome, in exchange for Milan. A few of these families managed, at considerable expense in military and diplomatic activity, to 'hold' some or most of what they had 'gotten' during the preceding century – families like the Gonzaga in Mantua, whose family head served alternatively as a general in whatever army happened at the moment to be the most promising, and like the Este in Ferrara, whose skill in effecting timely changes of sides won them the admiration of all Italy. Several others, like the Bentivoglio, the Baglioni, the Borgia and the Varano, were permanently eliminated from the competition. Many others were still, or had recently become, active candidates: the Colonna, the Orsini, the Fieschi, the Adorno, the Strozzi and, somewhat later, the Farnese. And the longer the chaos could be protracted, the greater were their chances for success.

The notion of borders between political entities vanished as well. No one knew exactly where Florentine, Lucchese, Este and Malaspina territories lay in the Garfagnana, as the poet Lodovico Ariosto discovered to his sorrow during his term as governor in the 1520s – no one, that is, except smugglers and bandits, who profited from the confusion. No one knew where the Kingdom of Naples really ended and the Papal State really began, since many of the same feudatories held contiguous domains on both sides of what was supposed to be the border. The Venetians continued to regard whatever their borders were at any one time as merely provisional, in anticipation of the next opportunity to push them still further outward. Having solemnly surrendered their former possessions in the Romagna to Pope Julius in 1510, they took them back the moment they heard that Pope Clement was safely locked up in Castel Sant'Angelo.

Some of these 'states' were scattered all over Italy – from Altamura in Puglia to Novara in western Lombardy in the case of the Farnese 'state' in the 1540s, all over the Kingdom of Naples and the Papal State in the case of the 'state' of the Medici, who stationed a permanent 'viceroy' at Naples to administer it. Others were concentrated in one area, like that of the Rossi in the Val di Taro and of the Pico at Mirandola. All of them varied in size and shape as their sovereigns won or lost the interminable legal or armed quarrels that went on for much of the century or as they exchanged territorial dowries in accordance with marriage alliances among one another – their chief means of collective defence against the 'established' states that claimed jurisdiction over them. So well did they succeed that by the 1530s the three-century process by which the countryside had gradually come under the dominion of cities seemed to have been definitively reversed. In much of the land between eastern Liguria and the Po delta the authority of urban magistrates had been confined within limits no larger than those of the corresponding modern *comuni*. And much of the rest of Italy was on the verge of dissolving into an amorphous collection of rural and urban areas much like contemporary Swabia and Franconia, without any effective central political authority at all.

In the absence of governments capable of offering some measure of protection – or, for that matter, of doing anything but oppressing their subjects with ever more ruinous exactions in kind and money – political disintegration was inevitably accompanied by economic disaster. The systematic destruction of crops carried out in accordance with the fifteenth-century tactic of scorched earth greatly increased the frequency of famine, particularly in those parts of northern Italy that had long imported much of their food. The constant interruption of commercial routes – like that experienced by Florence after the secession of Pisa and by Venice after the closing of the Brenner – ruined the export business upon which the industrial and commercial cities depended for a living. Most of the textile plants that maintained the small and middle-sized cities of Lombardy and the Veneto were destroyed; and most of the capital that otherwise might have been available to rebuild them was drained off in the form of ransoms and special levies.

Natural disaster followed man-made disaster. The plague returned with new virulence in the mid-1520s, killing as much as a third of the population of Florence and almost half the population of Genoa. The entire army of the League. of Cognac camped outside Naples in 1528 and was destroyed with such rapidity and amid such unhygienic conditions that even the hardened defenders on the walls were moved to pity. The arrival of syphilis, which was imported from the New World, wreaked havoc on a population possessing neither natural nor acquired immunity to the new disease. They filled up the hospitals, or *lazzaretti*, with which private charity sought to meet the disaster as fast as they could be built. Thus the slow demographic recovery in the second half of the fifteenth century was suddenly reversed. Verona dropped from 47,084 inhabitants – according to contemporary estimates – in 1501 to 26,014 in 1518. Pavia dropped from some 16,000 in 1500 to less than 5,000 in 1535. 'Of the misery and ruin of the city and countryside', wrote one authoritative observer upon his return to Florence on the morrow of the siege of 1530, 'there is little I need say'.

It is far worse than anything I had imagined. The wealth of the inhabitants has been used up. All the houses around the city . . . have been destroyed. . . . There is very little grain left to eat this year. There is very little prospect of there being any more next year.[8]

And Florence had been, just a few years before, one of the wealthiest cities in Christendom.

Still worse than the physical effects of war and disintegration were the psychological effects. Italians tried to fix the blame on one or another individual or group of individuals – on Pope Alexander VI, on the Venetian Senate, on Cesare Borgia, on Ferrante d'Aragona, on the Florentine Piagnoni (Savonarola's followers) and above all on Ludovico 'Il Moro' Sforza of Milan. In vain: the list multiplied so rapidly that the question of individual culpability soon became meaningless. They tried to fix the blame on those of their ancestors who, ever since a pause in the Hundred Years War, had begun filling Italy with unemployed veterans and had substituted professional armies for citizen militias. But Machiavelli's militiamen were no more willing than Vitelli's mercenaries to walk through the hole in the walls of Pisa; and Machiavelli's spiritual heirs in the Florentine government in 1529–30 took care to let their hot-headed patriots parade around the piazza while entrusting all serious military operations to the hired soldiers of the professional general they had imported from Perugia. Some humanists tried to revive Cicero's identification of modern Gauls and Germans with the 'barbarians' of antiquity. Moreover, few Italians of any experience could say that Italian soldiers behaved any less 'barbarously' than 'foreign' soldiers, that 'foreign' armies were not often led by 'Italian' generals and invariably paid for by 'Italian' bankers, that such 'Italian' armies as those of the Venetians were not made up of soldiers recruited in Greece rather than those recruited in the Veneto, and that the most self-consciously Italian of all the armies in Italy, the famous Black Bands (*Bande Nere*) of Pope Clement's distant cousin Giovanni de' Medici, served any less efficiently and enthusiastically in French or Imperial than in Papal service.

Indeed, whatever it once may have been, the notion of a distinction between Swabians, Burgundians, Andalusians, Gascons, Swiss and 'Illyrians' on the one hand and all the various 'nations' that somehow qualified for the denomination 'Italian' on the other all but disappeared. 'Foreign' armies from the beginning were acclaimed with shouts of *Francia!*, *Impero!* or *Spagna!* by populations utterly indifferent to the supposed 'Italian' character of the regimes the foreigners had come to rid them of – and just as indifferent to such operatic extravagances as the *disfida* ('challenge') hurled in 1503 at Barletta against the 'French' *cavalieri* by an 'Italian' captain in the Spanish service. The most glorious of all the generals of modern Italy, proclaimed the biographer Paolo Giovio, was Gonzalo del Cordoba, 'el Gran Capitan'; that he was really a Spaniard, not any kind of Italian, and that he helped the king of Spain pension off the last resident monarch and turn Naples from a kingdom into a viceroyalty, made no difference whatever. Similarly, all common soldiers were equally despicable – or pitiful – the products as well as the victims of a military system that rested upon eternally overextended treasuries and upon the existence of such pockets of overpopulation as

Swabia, the Marche, the Alpine cantons and Andalusia. All soldiers, wherever they may have been born, were equally *déracinés*, equally dependent for survival upon the booty that followed victory, equally despondent after being defeated, equally innocent of any ideological commitment, equally helpless the moment they became sick or mutilated.

Not being able to blame anyone in particular, some Italians blamed 'Fortune', that increasingly commonplace scapegoat of the humanists. But as Fortune became increasingly ungenerous of the favourable 'occasion' that Machiavelli had perceived in its behaviour in the past, they came to look upon it as congenitally inimical, a force which could never be anticipated with a timely dike or seized at the right moment by an individual of extraordinary *virtù*. Even Guicciardini, who had done more than anyone else in his generation to change the course of Fortune, was eventually led to admit that it was now totally out of control. No one could do anything about the calamities that Fortune inevitably and invariably engendered except escape into the contemplation of a hopelessly lost golden age in which it had once been subject to human will. Other Italians blamed the stars, or whoever used the stars as oracles. A conjunction of planets in Pisces in February 1524 persuaded the leading astrologers, from Agostino Nifo and Niccolò Peranzone to Silvestro Rucarelli and Francesco Ruffo, that the worst was still to come – floods, heresies, conflagrations.

Most Italians, however, blamed themselves – even for syphilis, which, according to the leading authority on the disease, was a consequence of the *discordia* that had robbed 'Ausonia infelix' of its 'ancient valour'.[9] Or, rather, they blamed their sins, which had apparently provoked God's wrath in modern times just as automatically and just as violently as had the sins of the ancient Israelites about which modern prophets read in what they thought to be a timeless Old Testament. But as the prophets of doom electrified crowds in one piazza after another all over Italy, notwithstanding the express prohibitions of popes, bishops and civil governments, Italians became convinced that they could no more assuage God's wrath than they could change the course of the planets. Two centuries of gentle satires, biting moral treatises and thundering sermons had obviously failed to diminish the addiction of at least a sizeable minority of Italians to what they regarded as the greatest of sins: blasphemy, usury and sodomy. Hence, their only hope lay in waiting patiently until God finally tired of punishing them and – wholly on His own initiative and according to His unfathomable schedule – ushered in the new Age of the Holy Spirit.

NOTES AND REFERENCES

1. An anonymous description of the event partially published from the Madrid manuscript by Vicente de Cadenas y Vicent in *El Saco de Roma de 1527*, Madrid 1974, p. 334. The most famous contemporary discussion of the event, that by

Alfonso de Valdés (d. 1532), is available in English translation by John E. Longhurst and Raymond MacCurdy, *Alfonso de Valdés and the Sack of Rome: Dialogue of Lactancio and an Archdeacon*, Albuquerque 1952; and by the same author, *Dialogue of Mercury and Charon*, tr. Joseph V. Ricapito, Bloomington 1987. For modern reconstructions, see Maria Ludovica Lenzi, *Il Sacco di Roma del 1527*, Florence 1978; and André Chastel, *The Sack of Rome, 1527*, Princeton 1983. For new perspectives, see A. Asor Rosa, V. De Caprio and M. Miglio, 'Il Sacco di Roma del 1527 e l'immaginario collettivo', *Rivista di studi italiani*, 4, 1986.

2. Lodovico Guicciardini, *Il Sacco di Roma*, Paris 1664, pp. 203, 223.

3. Francesco Guicciardini to Gian Matteo Giberti, 24 May 1527, in Francesco Guicciardini, *Carteggi*, ed. Pier Giorgio Ricci, Rome 1969, vol. 14, p. 3, n. 1.

4. Quotations from anonymous sixteenth-century *Vitae* of the bishops of Ravenna cited by Pietro Paolo Ginanni in *Memorie storico-critiche degli scrittori ravennati*, Faenza 1769; Jacopo Modesti, *Il miserando sacco dato alla terra di Prato dagli Spagnoli*, *ASI*, 1, 1842; Paolo Giovio, *Vita del Marchese di Pescara*, published with *Vita del Gran Capitano*, tr. Ludovico Domenichi (1550), ed. Costantino Panigada, Bari 1931, p. 273; Francesco Guicciardini, *Storia d'Italia*, ed. Silvana Seidel Menchi, Turin 1971, Book 14, Ch. 14, and Book 18, Ch. 13.

5. Paolo Giovio quoted by Gino Franceschini in 'Le dominazioni francesi e le restaurazioni sforzesche' in the Treccani *Storia di Milano*, Milan 1957, vol. 8; Galeazzo Capella, *Commentarii delle cose fatte per la restituzione di Francesco Sforza secondo, duca di Milano*, tr. Francesco Philipopoli, Venice 1539; Antonio Campi, *Cremona fedelissima città*, Cremona 1585.

6. Giovanni Pillinini, *Il sistema degli Stati italiani, 1454–1494*, Venice 1970; Piero Pieri, *Il Rinascimento e la crisi militare italiana* (2nd edn), Turin 1970.

7. On this and what follows: Augusto Vasina, 'La Romagna Estense. Genesi e sviluppo dal medioevo all'età moderna', *Studi Romagnoli*, 21, 1970; Renato LeFevre, 'Il patrimonio cinquecentesco dei Medici nel Lazio e in Abruzzo', *Archivio della Società Romana di Storia Patria*, 98, 1975; Giorgio Chittolini, 'Il particolarismo signorile e feudale in Emilia fra Quattro e Cinquecento', and Letizia Arcangeli, 'Feudatari e duca negli Stati farnesiani, 1545–1587', both in Paolo Rossi (ed.), *Il Rinascimento nelle corti padane*, Bari 1977; Gennaro Incarnato, 'L'evoluzione del possesso feudale in Abruzzo Ultra dal 1500 al 1670', *Archivio storico per le provincie napolitane*, 89, 1972; Alfonso Prandi, 'Il patrimonio fondario dei Pio', in *Società, politica e cultura a Carpi ai tempi di Alberto III Pio* ('Atti Convegno 1978'), Padua 1981.

8. Francesco Guicciardini quoted by Furio Diaz in *Il Granducato di Toscana* ('Storia d'Italia', ed. Giuseppe Galasso, vol. 13), Turin 1976, p. 39.

9. Girolamo Fracastoro in *Della sifilide, ovvero del morbo gallico*, Verona 1530. In general, Cesare Vasoli, 'Temi mistici e profetici alla fine del Quattrocento' in his *Studi sulla cultura del Rinascimento*, Manduria 1968, and Ottavia Niccoli, 'Profezia in piazza. Note sul profetismo popolare nell'Italia del primo Cinquecento', *QS*, 41, 1979, republished in her *Profeti e popolo nell'Italia del Rinascimento*, Rome and Bari 1987. Quoted by Paola Zambelli in her indispensable study, 'Fine del mondo o inizio della propaganda?', in *Scienze, credenze occulte, livelli di cultura* (Istituto Nazionale di Studi sul Rinascimento), Florence 1982.

CHAPTER THREE

Monuments of the High Renaissance

Fortunately, Italy was not just a system of states and families nor just a collection of miscellaneous cities, fields, armies and merchant bankers. It was also – or at least several of its major cities were – the site of what had been for almost a century the epicentre of the most productive and vivacious culture in Christendom. Indeed, the years of the 'calamities' corresponded with the appearance of the great monuments of what is today called the 'High Renaissance' and what then was referred to as the 'Age of Leo x', in deference to the pope who received credit for sponsoring it. When judged from the point of view of the history of culture, rather than from that of the history of politics and war, this age represented not the nadir but the apex of a long historical process. 'If you ask me in what age good letters have most flourished since the fall of the Roman Empire', noted one of the many observers who did judge it in this manner, 'none will appear to be comparable to the one that is now passing.'[1]

One of these monuments falls into a category that today would be called linguistics and philology: the *Prose della volgar lingua*, which the author, Pietro Bembo, presented to Pope Clement VII in 1524.[2] Bembo (1470–1547) was a Venetian patrician who, after a rather unsuccessful career in the papal diplomatic service, settled down in his country house at Villabozza on the Brenta near Padua to enjoy his newly won reputation as the linguistic arbiter of Italy. He had already solved one of the 'language questions' that had been debated ever since the advent of humanism: which of the various forms of Latin revealed in the many newly discovered or edited texts of antiquity should take the place of the medieval Latin that the humanists all agreed on rejecting. He began by posing an axiom: that all great literature is engendered by one of those few languages that, after a long development, reaches a stage of 'perfection'. According to the Romans themselves, the greatest Latin prose was written by Cicero and the greatest Latin verse by Virgil. Whoever, then, in modern times wants to write good Latin should adhere strictly to the vocabulary, style and syntax found in Cicero's and Virgil's surviving works. He should borrow from later Latin writers – including Quintilian, the school-master of the mid-fifteenth century as well as the second century AD – only those words that those writers in turn may have borrowed from now lost works of the great age.

Bembo then turned to the other outstanding language question: the one raised by the Florentine and Ferrarese 'vernacular' poets of the late fifteenth century. He solved this question in the same manner. The greatest vernacular poet, Bembo asserted, was Petrarch, and the greatest vernacular prose writer was Boccaccio – if not in all, at least in some of his tales. Whoever wants to produce works of comparable value in the sixteenth century should there-fore write in the same fourteenth-century Florentine that had been used by Petrarch and Boccaccio and that Bembo, to distinguish it from the many different languages then currently spoken in Italy, called the 'Volgare'. The Volgare was just as 'noble' as Latin because, as Bembo demonstrated in a series of well-documented historical and philological arguments, it was as independent of Latin in its origins as Latin had been of the other 'creative' ancient language, Greek. To demonstrate how effective it could be in those literary genres like love poetry and philosophical dialogues about love for which there was no ancient precedent, he published a revised version of his immensely successful *Asolani* of 1502, and he put together a *canzoniere* of his own original, but impeccably Petrarchan, *rime*. To demonstrate how effective both languages could be in a literary genre that was amply sanctioned by both ancient and modern humanist precedent, he accepted a commission from the Senate to write a history of contemporary Venice; and he then translated his own Ciceronian Latin into equally rigorous Volgare.

Bembo's solutions to the language questions at first met with considerable opposition. Many Latinists feared that freezing classical Latin into a Cicer-onian mould would destroy forever its chances of becoming the living, spoken language of the new universal empire just then being restored by Emperor Charles V. They warned of the danger of letting Christendom break up into as many separate political fragments as there were mutually incomprehensible 'vernaculars'. And they denounced certain 'arrogant men' who, excusing themselves as incapable of Bembo's rigorism, were abandoning altogether a 'fixed language bound by its own rules' for languages which, born of 'barbarian invasions and the ruin of the [ancient] Empire', were by nature inimical to the maintenance of political order.[3] The leading Latinist of Chris-tendom, Erasmus of Rotterdam, poured ridicule upon the 'Ciceronians' in one of his best-selling colloquies; and he did so with such rhetorical force that even Bembo, his main target, continued to respect him. One Italian Erasmian accused the 'Ciceronians' of denying the humanist principle of *imitatio*, which obliged the 'imitator' to elaborate upon his linguistic as well as his literary 'models'. Another complained that had he followed Bembo's rules, he would never have been able to read Poliziano, translate Savonarola, correspond with his Polish friend Nicolaus Copernicus and help his Netherlands friend Erasmus hunt down 'that ferocious bear', Martin Luther.[4] Another, more virulent Erasmian turned against Cicero himself and accused him of resorting to 'cacophony, incoherence and dirty, obsolete, horrid, uncouth and strident words', worthy only of perpetual exile in Scythia. Even those moderate Ciceronians who admitted the authority of Cicero and Virgil in such genres as rhetoric and epic poetry were often willing to admit other ancient authors as linguistic authorities in other genres. If no ancient authorities could be found, they recommended turning instead to 'Erasmus, Budé, Vives' or any of the other modern authors 'who have shown us the road to follow in order to become Latins'.[5] They consequently applauded the fifteenth-century poet Daniele Fini of Ferrara for having plundered all the fifteenth-century humanists in order to discourse, in perfect Horatian stanzas, on such un-Horatian subjects as why lightning produces thunder, why cheeks turn red from embarrassment, why tides change every six hours and why hair does not grow on scarred skin tissue.[6]

Bembo's Volgare aroused even stronger opposition. Some of it came from proponents of those many local vernaculars that were at the time aspiring to the status of written as well as spoken languages. Venetian had long served as the lingua franca of the Venetian dominions in the Adriatic and the Aegean; and it was just then producing, if not works of literature, at least two indispensable historical reference books: the diaries of Girolamo Priuli (1476–1547) and Marino Sanudo (1466–1536). Perugian had long been used in the official records of the commune; and the leading Perugian dramatist, Mario Podiani (1501–1583), who also spoke Latin worthy of the papal court, did not hesitate to give the vocalism of his dialect to Tuscan when writing comedies for the benefit of his fellow citizens.[7] Paduan was commonly spoken in much of the Marca Trevigiana, as the Veneto was then called. In the 1520s it generated one comedy, *Il Reduce*, that Venetians themselves acclaimed as 'the most beautiful play that has been put on in this country in the memory of living men'[8]; and it subsequently produced several others that were found worthy of well-paid performances in Venice and Ferrara as well as in Padua. The author of these comedies, Angelo Beolco (1502?–1542) – better known as Ruzante from the personage he himself represented on the stage – was perfectly conscious of the significance of his choice of language. He was a well-educated humanist, one who took care to base his plays on those of Plautus and Terence and to imitate Virgil in his eclogues. He was also an expert actor and entrepreneur, one who directed a profitable professional company and knew how to charm his audiences by sprinkling his speeches with samplings of the different levels of speech he collected while touring the countryside in search of poignant popular expressions.

Some of the opposition came from proponents of the several local vernaculars that had proven to be sufficiently absorbent of other vernaculars to qualify as regional languages. A 'hybrid, composite . . . formless' variety of Milanese had been refined by contact with Latin and Trecento Tuscan to the point of becoming 'a semi-literary koiné' with 'a measure of regularity' for all of Lombardy. The *Volgar pugliese* adopted for administrative purposes a half-century earlier had since been sufficiently 'laced with Tuscanisms, Latinisms, Hispanicisms and Gallicisms' to serve as a means of communication all over the polyglot Kingdom of Naples.

Indeed, one vernacular was already endowed with such a rich literary heritage that it could seriously contend with the Volgare all over Italy. The Sienese called this language 'Tuscan' and insisted that good literature could be generated only by a living language spoken throughout a wide area like Latium or Tuscany. The philologist and playwright Claudio Tolomei (1492–c. 1555) called upon Italians everywhere to stop wasting time with archaic words and dead languages and learn Tuscan instead. Florentines called this language 'Florentine'; and they turned Tolomei's argument upside down by declaring the metropolis, not the hinterland, Athens, not Attica, to be the generator of great languages and thus great literatures. Such a language, they proclaimed, is one in which structure and regularity are continuous, not static, evolving, not fixed. Without changing its basic nature, Florentine could borrow freely, in the sixteenth as it had in the fourteenth century, from administrative jargon, from plebeian slang, from Latin (*preterire*) and from French (*fauta d'argento*). It could therefore be expanded to accommodate any thought that anyone might ever have about any subject. At the same time, Florentine constantly renewed itself by returning to its literary sources. These sources included not only Bembo's Petrarch and Boccaccio, but also all the 'ancient authors' he relegated to the limbo of precursors; and the Florentine printer Bernardo di Giunta published a ten-book selection of their writings in 1527 as proof that 'this language of ours is not a bit inferior to any other including Greek and Latin'.[9] Hence, living Florentine, which constituted 'the true wellspring and foundation' of all other Italian idioms, should alone be recognized as 'the common language of Italy'. Such was the commitment of Florentines to these arguments that some of them gathered them together in the 1540s in a *Dialogue on Our Language* ('Dialogo della nostra lingua') that was later attributed to the author of the most recent masterpiece of 'Florentine' literature, Niccolò Machiavelli.[10]

Still other alternatives were offered in the form of composite languages in which a Tuscan base was expanded to include many more words and expressions borrowed from all the more developed vernaculars. One such language was currently used in the pan-Italian courts of Rome and Urbino and in diplomatic correspondence all over Italy; it had the further advantage of being advocated by one of the highest ranking diplomats at the time as well as one of the greatest High Renaissance literary figures, Baldassare Castiglione (1478–1529). Another such language was the one used by another High Renaissance literary figure, Gian Giorgio Trissino (1478–1550). Trissino imitated Petrarch to the extent of restricting his poetic vocabulary to only 1,600 different words in 2,126 verses. But he maintained the Latin (*advenire*) and Venetian (*addoprando, dureza*) forms of many of the 25 percent of his words that were not in Petrarch. He justified his preferences by appealing to the recently discovered treatise *De vulgari eloquentia* of Dante. And he sought to render his preferences more accessible to others by adding Greek letters to the Latin alphabet corresponding to its phonetic peculiarities.

There was the low-life jargon, a sort of cipher called *lingua zerga*, the most widely used version of which was based on the Veneto dialect.[11] This language, shared by a restricted group of practitioners, was used in their comic poetry and letters; Bembo's disciple Antonio Brocardo (1500?–1531) compiled a dictionary and a grammar in the 1520s to make it intelligible to the 'uninitiated'. An even more formidable alternative was the Latin-based jargon spoken by the polyglot student body at Padua. One form of this jargon had already been proposed as a literary language in the late fifteenth century by the Paduan Tifo Odasi, who gave it the name *maccheronico*. It was then made into a literary language in the early sixteenth century by the masterful author of several anti-High-Renaissance literary monuments, the Mantuan Benedictine Teofilo Folengo (1491–1544). Macaronic, Folengo found, had ample ancient precedent in the lexical liberties taken by Plautus and the Latin Church Fathers. It had the great advantage over the Volgare of not having any rules at all. It could move up and down the social scale for the benefit alternately of learned professors and illiterate peasants. It could form sentences out of Paduan, Tuscan, Latin, Bergamasco and German and thus be made intelligible to whoever spoke any one or more of those languages. It could be turned upside down in the form of macaronic Tuscan, as it was by Camillo Scrofa of Vicenza (1526?–1565), who ridiculed Bembo's themes as well as his language by putting a homosexual pedant and his adolescent boyfriend in the place of Petrarch and Laura. It could be converted into macaronic French, as it was by one of Folengo's most ardent admirers, François Rabelais, who recreated Folengo's Cingar as Panurge, one of the greatest literary heroes of all times. Above all, it was fun to read, and it was even more fun to write.[12]

The opposition to Bembo's solutions was certainly formidable. But it was no match for the concerted campaign launched immediately on Bembo's behalf. Bembo's credentials as a Latinist were impeccable; and during his student days in Messina he learned Greek, that indispensable corollary of good Latin, well enough to use it in corresponding with the Greek refugee scholars for whom he found jobs in Venice and Padua.[13] His Ciceronian Latin was forthwith adopted in most of the popular dictionaries of his and the following generation – from Mario Nizoli's *Thesaurus Ciceronianus* to Lazzaro Bonanimo's *Concetti per imparare la lingua di Cicero* ('Concepts for Learning the Language of Cicero'). It was adopted as the official language of the Roman Church, which entrusted the wording of all its more important pronouncements to such eminent Bemban Latinists as Jacopo Sadoleto (1477–1547), the author of the bulls of convocation for the Council of Trent. Medieval Latin, on the other hand, was left to the lawyers, whose jargon was meant to be obscure, and to the more obscurantist religious orders, from which no one expected anything better. Departures from a strict Ciceronian vocabulary were permitted only in the case of such marginal literary exercises as the 'medical poetry' of Paolo Dionisi of Verona, which relied on Lucretius' *De rerum natura* as well as Virgil's *Georgics* in order to explain the anatomy of the eyeball in verse.

Similarly, Bembo's Volgare was accepted as early as 1526 in Perugia, at least by one conscientious editor who took care to translate the mid-fifteenth century vernacular poem *La Fenice* before handing it to the printers. It was accepted in Naples in 1527, since it was found to coincide almost exactly with the language extracted from the same Trecento classics by the current dean of the Neapolitan poets, Jacopo Sannazaro (1458?–1530), and since his *Arcadia*, soon to become the model for 'Arcadian' literature all over Europe, was found to coincide thematically with Bembo's *Asolani*. It was accepted by the Florentine poet Francesco Berni (1497?–1535), even though Berni's own bagatelles were often read as polemical antitheses to Bembo's solemn sonnets. For Berni realized that the fifteenth-century Ferrarese poet Matteo Boiardo could be saved from the oblivion to which Bembo condemned all his contemporaries only if his *Orlando innamorato* were translated into one of the two languages which Italians would now deign to read.

The Volgare was also taken up by such linguistic theorists as Girolamo Muzio of Padua (1496–1576), who excoriated the Florentines for saying *mia* instead of *miei, volevi* instead of *volevate, anco* instead of *anche*. When Muzio threatened to remove Machiavelli himself from the bookshelves of Italy, even the Florentines at last succumbed. If isolated from the rest of Italy, they realized, Florentine would inevitably be corrupted by the Florentines themselves, and they would lose forever the rank of linguistic arbiters to which they aspired. They proclaimed the Volgare to be identical with the language spoken not by all, but by educated Florentines. They sacrificed all of their own authors 'who wrote between the times of Dante, Petrarch and Boccaccio and the time of Bembo' and who, 'having ceased to imitate the first three, wrote in a manner deserving of no praise whatever'.[14]

The other languages of Italy did not, of course, disappear. But without the grammars, vocabularies and samplers that soon buttressed the Volgare, they eventually became as unintelligible to their heirs as they were at the time for the 'foreign' compatriots of those who spoke them. When an anthology of Ruzante's comedies toured northern Italy in the winter of 1981–82, it had to be translated into the twentieth-century version of the Volgare.

That one of Bembo's two languages won out over the other as a language of speech as well as of prose and poetry, that Italy eventually became monolingual rather than, as Bembo hoped, bilingual, was due in large part to the adoption of the Volgare by the authors of most of the literary monuments of the High Renaissance. One of these monuments was Ludovico Ariosto's *Orlando furioso*, a long sequence of 'pleasant and delightful feats of arms and love', as the author described it,[15] performed by passionate knights and ladies as they romped back and forth across a fantastic map of three continents and through forty-six cantos of exquisitely balanced eight-line stanzas. Ariosto raised to the level of a literary genre consonant with humanist standards the medieval romances recently imported from France for the amusement, rather than the instruction, of their un-Horatian audiences in Ferrara and Florence. He did so by combining borrowings from such respectable ancient sources as Apuleius, Virgil, Justinus and Valerius Maximus with the basic material provided by the Arthurian and Carolingian cycles. When he revised an earlier version in accordance with Bembo's linguistic prescriptions, and when he omitted six subsequent cantos from the definitive edition of 1532 out of respect for the harmony he had managed to impose on an apparent 'labyrinth', his *Orlando furioso* was hailed as one of the greatest poems of all times. As edition followed edition, it became a source of inspiration not only for scores of other poets, but also for the painters who converted its episodes into fresco cycles and copper engravings.

Whenever Ariosto was not writing romances, and whenever he was not burdened with such ungrateful administrative chores as governing the Garfagnana, he was usually engaged in the frenetic activity of organizing spectacles for the duke, the cardinal or one or another of the court gentlemen at Ferrara. He had already shown in his *La Cassaria* of 1508 that the recently recovered comedies of Plautus, Terence and Aristophanes need not simply be copied as archaeological relics. They could also be used as models, in conformity with the humanist principle of *imitatio*, for comedies pertinent to and reflective of the daily experiences of modern audiences. Between 1528 and 1532 he rewrote his already successful *La Lena, La Cassaria* and *Il Negromante* and supervised construction of the stage sets and production of the musical interludes that made the performances an indispensable part of all public and private celebrations.

What Ariosto did at Ferrara, Niccolò Machiavelli did at Florence.[16] He took situations from the Volgare classic, Boccaccio's *Decameron*, and personages from his observation of current life in Florence, combining them in a typically Plautan plot. He thus sought to impress upon his applauding audiences in Bologna and Florence the lessons about 'corruption' and 'virtue' that were buried in his still unpublished political treatises. And he at least succeeded in pleasing them. The *Mandragola* was provided with musical scores and performed over and over again before and after the first printed edition of 1526[17]; and it remains today the most frequently performed play in Italian literature written before the age of Carlo Goldoni (1707–1793). What Machiavelli did for the Florentines, Pietro Aretino (1492–1556) did for the Romans, whose scurrilous *pasquinate* ('lampoons') provided him with innumerable jibes.[18] By fixing the scene of *La Cortigiana* unmistakably on the streets of Clementine Rome – before the Sack in the first version, after the Sack in the second – he used realistic situations and well-known Roman type-figures to pour ridicule on the pretentious pedants, the whoring priests and the avaricious friars that he then excoriated in his bitterly satirical *Ragionamenti* of 1533.[19] He did the same thing for the Mantuans, weaving a number of apparently disconnected situations created by credibly portrayed personages of the ducal court around the not very important *beffe*, or practical jokes, played by the duke upon his homosexual 'stablemaster' (*Il Marescalco*).

What Ariosto, Machiavelli and Aretino did for comedy, Trissino – the alphabet inventor – did for tragedy. Rather than just translate or paraphrase Sophocles, as the Florentine classicist Giovanni Rucellai (1475–1525) had done in his enthusiasm for the newly recovered texts, Trissino put a story from Livy into a Sophoclean framework. By removing the scene of action as far away in space and time as he could without resorting to no-longer-credible gods, he managed to 'move' his audiences (or at least Pope Leo X, who accepted the dedication) to 'compassion' as effectively as the comedians moved them to laughter – notwithstanding the endless streams of unrhymed hendeca-syllables reinforced by superfluous comments from the chorus that would probably move twentieth-century audiences to sleep. His *Sofonisba* was soon found to be perfectly in accord with the rules Aristotle had extracted from Sophocles. It was performed and republished over and over again for almost a century after the first printed edition of 1524.[20]

Other High Renaissance monuments fell into such well-established hu-manist genres as Ciceronian dialogues, prose treatises and Livian-Thu-cydidean histories. In 1515 Baldassare Castiglione – the proponent of the language of the Italian courts – began writing down what he claimed to recall of conversations that had taken place among the residents and guests of the court of Urbino ten years earlier.[21] In 1520 he revised what he had written on the basis of what he had since observed in travels between Rome and Milan and what he had since read in the humanist ethical treatises of the fifteenth century: those of Leon Battista Alberti, Matteo Palmieri, Giovanni Pontano. In 1527 he revised it once again after getting help from a member of Bembo's circle (Francesco Valier) in weeding out most of the remaining Lombardisms. The *Cortegiano*, or 'Book of the Courtier', thus succeeded in raising to the level of an ethical ideal the *modus vivendi* worked out in practice by all those of his compatriots who hoped someday to replace barbarism with civility and fighting, quarrelling and intransigence with polite, non-committal, in-conclusive, but marvellously pleasant conversations about language, painting, music, principalities, costumes, feminine virtue, Platonic love – and indeed about anything other than war, religion, crime and taxes.

While Castiglione was showing how to escape the calamities, Machiavelli was busy – before returning to his long-interrupted projects as a dramatist – figuring out a way to stop the calamities through political action. Having summed up the lessons of his twelve years of service in the Florentine chancery in the first twenty-five chapters of his first major work, *Il principe* ('The Prince') in 1513, Machiavelli used his enforced leisure to study more method-ically the ancient historians – no longer just Livy, whom he had been anno-tating for years, but also Sallust, Tacitus, Plutarch, Thucydides and above all Polybius. Remembering the humanist precepts about the practical appli-cability of learning and about the fruits to be expected of *imitatio* (and unaware that he would one day be hailed as an anti-humanist), he concluded that what the Spartans and Romans had done in antiquity, Italians, profiting from the ancients' errors, could do even better in the sixteenth century. One single man of extraordinary wisdom, determination and courage (*virtù*), said Machiavelli, should seize the first favourable occasion to destroy all existing political institutions. He should then promulgate a new constitution and invent new gods to back it up. Finally, he should yield his absolute power to an aristocratic senate and a plebeian army. Law would thus replace men as the source of political authority, and the state that emanated from the laws

26

would be invincible and indestructible – just the opposite of all the current states of Italy. Having been totally immunized against the 'corruption' that was the chief cause of the current calamities, the citizens would enjoy forever a perfectly virtuous (*virtuoso*) paradise, interrupted only by an occasional quarrel between the two classes and by an occasional war beyond their own boundaries – a paradise something like the one Machiavelli had read about in the all too short-lived Age of the Antonines.

That Machiavelli's solution was even more utopian than Castiglione's – which, after all, could be and was in fact realized in the many conscious imitations of his idealized court of Urbino that cropped up all over Europe during the following century – bothered no one. It did not bother those of Machiavelli's own close friends who were his first critics – for example, those who insisted instead that all governments were inevitably tyrannical or that ancient examples were irrelevant to the problems of the modern world. Even Machiavelli was willing to compromise after the future Pope Clement declined his offer to assume the role of prince-founder of a new Republic of Florence. In his *Storie fiorentine* ('Florentine Histories') of 1522–25 he sought to show – with almost the same indifference to historical veracity that he had revealed in his specifically historical works – how the most imperfect state of all time could be transformed, not indeed into a perfect mixed *res publica*, but at least into a somewhat less imperfect constitutional monarchy.

What was correctly recognized as the most striking innovation in the *Discorsi* ('Discourses on Titus Livy'), particularly by the Florentine men of letters who gathered in the Rucellai Gardens to hear Machiavelli read chapter after chapter aloud between 1515 and 1517, was the method. The laws of politics, said Machiavelli, could not be deduced from theology or moral philosophy. Rather, they had to be induced from the observation of the relevant phenomena. That, after all, was how modern jurists, artists and physicians, inspired by ancient prototypes and enriched by the accumulated experience of ancient and modern times, had discovered the laws of justice, aesthetics and medicine. If the laws of politics turned out to be irreconcilable with the laws of Christian morality, which they did more often than they fortuitously coincided with them, that was too bad. But it came as no surprise to the politicians of Italy who had long been acting as if the two spheres were wholly unrelated; and Machiavelli wasted no time trying to imagine a primordial Eden of Apostolic or Franciscan Christianity in which Mars and Jehovah, Romulus and Jesus, had lived together in happy harmony. Machiavelli bequeathed to his successors the challenge of trying to put religion and politics, or religious and political ethics, back together. He also dictated to them the literary form in which they were forced to accept his challenge: a close commentary on one historiographical text enriched by a knowledge of many others. Much as they might denounce him, and as often as they might laugh at his anachronistic recommendations concerning fortresses and cannons, they had no choice but to accept the transformation of political philosophy into 'political science' and to support their views on the basis of what had really happened, not on what ought to happen.

Fortunately, Francesco Guicciardini's *Storia d'Italia* ('History of Italy') provided Machiavelli's successors with a substantial body of relevant information concerning the very years of the calamities that most concerned them.[22] Guicciardini had learned to write history in the same way that Machiavelli had learned about politics – that is, by reading earlier historians. He did not, however, establish a new form of literary expression, as Machiavelli was forced to do, when he relegated the ancient political writers to the realm of ethics. Guicciardini wrote first a complete history of Florence and then the first draft of another in accordance with the models perfected by his humanist predecessors since the time of Leonardo Bruni. Later, in the *History of Italy* begun in the early 1530s and finished on the eve of his death in 1540, Guicciardini surpassed his models. By taking as his point of reference all the various events that were causally linked to his point of departure, the invasion of 1494, he managed to encompass in a cohesive narrative all the histories of the different political entities, the myriad personages and the many military campaigns on which works of humanist historiography had been centred. He also followed the humanist historiographical precept of drawing political lessons from the events he recounted, even though his lessons invariably led to the unhappy conclusion that effective political action was no longer possible. He reinforced these lessons by mastering the art of rhetoric in impeccably unified expository prose, in the carefully composed orations he put into the mouths of the 'agents' of historical action and in recasting the Florentine vernacular he normally used in his correspondence into Bembo's Volgare. Finally, he took such care to base his account on archival as well as on narrative sources that it was accepted by subsequent generations as a trustworthy source from which students of politics as well as historians could draw without fear of error.

Thus, during the years of the calamities the writers of Italy produced a number of literary monuments of such quality, when judged by the humanist standards spreading rapidly to the whole of Christendom, that they gave promise of being able to survive the most severe of political and economic crises. So also did the artists: Baldassare Peruzzi with the villa (Farnesina) he built for Agostino Chigi on the banks of the Tiber in 1508–11, Bramante with the circular tempietto he placed in the courtyard of S. Pietro in Montorio in 1502, Raphael in the cycle of frescoes he painted in the Stanza della Segnatura in the Vatican in 1509–11, and Michelangelo Buonarroti with the ceiling of the Sistine Chapel – 'than which', exclaimed the leading art critic of the following generation, 'nothing more excellent has ever or ever can be done'.[23]

High Renaissance art in Rome brought to full realization the potentialities of the aesthetic revolution that had been launched by Brunelleschi, Masaccio and Donatello in Florence in the 1420s and 1430s and that had been codified shortly afterward in Leon Battista Alberti's treatises *On Painting* and *On Architecture*. This revolution consisted in the substitution of ancient, or rather pre-Constantinian, forms, structures, styles and decorative motifs for those previously borrowed from Byzantium, France and Germany; and it was based upon the same principle that was accepted by the writers of the 'imitation' of accepted classical models as the key to creativity. If ancient architects were known — either through the observation of surviving monuments or through the descriptions of them given in the recently discovered textbook by Vitruvius — to have constructed semicircular rather than pointed arches, barrel vaults rather than ribbed vaults, Doric, Ionic and Corinthian capitals rather than capitals with gargoyles and dragons, so should modern architects. But if ancient painters painted as well the fantastic combinations of totally unrealistic human, vegetable and geometric forms that Raphael called *grotteschi* after the *grotte* in which he discovered them, so could modern painters — even though this form of decoration did not correspond with what Pliny had said about all the ancient painting that had since been lost.

The Sack of Rome may have put an end to the Age of Leo x in Rome — or to what was left of it after the interruption imposed by Leo's parsimonious Flemish successor, Adrian vi, and the considerably scaled-down level of patronage imposed by Leo's self-proclaimed follower, Clement vii. But the Sack inadvertently facilitated the continuation of the Age in several other cities of Italy. Michelangelo had been commissioned as early as 1523 to build a funeral monument worthy of Pope Clement's family in Florence[24]; and thanks to the proximity of a stimulating model in the Old Sacristy built in the contiguous basilica of S. Lorenzo by Brunelleschi, the precursor he admired most, the building was finished in two years. He took time off to draw up the plans that Bartolomeo Ammannati (1511–1592) was to carry out for the staircase and reading room of the Laurenziana Library on the opposite side of the basilica, to strengthen the fortifications of the city in anticipation of the siege of 1529–30 and then to leave town in protest against the increasing oppression of the current government. But he soon turned his attention to sculpture; and by the time he left definitively for Rome in 1534, he had finished the idealized, although still recognizable, images of Giuliano and Lorenzo de' Medici (Machiavelli's first two candidates for the role of prince-founder), most of the figures representing *Night, Day, Dawn* and *Dusk* and at least a sketch for one of the four river gods for the New Sacristy. When his disciples finally completed his work, they discovered that two of what Giorgio Vasari (1511–1574) was to categorize as 'fine arts' (*arte di disegno*) — namely, sculpture and architecture — and one of what consequently became a minor or auxiliary 'craft' (*arte*) — floor mosaic — had been brought together in a single aesthetic whole. Each of the parts was admirable in itself alone; but each also contributed to the total impression of classical perfection and timeless melancholy. Michelangelo had clearly surpassed his ancient 'models', the Belvedere torso and the Leda sarcophagus. He had surpassed all the funeral monuments upon which wealthy Florentine families had been staking their public images for almost two centuries. By stretching Giuliano's neck to the limits of natural length, by making the infant Jesus considerably bigger than most nursing infants and by endowing the female figures with almost masculine muscles he had surpassed nature itself. No more had been or could be asked of a Renaissance artist.

What Michelangelo accomplished in sculpture and architecture in Florence, Titian (Tiziano Vecellio, d. 1576) accomplished in painting in Venice. Instead of imitating Raphael's soft-coloured frescoes and Michelangelo's sharply outlined forms – both of which, however, he was well aware of – Titian sought to perfect the new technique of oil on canvas that had recently been imported into Venice from Flanders. He learned to make night emerge from darkness, to use colour as a means of heightened dramatic tension (as in the *Assumption of the Virgin* completed in 1518 for the church of S. Maria Gloriosa dei Frari), to use nature 'in its apparent reality, just as it is revealed to our eyes',[25] rather than 'architecture' (painted buildings) to give an impression of three-dimensional depth, to invite the participation of the viewer with contemporary references (e.g., the text of Adrian Willaert's musical score in the *Bacchus and Ariadne*) rather than a pair of Albertian beckoning eyes. All these lessons culminated in the vast narrative scene of the *Presentation of the Virgin in the Temple* (1534–38) for the Scuola della Carità in Venice (now in the *Accademia*) – a scene in which the symbolic significance is revealed not by the narrative itself, but by a group of recognizable patricians on one side and, on the other, an old woman gazing in the opposite direction (the 'Old Testament'). These lessons also culminated in the portrait of Charles v of 1533 (Madrid: Prado). Titian freed his subject from any dependence upon a *storia* – like the *Adoration of the Magi* in which Benozzo Gozzoli and Botticelli had situated members of the Medici family. He freed the face and body of any overtones of abstraction, and he confined indications of rank, function and station to the margins. He thus made Charles (not 'the emperor') – and all the other privileged clients whom he permitted to sit before him thereafter – into a complete, uncategorizable individual, with his own peculiar physiognomy, psychological makeup, mood and character, just like the historical agents in Guicciardini's *Storia d'Italia*. Fully conscious of the magnitude of his accomplishment, he took advantage of another recently improved mechanical innovation, copper engraving, to broadcast his work to the whole of Italy.

NOTES AND REFERENCES

1. Piero Valeriano in *De litteratorum infelicitate*, quoted by Vincenzo De Caprio, 'Intellettuali e mercato del lavoro nella Roma medicea', *Studi Romani*, 29, 1981, p. 30.
2. On Bembo: the introductions of Mario Marti to his edition of Bembo, *Opere in volgare*, Florence 1961; of Carlo Dionisotti to his edition of Bembo, *Prose e rime*, Turin 1966; and of Daniele Ponchiroli to his anthology, *Lirici del Cinquecento*, Turin 1958. In general, Ettore Bonora, 'Il classicismo dal Bembo al Guarini' in *Storia della letteratura italiana*, Vol. 4: *Il Cinquecento*, ed. Emilio Cecchi and Natalino Sapegno, Milan 1966; Carlo Dionisotti, *Gli umanisti e il volgare fra Quattro e Cinquecento*, Florence 1968; and Nino Borsellino and Marcello Aurigemma, eds, *Il Cinquecento: Dal Rinascimento alla Controriforma*, Bari 1973.
3. Quinto Maria Corrado quoted by Aldo Vallone in *Civiltà meridionale: Studi di*

storia letteraria napoletana, Naples 1978, p. 76. On Romolo Amaseo, one of the most adamant proponents of Latin as a pan-Imperial language, see Giancarlo Mazzacurati's *La questione della lingua dal Bembo all'Accademia Fiorentina*, Naples 1965.

4. On Bartolomeo Ricci's *De imitatione* of 1541–45 and on Celio Calcagnini: G. W. Pigmann III, 'Imitation and the Renaissance sense of the past: The reception of Erasmus' *Ciceronianus*', *Journal of Medieval and Renaissance Studies*, 9, 1979. Calcagnini is quoted here from the article on him by Valerio Marchetti, Augusto De Ferrari and Claudio Mutini in *DBI*, vol. 16 (1973), pp. 492–98.

5. Ortensio Lando in *Cicero relegatus, Cicero revocatus* (1533–34), quoted by Donato Gagliardi in 'Il Ciceronianesimo nel Cinquecento e Ortensio Lando', in *Le parole e le idee*, 3, 1961, p. 19.

6. Pietro Lauro in *Delle lettere*, Venice 1553, vol. 1, p. 108; on whom: Silvio Pasquazi, *Poeti estensi del Rinascimento*, Florence 1966.

7. Francesco Ugolini, *Il perugino Mario Podiani e la sua commedia 'I Megliacci' (1530)*, Perugia 1974.

8. Marino Sanudo quoted in Emilio Lovarini, *Studi sul Ruzzante e la letteratura pavana*, ed. Gianfranco Folena, Padua 1965, p. 81.

9. In his preface to *Sonetti e canzoni di diversi antichi autori toscani*, Florence 1527.

10. Quotations from the *Dialogo* as published in Machiavelli, *Tutte le opere*, ed. Guido Mazzoni and Mario Casella, Florence 1929 (now in offset edition without title page by Giunti Barbèra, Florence). The doubts of Fredi Chiapelli in *Nuovi studi sul linguaggio del Machiavelli*, Florence 1969, and in *Machiavelli e la lingua fiorentina*, Bologna 1974, about the attribution have been substantiated by Sergio Bertelli in 'Egemonia linguistica come egemonia culturale e politica nella Firenze cosmiana', *Bibliothèque d'humanisme et renaissance*, 38, 1976.

11. Franca Ageno, 'A proposito del *nuovo modo de intendere la lingua zerga*', *Giornale storico della letteratura italiana*, 135, 1958, pp. 370–91 and 'Ancora sulla conoscenza del furbesco antico', in *Studi di filologia italiana*, 18, 1960, pp. 79–100.

12. Still fundamental is Ettore Bonora's *Le maccheronee di Teofilo Folengo*, Venice 1956. On *lingua zerga*, macaronic Latin, and other forms of linguistic expressionism, especially in northern Italy, see Ivano Paccagnella, *Il fasto delle lingue. Plurilinguismo letterario nel Cinquecento*, Rome 1984, with references to the standard literature on the subject, including the important contributions of Cesare Segre.

13. P. D. Mastrodimitis, Ἀνέκδοτη ἐπιστολῆς τοῦ Ἀντωνίου Ἐπάρχου Pietro Bembo, Athens 1973–74.

14. Benedetto Varchi quoted by Francesco Bruni in his *Sistemi critici e strutture narrative*, Naples 1969, p. 58.

15. In his letter to the doge of Venice of 7 January 1528, edited on p. 342 of Angelo Stella's edition of the *Lettere*, Milan 1965. The current standard edition of the *Orlando furioso* is that of Lanfranco Caretti, 1963; in English, that of Barbara Reynolds in Penguin Classics (Harmondsworth 1975). On Ariosto and his predecessors see Ernest W. Edwards, *The Orlando Furioso and Its Predecessors*, Cambridge 1924; on the poem and its cultural milieu, John Addington Symonds' *Renaissance in Italy: Italian Literature* (2 vols), New York 1981 is still a useful and very detailed introduction; a good bibliography in English can be found in the notes of A. Bartlett Giamatti's 'Headlong Horses, Headless Horsemen: An Essay in the Chivalric Romances of Pulci, Boiardo and Ariosto', in K. Atchity and G. Rimanelli (eds), *Italian Literature: Roots and Branches: Essays in Honor of*

T. Bergin, New Haven and London 1976, pp. 265–307, and in Vincent Cuccaro, *The Humanism of Ludovico Ariosto: From the 'Satire' to the 'Furioso'*, Ravenna 1981.

16. Luigi Vanossi, 'Situazione e sviluppo del teatro machiavelliano', in his *Lingua e struttura del teatro italiano del Rinascimento*, Padua 1970.

17. For the text: Niccolò Machiavelli, *Mandragola*, ed. Gennaro Sasso and Giorgio Inglese, Biblioteca Universale Rizzoli, 1980; tr. David Sices in the bilingual edition of the *Comedies of Machiavelli*, ed. David Sices and James B. Atkinson, Hanover and London 1985.

18. I follow Giorgio Petrocchi, 'Le Pasquinate dell'Aretino' (1961), in his *I fantasmi di Tancredi*, Caltanissetta 1972. An extensive bibliography through 1976 is in Maria Beatrice Sivolesi's edition of *Sonetti lussuriosi pasquinati*, Rome 1980. See also the massive edition of *Pasquinate romane del Cinquecento*, ed. Valerio Marucci, Antonio Marzo and Angelo Romano, Rome 1983, which should be read with the strictures proposed by Massimo Firpo in his review in *RSI*, 96, 1984, pp. 600–21.

19. The *Ragionamenti* are edited as *Sei giornate* by Guido Davico Bonino, Turin 1975.

20. Trissino's *Sofonisba* is published by Marco Ariani in *Il teatro italiano*, 2: *La tragedia del Cinquecento*, Turin 1977.

21. See Sidney Anglo, 'The courtier: The Renaissance and changing ideals', in *The Courts of Europe: Politics, Patronage and Royalty 1400–1800*, ed. A. G. Dickens, 1977; and Cesare Vasoli, 'Il cortigiano, il diplomatico, il principe', in his *La cultura delle corti (Riflessioni su 'Il libro del cortegiano')*, Bologna and Florence 1980.

22. See my *Historians and Historiography in the Italian Renaissance*, Chicago 1981, and 'L'eredità del Guicciardini: Dalla storia 'nazionale' alle storie 'definitive', in *Francesco Guicciardini, 1483–1983: Nel v centenario della nascita*, Florence 1984.

23. Giorgio Vasari quoted from *Vite*, ed. Guglielmo Della Valle, Siena 1973, vol. 10, p. 82.

24. James Ackerman, *The Architecture of Michelangelo* (rev. edn), London 1970; Leonardo Benevolo in *Storia dell'architettura del Rinascimento*, Bari 1968, pp. 449–53; Frederick Hartt, *Michelangelo: The Complete Sculpture*, New York 1968, esp. p. 172; Howard Hibbard, *Michelangelo* (2nd edn), New York 1987.

25. Quoted by Pietro Zampetti, 'Tiziano e la pittura veneziana' in Galleria nazionale delle Marche, ed., *Tiziano per i duchi di Urbino: Celebrazione del IV centenario della morte di Tiziano: Mostra didattica*, Urbino, 1976. See also Harold Edwin Wethay, *The Paintings of Titian*, New York 1975; Cecil Gould, *Titian as a Portraitist*, London 1976; David Rosand, *Titian*, New York 1978; William Hood, 'The narrative mode in Titian's *Presentation of the Virgin*', in *Studies in Italian Art and Architecture* (Memoirs of the American Academy of Rome, 35), Rome 1980; and Augusto Gentile, *Da Tiziano a Tiziano. Mito e allegoria nella cultura veneziana del Cinquecento*, Milan 1980.

CHAPTER FOUR

A New Political Order

THE IMPERIAL ALLIANCE

Italy in 1527 may have been politically, demographically, economically and psychologically in ruins. Culturally, it had never been stronger. For the first time since the fall of the Roman Empire it possessed a national language, the foundations of a national literature, and an aesthetic standard that had been created by Italians themselves rather than imported from abroad or from the distant past. That the monuments of High Renaissance culture were not still-born, that they were not left simply to be admired by contemporaries abroad and by future generations in Italy and that they became instead 'models' for creative 'imitation' in a dynamic national culture, was the result chiefly of two unforeseen events: a sudden cessation in the seemingly endless chain of calamities, and the gradual, but equally unexpected, creation of a new political order.

The principal agent of peace and the principal architect of the new political order was the Emperor Charles v. Charles was the direct ruler of the Kingdom of Sicily and Naples and the indirect feudal overlord of all the rest of Italy north of the Papal State and west of the dominions of the Venetians. He thus held title to as much territory in Italy as any of his precursors, aspirants to hegemony over all of it – Frederick ii, Carlo and Robert d'Angiò (d'Anjou), Giangaleazzo Visconti. But unlike his precursors, his power base was not confined to Italy. He was the ultimate feudal overlord of all the princes and cities of the Holy Roman Empire, which had recently been endowed with somewhat more effective central judicial and administrative organs. He was the immediate hereditary ruler of the Hapsburg dominions in Germany, most of the former Burgundian dominions in eastern France and the Low Countries, the Kingdom of Aragon with its Mediterranean dependencies and the Kingdom of Castile with its rapidly expanding empire in America. He was also a close ally, through his wife and colleague in government, of her father, the king of Portugal and head of the other rapidly expanding overseas empire. He thus held title to a greater part of the lands of Christendom than any of his Imperial predecesors since the time of Charlemagne; and he could bring to bear on the Italian parts of his vast domain the authority he derived from all of it. He could at last enforce the Imperial feudal rights in northern Italy that had been all but forgotten since the mid-thirteenth century; and he could at last settle the dynastic question that had been used to justify rebellion in Naples ever since the mid-fourteenth century.[1]

That Charles was not an Italian by birth made very little difference in a country long accustomed to absorb, and to submit to, Angevins, Valois, Aragonese and Borgias. Charles learned to speak Italian as rapidly as he had all the other major languages (except German) of his far-flung empire, and he invariably used it – rather than Castilian, the language of his correspondence – whenever he wanted Italians to understand clearly his replies to their petitions, and when he was not annoyed with them. He was also the beneficiary of the medieval ideal of a universal Christian monarchy – an ideal that blended nostalgic reminiscences of Caesar, Augustus, Trajan and Constantine with a Pauline, or Eusebian, concept of a *Corpus Christianorum*. This ideal had survived the attacks of the Florentine civic humanists and of the Venetian propagandists; and it was just then being refitted in Erasmian humanist garb by the emperor's chief counsellors, the Piedmontese Mercurino di Gattinara and the Spaniard Alonso de Valdés. The humiliation of the papacy in 1527 then transferred to Charles most of what was left of the pope's prestige as a colleague in, or a rival for, the post of 'head' of the 'body'. And Pope Clement quietly acquiesced in his new role as a purely spiritual 'father' of a 'faith' of which Charles was the 'foundation'.[2]

According to Charles himself, the chief aim of the universal Christian monarchy was the promotion of 'peace among Christians and war against the infidels'.[3] In the fall of 1529 Charles took a first step toward realizing the first aim. He persuaded King Francis to admit as irreversible the results of the disasters of Pavia and Naples and to limit his intervention in Italy to what could be attained by diplomatic means alone. In eulogy after eulogy, Charles was proclaimed to be the incarnation of the virtues and the staunch opponent of the vices manifested by the heroes of antiquity. He was compared favourably with Justinian – by none other than the tragedian Trissino – for having 'corrected the abuses . . . of the laws of the Christian religion' and for having 'brought peace to Italy and freed it of wars'.[4] The citizens of Lecce erected an enormous arch in anticipation of his visit, featuring a double-headed eagle and a two-metre-high shield with all his coats of arms. The citizens of Milan professed themselves to have been 'in all times past totally devoted to the Holy Roman Empire'.[5] On the morning of the siege of Florence, the poet Mambrino Roseo da Fabriano celebrated in long heroic stanzas the 'concord' that had suddenly put an end to 'so much sedition', and he hailed the 'praiseworthy accord' between pope and emperor as assurance that 'this tranquil state will last forever'. On 22 April 1531 three suns appeared in the sky over Modena, the same three suns that, according to a local chronicler, had heralded the advent of 'universal peace . . . in the time of the Emperor Octavian'.[6]

The foundation of the new Italian political order was laid at Bologna between November 1529 and February 1530, when 'many princes and principal persons' and the rulers or representatives of the big and minuscule states 'of all Italy' gathered to behold 'the greatest and the best court that has ever been assembled in any part of the world'.[7] Amid the almost interminable round of balls, processions and hunting parties culminating in his well-staged coronation in early February, Charles took time to settle the outstanding differences among the participants. In exchange for recognizing his supremacy in temporal affairs and the value of his advice in spiritual affairs – and in exchange for accepting the much more expedient explanation of the Sack as the work of insubordinate lieutenants – Charles pledged Pope Clement his continued support in the enterprise he knew to be closest to the pope's heart, the siege of Florence. In exchange for the duke of Ferrara's abandonment of his family's traditional Gallophile foreign policy, despite his recent marriage to a French princess, Charles recognized his reconquest of Modena and Reggio and confirmed his annexation of Carpi. He persuaded the Venetians to give up their cities in Puglia and to return Ravenna and Cervia to the pope – who was thus compensated for the loss of his land corridor to Parma. In return, he made the pope recognize the restoration of the Venetians' protégé, Francesco Maria Della Rovere, as duke of Urbino; he gave Milan back to their erstwhile ally, Francesco II Sforza, whose act of penance at Bologna brought tears to the eyes of all the connoisseurs of humanist rhetoric; and he promised support in the defence of the remaining Venetian possessions in the Aegean. He rewarded his new ally Duke Carlo II of Savoy with the city of Asti, which he had recently conquered. And he distributed privileges, jobs, titles and favours to all the scores of petitioners who were willing to pay for them.

The new political order rested primarily on the authority of the emperor himself. Charles returned to Italy in the winter of 1533–34 to reward the loyal general, the marchese of Mantua, with the title of duke and to summon the states of Italy to another meeting at Bologna – this time for the purpose of redrafting the arrangements of the previous meeting in the form of a solemn alliance. He returned once again in 1535–36, with his prestige still further enhanced by his recent victory in Tunisia, to check on the defence of Sicily, to hear the complaints of the opponents of the current regimes in Naples and Florence, to test the loyalty of the new pope (1534), Paul III, and to summon the support of the new alliance for the most recent round in his by now endemic wars with the king of France. Between visits, he continued to exercise his authority from afar. He received petitioners and counter-petitioners in Augsburg, Brussels or Valladolid, confident that as long as they were petitioning they would not resort to violence. He let an unruly vassal of the duke of Savoy carry an appeal against his lord all the way to the Imperial Council of Vienna, thus being assured of the fidelity both of the vassal, who had no other hope, and of the duke, who preferred to make good his rights as a prince of the Holy Roman Empire rather than insist upon his legal rights as a court of final appeal.

Most of these measures were reflections of the one principle of government Charles adhered to rather scrupulously: never to 'occupy' anything that was not his by right of inheritance, as he explained to the relieved Venetians as he passed through their territory in 1532,[8] or at least never to use anything that might accidently be occupied for him (as he was careful not to explain to them) except for what immediate financial or diplomatic profit he might exact from it. He relinquished the Tuscan fortresses that had been seized in his name as soon as the staunchly loyal Duke Cosimo came up with an irresistible donation. Instead of keeping Milan after it fell to him by devolution upon the death of the last Sforza duke in 1535, he left it dangling before the concupiscent – and therefore tractable – eyes of various candidates for over ten years before at last giving the investiture, to the consolation of the Milanese, to his son Philip.

Charles left the formulation of policy and the statement of principles to his lieutenants, never 'considering any of the implications' of the policies they adopted and never 'producing any system of priorities' by which those policies might be implemented.[9] It was therefore not he who directly ruled Italy, but rather his lieutenants: his ambassadors in Venice, Rome, Florence and Genoa, his generals – who after 1535 were also his governors – in Milan, his viceroys in Naples and Palermo. Since he all but assured his lieutenants of life tenure after he appointed them, they were free not only to formulate, but also to carry out policy – even at the risk of occasionally coming into conflict with their colleagues and even at the greater risk of adopting policies reflective of the interests of the people they ruled rather than of the emperor in whose name they ruled. Pedro Alvarez de Toledo (1532–1553), marqués de Villafranca, whose accent in Italian betrayed the homeland he left in his youth and never saw again, took a Neapolitan mistress, to the delight of the Neapolitans, as soon as his Spanish wife died. The melodramatic Alfonso d'Avalos, marchese del Vasto, 'the most handsome man in the world', who once pawned his wife's jewels to pay his master's debts in an anachronistic display of chivalric fidelity, let himself be persuaded by the Milanese Senate to use Imperial troops in order to 'make subject to their obedience as they had been in the past' the rebellious city of Vercelli and the former Milanese dependencies in the Lunigiana.[10] Ferrante Gonzaga, the Italian general 'of an extraordinarily ferocious spirit',[11] who once urged Charles to conquer the rest of Italy and rule it with Spanish functionaries, took the protests of his overtaxed Sicilian subjects with him when he went to report to the emperor in Brussels. After he succeeded Del Vasto as governor of Milan, he decided that the borders of the duchy in his day ought to correspond to the borders established by one or another of the Visconti; and he was willing to upset the whole Imperial alliance in order to pursue his often violent intrigues in Genoa, Piacenza and the Valtellina.

The Imperial lieutenants, however, could exercise direct authority only in the domains the emperor 'occupied'. For the rest of Italy they depended upon the cooperation of the rulers of those states which still retained as great a degree of independence as could be expected of small and middle-sized members of a multi-state polity dominated by two or three much larger powers. Some of these rulers were the descendants of ancestors who had long since transformed themselves from *signori* (lords) into dynastic monarchs and by now had freed themselves of competition from either rival candidates for the *signoria* or jealous brothers and cousins. Duke Federico Gonzaga of Mantua, the cousin of the governor Ferrante and a professional general, enriched his small duchy with the profits he had made in the service of one or another of the contending powers during the calamities. Ercole II and his successor Alfonso II d'Este ruled Ferrara, which was still legally a feudal dependency of the Papacy. Carlo II fell heir to the amoeba-shaped Savoyard dominions that stretched across the Alps from the Saône on the west to the Po on the east, from Lausanne on the north to Nice on the Mediterranean. Others of these rulers were oligarchs that had succeeded in blocking or reversing in their own domains the evolution common to most late medieval Italian cities from oligarchy to monarchy. Such were the members of the various *monti* at Siena, the political and economic factions that had dominated the others at one or another time in the past and that had united to overthrow the *signoria* of the Petrucci in 1521. Such also were the landowners and manufacturers of Lucca, who had rid themselves of one last aspirant to the *signoria* in 1524 and who in 1531 put down a still more dangerous revolt of the silkworkers, the *straccioni*, upon whom the prosperity of the industrial city depended.

The pope and the Venetian Senate, the two powers with extensive extra-Italian commitments, were less dependable allies. Outside the Papal State, which extended from the Neapolitan frontier on the south and east to Bologna on the north, the pope was temporal sovereign of the enclaves of Benevento north of Naples and Avignon on the Rhône. But he was also the spiritual head of all those parts of Latin Christendom that had not seceded with the Protestants. What he did in Italy or in his pan-European relations with the emperor was often conditioned by his attempts to pursue what he considered to be the good of all Catholic Christianity. Outside the *terraferma* dominions, which extended from Istria and Friuli on the east to Brescia and the enclave of Crema on the west, the Venetian Senate was ruler of Dalmatia, the Ionian Islands, Crete, Cyprus, and occasionally a scrap of the Greek mainland; and it depended for the preservation of this thalassocracy upon maintaining viable relations with the Ottoman Turks, who, whatever the emperor might think about their religious commitments and their territorial ambitions, were among the Venetians' best commercial customers.

Far more dependable, on the other hand, were the two rulers who had just recently triumphed over rival claimants to the *signoria* in their respective oligarchical republics and who needed the emperor's support in consolidating their positions: Andrea Doria in Genoa and Cosimo de' Medici in Florence. In 1528 Andrea made use of the prestige and power he enjoyed as owner of the largest fleet in Imperial service to 'liberate' his native city from the alternating regimes of the domestic protégés of the emperor or the king of France, and made himself the guarantor and arbiter of the oligarchical regime he had put into power. In 1537 Cosimo was elected, at the age of seventeen, to be 'head of the Florentine Republic' after the assassination of Pope Clement's nephew and his own distant cousin, Duke Alessandro.[12] After sending into retirement the 'counsellors' appointed to supervise him, and after destroying the army of irreconcilable exiles sent across the Apennines to depose him, he was officially recognized as 'duke of Florence' in his own right and the most *devoto y aficionado* of all the emperor's Italian allies.

The preservation of the alliance still required the presence of an armed force – namely, the Imperial army that was permanently stationed in Lombardy and the detachments of Spanish troops stationed in Siena, Naples and Sicily. As the generals and viceroys succeeded in putting a stop to periodic mutinies (the last serious one took place in Sicily in 1535), in mercilessly punishing all acts of violence against civilians and in taking full and much publicized credit for both, hostility toward the soldiers rapidly diminished. Their presence in Italy came to be regarded as an indispensable deterrent against another French or Turkish invasion. But far more important for the preservation of the alliance was the growing recognition among all the members that 'the defence of Italy', 'the good of Christianity' and 'the conservation of the lands' could be achieved only by peaceful collaboration.[13] In practice, this rule of behaviour meant settling internal differences by negotiation or by law rather than by force, even when legality was determined by the complicated marital gymnastics that enabled Federico Gonzaga to double the size of his domain by marrying the last heir of the Paleologo family of Monferrato. The rule also meant giving up the century-old expansionist aims of all the larger Italian states and accepting as definitive the *status quo* of 1530. Once they had restored their frontier on the Adda and recovered Rovigo in the Polesine, the Venetians declared themselves satisfied; and their publicists were charged with changing their 'image' from one of prospective *signori* to one of the guardians of the 'liberty' of Italy. Similarly, Duke Cosimo rejected the 'image' inherited from the Albizzi and Savonarola of Florence as the *ombelico d'Italia*. He declined to intervene in Lucca, which so many of his predecessors had tried to conquer, as soon as he was assured that it would not engender any more dreamy Brutuses like the short-lived Francesco Burlamacchi. He gave up trying to buy the minuscule Appiani state at Piombino when he was assured that the Turks would not land there. He put off intervening in Siena until he realized that it was becoming a French-protected haven for die-hard Florentine rebels. And he turned Pitigliano back to the Orsini, after a promise of good behaviour, instead of accepting the city council's request that he annex it.

Far, then, from being a 'foreign' or a 'Spanish' dominion imposed upon Italians against their will, the new political order rested upon a voluntary alliance among members of various sizes and degrees of external autonomy. It differed from the previous pan-Italian alliance of Lodi chiefly by recognizing the emperor as ultimate arbiter of internal differences and by extending to the whole of what had traditionally been called the 'province' of Italy. The main institution of this alliance was a refined version of the corps of resident ambassadors (or nuncios in the case of the papacy) that now included the ambassadors of Siena and Lucca at Florence and those of all the cities in the Papal State at the papal court. This corps was reinforced by the extension even to small states of another fifteenth-century Italian institution: the one by which all ruling families (in the case of oligarchies, one family designated by the oligarchy) were assured of a place in the College of Cardinals, and hence a voice in the election of popes, the distribution of ecclesiastical benefices and the determination of general papal policy. The Este were represented by Cardinals Ippolito I and II; the Gonzaga by the duke's brother and bishop of Mantua, Cardinal Ercole; Pedro de Toledo by his brother Cardinal Juan Alvarez, one of Michelangelo's protectors; and Duke Cosimo – as soon as he was rid of such hostile survivors of the former oligarchy as Cardinal Niccolò Ridolfi and his maternal uncle Cardinal Francesco Salviati – by his son Cardinal Ferdinando and his distant cousin Cardinal Alessandro de' Medici. Both ambassadors and cardinals were reinforced by an institution that had first been introduced from northern Europe, with limited success, in the age of Gian-galeazzo Sforza and Lorenzo de' Medici: marriage alliances. Charles' cousin was married to Francesco II Sforza. His sister-in-law was married to Carlo of Savoy. His illegitimate daughter was married first to Duke Alessandro de' Medici and then to Pope Paul III's grandson Ottavio – whence the name by which she was later known in her heroically unpleasant life as governor of the Netherlands, Margherita of Parma. Similarly, Pedro de Toledo's daughter was married to Duke Cosimo and his son to the daughter of Ascanio Colonna, and Eleonora Gonzaga of Mantua was married to Francesco Maria Della Rovere of Urbino.

During the first thirty years of its existence, this alliance underwent a series of increasingly severe crises. In 1536 King Francis suddenly seized all the transalpine and half the cisalpine dominions of Duke Carlo; and when a counter-invasion of Provence failed to dislodge him, Carlo was forced, even at the cost of belying one of the principle aims of the alliance, to acquiesce in the subsequent annexation of the occupied territories, with French-style *parlements* at Turin and Chambéry. In 1540 the citizens of Perugia declared themselves to be 'willing to endure every great injury' rather than pay Pope Paul's new salt tax, just at the moment when Cosimo declared himself to be willing to endure an interdict rather than let Pope Paul tax the Florentine church. Only the passivity of the other papal cities and diplomatic pressure on the part of Cosimo's father-in-law at Naples prevented the outbreak of war between two of the principal allies. In January 1547 Gian Luigi Fieschi, the head of one of the four big families of Genoa, sent the henchmen he had brought in from his Apennine 'state' screaming 'popolo et libertà' through the streets in an effort to overthrow the Doria regime. In May 1547 the nobles and citizens of Naples suddenly stopped quarrelling among themselves in order to block Toledo's attempt to substitute a Spanish for a Roman inqui-sition; and so successful were they in bottling up Toledo's Spanish soldiers in the castle that he is said to have exclaimed: 'Let's go enjoy ourselves; for I am viceroy no longer and can do nothing!'[14] In September 1547 a band of disgruntled feudatories murdered Pier Luigi Farnese, the ruler of the new duchy Pope Paul III had created for him at Parma and Piacenza. Encouraged by the emperor's recent victory over the Protestant states at Mühlberg,

Governor Ferrante Gonzaga occupied Piacenza, forcing Pier Luigi's son Ottavio to turn for help to the French in Piedmont and provoking a three-way war with Pope Paul's anti-Farnese successor that soon 'scorched the earth' all around Mirandola and Parma.

A graver crisis was precipitated in 1552, when the citizens of Siena, alarmed by the news that the fortress under construction along their walls was to be billed to their already overdrawn treasury, expelled the Imperial garrison and invited in a French garrison to make sure it did not come back. The crisis deepened the next year, when a French expeditionary force, responding to an appeal from the local rebel, Sampiero della Bastelica, seized Ajaccio and Bastia in Corsica and threatened to remove the whole island from the jurisdiction of the Genoese Banco di San Giorgio, to whom the Corsicans themselves had submitted in 1453 and 1485. With his troops suddenly advancing into the very heart of Italy, the king of France informed the anti-Medici colony in Rome that 'having liberated Siena', he was prepared 'to do the same in Florence, restoring it to its former status and government'.[15] As the Florentine exiles raised money in Venice and Lyon, the new pope, Paul IV, decided that the great days of family 'state-getting' had suddenly returned. Since the last available 'state' had been 'gotten' by the Farnese, his own Carafa family was forced to turn to their homeland, the Kingdom of Naples. And since the Kingdom happened to be 'occupied' by the emperor's heir, King Philip II of Spain, he concluded an offensive alliance with the king of France for the purpose of partitioning it between himself as pope, his nephews as secular rulers and one of the king's sons. Toledo's successor as viceroy, the duke of Alba (later conqueror of the Low Countries), thereupon marched into Rome; and instead of letting his troops repeat the gesture, in almost identical circumstances, of their predecessors of 1527, he graciously asked the pope's pardon for undoing the master plan that had been directed principally against him.

Grave as these crises were, the alliance managed to survive them. Cosimo eventually compromised on the tax issue; and in 1549 he procured the election of a new pope, Julius III, who was as favourably disposed toward him as Paul III had been hostile. The Fieschi estates in Liguria were confiscated. Sampiero was killed in an ambush five years after the final withdrawal of the French in 1559, and two years later his son was persuaded to go into permanent exile. The Farnese domains in the Papal State were restored and Piacenza was reunited with the duchy of Parma. Toledo withdrew the inquisition decree and directed his wrath solely at the ambassadors the Neapolitans had sent to the Imperial court; and they wisely decided to remain abroad until after his death. The pro-Carafa barons realized that 'throwing the Spanish out of Italy' could be accomplished only by submitting to 'the terrible and arrogant government of the French',[16] and they left Paul IV to devour his nephews, Saturn-like, blaming them for all his errors. After a year-long siege, the Sienese surrendered. Their 'state' was divided between Philip II, who kept the ports in Monte Argentario and Talamone, and Cosimo, who kept the rest. What one sixteenth-century observer called 'a mishmash (*guazzabuglio*) and confusion of republics' became a 'well-ordered and well-organized' regional state.[17] The joint states of Florence and Siena were elevated to the rank of the Grand Duchy of Tuscany by decree of Pope Pius v in 1569.

A major aim of the alliance, removal of French forces in the peninsula, was suddenly attained in 1559. After having lost still another army at the Battle of Saint-Quentin, King Henry II agreed to withdraw from Savoy and Bresse; and by the Treaty of Cateau-Cambrésis – the most important landmark in Italian history since 1530 – he formally put an end to the forty-year war against Habsburg encirclement and to two and a half centuries of intervention in Italy. The corollary of this aim was almost attained: keeping out the Turks, the ally of the French on the Mediterranean. The price of this attainment was the abandonment of the dreams of the previous kings of Naples to reconquer the whole of the former Byzantine Empire. After a Neapolitan–Spanish army was obliged to evacuate the provinces in the Peloponnesus it had occupied in 1532, and after the Venetians were obliged to abandon their outpost at Navpaktos (Lepanto), Toledo became markedly less receptive to the assurances brought him by the usual stream of Greek refugees that the Orthodox bishops of Mani and Epirus were ready to rouse the whole population the moment he returned.[18] But abandoning an offensive policy merely increased the effectiveness of a defensive policy. As Andrea Doria kept the Genoese–Neapolitan–Spanish fleet hovering around the Straits of Messina, and as the Venetian fleet guarded the approaches to the Adriatic, the Genoese began erecting a string of fortresses all along the coast that bordered on the Turkish sea route to Toulon. In order to protect his point of greatest exposure to the same sea route, Cosimo reproduced at Porto Ferrato on Elba the revolutionary cannon-proof Fortezza da Basso designed by Antonio da Sangallo in 1554. Similarly, the Venetians blocked both the passes in Friuli through which Turkish armies had passed twice before and the routes of former invasions from Germany with similar fortifications at Brescia, Peschiera and Verona.

As military architecture was raised to the rank of an exact science and expounded in such manuals as Girolamo Cattaneo's 'Euclidian' *Opera nuova di fortificare* of 1564,[19] the new bastions, with their star-shaped projections into a surrounding moat, became increasingly impossible even to approach, much less to take. Although they were more expensive to build than the tall pre-artillery crenelated walls of late medieval towns, they were less expensive to operate. Ferrante Gonzaga brought in the military architect Antonio Ferramolino from Brescia to ring Sicily with them in the 1540s, making Palermo completely 'inexpugnable' by 1546. The Turks still managed occasionally to raid an isolated town along the Tyrrhenian coast, and in 1553 they even captured the city of Bonifacio in Corsica. But after two abortive, if strenuous, attempts to get past the bastion built with Ferrante's help on Malta, they gave up their grandiose plans for erecting a Muslim version of the empires of Augustus or Justinian in the western Mediterranean. By 1558 many Italians felt free enough of imminent danger to think seriously about imitating the Venetians in their decision of 1540 to withdraw from Charles' anti-Ottoman crusade; and a Florentine ambassador, bearing samples of Florentine manufactured goods, was received with 'clear expressions of good will' at Constantinople.[20]

THE ITALIAN STATES

At the same time, the second aim of the alliance, that of internal peace, was realized at least to the extent of permitting a revival of whatever constructive political forces had survived the calamities. Remarkably enough, some had indeed survived. While admitting that their incurable sins were the cause of the 'so many and such manifestly great calamities' they had suffered in the past, members of the Senate of Genoa declared themselves prepared, in April 1526, 'to make one more try in providing for our difficulties', in the remote hope that 'guided by divine favour' they might somehow defend themselves against even more 'unbearable calamities in the future'. In 1534 the *Reggimento* of Bologna declared itself still sufficiently confident in the ability of the Papal State to 'preserve quiet and security' that they themselves took the initiative in preventing a repetition after the death of Clement VII of what had happened after his imprisonment in 1527; and to Guicciardini's amazement their initiative was immediately 'approved with every expression of good intentions and [concrete] offers of assistance . . . by all the other gentlemen [of the city]'.[21] The citizens of other subject cities recognized that what remained of the territorial states was still preferable to the only alternative, chaos.

Encouraged by such expressions of confidence – and by the well-publicized success of the Venetians in rebuilding their territorial state within fifteen years of its almost total destruction – the rulers of the Italian states set out to pick up the pieces. Unfortunately, they received very little help from those who proclaimed themselves to be the most authorized to give it: the heirs of the humanist political philosophers of the fifteenth century. For the sixteenth-century political philosophers continued to concern themselves with only three modern states: Venice, Florence and, after 1552, Siena. Moreover, after the death of Machiavelli they split into three irreconcilable camps. There were the idealists, like the Florentines Donato Giannotti (1492–1573), Bartolomeo Cavalcanti (1503–62) and Antonio Brucioli (c. 1498–1566), who were so busy inventing perfect republics that they forgot about the notoriously imperfect versions of Castiglione's 'court' most of them inhabited. There were the realists, like Francesco Vettori (1474–1539), Lodovico Alamanni (1488–1526) and even Guicciardini in his later famous *Ricordi*, which declared the traditional slogan 'liberty' to be merely a screen for the 'ambition and utility' of those interested in 'nothing but money'.[22] Finally, there were the apologists, like Gasparo Contarini (1483–1542), Filippo de' Nerli (1485–1556) and Tommaso Diplovatazio (1468–1541), who declared all the noblest aspirations of the Greek philosophers and the Hebrew prophets to have been fully realized in one or another perfect *polis* or New Jerusalem of which they happened to be citizens. These theses often seemed to be subversive of the order the rulers were desperately trying to establish. The Florentine government therefore banned the century-old pastime of constitution drafting; and after holding up the publication of Contarini's apology until 1543, the Venetian government prohibited even private discussions of politics. Political philosophy in the Brunian–Albertian tradition went into exile, still further removed from contact with the political reality to which it was supposedly directed, and ever less protected against the temptations of Utopia.

Bereft of help from the theorists, the rulers of the Italian states fell back on platitudes about the 'prudence, magnificence and incredible felicity' of Augustus, that archetype of a prince who extracted order from chaos.[23] They mixed maxims from Bruni and Alberti with maxims from Erasmus, whose *Enchiridion* the Genoese humanist-partician Lodovico Spinola held to be a complete guidebook of political behaviour. They redefined the traditional catchword 'liberty' to mean a condition in which 'the laws and public order prevail over the appetites of single men' and in which 'all subjects are treated equally'. They redefined 'justice' to mean that 'the ordinances, both criminal and civil, [should] be regarded as sacrosanct and [should] be strictly observed . . . without regard to quality of persons'.[24] As formal treatises gave way to informal letters and occasional orations as the normal vehicle for the expression of these concepts, the purpose of government came to be defined in such a way that it could be applied either to a 'republic', like the one of which the Genoese orator Lorenzo Cappelloni was a participating member, or to a 'principate', like the one ruled by the object of his eulogy, Prince Philip of Spain – and of Milan, Naples and Sicily. A good government, said Cappelloni, is one in which 'a prince or lord . . . governs in such a way that the weak are not oppressed by the strong, the timid are not offended by the proud, the lesser are not taxed more than the greater and everyone is left to enjoy in peace and security the higher or lower fortune God has given him'.[25] And since all of his colleagues were 'republicans' simply because they could not stand the thought of any one of them becoming a 'prince' – rather than for the ideological reasons attributed to other sixteenth-century oligarchs four centuries later – not one of them objected to his blurring the distinction between two theoretically antithetical forms of government.

Most rulers identified as the chief shortcoming of all preceding regimes the suspicion of illegitimacy. Almost all of them took pains to legitimize their regimes with new or revised constitutions drawn up with the help of committees of experts[26] – the Genoese constitution of 1528 revised in 1547 and 1576, the Venetian constitutional statutes of 1528–29, the judicial and commercial decrees of Lucca of 1532, the constitution of the Florentine Principate of 1532, the *Novae constitutiones* of Milan of 1541, the statutes *De civibus* and *De officiis sindicorum* (1528) and the *Constitutiones excelsae superioritatis Tridentini* of the prince-bishop Cristoforo Madruzzo of Trent in the 1540s, the thirty-five articles of the Kingdom of Naples approved by Charles v and explained in Giulio Cesare Caracciolo's *Discorso sopra il Regno di Napoli* in

1554, the *Decreta* adopted by the estates of Savoy and Piedmont after the restoration of the duchy in 1568. So carefully, indeed, were these constitutions drawn up that most of them lasted, with very few changes, until the reforms of the late eighteenth century.

These constitutions differed from one another in where they located the official or symbolic centre of political authority – whether in a lifetime doge and a Council of Ten (*Dieci*) as in Venice, in a duke and his 'four counsellors' as in Florence, in a two-year elected doge with a 'regal' bodyguard of 500 German soldiers as in Genoa, or in a single Council of Elders (*Anziani*) as in Lucca. Nevertheless, they all provided for one or more intermediate bodies of varying composition and degrees of authority between the source and the object of political power. The Council of Forty-Eight and the Council of Two Hundred in Florence became largely honorary shadows of the Savonarolan Great Council after 1537. Much ordinary administration was still carried on even by such anachronisms among the traditional elected magistracies as the *Parte Guelfa* and the *Ufficiali dell'Onestà*. The *Collegio dei Governatori*, the *Minor Consiglio*, the *Maggior Consiglio*, the *Supremi Sindicatori* and the *Collegio dei Procuratori* at Genoa were balanced against one another by an almost unfathomable system of multiple elections, and all of them were limited in fiscal and financial matters by the wholly autonomous Banco di San Giorgio, which controlled the public debt. In Milan, the governor appointed by the absent emperor-duke shared political power almost equally with a self-perpetuating Senate, inherited from the time of Louis XII and confirmed by Philip II, and with two councils, one of the Sixty *Decurioni* and the other of the *Giurisconsulti*, inherited from the time of the Visconti; and so even was this *de facto* as well as *de iure* division of powers that the regime has been accurately described as a 'diarchy' or a 'monarchy tempered by aristocracy'. Even at Ferrara, the duke delegated some of the all but absolute power acquired over a century of interrupted rule to a *Consilium Domini*, a *Iudices Curie* and a *Consiglio Segreto*. And in the Savoy dominions the duke constantly had to negotiate with two traditional 'sedentary' councils in Chambéry and Turin and one mobile council *cum domino residens*.

Two of the most powerful of these intermediate bodies were the *Parlamento*, representing the barons and the demesne cities of the kingdom, and the *Seggi* (or *Sedili*) of one 'popular' and five 'noble' *eletti*, representing the city of Naples. Both of these bodies remained 'dynamically operative' throughout the century. They did not hesitate to appeal, in moments of constitutional conflict with the viceroy, directly to the king-emperor, who scrupulously 'respected the autonomy of the kingdom and the attributes of its institutions'.[27] Even more powerful was the three-house *Parlamento* of Sicily, partly because the Sicilians could always remind the king that his power was limited to what they had voluntarily bestowed upon his ancestors after the Vespers of 1282 (when they killed the entire French army of occupation in a single night), partly because a permanent committee of the *Parlamento* continued to sit between one almost annual session and the next. 'The Sicilians act with unbearable temerity in everything that concerns the management of public business', one viceroy warned his successor in 1577.[28] They soon learned even to undercut the extra power the viceroy enjoyed by virtue of the rights of papal legate in the Sicilian church, concerning which recently discovered historical documents were put together between 1547 and 1557 in a *Liber Regiae Monarchiae* by the viceroy Juan de Vega, to the lasting annoyance of the papacy. All they had to do was play off the viceroy and the bishops he appointed against the Inquisition, which, being organized on a Spanish rather than on a Roman model, was independent of both.

In order to assure the efficient functioning of these constitutional bodies and to avoid conflicts among them, most of the rulers relied on another traditional institution, that of the notary-chancellors of the fourteenth century and of the humanist secretaries of the fifteenth; and they remodelled this institution in accordance with job descriptions similar to the one prescribed by the duke of Mantua: that applicants be men of learning and integrity who had received a doctor's degree at least ten years earlier and had been occupied with the discipline of law since then. Unlike the occupants of the constitutional bodies, these *auditori*, as they were often called, did not have to be nobles or citizens of a dominant city. Some of them were indeed patricians, like Cassiano del Pozzo, who drew up the blueprint for the reconstruction of Savoy-Piedmont after the restoration; and increasing numbers of patricians began enrolling in the law faculties for the express purpose of qualifying for state appointments outside the magistracies reserved for their fathers. However, most of the *auditori* were citizens of subject or even 'foreign' cities. Many of them were men of modest or even humble origin, for whom civil service provided a means of social advancement – men like Francesco Campana, who retired to the palace he built in his native Colle Valdelsa with the bundle of ecclesiastical benefices accumulated during a lifetime of hard work for Pope Clement, Duke Alessandro and Duke Cosimo in Florence.

Since the *auditori* were promoted, retained or transferred largely on the basis of talent and performance, their loyalty to whoever hired them was unqualified and unquestioning. Since they remained in office while the elected magistrates changed every three, four, six or twelve months, it was often they who made the decisions – or who transmitted to the magistrates the 'decisons' that their employers 'recommended'. Since they were experts in Roman law, the standard by which all statutory law was measured, they were usually entrusted as well with the task of drafting constitutions and assigning functions – as were, for example, Girolamo Scopulo, president of the High Court of Mantua, Andrea Ardoino, author of Ferrante's Council of State in Sicily, Bernardino Ploti, author of the 1543 decision on the relations between metropolis and *dominio*, and Egidio Bossi, the 'passionate defender of the rights of the state', who wrote the *Novae constitutiones* of Milan. Since they customarily thought in terms of law rather than of politics, they took care to keep written records of their transactions on pages of standard format bound in covers of different colours according to category, which were preserved in archives for future consultation. Since the *auditori* were rewarded chiefly in money, they sought to decrease waste and centralize tax collecting in a single office – that of the *auditore fiscale* in Venice and of the *tesoriere generale* in Mantua – in which the incumbent had full authority 'to intervene . . . in the affairs of all the other ministers . . . so that no expense of any sort will be incurred without his approval'.[29] As the *auditori* developed among themselves a certain *esprit de corps*, they became increasingly powerful. In Milan they gradually filled all the Senate seats once reserved for patricians and men of arms. In Naples they expelled the *cappa corta* ('nobility of the sword') members of the Supreme Council (*Collaterale*). And without being conscious of introducing the slightest novelty, they laid the foundations of the 'administrative state'[30] of the seventeenth century.

The same method of experimenting within a framework of inherited institutions guided the formation of policy toward the *dominio*, the subject territories. The statutes and treaties by which single cities and towns had originally submitted to a *dominante* were left standing, for the obvious reason that local governments usually survived the calamities far more intact than the territorial governments. But the calamities also endowed the subject cities with a much greater sense of their own dignity: they, after all, had suffered as many disasters and had been visited by as many great generals as any of the *dominanti*. 'Such is my homeland', one patriotic poet of Modena pointed out to the Romans after its definitive incorporation into the state of the dukes of Ferrara,

that there is no reason to hide it or be ashamed of it. It has generated many great men in various professions (*arti*), and many famous men have bestowed upon it honour, fame and glory.[31]

The citizens of the subject cities also followed the example of their territorial princes and drafted or revised constitutions of their own: i.e., the *Ius civile* of Vicenza (1529), the *Ordinamenti di Madama* of Aquila (1541, amended in 1548, 1558 and 1568), the 'Thirty-One Articles' of Apice (1546), and the *Statuta di Feltre* (1551). Whether these constitutions were drawn up by towns subject directly to a territorial prince or subject indirectly through a feudal intermediary – as happened frequently in the Duchy of Milan and the Kingdom of Naples – made little difference. 'Vassals' looked upon 'barons' in much the same way as 'subjects' looked upon 'princes', even though the former had the advantage of being able to negotiate amendments every time the feudal title passed by inheritance or purchase from one baron to the next. All the constitutions aimed at promoting the 'fidelity' of the subjects to the superior power and the 'utility, comfort, pacific state, tranquil administration and protection of the interests of the town, its government (*universitas*) and all its inhabitants individually and collectively'.[32] All of them provided for the election of a large number of councils and magistrates – four *eletti* and two *sindaci* in the small Neapolitan town of Massa Lubrense and four *priori*, thirty *senatores* and seventy councilmen in the minuscule Marche town of Montemilone.

In many larger cities, the constitutions reserved the higher magistracies for patricians. Guided by their own class prejudices, the Venetians restored the patriciate of the subject cities to their former privileges soon after the reconquest, even though the *popolo* and the peasants had been much more loyal.[33] More often, offices were divided between two upper classes, as were those of Sulmona between forty-five *casate nobili* and sixty-five *delli honorati del popolo*. But in smaller towns such distinctions were more difficult to observe. San Ginesio in the Marche excluded landowning nobles. Nearby Roccastrada divided its two councils between artisans and resident peasants (*rurali*), far-off Friuli between landowners and *plebi rurali*. Most small towns made no distinctions at all and admitted to a *parlamento* all male heads of households, as did Castiglione di Garfagnana. Montepulciano in Tuscany admitted 'one man per household' to its *Consiglio del Popolo* on the sole condition that he had been born in the city or the *contado* or that he had lived there for thirty years; and even Pistoia, that traditional battleground of warring nobles, admitted new residents on the sole condition that they 'be approved and declared eligible' by a simple act of the council.

Seen from the top down, the new political order was almost universally monarchical, since subjects had no part whatever in the selection of their individual or collective 'princes'. They employed the term 'prince' indifferently without making any distinction with regard to the constitution of the central government. Since most cities were subject to 'princes' who did not reside there, and since the terms *patria* and *nazione* referred exclusively to the city of birth or residence, not to the territorial state, the new political order can also be described as one of 'foreign' domination – at least outside of such *dominanti* as Palermo, Piombino, Venice and Sabbioneta. After all, Duke Federico Gonzaga was even more of a 'foreign ruler' at Casale, which rebelled against him, than Charles v was at Naples, which rebelled against the viceroy to the cries of *Impero* and *Spagna*. When seen from the bottom up, however, in much of Italy the new political order was as democratic as any before the institution of universal male suffrage in 1911. And since the popular *parlamenti* were often as 'crowded and frequently convoked' as that of Aquila, where in 1557 those present 'could not be accurately counted because of the multitude',[34] such democracy was sometimes more active and participatory than any before the Liberation of 1945.

While leaving the subject cities to govern themselves, the 'princes' took all the steps they deemed necessary to prevent conflicts between the actual practice of self-government and the rather hazy theory of equal justice for all subjects. In all the larger territorial states a governor (a *rettore* in the Venetian cities, 'cardinal legates' in the papal cities) responsible directly to the prince resided in all the major subject cities with the authority to veto any act of the local government. A system of appellate courts was instituted on behalf of possible victims of local injustice – a particularly important measure in the Venetian cities, where the courts too were dominated by patricians. Conflicts among local laws were ironed out where possible in order to make sure, as Cosimo put it, that 'more serious offences are punished in same manner' throughout the *dominio* and that 'justice is administered equally to all subjects in accordance with their merits and demerits'.[35]

The enforcement of justice presented particular problems in those areas where big feudatories maintained a relatively high degree of autonomy. Without being at all prejudiced against the notion of feudal holdings, the princes were often very severe in cases of flagrant abuses – as the Petrarchan poet Galeazzo di Tàrsia (fl. 1520–1553) found out when Toledo put him on the island of Lipari for browbeating his peasants. Whenever feudal autonomy posed a threat to the cohesion of the territorial state, the princes did not hesitate to confiscate entire holdings – as the Genoese did in order to get the Fregoso out of Novi Ligure in 1528 and as the Farnese did in 1578 in order to prevent Claudio Landi from using the title 'prince' he obtained from the emperor to found a separate 'state' at Borgo Val di Taro. For those whom poverty exposed to injustice in the courts, the princes occasionally imposed statutory limitations on the length of proceedings; and for 'those who do not have the [financial] means for carrying on litigation' in civil cases, they sometimes provided free legal counsel.[36] For those, on the other hand, in whom wealth was joined with a suspicion of disloyalty, they prescribed exile, confiscation or death – the latter executed by paid assassins if the guilty one escaped across a border. For those whose acts seemed derogative of their authority, the princes were often very severe – as the Venetians were in 1554 when they confined an indiscrete Brescian for two years in distant Capodistria merely for having uttered an offensive word about the governor of Brescia. For those caught committing any act capable of provoking 'the ire of the high and all-powerful God', they prescribed imprisonment, mutilation, quartering or the galleys.[37]

Few of these innovations were ever carried to their logical conclusions – for the very reason that the motivation of the innovators was always pragmatic or experimental, not logical or systematic. Ferrante's program of bringing law, order and efficiency to Sicily foundered on the pressing needs of his other programmes to make the island a bastion against the Turks. He reluctantly accepted the huge bribes offered for the release of the high-born criminals he caught *in flagrante*, and he borrowed still more money from the local banker from whom he hoped to buy back the tax revenues of Noto. Doge Andrea Gritti's project to revise all the Venetian statutes in conformity with the principles of 'clarity, simplicity and rationalization' bogged down in endless debates in the Great Council; and the *terraferma* continued to be ruled according to Roman law codes very different from the law observed in the metropolis.[38] Princes who confiscated feudal domains did not shrink from creating new ones elsewhere, as Cosimo did for the family of Pope Julius III at Monte San Savino. Even potentially dangerous barons were left alone to enjoy the castles they built ostensibly 'for the defence of our peaceful population', particularly if they made the castles a little less offensive by covering the raw brick with plaster Doric columns.

Once the borders of territorial states were made safe, they were left in all the illogical serpentine shapes that history had bequeathed to them. The prince-bishop of Trent pushed his western borders to their 'natural' limit on Lake Garda and absorbed Rovereto, Castelbarco and Pergine, while he ignored the anomaly represented by several unoccupied valleys along his eastern borders and by his semi-sovereign rights in distant Brixen. The duke of Savoy added Cherasco to his domains in 1559, while he left Alba, which his domains surrounded on all sides, as an isolated outpost of Monferrato. The duke of Mantua settled his eastern borders with the Venetians, while he padded his western borders with autonomous appanages for his relatives. Similarly, Cosimo persuaded the inhabitants of the Florentine Romagna to put up stone markers all along the jagged papal frontier at their own expense. But he left the Cybo-Malaspina to fight among themselves for the possession of the tiny principality of Massa Carrara, where only 128 'citizens' could be rounded up for an oath of allegiance in 1553. 'Keep the state for yourselves', he told them, 'but take care that you do not look for a chance to put it into someone else's hands'.[39] Pope Pius V severely limited the autonomy of extant feudal domains and prohibited the creation of new ones. But he left the nephew of Pope Julius III to enjoy his 'principality' at Castiglione del Lago, complete with a 'ducal palace' and several pretentious Renaissance avenues.[40]

The map of Italy continued to be pockmarked with mini-states, autonomous Imperial feudal estates and detached enclaves. The maps of the larger states continued to look much like the multi-coloured jigsaw puzzles recently reconstructed for Tuscany and the Marche.[41] The domains of the dukes of Savoy continued to be divided into wholly separate jurisdictions without even an overall name: Bresse, Savoy, Piedmont, and the Val d'Aosta, the latter still governed by the *Assemblée des Etats* and the *Conseil des Commis* established during the years of *de facto* independence.

At the same time, the age-old barriers between privileged and underprivileged and between *dominante* and *dominio* had been substantially lowered in favour of the latter. The subjects of southern baronies 'no longer felt themselves isolated, face to face with a baron', and they had acquired 'a sense of belonging to the state' that kept the baron in check. The citizens of Gubbio themselves took the initiative in 'suggesting ways by which the city might be made still more closely subject to the duke [of Urbino]'. 'The multitude of inhabitants . . . of good quality' in Fano grew to the point where they themselves requested an enlargement of the city's fortifications. The communities of the Castelli Romani voluntarily collaborated with the officials of the Camera Apostolica in Rome to promote what was later recognized as 'the definitive consolidation of the Papal State in modern structures' right in the heart of one of the most feudalized areas of Italy.[42]

The new political order was clearly established on much broader social bases than those of any of its predecessors. Revolts, revolutions and secessions all but vanished. The borders between the various states remained unchanged, with few exceptions, until the Austrian invasion of 1707, if not until the French invasion of 1797. The first essential steps had been taken toward transforming a hodgepodge of semi-autonomous communes, feudal domains and *castelli* into the rationally organized and clearly defined regional states of the political and economic reformers of the Age of the Enlightenment.

NOTES AND REFERENCES

1. Salvador de Madariaga (ed.), *Charles Quint: Textes de Charles Quint, Alonso Manrique, Gasparo Contarini, Niccolò Mocenigo*, Paris 1969; Manuel Fernandez Alvarez, *Política mundial de Carlos V y Felipe II*, Madrid 1966.

2. Aretino to Clement VII, 31 May 1527, in his *Lettere*, ed. Francesco Flora and Alessandro Del Vita, Milan 1960, p. 18, n. 7.

3. Quoted by Ramón Menéndez Pidal in 'Formación del fundamental pensamiento político de Carlos V', in *Charles Quint et son temps*, Paris 1959.

4. Lodovico Dolce, *Vita dell' invitiss. e gloriosiss. imperador Carlo Quinto*, 1561; Giovanni Battista Adriani, *Oratione recitata in Florenza nell' ossequie di Carlo Quinto Imperatore, fatta uolgare, nella quale si contengono tutti i fatti, e le laudi di sua Maestà Cesarea*, Bologna 1559; Trissino in the dedication to *Italia liberata dai Gotti*, in *Tutte le opere di Giovan Giorgio Trissino*, Verona 1729, vol. 1.

5. Quoted by Federico Chabod in *Storia di Milano nell'epoca di Carlo V*, Turin 1971, pp. 11 ff.

6. Roseo, *L'assedio et impresa di Firenze*, Perugia 1530; Tommasino Lancelloti quoted by Ottavia Niccoli, 'Profezie in Piazza. Note sul profetismo popolare nell'Italia del primo Cinquecento', p. 517 (above, Chapter 2, n. 9).

7. Pedro Mexia, *Historia del emperador Carlos V*, ed. Juan de Mata Carriazo (Colleción de Crónicas Espanolas, 7), Madrid 1945, p. 548.

8. Dolce, *Vita* (above, n. 4), p. 52.

9. John Lynch, *Spain under the Habsburgs*, Oxford 1964, vol. 1, p. 69.

10. Alonso de Santa Cruz, *Crónica del emperador Carlos V*, Madrid 1923, vol. 4, pp. 36 and 391.

11. Giuliano Gossellini, *Vita del principe Ferrando Gonzaga*, Venice 1579 (no pagination).

12. Giorgio Spini's *Cosimo I e l'indipendenza del principato mediceo* of 1945 has been reprinted with additional bibliography, Florence 1980.

13. Pedro Girón, *Crónica del emperador Carlos V*, ed. Juan Sanchez Montes, Madrid 1964, p. 27.

14. Quoted by Pietro Giannone in his *Storia civile del regno di Napoli*, Milan 1846, vol. 4, p. 572 (first published in 1723).

15. Antonio de Herrera y Tordesillas, *Historia general del mundo del tiempo del Señor rey Don Felipe II el Prudente*, Valladolid 1606, Book I, p. vi.

16. Alessandro Andrea, *Della guerra di Campagna di Roma e del regno di Napoli*, ed. Girolamo Ruscelli, in his *Raccolta di tutti i più rinomati scrittori del'istoria generale del regno di Napoli*, Naples 1769, vol. 7.

17. Benedetto Varchi, *Storia fiorentina*, Trieste 1858, Book VI, p. xxx.

18. Ioannis Hassiotis, ᾽Εκθέσεις ῾Ελλήνων . . . τουρκοκρατίας, Thessaloniki 1964.

19. Analysed by Lanfranco Franzoni in 'Due architetti veronesi . . .', *Atti e memorie dell'Accademia d'Agricoltura, Scienze e Lettere di Verona*, 31, 1981. On military architecture, see J. R. Hale, 'The end of Florentine liberty: The Fortezza da Basso', in Nicolai Rubinstein (ed.), *Florentine Studies*, London 1968; 'The early development of the bastion', in J. R. Hale, J. R. L. Highfield and B. Smalley (eds), *Europe in the Late Middle Ages*, Evanston, Ill. 1965; J. R. Hale, *Renaissance Fortification: Art or Engineering?*, London 1977, and the same author's 'Terra ferma fortifications in the Cinquecento', in Sergio Bertelli, Nicolai Rubinstein and Craig Hugh Smyth (eds), *Florence and Venice*, Florence 1979–80. After all Hale

has said, little can be, and little is, added by Mauro Gianeschi and Carla Sodini in 'Urbanistica e politica durante il principato di Alessandro de' Medici', *Storia della città*, 19, 1980: whoever assigned them their *tesi* apparently had never heard of Hale either. More informative are the essays edited by Paolo Marconi, Francesco Paolo Fiore, Giorgio Muratore and Enrico Valeriani in the splendidly illustrated *I castelli: Architettura e difesa del territorio fra Medioevo e Rinascimento*, Novara 1978.

20. Archivio di Stato, Florence, Mediceo del Principato, 49, f. 503.

21. Quotations from an anonymous diary in the Archivio Civico of Genoa, Cod. 92, f. iii, and Guicciardini in a letter to Innocenzo Cybo, 16 October 1534, Guicciardini *Carteggi*, p. 17 (above, Chapter 2, n. 3), p. 299. Basic to what follows are the volumes in the series *Storia d'Italia* edited by Giuseppe Galasso and published in Turin; Furio Diaz, *Il Granducato di Toscana*, Vol. 1: *I Medici* (1976); Mario Caravale and Alberto Caracciolo, *Lo Stato Pontificio da Martino V a Pio IX* (1978 – which, however, should be read with the reservations expressed by Paolo Prodi in his major work on the Papal State, *Il sovrano pontefice: Un corpo e due anime, la monarchia papale nella prima età moderna*, Bologna 1982; Claudio Costantini, *La Repubblica di Genova nell'età moderna* (1978); and Lino Martini, Giovanni Tocci, Cesare Mozzarelli and Aldo Stella, *I ducati padani–Trento e Trieste* (1979), as well as previously published regional histories: *Storia di Napoli*, Naples 1967–, particularly for this period vol. 5 by Guido D'Agostino *et al.*; the Treccani *Storia di Milano*, from which the part by Federico Chabod is published separately (above, n. 5); Dino Gribaudi *et al.* (eds), *Storia del Piemonte*, 2 vols, Turin 1960; Ernesto Sestan, 'Gli Estensi e il loro Stato al tempo dell'Ariosto', *Rassegna della letteratura italiana*, 79, 1975; Giuseppe Giarrizzo, *La Sicilia dal Viceregno al Regno* (Storia della Sicilia), Naples 1978, vol. 6.

Equally essential are the several histories of single cities: Marino Berengo, *Nobili e mercanti nella Lucca del Cinquencento*, Turin 1965; Francesco Cognasso, *Storia di Novara*, Novara 1975; Judith Hook, 'Habsburg imperialism and Italian particularism: The case of Charles V and Siena', *European Studies Review*, 9, 1979; and Ann Katherine Chiancone Isaacs, 'Popolo e monti nella Siena del Cinquecento', *RSI*, 82, 1970. See also my own *Florence in the Forgotten Centuries, 1527–1800*, Chicago 1973.

22. Vettori quoted by Diaz in *Il Granducato di Toscana* (above, n. 21), p. 36, in the course of the best current survey of post-Machiavellian political thought; Alamanni quoted from his 'Discorso' in the text published by Diaz' principal predecessor, Rudolf von Albertini, in the appendix to his *Das florentinische Staatsbewusstsein im Übergang von der Republik zum Prinzipat*, Bern 1955. The standard edition of the *Ricordi* is the heavily annotated one edited by Raffaele Spongano, Florence 1951. The standard edition of Giannotti is Furio Diaz' *Opere politiche*, Milan 1974, on which: Giorgio Cadoni's two articles, 'Donato Giannotti: Il "Discorso di armare la città di Firenze" e il "Discorso sopra il fermare il governo di Firenze"' and 'Intorno all'autografo della "Repubblica fiorentina" di Donato Giannotti', in *Storia e politica*, 16, 1977; and Giuseppe Bisaccia, *La Repubblica fiorentina di Donato Giannotti*, Florence 1978. In general, Felix Gilbert, The Venetian constitution in Florentine political thought', and Carlo Pincin, 'Machiavelli e gli altri', both in Rubinstein (ed.), *Florence and Venice* (above, n. 19).

23. Cosimo to Prince Francesco, 30 May 1563, *ASI* (Series 4), 11, 1883, p. 83.

24. Quotations from Cosimo's letter to Pietro Aretino, 3 February 1548, in his *Lettere*, ed. Giorgio Spini, Florence 1940, p. 113; Serristori in *Legazioni di*

Averardo Serristori, ambasciatore di Cosimo I a Carlo Quinto e in Corte di Roma, 1537–1568, ed. Giuseppe Canestrini, Florance 1853, p. 66; Guicciardini quoted by Emanuella Scarano Lugnani in *La ragione e le cose: Tre studi su Guicciardini*, Pisa 1980, p. 22, and by Roberto Ridolfi in *Studi guicciardiniani*, Florence 1978, p. 26; see also Silvana Seidel Menchi's 'Passione civile e aneliti erasmiani di riforma nel patriziato genovese del primo Cinquento: Ludovico Spinola', *Rinascimento*, 18, 1978, pp. 87–134.

25. Lorenzo Cappelloni, *Orazione al principe di Spagna nella sua venuta a Genova*, Florence 1549.

26. Gaetano Cozzi, 'Considerazioni sull'amministrazione della giustiza nella Repubblica di Venezia (secc. XV–XVI)' in Rubinstein (ed.), *Florence and Venice*, vol. 2, p. 116 (above, n. 19). On this and what follows: Giuseppe Maranini, *La costituzione di Venezia*, Florence 1974; Edoardo Grendi, 'Un esempio di arcaismo politico', *RSI*, 78, 1966; A. Petracchi, 'Norma e prassi "costituzionale" nella Serenissima Repubblica di Genova. I: La riforma del 1528; II: Modifiche al sistema: "Garibetto" e "Leges novae"', *Nuova rivista storica*, 64, 1980, pp. 41–80, 524–64; Furio Diaz (who justly corrects my thesis about the debt of the new government to its predecessors), 'Cosimo I e il consolidarsi dello Stato assoluto', in his introduction to Elena Fasano Guarini (ed.), *Potere e società negli Stati regionali italiani fra '500 e '600*, Bologna 1978; J. R. Hale, *Florence and the Medici: The Pattern of Control*, London 1977; Franco Arese, 'Le supreme cariche del Ducato di Milano', *Archivio storico lombardo*, 97, 1970; Ugo Petronio, *Il Senato di Milano: Istituzioni giuridiche ed esercizio del potere nel Ducato di Milano da Carlo V a Giuseppe II*, Milan 1972 (on which see the authoritative review article by Raffaele Ajello in *RSI*, 85, 1973); Antonio Marongiu, *Il Parlamento in Italia nel Medio Evo e nell'età moderna*, Milan 1962; Manlio Bellomo, *Società e istituzioni in Italia tra Medioevo ed età moderna*, Catania 1982; Paolo Brezzi, 'Barbari, feudatari, comuni e signorie fino alla metà del secolo XVI', and Guido Astuti, 'Gli ordinamenti giuridici degli Stati sabaudi', in Gribaudi *et al.* (eds), *Storia del Piemonte* (above, n. 21); Filippo Valenti, 'I consigli di Governo presso gli Estensi dalle origini alla devoluzione di Ferrara', in *Studi in onore di Riccardo Filangieri*, Naples 1959, vol. 2. The Milanese councils are described by Dante Zanetti in *La demografia del patriziato milanese nei secoli XVII, XVIII, XIX*, Pavia 1968, pp. 16–17.

27. Marongiu, 'Pagine dimenticate della storia parlamentare napoletana cinquecento', quoted in *Studi Filangieri* (above, n. 26), vol. 2, 326–27. Further: Guido D'Agostino, 'Il parlamento napoletano nell'età spagnuola', *Archivio storico per le provincie napolitane*, 11, 1973; and H. G. Koenigsberger, 'The parliament of Sicily and the Spanish empire', in *Mélanges Antonio Marongiu: Studies Presented to the International Commission for the History of Representative and Parliamentary Institutions*, XXXIV, Palermo 1967.

28. Don Scipione de Castro quoted by Maria Giuffrè in *Miti e realtà dell'urbanistica siciliana*, Palermo 1969, p. 9. A full description of the Sicilian government is in Alfonso Crivella, *Trattato di Sicilia* (1593), ed. Adelaide Baviera Albanese, Caltanissetta and Rome 1970. On the 'Regia Monarchia': Mario Caravale, 'Dottrina siciliana sulla potestà regia', *Annuario ISIEMC*, 29–30, 1979, and Mario Scaduto, 'La vita religiosa in Sicilia secondo un memoriale inedito del 1563', *RSCI*, 28, 1974.

29. Quoted by Roberto Navarrini in 'Una magistratura gonzaghesca del XVI secolo: Il Magistrato Camerale', in *Mantova e i Gonzaga nella civiltà del Rinascimento*, Segrate 1978.

30. The term is Salvio Mastellone's in 'La naissance de l'état administratif', in *Théorie et pratique politiques à la Renaissance:* XVIIe *colloque international de Tours*, Paris 1977.

31. Alfonso Guarini in *Il pratico*, quoted by Marina Calore, 'Il teatro ferrarese tra Ariosto e Giraldi', *Atti dell'Istituto Veneto di Scienze, Lettere ed Arti*, 138, 1979–80, p. 156. On the distinction between *dominante* and *dominio*: Marino Berengo, 'La città di antico regime', *QS*, 27, 1974. On what follows: Carlo De Stefani, 'Ordini amministrative dei comuni di Garfagnana', *ASI*, Series 5, vol. 9, 1892; Gianni Jacovelli, 'Manduria nel Cinquecento', in Michele Paone (ed.), *Studi di storia pugliese in onore di Giuseppe Chiarelli*, vol. 2, Galatina 1972–80; Elena Fasano Guarini, 'Città soggette e contado nel dominio fiorentino: Il caso pisano', in *Ricerche di storia moderna*, 1, 1974; Amelio Tagliaferri, *Struttura e politica sociale in una comunità veneta del '500 (Udine)*, Milan 1966; Gian Maria Varanini's report of 'Venezia e la Terraferma nel Quattrocento e nel Cinquecento', in *CS*, 17, 1980; Lino Marini, *Libertà e privilegio: Dalla Savoia al Monferrato, da Amedeo* VIII *a Carlo Emanuele* I, Bologna 1972; Giuseppe Coniglio, *Aspetti della società meridionale nel secolo* XVI, Naples 1978; André Zanotto, *Histoire de la Vallée d'Aoste*, Aosta 1968; Raul Merzario, *Il paese stretto: Strategie matrimoniali nella diocesi di Como*, Turin 1981, p. 35; Gaetano Ramacciotti, 'Il governo farnesiano-borbonico nello Stato di Abruzzo', *Bolletino della Deputazione Abruzzese di Storia Patria*, vols 44–46, 1953–55; 44–46, 1961; Raffaele Colapietra, 'Gli organismi municipali dell'Abruzzo', *Bolletino della Deputazione Abruzzese di Storia Patria*, 66, 1976.

32. Statutes of Apice, 1546, art. 2, published by Michèle Benaiteau in 'I capitoli della terra di Apice', *Samnium*, 53, 1980.

33. Angelo Ventura, *Nobiltà e popolo nella società veneta del '400 e '500*, Bari 1964.

34. Cited by Raffaele Colapietra, 'Prestigio sociale e potere reale nell'Aquila d'antico regime (1525–1800)', *CS*, 16, 1979.

35. From the law of 9 February 1542 *sopra gli stupri*, which I found in the collection of statutes at the Newberry Library of Chicago, and from the *deliberazione* of 1545 quoted by Elena Fasano Guarini in 'Considerazioni su giustizia e società nel ducato di Toscana del Cinquecento', in Rubinstein (ed.) *Florence and Venice* (above, n. 19), vol. 2.

36. Giuseppe Pansini, 'I Conservatori di leggi e la difesa dei poveri nelle cause civili durante il Principato Mediceo', *Studi di storia medievale e moderna per Ernesto Sestan*, Florence 1980, vol. 2.

37. Quoted by Renzo Derosas in 'Moralità e giustizia a Venezia nel '500–'600 . . .', in Gaetano Cozzi (ed.), *Stato, società e giustizia nella Repubblica veneta (secc.* XV–XVI), Naples 1980. On the Bresciano, from Sergio Cella's synopsis of 'Documenti veneziani' about Istria in *Atti e memorie della Società Istriana di Archeologia e Storia Patria*, 25, 1977, p. 391.

38. Gaetano Cozzi in 'La politica del diritto nella Repubblica di Venezia', in Cozzi (ed.), *Stato, società e giustizia* (above, n. 37).

39. Elena Fasano Guarini, 'Alla periferia del granducato mediceo: Strutture giurisdizionali ed amministrativi della Romagna toscana sotto Cosimo I', *Studi Romagnoli*, 19, 1964; Cosimo to Lorenzo Cybo, *c.* 1546, in Luigi Staffetti, *Giulio Cybo-Malespina*, Modena 1892, p. 299 (2nd edn, Modena, 1974).

40. The report of the *custode*, Giovan Bernardino Carbone, is published by Scipione Volpicella in *Archivio storico per le provincie napolitane*, 2, 1877.

41. See the map prepared by Elena Fasano Guarini in a supplement to the *Journal of Italian History*, 4, Spring 1981; and the frontispiece to Bandino Giacomo Zenobi, *Ceti e potere nella Marca pontificia*, Bologna 1976.

42. Ruggero Moscati, 'Le università meridionali nel viceregno spagnuolo', *Clio*, 3, 1967, p. 34; Renzo Paci, *Politica ed economia in un comune del Ducato d'Urbino: Gubbio tra '500 e '600*, Urbino 1967; Francesco Laparelli, *Visita e progetti di miglior difesa in varie fortezze ed altri luoghi dello Stato Pontificio*, Cortona 1970; Renato Lefevre, 'Le comunità dei "Castelli Romani" e i loro Statuti (secc. XVI–XVII)', *Studi Romani*, 26, 1978.

CHAPTER FIVE

Institutions of Culture

The gradual attainment of peace, public order and political stability made possible the survival of the arts and letters in those cities, like Ferrara, Mantua and Venice, that had either escaped or anticipated the end of the calamities; and it made possible their revival in those cities, like Naples, Milan, Rome and Florence, from which the last of the calamities had all but banished them. 'In the years recently gone by', noted Ruzante, in the prologue of a pastoral comedy, 'the holy muses have been silenced by martial and bellicose furore'. Now, however, 'Minerva has decided to return to her beloved domicile, and she has come in still greater triumph and glory'.[1]

The first and in some cases the most important customers of the artists and men of letters in the decades after 1530 were the princes. They were obliged to make the best possible impression on the head of the alliance whenever he deigned – at their expense – to pay them a visit; and they dared not find themselves in the embarrassing situation of the *Conservatori* of Rome in 1536, who had to appeal to 'the people of the city to adorn Porta San Sebastiano at their own expense, to decorate the Campidoglio with painted scenery (*prospettive*) and to build triumphal floats (*carri*)', or of the Senate of Milan in 1541, which had to call in Giulio Romano from Mantua in order to cover the entrance route with statues and temporary arches consonant with the latest art styles. The princes were also obliged to impress their colleagues in the alliance whenever the conclusion of a marriage alliance afforded them the welcome opportunity of sending invitations all over Italy and Spain.[2]

Only humanist scholars, moreover, could enable the princes to justify their pragmatic innovations as the fulfillment, rather than the contradiction, of their subjects' age-old aspirations – scholars like Daniele Barbaro (1513–1570), who was called upon to 'invent' subjects for the ceiling of the Hall of the Ten in the Palazzo Ducale of Venice in 1552. Only humanist philologists could prevent the rhetorical impact of a decorative programme from being ruined by 'anything that might give rise to doubts about its historical veracity or be recognized as manifestly false', as Cosimo put it. While allowing Cosimo himself, rather than 'Florence', to be placed at the apex of 'Florentine history', the philologist Vincenzo Borghini (1515–1580) pushed Charlemagne, whom Cosimo might have welcomed as an 'ancestor', off to the side after re-reading the relevant historical documents.[3] Only skilled sculptors could immortalize the accomplishments of the present by associating them with the accomplishments of antiquity that the humanists held to be eternally valid. They alone could make Cosimo or Duke Vespasiano Gonzaga of Sabbioneta (d. 1591) pose forever in the well-known stance of Augustus. They alone could create a perfect 'metaphor', as Benvenuto Cellini (1500–1571) did when he imitated an ancient bust of the emperor Hadrian. Only skilled numismatists, like Alessandro Maggi, could provide the captain and the *rettori* of Padua with historically accurate portraits of the Twelve Caesars, who assured, from the walls of the Sala dei Giganti, the permanent resurrection of the city from the calamities of the Cambrai Wars. Only expert bronze casters like Leone Leoni (*c.* 1509–1590) could make a life-size Ferrante Gonzaga trample forever on a horrible 'Envy' in front of the main church of Guastalla and identify his wife and daughter respectively as a vestal virgin and as Diana on commemorative medals.

The most pressing need of the princes, in retrospect, was for technical assistance. They needed engineers – '*un inzegnier* skilled in fortifications' like Michele Sanmicheli (1484–1559), who built the fortresses at Lodi and Alessandria for Francesco II Sforza of Milan (1521–1524) and the walls of Verona for the Venetians. And since engineers were also artists, their walls were adorned with portals as magnificent as Sanmicheli's at the main entrance to Verona. Even more, the princes needed 'reputation', since what others thought of them in the sixteenth century was an essential ingredient of what they actually were and since what reputation they gained personally inevitably devolved – in an age in which collective entities were not yet recognized as active historical agents – upon the states they ruled. Hence, painters were charged with representing them figuratively as Camillus, the saviour of Rome from the 'calamities' of the fourth century BC, to whom Salviati (Francesco de' Rossi, 1510–1563) dedicated the Sala delle Udienze in the Palazzo Vecchio.[4] Poets were charged with acclaiming them as 'the bright sun of Italy' or, in Lodovico Dolce's (1508–1568) verses, as 'the victor over both fate and fortune'.[5] Sculptors were charged with placing their coats of arms – St Mark's lions, Medici balls, Farnese lilies, Della Rovere trees – on fountains, façades and palace entrances all over the remotest corners of their domains – thus assuring their psychological presence wherever and whenever they could not be present physically. Painters and sculptors together were charged with enabling them to gaze ceaselessly down or out at their subjects, their guests and their actual or potential allies.

Still more important in bestowing 'reputation' upon a prince was the size and magnificence of the palace he inhabited. The duke of Mantua already had a palace, which he promptly set out to enlarge and redecorate. But since its undisguisably 'Gothic' structure could express only transitory might, not eternal glory, he commissioned Giulio Romano (1492–1546) to build the new Palazzo del Te on the outskirts of the city. The duke of Urbino already had a palace too – indeed, one of the greatest architectural monuments of the early Renaissance. But he preferred to move to Pesaro, where the Urbino architect Girolamo Genga (d. 1551) and the most promising members of the new generation of painters in Rome and Florence, Perin del Vaga (1501–1547) and Angelo Bronzino (1503–1572), could properly celebrate him, in the completely remodelled Palazzo Ducale and in the new suburban Villa Imperiale, as the restorer of the duchy.

Cosimo de' Medici, on the other hand, did not have a palace, since the ownership of Michelozzo's Palazzo Medici was contested by his predecessor's widow. He moved into the Palazzo dei Signori (renamed Palazzo Vecchio when he subsequently moved out of it), and he commissioned first Giovanni Battista Del Tasso (1500–1555) and then Giorgio Vasari (1511–1574) with obliterating all traces of the former republican regimes and completely remodelling it as a monument to the new prince. The Genoese admiral and statesman, Andrea Doria, did not have a palace either. He brought to Genoa the same Perin del Vaga who decorated the palaces at Pesaro to build him one on the west end of the city – with a stately entrance that could be admired from an approaching avenue and with a series of high porticoes from which the port could be admired across a descending garden. Ottavio Farnese followed Andrea's example. Instead of trying to accommodate his recently won status as duke within the narrow streets of Parma, of which almost all the former lords had been non-resident outsiders, he moved across the river; and there, at the end of a large park, the architect Giovanni Boscoli of Montepulciano (*c.* 1524–1589) built him a stately Tuscan villa, with rusticated stone (*bugnati*) around the ground floor windows, delicately undulated capitals over the *piano nobile* windows, a white balustrade over the main entrance and a large clock projecting above the roof.

Magnificent palaces in turn had to be located in or near magnificent cities. Alas, the stalls and awnings that made the narrow streets of Naples dark, dank and impassable to all but thieves were anything but elegant. The viceroy Pedro de Toledo, in two decrees of February and May 1533, ordered them all torn down – to the annoyance, and then to the delight, of the shopowners. The tangle of tiny streets that separated the new viceregal palace, built for him by the Italianized Spanish architect Pedro Luis Scrivà, from the military and commercial centres of the city was militarily as well as aesthetically unacceptable; and Toledo charged his urbanist-in-chief Ferdinando Maglio with resurrecting the urban renewal schemes of his short-lived predecessors Alfonso II (1494–1495) and Ferdinando II (1495–1496), with extending the horizontal axis known ever thereafter as Spaccanapoli ('Cut-Naples-in-Two') and with creating as a perpendicular axis the broad, straight street that still bears his name – with the happy side-effect that private builders then laid out a grid plan of new houses on the slopes of Monte San Martino and thus turned Naples into an amphitheatre. In Rome, the tiny alleys that wound around the Terme Agrippina and that blocked the view of, as well as the access to, the nascent Palazzo Farnese were equally unacceptable, particularly in light of the example left by Paul III's predecessors in the three-pronged approach to the city from the Piazza del Popolo and in the rapidly growing Via Giulia. Unconcerned with the archaeological qualities either of ancient ruins or of medieval rubble, Paul charged his urbanist-in-chief Antonio da Sangallo (c. 1453–1534) with carving one street from his family's future residence right across the Campo de' Fiori toward what was later called Piazza Navona and two others from what is today Largo Argentina to either side of the Pantheon.

Equally incompatible with 'the convenience and ornamentation of the city' of Florence was 'the vile, low-lying area between the public palace (Palazzo Vecchio) and the Arno, inhabited by vile persons of sordid occupations and frequently covered by flooding from the river'. Almost as incompatible with Cosimo's notion of bureaucratic efficiency were the difficulties in communication among the various magistracies still scattered about the centre of the city. Hence, the moment he was rid of the Siena War, he persuaded the guilds to 'buy all the houses [in the area] and tear them down'. He then invited the magistrates to bid for the new quarters designed for them by his chief urbanist, Vasari. And the very next year construction began on what was soon to be one of the greatest Renaissance monuments of administrative coordination as well as of architecture and urban planning, the Palace of the Uffizi ('Offices', or 'Bureaux'). Equally incompatible with the new status won by the collective 'princes' of Genoa in 1528 were the black and white striped fortresses with purely ornamental window casings in which most of them lived – particularly after their *primus inter pares*, Andrea Doria, had identified princely status with Roman, not 'Gothic', design. They quickly followed his example in their suburban residences – the Grimaldi at Meridiana, the Pallavicino at the Piazza Fossatello. A few of them then tried to open up new spaces for respectable approaches to enlarged urban residences – as Vincenzo Imperiale did in 1555–63 with the help of the Bergamo architect Giovan Battista Castello. But after the completion of the new walls, about the only uncluttered area within the city was the strip at the base of the steep hill under the former *Castelletto*. In 1551, the *Governatori*, under the leadership of the doge Luca Spinola, expropriated the land from the furious Franciscans. And by 1558 the first of the 'very beautiful edifices that will bestow not only utility but also beauty on the city' began to rise along the most consistently magnificent of all the magnificent Renaissance geometrical streets, the Via Nuova.[6]

Obviously, many of these projects cost far more than any prince could afford on his own. Indeed, one prince, the bishop of Trent, after a few minor repairs to make his capital somewhat less unworthy of an ecumenical council, stopped rebuilding altogether and instead issued an elegantly coloured 'perspective map' on which what were really (and still are) portico-lined cow-paths were made to look – for the enlightenment of the friends of the departing council fathers back home – like the radii of a perfect amphitheatre. Some governments hit upon ways of passing off the financial burden onto private citizens – by giving rights of eminent domain to 'whoever [might] wish to build or enlarge their palaces in a manner [more] befitting their status', as a decree of the Florentine Senate put it in 1559.[7] Genoa even made money from its projects. It auctioned off the plots it had acquired around the Via Nuova one at a time and thus assured itself ever higher prices for the plots that remained. Most governments showed a lack of respect for historical tradition approaching that of the city council of Fermo, which ruthlessly tore up the centre of the city and replaced it with a perfect rectangle enclosed within a perfectly Vitruvian arcade. All of them insisted that every new stone laid in every gutted-out lot fit into a predetermined plan – like the one drawn up by the *ingegnere* Alessandro Bolzoni in Piacenza in 1546 and rigorously enforced by 'The Lord-Governor of the Upkeep and Decor of Buildings'.

Even though the greatest monuments of urban reconstruction – like Michelangelo's Campidoglio in Rome – had to be completed by future generations, the process initiated at Ferrara and around the Annunziata of Florence in the mid-fifteenth century by which medieval cities were transformed into Renaissance and later into Baroque cities had now, after the thirty- or forty-year interruption imposed by the calamities, become irreversible; and by the middle of the sixteenth century it had proceeded far enough to evoke expressions of wonder on the part of visitors. Florence, noted the Bolognese geographer Leandro Alberti (*c.* 1479–1522), 'is so beautiful that it well deserves the name it has obtained, "Beautiful Florence". If I had to describe all its amenities, natural as well as man-made, I would have to write volumes'. 'Have you ever seen a more beautiful view than this?' exclaimed the Greek refugee scholar Giovanni Tarcagnota (d. 1566), after a visit to Naples. 'What refreshment for the spirit and the soul to behold at one moment so many grand edifices, so many ornate churches, such magnificent houses, fresh fountains and streets frequented by so many nobles and by such an honoured citizenry!'[8] The process had also advanced far enough to afford some satisfaction to the builders. Federico Gonzaga at last felt himself worthy of Alexander, whose example he followed in patronizing his 'Apelles', Giulio Romano. Cosimo was at last worthy 'of his most illustrious progenitors', from whom he had learned 'that the protection of good letters confers glory upon princes and that the pursuit of good arts brings great utility to their people'.[9]

So successful, indeed, were these initial forays into the realm of the arts and letters that many princes sought to organize them more methodically. Occasionally they employed talent scouts like Filippo Del Migliore who, having saved the Biblioteca Laurenziana from rats during the last years of the oligarchy, was sent around northern Italy in search·of candidates for Cosimo's favours. Occasionally they centralized patronage under a single cultural commissar – Francesco Campana and Vasari in Florence, Giovan Battista Bertini in Mantua, Jacopo Sansovino in Venice and, somewhat later, Giovan Battista Pigna in Ferrara – the forerunners of the ministers of culture in twentieth-century western European governments. Above all, they hastened to reopen, revive or expand the universities, or *studia generalia*, that they had inherited from the distant or recent past but that had been gravely damaged during the years of the calamities. Aware of the economic benefits to be expected from the influx of students, particularly in some of the harder-hit subject cities, they erected new buildings and *collegi* for classrooms and dormitories. Aware of the importance of a highly qualified faculty in attracting students from abroad – from France, Germany and Spain as well as from neighbouring Italian states – they bid with ever higher offers on the highly competitive pan-Italian market until professors' salaries outstripped even those of military captains. They modified or reformed statutes to assure their control – or the control of such special boards as the *Riformatori* of Padua – over appointments and curricula, and to undercut possible opposition from entrenched interests to the introduction of new subjects more consonant with the demands of a new age – like Platonic philosophy, botany, and rhetoric. Soon the once famous universities of Padua, Ferrara, Bologna, Pavia, Pisa, Rome and Naples had fully recovered their former pan-European reputations, which came to be shared somewhat later by such new or newly refounded universities as Parma and Mondovi-Turin and by such smaller and now somewhat provincial universities as Siena, Perugia, Macerata and Camerino. Enrolments climbed appreciably. By 1549, 1,200 students were present at the University of Padua, to the delight of the Venetian *rettore*, making it seven times larger than its German equivalent, the University of Tübingen, at the height of its expansion twenty years later.[10]

If mid-sixteenth-century Italian culture was thus considerably indebted to government support, it was by no means restricted within the limits of what governments saw as its political utility. It can therefore no more justly be called a 'court culture' than can the culture of Paris under the much more aggressive direction of André Malraux in the 1970s or the culture of Bologna in 1967 under the direction of an assessor with 7.2 per cent of the annual budget at his disposal.[11] Few of the princes were any better informed about the arts and letters than had been that patron of fifteenth-century city planners, Pope Sixtus IV[12]; none of them even approached the competence of such energetic organizers of culture as Lorenzo Il Magnifico and Lodovico Il Moro at what is often considered to be the apex of Renaissance civilization. Cosimo had to take lessons in aesthetics from Vasari and Cellini, to whom he invariably yielded in all such questions that did not concern his wife's momentary passions. Pope Paul III thought he was getting no more and no less than another Raphael when he hired – and when he thereafter supported – Raphael's erratic disciple Perin del Vaga. And both of them waited trembling before what they knew to be the final judgement of the quality of the works they paid for: that of the ordinary people of Rome and Florence as they jammed into the Sistine Chapel or into the Piazza dei Signori for the unveiling of Michelangelo's *Last Judgement* and Cellini's *Perseus*. Except for Ercole II and Cardinal Ippolito II d'Este, who made Ferrara a centre of music as well as of poetry and drama, and except for Ferrante's daughter Ippolita, who brought the musician Orlando di Lasso and the painter Bernardino Campi (1522–1591) to Milan, none of them had anything resembling what Italians of the age defined as a 'court' – that is, the one they read about in Castiglione. The artists were left to do what they pleased, subject only to an occasional visit to their *botteghe* or a summons to the palace by their respectful patrons.

Quite as important for the support of the arts and letters were the many private patrons who followed – or anticipated – the example of the princes, sometimes for the very similar purpose of glorifying their own families, sometimes for the more altruistic purpose of encouraging culture for its own sake. Ottaviano de' Medici, not his distant cousin Duke Alessandro, was largely responsible for maintaining what little cultural life survived in Florence in the first years after the siege. Bernardino Martirana in his villa at Portici, not Toledo at his villa at Pozzuolo, was the patron of Luigi Tansillo and most of the other Neapolitan poets in the 1530s and 1540s. Giovan Battista Cavalcanti, not Cosimo, paid Bronzino for the *Noli me tangere* at Santo Spirito, a work that incorporated most of the elements sometimes identified with 'court' painting: the impossibly spiralling body of Jesus, the protruding eyeballs of Mary Magdalene, and the brand-new long-handle shovel that serves as the left frame of the composition. Even more important as patrons were the confraternities and religious orders, most of which insisted upon being served in accordance with the most advanced standards of artistic taste. The most admired works of art in Milan in the 1530s were commissioned by the Confraternity of Santa Corona and the Benedictines of San Maurizio, those in Cremona by the Gerolomini, those in Parma before the arrival of the Farnese by the Benedictines of San Giovanni Evangelista; and many of the most remarkable works of art in Venice throughout the century were commissioned by the charitable institutions know as *scuole grandi*.

So varied, indeed, were the kinds of commissions available that many artists and men of letters freed themselves from any particular patronage pattern and lived by free-lancing. A few of them were men of means by birth who did not need a salary from anyone – Florentines like Michelangelo, Pier Vettori (1499–1585) and Giovan Battista Adriani (1511–1579). A few others managed to procure irrevocable ecclesiastical benefices, as did the biographer-historian Paolo Giovio (1483–1552), and were assured of enough regular income to become themselves patrons of the arts. Many others rose from rags or moderate poverty to sufficient riches to enable them to purchase land and shares in mercantile companies, as did the historian-philologist Carlo Sigonio (c. 1520–1584) at Bologna and Modena. The phenomenon of artists' or writers' houses as plastic manifestations of the owner-builder's talents and tastes became ever more common in the wake of the classic examples set by Vasari in Florence and Arezzo, by Giovio in his museum-villa at Como and by Leone Leoni in Milan, where gigantic stone torsos still lean menacingly out of the façade of his palace.

Culture assumed, much more widely in the sixteenth century than in the fifteenth, the function of permitting its practitioners to climb upward along the social scale. Its effectiveness in this regard was recognized by Anton Francesco Doni of Florence (1513–1574) when he mocked those whose honourable social status was due to inheritance alone – and then invented a genealogical chart in his *Zucca* of 1565 that made him the descendant of a thirteenth-century noble family with two popes, Donus I and Donus II. He, after all, and all on his own, had survived the bankruptcy of one printing firm; and after failing to get a permanent patronage job at Pesaro, he made enough money churning out stories and comedies from a second printing firm eventually to retire to the villa he had bought at Monselice. The social position of artists was recognized as well by those painters who did portraits of each other according to the same schemes they adopted for princes: for example, the portrait of Bandinelli (Bergamo: Accademia Carrara) by Pontormo (1494–1556) and that of the poet Luigi Borra (Parma: Galleria Nazionale) by the Farnese court portraitist Girolamo Mazzola Bedoli (c. 1500–1569).

Social mobility benefited even those men of letters who did serve one patron at a time – men like Annibal Caro (1507–1566), the son of a modest merchant in distant Civitanova in the Marche, who worked as an ambassador, judge and administrator for Cardinal Guidiccioni and for Pier Luigi and then Cardinal Alessandro Farnese, and who in the end turned down still another offer from Duke Emanuele Filiberto of Savoy in order to retire in affluent tranquility to his town house in Rome and his 'Villa Piscina' at Frascati. Far from being conditioned or intellectually compromised by their patrons, these 'courtiers', as they were called by the several sixteenth-century continuers of the fifteenth-century literary genre of anti-curial treatises, had no trouble changing loyalties and even ideologies with each change of patrons. Pontormo passed from the anti-tyrant symbols of the current *popolo* regime in his *Virgin, Child and St Anne* of 1529 (Paris: Louvre) to the obviously pro-principate overtones of his official portrait of Duke Alessandro (Lisbon: Museu Nacional) in less than five years. Sansovino, having 'shown forth the forces that the Most Serene Republic [of Venice] has on land and sea' with his Neptune and Mars on the staircase of the Palazzo Ducale, then 'made a beautiful statue of Hercules' representing the equally serene – and wholly monarchical – duke of Ferrara.[13]

Private patrons, like Pietro Aretino in Venice and Agostino Giunti in Verona, anticipating the salons of the eighteenth century, associated as equals with the artists and writers they regularly invited to their houses. Theatrical productions, which required the collaboration of architects, painters, actors, musicians, dancers, writers and directors, were supported by professional or semi-professional *compagnie*, like the some forty-three organizations with that name recorded in Venice alone, which had written statutes, periodic meetings and rehearsals, regularly elected officers and fines for infractions of the rules. Some thirty-four plays were put on by the Venetian Compagnia della Calza before its dissolution in 1545 and as many more by its successor, the Sempiterni, thereafter. Similarly, those of Lodovico Dolce were put on by the Accademia Virtuosa, those of Andrea Calmo (1510–1571) by his own troupe, the *Egle* of Giambattista Giraldi (Cinthio; 1504–1573) 'in the author's house' at Ferrara 'at the expense of the student body of the law faculty',[14] and all those of the many playwrights of the third major dramatic capital of Italy, Siena, by the two theatrical 'academies', the Intronati and the Rozzi. Only in rare instances did these companies have fixed quarters – in Ferrara, for instance, where Ariosto himself built a theatre in the ducal palace, and in Padua, where the architect Giovan Maria Falconetto of Verona (1468–1535) converted Alvise Cornaro's *loggia* into a permanent stage. Often they were called upon to perform as part of nightlong parties in private houses that ended in banquets and dancing. More often they performed in public squares specially arranged to accommodate paying spectators. Occasionally they performed on a barge floating in the Grand Canal. They therefore had to buy or rent storage space for their movable equipment, particularly after Sebastiano Serlio (1475–1554), the leading current expert on ancient architecture, decided that painted scenery too was a work of art – or at least that the scenery he painted was – and ought not to be simply thrown away at the end of each series of performances.

The most widespread form of cultural organization, however, was the academy. The sixteenth-century Italian academies were not wholly without precedent. At least the first of them were inspired by the literary models proposed in the works of Cicero and Boccaccio and by the concrete examples of Marsilio Ficino's reincarnation of the Accademia Platonica at Careggi and the informal gatherings in the Rucellai Gardens at the time of Machiavelli.[15] But after 1540, the academies were all based on one or two specific models: the wholly private Accademia degli Infiammati founded by the philosophers and humanists of Padua under the leadership of Sperone Speroni (1500–1588), or, less frequently, the semi-public Accademia Fiorentina, reformed on the basis of a preceding private academy at almost the same time in Florence and subsidized to the extent that the duke paid for one or two regular lecture series and assured the consul, or president, of a partial salary as director of the *Studium* (a group of public lectureships) and as a member of the Council of the Two Hundred.[16]

Academies sought to guarantee their longevity by imitating the well-tried organizational structure of the guilds and confraternities. They arranged for permanent quarters, established procedures for the admission of new members, and drew up written statutes that provided for periodic meetings, for posting lists of subjects for discussion and for the regular election of a large number of officers. They also took care to combine business with various amenities that invariably included an annual banquet and occasionally a *lezione giocosa*, in which the members made fun of a serious subject or took a frivolous subject seriously. The academicians were thus assured, in the words of one member of the Accademia degli Ortolani of Piacenza, of 'spending their time honourably conversing with one another to the great profit of all'.[17] Similarly, a few of the academies were dedicated to particular disciplines – Petrarchan poetry, for instance, in the case of the Accademia degli Argonauti of Casale. More often, however, they specifically rejected disciplinary limitations. Even the Accademia Olimpica of Vicenza, which had originally been founded for the purpose of promoting the composition of drama in Palladio's new theatre, ended up admitting the discussion of 'poetry, logic, philosophy, oratory, humane letters both Latin and Volgare, metaphysics, mathematics, music, geometry, arithmetic, painting, sculpture, architecture, ancient and modern history . . . and all other praiseworthy professions'.[18] They welcomed painters, poets, physicians, secretaries, magistrates and even, in the Accademia della Valle di Blenio in Milan, embroiderers (*ricamatori*). They thus provided an unprecedented opportunity for the awakening intellects of even the smallest and most remote towns to exchange new ideas and information. Academies therefore sprang up all over the peninsula with titles suggestive of an unending variety of moral qualities – from the *Addormentati* ('Fallen Asleep') of Genoa to the *Irresoluti* of Galatina, the *Infimi* of Nardò, the *Erranti* of Brindisi and even the *Confusi* of the Genoese colony at Antwerp.

The efforts of the academies to encourage the productivity and diffusion of culture were greatly facilitated by the rapid expansion of two other institutions of fifteenth-century origin: preparatory schools and the printing press. The first of these institutions is still known only indirectly, through the careers of former pupils. In the 1520s one Gregorio Amaseo, disappointed in his quest for a chair of literature in Venice and compromised by an affair with a nun, left his subsequently more famous son Romolo in Bologna and returned to his native Udine. He spent the rest of his life there imparting to the sons of his fellow citizens what he had learned from the great Sabellico in Venice. From the 1530s on such cases multiplied rapidly. Some of the *maestri pubblici*, as the teachers were often called, seem to have taught all subjects at all levels in their own houses. Many of them were supported or subsidized by the town or village councils that called them in or granted them official recognition. All these schools followed a programme similar to that of their best known surviving archetype, the school of Battista Guarini (1538–1616) in Ferrara, 'from which men excellent in every kind of literature and good studies have gone forth to all Europe as from a Trojan horse', as Lelio Gregorio Giraldi recalled many years later, with a surprising tolerance for this overworked simile.[19] As they spread all over the peninsula, ever greater numbers of young men from the most remote towns were able to descend upon the big cities fully prepared to compete with the best educated of their contemporaries.

Much more is known about the printing presses. Scholars now generally accept that almost all of them were from the very beginning ventures organized according to the normal patterns of Italian commercial enterprises for the purpose of making money.[20] To be sure, many printers were also men of learning – like Aldo Manuzio at Venice in the first decades of the century and Francesco Priscianese at Rome in the middle decades. Conscious that standards of layout were still set by elegant manuscript copiers, many of them were also committed to the aesthetic quality of their products and to refining the appearance of the classical and Carolingian letters that were rapidly obliterating any trace of the once universally used 'Gothic' alphabets. Initially, the printing business benefited economically from its novelty and from the revolutionary nature of its technological base. It could pay wages lower than those set by the guilds in older industries. It could attract a steady flow of apprentices among sons of fathers optimistic about its future. And even the most expensive of its products could easily undercut the manuscript equivalents. But as competition increased, and as new entrepreneurs in one city after another rushed in to take the place of the many firms that dissolved in bankruptcy, the printers learned to adapt themselves to the demands of a market that became ever more varied as it increased in size.

Printers covered more risky ventures with sure-selling textbooks – the hundreds of law books that finally permitted university students to own copies of their own, and the Volgare-Latin grammar that for a century thereafter continued to bear the name of the printer of the first edition, the *Priscianello*. They persuaded governments to issue copyright (*privilegio*) laws to protect them from pirated editions. Since most printers were also booksellers, they occasionally formed inter-city associations to promote the sale of one another's books outside the city of origin as well as to facilitate the distribution of books imported from outside Italy. Since some readers found it easier to read what they were taught to write by hand in the humanist schools, they invented italic (*corsivo*) script as a variant of the more common roman script. When the demand for texts in ancient Greek turned out to be smaller than anticipated, they used their Greek characters to fill up the market created by the Ottoman conquest for modern Greek texts – from psalters and books of liturgy to translations of Aesop. They created still other profitable markets by setting type in Cyrillic characters. Publishers also sought to turn purchasers of a first book into purchasers of a second by printing serially a number of similar titles in the same format, as Michele Tramezzino did with his 'histories'. To cut costs, they ordered ever thinner paper – until at times the print on one side of a page showed through on the other – moved chapter headings forward to no more than a line or two below the end of the preceding chapter, pushed margins almost off the page or filled them with rubrics or references, and reduced large folio volumes to pocketbooks in 16°. And they provoked howls of protest from their authors by shortening the time allotted for proofreading.

Whether all this activity on the part of schools, universities, academies and printers also had the wholly favourable side-effect of raising general levels of literacy is a difficult question to answer. Indeed, it has been suggested, on the basis of the records of the Orphans' Office in Florence, that literacy levels actually declined in the sixteenth century.[21] What is certain is that the number of books in circulation multiplied over and over again. It is also highly probable that the number of private book collections increased.[22] Volgare translations outstripped Latin editions of the classics, just as the Accademia Fiorentina hoped they would when it launched its translation campaign. To make translations more acceptable to less exigent audiences, the translators heeded Lodovico Castelvetro's (*c.* 1505–1571) warning against word-for-word renditions (a red cloak won't turn a soldier into a cardinal!). They followed Doni's admonition that 'translations take into account the cities, customs and habits of modern times'; and they paraphrased, explained, or substituted modern for ancient references whenever they thought the original to be somewhat obscure.[23] Philologists could write for philologists with all the rigour demanded by their discipline. But the Sienese Intronati had to use a very different style when making the *Aeneid* comprehensible to 'illustrious and honourable ladies'.[24]

As government-appointed boards of governors continued to introduce still other university chairs of Latin and Volgare literature, and as more and more 'poets' were attracted by the growing prestige of the universities as intellectual centres rather than just professional schools, the former wall between the university disciplines on the one hand and the humanistic disciplines on the other began to crumble. Aristotelian metaphysicians, Galenic physicians and even Bartolist lawyers began to expound their *quaestiones* before lay audiences in the same humanist Volgare free of jargon and technical terms that had become the official language of the historians, the literary critics and the Platonist philosophers. Even the disciplinary barriers suggested by the division of ancient literature into canonical genres weakened before the onslaught of the 'polygraphs' – writers like Michelangelo Biondo (1500–1565) of Venice, who jumped from a treatise on 'The Origins of the French Disease' to a 'Dialogue on Envy', and translators like Lodovico Domenichi (1515–1564), who moved from Lucian and Pico to Erasmus, Augustine and even a disguised Calvin in accordance with what he thought the market could absorb. While respecting the special role of the creators of culture, the popularizing polygraphs exploited them for the immediate purpose of earning a living. The long-term effect of their activity made what had once been reserved to a Latinate elite available to whoever could read the Volgare. Florence thus became 'a city with a good eye and a bad tongue, where everyone gives his opinion' on everything, and where 'farm managers, barbers, shoemakers and even cobblers and ironmongers' talk about what the historian Benedetto Varchi (1503–1565) expounds in his public lectures[25] – to the distress of those who lamented the deleterious effects of consumerism.

NOTES AND REFERENCES

1. Ruzante quoted by Giorgio Padoan in 'Angelo Beolco da Ruzante a Perduocimo', *Lettere italiane*, 20, 1968, p. 124. Basic to what follows are such still-current 'classics' as Walter F. Friedlaender, *Mannerism and Anti-Mannerism in Italian Painting* (1941), New York 1965; Riccardo Scrivano, *Il manierismo nella letteratura del Cinquecento*, Padua 1959, and 'La discussione sul Manierismo', *RLI*, 67, 1963; Ettore Bonara, *Critica e letteratura nel Cinquecento*, Turin 1964; Peter Murray, *The Architecture of the Italian Renaissance*, New York 1966; Ezio Raimondi, 'Per la nozione del manierismo letterario', in his *Rinascimento inquieto*, Palermo 1965; John Shearman, *Mannerism*, Penguin Books, Harmondsworth 1967, and '*Maniera* as an aesthetic ideal', in Creighton Gilbert (ed.), *Renaissance Art*, New York 1970; Georg Weise, *Il manierismo, bilancio critico*, Florence 1971, and *Manierismo e letteratura*, Florence 1976. The debate continues in such collective endeavours as Franklin W. Robinson and Stephen G. Nicholas, Jr. (eds), *The Meaning of Mannerism*, Hanover, New Hampshire 1972 – one of many recent titles. For general surveys: Paul Renucci, 'La cultura', in the *Einaudi Storia d'Italia*, 1974, vol. 22, and Antonio Pinelli, 'La maniera', in the *Einaudi Storia dell'arte italiana*, vol. 61, 1981. For a manageable survey of Venice: Oliver Logan, *Culture and*

Society in Venice, 1470–1790, London 1972; for Florence, my own 'Firenze dal 1527 al 1630' in *La Rinascenza a Firenze: Il Cinquecento*, Rome 1981.

2. Rome decree of November 1535, in Cesare d'Onofrio, *Renovatio Romae*, Rome 1973, p. 144; Giulio Bora on this incident and in general on Milan in 'La cultura figurativa a Milano, 1535–1565', in *Omaggio a Tiziano: La cultura artistica milanese nell'età di Carlo v*, Milan 1977.

3. Vasari quoted by Nicolai Rubinstein, 'Vasari's painting of the *Foundation of Florence* in Palazzo Vecchio', in Douglas Fraser, Howard Hibbard and Milton J. Lewine (eds), *Essays Presented to Rudolf Wittkower on His Sixty–fifth Birthday*, Part I: *Essays in the History of Architecture*, London 1967.

4. Ettore Allegri and Alessandro Cecchi, *Palazzo Vecchio e i Medici*, Florence 1980, pp. 40–48 (from which I take most of what I say hereafter about the palace and its artists).

5. Lodovico Dolce in the preface to Enea Vico, *Discorsi sopra le medaglie degli antichi*, Venice 1558. Many more details in K. W. Forster, 'Metaphors of rule: Political ideology and history in the portraits of Cosimo I de' Medici', *Mitt Kunst F*, 15, 1971.

6. Decree of the Padri del Comune of 1550, quoted by Ennio Poleggi in *Strada Nuova. Una lottizzazione del Cinquecento a Genova*, 2nd edn, Genoa 1972.

7. Decree of 28 January 1550 of the Consiglio de XLVIII, in the Newberry Library, MS Case F36, 106, i.

8. Leandro Alberti, *Descrittione di tutta Italia*, Venice 1550, p. 41. Giovanni Tarcagnotta, *Del sito et lodi della città di Napoli*, Naples 1566, pp. 8–9.

9. Cosimo in the introduction to the *Provvisione* for the University of Pisa, 9 February 1542–43, in Lorenzo Cantini, *Legislazione toscana*, Florence 1800–1808, vol. 1, p. 221.

10. Among recent studies on Italian universities: Paolo Colliva, 'Le "nationes" a Bologna in età umanistica: I privilegi degli studenti germanici (1530–1592)', *Annali dell'Istituto Storico Italo-Germanico in Trento*, 5, 1979; Marina Roggero, 'Professori e studenti nelle università tra crisi e riforme', in *Storia d'Italia: Annali 4*, Turin 1981; Giuseppe Ricuperati, 'Università e scuola in Italia', in Alberto Asor Rosa (ed.), *La letteratura italiana*, Turin 1982, vol. 1; Richard I. Kagan, 'Universities in Italy, 1500–1700', in Dominique Julia *et al.* (eds), *Les universités européennes du XVIe au XVIIIe siècle* (Histoire sociale des populations étudiantes), Paris 1986, vol. 1.

11. Marcel Landowski in *Le Monde*, 26–27 April 1981; Olga Danosi and Giorgio Ghezzi in *Il Mulino*, 239 (anno XXIV), 1975.

12. Cf. Egmont Lee, *Sixtus IV and Men of Letters*, Rome 1978.

13. Vasari on Sansovino in *Vite*, IX, pp. 312–13.

14. I quote from the title page of the offset edition of the original published by Edizioni 'Quattro Venti', Urbino 1980. For the rest: Ludovico Zorzi, 'Elementi per la visualizzazione della scena veneta prima del Palladio', in Maria Teresa Muraro (ed.), *Studi sul teatro veneto fra Rinascimento ed età barocca*, Florence 1971; Muraro herself in 'La festa a Venezia', in *Storia cult ven*, 3, III; Marina Calore, 'Il teatro ferrarese tra Ariosto e Giraldi', *Atti dell'Istituto Veneto di Scienze, Lettere ed Arti*, 138, 1979–80; Elena Povoledo, 'Scène et mise-en-scène à Venise dans la première moitié du XVIe siècle', in *Renaissance, maniérisme, baroque* ('Actes du XIe Stage International de Tours'), Paris 1972.

15. For the Florentine academies in particular and for recent bibliography: my 'Le accademie', in *Firenze e la Toscana dei Medici nell'Europa del '500*, Florence 1983,

vol. 1, pp. 3–17. In general: Alessandro Lazzeri, 'Recenti studi sulle accademie', *Ricerche storiche*, 10, 1980.

16. Michel Plaisance, 'Culture et politique à Florence de 1542 à 1551', in André Rochon (ed.), *Les écrivains et le pouvoir en Italie à l'époque de la Renaissance*, Centre de Recherche sur la Renaissance Italienne, Paris 1974, vol. 3.

17. Lodovico Domenichi (1562) quoted by Riccardo Scrivano in *La norma e lo scarto: Proposte per il Cinquecento letterario italiano*, Rome 1980, p. 107.

18. Quoted by Lionello Puppi in *Il Teatro Olimpico*, Vicenza 1963, p. 16.

19. Giraldi's dedication of his *Syntagma* in his *Operum quae extant omnium . . . tomi duo*, Basel 1580, vol. 1, p. 127.

20. Carlo Dionisotti, 'Aldo Manuzio umanista', in Vittore Branca (ed.), *Umanesimo europeo e umanesimo veneziano*, Florence 1963; Luigi Balsamo, 'Tecnologia e capitali nella storia del libro', in Berta Maracchi and Dennis E. Rhodes (eds), *Studi offerti a Roberto Ridolfi, direttore de La bibliofilia*, Florence 1973.

21. Leandro Perini, 'Libri e lettori nella Toscana del Cinquecento', *Ricerche storiche*, 11, 1981.

22. Christian Bec, 'I libri dei fiorentini (1413–1608) (Ipotesi e proposte)', *Lettere italiane*, 31, 1979. See also his *Les livres des Florentins (1413–1608)*, Florence 1984.

23. In general: Carlo Dionisotti, 'La letteratura italiana nell'età del Concilio di Trento', in his *Geografia e storia della letteratura italiana*, Turin 1967.

24. *I sei primi libri dell'Eneide di Vergilio tradotti a più illustri et honorate donne*, Venice 1540.

25. Vincenzo Borghini quoted by Eve Borsook in 'Art and politics at the Medici court II: The baptism of Filippo de' Medici in 1577', *Mitt Kunst F*, 13, 1967; Varchi in Diaz, *Opere*, vol. 1, p. 342.

CHAPTER SIX

Mannerism

THE SURVIVAL OF THE MODELS

Encouraged by their patrons and clients and by new as well as older cultural institutions, the men of arts and letters set forth to carry on or, depending upon local circumstances, to revive what they all recognized as the greatest cultural achievement of all times: the High Renaissance. Like their mentors, they continued to pay tribute to the ancients as dependable guides for their own creative efforts. Quintilian and the fifteenth-century imitators of Quintilian remained their masters of pedagogy: to their reading lists the Neapolitan pedagogue Cesare Benenato was willing to add only one or two Neapolitan High Renaissance classics, like the pastoral poet Jacopo Sannazaro (1457–1530); and Cicero remained their master of oratory – both for Bernardino Tomitano of Padua (1517–1576), who repeated Cicero's identification of effective speaking with profound knowledge, and for the anti-*Infiammati* critic Mario Nizolio (1498–1576), who attacked the pseudo-philosophers 'in the name of the Ciceronian ideal of learned and eloquent philosophy'. Bartolomeo Cavalcanti accordingly took from Cicero 355 of the 680 examples of perfect periods that he selected for imitation in his *Retorica*.[1]

Similarly, Horace remained their master of literary criticism. Only the strictest adherence to his rules, warned Marco Girolamo Vida of Cremona (1485–1556) in his oft-reprinted *Poeticarum libri*, would eventually win for Volgare literature the Virgilian epic poem it still lacked. These rules were therefore read even into Aristotle's *Poetics* – the very text, that is, which was soon to provide a very different set of rules.[2] Euripides and Sophocles were prescribed as required reading for anyone seeking to compose tragedy out of his own fantasy.[3] Theocritus was added to the authorities on ancient painting, at least for those ancient paintings that survived only in his verbal descriptions of them. When neither a visual nor a verbal model survived, painters were admonished to follow the example of one of Pliny's hero-painters, whose Diana, it seems, was a composite of the most beautiful features of each of the five winners in a beauty contest he had sponsored in ancient Agrigentum. Vasari had his *Artist in the Studio* (Florence: Casa Vasari) paint his Juno while surrounded by three women – one posing completely in the nude, the other two removing their clothes in anticipation of taking her place.

Indeed, the stature gained for the ancients by the humanists of the fifteenth century was even further enhanced by the success of the philologists of the mid-sixteenth century in refining their predecessors' methods of textual criticism – in particular that of Pier Vettori, 'the educator of a whole generation of Florentines, [whom] in the knowledge of languages no one has ever surpassed'.[4] Teams of colleagues and disciples were dispatched to search through libraries for manuscripts and, although neither they nor any of their successors ever stumbled upon anything resembling the riches of the great treasure houses of the early Renaissance text hunters, they did manage to recover at least one long-lost literary work – the *Agamemnon* of Aeschylus – and to locate many more manuscripts of already known works. By organizing these manuscripts into chronologically arranged 'genealogies', they no longer had to rely upon well-informed guesses, as did Lorenzo Valla and Angelo Poliziano a half-century earlier, in order to fill in gaps and correct faulty readings. They could now climb back up the 'family tree' to the earliest surviving manuscript, the one nearest the lost original and less subject to subsequent scribal errors. They 'castigated' all extant editions accordingly – even when ancient spelling defied modern pronunciation, as it did apparently for Trissino when he transliterated *dianoia* as *djanea*. As these castigated Latin and Greek texts were broadcast to all Europe for the guidance of the learned, they were made accessible to the non-Latin reading public of Italy in scores of new translations. And to assure the widest possible diffusion of the translations, the translators generally followed the advice of the technical authorities – of Fausto da Longiano, who denounced inevitably awkward word-for-word renditions on the authority of Cicero, and of Antonio Minturno (d. 1574), who made ancient choruses sing in more familiar Petrarchan stanzas.

The men of arts and letters in the decades after 1530 also continued to regard their mentors of the Age of Leo x and Clement vii as the equals, if not the superiors, of the ancients. Castiglione still provided them with the framework for their literary and philosophical dialogues – even when he obliged the sedentary academicians of the *Infiammati* to move out of Padua to the properly atemporal, aspatial villa of Beatrice degli Obizi in the nearby Euganei hills. Machiavelli still provided them with the laws of politics and the method by which the laws could be discovered; and when one Giovan Maria Memmo became nervous concerning the wrath of the anti-Machiavellians, he disguised his numerous plagiarisms so skilfully that no one noticed them for another four centuries. Machiavelli also continued to furnish personages for comedy writers. His fra Timoteo reappeared as Anton Francesco Grazzini's *Frate* in 1540 and as fra Girolamo da Pesaro, the stand-in for a war-bound husband, in Lodovico Dolce's *Il marito* in 1548. Messer Nicia reappeared as missier Despontao in Andrea Calmo's *Pozione* of 1552. And whole passages from the *Mandragola* (1518) and the *Clizia* (first performed in 1525) reappeared in the conversations of the down-to-earth artisans that Anton Francesco

70

Doni picked up on the marble steps (*I marmi*) of the cathedral of Florence in 1552–53.[5]

Ariosto still provided the comedy writers with structures and stage directions. His complicated plots were reproduced in the equally Plautan plays of his successor at Ferrara, Alfonso Guarini (1538–1616), the son of the famous pedagogue Battista, the hero of whose *Il pratico* must overcome interminable obstacles before seducing the wife of a peripatetic Roman gentleman. His rule about choosing contemporary settings was scrupulously observed by Annibal Caro (1507–1566). He enlisted his friends in Florence to collect colloquial proverbs for the speeches of his Florentine characters. By emphasizing the contingent character of a single moment, he overcame the challenge of time.[6]

In some cases, the lasting influence of the High Renaissance mentors can be explained by their own longevity. Michelangelo lived until 1564, fourteen years after he had been canonized as the greatest artist of all times in the first edition of Vasari's *Lives*. Hence, Gianbattista Franco of Venice (*c*. 1498–1561) was not guilty of an anachronism when he copied figures on the Sistine ceiling for his own use in the 1530s; nor was the Florentine Alessandro Allori (1535–1607) when he borrowed the Christ and the pale tones of the *Last Judgement* for his own version of the same theme in the Annunziata of Florence in the early 1560s. In other cases, this influence can be attributed to the unswerving devotion of long-living disciples. The great Vicentine architect Palladio lived until 1580, ten years after he had canonized himself, in his *Quattro libri dell'architettura*, as the reincarnation of Bramante, 'that most excellent observer of ancient edifices'. He reproduced almost exactly, except for the roof, the structure of an ancient Roman theatre in the one he built for his colleagues of the Accademia Olimpica of Vicenza, wholly insouciant about the warnings of Serlio, his guide in reading Vitruvius, that ancient theatres were unsuitable for modern comedies, and just as insouciant about the efforts of the Sienese painter Baldassare Peruzzi (1481–1556) to find help in Vitruvius to overcome the empirically verifiable defects of the 'Pomponian' model inherited from the fifteenth century. So carefully did he achieve his goal that his theatre was imitated only once – in the ducal theatre at Sabbioneta – even though it had been inaugurated in 1585 with no less a manifesto of unbending classicism than a performance of *Oedipus Rex* and with 'such grandeur and pomp that even the majesty of a king could not have done better'.[7]

Frequently the longevity of High Renaissance styles was imposed by the original plans for a long-term project. The triumphal arches and high reliefs erected much later for the facing tombs of Leo x and Clement vii on either side of the apse of the Minerva in Rome look as if they had been built by Raphael or Antonio da Sangallo the Younger (1483–1546) largely because the sculptors were consciously trying to evoke the great age to which the popes had given their names. The decoration of the courtyard of the Palazzo Sacchetti was limited to simple arches without keystones and that of the Via Giulia façade to a small fountain on the far left, probably out of respect for the same Sangallo, who lived there, as the inscription still points out, in

1543. All the successive architects of the second biggest architectural undertaking of sixteenth-century Rome, the Palazzo Farnese, remained faithful to the original designs of 1514; and although it was completed long after the death of Pope Paul III, it became, if belatedly, one of the greatest monuments of High Renaissance architecture.[8]

Fidelity to the norm was even more marked in the centres more recently converted to humanism. In Milan, Giovan Pietro and Aurelio Luini reproduced in their Capella Bergamina of the Monastero Maggiore in 1555 almost exactly the same impenetrably statuesque figures that their father Bernardino had taught them to paint in his Cappella Besozzi of 1530; and they permitted themselves no greater departure from his rules than a playful cupid holding up a curtain in the corner of the Cappella Bentivoglio. In Parma, the painter Girolamo Mazzola Bedoli (the cousin of Parmigianino) adopted in his *Transfiguration* (1556) the same spacial patterns – with two prophets on a cloud and the three disciples spread out along an ascending foreground – that Correggio (1494–1534) had canonized on the ceiling of San Giovanni Evangelista; and when Correggio's *Coronation of the Virgin* was destroyed in 1587 to make way for a much enlarged apse, Cesare Aretusi (d. 1612) was commissioned to make another one exactly like it – with results that can be appreciated by comparing his work with the fragments of his model preserved at the National Galleries of London and Parma. When Gaudenzio Ferrari (d. 1546) arrived from Vercelli in Milan around 1539, he had already been converted to Titian. He was then converted to Leonardo da Vinci as well. He put the cross of his *Crucifixion* (Turin: Galleria Saubada) in the geometric centre with the two women in the foreground equidistant on either side. He put two immobile saints on either side of a perfectly centred, immobile *Virgin and Child* (Galleria Sabauda). He admitted no other alteration in the *Last Supper* (Milan: S. Maria della Passione) than an idealized temple outside the luminous window directly behind Jesus' head and a square, rather than an oblong, table in the front.[9]

The most faithful of all the disciples were the Bemban–Petrarchan poets and the Boccaccian short story writers. Their fidelity was encouraged in part by the appearance of several Platonic–Horatian treatises on *ars poetica* – beginning with the one by Bernardino Daniello (*c.* 1500–1565), the translator of Virgil's *Georgics*, and culminating in the six-book Latin dialogue by Antonio Minturno, which reconciled Quintilian and Cicero with every possible reference to poetry in all the works of Plato. Their loyalty was still further encouraged by the continuing presence of Marsilio Ficino's Neo-Platonism as the semi-official philosophy of most of the academies. Ficino's own Florentine version of his *Symposium* commentary, executed in accordance with the author's own anticipation of sixteenth-century translation standards, was published in 1544. The translation he had entrusted to Tommaso Benci of his Latin version of Hermes Trismegistos was published in 1548. Meanwhile, one after another writer of dialogues *dell'amore* – from Giuseppe Betussi in *Il Raverta* (1544) to Andrea Sansovino (1521–1586) in the *Ragionamento* 'in which young men are taught the beautiful art of love' – popularized in the Volgare the themes of

Ficino's works that were frequently reprinted in the Latin original. These themes were applied to Petrarch in the many current editions of, and commentaries on, the *Canzoniere*. One Platonic philosopher, the theologian and Old Testament scholar Agostino Steuco (1496–1549), went so far as to hail Ficino's Christianized Platonism as the 'perennial philosophy', the one that would finally exorcize the Christian faith of such inelegant writers as Thomas Aquinas and Duns Scotus and replace them with such elegant writers as Ovid, Virgil and Proclus.[10]

What made fidelity to the models particularly productive, however, was the flexibility of one of them and the inflexibility of the other. The prestige of Boccaccio's *Decameron* was reinforced during the course of the century by the publication of his other vernacular works and the translation of his Latin works, the latter by one of the chief authorities on *amore*, Giuseppe Betussi.[11] Sebastiano Erizzo of Venice (1525–1585) was thus able to borrow from the *Filocolo* and the *Famous Women*; and, as Boccaccio's first editor (Lodovico Dolce) observed, 'he managed to convert the food he consumed into his own flesh and blood'.[12] If in some details he appeared to be somewhat less than Boccaccian, it was for the impeccably orthodox reason that he sometimes read the *Decameron* not in the original, but as it had been 'pulled apart and interpreted in the *Prose* of Pietro Bembo'.[13]

The *Canzoniere*, on the other hand, admitted far fewer liberties. Originality had to be achieved solely by taking words, phrases and conceits from Petrarch or from an orthodox Petrarchan and arranging them in a slightly different order. That is what Galeazzo di Tàrsia did in his *Chiaro e di vero onor marmo lucente*, almost all of which consists of quotations from Petrarch, Bembo and Galeazzo's Bemban-Petrarchan colleagues in Naples.[14] The Petrarchan model prescribed only four or five primary colours, with no other shadings than an occasional diminutive like *pallidetto* (softly pale). It limited birds to only two kinds, big ones and small ones – like the *augellin* that carried Giovan Battista Strozzi's heart up into an otherwise unspecified 'air' (*aere*). It allowed poets to play on the same set of simple antitheses ('cry'/'laugh'; 'dead'/'alive'; 'the snow burns'), the same stretched-out similes ('As the . . .') resolved in the final *terzina* ('so I . . .'), the same conventional metaphors and personifications, such as *pasceste l'alma pur, lacrime mie* (tears of mine, you nourished my soul indeed [Tansillo]), or, more frequently, *Amor* (Love) and *Canzon* (Song). It allowed them to ignore ninety percent of the adjectives in current use: valleys were never anything more nuanced than *erbose* ('grassy'), pearls (or teeth) were always *candide* ('white'), a soul was always either *beata* ('blessed') or *infelice* ('unhappy') [Tàrsia]. Even those poets like Bernardo Tasso of Venice (1493–1569) who tried to disassociate themselves from a 'Bemban school' usually did so on behalf of a still more 'intransigent faith . . . in Petrarchan stylistics', and they were therefore even more obliged to translate 'her matutinal ablutions' as

Chiare fontane, ove a madonna piacque
col netto avorio e man gentili e schiette

nelle vostre gelate e lucid'acque
lavarsi il viso e quelle perle elette

Limpid streams, where my lady pleased,
with clear ivory [her arms] and pure and elegant hands
in your bright icy waters,
to bathe her face and those rare pearls

Furthermore, poets never had to bother about the complexities of love as an intimate physical and emotional relationship between two real persons. Love was nothing other than a predetermined set of psychological reactions of a lover-poet to an equally predetermined set of qualities supposed to exist in a wholly imaginary, or metaphysical, loved one – reactions that fascinated sixteenth-century writers as much as they seem to some twentieth-century critics to be expressions of a 'cold, hyperuranic intellectualism'. Specific places and times were also excluded: indeed, what appears to be a reference in a poem by Tansillo to an earthquake at Campi Flegrei on 29 September 1538 is actually a barely disguised paraphrase of Virgil (*Aeneid*, vii, 312).

To be sure, some individual and local variants of the formula were occasionally tolerated. Luigi Tansillo, whose greatest regret in life was not having met 'mio gran Bembo', added to the canon some lines from Ovid and Giovanni Pontano; and he produced a few new colours, a few apparently new metaphors and a few further specimens of 'virtuous counterpoint':

Dolce mio duol, novo nel mondo e raro, . . .
Se 'l remedio m'è noia e il mal diletto[15]

Sweet suffering of mine, strange to the world and rare, . . .
If the soothing hurts and the pain delights me

The paragon of women poets, Vittoria Colonna (1490–1547), who worshipped Bembo as much as he and all the other male poets of Italy adored her, sublimated Petrarch's Laura into *L'amor superno* ('celestial love'), which guided her 'out of [her] cold, arid winter and into His green, warm Spring', as in Bembo's *Se già ne l'età mia più verde e calda* ('If then in my greenest, warmest years'). For it was unthinkable that she, or any other of the many female Petrarchan poets of the age, should try to get even with men by turning them too into passive abstractions. Since apparently even the Holy Spirit did not mind being compared for the hundredth time to a mother bird feeding her chicks, Vittoria's poems spread across Italy in some multiple of the fifty-three manuscript copies that have survived and in some 340 known printed volumes of collected works.[16]

VARIATIONS UPON THE MODELS

The High Renaissance thus continued to be present well after the decades of the 'calamities' – indeed, until as late as the 1580s, when one Luca Marenzio felt moved, while setting to music the post-classical verses of contemporary Ferrarese poets, to profess once again his loyalty to his 'beloved classics'.[17] Yet most such professions of loyalty were made with one important, if usually tacit, reservation: that what the mentors had assumed were absolute and eternally valid principles be regarded instead merely as hypotheses for further experimentation or elaboration. For example, Rosso Fiorentino (1495–1540) left the arrangement of the figures in his *Virgin and Child Enthroned* (Volterra: Villamagna) just as it had been established by fra Bartolomeo; but he shoved them upward until all their heads were confined within the upper eighth of the frame and toned down the lines on their faces until they were unrecognizable as individuals (Volterra: Pinacoteca). Camillo Boccaccino (1501–1546) put his Mary in exactly the same statuesque pose prescribed for her by the dean of High Renaissance painters in Cremona, Gian Francesco Bembo (d. *c.* 1526); but he made her grin sarcastically at the angel at her feet whose wing had just been cut off by an archangel (Cremona: Museo Civico). Pordenone (1483–1539) combined the canonical three successive scenes of Christ before Pilate into one, and he exercised his 'complete anatomical control' with such 'dynamism, passion and violent movement' that the figures all seem 'to turn and bend at each joint'.[18]

Similarly, Giovan Battista Fornovo (1521–1575) maintained Bramante's temple in his Annunziata at Parma; but he turned the keystones into diamonds and let them cut up through the cornice above the windows. The Veronese architect Michele Sanmicheli left the standard Corinthian columns on either side of the arch in the Palazzo Bevilacqua at Verona; but he alternated the prescribed perpendicular fluting with spirals and topped the columns with a frieze of twisted leaves and flowers. Francesco Beccuti (1509–1553) rearranged quotations from Petrarch's *Italia mia* and *Chiare, fresche e dolci acque* in strictest obedience of the rules of Bembo, whose death later inspired him to write a tearful Latin *carmen*: but when he finished, the Petrarchan pain he felt turned out to have been provoked by the loss not of a Laura, but of his cat.[19] Jacopo Bonfadio (b. 1509) professed to having only two goals in life: 'displeasing God as little as I can' and 'pleasing Your Reverence [i.e., Bembo] as much as I can'; but he then went on to do so in a rather un-Beyman manner: by writing a poem in praise of 'roguery' (*furfanteria*) and dedicating it to 'King Rogue of most roguish Roguery'.[20]

Such 'bizarre, capricious, fantastic inventions'[21] scandalized the Neoclassic critics of the eighteenth century, who loaded Vasari's purely descriptive term *maniera* with pejorative critical judgements and applied it to whatever in the otherwise Augustan sixteenth century violated Winckelmann's ideal of *grande stile*. Critics of the sixteenth century, on the other hand, avoided being scandalized. They did so by ignoring the phenomenon altogether and simply repeating the formulas that their High Renaissance mentors had borrowed from their ancient mentors. If a modern painter could not find just the right model for 'a beautiful woman' in a classical painter, advised Lodovico Dolce, 'he needed only read those stanzas of Ariosto [that] marvellously describe the beauties of the fair Alcina'; for, as Horace had pointed out, poetry is verbal painting and painting is visible poetry.[22] If the painter had doubts about entrusting himself to a purely literary critic, he could turn to a painter-critic, like Paolo Pino of Venice (fl. 1534–1565), with full assurance of finding the rules of painting backed up by the rules of rhetoric: Vasari's 'drawing', 'invention' and 'colour', said Pino, correspond exactly to Cicero's 'invention', 'disposition' and 'elocution'.[23] If an architect could not find guidance for some detail in Vitruvius, he could look it up in Alberti, that 'great lover of ancient edifices', whose *De architectura* appeared in two different Volgare translations between 1546 and 1550. If he could not find it in Alberti, he could look it up in Trissino or in Alvise Cornaro, who pretended to do no more than explain the obscure passages in the text of 'the divine Vitruvius' and add a few points concerning 'the houses and rooms of [private] citizens' that 'the great Leon Baptista' had not had time to elaborate fully.[24] If he needed further guidance, he was certain to find it in the precise mathematical observations that Sebastiano Serlio had abstracted from Baldassare Peruzzi's measurements of ancient structures in Istria and Dalmatia as well as Rome.[25]

Alas, repeating the formulas made the critics ever less able to grasp what the artists and writers of their day were actually doing. They occasionally invented a new term – like Vasari's *facilità* ('ease'), Dolce's 'I don't-know-what (*non so che*) which fills the soul with infinite delight' and Girolamo Fracastoro's (1478–1553) commendation of whatever is expressed 'well and ornately', which threatened to throw Virgil and Lucretius off Mt Parnassus.[26] One well-qualified literary critic, Benedetto Varchi, decided to ask the artists themselves what they were up to. But his poll of Florentine *botteghe* produced only still another strange term, *grazia* ('grace'), which he was unable to define. Another, Bernardo Tasso, suggested that poets and rhetoricians abandon the role of judges altogether and turn it over to the general public. 'If it was all right for Doric painters to paint other than what was then considered to be properly Attic', he continued, 'why can't Italian poets compose their works in whatever manner' guarantees that their works will 'give pleasure [to] and be read' by others? What is good, proposed that prolific translator of the classics, the Dominican Remigio Fiorentino (*c.* 1521–1581), is what 'conforms to the customs' of the day. Ancient Athenians, he recalled, did not reproach Cimon for marrying his sister, even though modern Italians do; and 'there are things that [the ancients] held to be dishonest and ugly that we think honest and beautiful'.[27]

The attempts of the critics to comprehend current practice thus brought them to the brink of relativism; and since admitting even the possibility of different kinds of goodness and beauty would have ruined their common quest for absolute norms, they retreated. Instead of trying to explain what could not fit into their categories, they went on applying such uncompromisingly vague Vasarian terms as *bello*, *divino* and *meraviglioso* to whatever in the works of their contemporaries happened to correspond to High Renaissance conventions; and they quietly passed over all the rest.[28]

That left the artists and writers free to do what they pleased without fear of what the critics might say. Pontormo began as early as 1515 to take slight liberties with the patterns prescribed for him by his master Andrea del Sarto (1486–1531) – for instance, by making the woman sitting on the steps of his *Visitation* (Florence: Annunziata, 1514–16) stare anxiously, rather than look invitingly, at the spectator. He went on to turn Andrea's clear, nuanced colours into monochrome washes, to change his shaded-black shadows into stark red shadows in the *Supper at Emmaus* (Uffizi: Santa Maria Maggiore, 1525) and to separate the figures represented until they no longer touched each other in *Vertumnus and Pomona* in the Medici Villa at Poggio a Caiano. He shortened the legs of the dead Christ of the *Deposition* (Florence: Santa Felicita, 1526–28) until no weight at all fell on the shoulders of the light pink figure squatting on four deformed toes beneath them. He let the baby Jesus slip off Mary's lap and join her in grinning condescendingly at the vain efforts of Jerome to participate in their *Holy Conversation* (Empoli: Collegiata, 1519) by his intellectual powers alone. Pontormo's disciple Angelo Bronzino followed his master's example – first in Pesaro, then, after 1532, in his native Florence. He placed Orpheus' full face in the upper centre of the frame (*Venus, Cupid, Folly and Time*, London: National Gallery), just where Andrea del Sarto would have put it, and he placed Venus' profile head in exactly the same position. But he doubled the natural size of Orpheus' shoulders and thighs so that they fill up almost the whole right half and bottom one-fourth of the picture, and he slung a giant arm across the top to match Venus' weightless legs bent at right angles to form a corresponding frame at the bottom.[29]

Similarly, the reputation of Perin del Vaga as a disciple of Raphael increased to the point where he was appointed head of Paul III's project to re-design the interior of Castel Sant'Angelo – and asked to assemble assistants from all over Italy in what became the largest *bottega* of Pauline Rome. But when called upon to produce a Raphaelesque *Mother, Child and St John* (Rome: Galleria Borghese), he proceeded to press in the sides of Raphael's triangle until it became an isosceles and to leave Elizabeth outside in almost total darkness. When called upon to produce another Vatican *stanza*, he employed Raphael's famous techniques for un-Raphaelesque *trompe-l'oeil* effects: a life-size courtier pushing his way through a half-open door on one side, a squashed-down pile of aging muscles trying to escape up a spiral staircase on the other, and a zoo full of various kinds of birds and playful baboons running all around the walls – none of which could have served any other purpose than that of amusing the spectators.[30]

In like manner, Parmigianino (Girolamo Francesco Maria Muzzuoli, 1503–1540) began experimenting with the forms taught him by his master Correggio as soon as he returned, after several years of study in Rome and Bologna, to succeed him at San Giovanni Evangelista in Parma (1531). He had already introduced minor modifications before his departure – e.g., elevating a dog's hind legs so that its back would continue the diagonal line of St Vitale's sword. Now, he became still more courageous. On canvas, he doubled the size of his own hand in a *Self-Portrait* (Vienna: Kunsthistorisches Museum, 1524), using a convex mirror to avoid infringing upon the rule of natural reality; and he stretched out Baby Jesus' body to match the equally stretched-out long neck of His Mother (*Madonna dal Collo Lungo*, Florence: Uffizi, 1535). In fresco, he turned birds upside down, let cupids play on a floating platform, transformed the *Four Temperaments* into a string of fish, shields, swords, tridents and lutes, and flattened out the forehead of the tormenter of a muscular St Agatha (Parma: S. Giovanni Evangelista *c*. 1522–24). He did so with such a 'restless spirit' that it took all the ingenuity of his equally 'Mannerist' colleague Michelangelo Anselmi (d. 1554) to preserve the unity of the church – with gently coloured chiaroscuro arabesques all around the nave and with strings of flowers, vases and vines stretching down from the artificially elevated ceilings.[31]

The writers treated their masters in much the same way. Castiglione's dialogue form was given theoretical sanction soon after its appearance in final form – both by the lay philosopher Speroni, in his *Apologia dei dialoghi* (1543), and by the academic philologist Carlo Sigonio, in his *De dialogo*. It was adopted for a wholly different subject matter by one of the most universal encyclopaedic writers of the day, Alberti's translator Cosimo Bartoli (1503–1572) – namely, for questions regarding the structure of the eye and the nature of vision and for all the mass of miscellaneous erudition culled by the omnivorous author from scores of ancient, modern, Italian and transalpine authors. The same form was then adopted by the historian Paolo Giovio in order to treat systematically a subject that had been brought up and then dropped at the beginning of the *Cortegiano*: *imprese*, 'the emblems that great lords and noble knights are accustomed to wear on their garments . . . or fix onto their banners to signify one of their generous thoughts'. Giovio thereby sanctioned still another organizing principle about which to gather the encyclopaedic learning of the age – namely, the one that had been launched twenty years earlier by Andrea Alciato's *Emblemata* of 1531, one of the most frequently reprinted reference books of the entire century.[32]

Finally, the Castiglione dialogue form was adopted by the diplomat-poet Giovanni Della Casa (1503–1556) specifically for the purpose of reducing Castiglione's luminous utopia to chiaroscuro reality and of replacing his ethical ideal with an empirical investigation of current behaviour. Della Casa had already ridiculed unpragmatic ideals in an eloquent defense of the celibate life – a vocation which he never had and did not intend to observe himself, despite his clerical status. He had also explained to servants and secretaries how they could put up with disagreeable or incompetent employers whom they could neither reform nor abandon. Then, in his famous *Galateo* (1558), he replaced Castiglione's polished courtiers with an uneducated old Tuscan rustic; and he let his world-wise protagonist lecture at random to a young man, in impeccable Bemban Tuscan, on how to accommodate himself to the rather imperfect society in which he lived. For Della Casa the various rules by which civil society was maintained consisted of conventions over which the members of the society had no control whatsoever. Manners thus had no more to do with morality than Machiavelli's laws of politics with Christian theology. This discovery was presented with magnificent rhetorical skill – the subtle playing on different levels of language, the cleverly disguised references to Aristotle, Cicero, Theophrastus, Horace and a number of other ancient and modern authors whom the protagonist had never heard of, as well as the judicious use of apparently irrelevant asides, 'redundant similes' and 'epanorthoses' ('they don't like it, indeed, they detest it'). The *Galateo* was immediately acclaimed as 'one of the best prose works of the best age of literature and certainly second to none other' – to none, that is, except to the *Cortegiano*, the model that illuminated all its experimental variations.[33]

THE DRAMATISTS AND THE NOVELLA WRITERS

What the dialogue writers did with Castiglione, the tragedians did with Trissino.[34] They attempted – unsuccessfully – to displace the *Sofonisba* after the failure of such modern classical tragedies as those of Trissino's contemporaries in the Age of Clement VII, like the Florentines Luigi Alamanni (1495–1556), Ludovico Martelli (1503–*c*. 1531) and Alessandro de' Pazzi (1483–1530), as well as those of his immediate successors in the Age of Paul III, like Sperone Speroni in his *Canace* of 1540 and Pietro Aretino in his *Orazia* of 1546, which almost all critics from the sixteenth to the twentieth century have chosen quietly to ignore. The most successful of the mid-sixteenth-century tragedians was thus free to build on the *Sofonisba* alone – namely, Giambattista Giraldi (Cinthio), the leading dramatist in Ferrara in the decades after the death of Ariosto.

Giraldi added to Trissino's Sophoclean base elements borrowed from Seneca – who, he insisted, 'surpassed all the Greeks in prudence, gravity, decorum and majesty' – a prologue, for instance, and a division of the action into five acts of almost equal length. He then conscientiously put into practice the typically Mannerist critical principle he proclaimed in his *Discorsi* on comic and tragic drama. The tragedian's chief aim, Giraldi insisted, was 'to make his work pleasing to the spectators' by 'accommodating himself to the usages of the times' and by trying 'to satisfy those who listen, [even if that meant] writing something a bit less excellent whenever something too grand apparently displeased them'.[35] If strictly following Aristotle's rules for creating suspense failed to produce the desired effect, he could stretch out to un-Aristotelian lengths the time allotted for prying bad news out of a reluctant messenger. If they failed to sympathize fully with aristocratic heroes, he could transfer the role of protagonists to servants or to personages reduced to the tenor of everyday life, as Giraldi himself did in his *Didone*. If their responsiveness to Horace's aim of moral improvement was dimmed by a steady diet of tragic endings, the tragedian could experiment with a happy ending, as Giraldi did in his *Altile*. If they were more moved by the sight of horror than by descriptions of horror, he could let blood flow right on stage. He had Orbecche, daughter of the king of Persia, kill her father and then herself because he had killed her mother, her husband and her two children. Several spectators were reported to have fainted on the spot when the bloody remains of husband and children were displayed on stage.

What Giraldi did with Trissino, the Sienese playwright Alessandro Piccolomini (1508–1578) did with Aretino – or at least with Aretino's notorious
dramatic dialogues (*Ragionamenti*) of a nun, a married woman and a prostitute.
He moved the scene of his *La Raffaella o delle belle creanze delle donne* (1539)
from Rome to Siena, where moral standards were at least less debased, if no
less de-Christianized. He endowed his protagonist with characteristics
borrowed not only from Boccaccio, but also from the contemporary Spanish
comedy writer Fernando de Rojas, whose *Celestina* was published in at least
thirteen editions of Alfonso Hordognez' Italian translation between 1506 and
1543. He toned down Aretino's sense of revulsion before the more scabrous
aspects of contemporary life – to the point where Raffaella's exposition of the
difficult life of the beautiful young wife of an ever-absent aging husband
became a defence of women in general against 'those malicious men . . . who
hold them to be incapable of creating great and profound thoughts, . . . only
frivolous and feeble ones'.[36]

The comedy writers conducted similar experiments with the models
provided by Ariosto and Machiavelli. Marcantonio Epicuro (1472–1555) had
already anticipated Aretino's *Ragionamenti* in the *Cecaria* of 1523, a dramatic
dialogue among several old blind men whose ridiculous recollections of all
the corporeal parts of their former sweethearts, from the hair down to 'the
even more precious members that the clothes do not wish to make manifest',
constitute a clever parody of Bembo's Petrarchan themes. He then moved
classical comedy out of the city and into the woods, among Petrarchan 'lovely
hills' and Sannazaran 'murmuring, fresh, clear streams', inaugurating what
soon became a prolific sub-genre, the *Commedia boscareccia* ('rustic comedy').[37]
Similarly, Andrea Calmo, the most successful comedy writer in Venice in the
years after 1545, took the classical principle of realism in contemporary
settings to its logical extreme. He introduced not just Venetian, but also half-
Italianized non-Italian lowbrow characters into his plots and let them speak
on stage exactly as he had heard them speak in the *piazze* and on the canals
of the polyglot international emporium he had known as the son of a poor
fisherman. The Paduan rustics in *La Rhodiana* spoke in Paduan sentences that
he lifted out of Ruzante. The 'Todesco' in his *Las Spagnolas* spoke a mixture
of dialect German and Venetian. His Ragusan salted his speeches with Slavic
words. Even when comic figures were made to speak correct Volgare, as were
Annibal Caro's Roman *Straccioni* ('scruffy scoundrels'), and when they were
made to move in patterns borrowed from the Alexandrian romancer of the
second century, Achilles Tatius – the most recent addition to the repertoire
of ancient novella writers – they remained on the stage exactly as the author
had observed them while wandering around Rome's Campo de' Fiori. So faith-
fully did they reflect the real situations of a particular time and place, even
when they were occasionally transformed into 'emblematic personages' in
accordance with the prescriptions of the literary genre, that for years Caro
refused all the numerous requests to have his comedy performed in other
cities.[38]

The Mannerist playwrights thus succeeded in avoiding the tedium of such post-classical attempts at pure classicism as Donato Giannotti's *Il vecchio amoroso* of 1533–36, which amounted to little more than a paraphrase of Plautus' *Mercator*. Instead of attempting to create new classics themselves, they applied the formulas of the established classics to new subjects, like the generation gap between the shopkeeper's son Alamanno and his straightlaced mother in Giambattista Gelli's *Sporta* of 1543.[39] They mixed literary and scientific reminiscences, like those that were soon to turn Alessandro Piccolomini from a playwright into a philosopher, with the practical experiences of such performing companies as the Accademia degli Intronati. They placed Spanish-speaking captains, haughty Neapolitan noblemen and German students ignorant of Italian verb conjugations alongside Volgare-speaking Tuscans. They introduced political messages – like Piccolomini's appeal to his first distinguished spectator, Emperor Charles v, regarding the importance of an ecumenical council – into standard love intrigues. They thus assured the lasting popularity of their works – in the case of Piccolomini's *Amor costante*, some twelve editions between 1540 and 1600.[40] In order to underscore the contrast between a Mannerist variation and its High Renaissance model, at least one attempt was made to put them both on at the same time. The single acts of Giovan Maria Cecchi's masterpiece, *L'assiuolo* (*The Horned Owl*) of 1550, were separated by the corresponding acts of Machiavelli's *Mandragola* on an opposite stage in the same hall, with the *intermedi* suppressed and with stage designs by the most popular painters of the moment, Angelo Bronzino and Francesco Salviati. 'Never before', remarked one well-qualified spectator, 'have I ever seen such a remarkable invention'.[41]

Almost as bold as the dramatists were the writers of *novelle*.[42] All accepted Boccaccio as an infallible guide. But some of them stretched out his *cornice* (the 'setting' established by the refugees from the plague of 1348) until single *novelle* became merely specific illustrations of themes sustained by one or another of the personages of the *cornice* – as they are, for example, throughout Silvano Cattaneo's *Dodici giornate* ('Twelve Days') of 1553 and in Girolamo Parabosco's story of the young widow of Piacenza (*I diporti*, 1550), which is followed by three pages of moral debate among the listeners.[43] Others abolished the *cornice*: what holds together Matteo Bandello's (1485–1561) otherwise unrelated stories are the prefatory accounts of the situations in which he had first heard them – since he, the most prolific of sixteenth-century storytellers and the best-known of them in the twentieth century, never pretended to do other than collect stories supposedly invented by others.

Some writers populated their stories with characters taken from social classes well below the level of Boccaccio's princes, merchants and artisans – characters like Gian Francesco Straparola's (d. 1557) Pietro Pazzo and Adamantina; and they treated them with far more sympathy than Ruzante or the *Intronati* had ever shown their Paduan and Sienese rustics.[44] Some worked over Boccaccio's rather sensuous exposition of sexual relations until all traces of love and affection vanished and nothing was left but a purely physical passion – like that of Bandello's nymphomaniac Lucrezia Vicentina.

Others dwelt upon the morbid aspects of Boccaccio's stories until nothing was left but the unmitigatedly lugubrious – as in Anton Francesco Grazzini's accounts of a girl hanging from a bell rope and of dead bodies making amorous gestures. Satire, particularly when directed toward the clergy, often degenerated into tirades as bitter as those of Aretino. *Beffe* – the 'practical jokes' of the traditional Florentine storytellers – often turned into something approaching acts of sadism.

Seldom did the achievements of the short-story writers fully correspond to the authors' expectations. Francesco Maria Molza finished only five stories of what he had projected as a new *Decameron* before being distracted by his many other literary interests. Grazzini finished only about half of the *cene* ('suppers') he had hoped to write, in part because he preferred to repolish the stories he had already written before proceeding to write new ones, leaving his incomplete collection to be discovered two centuries later. Some of the tales amount to little more than paragraph-long accounts of incidents as tasteless as they are improbable – like Bandello's story about the ten-year-old girl who ate a castrated priest's testicles thinking they were figs.

Giraldi was certain that he had written a work of literature fully consonant with his doctrine of the perfectibility of models. 'Things in their beginnings are not perfect', he noted; 'they have need of our industry and diligence to be made better written' – as the experience of the Romans with their Greek models had proven in the past and as his own correction of Boccaccio's erroneous attribution of disaster to pure chance was meant to prove in the present. What he ended up with, however, was the *Hecatommithi* (1565) – a work impossible to read. Still, the *novella* writers contributed to the realization of the goal implicit in their experiments: that of exploring the possibilities of one or another aspect of their chief model, of travelling along new roads without breaking with the tradition and of innovating within the structural rules the model prescribed. Rather than eclipsing the *Decameron*, they assured its stature as a classic, to be imitated as well as admired among all their successors between the age of Giraldi and the age of Italo Calvino.

THE FAITHFUL REBELS

At times, the Mannerists took freedoms with their models that went well beyond the limits set by Grazzini's reservations. Some put aside the masters momentarily and imitated previous imitators instead. Rosso Fiorentino followed not Raphael, but Raphael's disciple Francesco Sansovino in the frescoes and canvases he painted at Arezzo in the late 1520s; and that is perhaps why many of them are so un-Raphaelesque or even anti-Raphaelesque in appearance. Bronzino borrowed not from any of the colleagues of Andrea del Sarto, but from Francesco Salviati in designing his *Justice Rescuing Innocence* (Florence: Palazzo Vecchio). Armed with the iconographic sanction of no less an authority than Annibal Caro, Bronzino turned the two principal figures

Plate 1. (*overleaf*) Taddeo Zuccaro, *The Armistice between Francis I and Charles V*. Detail from the Sala del Concilio di Trento, 1565, Villa Farnese, Caprarola (Alinari).

Plate 2. (*above*) Titian, *Paul III and his Nephews*, 1546, Capodimonte, Naples (Bridgeman Art Library/National Museum, Naples).

Plate 3. Titian, *Venus and the Organ Player*, Prado, Madrid (Mansell Collection).

Plate 4. Jacopo Pontormo, *Deposition*, *c.* 1525, Chiesa di Santa Felicita, Florence (Mansell Collection).

Plate 5. Rosso Fiorentino, *The Deposition from the Cross*, 1521, Pinacoteca, Volterra (Scala).

Plate 6. (*above*) Angelo Bronzino, *Venus, Cupid, Folly and Time, c.* 1545, National Gallery, London (Bridgeman Art Gallery).

Plate 7. (*right*) Francesco Parmigianino, *Madonna dal Collo Lungo, c.* 1535, Uffizi, Florence (Bridgeman Art Gallery/Ufizzi Gallery).

Plate 8. (*above*) Giorgio Vasari, *Studiolo* of Francesco I, 1570–73, Palazzo Vecchio, Florence (Alinari).

Plate 9. (*right*) 'Goldsmiths', detail from the *Studiolo* of Francesco I (Mansell Collection).

Plate 10. (*above*) Caravaggio, *The Calling of Saint Matthew, c.* 1599–1603, Santa Luigi dei Francesi, Rome (Alinari).

Plate 11. (*right*) Annibale Carracci, *Butcher's Shop, c.* 1582–83, Christ Church Gallery, Oxford (reproduced by kind permission of the Governing Body, Christ Church, Oxford).

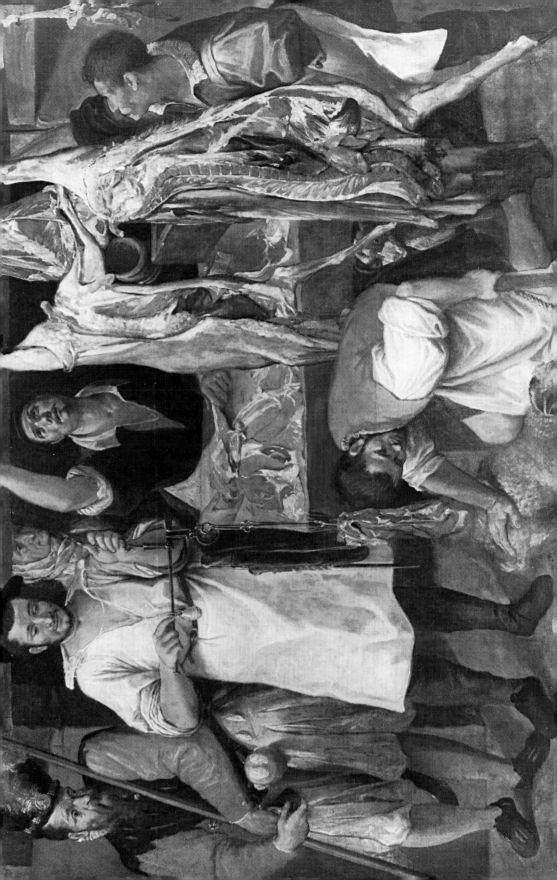

Plate 12. Stefano della Bella, title-page for Galileo's *Dialogo dei Massimi Sistemi*, 1632 (The British Library).

around backward, moved the dog to the foreground and strengthened the lines until they looked like 'puzzle pieces'. Giulio Romano's rather hazardous exaggeration of Raphael's perspective technique, the charioteer viewed *sotto-in-su* with bare buttocks and hanging testicles matching those of the horse, reappeared in Francesco Primaticcio's (1504–1570) sketch of Apollo (Uffizi: Gabinetto dei Disegni), in one of Vasari's frescoes in the Palazzo Vecchio, in Domenico Brusasorci's (*c.* 1516–1567) scenes in the Palazzo Chiericati at Vicenza and, most spectacularly, in Alberto Cavalli's *Apollo* in the main hall of the Palazzo Ducale at Sabbioneta.[45]

Occasionally, imitation verged on parody. Camillo Boccaccino's Christ in the scene with the adulteress at San Sigismundo at Cremona is framed by a receding barrel vault almost identical to the one in Raphael's *School of Athens*: but the expression on his face is both effeminate and drugged, and his body is so contorted that he appears to be blessing an equally fantastically shaped brown dog trying desperately, in spite of haunches twice the breadth of his shoulders, to climb up the steps. The reconstruction of the Palazzo Spada in Rome was undertaken in 1563 according to a 'substantially Sangallesco' (i.e., Antonio da Sangallo) model, with plain Tuscan arches, unadorned capitals and 'simple, bidimensional rhythms' on the court façade; but the architect and the stucco artists went on to intersperse the windows with struggling nudes trying to hold up coats of arms and to twist the vines in the frieze into spirals, all in a manner sharply in contrast with the orthodox Sangallesco Palazzo Farnese nearby.[46]

A few writers and scholars occasionally leapt beyond parody to direct confrontation. In revenge for having been expelled from Aretino's circle in Venice, Aretino's former secretary Niccolò Franco launched 'an attack of unheard-of verbal violence' against the whole school of sixteenth-century Petrarchism in general (*Il Petrarchista*, 1539) and against his former employer in particular. So violent was it, indeed, that the intended victim responded, with the quiet acquiescence of the government of the 'free' republic, by having a purported assassin frighten him into leaving Venetian territory. Niccolò Leonceno, a professor of medicine who built a new anatomical 'theatre' in 1551 with the money his students had saved by giving up carnival, rejected the authority of Pliny. His colleague Andreas Vesalius undermined the authority of Galen by pointing to muscles and organs that Galen had not mentioned. Meanwhile, the authority of Bembo was challenged by none other than a secretary of the Venetian Council of Ten, Gaspare Dalla Vedova, who published an anthology of poems in various *terraferma* dialects for the purpose of demonstrating the superiority of their phonic systems to that of Bembo's Volgare.

One of the hottest literary wars was the one provoked by Lodovico Castelvetro when he questioned certain uncanonical passages in one of Annibal Caro's occasional verses ('Petrarch would not have invited the Muses with such words'). Caro replied with an *Apologia* that broke with the established form of rhetorical treatises. It placed Caro's slanderous epithets in the mouths of 'Pasquino', 'Predella' and an equally inanimate 'Buratto', and it thus enabled the author to present explicitly his own modification of Bembo's rules for the Volgare. 'I am not', said Caro's mouthpiece, 'one of those who thinks that this language [of ours] came to an end . . . in Petrarch and Boccaccio; . . . for it is still not dead'. Equally intense was the battle waged by Ortensio Lando (1512–1553). Lando used a 'whip' (*sferza*) to excoriate all the writers of antiquity, from Thucydides and Aristotle to Cicero and Quintilian. He then went on, in a series of *Paradossi* ('Paradoxes') that were immediately translated into Latin and French and frequently imitated in Italian, to excoriate all the Renaissance classics as well – particularly Boccaccio, 'that miserable, adulterous, unbelieving ruffian Epicurus', whose works 'could have been written by any uncouth little pedant'. Finally – in a somewhat pale, forty-five-page adaptation of his translation of Thomas More's *Utopia* – he summoned up an ambassador from 'The Land of the Lost Ones' (*Sperduti*) to pour ridicule on all Italians of his day – on all of them, that is, with the possible exception of the Florentines, who were found to be skilful at least in planting carrots.[47]

Such statements as these have led some historians to posit an 'anti-' or 'counter-' Renaissance beginning somewhere in the second or third decade of the century, a general rebellion against all 'Renaissance learning and values' that they attribute varyingly to the effect of 'suffocating courts', to 'a ruling class that formally and juridically turned itself into a caste', to a 'depressing political situation', or to a predetermined biological cycle in which the 'weakness engendered by strong [political regimes]' periodically promotes 'a headlong search for self-identity'. The 'continued presence of corrupt rationalist remnants and of pre-organic and suppressed organic phenomena' supposedly produced 'a flood-tide of intellectualistic, pseudo-structuralistic and exotic evasions and exasperations', which can be attributed either to the currency of crypto-Protestant ideas supposedly hidden behind certain of Pontormo's frescoes or to an irreversible migration of 'the major centre of the Renaissance . . . outside of Italy'. An 'exasperating, empty and unproductive search for norms' must have been the expression of 'hopeless, unrealizable moral nostalgia [of minds] by now incapable of theory or concrete history', of an inevitable 'decline' that invariably 'follows an apex', of an 'epoch of crisis' in which 'the contemplation . . . of reality [had] become so impractical as to throw the intellectual and the artist back into the ghetto of his own metaphors' or, finally, of 'an anti-humanist culture' composed of 'purely formal values totally devoid of cognitive and ethical validity'.[48]

Few of these explanations are now tenable on the basis of the available evidence. Mannerism had nothing to do with the presence or absence of a 'court'. It flourished as well in Ferrara and Parma, where a knowledgeable prince took an active interest in the artists and writers he nourished, as it did in Florence, where the 'court' of Lorenzo the Magnificent had long since disappeared; and it continued to flourish in Florence long after Duke Cosimo, who admitted to being culturally illiterate. Nor can Mannerism be traced to the importation or the imposition of contemporary non-Italian cultural forms. Italian Mannerist painters learned to admire the woodblock prints of Albrecht

Durer; but they absorbed – they were not absorbed by – what they admired. The principal Spanish painter resident in Italy, Pedro de Rubiales, or Roviale Spagnuolo, learned his craft in Rome; and he was hired by the Spanish viceroy of Naples because of the Vasarian, not because of the possible Spanish, character of his painting. The principal resident Spanish writer, Alfonso de Ulloa, learned to write impeccable Italian as secretary to the Imperial ambassador in Venice and as an employee of the Venetian publishing house of Giolito de' Ferrari. His Italian translations of contemporary Spanish travel literature as well as his own history of the reign of Charles v were thus accepted as genuine contributions to Italian humanist historiography.

Mannerism had little if anything to do with one or another kind of political regime. It flourished after, as well as before, the consolidation of the Imperial hegemony in Italy. It prospered under the moderate tyranny of the Petrucci in Siena, under a Medici proconsul and under a government of radical anti-Mediceans in Florence, under a subject-city oligarchy in Cremona, and under a closed patriciate in the Imperial city of Venice. Vasari placed the same huge horses' rear-ends in the centre of his scenes and the same middle-aged nudes sprawled along the bottom wherever he worked – in viceregal Naples, in papal Rome, in ducal Florence.

Even less did Mannerism have any visible connection to psychological states, either individual or collective. Admittedly, Francesco Salviati was a megalomaniac who 'had no respect at all for [his colleagues] . . . and blasted their works while raising . . . his own above the stars'. And Pontormo was a solitary agoraphobe – to judge from the diary he kept – who pulled the ladder up behind him when he closed himself for days on end in an attic. But the works they produced represented no greater departure from the classic norms than did those of the 'straight' Bronzino, who saved Pontormo from starvation by dragging him out for a decent meal every week or so. They were not any more radical than those of Parmigianino, whose 'gracious manners and vivacious spirit' were marred only by a fascination with 'the nonsense of the alchemists', notwithstanding one recent attempt to blame him as well for anticipations of 'the pictorial culture of the Counter-Reformation'.[49]

Mannerism should not, therefore, be associated with a spirit of rebellion. Ortensio Lando's proposition that the works of Boccaccio are not worth reading is preceded and followed by such propositions as 'It is better to be crazy than wise' and 'to be drunk rather than sober'. To demonstrate that his irreverent comments were made solely to give 'extreme pleasure' to his readers, he then wrote – under a pseudonym that matches the abbreviated name concealed in the publisher's postscript to the anonymous first edition of his *Paradossi* – an equally violent attack upon himself, an author, it seems, 'devoid of judgement and with a tongue dyed in poison, a beast born in a latrine'. His rigorously Boccaccian *novelle* were meant to sustain no more lofty ethical principles than 'Better an egg today than a hen tomorrow' and 'Step-mothers should be nice to their stepsons'. They were not meant to be taken any more seriously than his pompous funeral orations for deceased cats, grasshoppers and fleas.[50] For Mannerist criticism was habitually tempered by another essential element of Mannerist culture: humour, which in the age of Mannerism was usually produced by suspending for a moment the norms that everyone assumed could never be suspended.

To be sure, most of the Mannerists at one time or another criticized aspects of contemporary culture and customs. They poured contempt on the dishonest pedants who passed off as their own the barely rescrambled learning of others and for whom Anton Francesco Doni prescribed the penalty of castration. They denounced the lawyers and clerics who used their barbarous Latin merely as a way of squeezing money out of the uninitiate. 'The avarice of [some] priests and friars is such', noted the 'soul' of Giambattista Gelli's (1498–1563) wise Volgare-Florentine-speaking shoemaker, that 'not satisfied with the portion of tithes ordered for them by God, they keep the faith hidden in order to sell it bit by bit at retail . . . and so live sumptuously'. He therefore demanded, in the name of David in Psalm 27, that manual labour be accorded the same value as intellectual labour and that the church's liturgy be celebrated in the Volgare, the modern Italian equivalent of Jerome's Vulgate. For only thus would Christians at last become as well-informed about their religion as Jews and Muhammadans were about theirs.[51]

Such criticism was always reformist, never revolutionary. When they chided the 'humanists' of their age, the critics were referring to the effeminate schoolteachers mocked in Sebastiano del Piombo's (c. 1485–1547) famous *Portrait of a Humanist* (Washington, D. C.: National Gallery) and in Camillo Scrofa's comedies, of which at least twenty imitations have been counted. They were not referring to the 'grammarians' of the generation of Valla and Poliziano, nor to the philologists of the age of Carlo Sigonio and Pier Vettori. Their denunciations were made in the name of the same principles with which Petrarch had confronted the pseudo-Aristotelians two centuries earlier. And as remedies they prescribed the strengthening of those principles in typically Petrarchan and traditionally fifteenth-century fashion: through a more serious, more philologically sound study of the ancient and High Renaissance classics.

FROM IMITATION TO INNOVATION

Indeed, many of the critical, experimental and reformist efforts of the Mannerists were inspired by the High Renaissance masters themselves. Raphael himself had recognized as aesthetically canonical – if only because they were sanctioned by ancient prototypes – what immediately became the leading decorative art of the High Renaissance: arabesques, or *grotteschi*, as they were called after the vaults (*grotte*) of the Domus Aurea in Rome where they had recently been discovered. Since *grotteschi* were not expected to perform any rhetorical function at all, the fantasy of the ancient painters could work directly upon the still greater fantasy of their Mannerist emulators; and to the standard vases, vines and vegetable-men were soon added Bernardino

Campi's dogs, dragons, beetles and turtles, Marco da Faenza's (d. 1588) 'terrible, fierce' monsters (Florence: Palazzo Vecchio) and Luzio Luzzi's (1528–1576) half-submerged merman pointing a huge erection in the direction of two placid swans (Rome: Castel Sant'Angelo).[52]

Similarly, Andrea Mantegna (d. 1506) set an example for later Mannerist departures from the natural in and around Venice with the zucchini-shaped breasts of his 'Avaritia', the shrivelled feet of his 'Ignorantia', the armless hermaphrodite being pulled into the water and the obviously unstable orange cliffs in the background of his *Minerva Expelling the Vices from the Garden of Virtue* (Paris: Louvre). Michelangelo set an example for later 'inconsistencies' by incorporating those of his predecessors in the New Sacristy of San Lorenzo in Florence: a ceiling out of proportion to the objects below it, *pietra serena* borders that seem to squeeze the tombs they contained, a lack of formal correspondence between the interior and the exterior.[53] Bembo's 'substantial alteration of the Petrarchan form' set an example for a 'real revolution in the realm of poetical technique' among his orthodox Venetian followers, a revolution that was to culminate in Celio Magno's (1536–1602) synthesis of the sonnet and the *canzone*. His 'taste for mirrorlike correspondences' and his Volgare adaptation of Quintilian's analysis of the emotive effects of spoken sounds set an example for Della Casa and Bernardino Daniello – the first when he sought to mirror painted portraits in a series (*corona*) of verses, the second when he established a theoretical distinction between the pleasing quality of words accented on the third last syllable (*sdrucciole*) and the loftiness of those accented on the last (*tronche*).[54]

It was thus the classical patrimony inherited from High Renaissance humanism that provided the Mannerists with a warehouse full of material for critical analysis and with the single pieces that could be combined and arranged in a process of continual reinvention. Hence, what may seem four centuries later to reflect an eternal sense of conflict and the instability of something not resolved either in expression or in theory was actually the result of taking one by one the various pieces out of their originally harmonious context while at the same time being careful never to 'call into question the unity that had once held them together'.[55]

One such 'piece' was realism, or the principle that prescribed an exact correspondence between what was represented and what could be observed in nature. In accordance with this principle, Giovanni da Nola, the leading sculptor in Naples in the 1530s and 1540s, occasionally abandoned his usual 'squashed down and flattened out' figures; and in one instance – the funeral monument for Pedro de Toledo at San Giacomo degli Spagnuoli – he tilted the head of Pedro's wife exactly to the point where the line of her eyesight formed a perfect right angle with the page propped up by the finger she had placed in the middle of the volume she was reading. Similarly, Vasari had a Florentine friend send him a hound so that his St Rocco would be assured of the services of a real dog – although in the end he gave St Rocco three other dogs and kept this one for St Eustachius (Lucca: Villa Guinigi). Vincenzo Borghini was prevented from falling back on abstractions and intellectualist schematizations in his studies of language by a need for concreteness, objectivity and adherence to reality.

Idealization soon disappeared from many of the Mannerists' works – for instance, in the life-size terracotta figures of the Passion scene at San Sepolcro in Milan, where the soldiers are dressed in historically impeccable Roman uniforms and where Jesus looks no different from any handsome thirty-year-old as he washes the feet of an older companion. Similarly, physiognomies became solely a function of the individual personalities that might be revealed in them. Giovan Battista Fornari's (d. 1540) *Ottavio Farnese* (Parma: Galleria Nazionale), with his hooked nose and bald head, clearly manifests the firm character that enabled the subject to rescue his newborn state from so many internal and external foes. Francesco Sangallo's *Angelo Marzi* tosses anxiously on his tomb (Florence: SS. Annunziata), with his eyebrows strained and his mouth turned sharply down – just as he may well have appeared to the sculptor while making the final arrangements for assuring his earthly immortality. Tintoretto's (1518–1594) portrait of *Sebastiano Venier* (Vienna: Kunsthistorisches Museum), with his short-cropped hair and a full grey beard, gazes outward with such calm intensity that the paraphernalia that identify him as a senator and a general fade away into the background. The 'two clear pupils in the damp eyes' of Lorenzo Lotto's (*c.* 1480–1556) *Young Man* (Bergamo: Accademia Carrara) so startlingly reveal a 'precocious melancholy' that they still disturb twentieth-century historians. Even Bronzino, whose official portraits bear the mark of the artist's predilection for oval shapes and distracted stares, painted Cosimo, Eleonora and their children (Florence: Palazzo Vecchio) so accurately that the subjects immediately identified with them; and they can be easily identified even four centuries later by whoever has read the corresponding passages in Benvenuto Cellini.[56]

Verse portraits, it is true, usually remained trapped in Petrarchan platitudes and thus confined to the realm of abstractions – even those that Alessandro Piccolomini wrote in honour of Titian's *Diego de Mendoza*. All that the poet Antonio Rambaldo could find to say about Titian's *Gaspara Stampa* was:

> Her forehead is whiter than snow,
> Her cheeks more lovely than fresh roses.

And all Molza could say about Sebastiano del Piombo's *Giulia Gonzaga* was to exclaim:

> Her beautiful locks! Her braided, blond hair!
> Her forehead! Her tranquil eyebrows!
> Her beautiful, youthful breast!

Prose portraits – like those by Ludovico Beccadelli and Giovanni Della Casa and even the massive *vite* of the military heroes of the age of the calamities by the dean of the Mannerist biographers, Paolo Giovio – were usually limited by their ancient models to *res gestae* ('deeds done by') and by the requirements of current political or ecclesiastical polemics. But the painted portraits that further developed the models provided by Titian multiplied in response to an ever-growing public demand. And some painters, like Giovan Battista Moroni of Milan (c. 1520–1578), eventually gave up all other kinds of commissions in order to devote themselves to portrait painting alone.[57]

Another of the 'pieces' in the 'warehouse' picked up by the Mannerists was individuality, or the recognition of the value of purely individual variants from classical norms. Leone Leoni's 'windows and cornices all very different from what is usually done' that protrude from his house in Milan were held to be aesthetically justifiable even though they had no other apparent purpose than that of 'showing off the magnitude of his [the sculptor's] great spirit' (Vasari). The same drawings by Salviati could be used for very different subjects, first in the church of Santa Maria dell'Anima and then in the Palazzo Sacchetti in Rome. What counted was not what they represented or how they represented it, but simply that they came from the hand of Salviati. Girolamo Santacroce (d. 1556) developed 'a formal language and a spiritual attitude so absolutely personal and *sui generis*' – with 'thin, emaciated bodies . . . and ascetic, visionary, spiritualized faces' – that the altar of the Madonna della Neve at San Domenico Maggiore in Naples long attributed to his colleague Giovanni da Nola (d. 1558) has at last been restored to him, despite the absence of corroborating written records.[58]

In at least one case, nascent individuality of expression was encouraged by the sudden interposition of a physical separation between emulator and model – namely, in the case of Giulio Romano. Despite certain liberties that his master had subsequently been obliged to paint over, Giulio remained unswervingly faithful to Raphael during the years of his apprenticeship in Rome – so faithful, indeed, that Raphael charged him with supervising the projects left incomplete upon his premature death in 1520. But an invitation to build a hunting lodge – and to build whatever else he wished – in Mantua suddenly enabled him to display 'the abundance and fertility of his imagination', free even from the restrictions that might have been imposed by local examples of early and High Renaissance art. Giulio boldly juxtaposed motives that he had borrowed indiscriminately from early and from late Roman imperial arches, disregarding the stylistic differences separating the age of Augustus from the ages of Septimius Severus and Constantine. He capped ground-floor windows with massive trapezoids, separated second-floor windows with clusters of delicate Doric columns and filled courtyard loggias with brightly coloured *grotteschi*. Inspired by the ancient writer Apuleius, he cast aside Raphael's one-point perspective, pushed three-dimensional space into a completely separated background, reduced the dominant figures in the foreground to a single plane, and dissolved painting into architecture by making them appear to fall away from the wall. So effectively, indeed, did he display his idiosyncratic innovations upon his master's themes that the Palazzo del Te became the principal showpiece by which the marchese and his ducal successors enticed distinguished visitors to Mantua; and among French architects it soon replaced both its ancient and its High Renaissance archetypes – like the Farnesina in Rome – as the model to be followed in transforming defendable fortresses into livable chateaux.[59]

This principle of individuality enabled several Mannerist writers and artists to introduce novelties into the accepted forms. First Aretino, in the many successive editions of his published correspondence, then Annibal Caro, in the *Familiar Letters* that circulated widely in manuscript well before they were published in 1572, did away with many limitations still accepted by Bembo, whose own ceaseless efforts to perfect the Ciceronian and Plinian models of his fifteenth-century predecessors made the final, and posthumously published, texts of his letters very different from the original missives. They learned to revise and elaborate before they dictated and to oblige recipients to destroy anything that on further reflection seemed to be literarily imperfect – lest, as Caro observed, it fall into the hands of 'one of those clever booksellers [who] print all kinds of rubbish'. They bestowed upon the art of letter writing a sense of immediacy and familiarity that made their letters rhetorically far more effective (Bembo is said to have been cured of a fever after reading one from Giovio) and far better mirrors of the real concerns of the letter writers.[60]

Similarly, Benedetto Varchi, whose conversion from poetry to history had been belated, followed Guicciardini into the archives in search of information. What he found seemed to be such eloquent testimony of the truth that he frequently substituted documents for Guicciardini's Thucydidean orations; and he accomplished the first major step in the conversion of rhetorical history into documentary, although still literary, history. To written records Paolo Giovio added the testimony he gathered from interviews with generals, diplomats and heads of state all over the peninsula; and while amply by-passing Guicciardini's professed geographical limitation to one part of Christendom, he converted Guicciardini's unqualified pessimism – in anticipation of the first posthumously printed edition of the *Storia d'Italia* – into a view of recent history that better reflected the first positive achievements of the post-calamities state-builders.

Meanwhile, Carlo Sigonio, 'a man of firm judgement and very well versed in history' (according to his Florentine collaborator and fellow philologist Vincenzo Borghini), dared incur the wrath of his fellow citizens of Bologna by refusing – as Borghini was to do in Florence – to cite their favourite stories about the remote past of their city; he recuperated for historiography the main function of myth-smashing which in the fifteenth century had usually been sacrificed to its celebrative function. Giovan Battista Ramusio (1485–1557), an associate of the Aldine Press in Venice, a correspondent of Bembo in Padua and a frequent secretary to Venetian ambassadors abroad, cemented both the documentary base and the increasingly universal scope of Italian humanist historiography by publishing hundreds of accounts of former and current voyages of overseas discovery – Spanish, French and Portuguese as well as Venetian. These accounts, appearing in one huge folio volume after another, finally severed the last remaining bond between modern Italians and the authoritative ancient geographers, Ptolemy and Strabo.[61]

Some of the artists and writers, on the other hand, managed to combine several pure or modified classical forms into what became a substantially new form. The authority of Serlio and Vitruvius and a few surviving pieces of decorative motifs from the time of the emperor Claudius encouraged Antonio Sangallo the Younger, Giulio Romano and even Giacomo Barozzi da Vignola (1507–1573) to elevate Tuscan columns and decorated, crystal-shaped *bugne* (rustications) from an accessory (which is how Michelangelo defined them in his plans of 1544) into independent architectural styles – namely, the 'rustic' and the 'gigantic' orders. These orders were applied to such buildings as the Palazzetto della Zeccha Vecchia in Rome and the Palazzo Brocchi in Bologna; and they were carried off to France by Philibert de l'Orme after his three-year visit to Rome in 1536.[62] Benvenuto Cellini was as respectful of Leonardo and Michelangelo and as careful to observe the linguistic prescriptions of the Accademia Fiorentina as any of the other Florentine humanists of his age. But when, at the height of his spectacular career as a goldsmith and sculptor, he set out to apply the *res gestae* format of classical biography to himself, he produced a unique kind of autobiography. It was one totally untouched by Petrarch's Augustinian introspection and largely free of the topical organization characteristic of the famous contemporary autobiography of the Milanese physician and mathematician Girolamo Cardano (1501–1576). Rather, it was a defence of his own 'great deeds' and a condemnation of all his enemies. It was dictated with such verve and literary skill that it has been one of the most widely read works of Italian Renaissance culture ever since its rediscovery in the early eighteenth century.[63]

Similarly, Giorgio Vasari combined the form of a series of biographies of a single category of subjects inherited from Suetonius, Plutarch and Diogenes Laertius with his own revision of Alberti's theories about art. Hence, the first and then the second enlarged edition of his *Lives of the Painters, Sculptors and Architects* presented not only a wealth of detail about the characters and the works of hundreds of individual artists, but also a view of the progress of the arts in general from the time of Giotto to the present. They became the model according to which the future discipline of art history was to be written for another three centuries.

FROM PALACES TO CITIES

Perhaps the greatest innovation of the Mannerists, however, consisted in the transformation of architecture into urban planning – or rather, in the transformation of the function of facades from that of setting off the building behind them to that of organizing the space in front of them. This transformation had been underway in the fifteenth century – theoretically in the treatises of Alberti and Filarete, practically in the colonnade-lined *piazze* borrowed from Brunelleschi's model at the Piazza Annunziata in Florence and then imposed arbitrarily by enlightened autocrats upon the medieval centres of Ferrara, Vigevano and Carpi. But the greater flexibility of Mannerist variants upon High Renaissance themes enabled sixteenth-century architects more easily to adapt new forms to an older environment. That is what Jacopo Sansovino set out to do with the support of the Doge Andrea Gritti as soon as he arrived in Venice after the Sack of Rome, just one step ahead of the *Landsknechte*, to become chief architect to the Procuratori di San Marco.

Sansovino covered the elegant Loggetta at the base of the Campanile with impeccably classical bas-reliefs and placed it so that it was centred by the entrance arch when viewed from his grandiose, statue-lined staircase in the courtyard of the Palazzo Ducale. But he left the Fabbriche Nuove in the Rialto with no more ornamentation – respecting its function as a warehouse – than triangular cornices over two long rows of perfectly rectangular windows. He divided the façade of the Palazzo Corner into equidistant arches separated by clusters of classical columns. But he set the four centre windows on the Palazzo Dolfin apart from the two pairs of lateral windows, so they would match the traditional lines of the Palazzo Bembo next door. He put a statue over each cluster of columns along the balustrade of the Library. But – as if to emphasize the different purposes of the two buildings – he built the adjacent Zecca (Mint) entirely out of the heavy rough *bugne* that Raphael had approved only for ground floors and corners. After a temporary setback brought on by the collapse of the Library roof and a consequent term in prison, he went on to clear out a rubble of old houses at one end and to turn the rest of Piazza San Marco into a perfect, if gigantic, trapezoid. He thus initiated, in the political and economic centres of the city and along its main commercial artery, the Grand Canal, what soon was to be accomplished by his many disciples and imitators: the metamorphosis of a Byzantine-international Gothic city into a Venetian version of a Roman-Florentine Renaissance city.[64]

What Sansovino did for Venice was done for Florence first by Giovanni Battista Del Tasso in the Mercato Nuovo (known to modern tourists as the 'Straw Market') and later by Vasari in one of the most spectacular of Mannerist urban renewal projects, the Uffizi. The old slum (and one ancient church) between the Palazzo Vecchio and the Arno was replaced with a long narrow *piazzale* bordered by symmetrical colonnades: and what became the administrative centre of the new state was connected to the prince's new residence across the river by a closed corridor. In Arezzo, the zone opposite the cathedral was widened into the *Piazza Grande* (now appropriately called Piazza Vasari), which terminated in the new Palazzo delle Logge. In Pisa, the medieval Piazza delle Sette Vie was doubled in size to accommodate, and to afford a full view of, Vasari's new Palazzo dei Cavalieri (now the Scuola Normale Superiore) and the adjoining church. In Padua, a Roman triumphal arch – appropriately bearing the arms of Sansovino's patron, Andrea Gritti – was placed beneath the ornate fourteenth-century clock, establishing the rectangular form for the civic centre of the city that was fully carried out a half-century later; and the civic centre was joined to the religious centre with Giovan Maria Falconetto's palace of the Monte di Pietà (1531–35).

The rebuilders of older cities inevitably ran into opposition, particularly from among the victims of the ever more stringent laws of eminent domain. 'Sumptuous and excessive building . . . adds only to the honour and glory of princes', complained one disgruntled Roman. '[For the rest of us] it's the cause of the ruin of our poor families'.[65] The rebuilders were frequently thwarted by financial restrictions as well. Of Michelangelo's grandiose plans for the Campidoglio in Rome, only the façade of the Palazzo Nuovo was actually undertaken in his lifetime. The long approaching staircase was entrusted to Michelangelo's successor, Giacomo Della Porta, only in 1578. The palace itself, begun in 1603, was not completed until 1645. And the star-shaped pavement so admired by modern tourists was not actually installed until 1940.

But in wholly new cities – and in cities like L'Aquila that had been destroyed by an earthquake – the architect-urbanists could impose their aesthetic ideals without restraint: Carlentini on the east coast of Sicily (1551), which the viceroy designated for habitation only 'by persons of some means' capable of defending themselves in case of a Turkish attack; Valetta in Malta (1565), which was entrusted to the same architect, Pietro Prado; Massa Nuova, or 'Massa Cybea', with its gardens, fountains and palace, which Alberto Cybo built on the plain below the fortified village in 1554; Cherasco in Piedmont, which Duke Emanuele Filiberto had totally rebuilt in 1559 to guard the western border of his newly recovered domain; Cosmopoli (from both 'Cosmos' and 'Cosimo', now Portoferraio) in Elba; and the 'City of the Sun' (*Terra del Sole*) in the Florentine Romagna. These 'perfect' cities were laid out as projections of the new star-shaped bastions, and their geometrical grid plans were forthwith infused with Neo-Platonic qualities by such theorists as Pietro Cataneo of Siena, whose 'First Four Books' appeared in Venice in 1554. In 1549 Ferrante Gonzaga began constructing a capital for his minuscule titular duchy at Guastalla, with two blocks taken out of the rectangular grid to form piazze equidistant from the geometrical centre. And in 1554 his megalomaniac cousin Vespasiano laid the cornerstone for what soon became the most perfect of all the Mannerist cities. He called it Sabbioneta as if to demonstrate that only the will of a glorious prince could make a city rise out of sand (*sabbia*), on which it was indeed built. The circular walls were twisted one clock-hour to the right so that an enemy entering one of the gates would arrive not on a major artery, but on a perpendicular side street. A long covered portico with a second-storey gallery reached into a large garden at the end of one axis. A ducal palace, topped with a Tuscan lookout tower, dominated the main piazza halfway along the opposite radius. All the variants of Mannerist themes displayed on private façades were harmonized by the all-powerful chief architect, Domenico Giunti (1506–1560) of Prato.

TOWARD A NATIONAL CULTURE

Still another 'piece' picked up by the Mannerists for special emphasis was the principle of the hierarchical equality, and hence the interchangeability, of all of what only later came to be identified as separate and qualitatively unequal disciplines. Vasari, it is true, tried to elevate painting, sculpture and architecture to a level superior to that of the other arts. He forced most art theorists of his day to squeeze their theoretical reflections about art into the debate over which of the three 'noble' arts was superior to the other two. Yet he gave no persuasive reason for doing so; and his distinction broke down when he at last yielded to evidence and included jewel and cameo makers as well. Alberti's distinction between artists and artisans was occasionally translated into law – e.g., in Paul III's edicts of 3 March 1539 and 14 July 1540 and Cosimo de' Medici's edict of 1570. But these edicts were always directed toward individual persons, not categories. None of the beneficiaries ever hesitated to concern himself with all the 'arts' ancillary to their noble 'art' (the word in Italian remains the same), being wholly dismissive of Plutarch's strictures against manual labour that were to weigh so heavily upon the consciences of their successors. Indeed, several of them – notably Parmigianino – took pains to learn and employ the new techniques of copper engraving being perfected by such proficient 'artisans' as Jacopo Caraglio of Verona (c. 1505–1565) and Ugo da Carpi (c. 1450–1525). They thus were able to promote the diffusion of their own works throughout Europe and to pave the way for the formal elevation of engraving to the rank of an art form in its own right later in the century.

Mannerist motifs permeated all the forms of art with equal facility and celerity. Mantuan woodcarvers abandoned the strictly classical lines they had adopted in the age of Mantegna as soon as Giulio Romano arrived with an alternative. Their 'structures . . . became more imposing', their 'projecting planes became more accentuated' and 'carving [in their work] came to prevail over inlay (intaglio/intarsio)'.[66] Their example may have spread as far as Perugia through the itinerant Bergamo woodcarvers Stefano and Damiano Zambelli, whose fantastic winged horses, acanthus-leaf old men, yawning snakes and grinning griffins adorn the stalls of the basilica San Pietro. So skilfully did their colleagues at Sabbioneta combine advanced design with technical virtuosity that even Napoleon's art-hungry soldiers were unable to dislodge Giovan Battista Brizziano's elaborately decorated panels (1516–17) from the ceiling. For he had fitted them into place while the wood was dry in anticipation of the expanding effects of the usual Po Valley humidity.

The other 'minor' arts benefited in the same manner. Maffeo Olivieri and fra Giulio combined parts of ancient imperial coins – with anachronistic effects similar to those of Giulio Romano's mixtures of imperial arches – in composing their own bronze medallions. A long series of calligraphers elaborated upon the achievements of the fifteenth-century students of inscriptions and column capitals and upon the formulas of the High Renaissance geometricians to produce 'fantasy alphabets'. The Franciscan Vespasiano Amphiareo made Roman letters grow into human bodies and tree trunks. Giovan Francesco Cresci perfected the handwriting patterns used in state chanceries and provided the presses with what has ever after been their second standard alphabet, corsivo, or, in English, 'italics'.[67] Miniature painting survived the invention of printing, particularly in books of liturgy and piety, like the Pauline commentaries and the 'Book of Hours' presented to Pope Julius III by Giulio Romano's close friend, Giorgio Giulio Clovio (1498–1578). And such famous 'noble' artists as Bronzino and Veronese adapted the miniature to bronze and glass in a form that was to make the product a standard luxury gift for the next two centuries.

Mannerist motifs became particularly prominent along the borders of Bronzino's and Salviati's tapestries, which Flemish weavers were brought in to make, and to teach natives to make, in what soon became one of Florence's chief domestic industries. They were also adopted in title page designs – e.g., in the caryatids with fruit clusters, sibyls with pointed breasts, torches and winged cupids that adorn the publications of the Torrentino. From title pages they penetrated into the volumes – for instance, in Giovan Andrea Valvassori's illustrations for Ariosto's *Orlando furioso*, which cleverly combine several episodes into one scene, and in the crowd of flexuous, elongated, serpentine figures that were constantly refined in successive editions of the *Decameron*.

Given the common Mannerist inspiration of all these art forms, they could easily be brought together in one place – as they were very effectively at the Cappella Taverna in Santa Maria della Passione in Milan by the fresco painter Carlo Urbino, the lacemakers Cesare Pusterla and Scipione Delfinone and the goldsmith-stucco worker Gian Pietro Mariani. Given the availability of many different classical models, moreover, any one artist or writer could, without too much difficulty, master a number of them. Hence the achievements of such polymaths – or polygraphs – as Francesco Sansovino and Lodovico Domenichi, who, with equal facility, and occasionally with equal superficiality, kept the Venetian presses supplied with a constant stream of translations, Horatian odes, Petrarchan sonnets, Ciceronian orations and Sallustian histories. Rather than being an exception to the rule, Michelangelo's famed versatility became ever more typical of this increasingly versatile age.

Provided with a common classical heritage of all Mannerist experiments, a single project too large for any one artist could be entrusted to several of them without endangering the aesthetic unity of the whole. One such joint project was the funeral ceremony for Michelangelo, which involved nearly the whole of the literary and artistic community, and his tomb, which involved two programme directors and three different sculptors. Another such project was the church of the Madonna della Steccata in Parma, where all the varied experiments of the heirs of Correggio were held together by continuous chiaroscuro friezes along the pilasters and vault ribs. Still another was the remarkable sanctuary of SS. Severino and Sossio in Naples, which was designed by one Roman and one Brescian architect and then filled with acanthus leaves and *putti* by several different Neapolitan woodcarvers. Painters and architects typically consulted men of letters on matters of iconography and programming – Annibal Caro for Vasari's frescoes at Palazzo Altoviti, Vincenzo Borghini, with a copy of Guicciardini in hand, for the mural cycle in the Salone de' Cinquecento in Florence.

In several such projects, the basic harmony was maintained by a happy conjunction of several separate strands of Mannerism in one place – for instance, in Cremona. There, Gian Francesco Bembo (d. c. 1526) and Altobello Melone brought the heritage of the disciples of Raphael from Rome, Bernardino Gatti (d. 1575) that of Parmigianino from Parma, and Pordenone brought his own experiments with Mannerism in the Veneto. The result was the series of massive nave frescoes that turned the Lombard-Romanesque cathedral into one of the earliest of the great Mannerist temples. The initiative of these artists was carried forward by Giulio (d. 1572), Bernardino (1522–1591), and Antonio (d. 1587) Campi of Cremona, who had also studied at Mantua and Rome and who were largely responsible, along with the local architect Francesco Dattaro, for transforming both the exterior and the interior of the suburban churches of San Sigismondo and San Piero al Po into 'fertile workshop[s] of Mannerism', with 'daring composition' and 'chromatic violence' and with a host of elongated figures whirling in a vortex toward the lantern of the cupola.[68]

In other projects, the harmony was maintained by the patrons' commitment to an original design. Such was the case of the two facing transept chapels of the Nardi family in San Pietro in Montorio in Rome, where the basically Vasarian motifs were scrupulously respected by Vasari's successors, Bartolomeo Ammannati (1511–1592) and Daniele da Volterra (c. 1509–1566). In still other projects, harmony was maintained by the continued presence of the original designers. After his return to Rome from Genoa, Perin del Vaga managed to impose 'an overall impression . . . of great strength, logic and harmony' on the interior of Castel Sant'Angelo, where even the gilded stucco is 'so varied, complex and elaborate as to defy coherent description', at least by modern art historians. Giovanni Battista del Tasso (1500–1555) and then Vasari managed to coordinate the work of a 'crowd of high-level artists' – painters, architects, sculptors, tapestry weavers, glass and stucco workers – in transforming the expanded Palazzo Vecchio in Florence into a residence worthy of one of the outstanding patrons of Mannerist art.[69]

If not the largest, certainly one of the most successful of these joint projects was the confraternity of San Giovanni Decollato in Rome, where the members had themselves painted as the 'audience' in front of several of the large murals. Pirro Ligorio's (d. 1583) archaeological anachronisms were juxtaposed with Jacopino del Conte's (1510–1598) Mary with her mouth open in anguish, with Francesco Salviati's weightless woman twisted 180 degrees and with a huge Vasarian Father Arno pouring water over his groin. These daring experiments were then carried over into the adjoining church, where blood gushes from Vasari's beheaded John while Battista Naldini's (1537–1591) Christ pulls a flexuous hip away from Mary Magdelene. But the contrasts are perfectly counterbalanced, and nothing is either superfluous or lacking.[70]

This felicitous combination of unity and diversity, uniformity and adaptability, enabled Mannerist culture to spread far more rapidly and to permeate far more deeply than any of the much more precisely circumscribed forms of High Renaissance culture. Mannerism had been launched in Rome, Florence, Siena, Mantua, and Cremona in the 1520s and in Parma in the 1530s. It was introduced in Venice by Sansovino; and his revolution in architecture and sculpture was instantly accepted by such native Venetian artists as Giovan De Zan, in his Scuola di San Giorgio, Vincenzo Scamozzi (1522–1616), in his Procuratie Nuove, and Alessandro Vittoria, who worked in Sansovino's *bottega* until 1543. Venetian painting succumbed after the arrival of Salviati and Vasari in the late 1530s and early 1540s. The 'placid world of classic serenity' gave way to Mannerist diversity, just at the moment when the Republic itself was basking in self-satisfaction over its successful recovery from the disaster of 1509. Even Titian's portrayed personages lost their 'interior serenity'; and the 'heroic ideality' of Titian's follower Jacopo Bassano (*c.* 1510–1592) gave way, particularly after his 'liberating' encounter with Pordenone, to a much 'more extreme expression of emotion' and 'an undulating rhythmic pattern'. The way was open for Tintoretto to usher in a wholly new period in Venetian painting with his gigantic canvases in the Palazzo Ducale and the Scuola di San Rocco. Venice had already become the capital of the Italian publishing business, one from which books written not only in Venetian and not only in Bemban Latin but above all in Bemban Volgare were manufactured for distribution to all Italy. It had also become more than half Italian politically after its adherence to the Imperial Alliance in 1531. It now became a part of Italy visually as well.[71]

Mannerist culture then proceeded to Genoa, which the Revolution of 1528 had at last detached from its century-long political dependence upon France and turned into a powerful, independent member of the Italian alliance. While Bembo's disciple Jacopo Bonfadio taught the Genoese to write even their local chronicles in the forms prescribed by humanist historiography and to express themselves in the language, very different from their own, prescribed by Bembo, Galeazzo Alessi (1512–1572) arrived from Rome to consolidate the artistic toe-hold established two decades earlier by Perin del Vaga at Andrea Doria's villa at Fassolo. He put an end once and for all to the proliferation of black and white horizontal marble stripes interspersed with Gothic windows that Genoese patricians had long thought proper expressions of their elevated status. He imposed instead the fruits of the 'extraordinary inventive capacity' that he had learned to apply to the models of his master, Antonio da Sangallo the Younger.

While Alessi's Genoese converts set forth to extend the lines of his Palazzo Cambiaso on the corner of the Piazza Fontane Marose down the Strada Nuova and out into the increasingly villa-dotted countryside, he himself moved on to Milan. There the erection of the palace of the Genoese merchant Tommaso Marino – with its courtyard crowded with stone masks and trophies and its monumental 'Sala Alessi' guarded by twisted musicians leaning over the painted balcony on the ceiling – coincided with the arrival of the Cremonese painter Giulio Campi and the Tuscan sculptor Leone Leoni. Realizing that antiquated Lombard structures could be 'modernized' merely by adding a balustrade over the entrance and covering the raw brick with painted stucco – as can be observed in the Palazzo Greppi in Via San Maurilio, where the stucco has peeled off – the descendants of those who had been forced to submit to the previous aesthetic importations from the capitals of High Renaissance culture now willingly embraced what they perceived to be not a Roman or a Florentine but a pan-Italian culture. Milan became a capital in turn, charged with diffusing the national culture within its traditional area of domination. And it finally succeeded, after several vain attempts by its chief High Renaissance painter Gaudenzio Ferrari, in breaking down the opposition even in Casale: after 1550 most important commissions were given to outsiders rather than to the local artists obdurately wedded to the 'Italo-Flemish' styles of the 1520s.

The march of Mannerism was equally triumphant as it moved southward. Alessi himself took charge of carving two broad thoroughfares through the centre of his native Perugia, to the delight of the city council; and he distributed his 'alteration of simplicity and exuberance' on façades all over the city, even, it now appears, on the church of Santa Maria del Popolo, which archaeologists have finally rescued from centuries of remodelling.[72] Naples had already been converted to High Renaissance architecture with the construction of the Palazzo Filomarino and the Palazzo Orsini di Gravina in the years after 1513. It was now converted to Mannerist painting – first by Vasari, who arrived in 1544 'to remove all that awkward old stuff' in the refectory of Monte Oliveto, and then by Marco Pino of Siena (d. c. 1587/88), with his 'grandiose plastic formations' and his 'daring inventions'. So thorough was the conversion that Naples soon generated its own school of Mannerist culture, one represented in poetry by the most prolific of the mid-century Petrarchan poets, Bernardino Rota (1508–1575), and in painting by Giovan Battista Lama.[73]

After the capitals, the provinces. On the outskirts of the chequer-board within which Viceroy Toledo made the citizens of L'Aquila rebuild their ruined city, the church of San Bernardino was endowed with a square façade – one of the boldest of Mannerist adaptations to local architectonic traditions, with two Doric columns on either side, a huge cornice over the top and three large round windows. Lecce was won for Italian letters when its Florentine bishop, Braccio Martelli, arrived from his former see of Fiesole to organize aspiring men of letters into the Accademia dei Trasformati. It was won for Italian Mannerism by the local architect Gabriele Riccardi, who at San Marco dei Veneziani achieved the first fusion of Roman-Neapolitan styles with local Venetian and Byzantine styles that was, in the following century, to make Lecce one of the most spectacular variants of pan-Italian urban architecture. When he extended the sphere of his activity to the other cities of the Terra d'Otranto, the cultural boundaries that had separated Puglia from the rest of Italy ever since the days of the Lombards and the Greeks began to fade away.

After the peninsula, the island – Sicily, where continental architects and sculptors had followed in the footsteps of Ferrante's fortress-builders. The rectangular Piazza Garraffo in Palermo was laid out in 1545, halfway along the main axis running from the port to the royal palace. The Via Cassari was widened by order of the Senate in 1567, the same year in which the strong-willed Italianate viceroy Don Carlos de Aragona began construction on the monumental piazza that was subsequently named for him. When the Senate then commissioned a huge monumental fountain, not from local sculptors trained in traditional Siculo-Catalan styles, but from the Florentine disciples of Bartolomeo Ammannati, and when they installed a giant version of Ammannati's Fountain of Neptune in Florence, Sicily too joined Italy – almost three centuries after it had seceded on the morrow of the Vespers.[74]

Italy at last acquired what it had lost upon the dissolution of the Visigothic Kingdom a thousand years earlier: a single literary language and a single set of cultural norms. Both were accepted unconditionally in the major and many of the minor cities of the political units that had been brought together in a rudimentary form of national political organization by the Imperial alliance of 1533.

NOTES AND REFERENCES

1. In general, see Bernard Weinberg, *A History of Literary Criticism in the Italian Renaissance*, Chicago 1962, part 1, Ch. 4; and Riccardo Scrivano, 'Retorica e manierismo', *Rassegna della letteratura italiana*, 83, 1979.
2. Luciana Borsetto, 'Il furto di Proteo: Struttura e scrittura dell'imitazione nei *Poeticorum Libri* di M. G. Vida', *Rassegna della letteratura italiana*, 85, 1981. Vida's *Cristiad* is now available in the English translation by Gertrude C. Drake and Clarence A. Forbes, Carbondale, Illinois 1978, and his *De arte poetica* in the English translation of Ralph G. Williams, New York 1976.
3. Giovan Battista Busini in his letter to Benedetto Varchi of 10 August 1548, in Varchi, *Opere* (above, Chapter 5, n. 17), vol. 1, p. 446.
4. Peter Brown quoting Lionardo Salviati in 'M. Pier Vettori and Lionardo Salviati', in H. C. Davis (ed.), *Essays in Honour of John Humphreys Whitfield*, London 1975, p. 156.
5. Giorgio Padoan, 'La *Mandragola* del Machiavelli nella Venezia cinquecentesca', in his *Momenti del Rinascimento veneto*, Padua 1978. On what follows: Giorgio Padoan, *La commedia rinascimentale veneta*, Vicenza 1982.
6. Marina Calore in 'Il teatro ferrarese tra Ariosto e Giraldi' (above, Chapter 4, n. 31), and Aulo Greco in 'Annibal Caro e il teatro', *Cultura e scuola*, 18, 1966.
7. For biographical details, James Ackerman, *Palladio*, New York 1976. See the beautiful photographs by Philip Trager and the splendid text by Vincent Scully in *The Villas of Palladio*, Boston 1986.
8. In general, Christoph Luitpold Frommel, *Der römische Palastbau der Hochrenaissance*, Tübingen 1973.
9. In general, Giulio Bora, 'La cultura figurativa a Milano', in *Omaggio a Tiziano* (above, Chapter 5, n. 2).
10. Giovanni Di Napoli, 'Il concetto di "philosophia perennis" di Agostino Steuco nel quadro della tematica rinascimentale', in his *Studi sul Rinascimento*, Naples 1973; Charles Schmitt, 'Perennial philosophy: From Agostino Steuco to Leibniz', *Journal of the History of Ideas*, 27, 1966, and 'Prisca theologia e philosophia

perennis: Due temi del Rinascimento italiano e loro fortuna', in *Il pensiero italiano del Rinascimento e il tempo nostro* (*Atti del V convegno internazionale del Centro di Studi Umanistici, Montepulciano, 1968*), Florence 1970; Gino Belloni, 'Sul Daniello commentatore del 'Canzoniere', *Lettere italiane*, 32, 1980. The texts referred to here are published in Mario Pozzi's new edition of Giuseppe Zonta's (1912) *Trattati d'amore del Cinquecento*, Bari 1975.

11. G. Mutini on 'Betussi' in *DBI*, vol. 9, pp. 779–81. In general: Bruno Porcelli, *La novella del Cinquecento* (from *Letteratura italiana Laterza*, 22, Bari 1973); and Marziano Guglielminetti (ed.), *Novellieri del Cinquecento*, Milan 1972 (La Letteratura italiana: Storia e testi, vol. 24).

12. In the introduction to the 1567 edition of Erizzo's *Sei giornate*, published in Venice.

13. Giuseppe Checci's review in *Lettere italiane*, 31, 1979, p. 143.

14. Galeazzo di Tàrsia, *Rime*, ed. Cesare Bozzetti, Milan 1980. Most of the examples that follow can be found in Giulio Ferroni (ed.), *Poesia italiana del Cinquecento*, Milan 1978, pp. 103, 208, *et passim*; or in Daniele Ponchiroli (ed.), *Lirici del Cinquecento*, Turin 1958, pp. 282, 594, 648, *et passim* (rpt edn, ed. Guido Davico Bonino, Turin 1978).

15. Giorgio Petrocchi, 'Tansillo e il petrarchismo napolitano' (1968), republished in his *I fantasmi di Tancredi* (above, Chapter 3, n. 18), and in general his 'La letteratura del pieno e del tardo Rinascimento' in *Storia di Napoli*, 1972, v, part 1, pp. 271–336; Mario Scotti, 'Luigi Tansillo tra Rinascimento e Barocco', and Ezio Raimondi, 'Il petrarchismo nell'Italia meridionale', in *Premarinismo e pregongorismo* (Accademia Nazionale dei Lincei, *Quaderno*, no. 180, 1973, pp. 95–150).

16. Alan Bullock, 'Vittoria Colonna e i lirici minori del Cinquecento: Quattro secoli di attribuzioni contraddittorie', *Giornale storico della letteratura italiana*, 157, 1980; Mila Mazzetti, 'La poesia come vocazione morale: Vittoria Colonna', *Rassegna della letteratura italiana*, 77, 1973.

17. James Chater, 'Fonti poetiche per i madrigali di Luca Marenzio', in *Rivista italiana di musicologia*, 13, 1978, p. 70. On the hotly debated question of Mannerism as a stylistic and periodic term, see the recent survey of the abundant bibliography by Eugenio Battisti in *Renaissance et Maniérisme*, Brussels 1981. Among recent additions: Edoardo Taddeo, *Il manierismo letterario e i lirici veneziani del tardo Cinquecento*, Rome 1974, and Antonio Pinelli, 'La maniera', in Giovanni Preritali and Federico Zeri (eds), *Storia dell'Arte italiana*, Turin 1979–88, part II, vol. 2 (part 1).

18. Charles Cohen, 'Pordenone's Cremona passion scenes and German art', *Arte lombarda*, 42/43, 1975.

19. Paul Renucci, 'Giuoco e passione nella poesia del perugino Francesco Beccuti', in *L'umanesimo umbro*, Perugia 1977.

20. Quoted from his letter to Bembo of 1542 in *Le lettere*, ed. Aulo Greco, Rome 1972. On this edition, see the critical observations of Paolo Trovato, 'Intorno al testo e alla cronologia delle *Lettere* di Jacopo Bonafadio', *Studi e problemi di critica testuale*, 20, 1980. The poem here referred to, *Delle lodi della furfanteria*, is published on pp. 159 ff.

21. Luciano Berti quoted from p. 2 of his *Pontormo: Disegni* (2nd edn), Florence 1975.

22. Giorgio Padoan, 'Ut pictura poesis: Le "pitture" di Ariosto, le "poesie" di Tiziano', in his *Momenti del Rinascimento veneto* (the reference is to Orlando Furioso, vii, pp. 11–15); Mark W. Roskill, *Dolce's 'Aretino' and Venetian Art*

Theory of the Cinquecento, New York 1968. On literary theory, Weinberg, *A History of Literary Criticism in the Italian Renaissance* (above, n. 1) is still basic. Marc Fumaroli, *L'Age de l'éloquence: Rhétorique et "res literaria" de la Renaissance au seuil de l'époque classique*, Geneva 1980, does no more than paraphrase one work after another for a grand total of 882 pages.

23. Quoted by Luigi Grassi in *Teorici e storia della critica d'arte*, Rome 1970. Most of the art theory treatises mentioned below are published in Paola Barocchi (ed.), *Trattati d'arte del Cinquecento fra Manierismo e Controriforma* (3 vols), Bari 1960, i, which is more appropriate for my purposes than her *Scritti d'arte del Cinquecento*, Milan and Naples 1971, since in the latter the treatises are broken up under topical headings.

24. Trissino quoted by Lionello Puppi in his *Scrittori vicentini d'architettura del secolo XVI*, Vicenza 1973, p. 85; Cornaro by Paolo Carpeggiani in *Alvise Cornaro e il suo tempo*, Padua 1980.

25. A. E. Santaniello in the introduction to the reprint (New York 1970) of the London 1610 edition of Sebastiano Serlio, *The Book of Architecture*.

26. On which: Renato Barilli in his *Poetica e retorica*, Milan 1969, Ch. 2.

27. Donatella Rasi, 'Breve ricognizione di un carteggio cinquecentesco: Bernardo Tasso e G. B. Giraldi', *Bergomum*, 28, 1980; Remigio's introduction to *Degli huomini illustri di Grecia*, attributed to Emilius Probus, Venice 1550.

28. Bernard Degenhart and Annegrit Schmitt, 'Methoden Vasaris bei der Gestaltung seines *Libro*', in Wolfgang Lotz and Lisa Lotte Moeller (eds), *Studien zur toskanischen Kunst: Festschrift Heinrich Heydenreich*, Munich 1964; Luigi Grassi, 'Giorgio Vasari, scrittore e critico d'arte', *Cultura e scuola*, 49/50, 1974; the numerous contributions to *Il Vasari storiografo e artista*, Istituto Nazionale di Studi sul Rinascimento, Arezzo and Florence 1976; and to *Giorgio Vasari: Tra decorazione ambientale e storiografia artistica*, Istituto Nazionale di studi sul Rinascimento, Florence 1985. In general, T. S. R. Boase, *Giorgio Vasari, The Man and the Book*, Princeton 1979.

29. Craig Hugh Smyth, *Bronzino as Draughtsman*, Locust Valley, New York 1971; Charles McCorquodale, *Bronzino*, New York 1981.

30. Bernice F. Davidson (ed.), *Mostra di disegni di Perino del Vaga e la sua cerchia*, Florence 1966. In particular: *Gli affreschi di Paolo III a Castel Sant'Angelo*, Rome 1981; in general: John Gere, *Il Manierismo a Roma*, Milan 1971.

31. S. J. Freedberg, *Parmigianino: His Works in Painting*, Cambridge, Mass. 1950; Augusta Ghidiglia Quintavalle, *Gli affreschi giovanili del Parmigianino*, Milan 1968, and *Gli ultimi affreschi di Parmigianino*, Milan 1971; Maurizio Fagiolo dell'Arco, *Il Parmigianino, un saggio sull'ermetismo nel Cinquecento*, Rome 1970; Paola Rossi, *L'opera completa del Parmigianino*, Milan 1980; Eugenio Riccòmini, 'The frescoes of Correggio and Parmigianino: From beauty to elegance', in *The Age of Correggio and Carracci* (National Gallery of Art), Washington 1986.

32. Giovio, *Dialogo dell'imprese*, ed. Maria Luisa Doglio, Rome 1978.

33. These technical terms are those of Arnaldo De Benedetto in the introduction to his edition of Della Casa, *Prose* (2nd edn), Turin 1974. The *Galateo* has been translated by R. S. Pine-Coffin, Baltimore 1958 and by Konrad Eisenbichler and Kenneth R. Bartlett, Toronto 1986. Other information from Lanfranco Caretti, 'Della Casa, uomo politico e scrittore', in his *Antichi e moderni: Studi di letteratura italiana*, Turin 1976; Antonio Sole, 'La lirica di G. della Casa', *Giornale storico della letteratura italiana*, 154, 1977 (on his debt to the fifteenth-century poets); and the several studies by Antonio Santosuosso now summarized in his *Vita di*

Giovanni Della Casa, Rome 1979, and his *Bibliography of Giovanni Della Casa*, Florence 1979.

34. Carmelo Musumarra, *La poesia tragica italiana nel Rinascimento*, Florence 1972 (to be read with the strong caveat of Riccardo Scrivano in *RLI*, 77, 1973, pp. 168–69); P. R. Horne, *The Tragedies of Giambattista Cinthio Giraldi*, Oxford 1962.

35. Carmelo Musumarra quoted by Antonietta Porro, 'Volgarizzatori di drammi Euripidei a Firenze nel Cinquecento', *Aevum*, 55, 1981, p. 481. The text of the *Discorso* is published in Giraldi's *Scritti critici*, ed. Camillo Guerrieri Crocetti, Milan 1973.

36. Quoted from the author's preface to *La Raffaella*, ed. Diego Valeri, Florence 1942, p. 34. On Rojas: Kathleen Kish, *An Edition of the First Italian Translation of the 'Celestina'*, Chapel Hill, North Carolina 1973.

37. Marc'Antonio Epicuro, *I drammi e le poesie italiane e latine*, ed. Alfredo Parente, Bari 1942.

38. Caro's *Straccioni* is included in Nino Borsellino (ed.), *Commedie del Cinquecento*, Milan 1962. It has been translated by Massimo Ciavolella and Donald Beecher: *The Scruffy Scoundrels (Gli Straccioni)*, Waterloo, Ontario 1980. See Giulio Ferroni, '*Gli Straccioni* del Caro e la fissazione manieristica della realtà', in his '*Mutazione' e 'riscontri' nel teatro di Machiavelli e altri saggi sulla commedia del Cinquecento*, Rome 1972. What I describe here as model and variation upon the model is presented as two separate genres, 'erudite' and 'rebel', in the synopses of plots by Douglas Radcliff-Umstead, *The Birth of Modern Comedy in Renaissance Italy*, Chicago 1969. The expression *personaggi emblematici* is that of Aulo Greco in 'Postille all'edizione delle *Familiari*', *Arcadia*, 7, 1973.

39. Delmo Maestri, 'Le commedie di Giovan Battista Gelli e la *Polifila*', *Lettere italiane*, 30, 1978. The text is in Gelli, *Opere*, ed. Ireneo Sanesi, Turin 1952, and in the same *Opere* re-edited by Delmo Maestri, Turin 1976. The most comprehensive study is Armand L. De Gaetano, *Giambattista Gelli and the Florentine Academy: The Rebellion against Latin*, Florence 1976.

40. The text is in Borsellino (ed.), *Commedie del Cinquecento* (above, n. 38), II.

41. Anton Francesco Doni quoted by Sergio Bertelli, in Sergio Bertelli and Piero Innocenti (eds), *Bibliografia machiavelliana*, Verona 1979, pp. xxvii–xxviii. On Cecchi, see Douglas Radcliff-Umstead, *Carnival Comedy and Sacred Play: The Renaissance Dramas of Giovan Maria Cecchi*, Columbia, Missouri 1986. Cecchi's *L'assiuolo* has been translated by Konrad Eisenbichler, Waterloo, Ontario 1981.

42. In general: Giambattista Salinari (ed.), *Novelle del Cinquecento*, Turin 1976 (from the 1st edn of 1955), with a good selection of what the editor categorizes as 'minors'; and Bruno Porcelli, *La novella del Cinquecento*, reprinted from *Letteratura italiana Laterza*, 22 (above, n. 11); Marziano Guglielminetti in the introduction to his edition of *Novellieri del Cinquecento*, Naples and Milan 1972. Selections from Bandello with a very informative introduction in Riccardo Scrivano (ed.), *Cinquecento minore*, Bologna 1966. On Grazzini: the introduction of Giovanni Grazzini to Raffaelle Fornaciari's edition of *Scritti scelti*, Florence 1957, on which: Robert J. Rodini, *Antonfrancesco Doni, Poet, Dramatist, and Novelliere*, Madison, Wisconsin 1970, Ch. 5. On Bandello: the introduction by Francesco Flora to his edition of *Tutte le opere* (2 vols), Milan 1934–1966. An excellent collection in English translation of Italian *novelle* is Janet L. Smarr (ed., tr.), *Italian Renaissance Tales*, Rochester, Michigan 1983.

43. In Giuseppe Gigli and Fausto Nicolini (eds), *Novellieri minori del Cinquecento*, Bari 1912.

44. All thoroughly analysed by Roberto Alonge in *Il teatro dei Rozzi di Siena*, Florence 1967.

45. Eugene A. Carroll, 'Drawings by Rosso Fiorentino in the British Museum', *Burlington Magazine*, 108, April 1966; Catherine Monbeig Goguel, 'Salviati, Bronzino et *La Vengeance de l'Innocence*', *Revue de l'art*, 31, 1976; Abraham Ronen, 'The Chariot of the Sun – Variations on a theme by Guilo Romano', *Mitt Kunst F*, 21, 1977.

46. Lionello Neppi, *Palazzo Spada*, Rome 1975.

47. Giulio Muratori and Delfino Bighi, 'Andrea Vesalio, G. B. Canani e la scuola medica . . . ', *Atti e memorie della deputazione provinciale ferrarese di storia patria*, 162, 1964–65; Roberto Bruni, 'Polemiche cinquecentesche: Franco, Aretino, Domenichi', *Italian Studies*, 32, 1977 (here quoted); Riccardo Scrivano, 'Ortensio Lando traduttore di Thomas More' (1972), now in his *La norma e lo scarto: Proposte per il Cinquecento letterario italiano*, Rome 1980; Sebastiano Martelli, 'Nicolò Franco: Intellettuali, letteratura e società nel Cinquecento', in *Interrogativi dell'umanesimo* (Atti del convegno di Montepulciano 1973), Florence 1976, II; Ortensio Lando quoted from the Venice 1544 edition of *Paradossi, cioè, Sententie fuori del comun parere*, pp. 97 and 100; Castelvetro and Caro quoted from Caro, *Opere*, ed. (with a very helpful introduction) Stefano Jacomuzzi, Turin 1974, pp. 103 and 206.

48. Paul Grendler, *Critics of the Italian World*, Madison 1969, here quoted from pp. 3, 9, 13, 70; Claude-Gilbert Dubois, *Le Maniérisme*, Paris 1979, pp. 12–13; B. Zevi, 'Attualità di Michelangiolo architetto', in Bruno Zevi and Paolo Portoghesi, *Michelangelo architetto*, Turin 1964; G. C. Argan quoted by Margherita De Simone in *Manierismo architettonico nel Cinquecento palermitano*, Palermo 1968, p. 11; Achille Bonito Oliva, *L'ideologia del traditore: Arte, maniera, manierismo*, Milan 1976; Paolo Simoncelli (on Pontormo's Protestantism), 'Jacopo da Pontormo e Pierfrancesco Riccio' (i.e., Ricci), *CS*, 17, 1980.

49. Vasari quoted by Alessandro Conti in Previtali and Zeri, eds, *Storia dell'arte italiana* (above, n. 17), II, p. 201, and directly from the Della Valle edition of the *Vite*, VI, p. 361, and by Maurizio Fagiolo dell'Arco in '"Peritissimo alchimista": Analisi del Parmigianino', *L'arte*, 7–8, 1969, pp. 69–137.

50. Ortensio Lando, *Novelle*, ed. Guido Batelli, Lanciano 1916, novelle 1 and 2; Ortensio Lando, *Commentario de le più notabili e mostruose cose d'Italia . . . , nel quale prendesi estremo piacere*, Venice 1550; Ortensio Lando, *Dilettevoli orationi nella morte di diversi animali*, which I read along with Angelo Firenzuola's *Consigli degli animali* in the joint edition of Venice 1604.

51. Doni in *I Marmi*, ed. Ezio Chiorboli, Bari 1928, I, p. 156; Gelli quoted from *Capricci*, no. 5, in *Opere*, ed. Ireneo Sanesi, Turin 1952, pp. 220–29 and 208. On which: Amelia Corona Alessina in her introduction to Gelli, *Opere*, Naples 1969, and Alessandra Del Fante, 'Note sui *Mondi* di A. F. Doni', *Annali dell'Istituto di Filosofia, Università di Firenze*, 2, 1980.

52. Alessandro Cecchi, 'Pratica, fierezza e terribilità nelle grottesche di Marco da Faenza in Palazzo Vecchio a Firenze', *Paragone*, 18 (327), 1977. I admired Campi's drawings in the Uffizi, Gabinetto dei Disegni, photo 29567.

53. Caroline Elam, 'The site and early building history of Michelangelo's New Sacristy', *Mitt Kunst F*, 23, 1979.

54. Daniele Ponchiroli in the introduction to *Lirici del Cinquecento* (above, Ch. 3, p. 30, n. 2); Giuliano Tanturli, 'Una raccolta di rime di Giovanni Della Casa', *Studi di filologia italiana*, 39, 1981; Andrea Cristiani, 'Dalla teoria alla prassi: La *gravitas* di Giovanni Della Casa', *Lingua e stile*, 14, 1979, p. 53.

55. Riccardo Scrivano, in *Rassegna della letteratura italiana*, 83, 1979, p. 53, and 'La funzione teatrale nella critica del manierismo', *Biblioteca teatrale*, 23/24, 1979; Giulio Ferroni in Ferroni and Amedeo Quondam (eds), *La 'Locuzione artificiosa': Teoria ed esperienza della lirica a Napoli nell'età del manierismo*, Rome 1971, p. 19.

56. Angela Ottino Della Chiesa quoted in *Accademia Carrara*, Bergamo 1955, p. 135. See also Antonio Daniele, 'Un ritratto di Tiziano e un sonetto di Alessandro Piccolomini', *Arte veneta*, 33, 1979, pp. 126–27; on the portraits of Pontormo and Allori: Doris Wild, 'Le sembianze di Jacopo da Pontormo nel ritratto e nell'autoritratto', *Rivista d'arte*, 36, 1961–62, 53–64.

57. The verses here quoted are in Marianne Albrecht-Bott, *Die bildende Kunst in der italienischen Lyrik der Renaissance und des Barock*, Wiesbaden 1976, p. 31. On Beccadelli: Gigliola Fragnito, *Memoria individuale e costruzione biografica*, Urbino 1978. Paolo Giovio's *Le vite del Gran Capitano e del Marchese di Pescara* in the translation by Ludovico Domenichi is available in the modern edition of Costantino Panigada, Bari 1931.

58. Vasari quoted from p. 36 of the catalogue of the Arezzo exhibition of 1981: *Giorgio Vasari*, Florence 1981; Alessandro Nova, 'Francesco Salviati and the Markgrafen Chapel', *Mitt Kunst F*, 25, 1981.

59. Frederick Hartt, *Giulio Romano*, New Haven 1958; Giovanni Paccagnini, *Il Palazzo ducale di Mantova*, Turin 1969; Egon Verheyen, *The Palazzo del Te in Mantua: Images of Love and Politics*, Baltimore 1977.

60. Caro quoted by Aulo Greco in the introduction to his edition of *Lettere familiari*, Florence 1957, p. xix; for Bembo, see Carlo Dionisotti (ed.), *Opere in volgare*, p. 686 (see above, Chapter 3, n. 2).

61. Vincenzo Borghini quoted in his *Discorsi* (1584–1585), vol. 2, Florence 1755, p. 256. Massimo Donattini, 'Giovan Battista Ramusio e le sue *Navigationi*: Appunti per una biografia', *CS*, 17, 1980; Federico Chabod, 'Paolo Giovio', in his *Scritti sul Rinascimento*, Turin 1967; Eric Cochrane, *Historians and Historiography*, Chicago 1981, pp. 320 and 366 ff.

62. Lionello Puppi, 'Prospetto di palazzo e ordine gigante nell'esperienza architettonica del '500', *Storia dell'arte*, 38/40, 1980.

63. Alexander Perrig, 'Michelangelo-Zeichnungen Benvenuto Cellinis', in his *Michelangelo-Studien*, IV, Frankfurt-am-Main 1977; Dino Cervigni, *The 'Vita' of Benvenuto Cellini*, Ravenna 1979; Nino Borsellini in *DBI*, vol. 23, pp. 440–51; and John Pope-Henessy, *Cellini*, London 1985.

64. Manfredo Tafuri, *Jacopo Sansovino e l'architettura del '500 a Venezia*, Padua 1969, valuable particularly for its historical approach; Deborah Howard, *Jacopo Sansovino: Architecture and Patronage in Renaissance Venice*, New Haven 1975, valuable more for its splendid illustrations than for its *kunstgeschichtliche* disregard for historical context; Wolfgang Lotz, 'La trasformazione sansoviniana di Piazza San Marco e l'urbanistica del Cinquecento', *Bolletino del Centro internazionale di Studi di Architettura Andrea Palladio*, 8, 1966.

65. Marco Alteri in *Le nuptiali*, ed. Enrico Narducci, Rome 1873, quoted by Massimo Miglio in 'Il leone e la lupa dal simbolo al pasticcio alla francese', *Studi romani*, 30, 1982, p. 183.

66. Maria Giustina Grassi, 'Gli arredi lignei e l'intaglio negli edifici religiosi di Mantova e del Mantovano', *Arte lombarda*, 42/43, 1975, p. 101.

67. Emanuele Casamassima, *Trattati di scrittura del Cinquecento italiano*, Milan 1966. On High Renaissance alphabet writers, with full bibliography: Giovanni Mardersteig, 'Francesco Torniello e il suo alfabeto romano', in Gabriella Bernardoni Trezzini *et al.*, *Tra latino e volgare: Per Carlo Dionisotti*, vol. 2, Padua 1974, pp. 521–43.

68. Maria Luisa Ferrari, 'L'arte a Cremona', in her *Studi di storia d'arte*, Florence 1979; Franco Voltini, *La chiesa di S. Sigismondo di Cremona*, Cremona 1974; Silla Zamboni quoted from her article on 'Giulio' in *DBI*. In general: Giulio Bora, ed., *Disegni di manieristi lombardi*, Vicenza 1971.

69. Elena Parma Armani (ed.), *Villa del Principe Doria a Fassolo*, Genoa 1977; Bernice F. Davidson, 'The decoration of the Sala Regia under Pope Paul III', *Art Bulletin*, 58, 1976 (here quoted from p. 399); Ettore Allegri and Alessandro Cecchi, *Palazzo Vecchio e i Medici*, Florence 1980 (quoted). On another important Vasari project: Marcia B. Hall, *Renovation and Counter-Reformation: Vasari and Duke Cosimo in Santa Maria Novella and Santa Croce, 1565–1577*, Oxford 1979, which kindly refrains from explicitly criticizing the rather different picture of the age presented in my *Florence in the Forgotten Centuries, 1527–1800: A History of Florence and the Florentines in the Age of the Grand Dukes*, Chicago 1973.

70. Rolf E. Keller, *Das Oratorium von San Giovanni Decollato in Rom*, Rome 1976.

71. All this and much more in *Da Tiziano a El Greco: Per la storia del manierismo a Venezia*, Milan 1981. W. R. Rearick, 'Early drawings of Jacopo Bassano' (here quoted), and Jan Bialostocki, 'Le vocabulaire visuel de Jacopo Bassano', both in *Arte veneta*, 32, 1978.

72. Francesco Santi, 'La facciata originale dell'alessiana chiesa di S. Maria del Popolo a Perugia', *Bolletino della Deputazione di Storia di Patria per l'Umbria*, 73, 1976.

73. Vasari quoted by Mario Rotili, *L'arte del Cinquecento nel Regno di Napoli*, Naples 1972.

74. Giuseppe Spatrisano, *Architettura del Cinquecento in Palermo*, Palermo 1961 (with good photographs).

CHAPTER SEVEN

Tridentine Reform

THE RELIGIOUS REVIVAL

The triumph of the humanist culture of the Renaissance in the Age of Leo X and Clement VII and the extension of humanist culture toward the geographical confines of the Italian peninsula coincided chronologically with what, for want of a better term, may be called a religious revival – specifically, a demanding search on the part of an increasingly large number of persons for a more intense and more meaningful relationship with the supernatural.

This revival had nothing to do with a supposed 'subjection of Italy to Spain', as is sometimes claimed. Its first manifestations appeared well beyond the limits of the two states in which Spanish influence was most conspicuous in the late fifteenth century – Rome under the Borgia and Naples under the Aragonese; and its later manifestations appeared with equal frequency on either side of the confines of those states that eventually became dependencies of the king of Spain. Neither did it have anything to do with what is sometimes pictured as the efforts of an *Ecclesia triumphans* to substitute 'Christian' for political or cultural 'heroes'. It had even less to do with a supposed attempt by agents of 'Roman centralism' to wipe out 'the survival of ancient, deep-rooted . . . local culture' and to 'prevent the development of . . . a materialistic attitude toward work and the sciences', since their 'culture' was none other than the same humanist culture freely accepted everywhere else in Italy.

Nor can the revival be explained as a consequence of the 'crises that the cultural world was undergoing during the wars of Italy' or of a 'crisis without any possibility of a solution' that the 'principates of northern Italy' supposedly faced after having 'lost their autonomy'; for the word 'crisis' has been rendered almost meaningless by overuse in modern Italian political jargon. It cannot be blamed upon 'Italian intellectuals' who, in order to keep their 'status and wealth in this world' let themselves be 'suffocated and domesticated' by a 'Roman Church', or upon 'the ruling classes' who, 'in response to the collapse of humanist values', somehow 'became aware of the urgency of a doctrinal re-establishment capable of sanctioning and confirming their immutable privileges'. Nor can it be described as a psychological reaction to any natural or man-made 'calamities'. For it flourished most vigorously during the late fifteenth century in places where calamities were the least frequent – e.g., Florence and the Veneto – and it continued to flourish well after 1530, when calamities rapidly diminished in number and intensity. Indeed, its chief protagonists seldom mentioned even the famous calamities of their age except when they needed empirical verification for their interpretations of prophetic passages in the Bible.[1]

One of the principal manifestations – and one of the principal stimulants – of the religious revival was the ever increasing number of reported cases, starting in the middle of the fifteenth century, of persons who rose (or, as they put it, were raised) to the highest levels of spiritual experience. That is the level which the sixteenth-century codifiers of their experiences refer to as a 'state of union' with God, one in which, after a long period of preparation, the subject's will is made to harmonize perfectly, although without being absorbed by, the will of God. Such persons are today called 'mystics', and their collective experience is called 'mysticism', even though neither they nor any of their contemporaries ever used either this or any equivalent term.

The Italian mystics of the Age of the Renaissance came from all classes of society; and mysticism cannot therefore be described as the expression of any one class. Stefana Quinzani (1457–1530) was the illiterate daughter of a servant at a monastery in Soncino near Brescia who was herself hired as a house servant when she was left an orphan at the age of fifteen. Laura Gambara (fl. 1530s) and her sister Paola (1463–1505) were born into one of the first families of Brescia. Lodovica Torelli (1500–1569) was the countess of the autonomous appanage of Guastalla who, after one husband and two of her infant children died and after another husband was murdered before her eyes, sold her domain to Ferrante Gonzaga – thus happily strengthening his status in the state he governed for the emperor – and retired to a monastery she had built and endowed in Milan. Women outnumbered men among the known mystics of the age; and they in part account for the rise, in early sixteenth-century Italy, of the proportion of women to men subsequently beatified or canonized to the all-time high of 23:25.[2]

A few of these mystics remained relatively isolated from the world around them. Chiara Bugni's (1471–1514) battles with the Devil were known only to her fellow nuns in Venice until she was visited by a high-ranking committee of one cardinal, two bishops, and several medics. The constant stream of tears that almost blinded Caterina de' Vigri of Bologna (1413–1463) and the reward she got for them when the Virgin herself let her 'place her face into that of the most sweet Baby Jesus' became known only upon the publication of her *Spiritual Battle* in 1475. The chief service of such a secluded mystic to the cause of religion thus consisted largely in assuring her fellow citizens that God was in direct contact with one of them, and that she, like the Dominican Osanna Andreasi (1449–1505), was so consumed by 'the fire of the love of God that she desired [only] to become drunk with the precious blood of Christ' by 'placing [her] mouth on His most holy Side'. Far from being distracted by the Freudian overtones of these rather physical expressions of religiosity, the citizens so prized their local mystics that they were willing to fight for them – as Duke Ercole I d'Este discovered when he tried to buy the remains of the Dominican Lucia Brocadelli da Narni from Pope Alexander VI.[3]

But even those mystics who initially retired from the world were eventually forced back into it – not in spite of, but as a consequence of their contemplative experiences. Paola Antonia Negri (1508–1555) devoted so much energy to advising monks on how to reform their monasteries and bishops on how to govern their dioceses that she was eventually accused of being a spy for Ferrante Gonzaga and expelled from Venice. Cloistered nuns also spent much of their time giving spiritual – and sometimes political – advice to princes and potentates, who scrupulously deferred to them as a way of adding a bit of divine legitimization to their shaky political titles. Osanna Andreasi was the advisor of the Gonzaga in Mantua, the Augustinian Veronica Negroni da Binasco (1445–1497) that of the Sforza in Milan and Colomba da Rieti that of the Baglioni in Perugia. Thanks to the advent of the printing press, the advice they gave to their princely charges – as well as detailed descriptions of the spiritual road by which they had arrived at their rank as advisors – was made available to the whole Italian literate public, which could read about it in such popular works as the biography of Caterina of Bologna and the treatise *On the Contemplative Life* (1527) by the Augustinian Antonio da Crema, the protégé of Pope Alexander's daughter, Lucrezia Borgia.

Indeed, it was this urge toward the active life that most distinguishes the mystics of the early sixteenth century from their closest predecessors, the mystics of the mid-fourteenth century. Some of them, to be sure, seem to have been conscious of the precedent. They were certainly familiar with the prophecies of Brigid of Sweden and of Severus of Ravenna, which were described in numerous editions after 1500, and with the letters of Caterina da Siena, a copy of which was sent to Lucrezia Gambara by one of her disciples in 1504. But few if any of them paid much attention to this heritage. Indeed, the most famous of them, Caterina Fieschi of Genoa (1447–1510), appears to have traversed the entire long and painful course from initial purgation to final beatitude completely on her own. Many of them travelled extensively. Between 1522 and 1524 Angela Merici (1474–1540) went from Brescia to Mantua, to the Holy Land, back to Venice and to Rome, where Pope Clement tried in vain to detain her. In 1530 she was alternately in Cremona and Brescia; in 1532 she was in Milan as the guest of Duke Francesco II Sforza. And the organization she founded in 1535 was the opposite of the traditional cloistered order: the Company of St Ursula was composed of women of all social ranks who lived not in convents but in their own homes – in order better to serve the members of their own families and fellow citizens.

Some of the mystics were even married – a revolution in the history of mysticism at least since the time of that gamophobe, St Jerome. Caterina Fieschi and her patrician husband finally separated only after he too received a special vocation. Both of them spent the rest of their lives not as secluded contemplatives, but as highly competent hospital administrators. Even those who began or ended their careers as members of religious orders studiously avoided suggesting that their disciples follow their example. 'The habit of virtue is acquired by the grace of God and by our exertions', warned the Dominican Battista Carioni da Crema in his manual *Lo specchio interiore* ('The Interior Mirror') of 1540. 'Disciplines, vigils, fasts and other such macerations' are a matter for those with special gifts, but they are wholly extraneous to the real work of sanctification.[4]

Closely related to the mystics were the prophets. They too claimed to be recipients of divine revelations. But their revelations came to them through sudden or gradual illuminations concerning the current relevance of what had been written by or about other prophets in the past, not in ecstasies or visions. Occasionally these illuminations were corroborated by borrowings from such secular 'sciences' as astrology – as they were, for example, in the case of the Dominican scholar-theologian Annio da Viterbo. By observing the position of the stars, Annio was able, in 1480, to predict the imminent 'triumph of the Christians over the Turks and all other Muslims'.[5]

More often the illuminations relied upon the heritage of the preceding great century of prophecy, the thirteenth, particularly after the printing presses began resuscitating several of the more important literary expressions of that heritage – those of Angelo of Jerusalem, the Anchorite of Mt Carmel who had been martyred in Sicily in 1225, of Jacopone da Todi, whose *laude* first appeared in Florence in 1490 and, above all, of the Spiritual Franciscan Gioacchino da Fiore. Soon everyone was once again acquainted with Gioacchino's version of the traditional medieval scheme of historical periodization – one which added a third 'Age of the Holy Spirit', now enriched with humanist notions of a literary rebirth, between the 'Age of the Son' and the Last Judgement. All that remained to be done was to look for the signs of the purifying conflagration that all the prophets said would usher in the new age – signs like the invasion of 1494, the flood in Rome of 1495, the five meteorites that fell near Forli in 1507 and the butterfly invasion of Brescia of 1522. The passage from one historical age – the next time as well as the last time – was effected by God alone, the prophets pointed out. All men could do was make sure that they would be found on the side of the beneficiaries rather than that of the victims; and to do that they had no choice but to give up, and to make their fellow citizens give up, what the prophets identified as the worst and most widespread sins of the age: blasphemy, simony, sodomy and exaggerated ornamentation in female attire.

Some of these prophets were highly trained and highly regarded members of prestigious religious orders. Such, for example, was Giorgio Benigno (to use the Italianized form of his Serbian name), a protégé of Pope Sixtus IV and Lorenzo de' Medici and professor of theology at Santa Croce and at the Studio in Florence.[6] Others were consigned to the category of *ciurmatori del mondo* ('riff-raff of the world'), at least by those few of Francesco da Montepulciano's hysterical listeners in Florence in 1513 who could not bring themselves to believe that they would ever 'sail boats through blood, through lakes of blood, through rivers of blood'. Still others behaved like Francesco's companion Matteo da Bascio, who

> wandered about from city to village . . . with a cross in one hand and . . . a breviary in the other, shoeless with nothing on his feet, with a half-length, rough, narrow habit patched with sackcloth, all squalid and macerated from continuous fasting and penances, crying with a loud and terrifying voice: 'All sinners into Hell!' . . . scorned by many as a madman, revered by others as a saint.[7]

Yet whereas the mystics continued to flourish, the prophets eventually wore themselves out. When neither Charles VIII nor Louis XII chose to assume the task of scourging the Church of Rome, when Francis I declined the invitation to become the latest version of a modern Cyrus, when Clement VII rather than an 'Angelic Pope' returned after the Sack and when the Turks conquered Hungary instead of converting *en masse* to Christianity, more and more of the prophets' devotees decided to put off the Joachimite Third Age into the distant future and to settle for the more modest, but at least somewhat effective, Age of Charles V and Ferrante Gonzaga.

The one apparent exception to the general demise of prophecy proves the rule: the one associated with the most famous of all the prophets, Girolamo Savonarola.[8] Savonarola's political and ecclesiastical foes – the *Arrabbiati*, the Franciscans of Santa Croce in Florence and even one general of Savonarola's own Order of Preachers – did their best to obliterate the memory of him in the years after his execution in 1498; indeed, the nuns in one Florentine convent were threatened with a bread and water diet if they even mentioned his name. Savonarola's faithful heirs did their best to discredit his policy of using political action to speed up the course of metahistory – most particularly in 1529–30, when their attempt to revive his blindly Gallophile foreign policy ended in the disaster of the siege. They then lost their principal institutional base. In 1545 Duke Cosimo threw them out of their monastery of San Marco; and he let them back in only after they had promised to leave the millennium to God and politics to him.

In the meantime, however, many Florentine Savonarolans had emigrated to other cities – tactfully forgetting to take with them Savonarola's impolitic plan for the imminent submission of all Italy to the sanctified New Jerusalem at its 'navel'. Fra Modesto Masi, for example, moved about as prior of Dominican convents from Prato to San Gimignano, Lucca, Viterbo, Perugia and Montepulciano; and he was everywhere received as a 'father of good doctrine in all disciplines' – one 'modest not only in his name but in his works, his words and his gestures', who wore a hair shirt and regularly flogged his weak body with the whip he kept under his mattress. In Florence itself, Savonarola became a common subject for the iconographers: fra Bartolomeo painted him as St Peter Martyr with a gold halo (San Marco), and Taddeo da Fiesole carved two busts of him in porphyry. He continued to guide the careers of such minor state officials as Lorenzo Violi, who, while waiting for his ultimate deliverance, managed to stay quietly in office from one change of regime to another. Better yet, he continued to pay personal calls particularly on his female disciples. In 1510 Lorenza da Firenze was cured of a grave illness after 'putting on his relics'. In 1531 Beatrice Arnolfini got rid of her migraines by wrapping her head in his towel. And applications for admission to their convents rose proportionately.[9]

The most famous of these convents was San Vincenzo of Prato – not only because of its exclusively patrician inmates nor because of the excessive austerities they were forced to endure, but chiefly because one of them happened to be the most famous of all the Italian mystics of the mid-sixteenth century: the Florentine Dominican Caterina de' Ricci (1512–1590).[10] Savonarola's intercession enabled Caterina to pass thirty-two kidney stones without the slightest pain in 1540, to receive the stigmata in 1542 (with the chest wound in the left, not the right side, as a mirror image of the crucified Christ), to sleep no more than three hours a night and vomit every time she accidently tasted cheese or meat, to remain kneeling in rapture for up to ten hours at a time, to suffer all the pains of the Passion every year from Holy Thursday through Good Friday – all this while remaining 'always happy and of such grace that whoever looked at her knew there was something divine in her face'.[11] Duchess Eleonora adopted her as her personal line of communication with the supernatural, while the first prelates of Florence reported having watched as her body floated upward from the floor of the chapel to be embraced by Christ as he leapt from the Crucifix.

It was not until the 1580s that an an effective counterattack could be launched. By then Savonarola's role as a prophet had been thoroughly undermined: the same 'Age of the Son' that he insisted would soon give way to a wholly different 'Age of the Holy Spirit' continued to roll on, and the radiant opposite of the abysmal Alexander VI had been created by human, not divine, initiative. Savonarola's role as a miracle worker had also suffered from the appearance of many more up-to-date, and hence more effective, competitors. And the one role still left to him, that of a martyr, had become identified with a cause in which no one any longer believed. Archbishop Alessandro de' Medici confiscated all the altars dedicated to him in Florence. Pope Clement VIII, whose own mother had been one of his devotees, forbade Masses in his honor. And not even the threat of that eminent biographer of Florentine saints, Serafino Razzi (1531–1611), to walk all the way to Rome in support of his canonization could do anything to stop them.

RELIGIOUS ORDERS AND CONFRATERNITIES

The second principal expression of the religious revival of the late fifteenth and early sixteenth century is to be found in a number of separate and sporadic efforts to reform several of the older religious orders – those institutions that still bore witness to the religious revivals of the fifth, the tenth and the thirteenth centuries. 'Reform' for these religious orders meant nothing more nor less than returning to severe discipline and to a 'renewed observance of the original rules and to the ideals for which they had been founded'.[12] That is precisely what the monks of the Benedictine community of Santa Giustina in Padua sought to do as early as 1404. Their example was followed a few years later by the Benedictines of Pavia and enough of those at San Giorgio Maggiore in Venice to warrant the creation of a separate Benedictine congregation. The example was subsequently adopted by the entire Olivetani Congregation of the Benedictine confederation, then by those members of the Pavia Certosa who had not been overwhelmed by the transformation of their monastery into a showpiece for the ducal regime, and finally – thanks to the efforts of an emissary from Santa Giustina itself, the poet Angelo de Faggio – by the oldest and most revered of all the Italian Benedictine monasteries, Montecassino.[13]

Occasionally these reforms were inspired by extra-Italian models. That of the Neapolitan Carmelites, for example, was initiated by a visitor from Normandy in 1457 and by one from Catalonia in 1503; it was then completed in accordance with the example of the reformer of the Spanish Carmelites, Teresa of Avila (1515–1582). Occasionally the reforms resulted from the infusion of new expectations first formulated outside the order. The reestablishment of a strict cloistered life at Camaldoli was largely the work of a group of Venetian patricians who had begun meeting at Santa Giustina during their student days at Padua. The particular vocations that led several of them, from 1508 on, to abandon their palaces in Venice for isolated cells in one of the wildest and most windswept areas of the Tuscan Apennines, and the energy that then enabled them (and their politically powerful patrons) to override the objections of the bewildered old-timers among their new confrères – all this had been set down as early as 1506 in the *Pensieri quotidiani* ('Daily Thoughts') of the leading member of the group, Paolo Tommaso Giustiniani.[14]

More often, the demand for reform came from the members themselves, since they were the ones who were most constantly exposed to contrasts between the statement of ideals and actual practice. It was Agostino Bonucci who, upon his election as general in 1542, introduced a reform among the Servites, the butt of Machiavelli's satire in *La Mandragola*; and he got at least as far as saving many of their houses from the *magna penuria* into which they had fallen by borrowing on future revenues.[15] It was Girolamo Seripando (1492–1563) – a disciple of the former general Egidio Viterbo, a patron of the Neapolitan poets, and a man who joined 'the greatest moral probity and sanctity of life with a knowledge of the arts' – who drafted the new constitution of the Augustinians. Seripando then dedicated most of the remainder of his twelve-year term as general to travelling all over Italy and beyond the Alps in order to get the constitutions adopted by all the houses of the far-flung confederation. He rested from his ceaseless peregrinations *en route* only long enough to note, in his spiritual diary, the number of kidney stones he passed from time to time.[16]

Internal reform turned out to be particularly effective in the two major mendicant orders, the Order of Preachers (Dominicans) and the Order of

Observant Friars Minor (Franciscans). Even though they, more frequently than any others, had been the object of jokes and violent denunciations ever since the time of Boccaccio, the mendicant orders managed to preserve a considerable degree of popular esteem. Mendicants were still called upon to deliver Advent and Lenten sermon series in the major churches and basilicas of the peninsula. One of them, Bernardino da Siena, had been hailed as a second Francis in the early fifteenth century. Another, Bernardino Tomitano da Feltre, was hailed as a second Bernardino da Siena in the late fifteenth century. Mendicants continued to be sought after for moral advice by princes and republics as well as by other religious institutions; and their advice continued to be taken seriously. A Benedictine monastery in Genoa consulted Antonino, the Dominican archbishop of Florence and a leading moral theologian, to determine whether it could licitly sell at a discount deferred interest (*paghe*) payable on shares in its possession that had been emitted by the Banco di San Giorgio. The Cistercians of Sant'Andrea of Sestri Levante appealed to the Dominican theologian Raffaello de Pornassio (d. 1467) in order to decide whether their members could own their own books. In 1468 the city council of Rieti turned over to the Franciscan preacher Michele da Milano the task of writing its new laws against *incantatores et incantatrices* and Carnival transvestites.[17]

While insisting upon nothing less than a total return to the most recent age of perfect Christianity, the mendicants were not averse to updating the past in deference to the particular needs of their own times. Bernardino da Feltre declared a moderate interest payment to be legitimate: there was no other way, he contended, to finance the *monti di pietà* (pawnshops administered by laymen) upon which the poor were dependent for small, short-term loans of money. The Franciscan Bernardino Caimi of Milan was so excited by a pilgrimage to the Holy Land in 1477–78 that he resolved to share it with those of his fellow Lombards who could not afford the trip: he built replicas of the buildings he had observed while climbing up Calvary on a new 'Holy Mountain' near Varallo in Lombardy. He thus provided a model for the many other *monti sacri* that were to flourish in the Alpine foothills for another two centuries.

Consequently, these orders still managed to attract applicants of notable piety, talent, and even good birth – applicants like Cristoforo da Monza, a *cavaliere* in the court of the duke of Milan, who was converted by a sermon of Giovanni da Capistrano in 1441, or like the Genoese patrician Giovan Battista Cattaneo, whose heroic death in the service of plague victims in 1504 inspired one of the novelist Matteo Bandello's first literary efforts. They also generated several determined efforts at institutional reorganization – those of Vincenzo Bandello among the Lombard Dominicans in 1501 and 1505, those of the Brescian Franciscan Francesco Licheto in the province of Terra di Lavoro in 1514, and, above all, those of Savonarola, who, with the support of the influential humanists attracted by his philosophical and theological discussion sessions at San Marco, turned many of the Dominican houses in the new Dominican province of Tuscany into models of apostolic fervour and austerity.

But this was not enough to satisfy the most determined reincarnations of Francis and Dominic. Two of them went all the way to Damascus in 1548 'in order to suffer death for Christ' by shouting anti-Muslim blasphemies in public places; but they were cheated of their goal when, after their first arrest, the tolerant and urbane pasha decided instead to turn them over to the resident Venetian consul.[18] Several of them followed the hermit Matteo da Bascio (1495–1552) out into the hills of Umbria and the Marche, where they established a completely new branch of the ever-feuding Franciscan family – the one soon to be known as the *Cappuccini* (Capuchins) after the particular shape of the hood Matteo had noticed in an early portrait of Francis. After several of his famous about-faces, and after considerable pressure from his niece, the duchess of Camerino, Pope Clement finally approved the constitutions that had been drawn up by a committee composed, appropriately enough, of twelve of them. As other Capuchin congregations then sprang up all over Italy, the Observants too found it necessary to make special provision for their own *fratres strictioris vitae*, who otherwise might have defected to the Capuchins; and many of those who hitherto had hidden their reluctance to reform under the assurance that they were at least more reformed than their wayward rivals, the Conventual Franciscans, were subsequently moved to follow their example.[19]

The reform of the religious orders was accompanied by the revival and further elaboration of another traditional institution, the confraternities. Unlike religious orders, confraternities did not require their members to take permanent vows, although they generally screened them carefully before admission and put them through an initiation ceremony designed to strengthen their initial commitment. The confraternities were usually composed of persons actively engaged in normal secular occupations whose participation in collective activities was limited to the specific occasions established by statute. Moreover, their form of organization was patterned not upon a monastic rule, but upon those institutions with which the founders were most familiar: the magistracies and the guilds of the late medieval communes. And much of their energies thus went into writing and rewriting constitutions and electing large numbers of officers for correspondingly short terms of office.

However, none of the confraternities ever pretended to express a 'lay' – much less a 'secular' or 'burgher' – piety, as opposed to a 'clerical' or even a 'monastic' piety. Even those that boasted of being composed of 'mere seculars with lay and profane goods' and of having 'nothing to do with the clergy' still insisted upon having their statutes approved by their local ordinary, if not by the pope. Those which explicitly forbade or limited the number of clerical members always designated one or more priests as chaplains. Such provisions were no different in kind from those that restricted membership to specific categories of laymen – for example, to nobles or to citizens of one city resident in another. But even these limitations were exceptional. Most of the confraternities, in practice if not by statute, did not discriminate among 'plebeians, artisans and nobles' – like those who composed the Compagnia di San Girolamo at San Marco in Florence – or between those who could and those who could not read in, for example, the Confraternity of San Giovanni Evangelista in Padua.[20]

Indeed, many of the confraternities were originally organized by devotees of a member of a religious order in a manner similar to that of the 'third orders', or lay associates, of mendicant communities. The several associated confraternities of the 'Cinque Piaghe di Gesù' ('The Five Wounds of Jesus') were originally inspired by the sermons of the Observant Franciscan Cherubino da Spoleto (1414–1484), those of the Santissimo Sacramento at Santa Maria sopra Minerva by the Dominican Tommaso Stella (d. 1566), and the one of the same name in Naples – one which soon included some 6,000 members – by Stella's former colleague at the Minerva, Ambrogio Salvio da Bagnoli (1491–1577). The principal attraction of these particular confraternities lay in their promise to extend to *seculares* the special spiritual benefits generally reserved for their sponsors *in religione*.[21]

But confraternities associated with religious orders – and using space provided by the monks or friars for their meetings – were no different in structure and in spirit from those that had been founded and inspired by pious matrons – for instance, by Mariola de' Negri of Genoa, whose Opera della Pietà di Gesù e Maria (1551) took care of adult women with no means of support. These confraternites in turn were indistinguishable in purpose and scope from – for example – the Confraternity of San Rocco of the boatmen (*barcaioli*) of Rome, who built a hospital for plague victims, or from the Confraternity of Good Works (*Carità*), which – because one of its founders was Cardinal Giulio de' Medici, later Pope Clement VII – provides a classic example of the inextricable confusion between the realms of the lay and the clerical so characteristic of the age.

Many of these confraternities still showed signs of their thirteenth- or fourteenth-century origins. The remarkable growth of the 'Disciplinati' in the sixteenth century – from 9 to 202 in Lombardy, from 9 to 81 in Umbria – after an equally remarkable decline in the fifteenth century shows that the attraction of the Flagellants had not been permanently affected by the exaggerations of which they had been accused in the fourteenth century.[22] Equally medieval in its origins was the Company of Santa Maria della Pietà at the church of San Salvatore in Rome: it aimed at nothing more practical than promoting the veneration of an image of the Virgin that had cried when someone was murdered in front of it in 1546. The 'several devout persons' – one of them a member of the noble Spinola family, another a shoemaker, another a monk – who established the Congregazione della Venerazione del Santissimo Sacramento in Naples in 1554 sought to do no more than 'improve themselves in the service of God . . . for the spiritual good of the souls of their neighbours'. Their chief activity consisted in 'talking about the things of God' and making their own households as much as possible 'like those of the primitive church'.[23]

Yet without ever making programmatic declarations to that effect, most of the confraternities founded after the mid-fifteenth century, and many others of medieval origins that were subsequently revived or reformed, differed substantially from their distant progenitors in one important respect: they were much more committed to serving the material and moral needs of non-members. The *vita contemplativa* increasingly came to be linked with the *vita activa*, 'which consists in coming to the aid of one's neighbours in a spirit of fervent charity'; and it was supposed to be reflected in the *vita morale*, 'which consists in ordering one's self in honest living and virtuous conversation'. Such, for example, was the case of the thirteenth-century Confraternity of SS. Giacomo and Lazzaro in Verona, which greatly expanded its endowment in the sixteenth century in order to administer properly a lepers' hospital – at least to judge by the large quantity of medicines it ordered from local pharmacists. Such also was the case of the three-centuries-old Confraternity of the Annunziata in Perugia. In 1557 it accepted from the city the administration of a home for repentant prostitutes; and in 1587 it revised its statutes in accordance with its new obligations.[24] Moreover, the customary medieval exemplars of the spirit of charity frequently yielded either to modern or to ancient exemplars. 'Faith without works is dead', declared the statutes of the Company of the Misericordia of Genoa in 1464.

Neither [particular] places nor [the taking of holy] orders bring one closer to God, as St Gregory said, only good merits [*li buoni meriti*]. For this reason St John Chrysostom complained that there were many priests but few priests, it being insufficient, as St Ambrose said, to wish to do good unless you do it.[25]

Typical of this new kind of confraternity was the Oratorio of Divine Love founded in Genoa in 1497.[26] Its spiritual and moral model was the mystic and hospital administrator, Caterina Fieschi. Its members were citizens of Genoa, no more than four of whom could be in holy orders. Every year they elected a prior, three counsellors, a *sindaco* (secretary), several *massari* (administrators) and visitors to the sick according to a procedure almost as complicated as the one established by Andrea Doria's constitution of the Republic in 1528. They sought to 'root and plant in our hearts divine love' through frequent religious services. They sought to maintain a high level of personal morality by excluding blasphemers and adulterers and by imposing humiliating penances on anyone who backslid. Most of their free time was spent administering and servicing the Redutto (hospice) de' Poveri Incurabili.

So successful was the Oratorio in realizing these objectives that brief visits between 1517 and 1519 by its most prominent member, Ettore Vernazza, were sufficient to engender sister oratories at Santa Dorotea in Trastevere in Rome and in Naples. Soon some of the best-born prelates in Rome were busy cleaning beds and bedpans, a professor of metaphysics in Naples was caring for syphilitics and a duchess was supervising the day-to-day affairs of a hospital. Meanwhile, another branch of the Oratorio had been founded in Venice by the former companions of the refugees at Camaldoli, who founded a hospital for incurables on the Zattere in 1522; and others were founded shortly afterward in several cities of the Venetian dominion. What had begun as a purely spontaneous and unprecedented attempt of a small group of laymen to realize in their own lives some of the supernatural graces bestowed upon a still only locally known mystic had become a large charitable institution of national dimensions.

Italy thus came to be populated by 'myriad small and middle-sized, rarely large, institutions, polycentric enterprises of ecclesiastics, laymen, monks, bishops, gentlemen and pious gentlewomen', the main problem of whom consisted in finding some human or spiritual need that was not yet being cared for. The brothers of San Girolamo della Carità in Vicenza visited invalids confined to their homes. Those of San Giovanni Decollato in Rome (the builders of the homonymous 'temple' of Mannerist art) accompanied condemned criminals to the scaffold – and codified their experiences in a number of manuals for the benefit of whoever might wish to do likewise. Those of the Santissima Trinità dei Pellegrini e dei Convalescenti in Naples sought out only those daughters of prostitutes whose mothers had had them violated so that they would not be taken in by the Confraternity of the Bianchi, which accepted only virgin girls. Those of SS. Filippo e Paolo in Milan taught poor children how to read and write – not, to be sure, for the improvement of their minds, but for 'the salvation of their souls and the glory of God'. Those of Santa Maria della Pietà dei Pazzarelli maintained (as the title indicates) an asylum for the insane.[27]

Far from deploring the latest additions to Europe's already abundant list of lethal diseases – syphilis (*mal francese*) and typhus (*mal di petecchie*) – the confraternities welcomed them as still another opportunity for expressing their religious commitments. Specialized hospitals for the victims of these diseases quickly sprang up in one city after another: in Bologna in 1500, in Rome in 1515 (San Giacomo degli Incurabili), in Naples in 1519, in Savona, Vicenza and Verona in 1520, and so on. What the confraternities could not do, or what they turned out to do less well than they hoped, they frequently left to the civil governments. After discovering irregularities in the administration of their endowments, the city council of Como united all the existing hospitals into a central Ospedale Maggiore di Santa Anna in 1485 under a twelve-man board of directors. Fearing the mismanagement of its ample endowment, the government of Florence took over the Ospedale in Santa Maria Nuova in 1498; and it returned it to its former directors in the Confraternity of the Buonomini only after they had been purged of Savonarolan nostalgics. Duke Cosimo established a twelve-man commission in 1542 to oversee all of the some two hundred charitable organizations in the Florentine domains, as well as to administer directly the commission's own orphanage in Via San Gallo.

One problem was almost always left to the political authorities: what to do about beggars and vagabonds. The Venetian Senate commissioned the Provveditori alla Sanità to look into the matter in 1528 – with the result that by 1545 the number of beggars had fallen from 6,000 to 1,400. Pope Pius v got them out of the churches, at least during religious services. Pope Gregory xiii had the eminent architect Carlo Fontana transform a former Dominican convent into a home for those of them who were unable to work.

Political initiative in the realm of charity was motivated by the largely practical intent of solving a social problem, rather than by the purely religious intent of saving the souls of the agents and the recipients of charity. But that bothered no one – especially not the clerics who were frequently appointed to the corresponding magistracies. It seemed perfectly natural to adopt in the realm of public charity the same method of experimenting within the framework of past experience that was being used rather successfully in the realm of state building.[28]

THE CONTRIBUTION OF THE HUMANISTS

The reformers of the religious orders and the founders of the confraternities generally looked backward in time, not forward; and when in fact they did introduce something new, they carefully disguised it as a restoration of something old. What eventually enabled them also to envisage forms of religious life different from, or at least not sanctioned by, the inheritance of the Middle Ages was humanism – that is, the same cultural movement dedicated to the creative imitation of ancient models that had already effected an equally sharp break with the medieval inheritance in the realms of art, letters and politics.

The humanists had discovered in the remains of antiquity many aspects of human experience that had no apparent relevance to any kind of religion, Christian or pre-Christian; and given the normative character of all antiquity, these aspects could not lightly be discarded. But they had also devoted considerable energy to realizing Petrarch's aspiration for a more intimate, more personal relationship with God – or at least with the God of Augustine. To this end, Lorenzo Valla had sought to rescue the faith from philosophy and the papacy from politics. Maffeo Vegio had tried to make hagiography philologically sound and thus morally more effective. And Marsilio Ficino, a priest as well as a philosopher, had tried to shift the metaphysical foundation of the faith from an Aristotelian to what he believed to be a firmer Neo-Platonic base.

Moreover, the humanists frequently ran into what appeared to be contradictions between the sacred and the secular, between the inheritance of Christian and of non-Christian antiquity. Some of them – like Alberti – simply ignored these contradictions. Some of them – Castiglione's courtiers, for example – artifically suppressed them. Some of them – like Pietro Pomponazzi and Machiavelli – frankly exposed them and then passed the dilemma onto their readers. But none of them ever proposed discarding the religious in favour of the secular; and all of them were sustained by the hope, if not the conviction, that the apparent contradictions could eventually be overcome.

During the first decades of the sixteenth century, more and more men of the arts and letters became interested in religious subjects – even those whose other literary and artistic concerns were totally areligious, if not irreligious. When he was not writing comedies or letters, Pietro Aretino filled in lacunae in the Gospel narratives with details about how many cooks Mary and Martha had hired to prepare supper for their Houseguest and about how difficult it had been for the soldiers of the Flagellation to extract their ropes from Jesus' lacerated flesh. After a busy career as a diplomat and as the author of love lyrics in honour of his famous mistress in Rome, Girolamo Muzio suddenly started studying the Holy Scripture – all without changing the way of life (*costumi*) he previously had followed, thus scandalizing his prudish eighteenth-century biographer. He thereafter concerned himself with treatises on the Mass, on the saints, on the papacy and on the errors of heretics.[29]

Not all these literary contributions to the cause of Christianity proved to be successful either from a religious or from an aesthetic point of view. Marco Girolamo Vida, later bishop of Alba and one of the patrons of the Campi family of painters in Cremona, could write amusing verse instruction books on how to grow silkworms and how to play chess. But he did not really add much force to the meaning of the story of the adultress in the Gospel by making her the victim of a forced marriage to an old man. Poems 'On the Immortality of Souls' usually sounded like metered jargon. *Carmina sacra* in iambic pentameter sounded like archaeological remains of the Age of Ambrose. Epic poems with titles such as the *Cristiade* sounded like parodies of the *Orlando furioso*. But at least they were sincere; and in some cases – in that, for example, of the sacred poems and letters of Vittoria Colonna – they managed effectively to unite the aesthetic qualities guaranteed by current Petrarchan and epistolary models with clear, and rhetorically effective, expressions of genuine religious sentiments.

If these efforts were occasionally successful in elevating the general tone of religious life in Italy, it was in part because of the gradual conversion to humanism even of some of those ecclesiastical institutions that were initially hostile or indifferent to it. That the Scuola di San Rocco of Venice was decorated by Tintoretto, that the statues in the first 'Holy Mountain' of Lombardy were made by the current dean of Milanese artists, Gaudenzio Ferrari, that the headquarters of the Confraternity of San Giovanni Decollato was planned by Vasari, that the Ospedale di San Giacomo in Augusta was designed by Baldassarre Peruzzi and Antonio da San Gallo: none of this was particularly surprising. The patrons of these projects were the patrons, or friends of the patrons, of the same artists in their non-ecclesiastical walks of life.[30] On the other hand, that a Franciscan professor of theology trained to multiply Scotist syllogisms should also write an impeccably Vallan-Ciceronian dialogue full of references to Terence, Virgil, Horace and Jerome, and none at all to Scotus: that was rather exceptional. But it soon became the rule. By the 1530s the theological curriculum at the Benedictine Badia of Florence was totally biblical and patristic – which may be why it was frequented by so many prominent men of letters. In 1541 the Olivetani permitted the study of Greek and Latin literature that they had prohibited in 1476; in 1559 they made it obligatory. By the time he was invited to preach at the Council of Trent, the homiletic expert of the Conventual Franciscans, Cornelio Musso (1511–1574), had perfected a method of preaching 'based on ideas, not images, open and certain, not dubious'. It was one that forced him to rise 'above the common style of our times by following in the footsteps of the most eloquent Greek and Latin fathers'.[31]

The greatest support for religious humanism, however, was provided by the most important of the ecclesiastical institutions, the papacy. As early as the pontificate of Nicholas V (1447–1455), the papacy had adopted humanism as its official ideology – that is, as the supplier of the forms of expression most appropriate for the task of turning the Church Militant into the Church Triumphant. Humanists continued to be summoned to preach in accordance with humanist – that is, scriptural and patristic – standards even by such culturally illiterate of Nicholas' immediate successors as Paul II (1464–1471). Florentine artists and writers continued to flock to Rome even under such dynastic and military popes as Alexander VI and Julius II.

Under Leo X the humanists completed their take-over of the papal secretariat that had been initiated by Leonardo Bruni a century earlier. They did so with the backing and encouragement of the most genuinely humanist of all the popes, Paul III, the pupil of the renowned philologist Giulio Pomponio Leto (1428–1497) and the head of a family 'that participated brilliantly in the intellectual movement of the Renaissance'. The promotion to the cardinalate and to other high ecclesiastical offices of so many 'great, learned and well-mannered gentlemen' was celebrated by Vasari when he surrounded the pope with them in his frescoes at the Cancelleria. It was celebrated by one of the most learned of these gentlemen, Ludovico Beccadelli, when he had their portraits painted on the walls of his Villa di Giuppara. It was celebrated by the heirs of the most productive of them, Pietro Bembo, a bishop and a cardinal as well as the linguistic arbiter of Italy, when they buried his body halfway between the funeral monuments of the two Medici popes in the chancel of the Dominican basilica of Santa Maria sopra Minerva.

This support from ecclesiastical institutions encouraged what was soon recognized as the most important and potentially innovative contribution of humanism to the religious revival: the application of philological methods to the reading of the Latin Church Fathers and the recovery and propagation of the Greek Church Fathers. Since no one in the Renaissance ever contemplated the distinction between 'classical' and 'post-classical' authors canonized in the classics departments of twentieth-century universities, Basil was held to be as much of an 'ancient' – and hence as normative – as Plato, just as Augustine, Petrarch's favourite ancient author, was regarded as the peer of Cicero. Consequently, the early Renaissance text hunters were equally interested in both. So, for that matter, were the artists, who celebrated the efforts of the philologists in such paintings as fra Angelico's portraits of Athanasius and Chrysostom in the chapel of Pope Nicholas V (1447–1448) and the anonymous triptych of Augustine, Monica and Ambrose in Vigevano. So successful were these efforts that by the end of the fifteenth century all the principal writings of the Fathers were represented in the major, public repositories of ancient literature – the Vatican in Rome, the Marciana in Venice, and the Laurenziana in Florence.

120

That left the sixteenth-century text hunters free to dig up the still little-known works of already well-known Fathers – like Chrysostom's commentary on the Psalms, which was found in Greece in 1548. It left the translators with the task of rendering in the Volgare those texts that had already been published in Latin – as Giovan Francesco Zeffi did with Erasmus' edition of Jerome and as Pier Francesco Zini did with Gregory of Nyssa. And since no one in the Renaissance yet knew the difference between Greek and Byzantine, that left the Hellenists with the task of translating into Latin such late Greek spiritual writers as Nylus Ancyranus and Theophilatus, bishop of Bulgaria. All the Fathers were thus included in the grandiose scheme envisaged by one of the most scholarly and pious bibliophiles in the Farnese circle in Rome, Cardinal Marcello Cervini (1501–1555): to publish and 'broadcast to the whole world' all the Greek manuscripts in the Vatican Library.[32]

The reading of the Fathers encouraged a return to what had been their major source of inspiration: the Bible. 'Believing it better to spend his time studying the Sacred Scriptures than writing about speculative questions full of useless arguments', another Genoese patrician convert to the Dominican order, Agostino Giustiniani (1470–1536), was inspired by the memory of Pico della Mirandola to learn Hebrew, which he taught for several years at Paris. He was moved by the exhortations of Thomas More, whom he met in England, to apply his remarkable command of languages to a pentalingual edition of the Psalms. He then retired to the diocese that had been procured for him in Corsica, 'far from the pomp and ambitions of the world', to do the same for the rest of the Old Testament – while at the same time writing guide books for his unlettered clergy and translating Xenophon for his nephew.[33]

Similarly, the lyric poet Marcantonio Flaminio (1498–1550) prepared for Cardinal Alessandro Farnese an *Explanationes* and *Paraphrases* of the Psalms, with the help of rabbinical as well as of patristic commentaries. The Platonist-Hebraicist Agostino Steuco (1497–1548) consulted with the most learned Jewish scholars of the day – like Moses Ibn Habib – and concluded that Hebrew had much more in common with Italian than it did with Latin or Greek. Hence, the Psalms could much better be understood if they were treated as syllabic rather than metric or quantitative verse. The Latinist-prelate Jacopo Sadoleto replaced the four-fold interpretation of the scholastics with the rhetorical interpretation sanctioned by Chrysostom and codified by Photius and Euthymius Zigabenus – Greeks, all of them, and therefore authoritative. A certain Massimo Teofilo wrote a Volgare commentary to accompany his 'New and Eternal Testament' of 1551. Antonio Brucioli prepared a new translation of the New (1530) and then the Old Testament (1532); and in the 1540s he supplemented his translations with a historical and philological exegesis of the entire Bible.[34]

The study of the Scriptures and the Fathers suggested a kind of religious piety very different from that which had been inherited from the high Middle Ages. The new 'form of the perfect Christian man' – to borrow the title of a treatise by Gregory of Nyssa – was based not on the memorization of precepts or the performance of certain acts, but upon the 'imitation' of those individual persons, ancient or modern, who had reached high levels of piety. It was guided not by disputes among specialists, but by friendly dialogues, or *sacre conversazioni*, among inquirers. And it assumed an underlying harmony between secular and religious learning in accordance with the prescriptions of the most 'humanist' of the Church Fathers, Basil. Indeed, it was Machiavelli's questioning of this assumption that elicited the first major attack upon him, the one expounded in a 'dialogue' of 1535 between the anti-Savonarolan Ambrogio Catarino Politi (1484–1553) and the Spanish convert to Italian humanism, Juan Ginés de Sepùlveda (1490–1573). The validity of the assumption was forthwith restored by another Italophile Spanish humanist, Jeronimo Orosio, who redefined the term 'glory' so fundamental to the Ciceronian – and the Machiavellian – ethical system in a manner that made possible the realization of just what Machiavelli had said was impossible: a durable and viable political society that was also thoroughly Christian.[35]

This new piety was as accessible to laymen as to monks, as one of Giustiniani's friends discovered when an intense spiritual experience in 1511 resulted in a religious vocation not for a hermitage, but for a diplomatic career:

Why should I not rest in peace, even in the midst of the world? . . . I can sleep and be awake here just as securely and peacefully as if I passed my whole life up there [at Camaldoli].[36]

It gave no advantage to one sex over the other. Vittoria Colonna was found to be an imitable model for whoever, male or female, understood that the Grace of God was manifested 'not by hushed voices, not by downcast eyes, but by a pure mind, generous charity toward the poor and a true conscience'. It did not even distinguish between celibates and those whose sexual liaisons were sanctioned by custom rather than by law – like Pietro Bembo's life-long mistress: 'Lieta ed a Dio cara tanto, tutta infiamata di superno zelo. . . .'[37]

This piety turned out to be very similar to the Patristic-New Testament piety being propagated north of the Alps and south of the Pyrenees by the prince of the Northern humanists, Erasmus of Rotterdam. For Pietro Aretino, Erasmus was 'an abundant river of intellect and [the source of] an immense sea of writing'. For Paolo Giovio, who consulted him on difficult passages in the Bible, he was the 'Olympic Jupiter of good letters and all fields of learning'. The piety of the Italian humanists was greatly enriched by Erasmus. His *Enchiridion of the Christian Soldier*, the most popular and easily intelligible expression of this piety, was translated into Italian with the full backing of the Bemban-Erasmians of Padua; and much of it was incorporated into the manuals of piety of the Augustinian Ambrogio Quistelli. His *Praise of Folly*, the biting satire upon the various current antitheses of Erasmian piety, was published in Venice in 1515, then in Florence in 1518. It provided a model for the several poems and discussions about 'madness' (*pazzia*) composed in the 1530s by Antonio Fregoso and Ortensio Lando, among others. The *Colloquia*, in which various aspects of the Erasmian ideal of the pious Christian were inserted into charming vocabulary-building exercises, were widely used as textbooks in the original Latin and read for their contents in Pietro Lauro's Italian translation of 1545.

So effective was this publishing campaign that it inspired personal imitations of the author even among members of those religious orders for which Erasmus had little sympathy – like the Benedictines. The New Testament translator Massimo Teofilo, the product of the Erasmian theological curriculum at the Badia Fiorentina and later abbot of the prestigious monastery at Subiaco, also translated the works of Chrysostom for the benefit of those who could read only the language 'known and common to all Italy'. And he was rewarded for a successful defence of his guide to the Italian New Testament by being appointed papal plenipotentiary at Parma.[38]

THE NEW ECCLESIASTICAL INSTITUTIONS

Different as they were in character and origins, all these various aspects of the religious revival managed to cohabit in an atmosphere of relative harmony, or at least of mutual toleration. They did so first of all because of frequent personal contacts among their chief representatives. Vittoria Colonna was one of the chief backers of the Capuchins, even though her life-style, that of a retired but affluent widow, was the exact opposite of theirs. The humanist prelate Marcello Cervini was the cardinal protector of the Servites and the Augustinians, even though he had very little in common with the vast majority of the members of either order. Harmony was maintained also by the desire of all of them to share with as many people as possible the particular spiritual insights that they had acquired – or been granted. The mystics' long path to 'the union of the soul with God' was reduced to an 'art' in accordance with what was now revealed as its usefulness 'not only for regulars, but for secular persons as well' – for example, in the tracts of the Franciscan Giovanni da Fano (d. 1539). Even the technical confessors' manual composed by Antonino of Florence in the mid-fifteenth century was now judged to be of value not only for moral theologians, but also for 'simple priests who know no grammar [i.e., Latin]' and for 'all other persons who wish to know how to live in a Christian manner'.[39]

Similarly, all the various groups – including even some members of those orders that were frequently accused of preferring the founders of the 'religions' they adhered to by their vows to the founder of the 'religion' to which they were committed by baptism – were basically Christocentric in piety. They looked to Christ as 'the supreme intermediary between the Creator and all creatures' and as 'the synthesis of all things', as the ex-Scotist Talmudic prophet and biblical scholar Francesco Zorzi da Venezia put it in his *De harmonia mundi* of 1525. And they looked to the saints no longer as superhuman wonder-workers, but as fully human, and therefore imitable, models of pious living.

More important still, the mystics, the prophets and the confraternity brothers were all as little concerned as were the humanists with institutions in general and with ecclesiastical institutions in particular – with the exception, of course, of the ones they happened to belong to. Their indifference was well motivated. The Church in the Renaissance bore very little resemblance to the autocratic monolith imagined by anti-conciliarist polemicists in the fifteenth century and put in legislative form by anti-liberal popes in the late nineteenth century. It consisted rather of a loose confederation of a vast number of separate organizations with vastly different structures, origins and activities, most of them wholly independent of all the others except for their common loyalty to, and legal dependency upon, the papacy. In this multifarious 'Church', the line between the 'regular' and the 'secular' clergy was at best blurred, since seculars often held abbeys without spiritual obligations (*in commendam*) and since regulars were often appointed to secular sees. So was the line between the secular clergy and the laity: the higher clergy were almost invariably recruited from the same noble and patrician families that dominated Italian politics; the lower clergy were usually as little instructed in the essentials of the faith as laymen of the lower social classes from which they came. The line between the sacred and profane was almost invisible, as Savonarola complained when he noticed how many of his listeners talked during his sermons. The cathedral of Florence was an appropriate place for 'divine worship', as Leon Battista Alberti had noted long before. It was also a convenient place for 'walking about . . . and talking about pleasant matters of learning and of the investigation of worthy and rare things'.[40]

As a consequence, most ecclesiastics above a certain rank sought to transform their ecclesiastical offices into permanent family possessions – just as the Este and the Gonzaga had done with the once elective *signorie* of Ferrara and Mantua. They did so through a legal device by which a title could be yielded or held in reserve for a cousin or a nephew. One politically weighty Florentine patrician inherited the distant diocese of Saluzzo from one brother and traded it back and forth thereafter for the nearer diocese of Borgo San Sepolcro – neither of which he ever saw – with another brother and a nephew, all the while enjoying the revenue of one monastery and several canonries without ever being a monk or a canon. Similarly, accession to ecclesiastical office did not normally require a change in life-style. The cardinal-archbishop of Ravenna continued to spend his time 'hunting warblers, . . . eating massive meals (*adipaliter*) twice a day, drinking Greek wine in a cup without water with ostentation and as though it were the cup of Christ (*retorice et sacramentaliter*) . . . [and tasting] plates prepared by a female, but not a virgin hand'; and all this seemed amusing, but certainly not scandalous, to the Como patrician Paolo Giovio, whose distant southern diocese served to maintain his own refined culinary tastes and his abundant library. Not even the rule of celibacy constituted a barrier, since the campaign of the Gregorian reformers of the eleventh century to impose it on all the Latin rite churches had long since spent its force. Most secular priests had concubines. Giovanni Della Casa, by then archbishop of Benevento, arranged for an 'amorazzo' within weeks of his arrival as papal nuncio in Venice – provoking no negative comment among his hosts other than one concerning the inappropriate social class of the object of his favours. Pope Paul III was often portrayed as an incarnation of Aristotle's principle of paternal affection: he was 'full of sweetness and tenderness because of the arrival of his *nepoti*', as Giovio noted in 1535, making use of the Italian word that included not only his nephews, but also the children of his son Pierluigi and his daughter Costanza.[41]

An ecclesiastical office was generally defined as a 'benefice', that is, as a means by which the holder would be assured of a fixed income, not as an obligation to provide services to others. A good bishop was one like Ennio Filonardi, whose income from the see of Veroli enabled him to serve Popes Leo and Clement as nuncio to the Swiss – and to transmit to Erasmus Pope Clement's thanks for the dedication of the *Paraphrases of the New Testament*. A good bishop was also one like Fabrizio Marliani, whose main service to the diocese of Piacenza he inherited from an uncle consisted in supervising the translation of a number of relics, doubling the income due him as bishop, and otherwise leaving the Piacentines alone. If one benefice was insufficient for the proper maintenance of a worthy diplomat or scholar, it was only right that he should hold several – five dioceses and as many monasteries and canonries in the case of Cardinal Antonio Maria Del Monte in the 1510s. Cardinal Ippolito I d'Este was made archbishop of Esztergom and primate of Hungary at the age of seven, thanks to the influence of his aunt, Queen Beatrice. He was subsequently made bishop of Ferrara, of Modena and of Narbonne and archbishop of Capua and of Milan – all for the purpose of permitting him to carry out his principal obligation: to represent the interests of the king of France in Rome. Since benefices did not come vacant in any rational geographical order, Cardinal Innocenzo Cybo had to accept the archbishopric of Messina, even though it was so far from the seat of his family at Massa Carrara and from the centre of his political intrigues in Florence that he could not possibly have gone there. At the same time, his uncle Giuliano was the bishop of Agrigento. Pompeo Colonna, Toledo's predecessor as viceroy of Naples, was the archbishop of Monreale. And in the entire kingdom of Sicily there were never more then two or three sees whose bishops had ever even visited them.[42]

Administered in this manner and for these ends, the Church was often the object of considerable criticism. Giovanni Pico's nephew Giovan Francesco (1470–1533) complained bitterly that

among many of the leading men of our religion, . . . there is either no worship of God or, indeed, very little, no concern or disposition for living well, no shame, no modesty; justice has degenerated either into hatred or gratification; piety has been distorted into superstition and openly held blameworthy in all classes of men.[43]

Prophets regularly referred to the Roman court as the Whore of Babylon, destined to be overthrown by a new Cyrus. And many popes acknowledged the justice of these criticisms by refurbishing from time to time some version of the reform decrees announced by Pius II in the mid-fifteenth century.

Criticisms of this sort were invariably directed at churchmen, not at 'the Church as a divine institution'. They were often accompanied by equally violent, and equally vague, denunciations of all classes of the laity. And they never presented any other solution for the defects they lamented than the warning that God would or the admonition that the pope should do something about them. Still, there were good reasons for not changing anything at all, or at least for limiting change to merely the correction of obvious abuses. Most bishops may indeed have been non-residents. But many of them made sure that they were represented in their dioceses by vicars 'of learning and well-tried good sense', like those who actually governed the church of Pavia for a hundred years after 1453.[44] Vicars had one notable advantage over bishops: they were more willing to collaborate with the local secular governments in what was, after all, a joint responsibility. Distant bishops often had the advantage of being in a better position to obtain favours and jobs from the upper levels of both secular and ecclesiastical governments.

The office of vicar thus emerged as a professional category all its own, with standards of administrative, political and legal competence well beyond the range of most bishops – certainly beyond that of the last of the non-resident bishops of Pavia, Ippolito de' Rossi, whose chief qualification, according to Varchi, Bembo and Della Casa, was his ability to write Petrarchan sonnets and Livian history. The vicarage was a geographically mobile office, much like that of the notary-chancellors of the fourteenth- and fifteenth-century communes. But mobility stopped when the more successful professional vicars were rewarded with, and permitted to settle down in, a diocese of their own – the diocese of Padua in the case of the most famous of them, Niccolò Ormaneto (c. 1515–1577), formerly vicar of Verona, Milan and Rome.

Moreover, the system of recruitment by inheritance, by the purchase of a venal office or by raccomandazioni (the subject of much of the surviving correspondence of the age) managed to produce a number of office holders – in the Church as in the state – whose moral, intellectual and technical qualifications were consonant with the highest standards. Gaetano da Thiene, who was to become one of the most prominent religious leaders of the third decade of the century, first rose to prominence by purchasing a series of offices in Rome – and by using those offices to obtain a series of benefices for his well-born relatives in Vicenza. Gaetano's future colleague was Gian Pietro Carafa, later Pope Paul IV, whom Paolo Giustiniani judged in 1523 to be 'a man of letters of great modesty and sanctity of life', capable of 'reciting entire pages of Cicero and Virgil', of speaking Greek 'as if he had been born in the middle of Greece' and of 'knowing all the Sacred Scriptures by heart'. Gian Pietro had been launched into the Church through the influence of his uncle, Cardinal Oliviero Carafa, the 'most holy and learned' but still non-resident archbishop of Naples. He also inherited his first diocese from another uncle at the ripe age of twenty-nine. Luigi Lippomano (1500–1559) was one of Paul III's most able diplomats and one of the most conscientious sponsors of able vicars in the succession of dioceses that his busy schedule seldom permitted him to visit. Luigi was the illegitimate son of a Venetian nobleman who received his first episcopal appointment as coadjutor with right of succession to one of his many well-placed legitimate cousins, the bishop of Bergamo. The brothers Tommaso (1481–1564) and Lorenzo (1502–1554) Campeggi first brought their legal skills to the service of the papacy in exchange for their family's loyalty to the new papal regime in Bologna. The bundle of benefices they subsequently accumulated made it possible for them to undertake an unending series of arduous diplomatic missions on either side of the Alps. And the dedication with which both of them served the institution of which they were originally merely beneficiaries lessened much of the force of the criticisms they levelled against it in such tracts as Lorenzo's *De depravato statu ecclesiae*.[45]

The Renaissance Church had still other admirable qualities. Its prelates were expected to be 'lovable, handsome, jovial and pleasing to all', like Cardinal Girolamo Capodiferro, and 'learned and pleasant beyond belief, of good speech and gracious aspect and well experienced in the courts of great lords', like Galeazzo Florimonte, bishop of Aquino, from whose nickname Della Casa borrowed the title of his *Galateo*. If possible, they should also be 'very learned in the Greek and Latin languages and well versed in rhetoric, dialectic and mathematics', like Giampietro Grassi, whose skill as a tutor in mathematics and as a commentator on Aristotle earned him the diocese of Viterbo. Monks in the Renaissance Church were expected to be 'good spirited and literate persons' governed civilly by 'a gentle prior', such as the one Cardinal Giovanni Guidiccioni so admired at Ravenna in 1540. So successful was the Church in attracting persons of these qualities that at one moment it appeared to be capable of generating its own *papa angelico* all by itself, without the disagreeable holocaust predicted by the prophets. So at least thought the historian Paolo Giovio, when the most likely candidate to succeed the aged Paul III seemed to be Gasparo Contarini, a man 'so excellent in virtue, letters and goodness, and – better yet – *quasi vergine*'.[46]

Furthermore, the benefice system provided an indispensable cultural, if perhaps not spiritual, service in the form of what later would be called 'fellowships' for worthy men of letters – like one of Bembo's protégés for whom two cardinals were asked to assure 'the leisure for study' in return for 'the praise and good will of men of letters'. It enabled the Genoese patrician Stefano Sauli to study at Padua and to support a whole court of learned and pious men of letters in Rome. It guaranteed the Calabrian jurist, later cardinal (1539), Pietro Paolo Parisio the independence he needed – with a canonry at Cosenza – to escape the domination of the orthodox Bartolists in the law faculties of Rome and Padua and to modify his interpretation of canon law in the direction recommended by the proponents of humanist jurisprudence. Likewise, the 'personal recommendation' system permitted and made possible exceptions from the letter of the law for human and humane considerations – such as the leave of absence requested by Bembo for a Franciscan friend with urgent family problems. It allowed princes to provide for younger brothers and civil servants without paying them, prelates to get good jobs for lay relatives, monks to pray free of administrative chores, and painters and poets to paint and write as – although not what – they pleased and still be suitably paid for it. 'Illiteracy and immorality' at the lower levels and 'shamelessness at the higher levels' might shock modern heirs of those who broke with the Renaissance Church four centuries ago. But at least some recent historians have come to agree with the contemporary Italian critics of that church in noting that 'the Curia was less exclusively wrapped up in purely secular concerns . . . and much more serious in maintaining high standards' than has usually been admitted. They have discovered 'a world full of problems and contradictions, . . . but also one characterized by a receptivity to innovation and a sincere desire for renewal – in short, a world made of shadows but also of light'.[47]

Still, the greatest merit of the Renaissance Church was one that followed from its pluralistic constitution: its willingness to give legal approval to almost any initiative on the part of its members that did not threaten the tacit principle of mutual toleration. Typical was the permission given to one group by Pope Clement in 1533:

to live together in common in the same place that you may choose, to adopt all those statutes and rules that may be favourable to your well-being and the development of your principles, provided only that they be reasonable and not contrary to the sacred canons, and to change, annul or renew them freely . . . as it may seem proper to you according to the conditions of the times.[48]

Instead of complaining about the inadequacies of established Church institutions, the protagonists of the religious revival set out to create new institutions of their own. Being bereft of a theoretical framework concerning the nature of institutions, and being the victims of the ecclesiological chaos left over from the conciliar controversy of the preceding two centuries, they were forced to resort to the same method used by the state-builders after 1530: experimentation.

One solution was the one suggested by the Socratic relationship between a master and his disciples recently made flesh in the Platonic Academy of Marsilio Ficino. Such a solution was adopted by a group of graduates of the University of Paris who, having rid their minds of impediments to their divine calling under his direction, followed their master, the Basque mystic Ignatius of Loyola, to Venice. While waiting to see if they would be called to the Holy Land, they settled down to work in the local hospitals, where their faith was put to the test:

[a leper] called one of the fathers and asked him to scratch his back. The father diligently performed this service. While doing so, he was suddenly struck with horror and nausea. But since he wanted to master himself and suppress his rebellious spirit, . . . he put into his mouth a finger covered with pus and sucked it.[49]

The same solution was adopted by the pan-Italian disciples of the Spanish spiritual writer Juan de Valdés, the brother of the Imperial secretary Alfonso, who had followed Charles v to Bologna in 1530 and who then, rather than letting himself be caught up in the controversy provoked in his homeland by his *Dialogo de doctrina cristiana* of 1529, settled down for the last six years of his life in the free atmosphere of Pedro de Toledo's Naples. The disciples met informally – bringing along whichever distinguished friends from out of town happened to be passing through – either in Valdés' villa near Posillipo or in the apartment of his most distinguished disciple, the beautiful Giulia Gonzaga, at the convent of S. Francesco delle Monache.[50]

Another solution suggested by humanist institutional experiments – like the Orti Oricellari in Florence – was the one that ended up in the foundation of the academies: informal meetings among friends for the discussion of topics of common interest. Such was the group that gathered in the house of the Dominican patrician – and historian of his city and of his order – Achille Bocchi in Bologna in the 1520s. Such also was the group that met in the chambers of the Dominican theologian Ambrogio Catarino Politi – with Michelangelo as a frequent participant – at S. Silvestro al Quirinale in Rome in the 1540s. Such was the much more famous group – one that attracted many of the most learned and most pious persons of all Italy – that gathered at Viterbo during the residence there of Vittoria Colonna and the governorship of the English Cardinal Reginald Pole. Such also was the equally famous group modelled on the conversations recorded by Aulus Gellius in antiquity that met in the Noctae Vaticanae under the sponsorship of the adolescent archbishop of Milan, Carlo Borromeo (1538–1584), during the pontificate of his uncle, Pius IV.[51]

But neither of these solutions was capable of endowing the pursuit of common goals with the essential ingredient of longevity – as was demonstrated by the rapid dispersal of all these groups as soon as their leading members went away. That ingredient was furnished by combining *sacre conversazioni* with confraternities – and by thus creating a completely new kind of ecclesiastical institution. These institutions came to be called 'congregations of priests', and they soon assumed a role in the Tridentine Reform analogous to the one taken by the Cluniac Benedictines and the mendicant orders during previous ages of Church reform.

Typical of these congregations of priests was the Roman Oratorio. Its guiding spirit was the Florentine Filippo Neri (1515–1595), who had been brought up in the shadow of Savonarola – and of Tre- and Quattrocento Florentine literature – at San Marco and who, between one or another of the violent ecstasies that doubled the size of his heart by the time of his death, acquired the titles of both the 'Harlequin' and the 'Socrates' of Rome.[52] Although he had assisted in the founding of the Confraternity of the Trinità dei Pellegrini, Filippo himself was incapable of organizing, or being organized by, anyone. It finally took the intervention of his fellow boarder at the confraternity's church of S. Girolamo della Carità, Persiano Rosa, to get him to agree to provide some sort of structured service for the crowds that followed him around on his hiking tours to the ancient cemeteries and basilicas and that filled his chambers for the discussion and *laude*-singing sessions he directed. But even after its official recognition in 1574, the associates of what was at first called – in deference to the nationality of many of the members – the Congregazione di S. Giovanni dei Fiorentini were free to carry on whatever activities they judged consonant with their individual vocations. They thus left Filippo alone to follow his vocation and to transform the rather embryonic rite prescribed for the sacrament of Confession by the Fourth Lateran Council (1215) into an instrument of spiritual direction – one that involved an ever closer relationship between a director and a penitent and that came to constitute one of the most important liturgical innovations of the Tridentine Church.

That the Oratorio typified the new congregations was, according to the testimony of their founders, purely fortuitous. Their constitutions, they insisted, were derived not from a critical examination of the experience of other institutions, but from divine revelation. As Gerónimo Nadal (1507–1580) put it some years later,

Question: What was the origin of these religious organizations or states of perfection?
Answer: The doctrine and counsel and inspiration of God.
Question: Is the Society [i.e., of Jesus] such a religious organization or state of perfection?
Answer: Yes; for Father Ignatius [of Loyola] was inspired to erect this congregation in this manner, and everything has been approved by the Church.[53]

Ignatius certainly had plenty of opportunity to receive divine inspiration regarding such matters, for he suffered ecstasies as intense as those of Filippo – even though the outward manifestation of his ecstasies was tears, not fever.

Fortunately, inspiration was generally seconded by utility. It was as essential for Ignatius' comrades to prevent the dispersal of their activities as they spread all over Italy – and then over much of the world – as it was for Filippo's comrades to avoid bumping into each other in Rome. So dispersed from the very start were the Jesuits that Pope Paul had to make an exception to the usual rule for full attendance of all the constituent members at an initial 'General Congregation', or constitutional convention.

Thus the actual form of organization varied considerably from one congregation to another. The Chierici Regolari ('Regular Clerks') di S. Paolo, later called the Barnabites, began as a *conventus piorum hominum* who frequented the tirades of the patrician physician Anton Maria Zaccaria at S. Vitale in Cremona against 'the pestiferous . . . enemy of Christ, Our Lady of Lukewarmness'. Its first main activity consisted in giving counsel to married men – in order that they 'approach with trepidation a sacrament as great as matrimony and not get lost in it, as do the ignorant (*vulgari*)'. The Barnabites then joined with the followers of Jacopo Antonio Morigia (1525–1604) in the Oratorio della Divina Sapienza ('Divine Wisdom') of Milan in propagating all over Italy the devotion of the forty-eight hours, which had been invented in Milan in the late 1520s as a way of persuading God to put an end to the wars in Lombardy. And together they soon spawned a female branch among the disciples of the pious countess Lodovica Torelli, the Angeliche di S. Paolo – lay sisters who, like the Oblate at Tor' di Specchi in Rome and wholly unlike the traditional cloistered nuns, were free during the day to engage in whatever charitable activities were dictated by their consciences.[54]

The Theatines, on the other hand, originated among the refugees from the Roman Oratorio del Divino Amore who settled in Venice after the Sack – particularly those like Gaetano da Thiene and Gian Pietro Carafa, who took as their special mission the perfecting not of others but of themselves. The Somaschi originated among the followers of the Venetian patrician Girolamo Emiliani; and they divided their time between the spiritual exercises in their common house and the care of orphans. The Consorzio Mariano grew out of a fifteenth-century confraternity in Lombardy; when its members agreed to seek holy orders, they reorganized in 1589 as the Scuola del SS. Sacramento e dei Dodici Apostoli ('of the Twelve Apostles'), with the members ordinarily resident in their respective parishes and obliged to come together only for periodic communal spiritual exercises.

All the congregations resembled one another in their conscious departure from all previously established forms of religious life – the chanting of daily monastic hours, a uniform 'colour of dress or special habit' (as the Theatine rule put it) and the observance under vows of feasts and fasts other than those prescribed by the Church for all Catholic Christians.[55] They resembled one another in the absence of specifically stated aims in their constitutions and hence in their availability for any task that might suddenly be presented to them – like staffing a school for prospective members in Messina and then for candidates for the priesthood in Rome, as in the case of the Jesuits; like promoting historical research and new forms of church music, as in the case of the Roman Oratorians; and like teaching children how to read, as in the case of the Barnabites. Above all, they resembled one another in replacing the monk and the friar of the Middle Ages with the secular priest as a model of morality and piety for the guidance and inspiration of others.

The congregations thus provided the Church with a large pool of highly motivated and – thanks to the humanist education required of or imposed upon all their recruits – highly trained and very flexible labour just at a time that was to prove one of the most critical in its long history.

The other important institutional innovation of the religious revival was the diocese – the diocese, that is, conceived of no longer as an administrative subdivision of the universal Church or as a subdivision of a territorial state for the administration of its ecclesiastical offices, but rather as an instrument for the sanctification of all its members. To be sure, this new institution had some precedent in practice, at least in those territorial states where episcopal sees were taken over by the patriciate of the dominant city. Since their cousins and brothers had to reside in the subject cities to which they had been assigned as governors, some bishops found it appropriate to do so too – Matteo Bosso in Verona, Bartolomeo Visconti in Novara and, the most famous of them all, Pietro Barozzi in Padua. As long as they were residing, it occurred to them to check the prescriptions of canon law regarding their duties and privileges; and they accordingly established what came to rank among the most notable institutions of Tridentine churches: visitations and synods.

Such isolated experiments were invariably limited in scope by the legal exemption from episcopal control of most local ecclesiastical institutions – exemptions inherited from the battle of the regulars against the seculars during the Gregorian reform and from the centralization policies of the Avignon papacy. What finally furnished the experiments with a theoretical rationale sufficient to permit their adoption by other bishops was the philologists' reconstruction of the diocese as it had existed in antiquity. Chrysostom, Ambrose and Augustine, the text-editors revealed, had resided in their sees, and they had been distinguished as models of high moral life, as celebrants of common liturgies and as preachers capable of bringing to the service of the faith all the eloquence of Cicero and Demosthenes. They had seen to it that the secular priests committed to their charge were 'men graced by good morals and outstanding for learning', and they made sure that their regulars stayed inside their monasteries pursuing their own very special vocation. Therefore, concluded Gasparo Contarini in his *De officio episcopi* of 1516, let modern bishops do likewise.[56]

That two of the most prominent bishops of the age actually chose, and were also able, to do so was the result of chance: the Sack of Rome, which forced them to move, for want of a more appropriate seat, to their dioceses. For Jacopo Sadoleto, life in tiny Carpentras in the papal enclave of Avignon was a bit like a scene out of Sannazaro's *Arcadia* or a re-creation of Pliny's villa at Como. He welcomed it as a chance to read and write free of the distractions of Clementine Rome and as an opportunity to further the career of an ambitious cousin. But he too knew that ancient bishops had been much more than retired curial officials: the portrait of an ideal pastor he drew in his commentary on Psalm 93 was very close to Contarini's. As long as he was in Carpentras, he decided to make sure that the regular clergy lived according to their original rule, that papal temporal officials did not intrude upon the liberties of his flock and that exceptions to his episcopal authority were withdrawn.[57]

To Gian Matteo Giberti (1495–1543), on the other hand, life in Verona was a challenge. Armed with the considerable independent income he enjoyed from the large collection of benefices that he had no intention of relinquishing, and fortified with the special powers of an apostolic delegate and with the benevolence of the Venetian Senate, Giberti set forth to remake the Church of Verona according to the model of the ancient Church of Milan or of Constantinople. He brought a printer from Venice in order to illuminate his dependents with the same works of Basil, Chrysostom and John Damescene that had inspired him. He turned the episcopal household into a religious version of Castiglione's Court of Urbino, with lecture and discussion sessions conducted by some of the best humanist writers in Italy. As his disciple and successor Luigi Lippomano put it in his instructions to his own subordinates:

We wish to dine only in that place [the episcopal residence] and have with us only about twenty persons [*bocche*] and thirteen horses. Make sure to have a modest supply [of victuals] and not send outside for wines and other delicate and exquisite foods; but provide only things available in the locality, never exceeding two dishes [per meal].[58]

Giberti admonished parish priests in periodic assemblies to live up to the models described in such guidebooks as those written by his fellow bishop, Filippo Sauli. He commissioned his homiletics expert, Tullio Crispoldi (1510–1573), to demonstrate the effectiveness of sermons drawn not from theological abstractions but from the Scriptures. And he personally saw to the execution of his recommendations by visiting the many institutions that he managed to bring under episcopal control.[59]

The efforts of these pastoral bishops were frequently thwarted by internal opposition. The cathedral canons of Verona denounced Giberti to the Senate as a tyrant. The inmates of fashionable convents complained to their fathers on the city council. At one point, the priests of the city organized a 'strike' and barred him from the cathedral. Meanwhile, the frequent calls to Rome forced him to violate his own principle of residency and sharply reduce his expectations. Still, enough was accomplished to raise the Church of Verona to a rank similar to that celebrated in the literary and artistic masterpieces of the High Renaissance. It was acclaimed – in a series of panegyrics – as visible proof that what had been done in antiquity could also be done in modern times.

Such acclamations caused some serious crises of conscience, particularly among those prelates who had never questioned the thesis of the Lombard humanist Bartolomeo Platina (1421–1481) in his quasi-official history of the papacy: that the Church of Pius II (1458–1464), having reached the apex of its glory, was destined to last forever. 'What will you do with those of your benefices that include pastoral responsibilities?' asked one of them:

You can't turn them over to a vicar without legitimate cause, which you don't have. Treating them like a pension would be simony. . . . What then to do? You'll find some respectable poor priest in town and give it to him without further ado. 'And how will I manage without the income?' You'll do what many respectable persons do who are content with what God gives them, much or little. That's what St Paul advises: 'having food and raiment [1. Tim. 6:8]'.[60]

But many of them took the advice and made a serious attempt to follow the example of the 'Monsignor di Verona'. Cosimo Gheri did so with such enthusiasm at Fano – of which, in good Renaissance fashion, he had been made bishop-elect while still in his teens – that he died before he had had a chance even to receive holy orders. Braccio Martelli did so in Lecce, where Pope Julius III transferred him after he had quarrelled with his nephew. Seripando – when he was not occupied with the Augustinians – did so in Salerno. Giulio Pavesi did so in Sorrento – even though, as a Dominican, it may not have been easy so openly to promote the cause of seculars.[61]

In these instances the diocese ceased to be a benefice and became instead a *corpus fidelium*. As such it held promise of doing for all Christians, lay as well as ecclesiastic, what the reformed orders, the confraternities and the congregations were doing for their own select members.

ORTHODOXY AND HETERODOXY

Just as they were insouciant toward the traditional institutional aspects of religious life, so too the protagonists of the religious revival viewed with relative indifference the theoretical foundation of those institutions: theology.

Theology had never enjoyed a prestige in Italy comparable to that accorded it in the major universities of Northern Europe. Its reputation declined still further as the issues that until recently had provided it with some degree of relevance, like the Hussite Revolt and conciliarism, were contained, resolved or forgotten. Not until 1470 did the Venetian Senate at last consent to pay even nominal salaries to theology professors at Padua, in part because they taught almost no one but members of their own religious orders. Only 10 out of 72 students at the Studio Fiorentino, and only 12 out of 371 at Pisa, were enrolled in theology classes between 1505 and 1528. Deans were elected chiefly for the purpose of having an excuse for dinner parties. Statutes were revised – at least in the case of Florence in 1566 – chiefly for the purpose of keeping the faculties 'completely free and in no way dependent upon the archbishop'. Only at the Roman Sapienza was any effort made to introduce a programme compatible with the methods sanctioned by the humanists:

There are five [teachers] in the morning and afternoon who read the Gospels and the epistles of Paul, . . . and [the lectures] are based no longer on Scotus and St Thomas, but only on the true sense of the Gospel.[62]

Similarly, most preachers tried to avoid theological issues altogether. Those few who did not invariably embroiled themselves in 'turgid scholastic disquisitions' barely enlivened by 'questionable pulpit theatricality'[63] – to the annoyance of Bembo, for one, who scrupulously avoided them:

What should I do? What else does one hear there but contests between the Subtle Doctor and the Angelic Doctor that are resolved by bringing in Aristotle as the judge?[64]

They were generally left to talk about subjects far removed from current religious concerns, like 'the debates of the grey and black friars about the [Immaculate] Conception' ridiculed by Vasari and those portrayed by Raphael, without much sympathy, on the walls of the Vatican. Theology, concluded one pious humanist, was merely a tool by which 'an evil band . . . seduces simple minds and stirs up noise and heresies'. Since it was invariably expressed in a manner wholly 'out of consonance with the [rules of] the Tuscan language', advised another, it was best left to 'the schools of the friars'.[65]

Yet what might seem to have been a rejection of theology altogether actually amounted to the promotion of a very different kind of theology. The old theology was by no means dead. Indeed, it was actively promoted by one of the most prominent of the humanists, Prince Alberto Pio of Carpi (1475–1531). Tacitly accepting Pomponazzi's radical division of faith from reason, Alberto Pio held the final authority in all theological questions to be none other than the Franciscans' own John Duns Scotus, the Pomponazzi of the early fourteenth century and the nemesis of all the humanists since Petrarch. He sponsored the printing of numerous commentaries on Scotus' *Opus Parisiense* under the direction of an Observant Franciscan he had borrowed from the nearby university at Padua. And he violently denounced all those, like Erasmus, who pretended to bridge the gulf he strove to maintain between theology and humanism.[66]

But most of Alberto Pio's fellow humanists preferred to refer theological questions to the same sources to which they turned for inspiration in achieving a higher degree of religious piety: the Bible, the works of the Fathers and their own individual and collective religious experiences. Such a method in theology was far more consonant with Machiavelli's search for political laws in his 'long experience with modern affairs and continuous reading about ancient affairs'. It opened much greater possibilities for coordinating a commitment as a Christian with commitments as an artist, a statesman or a man of letters. By constantly refreshing the memory of 'those blessed fathers who first taught them', it held forth much greater promise for finally turning the dens of smelly adulterers denounced by the novelist Girolamo Parabosco into the 'enclosures of holy people'.[67]

Unfortunately, the Fathers did not always agree with each other, as Peter Abelard had discovered long before and as Paolo Cortesi (1465–1510) might have noticed had he bothered to compare closely the passages he reproduced in his Ciceronian Latin substitute for Peter Lombard's textbook in 1513.[68] Moreover, even the literal meaning of the Bible was often obscure, as Augustine had noted even earlier and as the team of Hellenists under the direction of Gian Francesco Virginio of Brescia discovered when they were forced to introduce 'interpretations in accordance with what they could agree upon among themselves' as they translated 'word for word' (*de verbo ad verbum*). Did Giorgio Siculo's (d. 1550) downgrading of external acts and his refusal of a theology presented *in abstracto et metaphysice* really encourage the faithful 'to think about divine things in a sincere and Catholic manner', as the humanists in Bocchi's circle at Bologna supposed? Or was it heretical, as a Neapolitan Franciscan announced from the pulpit in 1540? Was the Dominican Battista da Crema (d. 1534) right in supposing that 'every devout person can easily ascend to the fullness of perfection' and place his own 'free will' into a state of 'admirable union . . . with the will of God'? Or was he guilty of Pelagianism, as he seemed to admit when elsewhere he held that 'all our justice and good works are soiled and abominable like a menstrual cloth'?[69]

Similarly, was Valdés overly optimistic in his 'firm conviction . . . that divine power would certainly [effect] the regeneration and renewal of

mankind'? Was a suffragan bishop of Mantua or an Augustinian of Padua
right in their logomachy over the orthodoxy of Erasmus' *Enchiridion*? Was
Contarini too pessimistic when he accorded the principal role in justification
to faith rather than to works? Was his companion Sadoleto disrespectful of
divine omnipotence when he defended the ability of the yet unjustified man
to do good works? Was talk about an 'angelic pope' and a miraculous
'reformation of the Church . . . to be considered very suspect' at a time when
a man-made reformation seemed to be well under way, as the Jesuit Jacob
Laínez (1512–1565) supposed? Were the anti-Savonarolan Theatines being
unreasonable in their 'obsession with the primacy of the papacy', and were
the Savonarolans being illogical when they then joined the Theatines in
attacking Cardinals Pole and Morone?[70]

Equally puzzling were questions that regarded the consequences of theological statements in the realm of practical morality. Was the *vita contemplativa* really preferable to the *vita activa*, as Pole thought after failing to
persuade some of his colleagues of the virtues of his own theological formulas?
Was a pious man obliged to promote the spiritual and material welfare of
all his fellow Christians by actively joining in a campaign to reform the
Church as a whole? Or should he rather 'seek the salvation of his own soul
and nothing else', as the hermits insisted? Even more puzzling were questions
that regarded the delicate and ill-defined borderline between the religious and
non-religious areas of humanist endeavour. Was it theologically sound to
proclaim with Jacopo Bonfadio that 'to whoever gives aid to the fatherland
is assigned a place in heaven'? Did Michelangelo's *Last Judgement* constitute
not just an aesthetic triumph, as Vasari thought, not just a violation of
decorum, as Aretino thought, but also a 'theological revolution', one capable
of provoking the ire of subsequent Counter-Reformation apologists?[71]

Attempts to answer these questions occasionally led to harsh confrontations
even among those who recognized each other as collaborators. The head of
the Theatines objected to the Jesuits' practice of assigning to penitents a
permanent spiritual director. That, he said, was a form of 'tyranny' quite out
of keeping with ecclesiastical traditions. The head of the Jesuits denounced
the Theatines for tempting God by charging him with the entire responsibility for their financial support; and 'all the bones of his body shook' when
their head was elevated to the papacy. The Jesuits and the Theatines were
both accused of being purveyors of 'hidden poison' by a certain Giovanni da
Torano in 1547; they were equally 'contaminated', he asserted, 'by many blots
of heresy'.[72]

No clear answers to these questions could be found in the works of
Ambrose, Augustine, Anselm or Bernard. At least, that was the conclusion
drawn by the diocesan preacher of Verona, Tullio Crispoldi, when he searched
through them for arguments against those who, in order 'not to do anything
and to give themselves completely over to pleasure', asserted 'that to be saved
it is enough to have faith'. Neither could definitive answers be found in the
many scholastic texts that Cardinal Marcello Cervini added to his complete
collection of Greek and Latin Fathers. Recent attempts to bring together

under the title 'Evangelism' all the various answers that were suggested at the time have merely given a name to what was in fact 'a cultural and religious movement with no institutional forms, no orthodoxy and no unified doctrinal *corpus*'; and recent attempts to explain the obvious diversity among the so-called 'Evangelicals' have been forced to trace a fatal 'crisis' back to the very origins of the supposed 'movement'.[73] One of the best informed of recent historians of the religious revival has thus concluded that it produced not doctrine at all, but rather 'doctrinal *Unklarheit*' ('non-clarity'), and that its chief theological manifestation consisted not in any specific theological position, but in 'a laborious inquiry into doctrine, the elaboration and combination of [many different] themes and positions'.[74]

Still, an atmosphere of inquiry rather than of formulation, of debate rather than of consensus, was fraught with peril. The reading of the Fathers without a rigorous philological preparation could easily end up in theological premises that were increasingly difficult to resolve in terms acceptable to the majority of the protagonists of the revival. So could a purely empirical approach to theology, one based solely on the spiritual experience of a select number of persons in the sixteenth century without a knowledge of the similar experiences of other Christians during the fifteen previous centuries. If 'inquiry' and 'debate' were conducted not only by an educated elite but also by the other social groups which the popularization campaigns of the academies were incorporating into the domain of humanist culture – if 'everyone in the shops, houses and streetcorners' of Modena took it upon himself to talk continuously 'about Faith, Free Will, Purgatory, the Eucharist and Predestination', who would ever be able to figure out who was right? Who would be able to persuade the nuns of Reggio that God was not about to be incarnate in the body of a certain Basilio Albrisio? Who would be able to stop the Augustinian Ambrogio Cavalli from shocking the Cypriots with denunciations of Mariolatry, fasting, Confession and the Mass? Who could tell the translator of Thucydides, Francesco di Soldo Strozzi, that his condemnation of the abuses of the papacy was bordering upon a condemnation of the papacy itself? Not even the papal legate in Venice, who put the supposedly miracle-working body of one of them 'below the ground, where the other friars are', could prevent certain unlettered Capuchins from 'leading the people into superstition'. No one could say definitively that a certain fra Pagliarini was wrong when he declared at Palermo that 'the Mass ought not to be said' and that 'the Host does not contain the Body of our Saviour' or that a certain Massimo Massimi was incorrect when he announced at Venice that salvation could be gained merely by reading the Scriptures.[75]

Such statements might have been consigned to the hazy realm of *adiaphora* ('indifferent matters'), or left to wither in the limbo of lunatic fringes, had it not been for the gradual, then more rapid, spread in Italy of theological doctrines that had already provoked an open break with the Church of Rome beyond the Alps. When the more portentous of these doctrines were first announced – in the disputations of 1518–19 and then in Martin Luther's three great theological pamphlets of 1520 – most Italians had paid very little attention to them. The Venetian ambassadors in Germany wrote them off as merely a front for covetous princes anxious to lay hands on ecclesiastical properties. The Italian Franciscans ascribed them to 'the instigation of the Devil' and proposed to get rid of them by adding a few more prayers in honour of the Virgin to their daily hours. The Dominican Tommaso Radini Tedeschi (1488–1527) was offended by Luther's ignorance of his numerological–astrological explanation of the crucial role of St Dominic in the process of salvation; he therefore surmised that Luther's chief theological advisor, Philip Melanchthon, could be reconverted merely by sprinkling a few quotations from ancient and humanist authors on top of the ones he had already collected from Thomas Aquinas. Pietro Aretino was less optimistic, but he was just as unenthusiastic. Luther, he said, was merely a pedant, indeed, a *pedantissimo*, one who was trying to 'cover up his dishonest vices with the venerable name of learning'.

Pope Leo's view of the matter was not much different. He regarded the whole issue Luther had brought up as little more than a replay of the monks' quarrels about the Immaculate Conception. He therefore turned it over to the only one of his assistants who might have found it interesting, his incorrigibly scholastic and eminently verbose master of the sacred palace, Silvestro Mazzolini (1456–1527), called Prierias after the name of his birthplace in Piedmont. Once Prierias had buried the issue under several pounds of heady syllogisms, the pope turned over to God (in the Bull *Exsurge Domine*) the task of throwing them at Luther (who promptly burned the bull in public); and he turned over to other friars the task of digging out of 'Peter's breast even such questionable practices as selling indulgences'. *Roma locuta, causa finita*: 'Rome has spoken, and that's the end of it'.[76]

The spread in Italy of Lutheran and other doctrines of non-Italian origin encountered several formidable obstacles. Most Italians still accepted Pope Pius II's negative, if fairly well-informed, view of the German character. Almost none of them could speak any of the current varieties of the German language – not even such official emissaries to Germany as Tommaso de Vio (1469–1534), called Cajetan, who mistakenly thought that Luther's main doctrinal concern was to knock down his own favourite formulation of the doctrine of papal supremacy, and not even Pope Clement's representative at the Imperial diet, Lorenzo Campeggi, who thought that Luther could best be combated by convoking diocesan synods all over Germany.[77]

Moreover, almost all the humanists sympathized with the initial response of the learned translator of pagan and Christian classics, Raffaele Maffei Volterrano. They too feared that Luther's exaltation of the Scriptures at the expense of the Fathers would force his adherents to throw away the entire cultural heritage of pagan as well as Christian antiquity.[78] Similarly, Luther's exaltation of faith at the expense of hope ran counter to the unanimous experience of the mystics: that a deepened faith was the product of, not just the cause of, love and desire. His demotion of charity to the position of a consequence, rather than a constituent element, of the process of making sinners just ('justified') before God amounted to a condemnation of all the charitable institutions that they had created largely for the purpose of promoting their own justification. His condemnation not just of the sale of indulgences but also of indulgences themselves would wipe out their chief source of financial support.

Above all, Luther's denial of the role of the Church – or any church – in transmitting divine grace went far beyond the old Italian custom of associating current Church representatives with one or another of the several horrible animals mentioned in the Bible. It threatened to replace one Church with many: as one Isidoro Chiari noted, 'The Lutherans have already given rise to Pneumatics, Anabaptists, Sacramentarians, Iconomastics; and still others will soon follow'. Worse yet, it loosened the tie that still bound even the most critical Italians to the Church of their fathers and of the Fathers – the kind of untheological affection reflected in Galeazzo Florimonte's 'Credo' of 1543:

Here is one great boulder for those beasts of Lutherans to fall over: '[I believe] in one holy and apostolic Church'. And when they ask, 'What is this Catholic Church?' I'll put out another one: 'The Church of my father, my mother and him who answered for me at my baptism'.[79]

The prevailing atmosphere of theological confusion made it impossible to immunize Italy entirely from the theological controversies that were raging in the rest of Europe. Refugees from the abortive Tyrolean revolution of 1525 used the leisure provided them by subsidies from the Venetian government to inform some of their hosts' humbler subjects of their own special brand of Moravian Anabaptism: that political action is immoral, that the sacraments are worthless, that 'there is no Trinity but [only] a single God who dwelt in Christ'. These doctrines were soon supplemented by others brought back to Venetian territory by such temporary emigrants as the ex-Benedictine Francesco Negri, who had followed Zwingli to Marburg in 1530, and by such illegal immigrants as a group of German and Slavic prisoners who escaped before they could be consigned to Andrea Doria's galleys at Trieste. They were also supplemented by the anonymous publication in Italian translation of various of Luther's and Melanchthon's writings. When such doctrines were introduced into the speculative philosophic environment of Padua, they engendered still other doctrines – for instance, Psychopannychism, according to which all souls sleep until the Last Judgement, when only the elect will arise again. Converts to one or another of these doctrines became sufficiently numerous both to warrant their meeting in a sort of underground national convention, first at Vicenza in 1542, then in Venice in 1550, and to quarrel more or less openly about whose doctrine was the correct one.[80]

Similar doctrines soon began to circulate in Lucca, where they gave some comfort to the survivors of the abortive silk-workers' uprising of the early 1530s. They circulated in Ferrara, where the duke's French wife Renée played host to her fellow countrymen of admitted heterodoxy, and in Salerno, where in 1546 'not only gentlemen, citizens, artisans . . . and the canons of the cathedral . . . but even women from their windows' were found to be 'talking about this heresy'. They circulated even more freely in Siena, where their adherents organized themselves into study groups under the protection of influential patricians. One of the more significant results of their study was the rejection of the Nicaean–Chalcedonian definition of the Trinity and its replacement by the doctrinal formula subsequently known as Socinian, from the surname of the Sienese patrician Lelio Sozzini (1525–1562) who first proposed it. Similar groups were organized at about the same time in Modena, with memberships ranging from patricians to wool-workers, in conformity with the peculiar ecclesiology of their inspired fellow citizen, Pietro Antonio da Cervia:

They believed that the Church was the congregation of the faithful and the believers, that is, those who believe they are saved by the death and passion of Christ. This was the true Church; but those who believed they could be saved by indulgences, pardons, vows, pilgrimages and other such works did not truly believe and hence were not of the Church.

One such group appeared even in Florence, among the friends of the former ambassador to France, Bartolomeo Panciatichi, who busied themselves with reading Luther and promoting the translation of Calvin.[81]

After 1540, the epicentre of what in northern Europe was coming to be called Protestantism and what in Italy was still indiscriminately referred to as Lutheranism shifted from Wittenberg to Geneva; and there it assumed a much more proselytizing and much more cosmopolitan form under the leadership of John Calvin. The propaganda campaign first directed at Calvin's compatriots in France was soon turned toward Italy as well. Anonymous translations of the writings of Calvin and of his successor Theodore Beza crossed the frontiers in the bottom of boxes carrying other merchandise; and long passages from their writings were incorporated directly into books of piety compiled by Italians in Italy. The most famous case – at least to judge by the quantity of scholarship it has inspired in the late twentieth century – was the *Beneficio di Cristo* (1543), a pamphlet compiled by Benedetto Fontanini of Mantua with the help of the humanist Marcantonio Flaminio and devoured as a guide to orthodox spirituality by the most prominent personages in the world of Italian religion.[82] Some of these personages eventually recognized the doctrines contained in such works as essentially the same as the ones they had arrived at from their own reading and reflection – most notably, the Capuchin preacher Bernardino Ochino (1487–1564), the Lateran canon Pietro Martire Vermigli (1500–1562) and the Sicilian Minorite Camillo Renato (d. *c.* 1571). When requested or pressed to give an explanation of their doctrines, they fled abroad; and they thus initiated an exodus of religious dissidents, or at least several dozen of them, that was soon to transfer the scene of the most intellectually exacting Italian theological controversies from Italy to Geneva, Basel, Zurich, Krakow, Alba Iulia and, above all, Grisons, the first stop for most of them and the final stop for many of them.

These defections sent a shock wave throughout the Italian religious community. As soon as the defectors were safely out of Italy, they lost no time in making explicit what previously they had dared only suggest: that many of their convictions, when carried to their logical conclusions, were incompatible with the continued existence of the established Church. Consequently, the former associates they left behind in Italy found themselves obliged to give much closer attention to the possible heterodoxy or orthodoxy of their theological statements. If justification, and hence salvation, was accomplished solely by an act of faith; if that act of faith was produced by God alone without any initiative or collaboration on the part of the recipient; if justification had been decided upon before the beginning of time; if that decision was communicated to each of the already justified during the course of his life; and if these truths could be found clearly stated in the Bible without the help of ancient Church Fathers, medieval dialecticians or modern philologists and exegetes – then the papacy, the episcopacy, the religious orders and the confraternities were more than just useless. They were abominations. As Ochino pointed out to one of the disciples he left behind, 'The pope is the Antichrist. All the ceremonies of the Roman court are diabolical . . . [and] the Mass is . . . the greatest act of idolatry that can be performed'.[83]

THE INQUISITION AND THE INDEX

Something, obviously, had to be done – if for no other reason than to put a stop to the impassioned, usually ill-informed and potentially disruptive heresy-calling contests touched off by the defections. The unreformable clergy of Capodistria used just such charges in order to drive their reforming bishop, Pier Paolo Vergerio (d. 1565), out of his diocese. At least one prominent, but theologically illiterate, Franciscan charged all the members of his order's chief rival, the Augustinians – as well as everyone else whose complicated arguments he had difficulty understanding – with holding the doctrines professed by one of their former members, Martin Luther.[84]

One solution to the problem was the one suggested by the theologians, particularly by the humanists among them: study all the various opinions critically until orthodoxy and heterodoxy separate themselves out, and then promulgate the distinction in print and from the pulpit. That is what the Erasmian Latinist Celio Calcagnini (1479–1541) sought to do in his treatises *De trinitate, De libero animi motu, In sacramentum eucharistiae*, and others. That is also what the Dominican scholar Paolino Bernardini sought to do in his 'Ecclesiastical Concord against All the Heretics' of 1552. But treatises and sermons had not converted a single Waldensian in the valleys of Piedmont a half-century earlier. They had not since reconverted a single Lutheran, as Gasparo Contarini realized, despite his commitment to the humanists' faith in the power of the word, as he set off, in 1541, for what he knew would be a futile colloquy with his Lutheran counterparts at Regensburg. How, then, could they be expected to reconcile the even greater theological divergences then current in Italy?

Much more promising of immediate results was a second solution: let the political authorities fulfil their responsibilities. As the offended bishop Vergerio put it in an oration to the doge:

You are well aware of your vocation as a prince chosen by God. Look attentively upon this church. God has taken it from the hands of your predecessors, who ought to have reformed it, and placed it in the hands of Your Serenity.[85]

The first government to take measures against what it perceived to be heresy was that of the Florentine 'Republicans' of 1529–30, ever as intransigent in religious as in political matters: they banished the Bible translator Antonio Brucioli for having referred to Luther and Bucer in his commentary on the Old Testament. The second was the Republic of Siena: in 1541, it issued the first of several stringent decrees against the expression of opinions similar to those then being promulgated by their future apostate fellow citizen Ochino. The third was the Republic of Venice, oblivious of its future reputation as a bastion of freedom and secularism. In 1543 the Senate charged the Three Deputies on Heresy with suppressing everything 'contrary to the honour of the Lord God and of the Christian Faith'; and when the Deputies' efforts failed to produce the desired results, it made clear its intention of collaborating fully with, and even of anticipating the measures of, the papal nuncio, notwithstanding the risk of losing its military manpower base in the bordering heterodox domain of Grisons.

Similar measures were soon adopted by most of the other governments of the peninsula, local, diocesan and regional – by the city council of Como, for example, after the absentee bishop failed to respond to its complaints, and by the governor of Milan, who threatened to expel all the Augustinians from the duchy after one of them violated his general's order to stop preaching. Lists of 'poisonous' and 'bad' books were compiled for the protection of the faithful – in Lucca in 1545, in Siena in 1548, in Venice in 1549; and the books that appeared on the lists were confiscated and burned. Offensive passages in books then in the course of publication were removed from the manuscripts – e.g., one of the stories that the oligarchs of Lucca had objected to in the first edition of Bandello's *Novelle*. And preachers whose sermons appeared to echo what were generally held to be 'Lutheran' ideas were summoned for questioning before civil or diocesan courts. Still, Italian governments were at least twenty years behind governments elsewhere in Europe. The free republic of Augsburg, for instance, had imposed prior censorship on book publishers as early as 1523; and it had expanded its prohibitions in 1537 to include 'writing, possessing, buying, selling, singing and reading' as well as 'printing' all the 'songs and poems' as well as 'books' it had banned.[86]

At the same time, Italian governments were just as committed to the definition of liberty accepted almost universally – a definition according to which citizens and subjects had the right to live peacefully under the law, free of political obligations (the prince's business, not theirs) and immunized from polluting notions that might endanger either the salvation of their souls or the security and stability of the state. 'Freedom of speech' could be admired as an expression of 'strength of spirit', like that exemplified by Cardinal Francesco Piccolomini when he opposed Pope Alexander in the matter of an ecclesiastical fief for Cesare Borgia. Freedom of speech in religious or political matters meant 'licence', as it did for the nuncio Fabio Mignanelli when he complained about 'the great freedom that is current in this city [Venice]'. 'Freedom of conscience' invariably meant in Italy what it meant in Calvin's Geneva: 'the freedom to obey God, and that's that'.[87]

The proliferation of these governmental measures often failed to achieve its objectives. Some investigations dragged on so long that the accused were driven to desperation – which is what occurred most notoriously in the case of Pier Paolo Vergerio. Toward the end of 'one of the most lengthy and complex prosecutions ever conducted . . . against an Italian accused of heresy', Vergerio fled to Switzerland and Germany; and he spent the remaining sixteen years of his life no longer as a 'reformer', but as an isolated and involuntary exile.[88] Other investigations were thwarted by constant bickering among the authorities about the extent of their respective jurisdictions – bickering that finally led the Inquisitor of Milan to request the governor to 'order the said Senate and the governors [of the subject cities] that in cases regarding the extirpation and punishment of all pernicious heresies they leave [me] free to proceed without obstacle'. Modena, a centre of active religious dissent, experienced a controversy over an Italian translation of the Flemish 'Summary of the Holy Scripture' (largely a translation of Melanchthon), which eventually involved Cardinals Giovanni Morone, Reginald Pole and Gasparo Contarini, the Inquisition, the city council, and the duke. In the end, the controversy produced no more positive result than that of forcing one of the city's foremost men of letters, Lodovico Castelvetro, into exile and into apostasy – both of which he had long shunned.[89]

In the 1550s, to avoid the repetition of such scandals, the bishop of Modena, Egidio Foscarari, simply let all suspects go free after a private abjuration – and, alas, after jotting down their names in a personal log book that was discovered by his less tolerant successor soon after his death. The first Florentine governor of Siena followed much the same course after discovering that Duke Cosimo's new subjects were as contentious about religious issues as they had been about political issues, notwithstanding the recent devastations of the siege of the city. The local Jesuits accused the Accademia degli Intronati of being 'a hotbed of heresy'. The academicians responded by plastering the walls of the Jesuit college with posters denouncing the proprietors as 'liars, sodomites, adulterers, adulators, spies and fleecers of poor widows'. After publishing a decree 'Against Heretics and Lutherans', the governor decided 'not to make any more noise' than was absolutely necessary and to get back to his main job of reconciling all the various factions of the Sienese to the rule of their new master.[90]

These difficulties were partially overcome after 1542 by the re-establishment of a central Congregation of the Inquisition in Rome. In the beginning, the new congregation had very little idea of what it should do or how to do it and it kept its experts busy studying the records of its medieval precursor.

But eventually it adopted procedures that most observers at the time recognized as close to prevailing concepts of jurisprudence. Adherence to these procedures was guaranteed at Venice, for example, by the insistence that observers appointed by its government be present at all proceedings. It was guaranteed at the central level by the congregation's insistence upon reviewing all cases of a serious nature – and either transferring them to Rome or returning them for reconsideration if they were found to contain the least irregularity.

The first task the Inquisition set for itself was to find out who held or professed what appeared to be heterodox theological opinions; and to that end it adopted the practices generally accepted in other tribunals at the time of encouraging anonymous denunciations, of protecting witnesses against the often real danger of retaliation and of using torture, or the threat of torture, in order to track down accomplices of the accused. Its other principal task – and in this it differed most notably from the secular courts – was not to punish the guilty but to reconcile them with the Church. In other words, the accused were supposed to benefit as much as society as a whole – the latter by being spared further danger of contamination, the former by being assisted in recognizing errors that would eventually cost them their souls.[91]

Not even the well-trained technicians of the Roman Inquisition could avoid occasional slips. A textbook on Scriptural homiletics published in 1546 by a Spanish Benedictine graduate of the University of Bologna so impressed the cardinal Inquisitor to whom it was dedicated that he did not notice any of its numerous plagiarisms from the treatise of almost the same title by Melanchthon. Neither did anyone else for another four centuries. Many of the very passages that had led to the condemnation of their author, Giorgio Siculo, reappeared in Latin translation in the four volumes of sermons published by the Benedictine bishop of Foligno, Isidoro Chiari, in 1566; and they were not finally identified until 1973. One well-connected amateur theologian, a certain Aonio Paleario (b. 1503), was formally absolved in 1542 of all charges brought against him by what his modern biographer denounces as a representative of 'the most narrow-minded orthodoxy'. He then went on peacefully for the next twenty-five years working out a wildly anachronistic plan for an anti-papal ecumenical council – a plan that betrayed little more than a total ignorance of the experience of all former councils – and borrowing Melanchthon's doctrines of Grace and Justification in support of his notion that the popes were the subverters, not the successors, of Peter.[92]

The attempt of one of the Roman inquisitors, the Theatine archbishop of Naples, Gian Pietro Carafa, to overcome jurisdictional conflicts by elevating the office of the Inquisition to the apex of the curial hierarchy almost ended by totally discrediting it – along with 'religion, the faith and the authority of the Holy See', as one of its impeccably orthodox victims pointed out. The moment Carafa became Pope Paul IV, in 1555, he pulled out the notes he had quietly amassed during the pontificate of his predecessor, who could not stand him; and he forthwith presented them as evidence of theological deviationism in most of the more prominent religious leaders of the city – as well as, according to Duke Cosimo's ambassador, anyone whom he perceived to be more intelligent than he was:

He wants either to be obeyed or to destroy the whole world. Believe me, this is a man of steel, and the stones he touches turn to fire for ruining and burning [whoever] does not do as he wishes. He is [also] very precipitous; and you cannot put much trust in him.[93]

Cardinal Pole's mission to England on behalf of Queen Mary Tudor was compromised by a recall to Rome just as it was beginning to achieve its first positive results. He remained in England, where he died in November 1558, energetically defending Mary and her husband King Philip II of Spain. Even Philip would have been jailed had he shown up unprotected in Rome. To the violently anti-Spanish Carafa, he was nothing but 'the iniquitous Philip of Austria, currently acting as king of Spain, and the rival in iniquity of his father', Charles V, who, having failed to kill all the Lutherans in Germany, must certainly have been a Lutheran himself. The titles of half the books then in print were hastily inscribed on a 'Roman' Index, which the pope meant to substitute for what he thought to be criminally incomplete local indexes all over Italy. This Index accomplished little else than arousing the wrath of the booksellers, who would not easily consent to the confiscation of most of their stocks, and provoking the fury of the princes, who were offended by such a flagrant attempt to violate their rights as sovereigns.[94]

Pope Paul's wildly ambitious nepotistic and political schemes soon precipitated the disgrace of all his family and the disaster of the 'Carafa War'. His death in 1559 was greeted by the destruction of the palace of the Inquisition and by the liberation and rehabilitation of the persecuted prelates; and his Index was quietly laid aside until another one could be issued under the authority of the Council of Trent. When the megalomaniac Neapolitan was then succeeded by a civilized, cultivated Milanese, the short-lived pontificate of Paul IV proved to be not the model to which all succeeding 'Counter-Reformation' popes sought to adhere, as is sometimes supposed, but a brief, if ominous, interlude in the history of the papacy between the fifteenth and the nineteenth centuries.

THE COUNCIL OF TRENT

The greatest shortcoming both of the Inquisition (or inquisitions) and of the various indexes of heretical books lay in the persistent lack of consensus about what was orthodox and what was heterodox – outside explicit quotations from avowed apostates – as well as about what method to follow in distinguishing between the two. Neither humanist nor scholastic theologians, neither older religious orders nor new congregations, neither princes nor city councils, neither the bishops nor the pope, not even the great theological faculties of

Paris, Louvain and Salamanca, which had long represented the teaching authority (*magisterium*) of the Church but which were seldom any longer even mentioned south of the Alps – none of these possessed enough prestige or authority to impose a new consensus in the place of the one that had been irremediably shattered.

It became ever more urgent that at least some of the constituent parts of the Church regain their lost prestige. Since the prestige of one was inevitably linked to that of all the others, it became equally urgent that the spiritual level of the entire Church be substantially raised – and that this be done as quickly as possible. Yet during the three decades after the conclusion of the Fifth Lateran Council, which was supposed to have reformed the Church, the very protagonists of the religious revival who had done the most to raise expectations about an eventual reform of the Church proved to be ever less capable of implementing even the very limited and rather anachronistic measures the council had actually adopted. Ecclesiastical offices and benefices continued to pass into the hands of powerful families, who managed them 'for the honour and utility of the family' rather than for the purposes prescribed in the original endowments; in one case they were put under the control of the same four-man board of directors that also managed the family's non-ecclesiastical holdings. Ecclesiastical properties continued to be alienated to outsiders or mismanaged by incompetent insiders; and donations for the support of the corresponding institutions fell in response to increasingly specific rumours about misappropriated revenues. Leave your money 'for building chapels and celebrating Masses', warned one well-informed lawyer in 1522, and 'your descendants will beg while the chaplains have banquets; they will lie naked on cots while the prelates luxuriate in magnificent clothes'.[95]

Similarly, the self-reform of local churches frequently bogged down in the face of ever more discouraging obstacles – even in the 'model church' of Verona, where Giberti's successor discovered that some 5,000 people had not been to confession or communion for years. So did the self-reform of many of the older religious orders, especially after it became apparent that those orders which refused to reform, like the Jesuits, were being awarded the same signs of papal favour normally offered as a prize for reformation. The changes decreed for the most obdurate strongholds of unreformable privilege, the cathedral canonries, were often ignored – or else rescinded, as they were when Carpi was annexed to the Este dominions. Their members too continued to be selected 'in accordance with the most undisguised criteria of the patronage system'.

It is not surprising, therefore, that even the most ardent reformers at times became discouraged. Nothing can be done about the regular clergy, one of them lamented, until they are put under the control of secular 'prelates . . . [who] will follow [*imitari*, in the humanist meaning of the term] in the footsteps . . . of the Apostles . . . and be immune from all vices and act neither as lords nor owners but as ministers and dispensers'. Nothing can be done to assure the accession of apostolic bishops, noted another, until some means can be found to assure the election of popes who are cultivated men of letters and exemplary pastors — rather than coin-collectors, like Paul II, or nepotists, like Sixtus IV. Nothing can be done to correct the immorality of the lower clergy, insisted still another committed observer, until 'they either are given wives or are castrated' — and thus discouraged from 'running around hot' after the wives of laymen. Nothing can be done to elevate the religious life of the mass of the laity until the liturgies hidden in a strange tongue 'by the avarice of priests and friars' are recited in the Volgare. For only then will Christians too be able to praise God like 'the Latins in Latin, the Hebrews in Hebrew and the Slavs in Slavonic' instead of 'chirping like birds and prattling like parrots'.[96]

But who could finally decide which reforms were necessary, and who could then carry them out? Who, in other words, would be able to do many times more than what was contained in the never-fulfilled promises of half the popes and all the councils since the end of the Great Schism?

One possible solution to this question was to leave the responsibility to ordinary laymen. They, after all, proved capable of ostracizing unworthy priests and prelates, as the citizens of Messina did in 1563 when they flaunted their 'irreverence' by going off to arrange 'contracts and [other] secular business . . . during the hours in which Mass was celebrated'. They could throw rocks at misbehaving rich nuns with shouts of 'To the wolves! Go do some work, you lazy women!' as the construction workers once did in Modena. They could take over parish churches and force the episcopal vicars to confirm their choice of parish priests.[97]

But congregationalism, however well sanctioned by antecedents in the fifth century, was totally without theoretical foundations in the sixteenth century; and legally it could be instituted only in those parishes of which the congregations happened to be the patrons with rights of nomination — as were several in Milan. Thus a second answer to the question was more frequently proposed: let the princes assume the same responsibility for the reform of the churches under their jurisdictions as they did for rooting out heresy. That, after all, is what was demanded in innumerable petitions, like the one presented to the Venetian Senate by the residents of Valli del Pasubio in 1535 regarding the 'tyranny, thievery, rapine, violence, homicides and assassinations' committed by the 'satellites' of a local priest. That is what was recommended by the chief counsellor of the duke of Savoy in 1560 when he called upon his secular superior to 'provide curates of learning and good conscience' capable, as few were at the time, of 'explaining to their congregations the Christian life [as prescribed in] the Gospels and the Letters of St Paul'. Duke Cosimo's behaviour in this matter was exemplary. He made the priests of San Lorenzo stop lighting stoves in the Sacristy after Borghini pointed out that the smoke was staining Michelangelo's statues, among the chief tourist attractions of the city. He placed all monasteries with cure of souls under the jurisdiction of the bishops. He appointed a three-man commission to make sure that the exempt religious 'behaved correctly and did not shirk their obligations'. And he forbade the admission of any visitors except close relatives in female convents without written permission from the civil authorities.[98]

But however attractive they may have seemed to some of the subjects of the king of England or the elector of Saxony, in Italy a number of autonomous state churches would have succeeded no better than congregational churches in solving the problems of the Church as a whole. For one thing, none of the secular governments ever dreamed of proposing their necessary corollary: the abolition of the universal Church; and all of them were forced by their own consciences, as well as by the realities of political power, to respect all legally constituted limitations on their authority even with regard to ecclesiastical institutions within their civil jurisdictions. Duke Cosimo, for example, was motivated in part by his commitment not to yield one inch of what legally belonged to him, as he proved in his bitter jurisdictional quarrels with Pope Paul III. He was also motivated by the fear that the unacceptable conditions uncovered by his ecclesiastical survey of 1551 would diminish the efficacy of his clergy's prayers on his behalf. But he freely admitted that the ultimate solution was not his; and he accompanied his own reform measures with an appeal 'that Your Blessedness send a person [to every diocese] who has ample authority to reform and castigate [those who deserve it] in the affairs of the monasteries and [in questions] of heresy'.[99]

Thus the second solution was usually combined with the third: let the pope do it. Let him 'revoke all the reservations [heretofore] conceded and grant no more of them', urged Tommaso Campeggi, who became the regent of the Papal Chancery in 1540. Let him toss out of Rome 'like the plague . . . all those innumerable persons' who reside there only 'to look for benefices and to initiate lawsuits'. And let him appoint a commission of three cardinals and six to eight prelates of different 'nations' to see that his orders are carried out. Let him get rid of all those false theologians who blinded his predecessors to the deplorable state of the Church with flattering but hollow theses about papal omnipotence: so urged the Commission of Cardinals appointed in 1537 in their *Consilium de emendanda ecclesia* ('On the Reform of the Church' – the title of their famous report). Let him abolish all the old religious orders that prove incapable of reforming themselves. Let him thoroughly cleanse the *caput* of the Church; and the cleansing of the *corpus* will follow automatically.[100]

Unfortunately, not even Paul III was able to do much more than shuffle around a few posts in the Datary, the office that administered the distribution of papal benefices and that was widely held to be the chief source of corruption in the Curia; and Paul was probably more sincerely committed to the cause of reform than any of his predecessors since Gregory VII. Marcello II, as the humanist Cardinal Cervini was called after his election in 1555 – the first Renaissance pope who scrupulously 'sought the glory of God [rather than] his own glory in this world' and the one who showed the most promise of carrying through the programme Paul had begun – died within a few days of his election. There was then only one solution left: call an ecumenical council – a council held with the consent of the emperor, like the Councils of Nicaea and Constance, but summoned by and not against the pope (as the abortive Council of Pisa had been in 1511), a council presided over by papal legates rather than by the pope himself and still sufficiently independent of either to clear it of the suspicion of being dominated by anyone but the Holy Spirit. This council should also be capable, as none of its immediate predecessors had been, both of solving all outstanding theological questions of the day and of providing an institutional framework for assuring the acceptance of its decrees among all the various peoples officially or potentially in communion with the Church of Rome.[101]

This was the solution that Paul III formally adopted at the beginning of his pontificate and the one toward which he directed most of his diplomatic activity during the following decade. It was also the solution that many formerly ardent papalists, like Girolamo Aleandro, came to accept once they realized that all alternative means 'by which those who have left the Church can be called back' had failed.[102]

Yet even the conciliar solution was far from perfect. For one thing, the tiny city of Trent – where, after the failure of previous summonses to Mantua and Vicenza, the first small delegation constituted itself in December 1545 – had been chosen for its potential attractiveness to the Germans, 'Protestant' as well as 'Catholic' (the terms not yet having been defined). For while culturally within the borders of the Italian 'nation', legally it lay within the borders of what the Germans called 'The Holy Roman Empire of the German Nation'. Trent had not been chosen because of its attractiveness to Italians, who were accustomed to living in cities equipped with all the necessities of what passed at the time for comfortable living. And both the pope and the princes who supported him had to exert constant pressure to get their bishops to go there and then to keep them there once they had been installed in whatever dank monastic cells the legates could find for them. For another thing, to the extent that they were theologians at all, most of the Italian bishops were humanist theologians, and they reflected the whole spectrum of theological opinions that had been generated by the religious revival. They were thus forced at times to consult scholastic specialists, like the Dominican professor at Bologna, Placido da Parma, and the Sorbonne-trained Jesuit, Diego Lainez (1512–1565), whose language and formulas they often found either repugnant or incomprehensible. And they were frequently left trying to decide on the basis of their own little reading and less spiritual experience among Contarini's, Sadoleto's and Seripando's very different definitions of grace, faith and good works.

Moreover, all the bishops were subject at times to conflicts of loyalty between the pope, their conciliar colleagues and their political superiors. The Tuscan bishops, for example, were called upon by the duke's resident ambassador to represent to the Council the objections of their prince – who, after all, had nominated most of them to their sees – to undermining the monopoly of Florence's Wool Guild in the selection of Advent and Lenten preachers and to infringing upon the legal rights of lay (and therefore taxable) patrons of ecclesiastical benefices. At least twice the Council almost disbanded as a consequence of papal political measures that were wholly out of keeping with the norms of behaviour it was trying to formulate: first when Paul III provoked the wrath of the emperor by investing his son with Parma and Piacenza, then when Pius IV repaid his election debts by elevating to the cardinalate the eleven-year-old Ferdinando de' Medici. The Council was transferred to Bologna in 1547 and then was suspended when the Imperial bishops refused to follow. It was reconvened in 1551–52 in Trent by Julius III, forgotten during the pontificate of the anti-conciliar Paul IV, reassembled by Pius IV after interminable and ambiguous diplomatic negotiations with the kings of France and Spain and then threatened again with dissolution over the hotly fought issue of the divine origins (*de iure*) of the obligation of episcopal residence.[103]

Nevertheless, even though its attendance record was far below that of all previous councils, and even though its geographical distribution was far more restricted, no one in any of the churches still allied with Rome ever doubted its ecumenical character – that is, its right to make decisions binding on all of them. What grumbling still went on in the Roman Curia, which had the most to lose from the implementation of the disciplinary decrees, was quashed soon after the conclusion of the Council (December, 1563), when Pius IV officially accepted the decrees and nominated a commission of cardinals charged with promulgating and interpreting them. No one who looked carefully at voting records would have had any doubts either about the canonically indispensable freedom of the deliberations. For none of the papal subsidies paid to 42 percent of the bishops in attendance by 1563 was sufficient to cover more than half of their living expenses. Some 24 percent of those receiving subsidies dared to vote against the legates even on an issue so crucial to the pro-papal party as *de iure* residence. And they did so without suffering any cut in their subsidies.[104]

The Council was not able to accomplish all of the ambitious programme set forth for it by Jacopo Sadoleto in the original bull of convocation. It did not bring about the reconciliation of the Lutherans – for the obvious reason that the Lutherans consistently denied the legitimacy of any council convened by the pope. It did not persuade the Catholic princes to unite in destroying the Ottoman Empire. But it did accomplish more than was ever really expected. It consolidated the variant doctrinal theses generated by the religious revival – or at least persuaded those whose specific formulas it turned down to accept the ones it adopted in their place. It also provided a fair number of specific, yet flexible, answers to many of the pressing theological questions of the age. Henceforth, it intimated, orthodox Christians could direct their theological inquiries as much as they liked toward the Bible, providing that they recognize the inspired character of all the books the Council listed as canonical – including what many Protestants rejected as the 'Apocrypha' and those New Testament Epistles that Luther downgraded with respect to the 'key' Epistle to the Romans. They could exalt the Age of the Apostles as much as they liked, provided that they also respect what Cervini, Pole and Claude LeJay had dug out of the Fathers concerning a continuous 'tradition' of interpretation and clarification. They could ascribe as much as they liked to God's freely bestowed grace, provided that they grant at least some effectiveness, however small, to man's freely assenting to what God did for him. They could ascribe as much as they wished to good works, provided that they admit the solely divine origin of an original call and the necessity of grace in making the works wholly good. They could cultivate as much as they wished a direct, individual relationship with God, as long as they admitted that all seven sacraments, either administered or certified by properly ordained representatives of the hierarchical Church, provided an efficacious, even essential, support to that relationship.

While it was busy defining doctrine, the Council also gave its attention to making the Church worthy of the definitions. It raised to the level of universal norms many of the more innovative experiments of the Italian religious revival. It replaced a beneficed clergy with a pastoral clergy, one forbidden to hold more than one clerical office at a time and bound to permanent residence by the threat of severe monetary sanctions. It transferred to the secular clergy the preaching and sacramental functions previously all but monopolized by the regular clergy. It gave ordinaries the means to effect this transfer by cancelling all former exceptions to episcopal jurisdiction and by prescribing regular visitations and assemblies (synods) of all the clergy within a particular diocese or province. It made possible a regular supply of trained and dedicated secular priests by adapting in the form of diocesan seminaries the model of the new schools recently founded by the Jesuits in Rome. Finally, it set forth a new standard for clerical behaviour: for pomp and display, which served principally to glorify the Church, it substituted moderation and sobriety, which could serve as general guides to Christian living, in accordance with the assumption that

the behaviour of the clergy is so closely observed by the laity that, as their example often leads the latter into every sort of sin, so imitating them easily disposes laymen to obey the commandments of God.[105]

While spreading to the entire Universal Church the particular fruits of the Italian religious revival, the Council also provided special benefits for the churches of Italy. Its increasingly pan-European composition enabled the chief reformers among the Italian bishops to enrich their own experiences with those of their transalpine colleagues – with Josse Clichtove's descriptions of the diocesan visitations of Jacques Lefèvre d'Etaples at Tournai; with Johann Gropper's *Enchiridion*, which Giberti had republished for his priests in 1541; with Pedro de Soto's 'Treatise on the Institution of Priesthood' (1558), passages from which were reproduced *verbatim* in the corresponding conciliar canons.[106] The presence of so many other Italian bishops also enabled them to convert the initially reticent to the cause of reform – and to add a religious vocation where formerly there may have been only a political or financial vocation for the prelacy. Even more, it encouraged those who had previously thought of themselves only as Venetians or Neapolitans, or as the subjects of the Senate or of the King of Naples and Spain, to think of themselves also – for the first time in history – as members of a pan-Italian episcopacy. The enthusiasm generated in the last days of the Council by the prospect of its successful conclusion then endowed all the members of this embryonic collectivity with a common mission.[107] And the moment the Council was over, they returned – or went for the first time – to their sees, determined to put into practice the formulas for reform they had worked out together at Trent.

The Council of Trent created a new Church very different from the one out of which it had arisen – a Church that can with some justice be called the 'Tridentine Church' (from the Latin name for the city of Trent) in order to distinguish it from a preceding 'Renaissance Church'. At the same time, it created one further criterion for defining the nascent Italian 'nation'. After the conclusion of the Council, being Italian no longer meant just accepting the High Renaissance masterpieces as normative in the arts and letters and Bembo's Volgare as a common written language. It also meant accepting the particular formulas of religious faith that had been laid down at Trent and the Tridentine Church as the sole institutional manifestation of that faith.

Whoever objected to this additional criterion of nationality was faced with a choice between four alternatives. He could keep what had now been defined as heterodox opinions to himself and conform outwardly to what had been defined as orthodoxy. Without any sound theological or philosophical reasons for doing so, in other words, he could adapt himself to the realities of a difficult situation just like so many other sincere members of religious minorities in Europe at the time. Calvin had condemned such practices with the admittedly inappropriate label of Nicodemism.[108] On the other hand, he could approach the Inquisitors for clarification of his error, renounce the errors they pointed out to him, or try to persuade them that what sounded like error was really orthodox – as Antonio Brucioli did in 1555 when he 'emended' the meaning of the adjective *sola*, which he had once coupled with the noun *fide*, so as 'not to exclude works'. The penitent would then be absolved with an abjuration and an often abbreviated term of psalm-reciting in jail or at home. Or else, if the Inquisitors had reason to believe his profession of innocence or to doubt the motives of his accusers, the charges would simply be dismissed. That is what they did, for example, in the case of a former governor of Pavia who, upon his return from Switzerland, protested:

I do not know what purpose I would have in reading such books, not being of that profession and not being a theologian; [and] I am not and have never been such a simple idiot that I would not have avoided even the suspicion of adhering to the opinions of Luther or Zwingli.[109]

The recalcitrant could, or course, go on talking out loud, refuse all invitations to recant, and suffer the consequences – which meant just what it would have for anyone guilty of treason in a civil court: death, or, if the judges thought a bit of pressure might eventually result in a recantation, an indefinite term in prison or in the galleys. That course was taken by very few – some of them because they preferred death to infidelity, some of them because they hoped to convert their judges, and some of them, like Duke

Cosimo's long-term protégé Pietro Carnesecchi (1508–1567), because their protectors got tired of protecting them.

Finally, recalcitrants could emigrate. Outside Italy, they could still perform services on behalf of Italian culture. They could translate for distribution in the rest of Europe the past or current Italian literary classics. That is what Celio Secundo Curione (1503–1569) did for the printing firm of another religious émigré, Francesco Perna, in Basel. Or they could teach their hosts to read the classics. That is what the former friar and subsequently violently anti-Franciscan Michelangelo Florio did when he wrote 'The Rules of the Italian Language' (1553) for his pupil, Lady Jane Grey.

Many of the émigrés, however, spent the rest of their lives wandering about in a hopeless quest for a place where their peculiar doctrines might fit into some sort of orthodoxy – and denouncing their hosts as worse than Italian Inquisitors when they failed to accommodate them. Or they sought equally in vain for a place where their heterodoxies might be tolerated along the lines proposed by Mino Celsi in his treatise, *In haereticis coercendis quatenus progredi liceat* (1577), of which most of the copies, alas, remained unread in the publisher's warehouse. That is why so many of the émigrés ended up in Transylvania and Poland, where they were protected by a stalemate in a three-way struggle between Catholic, Lutheran and Calvinist orthodoxies. Some of them eventually accepted one or another local orthodoxy and gave up their Italian for another nationality. A few of them got tired of wandering and publicly accepted even the Tridentine creed in order to go back home. But more often they exhausted themselves in hair-splitting controversies over ever more intricate theological refinements – as even the Antitrinitarians did when they began accusing each other of being 'Modalists' or 'Tritheists'. They were even led at times to denounce each other before their hosts' theological tribunals – as Vergerio, Curione and Giovan Bernardino Bonifacio (1517–1597) did before a magistrate who turned out himself to be an Italian 'heretic'.[110]

Since almost none of their former compatriots ever heard of any of these quarrels, the exiles effectively excluded themselves as active members of the nation they had abandoned. Their accomplishments and adventures, heroic or tragic as they may have been, belong to the history not of Italy, but of the countries where they eventually settled. Since none of them managed to transmit his secret opinions even to his own children, and since few defendants felt any reluctance to supply their judges with full lists of their former acquaintances, the Inquisitors and the censors had little trouble wiping out all remnants of religious dissent. Actually, they managed to find very little of it – only five real 'heretics' in the diocese of Verona in the half-century after 1548, only ten in Bergamo in the six decades after 1527. Within very little time after the conclusion of the Council, Italy had become totally Tridentine – or at least totally non-Antitridentine.

NOTES AND REFERENCES

1. Here quoted: Albano Biondi, 'Aspetti della cultura cattolica post-tridentina', in *Einaudi Storia d'Italia Annali 4: Intellettuali e potere*, Turin 1981, pp. 259–60; Alessandro Pastore in *Marcantonio Flaminio: Fortune e Sfortune di un chierico nell'Italia del Cinquecento*, Milan 1981, 7–12; Maurizio Calvesi and Mario Manieri-Elia, *Personalità e strutture caratterizzanti: Il 'barocco' leccese*, ed. Franco Panone, n.p. 1966, pp. 28–29; Ludovico Zorzi, *I teatri pubblici di Venezia (secoli XVII–XVIII)*, Venice 1971, p. 25. In general: Pietro Tacchi Venturi, *Storia della Compagnia di Gesù in Italia* (2nd edn), vol. 1, i: *La vita religiosa in Italia durante i primordi dell'Ordine*, Rome 1950; Adriano Prosperi, 'Il Concilio di Trento e la Riforma Tridentina' (reporting on the Trent conference of 1963), *CS*, 6, 1967; Mario Rosa, 'Per la storia della vita religiosa e della chiesa in Italia tra il Cinquecento e il Seicento: Studi recenti e questioni di metodo', in his *Religione e società nel Mezzogiorno: Fra Cinque e Seicento*, Bari 1976; Giovanni Miccoli, 'La storia religiosa', in *Einaudi Storia d'Italia, 2: Dalla caduta dell'Impero Romano al secolo XVIII*, Turin 1974; Pier Giorgio Camaiani, 'Interpretazioni della Riforma cattolica e della Controriforma', in *Marzorati Grande antologia filosofica* (15 vols), Milan 1954, vol. 6.

2. Antonio Cistellini, *Figure della riforma pretridentina*, Brescia 1948; Gabriella Zarri, 'Pietà e profezia alle corti padane', in Paolo Rossi (ed.), *Il Rinascimento nelle corti padane: Società e cultura: Interventi*, Bari 1977; Massimo Petrocchi, *Pagine sulla letteratura religiosa lombarda del '500*, Naples 1956.

3. Massimo Petrocchi, *L'estasi nelle mistiche italiane della Riforma cattolica*, Naples 1958, pp. 26 and 49.

4. Umile Bonzi, *S. Caterina Fieschi Adorno*, Turin 1961–62; Pio Paschini, *S. Gaetano Thiene, Gian Pietro Carafa e le origini dei chierici regolari teatini*, Rome 1926, p. 19.

5. Cesare Vasoli in ch. 2 of his *I miti e gli astri*, Naples 1977, as well as, in particular, on Annio and Lorenzo Violi. Other related topics in the indispensable collective volume *L'attesa dell'età nuova nella spiritualità della fine del Medioevo*, Todi 1962, and in Ottavia Niccoli, 'Profezie in piazza: Note sul profetismo popolare nell'Italia del primo Cinquecento' (above, Chapter 2, n. 9).

6. Cesare Vasoli, 'Notizie su Giorgio Benigno Salviati', in his *Profezia e ragione: Studi sulla cultura del Cinquecento e del Seicento*, Naples 1974.

7. Francesco quoted by Donald Weinstein, *Savonarola and Florence: Prophecy and Patriotism in the Renaissance*, Princeton 1970 (to which the following paragraphs are heavily indebted), p. 349; Paolo da Foligno quoted by Melchiorre da Pobladura in 'La "severa riprensione" di fra Matteo da Bascio (?1495–1552)', *Archivio italiano per la storia della pietà*, 3, 1962, pp. 284–85.

8. In general: Domenico Di Agresti, *Sviluppi della riforma monastica savonaroliana*, Florence 1980; on Savonarolism at mid-century: Romeo De Maio, *Riforme e miti nella Chiesa del Cinquecento*, Naples 1973, Ch. 4; and Paolo Simoncelli, 'Momenti e figure del savonarolismo romano', *CS*, 11, 1974.

9. Masi's *Diario*, with a contemporary preface from which this quotation is taken (pp. 79–80), is published by Guglielmo Di Agresti in his *Santa Caterina de' Ricci*, Florence 1969; Cesare Vasoli, 'Note sulle "Giornate" di ser Lorenzo Violi', in his *I miti e gli astri* (above, n. 5).

10. Dionisia Trosa, *Prolegomeni alla spiritualità di santa Caterina de' Ricci*, Florence 1975.

11. 'Apologia di-Anonimo', published in Di Agresti, *Santa Caterina de' Ricci* (above, n. 9), here quoted from p. 47.

12. Gino Damerini in Ch. 9 of his *L'isola e il cenobio di San Giorgio Maggiore*, Venice 1969, p. 44.

13. Virginio Luigi Bernorio, *La chiesa di Pavia nel secolo XVI e l'azione pastorale del cardinale Ippolito de' Rossi (1560–1591)*, Pavia 1972, pp. 58 ff.

14. Gabriele Monaco, *La riforma tridentina nel Carmelo di Napoli*, Naples 1967; Hubert Jedin, 'Contarini und Camaldoli' (with all the relevant correspondence in the appendix), *Archivio italiano per la storia della pietà*, 2, 1959; Giuseppe Alberigo, 'Vita attiva e vita contemplativa in un'esperienza cristiana del XVI secolo', *SV*, 16, 1974; Innocenzo Cervelli, 'Storiografia e problemi intorno alla vita religosa e spirituale a Venezia nella prima metà del '500', *SV*, 8, 1966; Gregorio Penco, *Storia del monachesimo in Italia dalle origini alla fine del Medio Evo*, Rome 1961.

15. Boris Ulianich on Agostino Bonucci in *DBI*, vol. 12, pp. 438–50; report on the Servite house in Prato quoted by Guglielmo Di Agresti in *Aspetti di vita pratese del Cinquecento*, Florence 1976, p. 46.

16. Donato Giannotti quoted from his letter to Paul III, September 1544, in R. Starn (ed.), *Donato Giannotti and his Epistolae*, Geneva 1968, p. 177. Hubert Jedin, *Papal Legate at the Council of Trent: Cardinal Seripando*, tr. Frederic C. Eckhoff, London 1947. The 'Diarium de vita sua' of Hieronymi Seripandi is published by David Gutiérrez in *Analecta Augustiniana*, 26, 1963.

17. Julius Kirshner, 'The moral problem of discounting Genoese *paghe*', *Archivum Fratrum Praedicatorum*, 47, 1977; and Raymond Creytens, 'Raphael de Pornassio', *Archivum Fratrum Praedicatorum*, 49, 1979.

18. Report of the guardian of the community in Jerusalem, 20 September 1548, published by Agustin Arce, 'Dos Franciscanos de la Provincia de Basilicata mártires en Damasco (23 Agosto 1548)', *Archivum Franciscanum Historicum*, 71, 1978.

19. Father Cuthbert, *The Capuchins: A Contribution to the History of the Counter-Reformation*. (2nd edn), London 1971; The Capuchin Constitution of 1536 is published in English translation in John Olin (ed.), *The Catholic Reformation. Savonarola to Ignatius Loyola: Reform in the Church 1495–1540*, New York 1969.

20. Pio Paschini, 'Le Compagnie del Divino Amore e la beneficenza pubblica nei primi decenni del Cinquecento', in his *Tre ricerche sulla storia della Chiesa nel Cinquecento*, Rome 1945; for the statutes (1502) of the Confraternity of S. Giovanni Evangelista, see the appendix to the description by Giuseppina De Sandre Gasparini in *Miscellanea Gilles Gérard Meersseman*, Padua 1970.

21. Michele Miele on Salvio in *Miscellanea . . . Meersseman* (above, n. 20), p. 830.

22. The figures are given by Pier Lorenzo Meloni, 'Topografia, diffusione e aspetti delle confraternite dei disciplinati' in *Risultati e prospettive della ricerca sul movimento dei disciplinati*, Perugia 1972. In general: Giuseppe Alberigo, 'Contributi alla storia della confraternite dei disciplinati e della spiritualità laicale nei secoli XV e XVI', in *Il movimento dei disciplinati nel settimo centenario dal suo inizio*, Perugia 1962, which describes, among other things, the reasons for statute reform in the sixteenth century.

23. Antonio Fiori, 'L'archivio della arciconfraternita della Dottrina Cristiana presso l'Archivio storico del Vicariato: Inventario', *Ricerche per la storia religiosa di Roma*, 2, 1978. Pasquale Lopez, 'Una famosa congregazione laica napoletana

nel '600 e l'opera missionaria di padre Corcione', *Rivista di storia salernitane*, 3, 1970.

24. Carlo Marcora, 'La Congregazione dello Spirito Santo a Milano', *MSDM*, 15, 1968; Amelio Tagliaferri, 'Povertà e assistenza ospedaliera nel secolo XVI', in Amelio Taglioferri (ed.), *Scritti storici in memoria di Paolo Lino Zovatto*, Milan 1972; Canzio Pizzoni, 'La Confraternita dell'Annuziata in Perugia', in *Risultati . . . disciplinati* (above, n. 22). In general: Pietro Tacchi Venturi, *Storia della Compagnia di Gesù* (above, n. 1), I, Chs 18 and 19: 'La beneficenza nella vita italiana del Cinquecento' and 'Ancora della beneficenza nella vita italiana del Cinquecento'.

25. Giovanna Balbi, 'La compagnia della Misericordia di Genova nella storia della spiritualità laica', in *Momenti di storia e arte religiosa in Liguria*, Genoa 1963, here quoted from p. 172.

26. Many other examples appear in G. G. Meersseman, 'La riforma delle confraternite laicali in Italia prima del Concilio di Trento', *Problemi della vita religiosa in Italia nel Cinquecento*, Padua 1960.

27. Mario Rosa, 'Chiesa, idee sui poveri e assistenza in Italia dal Cinque al Settecento', *Società e storia*, 3, 1980, quoted from p. 782; Keller, *Das Oratorium* (above, Chapter 6, n. 70); Michele Miele, 'L'assistenza sociale a Napoli nel Cinquecento e i programmi della Compagnia dei Bianchi dello Spirito Santo', in R. Creytens and P. Künzle (eds), *Xenia Medii Aevi Historiam Illustrantia. Oblata Thomae Kaeppeli*, Rome 1979, pp. 860–61; Luigi Firpo on the 'Decollato' in *Eresia e Riforma nell' Italia del Cinquecento: Miscellanea I del Corpus Reformatorum Italicorum*, Florence and Chicago 1974, p. 311; Donatella Balani and Marina Roggero (eds), *La scuola in Italia dalla Controriforma al secolo dei lumi*, Turin 1976.

28. Anita Malamani, 'Notizie sul mal francese e gli ospedali degli incurabili in età moderna', *CS*, 15, 1978; Marco Bubini, 'Povertà e assistenza a Como', and Daniela Lombardi, 'Poveri a Firenze', in *Timore e carità: I poveri nell'Italia moderna*, Cremona 1982; Flavio Baroncelli and Giovanni Assereto, 'Pauperismo e religione nell'età moderna', *Società e storia*, 3, 1980; Paolo Simoncelli, 'Origini e primi anni di vita dell'ospedale romano dei Poveri Mendicanti', *Annuario ISIEMC*, 25–26, 1973–74, and 'Nota sul sistema assistenziale a Roma nel XVI secolo', in *Timore e carità*; Antonio Rotondò in a scholarship-packed review essay of Armando Saitta's edition of the first Italian translation of Ludovico Vives' *De subventione pauperum* (1545) in *Riv SLR*, 12, 1976, pp. 258–64. The most thorough treatment of this subject, as well as the source of the principal thesis presented here, is Brian S. Pullan, in 'The famine in Venice and the new Poor Law', *SV*, 5–6, 1963–64, and his *Rich and Poor in Renaissance Venice: The Social Institutions of a Catholic State to 1620*, Oxford 1971.

29. Georg Weise, 'Elementi manieristi e prebarocchi in Pietro Aretino', in Amedeo Quondam (ed.), *Problemi del manierismo*, Naples 1975.

30. Peter Cannon Brookes, 'The *Sacri Monti* of Lombardy and Piedmont', *Connoisseur*, 186, no. 750, August 1974 (I am indebted for this reference to Anne Crawford Grubb); Marianne Heinz, 'Das Hospital S. Giacomo in Augusta in Rom: Peruzzi und Antonio da Sangallo i.G. Zum Hospitalbau der Hochrenaissance', *Storia dell'arte*, 41, 1981, pp. 31–49.

31. Luigi Cervaro, 'Momenti di vita letteraria al Santo', in *Storia e cultura al Santo*, ed. Antonio Poppi, Vicenza 1976 (here quoted from p. 597).

32. Pio Paschini, 'Un cardinale editore, Marcello Cervini', in his *Cinquecento romano*

e Riforma cattolica, Rome 1958; François Fossier, 'Premières recherches sur les manuscrits latins du cardinal Marcello Cervini', *Mél EFR*, 91, 1979.

33. From his autobiography in Giovanni Battista Spotorno, *Storia letteraria della Liguria*, Genoa, 1825, vol. 4, 25–37.

34. Andrea Del Col, 'Il Nuovo Testamento tradotto da Massimo Teofilo e altre opere stampate a Lione nel 1551', *CS*, 15, 1978; Pastore in his *Marcantonio Flaminio* (above, n. 1) (to be read keeping in mind the many reservations of Anne Jacobson Schutte in her review in *Bibliothèque d'humanisme et renaissance*, 44, 1982, pp. 414–47, and those of Nelson Minnich in *American Historical Review*, 87, 1982, pp. 1128–29). The role of Renaissance scholars in reinterpreting the Psalms is fully described by James L. Kugel, *The Idea of Biblical Poetry: Parallelism and its History*, New Haven 1981, pp. 223 ff.

35. Adriano Prosperi, 'La religione, il potere, le élites. Incontri italo-spagnoli della Controriforma', *Annuario ISIEMC*, vol. 29–30, 1977–78, pp. 499–529.

36. Letters to Paolo Giustiniani, ed. Hubert Jedin, in *Archivio italiano per la storia della pietà*, 2, 1951; and Jedin's 'Ein *Turmerlebnis* des jungen Contarini', in *Historisches Jahrbuch*, 70, 1950 (p. 117). For the context: Felix Gilbert, 'Religion and politics in the thought of Gasparo Contarini', in his *History: Choice and Commitment*, Cambridge, Mass., 1977.

37. Pietro Aretino, *Lettere, il primo e il secondo libro*, ed. F. Flora and A. Del Vita, Milan 1960, pp. 301 and 447.

38. Aretino in *Lettere* (above, n. 37), p. 508; Paolo Giovio's letter to Erasmus published by Clarence H. Miller with notes and translation in *Moreana*, 53, 977, pp. 65–76; Silvana Seidel Menchi, 'Alcuni atteggiamenti della cultura italiana di fronte a Erasmo', in *Eresia e riforma* (above, n. 27), and 'La discussione su Erasmo nell'Italia del Rinascimento: Ambrogio Flandino vescovo di Mantova', in *Società, politica e cultura a Carpi ai tempi di Alberto III Pio*, Padua 1981; Nicola Badaloni, 'Erasmo e la diffusione del suo pensiero in Italia', in his *Cultura e vita civile tra Riforma e Controriforma*, Bari 1973. These references, however, represent only a small part of the considerable bibliography on this subject.

39. S. Antoninus, *Opera*, Venice 1557, quoted from the title page of his manual for confessors. Giovanni Pili da Fano, *Arte de la unione*, Brescia 1536, cited (with many other similar titles) by Paolo Simoncelli in 'Il "Dialogo dell'unione spirituale di Dio con l'anima" tra alumbradismo spagnolo e prequietismo italiano', *Annuario ISIEMC*, 29–30, 1977–78, pp. 565–601.

40. In *Opere volgari*, ed. Cecil Grayson, Bari 1966, II, p. 107. In general: Denys Hay, *The Church in Italy in the Fifteenth Century*, Cambridge 1977.

41. Paolo Giovio to Alessandro Farnese, 21 September 1549, in Guiseppe Guido Ferrero (ed.), *Opera, II: Epistularum*, Rome 1958, pp. 141–42; and to Francesco II Sforza, 16 February 1535, in Giuseppe Guido Ferrero (ed.), *Lettere del Cinquecento*, Turin 1967, pp. 216–17.

42. Franco· Molinari, 'Visite pastorali dei monasteri femminili di Piacenza ne sec. XVI', in *Il Concilio di Trento e la riforma tridentina*, Rome 1965; Heinrich Lutz, 'Kardinal Ippolito II d' Este (1509–1572). Biographische Skizze eines weltlichen Kirchenfürsten', *Reformata Reformanda: Festgabe Für Hubert Jedin zum 17. Juni 1965*, ed. Erwin Iserloh and Konrad Reppegen, Münster, Westf. 1965, vol. 1, pp. 508–30; Barbara McClung Hallam, *Italian Cardinals, Reform and the Church as Property, 1492–1563*, Berkeley–Los Angeles–London 1985.

43. Quoted by Charles Schmitt in 'Gianfrancesco Pico della Mirandola and the Fifth Lateran Council', *Archivum für Reformationgeschichte*, 61, 1970, p. 168.

44. Quoted by Virginio Luigi Vernorio in an article full of relevant information, 'La Chiesa di Pavia nel secolo XVI . . . ', *Quaderni del seminario di Pavia*, 7–8, 1971.

45. Paschini, *S. Gaetano Thiene* (above, n. 4), pp. 36, 39; Romeo De Maio, *Alfonso Carafa, Cardinale di Napoli (1540–1565)*, Vatican City 1961, pp. 1–4; Lorenzo Tacchella, *Il processo agli eretici veronesi nel '500: S. Ignazio di Loyola e Luigi Lippomano (carteggio)*, Brescia 1979, Ch. 1.

46. Giovanni Guidiccioni to Gasparo Contarini, in Guidiccioni, *Opere*, ed. Carlo Minutoli, Florence 1867, vol. 2, pp. 263–64; Giovio quoted by Gigliola Fragnito in 'Gli "spirituali" e la fuga di Bernardino Ochino', *RSI*, 84, 1972; Niccolò Del Re, 'Pier Paolo Parisio, giurista e cardinale (1473–1545)', *RSCI*, 24, 1970.

47. Bembo in *Lettere*, Verona 1743, I, pp. 71–72; Denys Hay, *Italian Clergy and Italian Culture in the Fifteenth Century: Annual Lecture of the Society for Renaissance Studies*, Occasional Papers, no. 1, London 1973, p. 3.

48. Bull of 28 February 1533, in *I Barnabiti nel IV centenario dalla fondazione*, Genoa 1933, pp. viii–ix.

49. Quoted from Simon Rodriguez, *De origine progressu Societatis Iesu, Lisbon, 25 July 1577*, by Brian S. Pullan in *Rich and Poor* (above, n. 28), p. 265.

50. José C. Nieto, *Juan de Valdés and the Origins of the Spanish and Italian Reformation*, Geneva 1970, to be read in light of the findings of C. Gilly, 'Juan de Valdés: Übersetzer und Bearbeiter von Luthers Schriften in seinem *Dialogo de Doctrina*', *Archiv für Reformationgeschichte*, 74, 1983.

51. The details in Carlo De Frede, *La restaurazione cattolica in Inghilterra sotto Maria Tudor nel carteggio di Girolamo Seripando*, Naples 1971; Dermot Fenlon, *Heresy and Obedience in Tridentine Italy: Cardinal Pole and the Counter Reformation*, Cambridge 1972, esp. Ch. 3.

52. Louis Ponnelle and Louis Bordet, *Saint Philippe Néri et la société romaine de son temps, 1515–1595* (2nd edn), Paris 1958.

53. Gerónimo Nadal, *Commentarii de instituto Societatis Iesu*, ed. Michael Nicolau, Rome 1962, pp. 241–42.

54. Giuseppe Cagni and Franco M. Ghilardotti, 'I sermoni di Sant'Antonio Maria Zaccaria', *Archivio italiano per la storia della pietà*, 2, 1959, here quoted from p. 250.

55. Theatine constitution quoted from the English translation in Olin (ed.), *The Catholic Reformation* (above, n. 19), pp. 130–31.

56. The text in English translation in Olin (ed.), *The Catholic Reformation* (above, n. 19); on which: Hubert Jedin, *Il tipo ideale di vescovo secondo la riforma cattolica*, Ital. tr. E. Durini, Brescia 1950, and Gigliola Fragnito, 'Cultura umanistica e riforma religiosa: Il *De officio, viri boni ac probi episcopi* di Gasparo Contarini', *SV*, 11, 1969. On Barozzi, see Giuseppina De Sandre Gasparini, 'Uno studio sull'episcopato padovano di Pietro Barozzi (1487–1507) e altri contributi sui vescovi nel Quattrocento', *RSCI*, 34, 1980.

57. Richard M. Douglas, *Jacopo Sadoleto, 1477–1547: Humanist and Reformer*, Cambridge, Mass. 1959.

58. Quoted by Tacchella in the article cited above at n. 45.

59. Adriano Prosperi, 'Di alcuni testi per il clero nell'Italia del primo Cinquecento', *CS*, 7, 1968, and in general, Adriano Prosperi, *Tra Evangelismo e*

Controriforma: G. M. Giberti (1495–1543), Rome 1969; Paola Pavignani, 'Tullio Crispoldi da Rieti e il suo *Sommario* di prediche', *RSCI*, 28, 1974.

60. Galeazzo Florimonte, letter of 12 August 1537, in Ferrero (ed.), *Lettere del Cinquecento* (above, n. 41), pp. 165–66.

61. Scipione Ammirato in *Vescovi di Fiesole*, Florence 1637, pp. 51–53; Hubert Jedin, 'Der Episkopalist Braccio Martelli, Bischof von Fiesole. Nova et Vetera', *Römische Quartalschrift*, 60, 1968.

62. Quotations by Aldo Stella in 'La lettera del cardinale Contarini sulla predestinazione', *RSCI*, 15, 1961, p. 415, and by Antonino Poppi in 'La teologia nell'università e nelle scuole', in *Storia cult ven*, III, 1980–1981, p. 31. Celestino Piana, *La facoltà teologica dell'Università di Firenze nel Quattro e Cinquecento*, Grottaferrata 1977; Armando Verde, 'Dottorati a Firenze e a Pisa, 1505–1528', in Creytens and Künzel (eds), *Xenia Kaeppeli* (above, n. 27) (my count from his tables).

63. Anne Jacobson Schutte, in 'Printing, piety, and the people in Italy. The first thirty years', *Archivum für Reformationgeschichte*, 71, 1980, p. 13.

64. Pietro Bembo quoted by Paolo Simoncelli, 'Pietro Bembo e l'evangelismo italiano', *CS*, 15, 1978, p. 4.

65. Letter to Varchi of 1547 in Barocchi (ed.), *Trattati* (above, Chapter 6, n. 23), vol. 1, p. 60.

66. Cesare Vasoli, 'Alberto Pio e la cultura del suo tempo', and Luigi Balsamo, 'Alberto Pio e Aldo Manuzio editori a Venezia e Carpi fra '400 e '500', in *Società . . . Carpi* (above, n. 38). On the theological controversy provoked by Pomponazzi: Felix Gilbert, 'Cristianesimo, Umanesimo e la Bolla *Apostolici Regiminis* del 1513', *RSI*, 79, 1967.

67. Girolamo Parabosco, *Le piacevoli notti*, ed. Manilo Pastore Stocchi, Bari 1979, p. 44.

68. Described by John D'Amico, 'Beatus Rhenanus, Tertullian and the Reformation: A humanist's critique of Scholasticism', *Archiv für Reformationgeschichte*, 71, 1980, p. 47.

69. Antonio Rotondò, 'Per la storia dell'eresia a Bologna nel secolo XVI', *Rinascimento*, 2, 1962; Andrea Del Col, quoted from 'Il Nuovo Testamento tradotto da Massimo Teofilo' (above, n. 34), p. 141; Battista da Crema, *Lo specchio interiore*, Venice 1540.

70. Domingo de Santa Teresa, quoted from José C. Nieto, *Juan de Valdés* (above, n. 50), pp. 230–33; Romeo De Maio in *Riforme e miti* (above, n. 8), p. 85, and 'Eresia e mito della potestà pontificia nel processo romano a Savonarola', in *Movimenti ereticali in Italia e in Polonia nei secoli XVI–XVII*, Florence 1974; Massimo Firpo and Paolo Simoncelli, 'I processi inquisitoriali contro Savonarola (1558) e Carnesecchi (1566–1567): Una proposta di interpretazione', *Riv SLR*, 18, 1982.

71. Paolo Giustiniani quoted by Innocenzo Cervelli in 'Storiografia e problemi intorno alla vita religiosa e spirituale a Venezia' (above, n. 14), p. 465; Jacopo Bonfadio in *Gli annali di Genova dall' 1528, che ricuperò la libertà, fino al 1550*, tr. Bartolomeo Paschetti, Genoa 1597; Romeo De Maio, *Michelangelo e la Controriforma*, Rome and Bari 1978, pp. 67 and 77.

72. Peter Quinn, 'Ignatius Loyola and Gian Pietro Carafa. Catholic reformers at odds', *Catholic Historical Review*, 67, 1981, quoted (in English) on p. 391; Torano quoted by Pietro Tacchi Venturi in *Storia della Compagnia di Gesù in Italia* (above, n. 1), I, ii, p. 276.

73. Massimo Firpo and Dario Marcatto, 'Il primo processo inquisitoriale contro il cardinal Giovanni Morone (1552–1553)', *RSI*, 93, 1981, p. 76; Andrea Del Col quoting Anne Jacobson Schutte (and giving his own opinion here quoted on p. 527), in *RSI*, 92, 1980, pp. 520–28; and Del Col on Simoncelli, 'Per una sistemazione critica dell'evangelismo italiano e di un'opera recente', *CS*, 17, 1980 – a review of Paolo Simoncelli's *Evangelismo italiano del Cinquecento*, Rome 1979. Schutte in general on the dangers of the term 'Evangelism' in 'The *Lettere volgari* and the crisis of Evangelism in Italy', *Renaissance Quarterly*, 28, 1975.

74. Mario Rosa in *Religione e società* (above, n. 1), p. 187.

75. Letter to Morone from his vicar in Modena, quoted by Adriano Prosperi in 'Le istituzioni ecclesiastiche e le idee religiose', in Paolo, Rossi (ed.), *Il Rinascimento nelle corti padane*, Bari 1977; Antonio Santosuosso, 'The moderate Inquisitor: Giovanni Della Casa's Venetian Nunciature, 1544–1549', *SV*, n.s. 2, 1978.

76. Gustavo Cantini, *I Francescani d'Italia di fronte alle dottrine luterane e calviniste durante il Cinquecento*, Rome 1948 (here quoted from the Capitolo Generale of 1521); Tommaso Radini Tedeschi, *Orazione contro Filippo Melantone*, tr. and ed. Flaminio Ghizzoni, Brescia 1973 (with the Latin on facing pages); Aretino to the Cardinal of Ravenna, 29 August 1537, in *Lettere* (above, n. 37), p. 224; Carter Lindberg, 'Prierias and his significance for Luther's development', *The Sixteenth Century Journal* 3, 1972; and for much more information, Friedrich Lauchert, *Die italienischen literarischen Gegner Luthers*, Freiburg-im-Breisgau 1912 (the quotation from Isidoro is on p. 206).

77. Barbara McClung Hallman, 'Italian "natural superiority: 1517–1546" and the Lutheran question', *Archiv für Reformationgeschichte*, 71, 1980; Jared Wicks in the preface to his edition of *Cajetan Responds: A Reader in Reformation Controversy*, Washington 1978; Campeggi in Gerhard Müller, *Die römische Kurie und die Reformation, 1523–1534: Kirche und Politik während des Pontifikates Clemens VII*, Gütersloh 1969, p. 279.

78. John F. D'Amico, 'A humanist response to Martin Luther: Raffaele Maffei's *Apologeticus*', *The Sixteenth Century Journal*, 6, 1975; Albano Biondi, 'La giustificazione della simulazione nel Cinquecento', in *Eresia e Riforma* (above, n. 27).

79. Florimonte's letter to G. Ariosto, 5 July 1537, in Ferrero (ed.), *Lettere del Cinquecento* (above, n. 41), p. 162.

80. Aldo Stella, *Dall'Anabattismo al Socinianesimo nel Cinquecento veneto*, Padua 1967, and 'L'ecclesiologia degli Anabattisti processati a Trieste', in *Eresia e Riforma* (above, n. 27). What is still considered to be the standard work on the subject in most English-speaking scholarly circles, George H. Williams, *The Radical Reformation*, Philadelphia 1962, must be read along with the corrections and supplementary information provided by Antonio Rotondò in his indispensable 'I movimenti ereticali nell'Europa del '500', *RSI*, 78, 1966.

81. Charmarie Jenkins Blaisdell, 'Politics and heresy in Ferrara, 1534–1559', *The Sixteenth Century Journal*, 6, 1975; Valerio Marchetti, *Gruppi ereticali senesi del Cinquecento*, Florence 1975; Michele Miele, 'La penetrazione protestante a Salerno verso la metà del Cinquecento', in *Miscellanea Gilles Gérard Meersseman*, Padua 1970; Cesare Bianco, 'La comunità di "fratelli" nel movimento ereticale modenese del '500', *RSI*, 92, 1980, from which the passage here quoted from Pietro Antonio da Cervia is taken (p. 625).

82. Critical reviews of the immense (and often polemical) literature on the *Beneficio* are given by Mario Rosa, '*Il Beneficio di Cristo*: Interpretazione a confronto', *Bibliothèque d'humanisme et renaissance*, 40, 1978; by Carlo Ginzburg and Adriano Prosperi, *Giochi di Pazienza: Un seminario sul Beneficio di Cristo*, Turin 1975; and by Paolo Simoncelli in 'Nuove ipotesi e studi sul *Beneficio di Cristo*', *CS*, 12, 1975. An English translation by Ruth Prelowski is published in John Tedeschi (ed.), *Italian Reformation Studies in Honor of Laelius Socinus*, Florence 1965 (which contains several other relevant studies). For the authorship: Salvatore Caponetto on 'Benedetto da Mantova' in *DBI* and in the introduction to his edition of Benedetto da Mantova's *Il Beneficio di Cristo*, Florence and Chicago 1972.

83. The standard work is still Delio Cantimori, *Eretici italiani del Cinquecento* (1939), Florence 1967, although it has since been extensively supplemented in the detailed essays of Antonio Rotondò in *Studi e ricerche di storia ereticale italiana del Cinquecento*, Turin 1974. On Ochino in particular: Roland Bainton, *Bernardino Ochino, esule e riformatore senese del Cinquecento, 1487–1563*, Florence 1940. Philip McNair, *Peter Martyr in Italy: An Anatomy of Apostasy*, Oxford 1967, is marred by the author's misgivings about Cantimori's Marxism and by his conviction that nothing so serious as the doctrines he describes could possibly have been adopted by Italians. See also Robert M. Kingdon, 'Peter Martyr Vermigli, scholastic or humanist?' in Joseph C. McLelland (ed.), *Peter Martyr Vermigli and Italian Reform*, Waterloo, Ontario 1980, p. 126. On Geneva: John Tedeschi and F. David Willis, 'Two Italian Translations of Beza and Calvin', *Archiv für Reformationgeschichte*, 55, 1964, and the several essays in *Ginevra e l'Italia*, ed. Delio Cantimori, Florence 1959, as well as in *Genève et l'Italie*, ed. L. Monnier, Geneva 1969. The quotation is from the deposition on p. 32 of Carlo Ginzburg (ed.), *I costituti di don Pietro Manelfi*, Florence and Chicago 1970.

84. Letter of Dionisio Zannettini to Cardinal Farnese, 25 June 1546, in Gustavo Cantini, *I Francescani d'Italia di fronte alle dottrine luterane e calviniste durante il Cinquecento*, Rome 1948, p. 44.

85. Quoted by Aldo Stella in 'L'orazione di Pier Paolo Vergerio al Doge Francesco Donà sulla riforma della Chiesa (1545)', *Atti dell'Istituto veneto di scienze, lettere ed arti*, 128, 1969–70. On Bernardini, see Benedetto Carderi, 'Il trattato della perfetta obbedienza di fra Paolino Bernardini O.P. (d. 1585)', in *Archivio italiano per la storia della pietà*, 2, 1959, p. 73. On Vergerio, see Anne Jacobson Schutte, *Pier Paolo Vergerio: The Making of an Italian Reformer*, Geneva 1977, p. 107.

86. Wolfram Wettges, *Reformation und Propaganda*, Stuttgart 1978, p. 62. In general: Antonio Rotondò, 'La censura ecclesiastica e la cultura', in *Einaudi Storia d'Italia*, vol. 5, part 2.

87. Girolamo Garimberto, *Delle vite, overo, fatti memorabili d'alcuni papi e di tutti i cardinali*, Venice 1568, pp. 278 ff.; Claudio Tolomei to Gabriel Cesano (n.d.), in his *De le lettere* (2nd edn), Venice 1549, pp. 202 ff. Alain Dufour quoted in *Bibliothèque d'humanisme et renaissance*, 45, 1983, p. 200; Mignanelli quoted by Benedetto Nicolini in 'Il frate osservante Bonaventura de Cento e il nunzio Fabio Mignanelli: Episodio di vita religiosa veneziana del Cinquecento', *Studi in onore di Riccardo Filangieri*, Naples 1959, II, pp. 373–74.

88. Schutte, *Pier Paolo Vergerio* (above, n. 55), quoted here from p. 216. On the trial itself: Antonio Santosuosso (as well as for the perceptive thesis on religion in Venice as a whole), 'Religion *more veneto* and the trial of Pier Paolo Vergerio',

in McLelland (ed.), *Peter Martyr Vermigli* (above, n. 83), and (particularly on conflicts of jurisdiction) 'The moderate Inquisitor: Giovanni Della Casa's Venetian Nunciature' (above, n. 75).

89. Mario Bendiscioli, 'Penetrazione protestante e repressione controriformistica all'epoca di Carlo e Federico Borromeo in Lombardia', in Erwin Iserloh and Peter Manns (eds), *Festgabe Joseph Lortz*, Baden-Baden 1958, quoting the inquisitor in vol. 1, p. 370; Susanna Peyronel Rambaldi, *Speranze e crisi nel Cinquecento modenese. Tensioni religiose e vita cittadina ai tempi di Giovanni Morone*, Milan 1979; Cesare Bianco, 'La communità di "fratelli" nel movimento ereticale modenese del '500,' *RSI*, 92, 1980; Massimo Firpo, 'Gli "spirituali", l'Accademia di Modena e il formulario di fede del 1542: Controllo del dissenso religioso e nicodemismo', *Riv SLR*, 20, 1984.

90. Pietro Pirri, 'Episodi della lotta contro l'eresia a Siena', *Archivum Historicum Societatus Iesu*, 32, 1963.

91. John Tedeschi, 'Preliminary observations on writing a history of the Roman Inquisition', in F. Forrester Church and Timothy George (eds), *Continuity and Discontinuity in Church History: Essays Presented to George Huntston Williams on the Occasion of his 65th Birthday*, Leiden 1979. The proceedings of a typical trial are published in English translation by John Tedeschi and Josephine von Henneberg in *Italian Reformation Studies in Honor of Laelius Socinus*, Florence 1965.

92. John W. O'Malley, 'Lutheranism in Rome, 1542–43', *Thought*, 54, 1979; Silvana Seidel Menchi, 'Le traduzioni italiane di Lutero nella prima metà del Cinquecento', *Rinascimento*, 17, 1977; Adriano Prosperi, 'Una cripto-ristampa dell'epistola di Giorgio Siculo', *Bollettino della Società di Studi Valdesi*, 134, 1973.

93. Girolamo Muzzarelli quoted by Massimo Firpo and Dario Marcatto in *RSI* (above, n. 73), p. 142; Averardo Serristori to Cosimo, 19 September 1555, in the edition of Serristori's letters edited by Giuseppe Canestrini, Florence 1853, p. 375.

94. Pio Paschini, 'Un vescovo disgraziato', in his *Tre ricerche* (above, n. 20); Massimo Firpo, 'Filippo II, Paolo IV e il processo inquisitoriale del cardinal Giovanni Morone', *RSI*, 95, 1983 (here quoted from p. 8). The trial records are now being published as *Il processo inquisitoriale del cardinal Giovanni Morone*, Rome, vol. 1, ed. Massimo Firpo, 1981; vols 2 and 3, ed. Massimo Firpo and Dario Marcatto, 1983 and 1985, respectively.

95. Gianfrancesco Ripa quoted from his tract *De peste* of 1522 by Mario Ascheri in *Un maestro del Mos Italicus: Gianfrancesco Sannazari della Ripa (1480–1535)*, Milan 1970, p. 49.

96. Michele Miele, 'La riforma dei conventi nel Cinquecento', *Memorie Domenicane*, 3, 1972 (here quoted); Ruzante here quoted from the *Prima orazione* to Cardinal Cornaro in *Ruzante, Teatro*, ed. Ludovico Zorzi, Turin 1967, p. 1200; Gelli quoted from *Ragionamento* 4 of his *Capricci del bottaio*, ed. Amelia Alesima, Naples 1969.

97. Mario Scaduto, 'La vita religiosa in Sicilia secondo un memoriale inedito del 1563', *RSCI*, 28, 1974 (here quoted from p. 577). Many other cases cited in Federico Chabod's great work, *Lo Stato e la vita religiosa a Milano nell'epoca di Carlo V*, Turin 1971.

98. Petition of Andrea Hertele quoted by Giovanni Mantese, *Memorie storiche della chiesa vicentina*, III, ii, Vicenza 1964, p. 255; Cassiano del Pozzo quoted from

his *Memoriale* of 1560 in Lino Marini's *Libertà e tramonti di libertà nello Stato sabaudo*, Bologna 1968, appendix, pp. 135–36; Borghini to Cosimo, 3 February 1563, in W. Gaye (ed.), *Carteggio inedito d'artisti dei secoli XIV, XV, XVI*, Florence 1839–40, vol. 3, p. 92; Decree of 17 April 1545, in Lorenzo Cantini, *Legislazione toscana*, Florence 1800–1808 (here quoted).

99. Cosimo quoted in the catalogue *Firenze e la Toscana dei Medici*, Florence 1983, pp. 51–52 (along with his detailed report on the conditions of the Church in his dominions). He describes his obligations in a letter of 26 August 1558 to the cardinal of Santa Fiora, in his *Lettere*, ed. Giorgio Spini, Florence 1940, pp. 170–73. In general, Arnaldo D'Addario, 'Il problema "De Vita et Moribus Clericorum" nella diocesi di Firenze', in *Chiesa e società dal secolo IV ai tempi nostri: Studi storici in onore di Ilarino da Milano*, Rome 1979.

100. Hubert Jedin on Tommaso Campeggi in *DBI*, vol. 17, pp. 472–74.

101. Lodovico Beccadelli to Cervini, 29 January 1544, in the crossed-out passage published by Adriano Prosperi in *Riv SLR*, 10, 1974, p. 197.

102. W. B. Patterson, 'The idea of renewal in Girolamo Aleander's conciliar thought', in *Renaissance and Renewal in Christian History*, ed. Derek Baker, Oxford 1977.

103. The standard study is still Giuseppe Alberigo's *I vescovi italiani al Concilio di Trento*, Florence 1959. On the *de iure* question: Alberigo's 'Le potestà episcopali nei dibattiti tridentini', in *Il Concilio di Trento e la Riforma tridentina* (Milan 1965, pp. 471–523), and Ch. 1 of his *Lo sviluppo della dottrina sui poteri nella chiesa universale*, Rome 1964.

104. Umberto Mazzone, 'Sussidi papali e libertà di voto al Concilio di Trento (1561–1563)', *Cristianesimo nella storia*, 1, 1980.

105. Quoted by Adriano Prosperi in 'Intellettuali e chiesa all'inizio dell'età moderna', *Einaudi Storia d'Italia, Annali 4*, Turin 1981, p. 222. On visitations: Umberto Mazzone and Angelo Turchini (eds), *Le visite pastorali*, Bologna 1985.

106. Gilles-Gérard Meersseman, 'Il tipo ideale di parroco secondo la riforma tridentina nelle sue fonti letterarie', in *Il Concilio di Trento e la Riforma tridentina*, Milan 1965.

107. All this from the Introduction of Alberto Marani to his edition of Muzio Calini's *Lettere conciliari (1561–1563)*, Brescia 1963.

108. Antonio Rotondò, 'Atteggiamenti della vita morale italiana del Cinquecento: La pratica nicodemitica', *RSI*, 79, 1967. The methodological and philological foundations of Carlo Ginzburg's much praised *Il nicodemismo*, Turin 1970, have been critically challenged by Carlos M. N. Eire in 'Calvin and Nicodemism: A reappraisal', *The Sixteenth Century Journal*, 10, 1979.

109. Brucioli's deposition of 11 June 1555 in the appendix to Andrea Del Col, 'Il secondo processo veneziano di Antonio Brucioli', *Bollettino della Società di Studi Valdesi*, 146, 1979, p. 92, and the deposition of the former governor quoted by Domenico Maselli in *Saggi di storia ereticale lombarda al tempo di San Carlo*, Naples 1979, p. 35.

110. Giuliano Pellegrini, 'Michelangelo Florio e le sue *Regole de la lingua thoscana*', *Studi di filologia italiana*, 12, 1954; Carlo De Frede, 'Un calabrese del '500 emigrato a Ginevra', *Archivio per le provincie napolitane*, 10, 1972, Peter G. Bietenholz, 'Mino Celsi and the toleration controversy of the sixteenth century', *Bibliothèque d'humanisme et renaissance*, 34, 1972, and in *DBI*, vol. 23, pp. 478–82; and Manfred E. Welti, 'Il progetto fallito di un edizione cinquecentesca delle opere complete di Antonio de Ferrariis, detto il Galateo', *Archivio*

per le provincie napolitane, 898, 1972. Of the more important of the many recent studies of the religious exiles in eastern Europe: Domenico Caccamo, *Eretici italiani in Moravia, Polonia, Transilvania*, Florence and Chicago 1970, and Massimo Firpo, *Antitrinitari nell'Europa orientale del '500*, Florence 1977.

CHAPTER EIGHT

Consolidation

PEACE

The disastrous defeat at Saint-Quentin (10 August 1557) finally dissipated the last of a half-century of dreams on the part of four successive kings of France about extending their dominions throughout the Italian peninsula. Financial exhaustion prevented the king of Spain, the bearer of equally universal and pre-nationalist dreams of empire, from following up his unexpected victory. After two years of fruitless skirmishing and five months of intense negotiations, the plenipotentiaries of the two European superpowers at last put their signatures to what, from the place in which they met, came to be called the Treaty of Cateau-Cambrésis. The French agreed to withdraw not only from their distant outposts in the Senese and at Mirandola, but also from those parts of the domains of the duke of Savoy and the Republic of Genoa that they had formally annexed. The Spanish agreed not to interfere in French internal affairs. King Philip, now the widower of Queen Mary Tudor of England, agreed to marry King Henry's daughter Isabelle. Duke Emanuele Filiberto of Savoy, the main beneficiary of the treaty, agreed to marry Henry's aunt Marguérite. The consequences of the Battle of Pavia of 1525, the Treaty of Barcelona of 1529 and the Alliance of Bologna of 1531 were recognized as definitive. And the wars of Italy came to an end.

The Treaty of Cateau-Cambrésis, of course, did not settle everything immediately. The 'great consolation and joy' felt by 'the afflicted people of Piedmont' upon the proclamation of peace was considerably dampened by the news that the French army of occupation was still ensconced in the fortresses of Turin and Pinerolo and that it was demanding still another extraordinary tax levy as the price of evacuating them.[1] Indeed, not until 1600, when he traded his Rhône province of Bresse for Saluzzo, did the duke finally manage to get the French completely out of Piedmont; and not until then did his dominions at last become the 'Italic Wall' which, according to the pastoral poet Battista Guarini, would take the place of the all-too-porous Alps in protecting Italy from from transalpine invaders.

Meanwhile, the eastern frontiers of Italy remained as insecure as ever. In

1567 the Turks almost managed to capture Malta – and thus to acquire a secure base from which they might raid the Tyrrhenian coast at will. In 1570 they responded to an appeal by Venice's subjects in Cyprus by invading the island – and by displaying all over Asia Minor the skin they had peeled off the still-living flesh of the Venetian commander. They then set out to make their conquest permanent – by encouraging the Greek-speaking nobility to convert to Islam and by guaranteeing the property of all Venetian women who married Turks. At that moment, fortunately, the tide began to turn. The loss of Cyprus was exactly what Pope Pius v needed to persuade Venice to join the Italo-Spanish coalition of Malta. When a huge Turkish fleet assembled off Navpaktos (which Italians called Lepanto and pronounced 'Lépanto') emerged from the Gulf of Corinth for the obvious purpose of launching a full-scale invasion of the western Mediterranean, it was met by the combined Spanish, Neapolitan, papal and Venetian fleets. After a day-long battle that left some 29,000 Turks dead or captured amid the 'frightful & horrible spectacle . . . of an infinite number of bodies floating in a blood-coloured sea', the Turkish fleet had been totally destroyed.[2] To the amazement of the allies themselves, what had long been considered the inevitable expansion of the Ottoman Empire into Italy had been definitively halted.

The religious wars in France, the division of the German states into mutually hostile leagues and increasing signs of administrative and economic breakdown in the over-expanded Ottoman Empire guaranteed the continuing observance of the terms of Cateau-Cambrésis and of the post-Lepanto peace treaties. Meanwhile, internal peace among the Italian states was assured by the smooth passage of hegemonic power from Emperor Charles v to his son, Philip, to whom Charles one-by-one turned over his titles to Naples, Sicily, Sardinia, and Milan. Upon his father's abdication in 1555, Philip became king of Spain as well. He settled down to administer his far-flung empire from his new capital in Madrid and entrusted the administration of his Italian dominions to one of the several councils that composed his central government (the Council of Italy).

What had been an Imperial hegemony – one in which Italians could feel themselves participants as well as subjects – thus became a Spanish or, more properly, a Castilian hegemony: one in which Italians could be only subjects. When Philip decided to choose his administrative representatives not from all parts of his empire, as his father had done, but exclusively from Castile, and to rotate them frequently from one post to another rather than leaving them on indefinite tenure in the same place, the hegemony assumed an even more pronounced non-Italian character. To be sure, some poets tried to emphasize the continuity between one hegemony and the other:

> You, holy Philip, before whose brow
> Fortune still trembles, as it did
> before your ever-invincible and eternal father.[3]

Some artists drew attention to one advantage of the new hegemony: the strikingly handsome appearance of the new hegemon, whom Titian painted during his homage-collecting tour of Italy with plain grey hose protruding from a suit of thigh-length armour (*Philip* II, Madrid: Prado). But the difference was clearly recognized on the occasion of the funeral ceremonies honouring Charles V in 1559. In Rome they were celebrated at the church of S. Giacomo degli Spagnoli. In Bologna they were celebrated at the Spanish College; and the usual round of processions, orations and concerts was accompanied by the distribution of a limited edition of a biography of Cardinal Albornoz, the Spanish conqueror of the Papal State in the fourteenth century, by the contemporary Spanish historian Juan Ginés de Sepùlveda.

To be sure, the Spanish were never popular in Italy, particularly not in those Italian states of which the legitimate ruler happened also to be the king of Spain. The Neapolitans resented being asked to pay for the wars their king was waging in the Netherlands, which did not in the least concern them; and the Milanese resented having to dedicate some three-quarters of their annual state budget to the wages and upkeep of a standing army in their territory – the last of the Spanish standing armies left in Italy. The king's local representatives did little to dissipate this resentment. They remained uncompromisingly Spanish during their short terms of duty in Italy. Only those few of them who then settled there – like Alfonso de Ulloa, who gave up a military career to join the publishing house of Gioliti de' Ferrari in Venice – ever became more than superficially acquainted with the culture and language of their host country. The Italians reciprocated. Few of them took advantage of the grammar Ulloa wrote for them in order to learn correct Castilian. Those who became interested in one or another of the current products of Spanish literary culture contented themselves with the many available translations.[4]

After the transfer of Spain's main military commitments from Italy to the Netherlands, and after the fiasco of Pope Paul IV's pseudo-patriotic project for driving them out, the Spanish at least became less unpopular. The few Spanish soldiers still in Italy usually stayed off the streets, and most of the Spanish officials in Naples stayed within the quarter of the city where most of them lived. Since they changed place so frequently, Spanish administrators were more dependent upon, and hence more disposed to collaborate with, their Italian colleagues. For only resident natives could furnish them with information they needed for discharging their duties – information like that contained in the several *Descrizioni* of the provinces and cities of the Kingdom of Naples published in the last decades of the century for the enlightenment of uninformed viceroys. Spanish governors often yielded to their native collaborators in pursuing foreign policies not necessarily consonant with those of the king – like the treaty the Milanese signed with the Swiss cantons on 15 May 1588. And the legal-minded King Philip guaranteed the autonomy of both by scrupulously respecting the rights granted in his subjects' charters. That is what he did most notably in the case of a new tax assessment in the Duchy of Milan: in order to protect the subject cities from possible exploitation by the metropolis, he waited until all of them had submitted recommendations before passing on his own recommendation to the governor.[5]

Sixteenth-century Italians, or at least sixteenth-century Sicilians, often found it convenient to make the Spanish scapegoats for their own failures. But what justifiable resentment they bore them was amply offset by their recognition that the government of Spain was in many ways an idealized version of their own post-1530 states. For the king of Spain was the most prudent, most hard-working and least corruptible of all contemporary monarchs, and the Spanish armed forces formed an indispensable link in their defence lines around the peninsula as a whole and, best of all, the presence of Spanish agents in Italy was the most effective guarantee of internal peace. When the Parma playwright Giuseppe Leggiardo Galliani tried to blame the Spanish for all the misfortunes suffered by his tragic heroes between the Sack of Rome and the Piacenza War, his audiences yawned; and he was permitted to pass his life in perfect tranquility under the benign protection of a most Spanish viceroy in Naples.

Thanks, indeed, to the Spanish hegemony, diplomacy finally replaced war as the normal means for settling the political problems of Italy. Diplomacy was also relatively expensive. Two Swiss embassies to Milan in 1587 cost the Milanese treasury alone some 23,577 *scudi* – for sixty-four gold neckbands, thirty-one medals, and full expenses for all 193 members of the delegation. The Florentine ambassadors sent to congratulate King Philip III on his marriage in 1599 brought along, among other gifts, a diamond-studded belt worth 150,000 *scudi* and twenty-two pieces of gold-embroidered cloth. But diplomacy was much less expensive than war. It had an added advantage for Italian governments in that it enabled them to ship off well-connected trouble-makers on a constant round of foreign missions. It also had the inestimable advantage for the king of Spain of permitting him to pursue his military commitments on the frontier of his empire without fear of being undermined by troubles in the interior.

Diplomacy, not force, finally put an end to the warmest of the mid-century cold wars, the one between the Medici and the Este. The contenders agreed to stop insulting each other's female ancestors (Duke Ercole's mother Lucrezia Borgia, said Cosimo, was a 'figliola di prete', a priest's daughter, which she certainly was),[6] to dissuade their subjects in the Garfagnana from raiding each other and to let the emperor, the pope and the king decide which of their ambassadors should appear first at ceremonious occasions. They then cemented the agreement in a double marriage. Duke Alfonso married Cosimo's legit-imate daughter Lucrezia. His illegitimate son and heir-apparent Cesare married Cosimo's illegitimate daughter Virginia. And their descendants lived happily side-by-side ever after. Diplomacy was also responsible for accomplishing the one important change in political jurisdiction of the entire half-century practically without a drop of blood. For so assiduously had Pope Clement VIII cultivated the good will of the Ferrarese, and so loudly had he advertised the succession agreement drawn up by Duke Ercole and Pope Paul III some fifty years earlier, that Cardinal Piero Aldobrandini's invasion of 1598, when Duke Alfonso II died without a legitimate heir, amounted to little more than a colourful parade – exactly the opposite of Julius II's invasion of Bologna, for much the same reasons, in 1506. Cesare d'Este became the duke of Modena alone – that is, of the half of his father's dominion that lay within Imperial rather than papal jurisdication, while retaining title to all his father's private property in Ferrara. A papal legate took the place of the former duke in what was now the papal province of Ferrara. And even the Venetians, whose own appetite for Ferrara had provoked a pan-Italian war a century before, quietly looked the other way.

At the same time, law took the place of violence in regulating differences between rulers and subjects within each state. Some princes won the confidence of their subjects by redistributing the tax burden in accordance with more equitable assessments – like the ones decreed in Florence in 1551 and 1561 and in Piacenza in 1575. Others launched 'public relations' campaigns aimed at augmenting not their glory, but their popularity: so graciously did Grand Duke Ferdinando distribute food to the stricken as he rowed around flooded Florence in 1589 that the unpopularity gained by his reclusive predecessor vanished into history. Still others took care to transmit the glory they won personally to the states they ruled. The delicate, stiff-lipped pre-adolescent Alessandro Farnese was prepared for his future military career not by any of his glorious ancestors, but by the painter Girolamo Bedoli's (d. 1569) well-fed Roman matron named 'Parma' (Parma: Galleria Nazionale). The citizens of Piacenza gratefully acknowledged the glory he later won for them as King Philip's military governor of the Netherlands by erecting a life-size equestrian statue next to that of Duke Ranuccio in front of the city hall. Still other princes skilfully toned down with timely gestures of reconciliation the violence they did exert. The Genoese Senate shifted the blame for its previous misrule of Corsica onto the Banco di San Giorgio and then, with the *Statuti civili* of 1569–71, stripped the Banco of all its previous political jurisdiction. It now assured the Corsicans of representation on all local councils while reserving the most important posts for mainlanders. Finally, it enlisted the bishops to persuade Alfonso, the son of the former rebel leader Sampiero, that 'much greater glory awaited him amid the honourable feats of war in France.' The notoriously rebellious Corsicans settled down for an unprecedented period of calm submission that was to last for over a century.

So successful were such measures that the few challenges to the Italian governments were easily contained. One challenge was checked by compromise: when the Piedmontese Waldensians were disowned by their chief foreign ally, John Calvin, and when the duke of Savoy realized that he would never be able to force his way into their impregnable mountain valleys, the two parties signed the Treaty of Cavour (1561). Another challenge, that of the peasants of the Valtellina against their non-resident Milanese landlords, was resolved by a decree of the high court at Coira in 1572 – notwithstanding a direct threat of peasant uprisings against the magistrates by a 'turba non modica rusticorum'.[7] Still another, that of the city of Urbino in 1572, was crippled from the start by the nature of the insurgents' programme. Forgetful of the almost identical experience of the Perugians some thirty years earlier, they persisted in believing that, with enough *virtù*, a single commune could overcome the greatest of odds; and they made no effort to obtain the support of the other cities of the duchy. Moreover, they attacked the effect, the new meat tax, rather than the cause, the spendthrift habits of the duke, of whom they never tired of proclaiming themselves the 'loving subjects'. Hence, peace was easily restored simply by chopping off the heads of a few ringleaders and pardoning everyone else.[8]

Only those with close ties to political power could hope to modify the established order. The discovery of several cases of election rigging and embezzlement between 1579 and 1582 whittled away still more of the prestige, already severely compromised by the Cyprus War, of the two main organs of the Venetian government, the Ten (*Dieci*) and the Zonta. The Senators deprived them of several of the functions, particularly in foreign affairs, that they had 'usurped' in the aftermath of the disaster of 1509. The other of these challenges was resolved with a minimum of violence. Annoyed by the constant complaints of the 'New' nobles over the paucity of offices reserved for them by the Doria constitution of 1528, the 'Old' nobles of Genoa seceded in 1575 – that is, they moved out to their estates in Liguria. Fortunately the secession was compromised by the good number of them who quietly remained behind. When both Gregory XIII and Philip II, to whom the two parties instantly appealed, decided to act, in good post-Cateau-Cambrésis style, not as dividers and conquerors, but as mediators, the two 'nobilities' agreed to a new constitution. The legal distinctions between them were abolished, along with the *alberghi* that made smaller families the subjects of more powerful ones. Ninety-four new families were added to the eligibility list. In good 'republican' style, a rigorous censorship was instituted to preclude any subsequent criticism of this arrangement.[9]

Of the two challenges that aimed at, but failed to effect, constitutional changes, the first was by far the more serious. For the revolt of Naples in 1585, not against 'the Spanish', as the name usually given it today implies, but in the name of the king of Spain against the maladministration (*malgoverno*) of local officials, was supported by the lowest as well as by the middle classes of the city. It was to some extent justified by the claim not to innovate, but simply to restore constitutional rights previously granted by Ferrante II and Charles V. And it was conducted in accordance with a long-established 'liturgy' of popular uprisings that had proved fairly effective as recently as the anti-Inquisition uprising of 1547. Consequently, it was put down with a display of cruelty surpassing even that shown by the insurgents: thirty-two persons condemned to death, seventy-one to the galleys and 300 to banishment from the kingdom. And it resulted not in a change in the constitution, but in the formation of a new political balance of power – one based on an alliance between the viceroy and the feudal barons that dominated the kingdom until the next uprising in 1647.[10]

The other unsuccessful revolt was indeed supported, or at least abetted, by several of the bishops and by most of the Dominican and Augustinian friars of Calabria. But since it aimed at nothing less than the earthly inauguration of the utopian 'City of the Sun' imagined by its sole ideologue, the famous philosopher Tommaso Campanella (1568–1639), and since the possibility of accomplishing this aim rested on nothing more than Campanella's prophesies about the millenarian events scheduled by the stars for the year 1600, it was put down simply by sending a boatload of friars off to Naples. Its sole lasting effect was a complete change of mind on the part of the philosopher-prophet. Italians were very fortunate, Campanella subsequently told the 'princes of Italy', to be subject to Spain. For 'being very few' yet 'governing two worlds', the Spanish are 'timid'; and this timidity 'makes them courteous, cautious, reserved, obedient and wise' and thus worthy of the mission entrusted by God to the universal 'Monarchy of Spain' on behalf of all Christians.[11]

The achievement of internal peace permitted the rulers of the Italian states to direct their attention to the most urgent problem they shared with the rulers of many other European states at the time: banditry. Why this problem should have become so acute at this particular moment is a question that still baffles historians, who are usually forced to fall back on that historiographical-ideological catch-all of all unexplainable phenomena, 'crisis'. By the 1570s, in any case, bands of armed robbers had become so powerful in the mountains of south and central Italy that the economic lifeline between Naples and Puglia was in danger of being completely severed. Through their famous leader, the Italian 'Robin Hood', Marco Sciarra, they offered stiff competition to the established authorities for the loyalty of the rural population. As one well-informed observer remarked:

Neither in the villages nor in the cities – almost not in Rome itself – was there security of persons or property. It is impossible to say how many men they killed or in how many places or how many things they stole.[12]

The governments finally decided to collaborate, rather than, as had been the custom, to continue using the bandits as trumps against one another. By the end of the pontificate of that most determined bandit hunter, Sixtus v, the problem had been, if not resolved, at least brought under control. And Italians were at last able to enjoy all the fruits of one of the longest periods of peace their country had known.

PROSPERITY

As war and plague had provoked the demographic disasters of the first decades of the century, so peace, and a rapid decrease in the frequency and the virulence of epidemics, established the conditions for a notable increase in population in the decades after 1530.[13]

Population statistics for the sixteenth century must be used with caution. Most civil censuses were conducted largely, if not exclusively, for the assessment of taxable property; and they undoubtedly passed up a good number of residents from whom no revenue could be expected. Ecclesiastical censuses were conducted for the purpose of enabling ordinaries to check on the progress of the Tridentine reforms; and the complexity of the items on the question-naires – which touched on everything from the reception of sacraments to the state of unhappy marriages – was such that it apparently surpassed the administrative talents of the 44 out of 79 parish priests who failed to respond even in the classically Tridentine diocese of Milan.

Still, the census-takers of the age of political reconstruction and ecclesi-astical reform had far more incentive to be accurate than any of their prede-cessors, at least since the famous Florentine catasto of 1427. Moreover, many of their inaccuracies in terms of absolute numbers are unimportant and show clearly that wherever war continued or reappeared for any appreciable length of time – as it did in Tuscany during the decade after the first Florentine census of 1551–52 – the population fell. On the other hand, wherever wars had been only temporarily disruptive, as they were in Pisa after 1509, the population quickly recovered.[14] Wherever even the threat of war disappeared, as it did in the Veneto after its reconquest by the Venetians, the recovery took place even more rapidly. Verona, which had fallen from 47,000 in 1501 to 26,000 after the Peace of Cambrai (1529), reached 32,574 in 1541. By 1558 it had well surpassed its pre-Cambrai population. The whole contado of Vicenza rose from 143,000 to 200,000 between 1558 and the next census of 1629.[15]

Usually the end of war was a more effective stimulant of population than the preservation of peace. The population of Lecce increased by 50 percent during the first fifteen years after the end of the last civil war, but only 20 percent during the next fifty years – from 30,000 to 36,000 in 1595.[16] Pavia grew by 120 percent in the first twelve years after 1529; another 45 percent increase – from 11,000 to 15,000–16,000 – took almost fifty-five years to accomplish.[17] Population losses were found in those areas that had served as refuges from war – like the mountains of Parma, which lost 1,791 of its wartime high of 10,490 during the half-century after 1593.[18]

Such, indeed, was the momentum of the demographic recovery that the only two demographic disasters of the late sixteenth century halted it only momentarily: the plague of 1575–76, which cut the population of Venice from considerably more than the 168,627 recorded in 1563 to only 134,871 in 1581, and the severe food shortages of 1590–92, which reduced the population of Modena from 19,911 to 15,451 in less than three years. By the end of the century, Italy had once again become the most populous part of Europe – much more densely populated than France, the Netherlands and Hungary, which had been devastated by invasions and civil war.

It had also become the most prosperous. Economic recovery seems to have begun in those same parts of Italy that first experienced demographic recovery, and probably for the same reasons. It also seems to have begun in those very enterprises, like wool and silk manufacturing, commerce and banking, that had been the mainstay of the northern Italian economy before the advent of the calamities. Largely in response to the ruin of former competitors on the mainland, the production of wool in Venice rose from

4,701 pieces in 1521 to 26,541 in 1569. The competitors then recovered as well, lowering but not reversing the pace of growth in Venice. Wool production in Bergamo climbed from 7,000–8,000 pieces in 1540 to 26,500 in 1561 and in Florence from 18,500 in 1527 to 30,000 in 1572.

The traditional centres of the more recent manufacture of silk cloth recovered in much the same manner. In Florence, applications for entrance into the guild rose from an average of 60–70 a year between 1490 and 1499 to 240–50 between 1540 and 1549. In Naples they rose from 195 a year during the decade of the 1560s to 255 after 1591. Meanwhile, silk manufacturing spread to other cities as well – to Como, for instance, where the pioneering initiative of the immigrant Pietro Boldoni to train 'our women' with the help of outside experts eventually attracted several other immigrant entrepreneurs. The growth of northern silk manufacturing stimulated the production of raw silk in Calabria. Notwithstanding the efforts of all northern governments to encourage cultivation of silk worms at home, the receipts from the Calabrian export tax rose from an average of 18,000 *ducati* a year in the 1490s to 55,362 in 1581–87; and the quantity of raw silk passing through one single toll station – that of Bisignano – rose from 378,240 pounds in 1550 to 811,483 in 1586.

Even more spectacular was the growth in banking. The Florentine firm of Zanobio Carnesecchi and Alessandro Strozzi was already large enough by 1570 to all but match the grand duke's own subscription to a large Spanish loan (564,667 *ducati*); and the proliferation of small banks was such that money available for lending managed to keep up with the demand – not only in the larger cities, but even in the small towns of Sicily, which used local capital to build most of the innumerable new palaces, fountains and aqueducts erected during the century with local capital. Thanks, probably, to this proliferation, interest rates remained relatively stable, notwithstanding the current inflationary cycle that everyone at the time blamed on the importation of precious metals from Spanish America. Interest varied between the 13 and 15 percent required for government loans by the Naples branch of the Florentine bank of Boffoli and Vecchietti in the 1570s and the 5 and 7 percent received for private loans in Florence.[19]

But big money in banking was made almost exclusively by the large international banks like the Spinola and the Grimaldi, with headquarters in Genoa. The Genoese bankers managed to organize and then dominate the annual 'clearing-house', or large pan-European accounts-settling 'fairs' held first in Lyon, then across the Rhône in Besançon (which Italians continued to refer to as 'Bisenzone') and finally in Piacenza. Since all the states of late sixteenth-century Europe lived largely on deficit financing, control of the fairs made them the financial masters of the most heavily indebted of all the states of the age, Spain. It was the Genoese bankers who advanced most of the money for equipping the transatlantic fleets. It was they who acquired title to most of each annual silver fleet as much as three years in advance of its arrival. It was they, in return, who furnished the gold with which King Philip's soldiers in the Netherlands insisted upon being paid. Since even the silver fleets were not enough to pay the interest or repay the loans, they also acquired control of the tolls and taxes of Castile that had been put up as collateral.

The Spanish may have clearly enjoyed political hegemony in Italy, but the Genoese enjoyed financial hegemony in Spain. King Philip could cause momentary havoc in Genoa whenever he decided to free himself from the hegemony by declaring bankruptcy. Havoc is indeed what he caused, for example, in 1575, when he declared himself unable even to pay interest on the some 13 million *ducati* he owed to the Genoese alone. But only they, not the Spanish banks he tried to substitute for them, could lend him the additional money he desperately needed to pay off the 6.5 million *ducati* he owed in back pay to his troops in the Netherlands. To overcome his remaining resistance, his Genoese financiers 'leaked' the news that they were negotiating with his arch-enemy, William of Orange. And that was enough to transform a renunciation into a renegotiation of all his outstanding debts.[20]

Since both banking and textile manufacturing in Italy was directed, then as before, toward foreign as well as domestic markets, their recovery also stimulated a revival of overland and overseas commerce. The calamities had left intact the ancient 'Florentine custom' praised by the historian Bernardo Segni (1504-1558)

of putting sons to work in a banking concern ('in una ragione di Banco') so that they may learn the mercantile orders and usages by which the Florentines, who are short on landed property, generally support their families and increase their fortunes.[21]

The heirs of Segni's hero, Niccolò Capponi, still operated one of the largest of the 22 Florentine firms which, along with 20 Lucchese, 19 Milanese and 11 Genoese firms, paid 28.5 percent of the total taxes collected by the city of Lyon in 1578. Similarly, the restoration of Mediterranean trade routes to the Far East, which followed rapidly upon the first shock of the discovery of the Cape route, made Venice once again the chief emporium for the cities of southern Germany. This emporium became still more important once the Peace of Augsburg (1555) proved to have the same effects in Germany as the Peace of Cateau-Cambrésis in Italy. Venice constituted by far the largest entry in the merchantman's guidebook (*Handelbuch*) of Lorenz Meder in 1558; and the number of Germans frequenting the Fondaco dei Tedeschi increased to the point where the Venetian government was forced to enlarge the building it rented to them during their business trips. When the sea route to Constantinople became less profitable — or rather, when competition from Ragusan merchantmen became too formidable — Venetian merchants opened up an overland route from Spalato (Split) through the Balkans; and they signed a formal agreement with the expatriot Spanish and Lombard Jews who had gained control over much of the internal commerce in the Ottoman Empire.

The pan-European scope of Italian business interests in the late sixteenth century is aptly illustrated by the last testament of a modest Florentine businessman, Piero di Niccolò Cambi, drawn up at Avignon in 1554. It locates Cambi's real estate holdings in the most serene dominions of the Venetians, in the State of the Church, in the domains of the duke of Ferrara and in the Comtat Venaissin and lists deposits in the Capponi bank in Lyon, one of whose partners, Francesco Nasi, was then doing business in Venice. Italians organized the exportation of beef cattle and leather from Hungary to Germany as well as to Venice. They organized the sale of Italian woollens and the manufacture of domestic glass in Transylvania. And they took advantage of the election of the prince of Transylvania, Stephan Bàthory, as king of Poland, to expand their interests northward – in military and domestic architecture as well as in commerce.

Meanwhile, commerce was stimulated at home by a notable improvement in communications. Regular postal services insured the delivery of letters sent from Venice to Florence in three days, to Rome in four and to Genoa in six – which compares favourably with the records set by the Italian state postal system in the late twentieth century. Post horses, food and lodging were readily available along the minor as well as the major routes, as a delegate of the town of Garessio in Piedmont discovered when he travelled to Rome in twelve days in January 1577.[22] Commerce was further stimulated by the elevation of Rome to the position of administrative as well as spiritual centre of the Tridentine Church and by the increasing recognition abroad of the position of Italy as the motherland of all European culture. 'Germans are we', responded one of Giuseppe Betussi's (c. 1512–1573) characters at Padúa in 1573:

We have come to Italy to learn your customs, language and manners and to see all the interesting things to be seen in all your provinces and cities.[23]

Cultural and religious pilgrims thus engendered a wholly new branch of commerce: tourism. The hotel keepers of Rome organized themselves as a *università* in 1595, just in time to prepare for the massive influx of 536,000 pilgrims, over four times the number of permanent residents, for the Jubilee of 1600. Those in Naples boasted that

our hosts are so perfect,/so polite, attentive and precise,/in performing their obligations, and/in inviting you to supper./They keep well-stocked/their noble kitchens/with partridges, Indian cocks and lamb;/and they will give you for the night/a room fit for a king, a good bed and better food/all for the reasonable price of 8 *carlini* a day.[24]

The principal agents of economic recovery were the same patrician-merchants and artisans who, as Duke Cosimo noted in 1538, 'had closed down their businesses' during the years of the calamities and had now, with the return of peace, 'opened them up again'.[25] Such, for example, were Carlo, Giovan Battista and Cosimo Martelli, the descendants of a family that had risen to moderate prosperity a century earlier under the shadow of Cosimo de' Medici the Elder. The Martelli revived the well-tried method of establishing several legally autonomous companies in each of the principal seats of their business: Florence, Valladolid and Lyon. They established a different set of partners, held together by a succession of three-year contracts, in each, always making sure that one of them was the principal capital-contributing partner. They continued to provide customers with the kind of financial services formerly provided by the Medici and still provided by the Medici's principal successors, the Strozzi. They also arranged for the importation and marketing abroad of Florentine wool cloth, Calabrian raw silk and Indian spices, and they sold insurance policies for the ships that carried the merchandise. The results were more than satisfactory. Profits averaged 25 percent a year in the 1570s, and the invested capital doubled in value during the three-year contract period that ended in 1572.[26]

Established entrepreneurs were soon joined by new entrepreneurs. The Usodimare di Rovereto, for instance, had been relative newcomers in Genoa in 1518, when the first of them finally achieved the status of public office. But his four sons, 'more sensitive to changes in the market than to the tradition of a specific activity', soon transformed their father's wool shop into a large-scale company that manufactured silk cloth in Genoa and sold it in Lyon. Such were their profits after a single generation that their heir in turn was able to enter the still more profitable business of high finance. Also among the newcomers were some twenty artisans from Bergamo and as many others from Lucca, Mantua, Milan and even Catalonia who were attracted by the revival of the wool industry in Florence in the 1540s – and who constituted the majority of applicants for admission to the guild by as early as the late 1540s. Indeed, the entrepreneurial spirit descended almost to the bottom of the social scale – for example, to the 'certain poor men' around Lago Maggiore who

hope to have found mines of silver, sulphur, lead and other metals in the mountainous places, where only poor persons live, who, in order to earn their living, have united themselves to look for such mines so they can work in them.[27]

Both old and new entrepreneurs were encouraged to some extent by the development of technological innovations. The diffusion of hydraulic silk mills *alla bolognese* added still another to the previously mechanized steps in silk cloth production and made possible both a notable improvement in the quality and a substantial lowering of the cost per unit of the finished product. A new kind of industrial furnace was invented by three Venetians in 1571 that consumed half the usual amount of burning wood. A new kind of incorporation contract, the *società in accomandita*, was introduced in Florence between 1577 and 1585, one that made possible greater diversification for big investors and much greater participation in business companies by small investors – bakers, storekeepers, silkworkers and priests. Indeed, the patent office of Palermo in the late sixteenth century recorded many ingenious inventions – new mills that promised to double the usual yield, new fish nets that would double the usual catch, a new kind of pitch for ship repairs that answered the problems caused by deforestation, a new way of making copper that would be far less dangerous to workmen.

Not all these innovations proved to be immediately applicable. The various kinds of automatic seed sowers invented almost simultaneously by Taddeo Cavallini and Ludovico Fieno of Bologna were never widely adopted, despite the constant and costly efforts of the rival inventors to improve and advertise them. None of the pumps that Italians tried to devise on models they had heard were used in Holland ever managed to raise water above the level of the dikes in the Polesine. None of the many schemes for dredging the Po succeeded in restoring Ferrara as a seaport, and the one scheme actually put into practice, that of the Jesuit engineer Agostino Spernazzati for changing the course of the Reno, effected little more than the destruction of some 45,000 hectares of formerly arable land around Bologna. All these innovations, moreover, were purely empirical in origin; for almost no one before the time of Galileo ever thought that technology had anything to do with theoretical science. But even the failures are good indications of what is more important than success: a mentality receptive to technological innovation. Indeed, the widespread attention the inventions received at the time is a good indication of the gradual disappearance of what had constituted the greatest impediment to innovation: secrecy, which the glass technician and maiolica maker Cipriano Piccolpasso (1524–1579) denounced in terms quite as severe as those used two centuries later by the authors of the French *Encyclopédie*.[28]

Much more effective in promoting economic recovery was the support all entrepreneurs received from their respective governments. Silk manufacturing flourished in Mantua in part as a result of Cardinal Ercole Gonzaga's efforts to reform the corresponding legislation in 1543 and 1545. Carrara marble became widely used as a building material in part as a result of the efforts of Prince Alberto Cybo Malaspina to attract Genoese capital into his minuscule principality. That wool manufacturing was even contemplated in the least industrial of all Italian cities, Rome, can be credited to the two rulers who are usually the most blamed for Italy's supposed economic 'decadence', Popes Pius v and Sixtus v. The first made a 10,000 *scudi* loan to prospective wool workers around the Fontana dei Trevi; the second drew up a scheme, as grandiose as it would have been archaeologically disastrous, for turning the Colliseum into a giant factory. These measures were given the blessing of the most prominent political philosopher of the late sixteenth century, Giovanni Botero, who formally added economics to the realm Machiavelli had reserved for politics. 'Nothing is more effective in elevating the power of a state', said Botero,

and for increasing the number of its inhabitants and assuring the abundance of all goods than the industry of men and the multitude of crafts. . . . Hence, the prince who wishes to make his state more populous must introduce every sort of industry and technique. He should bring in excellent craftsmen from other countries, receive them well and assure them of the conveniences they require. He should pay respect to bright minds and esteem inventions and encourage all singular and rare works by offering prizes for the best and most excellent.[29]

One of the most fruitful cases of collaboration between the public and the private sector is to be found in the construction of port facilities. In 1548 the papal legate and the Senate of Bologna gave approval to plans drawn up for them by the architect Giacomo Barozzi to build a canal between the city and the River Reno. By 1581 private entrepreneurs had enlarged the head-waters of the canal with several warehouses, artisan shops and an inn and had constructed a new road at their own expense. In 1592 Grand Duke Ferdinando de' Medici decided at last to put into effect the visionary project of his father Cosimo for rebuilding the tiny fishing village of Livorno. He dispatched architects to construct jetties, docks, canals and a fortress. He dispatched the sculptor Pietro Tacca (1577–1640) to portray him in bronze as the lord of the Mediterranean. He assured all prospective residents, of whatever nation and faith, of full tariff exemptions on goods in transit and of full respect for their ethnic and – notwithstanding the Tridentine fervour then sweeping through the rest of Italy – their confessional diversities. By 1622 Livorno had become one of the most prosperous cities of the age, and certainly the most rationally planned; and its bustling, polyglot population had risen from 700 to 10,454.

Another fruitful area of collaboration lay in the area of land reclamation. The Venetian patricians who by 1548 had bought up a third of the land around Padua first took the initiative in building bridges and canals and in forming consortia among themselves to pay for them. They then appealed for assistance to the state: 'Your authority', said one of the most dedicated of them, Ruzante's patron Alvise Cornaro, 'can get done in three years at two-thirds the cost what private persons could not do in twenty years at much greater expense.' The Senate forthwith set up a three-member commission (*Provveditori ai beni inculti*) to survey all the uncultivated lands in the *terraferma*. It bought up half the swamp land between Aquileia and Padua and began building dams and dikes. The entrepreneurial and capitalistic spirit of the private proprietors did the rest. By 1575 whole areas 'that once were not worth two *ducati* a field are now worth more than a hundred', as Cornaro reported, and over 100,000 such fields had been dedicated to cultivation.[30]

Just as often, however, economic prosperity was the consequence of the survival of what had been one of the chief virtues of Italian businessmen for over three centuries: versatility. When massive imports from America made silver mining unprofitable in the mountains of the Veneto, the miners turned instead to iron and copper, which an abundance of agricultural labour idle during the long winter months enabled them to transform into knives, swords and scissors for sale in Venice. When the loss of the last outposts in the Aegean and the introduction of protective tariffs in France undermined their traditional markets, Italian textile manufacturers shifted their operations to Spain. When a quick succession of bank failures in the 1580s threatened to rob the government of Milan of its principal source of credit, one of the bankers, Giovan Antonio Zerbi, took a tour of all the banks of Europe. On his return to Milan he expounded what he had learned on his tour, in typical humanist fashion, in a series of *Dialogues* aimed at persuading as well as informing the public. Having won the backing of the Senate, he then organized a semi-public bank under a board of directors that included several city magistrates as well as a number of experienced technocrats. Such was the confidence inspired by this formula that Zerbi was able to sell shares (in the place of deposits) for an annual return of no more than 3–5.5 percent.

Similar solutions to the same crisis were adopted in Rome, Siena and

Naples under the guise of that typical pre- and post-Tridentine charitable institution, the *monte di pietà*. This institution had already proven its potentiality for survival in the marketplace in the principal cities of Sicily, where eighteen of them had been founded between 1541 and 1561. The charm of good works continued to inspire confidence long after they had in fact been transformed into regular banking institutions, realizing a profit from the margin between the 4–5 percent paid for deposits and the 6 percent received from loans. Some of them did so well that they are still extant today – e.g., the Banco dello Spirito Santo in Rome (1605) and the Monte dei Paschi in Siena, founded in 1569, restructured in 1582, and recognized as the official bank of the city in 1622.[31]

This ability to adapt to new circumstances favoured the emergence of important profit-making enterprises in several relatively new branches of the economy. Book publishing, for example, continued to flourish in its primary centre, Venice. But it now spread to other centres as well – to Vicenza, where fifteen new presses were established in the decade after 1576, and in Ferrara, where the number of presses doubled and the number of titles published grew from 80 before 1550 to 400 by 1600. The manufacture of ceramics still remained the principal source of revenue in Faenza, thanks in part to the new fruit and flower designs and the ingenious bottle holders and boot-shaped pitchers introduced by such potters as Baldassare Manare and Battista Mazzanti. But the genius of the day-labourer Sforza di Marcantonio, who developed intense yellow and violet glazes, made Pesaro a manufacturing centre capable of attracting artisans from all over Italy. Stimulated by orders from such distinguished clients as the duke and duchess of Florence, ceramic manufacturing in Venice was reorganized on the model of the Murano glass works in order to sell its products in Germany; and the ceramic workers of Urbino made arrangements with the firms of Sanandrini in Livorno and Bernardo di Antonio Gondi in Lyon for exporting their products to France.

For much the same reasons that some old and new entrepreneurs invested in textiles and ceramics, others invested in agriculture. Agricultural investment by city dwellers had begun in many places a century earlier: already by 1498 Florentines owned 66.9 percent of the arable land in the Mugello, as opposed to 10.9 percent in the hands of peasant proprietors. This earlier tendency was strengthened after the 1530s by several motives that had little to do with economics – social climbing, escapism and, above all, the exquisitely humanist desire to imitate the ancients. All the ancient economic writers whose works were broadcast in Volgare translations carried the same message – from Varro and Columella to Rutilius Taurus Palladius, of whom a new translation was published in 1560 as an appendix to an epitome of ancient agricultural lore by the publisher himself, Francesco Sansovino. Agriculture, said the ancients, is the only economic occupation suitable for a gentleman, and it is a way of life, not a business. Most of the Italian agronomists took their models very seriously. Giovanni Rucellai's *Api* ('Bees') of 1529 was largely a paraphrase of Virgil's *Georgics*. The up-to-date practical information collected by Francesco Tommasi during his wander-years as a physician among

179

the towns of Tuscany and Umbria was buried in a mass of quotations, in part to fulfil the author's chief aim of getting Neapolitans to write correct Tuscan. The philologist Pier Vettori's *On the Cultivation of Olives* (1569) was basically a panegyric of the simple pleasures, not of the profitability, of country life – pleasures which the busy author himself seldom had a chance to enjoy.[32]

Yet even the most Theocritan agronomists knew very well that running an agricultural enterprise had little to do with Arcadia. As Isabella Guicciardini wrote to her husband, whose estate she managed while he was off serving the duke as commissioner for the Florentine Romagna:

Do you think it's much fun for me living here with two maids and almost no one else to see or talk to? I spend all my time writing, paying workmen, selling and keeping books. And all these things are looked down upon by people these days. If we want to be happy in this world, we'll have to get to like the things we dislike; otherwise we'll be constantly in torment.[33]

Peasants were no substitute for citizens as daily companions. As the polymath Tommaso Garzoni (1569–1589) wrote in one of his popular compendia,

The peasant, or villein, is less than a plebeian, for a plebeian at least rests on Sundays. . . . [The peasant] is dirty beyond imagination. He spits on his hands and wears slippers that smell of mildew, and he never changes his shirt.[34]

Hence, none of the non-economic reasons for investing in agriculture could compete with the two principal economic reasons: either to inspire confidence among the clients of a mercantile enterprise, or to make money. The first reason had prevailed ever since Leon Battista Alberti recommended it in his adaptation of Xenophon's *Oikonomia*. But the second was a product of sixteenth-century market conditions. The price of one feudal domain in the Kingdom of Naples rose from 3,556 *ducati* in 1553 to 8,500 in 1578, 17,000 in 1609 and 28,000 in 1624; and the frequency with which such domains changed hands even in Calabria suggests that capital gain was as much a motive in the minds of the buyers and sellers than any supposed desire to retreat from an 'Age of Capitalism' to an 'Age of Feudalism'. These property changes reflect not the retrograde, but 'the vivacious innovative spirit' of Calabrian agriculturalists – those who cleared forests and experimented with new crops in a manner totally inconsistent with the nineteenth-century stereotype of the Southern baron.[35] At the same time, prices for agricultural commodities rose even faster than those for industrial commodities – by 103 percent at Pisa during the last four decades of the century (to the delight, undoubtedly, of the Florentine and Pisan families who had bought up respectively 32 percent and 20 percent of the most fertile land in the area), by a proportion of 1:2.73 between 1530–39 and 1590–99 in Puglia (the chief source of grain for Naples), from 62.22 *soldi* in 1520–29 to 208.48 in 1610–19 in Parma, and from 80.10 in 1516–20 to 307.10 in 1589 in Friuli.[36]

It was thus not to advance his already secure social status that Grand Duke Ferdinando I commissioned the best Florentine architect, Bernardo Buontalenti, to design the practical but attractive farm houses, built 'no longer piece by piece but in a single block according to a precise order and plan', that are the delight of weekenders in the late twentieth century. It was not out of indifference to profits that the consciously aristocratic Knights of Santo Stefano reorganized according to 'rational and functional criteria of management' the estates that the previous owner, the unrepentant 'republican' Bartolomeo Cavalcanti, had used solely for pleasure. It was not in the hope of retiring from the city that one of the most 'noble' families in Lombardy, the Borromeo, built irrigation ditches and fertilized their idle fields by buying cattle to graze on them.

If separate 'enterprises' proved to be less efficient in promoting such new or specialized products as Pugliese steers, which were introduced into the Romagna in the 1540s, the agricultural entrepreneurs did not hesitate to adapt to their own needs the kind of corporate structure commonly used in commerce and industry – like the one formed by Lodovico Toffanino and four capital-owning colleagues, two of them Jews, in Ferrara. If the traditional forms of labour organization proved to be inadequate for the new tasks, they did not hesitate to change them – to replace sharecroppers with hired hands, to put several families under the direction of a single 'patriarch' and to construct the 'courtyards', with quarters for twenty to thirty persons, that are still the chief architectonic features of the Emilian and Lombard countryside today. If profits turned out to be less than anticipated, they did not hesitate to take capital out of agriculture and plough it back into industry. That is what was done by the Riccardi, the most upwardly mobile family in Florence. By 1599 the proportion of their investments had been reversed: 53,600 *scudi* in agriculture, 68,500 in industry. If the proprietors' own business talents seemed to be inadequate to their responsibilities, they hired professional managers – like the Paduan notary who leased a block of sixty fields from a newly arrived lawyer-proprietor, and like the merchants to whom Sicilian barons turned over entire feudal domains. Many of them then put down the results of their experiences and experiments for the guidance of others in such practical, and un-Arcadian, manuals as Innocenzo Malvasia's *Lessons in Agriculture Dictated to the Manager of His Lands around Bologna.*

Admittedly, all was not healthy in the Italian economy of the late sixteenth century. At least one important sector began declining seriously almost before it had recovered: shipbuilding. For the exhaustion of the Alpine and Dalmatian wood resources of the Venetian shipbuilders was only partially offset by the more favourable situation of their Ligurian competitors; and the increasing menace of Tuscan, as well as Turkish and Berber, piracy in the Mediterranean made costs spiral upward – by 250 percent between the 1530s and the 1590s. The government of Ragusa tried to halt the transfer of shipowners' capital into Italian state debts by taxing it. The government of Venice resorted to subsidies to assure the production of at least enough vessels to support the navy in emergencies; and in 1573 it finally withdrew its age-old monopoly in order to allow Venetian merchandise to be transported in foreign ships.[37]

Similarly, two other sectors were hard hit, first by the costs of the Lepanto war and then by their dependence upon the ever less secure economy of Spain.

Bans and tariffs on the exportation of high-grade Spanish wool were largely responsible for the rapid decline of the Florentine wool industry in the 1570s; and even if Spanish state bankruptcies really amounted to renegotiations, the lowered interest rates represented a real loss of capital. The biggest bank in Calabria folded in 1581. All the big banks of Venice collapsed within the next five years, dragging all the smaller banks along with them. And hope that they might be bailed out by the arrival of another Spanish silver fleet proved to be even less well-founded in the 1590s, when silver imports reached their height, than they had been in 1565, when one of the Martelli wrote to his partner in Seville:

Infinite thanks for the news about the arrival of the ships from India. That's really good news; and if now still more ships arrive from New Spain, so much more will our affairs flourish down there.[38]

Meanwhile, one other sector was threatened by a superabundance not of competitors, but of customers: agriculture. As the price curves indicate, Italian agriculture just managed to keep up with population growth in Italy; and as at least one figure for bread consumption suggests, most Italians still lived just barely above the level of subsistence – and therefore mostly on bread. Adults consumed an average of 650, and adolescents 1,500 grammes a day, which is far more than the 266 grammes a day consumed in 1981 in the greediest bread-eating region of Italy, Sicily, and the 156 in the least, Trentino-Alto Adige. But even greater population growth was taking place elsewhere in the Mediterranean basin – particularly in the Ottoman Empire. As peasants abandoned their fields to join the some 600,000 persons already jammed into Istanbul, Anatolia and the Balkans veered toward a Malthusian limit – as the Venetian *bailo* warned his government in 1573. That meant the end of the traditional reserve supply of grain in the Ukraine.[39] When three successive crop failures struck the entire Mediterranean in the early 1590s, filling the cities with starving peasants and exhausting the financial reserves of governments and confraternities, Italy too reached a Malthusian limit; and only Grand Duke Ferdinando's timely – and very profitable – plunge into the grain market at Danzig saved it from an even worse disaster.

The only remedy any of the governments could hit upon for any of these problems was, in the infancy of the discipline of political economy, simply an exaggerated form of the kind of remedy that had always been applied in the past: more regulations. 'Having heard that foreign carding machines are being used in the state of His Excellency', declared the Florentine Wool Guild (*Arte della Lana*), henceforth none but those 'that are made in Florence may be used there'. 'Having heard that for some time many persons have engaged, and are now engaged, in occupations subject to the said guild in the city, countryside and territory of Florence, without having paid the matriculation fee or taken the oath to the said guild', the *Arte di Por San Maria* gave all irregular gold and silversmiths, cobblers and dyers two months to adhere to regulations or suffer high fines and confiscations.[40] The laws of the Duchy of Milan stridently forbade any single subject from buying more than fifteen *some* of wheat and obliged every proprietor to bring a percentage of his harvest to the nearest city. The laws of the city of Bologna charged the *Annona* (sometimes called, ironically, 'Abbondanza') officials with fixing the price of bread without allowing for profits for the bakers – and they imposed a system of number juggling so complex that probably few of the bakers could understand it.

Only one or two isolated sceptics had the courage to question these remedies. 'With regard to free commerce', wrote the Perugian legate to Pope Gregory XIII,

wherever, since the world began, it has been permitted to carry grain and other things from one place to another without permission, there have never been many famines. But since free commerce has been prohibited, famines have been continuous.[41]

The guilds of Siena attributed the surprising survival of their wool industry for years after the collapse of its counterpart in Florence to the paucity of their regulations and demanded that tariff barriers inside the grand duchy be abolished.

For those Italians who were well off, however, the sun of peace and prosperity totally obscured these occasional clouds. For them, the daily food market resembled the cornucopia painted by Leandro Bassano (1557–1622): mounds of chickens, rabbits, eggs, doves and big round cheeses, with lambs being slaughtered off at the lower right and hanging from hooks in the centre.[42] The daily table at least approached the abundance and variety – and probably the unhealthy lack of balance – described in Cristoforo Messisbugo's *New Cookbook in Which is Taught How to Make Every Kind of Dish According to the Diversity of Times* of 1557, which also advised putting sugar on everything from capons to squid! Daily drinks approached the discrimination of the wine list of Sante Lancerio, former steward to Pope Paul III, which described with scientific precision the particular virtues of Giglio, San Gimignano and Monte Argentario – as well as, of course, of Montepulciano, which had been introduced to Rome by Cardinal Marcello Cervini, and of six- to eight-year-old *Greco di Somma*, which Pope Paul used to 'bathe his virile parts every morning'.[43] For most travellers, even Naples seemed to be a paradise. As Nicholas Audebert reported in 1576:

The fertility of the surrounding countryside in wheat, wine, fruit, oil and all other products necessary to man make this the most commodious city that ever could be, there being also a grand quantity of cattle and good pasturage in the mountains. Wool cloth here is excellent; . . . and there is nowhere else on earth where you can find a greater abundance of silk cloth.[44]

Sicily was not far behind. As the official historian of Noto pointed out in the last years of the century,

Never has Sicily lived so long in peace. In this age the Sicilians have made themselves richer. Their towns have increased by many hearths. They have erected many tall buildings, both public and private. And [better yet], they have shown themselves to be happy, not discourteous.[45]

THE RELIGIOUS ESTABLISHMENT

What the Peace of Cateau-Cambrésis meant in the realms of civil government, demography, and economics, the successful conclusion of the Council of Trent meant in the realms of religion and ecclesiastical institutions. By legalizing many of the numerous previous attempts to resuscitate one or another aspect of the normative Age of the Fathers, the Council gave assurance to its participants that its decrees would not either become a cause of future acrimony, like those of the Council of Basel (1431–47), or be quietly forgotten, like those of the Fifth Lateran Council (1512–17). Better yet, it provided them with a goal – indeed, no less a goal than that of transplanting the Heavenly Jerusalem to earth and remaking the City of Man in the exact image of the City of God. It also instilled in them an enthusiastic commitment to go out and realize the goal – rather than waiting, like the Joachimite prophets of the early sixteenth century, for the Holy Spirit to do it for them, or being content, like the hermits and cenobites of the Age of the Fathers, to realize it only within the narrow confines of a few isolated communities. As Girolamo Ragazzoni, bishop of Nazianzus, proclaimed in his magniloquent peroration delivered in the last session of the the Council in 1563:

This most happy day has dawned for the Christian people, the day in which the temple of the Lord, often shattered and destroyed, is restored and completed, and this one ship, laden with every blessing and buffeted by the worst and most relentless storms and waves, is brought safely into port.[46]

It was just this sort of over-extended metaphor that his listeners were prepared to accept.

The chief protagonists of this ambitious enterprise were the participants themselves. That they were as pleased with what the Council had done as their predecessors eighteen years earlier had been dubious about what it could do was not a consequence of any change in personnel. In social class, political status, education and career, the members who brought the Council to a close were all but indistinguishable from its initiators, for most of them had become participants in exactly the same way. Giulio Parisani, for instance, had inherited his see of Rimini from his uncle, Cardinal Ascanio, at the un-Tridentine age of sixteen; and as late as 1570 he still clung to the ante-Tridentine custom of bringing a woman along with him on a visit to Rome.[47] Giovan Francesco Gambara of Brescia had acquired his first major benefice at the age of fifteen. He had inherited several others from his uncle, Cardinal Umberto, of the powerful family of the Pallavicino. And he later assured himself of ante-Tridentine cardinalate comforts, whenever he needed a break from his usual routine in the palace his family had bought from Cardinal Rodolfo Pio da Carpi in Rome, by building an elegant villa at Bagnaia.

Most of the Italian bishops at the Council were also dedicated humanists. Antonio Minturno was well known as the author of two important treatises on poetics by the time he became bishop of Ugento in Puglia in 1559 and then of Crotone in 1565. Carlo Borromeo had been taught to pad a belated letter with quotations from half a dozen tardy correspondents in ancient Rome well before his uncle, Pope Pius IV, suddenly elevated him to the episcopacy. Antonio Puteo went on writing poetry long after his uncle Giacomo turned over the see of Bari to him in 1563; he also wrote plays, which he put on for the cultural as well as spiritual edification of his subjects.

The rather sudden genesis of so many enthusiastic Tridentine bishops can thus be attributed only to a conversion to conciliar ideals of the direct descendants of those representatives of the political, economic and cultural elite of Italy who had been administering the Church ever since the pontificate of Nicholas V. It was by his own choice that Girolamo Melchiori, the non-resident bishop of Macerata and papal courtier, finally earned the epithet 'doctrina pietate illustrissimus' ('most illustrious in teaching and piety') that was engraved on his funeral monument at Santa Maria sopra Minerva in 1583. It was by his own decision that the Genoese patrician Alessandro Sauli swept out his room and washed his dishes – and that he did so not at home in stately Genoa, of which he refused the archbishopric, but in his semi-civilized diocese of Aleria in Corsica; and this decision earned him a place of honour not in the chronicles of the great deeds of his fellow citizens, but in the *Acta Sanctorum* (October, V).

Similarly, it was his experience in the last days of the Council that led Antonio Altoviti to stop associating with anti-Medici exiles in Rome in order to associate instead with Savonarola's heirs at San Marco and Santa Maria Novella; and that experience turned him from the proponent of an anachronistic 'republic' into a proponent of Friday evening meditation sessions and frequent communion. It was a similar experience that induced Federico Cornaro, who had been made bishop of Brescia largely because three members of his illustrious Venetian family were already cardinals, to 'repair to my church . . . on the very day in which the Council of Trent came to a close. . . . From that day until 1572', he pointed out, 'I have absented myself no longer than thirteen months and a few days from the diocese'. Even after being transferred to Padua, 'he continued to tire himself out in body and spirit founding oratories, spiritual fraternities and a seminary . . . and [in general] cultivating the vineyard', not of his family or of his republic, but 'of the Lord'.[48]

But the Tridentine bishops alone could never have carried out so great an enterprise for the very reason that many of their non-Tridentine colleagues remained obstinately unconverted. One of them, Cornaro's fellow patrician Giovanni Grimani, who became bishop of Ceneda at the age of twenty and who inherited the patriarchate of Aquileia in 1546, spent most of his time quarrelling over feudal rights; and he had the bad taste to write a letter about grace and predestination without bothering to look up the relevant articles in the decrees of the Council. The bishops of Cefalù and Messina owed their positions respectively to descent from King Alfonso the Magnanimous and to string-pulling at the court of Pope Julius III; and both governed their churches 'with much avarice and little justice'.[49] Rather than yield to persistent orders to reside in his diocese, the bishop of Amelia in Umbria turned it over to his twenty-five-year-old nephew, who then did no more on its behalf than to have the Florentine sculptor Giovan Antonio Dosio (1553–c. 1609) build him a funeral monument. Such behaviour could even be justified, as late as 1558, by the portrait of a model prelate held up for imitation by Girolamo Garimberti. The artist's model was none other than the nephew of Pope Sixtus IV, Raffaello Riario, who 'showed forth the splendour of his high rank by spending no less judiciously than sumptuously' the income he received from 'several rich churches he had in the State of Milan . . . and in other places in Italy and Spain' and by 'supporting in his palace of San Giorgio in Genoa a noble and numerous family'.[50]

In such cases, the initiative passed to the civil authorities, whose cooperation the Council had explicitly requested. The viceroys Juan de Vega and Juan de la Cerda, duke of Medinaceli, undertook to 'Tridentinize' the Church of Sicily, backed by the legatine powers recently reinforced by the rediscovery of the eleventh-century chronicle of Goffredo Malaterra. 'Without this authority', they declared, 'Sicily cannot be governed'; and their declaration was fully supported by the provincial of the Society of Jesus, Giovanni Doménech, who was shocked as much by the ignorance of the Sicilian clergy as by the absence of schools.[51] Similarly, the Senate of Ragusa took the initiative in procuring a Tridentine successor to their impeccably Tridentine archbishop Ludovico Beccadelli upon his resignation during the last months of the Council; and they even picked the successful candidate, a Montecassino Benedictine – a man 'of excellent morals and doctrine' who had learned to speak the local Slavic language.[52] The mayor and the *Eletti* (councilmen) of Massa Lubrense took the initiative in getting rid of their un-Tridentine bishop; and they did so by listing, for the enlightenment not of the pope or the metropolitan, but of the viceroy of Naples, the 'crimes committed' by the incumbent:

He has extorted diverse sums of money from the ministers of the parishes . . . , spoken ill of the Sacred Congregation, declaring that it settles cases as it pleases for money, that it is composed of a bunch of ignoramuses, . . . seized and converted to his own use all the revenues of the benefice of Don Matteo de Turri . . . and publicly defamed the Jesuit fathers, saying . . . that they commit adultery with the women of the city.[53]

That what was gradually coming to be called the 'state' should have assumed responsibilities for what could still only with difficulty be separated out as the 'church' may be shocking to some observers in the anti-Eusebian twentieth century. But in the Tridentine sixteenth century, it bothered no one. The Three Deputies against Heresy, all of them experienced and powerful patricians elected by the Collegio, took the lead in investigating and prosecuting heresy in Venice. And Domenico Bollani, formerly ambassador to England, lieutenant in Friuli and *podestà* in Brescia, continued to work – and think – as a diplomat well after becoming the conscientious Tridentine bishop of Brescia. That, at any rate, is the role in which he is presented in the dialogue *On the Perfection of Political Life* that the Venetian political philosopher and historian Paolo Paruta dedicated in 1570 not to a statesman, but to one of the most dedicated and productive of the Tridentine bishops, Giovan Battista Valier.[54]

What neither bishops nor governors could do themselves was often undertaken by the Tridentine religious congregations, which forthwith transformed themselves from lone pioneers into well-organized executors of the new tasks suggested by the Council. The Capuchins rewrote their statutes in 1552 and again in 1557 in order to become preachers as well as hermits; and one of them, carefully avoiding the theological complications that had led his more famous predecessor, Bernardino Ochino, to apostasy, became indeed one of the most popular preachers of Italy: Lorenzo da Brindisi (1559–1619). Similarly, the Oratorians put aside their founder's predilection for informal groups of friends and disciples and, in 1575, transformed themselves into a formal congregation; and they established headquarters at the Vallicella in Rome, where Filippo Neri laid the cornerstone of a 'New Church', the Chiesa Nuova, the same year. The adherence of the wealthy nobleman Fabrizio Mezzabarba and of the talented administrator Pompeo Pateri then provided them with the income and the structural framework they needed to respond positively to the numerous requests for assistance. Affiliated congregations were soon founded in Naples, Milan, San Giorgio in Venere in Abruzzo, San Severino in the Marche and, somewhat later, even in France.

The Jesuits had changed as well. Some became preachers. Others – like Benedetto Palmio in Milan and Francesco Palmio in Bologna – became administrative assistants to reforming bishops. But most of them dedicated themselves to what Ignatius finally settled on as the principal activity of the Society: the training of a committed Tridentine clergy. Jesuit colleges were founded in one Italian city after another on the model of the first, and unexpectedly successful, colleges in Messina and Rome. Despite some disagreeable echoes in Italy of the squabbles among the Jesuits in Spain, which were quieted only by the timely intervention of Pope Pius IV on behalf of the third general, and despite even more painful growing pains in the last decades of the century, the Society prospered. In Padua, after an initial setback, its college rose from 60 students in 1555 to 450 in 1589. In Rome, its students and professors moved, just two years after the laying of the cornerstone, into the vast new quarters designed for them by the prominent architect Bartolomeo Ammannati. In Naples, the Society acquired, demolished and rebuilt buildings around its original headquarters at a rate that soon produced a housing shortage in the centre of the city. In Genoa it reaped a fortune through the conversion of the wealthy patrician Marcello Pallavicino: Marcello's brothers joined him, in 1589, in dedicating to the memory of their father and in paying for the new church of SS. Andrea and Ambrogio.[55]

Quite as important, particularly for the numbers and variety of the persons they attracted, were the confraternities. Armed now with a fully theological justification for their endeavours, the confraternities grew even more rapidly after the Council than before. So rapidly indeed did the Compagnia del Pellegrino of Prato grow, that it was forced to discourage applicants by requiring a year-long trial period. What made many of the confraternities especially attractive was the mixed character of their membership. The Compagnia del Pellegrino put carpenters and bakers on the same plane as nobles, while the Compagnia dei Bresciani in Rome made explicit provision for the admission of resident Brescians of all social ranks and of both sexes. The new confraternity 'della Pietà dei Carcerati' founded in 1575 by the penitents of the Jesuit confessor Giovanni Teller at the Roman Gesù included thirty women among the fifty-five new members it admitted in 1585, three years after it had been forced to move out of its once ample headquarters in the church of SS. Cosmo and Damiano in search of more space. By 1580, there were eight confraternities at Albona in Istria, which had a population of 2,000, twelve at Dignano, which had 6,000, and eleven – four of which explicitly included both men and women – in Assisi, which had 5,780. That represented an almost total mobilization on behalf of Tridentine ideals – so total, indeed, that the apostolic visitor to Assisi was able to come up with only one suggestion for improvement: that they consolidate some of their endeavours.[56]

What modern historians often depict as an arbitrary imposition by a few authoritarian prelates upon a reluctant, if not hostile, populace, was in reality the most universally popular movement in the whole history of Italy, one comparable in intensity – but not in duration and geographical extension – to such brief and locally circumscribed moments of enthusiasm as those in Milan at the time of Ambrose, Florence at the time of Savonarola and Emilia Romagna after the attempted assassination of Palmiro Togliatti. New or converted Tridentine bishops discovered that most of their administrative and many of their pastoral problems could be solved simply by adapting, collaborating with, or at least redirecting already well-tried organizations.

The first of the many tasks that all or at least some of these various collaborators were called upon to undertake was that of completing, or supplementing, the work of the Council. Some of these tasks could be entrusted, in accordance with the recommendations of the Council itself, to special commissions, or papal congregations, composed of former Council members and experts on the specific question to be resolved. One such commission was charged with answering questions about the meaning of the Council's published decrees on the basis of the diaries of the preparatory debates. Fearing that free access to these diaries would lead to appeals of its decisions, the commission locked them up in its reference library and let no one else look at them for another seventy years. Another commission was charged with determining which books currently in circulation actually fell within the Council's general categories of wholly prohibited, partially prohibited or prohibited until emended (*donec corrigatur*) – and with avoiding a repetition of the chaos that had ensued when Pope Paul IV unilaterally attempted to prohibit everything even slightly discordant with his own, not the Council's, notions of orthodoxy. Another commission was charged with deciding which of the many variants of the Latin Vulgate, which the Council rather vaguely declared to be theologically sound, were philologically sound and what to do in cases where they varied from the earlier versions preserved in the works of the Latin Fathers. Another commission was charged with replacing the many different local and corporate liturgies with a single Mass, Breviary, and Martyrology for all the churches of the Latin rite. Still another commission was charged with correcting the all-too-obvious errors in the fifteen-century-old Julian calendar – and thus with preventing moveable feasts from moving absurdly outside their proper seasons. So conscientiously did the Ptolemaic and Copernican astronomers work together with one of the leading mathematicians of the day, Christopher Clavius (1538–1612) of the Jesuit Collegio Romano, that, after Gregory XIII obliterated fifteen days in the middle of October, 1582, no day will have to be obliterated again until the year 3333!

At least one task, however, required the coordination of a much more extensive network of talents: the reinforcing and elaborating of the patristic bases of the Council's doctrinal decrees. For more manuscripts of still little-known Greek Fathers were constantly being discovered – like the *Eranistes* of Theodoret, which was first published in 1547. Each new manuscript had to be evaluated carefully in the light of one or another of the current humanist philological criteria. It also had to be examined in the light of the corollary to Trent's axiom about the collective infallibility of the Fathers: that any text not wholly in harmony with the Tridentine decrees must be corrupt. Similarly, many of the works of the Latin Fathers that had been issuing from Italian presses since the introduction of printing were as marred by errors of typography and transcription and by arbitrary choices among variant readings as were most of the other books published at the time.

Fortunately, the disciples and former protégés of Marcello Cervini, the pre-Tridentine director of the Vatican Library and one of the most energetic legates at the Council, were at that moment turning Rome into one of the most important centres of philological scholarship in all Europe. The leader of the Roman company of scholars was the Calabrian Hellenist Guglielmo Sirleto (1514–1585), whom Pope Pius IV appointed to Cervini's former post as director of the Vatican Library. Sirleto had already collaborated in a number of major editing projects – Basil, John Damascene and the apocryphal *Acta Beati Sylvestri* – when, in 1561, Aldo Manuzio's heir Paolo arrived in Rome with a commission from the pope to publish 'perfectly' correct books on the 'best paper', and, 'for the greater utility of the world and the greater glory of Rome', 'at the lowest possible price'.[57] Thereafter, with Sirleto's blessings, one great project followed another in rapid succession: Mariano Vittori's complete Jerome in nine volumes; Giulio Poggiano's translation of John Chrysostom's, and Pietro Galesini's translation of Gregory of Nyssa's, treatises on virginity; and Latino Latini's editions of Cyprian, the *Symposium* of Methodius of Olympus and the several new texts that Onofrio Panvinio and Francesco Davanzati brought back from a manuscript-hunting expedition to Sicily in 1564.

While the Roman presses served the Latin-reading public, the Venetian presses served Volgare readers with such popular publications as the sermons of Augustine, Basil and Chrysostom in the translations of another Tridentine scholar-bishop, Galeazzo Florimonte. Similarly, what the philologists did for the written remnants of the normative age, the architects did for its physical remnants. Several of them assisted post-Tridentine cardinals in fulfilling what came to be regarded as one of their most pressing obligations: restoring the ancient churches of Rome. When the fifth-century dome over the Constantinian church of San Lorenzo in Milan collapsed on 8 June 1573, one of them, Martino Bassi (c. 1542–1591), laid aside the Mannerist motives with which he had decorated – dutiful disciple of Alessi that he was – the new church of San Vittore al Copno; and he restored the plain walls, the unadorned arches and the Doric capitals, just as they had been in the days of Ambrose. Owing to these efforts, it was soon no longer unreasonable that all the parish priests of Milan be required to own a copy of Ambrose's sermons; and it was altogether fitting that Giacomo Della Porta introduced Gregory Nazianzen into the polychrome marble chapel he designed for Pope Gregory XIII in St Peter's.

Meanwhile, the task of demonstrating that the Age of the Council of Trent was at least potentially a faithful reincarnation of the Age of the Councils of Nicea and Chalcedon fell to the historians. Paolo Regio, bishop of Vico Equense, and the peripatetic polymath Girolamo Muzio assembled all the details they could find in all the known sources concerning the Church in the first century. Fausto Tasso and the first historians of the Society of Jesus, Niccolò Orlandini (1554–1606) and Francesco Sacchini (d. 1626), did the same for the Church in the late sixteenth century. The complementary task of demonstrating the historical continuity between the two ages fell, after several abortive starts by other candidates, to Cesare Baronio (1518–1607), the untiring and humourless archive explorer whom Filippo Neri sent to learn history from Sirleto. Fortified by the unequivocable vocation Filippo had discovered for him, comforted by assurances of collaboration from the whole Roman scholarly community, stimulated by the counter-project recently published by a group of Gnesio-Lutherans at Magdeburg and assured of unlimited research assistance from the historophiles of the Oratorio, Baronio set forth methodically to assemble, and to quote interminably from, every document that had any bearing on any aspect of the spiritual or organizational life of the Church, year by year, since the Incarnation. By the time of his death, just short of twenty years after the appearance of the first volume of his *Annales* in 1588, Baronio had filled over twelve huge folio volumes, all of which sold out as fast as they could be printed.

Baronio's work was still far from finished, and his successors had to fill in the gap he left between the early twelfth century and the present. But he had proved to the satisfaction of all Tridentine Christians – and of a few Protestant Christians as well – that, far from being novelties, the beliefs and practices sanctioned by the Council of Trent were precise versions of what had been sanctioned by the visible Church ever since the time of the Apostles. He had proved the theological utility of history by providing definitive answers to a host of major and minor questions – e.g., whether priests wore beards in the fourth century and whether therefore they should wear them in the sixteenth century.[58]

Similarly, the task of placing the single doctrinal decrees of the Council within a complete theological framework fell to a theologian: Roberto Bellarmino of Montepulciano (1542–1621), a close friend and collaborator of the historians and a nephew of their common mentor, Cervini. Bellarmino was well aware that theology in the few extant theological faculties of Italy, those of the mendicant orders, was still taught in accordance with the forms inherited from the scholastics of the thirteenth and fourteenth centuries. Filippo Gesualdo, for instance, the rector of his Conventual Franciscans' schools at Padua, Naples and Palermo, commented endlessly on the *Sentences* of Peter Lombard according to the directions of his order's chief. Even one of Bellarmino's fellow Jesuits, a certain Francesco Albertini, spent all the forty years of his academic career at the college in Naples defending not the authority of the Fathers, but the 'irrefragable philosophical and theological teaching of Saint Thomas Aquinas'; and he reminded Bellarmino of his efforts by dedicating to him the second volume of his massive *Theological Corollaries Deduced from Philosophical Principles* when it finally appeared in 1616.

Bellarmino was probably willing to admit that such intellectual exercises had been relevant in the days of the Augustinian theologians, Henry of Ghent, Giles of Rome and Gregory of Rimini, who were still the main protagonists in the debates of the sixteenth-century Italian scholastics. But he realized that they were almost totally irrelevant in an age in which questions about justification, free will and election had turned Gesualdo's favourite question, the Immaculate Conception, into a curious anachronism. Leaving scholasticism, therefore, with its logical and systematic rather than historical and philological approach to theology, to his better equipped and more daring contemporaries in Spain, Bellarmino turned instead to the Scriptures and the Fathers. He learned Hebrew well enough to compose and publish an oft-reprinted grammar of the language. He learned Greek well enough to read the texts directly, without the help of his Roman colleagues' recent translations. And he thereby accumulated an immense collection of passages from all the sources that the Council had acknowledged as authoritative; and he was ready to apply them to whatever question might arise concerning the Council's definitions.

Such a question was the one concerning Grace. That was a question that interested so few persons in Italy that Pope Pius v thought he could simply sweep it away with another of his cacophonous anathemas. But it was a question that interested everyone at the theological faculty of the University of Louvain, where Bellarmino was sent as a visiting instructor in 1570. On the question 'Whether the first man was created in [a state of] grace', Scotus and others, Bellarmino noted, had one opinion, Thomas and others another. Moreover, the usually cited Scriptural passages were not explicit, whatever former controversialists may have said on the basis of mere translations. But the Council of Trent, Session 5, Augustine, Epistle 106, Basil in *De Spiritu Sancto*, Chapter 10, Irenaeus in his first book, Chapter 37, Cyprian, Sermon

2, Hilary in a homily on Job, etc., etc., made it perfectly clear. One question settled, on to the next; and if Pope Sixtus v happened not to like the irrefragable pronouncements of the Fathers concerning the divine origin of civil government, so much the worse for him. Bellarmino went on adding article after article until Sixtus' successor withdrew his censures. His *Controversies*, by their own intrinsic value and persuasiveness rather than by fiat of anyone, were soon recognized as the most complete and most authoritative *summa* of the Tridentine church, the equivalent in theology of Baronio's *Annales* and the Gregorian calendar.[59]

All that needed to be done now was to make the great *summae* more accessible to a wider audience. That need was fulfilled for history by Francesco Panigarola, whose pocket-book *Compendio* was published in 1590 within two years of the first volume of the complete *Annales*. It was fulfilled for theology by the Roman, or Tridentine, Catechism. This work was compiled between 1564 and 1566 by another commission of experts on the basis of the decrees of the Council and of all the better-known pre-Tridentine doctrinal compilations, including Lippomano's *Confirmation of All the Catholic Dogmas* of 1553. It spread rapidly throughout Europe, with six separate new editions in 1567, two in 1568, four in 1570. And it was supplemented in several Italian dioceses by a number of Volgare abridgements, like the Augustinian Giovan Battista Antonucci's *Catechism for the City and Diocese of Naples* (1577), and by several up-dated versions of older manuals of confession, like the Dominican Bartolomeo Fumi's *Aurelia armilla* which made its debut in 1550.[60]

The Tridentine settlement was thus complete – at least on paper. But its protagonists were good enough humanists to realize that words were useless without deeds and that precepts were valueless unless they touched the will. The problem of how to make the ideal a reality was taken up initially in numerous practical manuals of piety. Agostino Valier, Achille Gagliardi and apparently Gabriele Paleotti wrote handbooks for bishops, with rules backed up by references to the 'model bishops' of ancient and modern times. The Senate of Milan drew up a list of its particular requirements: the bishop should be 'a man of authority and reputation' and rich enough not to be tempted into despoiling his church.[61] Valier also wrote a handbook for 'Christian women of all conditions of life'. Bernardino Caroli wrote one for small landed proprietors, of which he was one, and peasant farmers; and he made learning the latest agricultural techniques as much a requirement of holiness as being polite to landlords, teaching children to recite the Ten Commandments, making sure that a glass offered to a visitor is clean and getting wives to join a religious 'company'.

Most of the manuals, however, were written indiscriminately for everyone – for the high-born ladies who learned to chant Serafino Razzi's translations of Dominican liturgical hymns and for the 'simple and uneducated persons' to whom Silvio Antoniano made available all he had learned about matrimony and the rearing of children from Plutarch, Chrysostom, Sadoleto and the Roman Catechism.[62] The spiritual and corporeal adventures of the most famous of the post-Tridentine Italian mystics, Maria Maddalena de' Pazzi (1566–1607) of Florence and Caterina Vannini (1562–1606) of Siena, were invariably presented not as activities to which the great mass of Christians need or ought to aspire, but as 'demonstrations and signs [in which] the omnipotence, goodness and mercy [of God] can continuously be observed', as Federico Borromeo put it in his blood-chilling biography of Caterina.[63] Still, everyone could ascend to just short of the State of Union by following the rungs in the spiritual ladder enumerated in Mattia Bellentani's *Practice of Mental Prayer* (five editions from 1573 to 1586), Lorenzo Scrupoli's *Spiritual Combat* (1589), Vincenzo Bruni's *Meditations on the Mysteries of the Passion*, Bellarmino's own rather dull adaptation of Bonaventura, Luca Pinelli's updated version of Jean Gerson or Antonio Cordores' *Itinerary of Christian Perfection*, which was translated from Spanish in 1607 for the guidance of 'all persons of all walks of life desirous of serving God'.[64] New models more in harmony with Trent's concept of sanctity were put forward to take the place of the now anachronistic medieval models. The model soldier was now Bartolomeo Sereno, who later in life applied to spiritual combats in the monastery of Montecassino the military and diplomatic skills he had acquired during the battles of Tunis and Lepanto. The model wise man was the 'Christian Socrates', Filippo Neri, whose 'Lives and Deeds' Federico Borromeo painstakingly collected in anticipation of his imminent canonization. The model learned man was Bellarmino, who, according to one of his disciples, became holy 'by reading the lives of holy bishops and imitating their actions'.[65] But the model of all the models was Carlo Borromeo, by far the greatest iconographic success of the age. His portrait was painted by Guercino, Sante Peranda, Lodovico Carracci, Ambrogio Figino, Federico Zuccari, Lucio Foppa and Guido Reni. His body was reproduced in marble and in bronze by Giovan Battista Crespi. His life was chronicled by Agostino Valier, Carlo Bascapè, Giovan Battista Possevino and Giovan Pietro Giussano. His heroic actions were recaptured by Domenico Pellegrini in wall-sized murals all around his chapel in the episcopal palace of Milan.

With the manuals in their hands, and with the living models before their eyes, the reformers turned from individuals to institutions. The first institution that demanded their attention, in accordance with the formula 'from head to limbs' once again evoked in the last days of the Council by the conciliar orator Cornelio Musso, was the papacy.[66] The moment was propitious, for almost all the current cardinals were found to be acceptable according to the criteria adopted by the cardinal of Santa Croce in the poll he conducted in 1565: 'suitably cultured and compliant'. Accordingly, Pope Pius IV, once he had finished purging Rome of the last traces of his predecessor's reign of terror, took the first steps: cutting back the revenues of the Penitentiary, trimming down the jurisdiction of the Audientia and appointing a commission to screen candidates for the cardinalate. His successor, Pius V, took the other steps. According to Pius V, 'There is but one way to heal wounds as deep as these and to placate the wrath of God: the faithful and diligent observation of the Council of Trent.'[67] He therefore charged the professional diocesan reformers Niccolò Ormaneto and Giacomo Savelli with interviewing even women and children in every parish of Rome; and he himself made the rounds of the basilicas to make sure that their injunctions were being followed. He fired 130 members of his own staff, sent off *cura animarum* benefice holders to reside in their benefices and ordered the Swiss guards to marry their mistresses. He told the cardinals to stop taking vacations in the country, to put away all their silk drapes and to replace their silverware with tin or brass.

These measures helped save the papacy from the challenge of conciliarism. They also helped save it from tendencies toward oligarchy, particularly after 1588, when Sixtus v precluded any organized opposition in the College of Cardinals by dividing it up into separate congregations. These measures received apparent divine confirmation when, in the space of a year, the city's subsoil yielded the bodies of four martyrs, the body of one Church Father – Gregory Nazianzen, no less – and a 'most devout image of the Glorious Virgin', which accorded 'stupendous graces' to all who approached it.[68]

Better yet, these measures metamorphosed at least the image, if not the reality, of the popes themselves. Popes were still expected to be great patrons of the arts, and most of them were still members of powerful Italian families. But rather than glorious and magnanimous princes, like Leo x, they were now expected to be saints, like Pius v, who walked around barefoot while running a fever. They were supposed to be not generals, like Julius II, the conqueror of Bologna, but psalm-chanting defenders of the papacy's just territorial rights, like Clement VIII, the 'restorer' of Ferrara. Thus the 'Renaissance papacy', which had been inaugurated by Nicholas v over a century earlier, gave way to a somewhat, but not entirely, different 'Tridentine papacy'.

Another institution, or group of institutions, to demand the reformers' attention was the pre-Tridentine religious orders, or, more specifically, those orders whose impermeability to reform had given rise to recommendations for their total abolition on the eve of the Council and those whose non-Tridentine behaviour had justified the Council's decision to make them subject to local ordinaries – just what they had always feared the most. These threats were sufficient to persuade most of them to adhere at least to the spirit of the Council, in some cases even before its conclusion. The Dominicans adopted new constitutions in 1558 that raised the age limits and established stricter conditions for admission in conformity with the Council's concern for properly motivated professions. The General Chapter of 1580 ordered the provincials to keep accurate records of new members to make sure that the constitutions were being carried out. And soon the typical Dominican was one like Domenico Mansano of Palermo, 'a man of sharp mind and very well versed in Sacred Scriptures', who, despite his noble birth, studied at Paris, taught at Louvain and 'passed his whole life with pen in hand'.[69]

As for those orders, like the Basilians of Calabria, who could not reform themselves because they had alienated all their property, the initiative passed to representatives of already reformed orders – for example, the Benedictines of Montecassino, who arrived bearing recently printed copies of the rule composed by the greatest of the Greek scholar-émigrés of the preceding century, Cardinal Bessarion. As for those monasteries whose superiors resided beyond the reach of the authorities of the Tridentine Church, like those of the Venetian island of Cefalonia, the initiative fell to the local political administrators and to special papal emissaries – in this case a certain Giovanni Bonaré who was shocked to discover that at least one monk 'had stopped wearing his habit and, what is worse, slept in the same bed with his abbot, committing dishonesties and inconvenient operations'.[70] Such was the success of these initiatives that the old orders began to regain much of the lustre they had lost since the times of their founders.

The institution that most engaged the attention and energy of the reformers, however, was the diocese. For unlike most previous reform movements in the church, the Tridentine Reformation aimed at producing the saintly monk, the saintly friar and the saintly secular priest only as a means for producing its primary objective, the saintly layman. The Tridentine ideal of Christian perfection was best realized not in some hermit, celibate or mystic, but in someone like the saintly carpenter of Milan, Giambattista Casale, who recited a home liturgy he had composed every evening with his wife and children, supervised the marriage of his sons and daughters, built the benches for a school he founded for giving free lessons in reading and writing, helped organize the incessant parades sponsored by the bishop and rose to the position of prior not of a monastery or of a Tridentine congregation, but of the wholly lay Confraternity of Christian Doctrine.[71] This ideal was formalized liturgically on Holy Thursday of 1569, when the archbishop of Florence first washed the feet, no longer of twelve canons, but of twelve *poveri* recruited from the congregation.

Fortunately, the Council itself had given only general guidelines for how to turn what had become a mere administrative subdivision into a community of saints. Occasionally these guidelines alone appeared to be sufficient, as they were, for example, for Bishop Girolamo Vielmi of Padua, probably because he had already written a manual 'On the Good Bishop'. But most of their colleagues found that they had to fill in the guidelines in accord with the particular economic, political and historical circumstances of their churches. Gabriele Paleotti commissioned that master of humanist historiography, Carlo Sigonio, to write a history of the church of Bologna in order to preserve all that was still healthy in it. Carlo Borromeo, staunch Milanese though he was, imported specialists from abroad in order to extirpate what he judged to be unhealthy in the church of Milan; and to facilitate their work, he had the episcopal archives completely overhauled and catalogued. Alfonso Carafa, who needed a dispensation from the canonical age of twenty-seven before taking possession of the see of Naples, relied almost wholly on the advice of the local disciples of the famous pre-Tridentine reformer, Seripando, as well as on that of his Latin and Greek teachers. Braccio Martelli, the already seasoned bishop of Fiesole, relied on the men of letters of the see of Lecce to which he was transferred as a consequence' of his anti-curial stance at the Council. Alessandro de' Medici, later the short-lived Pope Leo xi, who alternated pastoral tours of duty in Florence with diplomatic tours of duty in France, won one battle against the remaining devotees of Savonarola, whose image he removed from all the churches; and he lost another battle against the non-cloistered nuns, whose dowries he was forced to pay back from his own pocketbook.[72]

Still, frequent correspondence among the reformers kept diversity always within the bounds of uniformity. Most of them used standard visitation questionnaires like those prescribed for the tiny southern diocese of Sarno in Paolo Fusco's treatise *On Visitations* of 1581. The questionnaires incorporated into the surviving eighteen volumes of visitation records for Reggio Calabria are almost identical with the sixty-six articles set forth by Giovan Battista Castelli at Rimini in the 1570s:

1. Describe the site and the material condition of the church [being visited].
2. Note the incomes from all benefices.
3. [Find out] whether the Council's decrees against clandestine marriages have been published.
4. Note which curates have been absent since last November. . . .[73]

Uniformity was also assured by the appointment of apostolic visitors – specialists sent by the pope himself to check on the progress of reform. Some visitors did the rounds of a score of dioceses in a few years – in the case of the Council orator Girolamo Ragazzoni, Famagosta in Cyprus, Chissamo in Crete, Ravenna, Cervia, Forlì, Pesaro, Urbino, Milan, Alessandria, Casale and Alba. They acquired considerable experience in overcoming obstacles that baffled the ordinaries – like the endemic quarrels among the various political jurisdictions that criss-crossed the diocese of Sarzana on the border between Liguria and Tuscany.

The principal means adopted for eliciting a positive response to the reforms were also very much the same. In anticipation of the full effects of the new seminaries, the clergy, rural as well as urban, were summoned to frequent instruction and discussion sessions; and they were ordered to reside in their benefices, memorize model sermons if they could not compose their own, get rid of their dogs and their concubines, wear clerical dress, stay out of taverns and in general behave as exemplars of virtue. Parents were informed that 'the Holy Council of Trent excommunicates all those of whatever state or condition who dare force their daughters into convents against their wills'. Nuns were warned against 'appearing too often at doors and windows and in reception rooms, . . . engaging in vain conversations, glances, laughter, jokes, hand-touching and other frivolities'; and they were enjoined to dispense with dowry requirements, and therefore with the class barriers that had usually been scrupulously observed, in order to make room for 'women poor in goods but rich in spirit and virtue'. Laymen were advised to abstain from 'the more lascivious kind of music' and to sing instead 'the spiritual *laudi* composed by various old and modern authors' and collected and published by that tireless popularizer of liturgies, Serafino Razzi, for use 'in the churches after vespers and compline . . . in monasteries, in confraternity meetings and in private homes'.[74]

Likewise, preachers of the religious orders – who turned out to be far more effective than the parish-priest preachers envisaged by the Council – were enjoined to familiarize themselves with the character and traditions of their audiences, to avoid any word or allusion that might not be understood by all, to eschew puns, archaisms and complicated metaphors, to stick to the Bible, the Fathers and the councils, to forget about scholastic jargon and to speak in neither Latin nor dialect, but in standard Bemban Volgare. Homiletic oratory became one of the most cultivated art forms of the age, and homiletic literature soon outdistanced all other categories on the book market – at least to judge from the remarkable editorial success of even so minor a preacher as Evangelista Marcellino (1530–1592) of San Marcello Pistoiese, who published some twenty-six collections of sermons during the course of two decades.

This art reached its apex in the sermons of the Observant Franciscan Francesco Panigarola (1548–1594). With the possible exception of the Capuchin Lorenzo da Brindisi, who could recall at an instant from his limitless memory any passage from the Bible and hundreds of passages from the works of Virgil, Homer, Ovid, Livy and Cicero, Panigarola was the most popular public speaker of all Italy since Bernardino of Siena. But he owed his popularity in part to presenting sermons that were totally different in form and content from those of his illustrious predecessor. As a faithful disciple of the Florentine linguist Leonardo Salviati, and as the author of a manual of preaching drawn from no less humanist authorities than Demetrios of Phaleron and Basil, Panigarola completely rejected the logic-chopping and story-telling sermons against which the early Tridentine reformers had railed; and he brought to perfection the biblical and patristic sermons that they had incessantly demanded.

Religious enthusiasm sparked in this manner was directed toward what were intended as means – sermons, prayer and hymn-singing sessions, masses, processions, canonical hours, fasts and feasts, which occupied an ever increasing proportion of the daily schedule of the residents of most cities – as well as toward organized pilgrimages to shrines abroad, particularly to Loreto, to the Holy Mountain of Varallo, which Carlo Borromeo completely reconstituted according to Tridentine criteria, and to Rome, at least for the immensely successful jubilees of 1575 and 1600. But most of this enthusiasm was directed toward good works; and good works, according to the Tridentine formula, meant making sure that all the residents, no matter how humble, were also citizens of the sacred community. The hospital established at Pavia in 1566 received an initial donation in urban and rural real estate sufficient to enable it to take care of all patients not accepted by the other hospitals of the city. In 1575 it received another cash donation of 1,192 *scudi* and an endowment yielding 429 *scudi* a year – enough to permit it to acquire an oratory and a garden. In 1584 still another endowment enabled it to found an orphanage and a widows' home as well. Similarly, the hospital of Santa Anna established by 'certain men' – and, in good Tridentine fashion, by certain women as well – 'of good spirit and of religious intentions' in Naples housed 400 prostitutes' daughters by 1587. Some 2,000 men and women bought the hospital of Nosadella in Bologna in 1576 and provided free medical care, medicines and dowries to all poor girls who applied.

At the same time, religious enthusiasm was directed away from what the Council had defined as the antitheses of biblical-patristic Christianity: heterodoxy and superstition. The first of these antitheses warranted much less attention than was actually given to it in the interminable trials of a few relics of pre-Council theological speculation: for example, the opinions of the philosopher-poet Giordano Bruno (1548–1600), whose doctrine of one truth for the intellectuals and another for the masses repelled the Venetian government and the Roman Inquisition as much as it has fascinated intellectuals since the mid-nineteenth century. Many of those who had been stigmatized at the time of Paul IV were quietly rehabilitated: the Waldensian mystic Bonsignore Cacciaguida, whose *Spiritual Letters* were republished in 1563 and 1583; the Neapolitan preacher Gabriele Fiamma, whom Gregory XIII made bishop of Chioggia; the Augustinian opponent of forced conversions, Girolamo Negri, who was elected head of his order's Piedmont province in 1573.[75] Several prominent exiles, whether through disillusionment with their former creeds or out of homesickness, retracted whatever the Council had meanwhile defined as error and came home: for example, Giovan Michele Bruto, Agostino Doni, Simone Simoni.

The word 'heretic' still bore an emotional response capable of transforming in an instant an entire population into soldiers of the Church Militant. That is what happened at Milan and Brescia in 1570 in response to rumours of an impending uprising or invasion of something called 'Huguenots'. Such a response was accurately captured by Giovan Battista Crespi when he painted a spotlighted Virgin holding her five-year-old son with one arm and, with the other, directing the slaughter of the Albigensians (Cremona: Museo Civico). For heresy was invariably associated with what was universally believed to be its unavoidable consequence: wars of religion, that 'madness with which we see ruined a great part of Christendom', particularly in France and Flanders.[76] And Italians had suffered too much through war in the first half of the century to want any more of it in the second.

The Inquisition was thus left with patiently listening to a semi-literate Friuli miller regurgitate undigested scraps of Paduan Aristotelian cosmographical speculations, with filing away ridiculous charges of personal enemies ('I say he's a filthy heretic: he denies the consecrated host . . . and says that the priest at mass plays with trifles like a cat . . .'[77]), with asking preachers to explain more clearly what an anonymous listener had objected to and then 'giving him full permission to continue his preaching', and with condemning a relapsed Spanish 'New Christian' to life imprisonment and then setting him free two years later.[78] The inquisitors therefore turned to the second of the Council's antitheses; and that gave them much more trouble. As cases of alleged heresy in Venice dropped from 6 a year in 1585–92 to 3 a year after 1615, witchcraft cases rose from 22 to 44; and charges of magic rose from 20 to 45 percent of the total in Naples between 1580 and 1620 while charges of heresy dropped from 40 to 11 percent.[79] Some witchcraft cases were fairly simple – like the one involving a certain Margherita d'Ambruos in the Canton Ticino, whose nocturnal wine-drinking parties in the church cellar broke up at the sound of an Ave Maria. Others were more difficult, like the one regarding a certain Caterina of Sicily, whose incantations appeared really to have helped several well-born Roman ladies overcome the after-effects of a miscarriage. Magic cases were just as varied. Some of them concerned merely the abuse of holy objects:

When you want to force a woman to do your will, smear [this chrism oil] on the middle finger and thumb of your right hand; while joking with her, touch her with [the two fingers] while saying these words: 'Quod Deus coniungit homo non separet'.[80]

Others could in one way or another be justified according to notions that still passed as scientific, or at least that could not yet be eliminated as unscientific, such as the 'books and tracts of onomancy, astrology, glomancy, hydromancy, pyromancy, chiromancy, necromancy' and other 'execrable incantations and superstitions' condemned by Sixtus v in 1586.[81]

The existence of such practices was commonly attributed to ignorance of Christianity – particularly in more remote parts of Italy, such as the mountains of Abruzzo and Corsica, which one horrified Jesuit missionary staked out as 'my India'.[82] At times they were traced to songs and stories that over the centuries had crept into local liturgies. One such was the 'vernacular office . . . that speaks of uncertain indulgences or the remission of sin or vain and superstitious observances' denounced by the bishop of Savona in 1565; others were the 'tales from apocryphal writers, the miracles not supported by writers of proven faith' and the 'inept and ridiculous fables' derided by the archbishop of Naples in 1597.[83] Never suspecting that such practices would ever be treasured as expressions of a 'popular' religion, the Tridentine reformers unanimously classified them as superstitions 'to be gotten rid of'.

The extent to which Tridentine bishops, visitors, carpenters, preachers, congregations and confraternities could 'get rid of' what they disapproved of and substitute what they thought better corresponded with the Tridentine ideals depended upon their overcoming a number of obstacles. One minor obstacle arose from the very lay constituency that generally gave them their strongest support. Members of parishes occasionally objected to what appeared to be unwarranted causal connections between one ideal and another – e.g., that only a celibate could be a good parish priest, which empirical observation often contradicted. In those areas where internal pacification was not yet complete, the 'great discord and civil enmity' was often such that 'it was impossible to perform God's service' – in the Dalmation city of Cattaro, for instance, where it killed one bishop and sent another flying to Venice.[84]

Much greater obstacles were occasioned by the often violent resistance of the local clerical establishment, particularly cathedral chapters, which were invariably dominated by powerful families for their own material interests, and monasteries and convents formerly exempt from the bishop's jurisdiction, which often housed the sons and daughters of those same families. One disgruntled monk tried to assassinate Carlo Borromeo right in his own chapel. One disgruntled monastery physically barred him from entering. When the suffragan bishop of Pisa in 1573 tried to force the convent of San Martino to admit two well-connected Lunigiana girls who did not fulfil the requirement of Pisan nobility,

a band of nuns furiously rushed from the convent into the church . . . tore to shreds the habits [with which the girls had just been vested], turned the altar upside down and filled the church with tumults and shouting. [When the bishop tried to put a stop to] flying fists and the enunciation of words that brought infamy upon the nuns and disgrace upon the whole convent . . . they turned on the poor man, who barely made it out alive, all beaten, broken and shaken up by the fury of those angry nuns.[85]

Even greater obstacles arose because of conflicts between ecclesiastical and political authorities. Carlo Borromeo quarrelled interminably with the governor of Milan over holiday markets and his right to have laymen charged with immorality arrested by his own armed guard, for the right to keep such a guard was never questioned. Each of them appealed alternatively for support to the king-duke in Spain, to the pope and to the Senate. So did Carlo's nephew and successor, Federico, who lost control over the lay charitable foundations (*luoghi pii*) when King Philip III turned cold toward him because of what his best friend, Baronio, had said about St James of Compostella in his *Annales*.[86] In the Kingdom of Naples, such conflicts were exacerbated by the viceroy's insistence upon maintaining the *exequatur*, that is, prior government approval for all actions of the clergy. The headstrong new bishop of Strongoli in 1566 was not able to conduct visitations in his diocese until after the king himself had calmed down both the pope and the viceroy. Such conflicts were further exacerbated by the overlapping between ecclesiastical and civil personnel and jurisdictions. The archbishop of Santa Severina consumed most of his revenues pursuing civil suits in Rome and Naples against the counts of Santa Severina. The bishop of Teramo was *ipso facto* prince of Teramo, an identity he celebrated by hanging the royal coat of arms over the door of the cathedral; his taxation rights in the city of Teramo had therefore to be settled in a royal, not an ecclesiastical, court. In 1570, Bishop Annibale Saracino won a tax exemption suit against the citizens of S. Pietro in Lama in Puglia concerning the olive orchards planted on ecclesiastical property after 1470; but the case he brought against the citizens regarding the *decima* (tithe) on their olive orchards was not settled until 1715.

Yet the most formidable of all the obstacles were those caused by conflicts among the ecclesiastical authorities themselves. In Milan, Carlo Borromeo's desperate attempt to carry out the Council's call for the restoration of metropolitan provinces broke down under the joint opposition of curial bureaucrats, who preferred to divide and conquer, and local patriots, who sought a painless revenge for their political subjection to the metropolis by having their churches made immediately subject to Rome. In Turin, the bishop obtained a bull from Gregory XIII making all the decisions of the inquisitor subject to his approval; but the inquisitor assured himself of the backing of the duke through an agreement barring the appointment of inquisitors who were not among the duke's subjects. All over Italy, much of the authority given to the bishops by the Council was given back to the religious orders by the Dominican Pope Pius V. Gregory XIII sought to reverse his predecessor's policy, but it was too late: the bishops themselves had already become dependent upon those who were supposed to be their dependants in carrying out many of their functions.

Soon also the demands of papal service began once again to take precedence over those of diocesan service. A diocese became a place for temporary retirement, as did Zara for the diplomat Minuccio Minucci when his diplomatic career ran into difficulty, to be abandoned as soon as it became unpleasant, as it did for Minucci when his ignorance of the 'Illyrian' language proved to be an embarrassment. More and more bishops began to aspire to careers like that of Filippo Sega, who was too busy as a papal legate in Flanders and Spain to visit either of his first two dioceses, and who abandoned his third nine years after going there to accept other legations in France and Germany. More and more of them looked forward to careers like that of Pietro Francesco Montoro: while still a layman, Montoro was given the diocese of Nicastro in Calabria as recompense for his services as governor of the Marche; but he resided there only until the advent of a more favourable pontificate turned him once again into a vice-legate at Avignon, a nuncio at Cologne and an assistant to the papal throne at Rome.

It is thus not surprising that results sometimes ran short of expectations. Compromise was often unavoidable. Most of the priests in the town of Bene in Piedmont were suspended when it turned out that they could not read Latin; but since there was no one to take their place, they were quickly reclassified as *scientia tolerabiles* and reinstated. An image of the Virgin at Vito began bleeding when a boy accidently hit it with a arrow in 1592; but since not even Pope Clement could stop the hordes of 'pilgrims' who flocked to see it, he finally approved a liturgy in its honour.[87] Refusal to compromise in time often made failure inevitable. Despite the large sums poured into Pellegrino Pellegrini's sumptuous building, the rigid rules imposed by Pius V on his Collegio Ghislieri in Pavia discouraged all but the most determined candidates from applying; and many of them were subsequently expelled for disciplinary irregularities. Carlo Borromeo's edicts against post-procession feasting and the *cavallaccio* (a sort of Trojan horse filled with presents) were simply ignored; and the moment he died, the student members of the Compagnia di Beatissima Maria at the Brera reintroduced all the 'lascivious images, clownish mimicry and other profanity' which he had blamed for 'inspiring the depravation of morals'.[88]

Often the obstacles were simply too great to be overcome. Even the apostolic visitors could not make the Benedictines give up their parishes and the Augustinians contribute to the seminary fund, and they could not stop the Franciscans and Dominicans from competing with each other's 'miraculous virgins' and the local barons from treating ecclesiastical property as their own. Most of rural Abruzzo and Basilicata thus remained totally untouched by the Tridentine Reformation.[89] The bishops of Ravenna and Faenza could insist that no couple be married without being able to recite the Decalogue and that their names be duly registered in a diocesan *liber matrimoniorum*. But they could not persuade parents that marriages were valid only if freely consented to by the parties and witnessed by a priest. They could repeat the Tridentine declaration that marriage was a sacrament; but they could not defend it against downgrading in the pronouncements on behalf of the equally Tridentine ideal of a celibate clergy by Filippo Neri and Baronio:

The Devil will say: 'Marriage is a holy thing. It is a sacrament. It is a state of life established by God himself . . .' Oh, what a diabolical deceit; oh, what infernal cunning![90]

The Tridentine ideal of the parish as the centre of religious life would ultimately lose out to the 'centrifugal force' exerted by religious orders, oratories, privileged altars and special shrines; and the behaviour of congregations even in such a Tridentine paradise as the cathedral of Verona was not exactly Gibertian or Borromean. During high Mass, Montaigne noted,

they chatted right in the choir, [strolled about] with hats on, stood with their backs to the altar, and gave no sign of following the service except at the elevation.[91]

Apart from these shortcomings, however, the Tridentine Reformation succeeded as well as could be expected given the instruments at its disposal. Knowledge of what the Council meant by Christianity was certainly much higher and much more widespread in 1600 than it had been in 1545.

THE AESTHETIC ESTABLISHMENT

Ars historica, already known in the early Renaissance, became almost a discipline unto itself in the later Renaissance. But the theoreticians of history – whether they also wrote history, like Uberto Foglietta (*c.* 1518–1581) of Genoa and Giovan Michele Bruto (1517–1592) of Venice, or whether they did not, like the philosopher Francesco Robortello (1516–1567) of Udine and the poet and free-lance editor Dionigi Atanagi (1505–1573) – derived their theories not from modern or ancient historians, but from ancient rhetoricians. Hence, the only advice they had for practitioners was to learn from Cicero, Aulus Gellius, Lucian or Quintilian how to make their prose more copious, more ornate, more turgid or more 'Tacitan' – and thus to make it better able to imbue its readers with the desired moral or political values.

Luckily, the practitioners did just the opposite – with the happy, although unintended, consequence of eventually assuring history 'an autonomous position among the sciences', even with respect to its age-old ally, rhetoric.[92] Spurred on by conditions of domestic tranquillity, the antiquarians set out to continue the work of their modern models, Flavio Biondo and Carlo

Sigonio; and the text editors – Bruno Latini, Gabriele Faerno (d. 1561) and the Romanized French scholar Marc Antoine Muret (1526–1585) – set out to refine (and fight about) the methods of their mentor, Pier Vettori. They learned, with the Roman antiquarian Fulvio Orsini (1529–1600), to distinguish between early and late, authentic and spurious inscriptions and to reject, as 'not worthy of the slightest attention', all those whose orthographic peculiarities proved them to have been composed at a different period.[93] Encouraged by governments like that of the city of Rome, which in 1573 increased the meat tax in order to pay for excavations around Trajan's Column, they demonstrated the importance of coins, medals and other archaeological remains for filling out the history of ancient Rome – for example, those illustrated by the engraver-scholar Enea Vico (1523–1567) of Parma in his *Images of the Empresses and of the Emperors . . . with their Lives Drawn from the Medals as well as from the Lives of the Ancients*. They also learned, with the botanist-minerologist Michele Mercati (1541–1593), to use analogies with pre-Columbian America in an attempt (alas, unsuccessful) to decipher the ideograms on the obelisks that Pope Sixtus v delighted in moving about Rome.

Meanwhile, the historians in the Livian or Polybian tradition quietly junked the rhetoricians' most prized literary device: formal speeches. Into a still impeccably Guicciardinian form they inserted instead exact quotations from the documents they laboriously dug out of the archives. They corrected in the works of their predecessors whatever they found to be inconsistent with archival evidence. They read widely – in search of a more meaningful context – in the by-now abundant historical literature about the other cities of Italy and the other countries of the world. They set to work composing a number of voluminous and 'definitive' histories of the cities in which they resided – Scipione Ammirato (1531–1601) in Florence, Pompeo Pellini (d. 1594) in Perugia, Giovan Battista Pigna (1529–1575) in Ferrara, Gianantonio Summonte (d. 1602) in Naples. So thoroughly did they carry out their tasks, so accurately did they record even the most minute political, diplomatic and military events, and so perfectly did they incorporate the aesthetic standards implicit in their ancient and modern humanist literary models, that their works remained authoritative for another two centuries.

The political philosophers – or, more accurately, the political scientists – followed the lead of the historians. Most of them, after all, were also historians – Pigna, Ammirato, Paolo Paruta; and they saw in history the only alternative to their own very limited experience as a primary source of information relevant to their quest. History, said Giovanni Botero, was 'the most beautiful theatre that can be imagined'. For in it

one can learn at others' expense . . . about shipwrecks without harm, about wars without danger, about the customs of various peoples . . . without the cost [of travelling, and thus] discover the beginning, the middle and the end of the rise and ruin of governments . . . and the causes for which some princes reign in tranquillity and others in trouble and for which some flourish with the arts of peace and others by the valour of arms.[94]

They followed Machiavelli – even while they avoided mentioning his name – in his method and his format: one thesis after another, each supported by two or three concrete historical examples and each connected to the other solely by the succession of events. They also followed Machiavelli in rejecting the authority of the theoreticians, modern as well as ancient, or in bringing them up in order to knock them down, as Pigna did with Polybius' notion of constitutional cycles. They considerably increased the geographical as well as the chronological scope of their sources of information – so much so, in the case of Botero, that he described them separately in his immense *Relazioni universali* of 1591. To Machiavelli's turbulent Roman Republic they added the relatively tranquil Principate – far more appropriate, thought the Jesuit theologian Antonio Ciccarelli (d. 1599), in an age in which peace had replaced turbulence in all the states of Italy. To his modern Italians, Swiss and French, they added the Egyptians, Incas and, most notably in Botero, Chinese; and they thus prepared for the exaltation of China as a model state in the works of political philosophers all over Europe during the following century.[95]

Thus prepared, the political philosophers set out to correct some of Machiavelli's more discomfiting theses – that civil discord is better able to rouse *virtù* than civil harmony, that men, not money, are the key to victory – and to confirm most of his other theses in the light of subsequent experience. They then went on to challenge Machiavelli's principal presupposition: that the pre-Gracchian Roman commonwealth was the best that had ever been instituted and that Livy provided an accurate record of its development. In its military organization, admitted Paruta, Rome did indeed excel. 'But in civil affairs, it was highly disorganized and confused'. It was therefore much inferior to post-Cambrai Venice, of which 'the form and the order of civil government is in every part well arranged and perfectly organized'.[96] Finally, they confronted the most disquieting of all the problems posed by Machiavelli: the irreconcilability of Christian and political morality. This problem they solved not by actually reconciling the two opposites, but by proclaiming Tridentine Catholicism to be much more effective than either ancient paganism or modern Protestantism – that most recent cause, proclaimed Tommaso Bozio's book title, *Of the Ruin of Nations and Kingdoms* (1589) – in keeping subjects obedient toward their governments and princes responsible toward their subjects. Any political actions that could not be sanctioned in terms of Tridentine Catholicism they swept into a totally amoral closet called 'Reason of State', which, being out of the sight of ordinary mortals, did not trouble their consciences.

Not even the 'Utopians' had serious objections to this solution. For instead of imagining the exact opposite of what they observed around them, as did their modern mentor, Thomas More, they simply added the perfecting touches to what they regarded as already near-perfect. Francesco Patrizi's *La Città felice* (1553) was based on contemporary Venice as much as on Plato's Republic. *La Repubblica immaginaria*, written by the jurist Lodovico Agostini

(1536–1609), had little to add to what the Senate of Venice, the grand duke of Tuscany and Agostini's own duke of Urbino had already accomplished. The author was left recommending what everyone else at the time recommended: that they get rid of lawyers, prohibit credit speculations and keep married women from dancing with other men. Even the most totalitarian of these latter-day Spartas, Campanella's *City of the Sun* (1623), was really an amalgamation of what fortunately remained separate in reality: the *virtù* of certain ancient Romans and the austerity of certain Tridentine puritans. And no one ever dreamed of actually effecting the amalgamation until certain Jesuit missionaries penetrated into Paraguay over a century later.[97]

In some other realms of Italian culture, on the other hand, the imitable examples were strongly reinforced by theory – for instance, in the three 'fine' arts of painting, sculpture and architecture. Unlike the *ars historica* writers, the art theorists were almost all practising artists. One of the non-practitioners, Giovan Paolo Lomazzo (1538–1600), had been forced to abandon painting for theory – and for poetry – when struck with premature blindness. Another of them, the botanist friend of the historian Ammirato, Michelangelo Biondo (1500–c. 1565), yielded to the practising theorists to the point of backing up his own well-informed evaluation of Titian with long paraphrases of their common model, Leon Battista Alberti.[98] All of them were thus well prepared to combine theory with practice. They could summon up everything all the poets and the orators had ever said about art since Homer – as Gregorio Comanini did in his *Figino, or On the Purpose of Painting* of 1591 – while giving specific instructions on how to draw a nose, an eye or a skull. They could speculate on the psychological, qualitative or metaphysical associations of colours while showing how or how not to juxtapose them in order to achieve the greatest effect: 'a soft green next to an acute, proud, flaming red' (Lomazzo, p. 2264).

Whether the art theorists drew their theories from Ficino's Plato or from 'the study of mathematics in that part which deals with what is a point, what a line, what a circle' (Alessandro Allori, p. 1960) made little difference. For they all addressed themselves not so much to specialists as to 'those noble gentlemen of whom [Allori was] such a good friend and [who] desired very much to learn how to draw' (p. 2263). Whether they let their theories emerge from informal conversations or whether they endlessly subdivided logical categories and single 'precepts', like those of Giovan Battista Armenini (1530–1609) of Faenza, made little difference either:

The art of painting is an imitator of nature. The first part is drawing, the second invention, the third and last colour. With regard to the first, I wish to divide it into four parts: judgement, circumscription, composition . . . (p. 758)

All of them took care to refer their readers to the High Renaissance exemplars in which the categories and precepts were perfectly illustrated. For Vincenzo Danti, that meant, as it had for Vasari, the masterpieces of Michelangelo, it being the opinion of almost all well-informed men that Michelangelo carried out his work with excellent perfection, more than all the moderns and perhaps all the ancients. (p. 1563)

For Lomazzo, whose secondary purpose was to vaunt the artistic merits of his own Milan, that meant those High Renaissance masterpieces which were accessible to his compatriots:

for an example of the true art of excellently arranging light, you can look at all those paintings of Leonardo Vinci . . . in San Francesco; . . . for excellence in the use of light, two paintings of the hand of Antonio Correggio here in this city are not less marvellous. (pp. 1993–94)

More important still, most theorists agreed that the arts had seriously declined since the completion of the masterpieces – that is, during the age of what later came to be called 'Mannerism' – and they drew attention to their own personal efforts aimed at reversing the decline:

> In those times I undertook diverse works,
> paintings, bizarre trifles and stories I painted,
> with friezes, grottesques and various panels,
> with cartouches, trophies, landscapes and fruits; . . . .
>
> But at a more mature age I would have done everything
> according to true, fixed and firm principles.
> (Lomazzo, Einaudi edn, vol. 9, p. xxvii)

As Federico Zuccaro's 'Painting' lamented,

> To such a state have I been reduced!
> Works of quality are no longer admired by anyone,
> and my eyes are wet with bitter mourning.
> Alas, grace and decorum have become extinct,
> of imitating nature there's not a sign,
> and a willow can't be distinguished from a laurel.
> Their eyes feed upon art without art,
> while the ignorant content themselves
> with pretty colours bereft of skill in drawing. (p. 1026)

The one theorist who did not share these qualitative judgements at least accepted the remedy: the Florentine Raffaello Borghini (c. 1537–1588). Borghini was unaware of any defects even in such manifestly Mannerist works as Baccio Bandinelli's (1488–1560) *Hercules*, Ammannati's *Neptune* and Francesco Salviati's *Deposition*. But he expressed his appreciation of them in terms borrowed directly from Vasari and Alberti; and his qualitative judgements were interspersed with very practical and completely up-to-date technical advice about how to prepare paper, make charcoal pens and use bread dough as an eraser.[99]

Some practising artists paid very little attention to the theorists' injunctions. Bernardino Poccetti (1549–1612), for example, was motivated chiefly by the ambition to paint something besides someone else's façade designs. He adopted the styles first of Raphael, then of Andrea del Sarto, then of Alessandro Allori and finally of his anti-Mannerist associates at the Certosa of Siena. And since he never rejected the previous style when he moved on to the next, his artistic development has been likened to a rolling snowball, rather than to a series of unrelated segments like a string of sausages.[100]

Some artists regularly deferred to the pre-Mannerist preferences of their patrons. Aurelio (1530–1593) and his brother Giovan Pietro Luini of Milan, for instance, continued to multiply 'calm and enticing images in the language of the first thirty years of the century' as long as they were working for Lombard confraternities. Once in the hands of more tolerant clients at Santa Maria di Campagna at Pallanza, they happily returned to their customary deformed old peasants, two-headed monsters, 'tasty cupids' and other such products of 'extreme freedom of invention' and 'animated expressivity'.[101] The Flemish-Italian sculptor Giambologna (1529–1608), who had been 'turned from a transalpine into a Florentine' by the leading patron of the Florentine Mannerists, Bernardo Vecchietti, seems not to have appreciated the artists admired by Vecchietti's favourite art therorist, Raffaello Borghini. There is not a trace of their influence in the classic stare of the Greek-nosed Venus he did for Vecchietti (Los Angeles: Getty Museum), in the unadorned Ionic columns framing the bronze Passion scenes in a chapel of the Annunziata or in the *Rape of the Sabine*, which turned the spectators into marble at the spectacle of marble turned to flesh when it was unveiled in the Loggia dei Lanzi in 1583.[102]

Yet most artists took full advantage of the rank of humanist won for them by their early and High Renaissance predecessors. Giacomo Barozzi da Vignola intentionally chose to follow the example of Antonio da Sangallo – rather than, say, of Giulio Romano, with whom he was well acquainted – in completing his greatest masterpiece, the Farnese villa at Caprarola. Federico Barocci (*c.* 1535–1612) decided to study not the works of other painters, but 'nature' – in many more than the some two thousand pastel drawings that are still extant. He drew grid lines across the sketch of his *Entombment of Christ* (Chicago: Art Institute) to make sure that all the figures corresponded to a perfect geometric pattern; and he arranged the colours according to their qualities 'so that they would be in concord and union and not conflict with each other'.[103] Lodovico Cigoli (1519–1613), a scholar as well as a painter, reverted to pre-Mannerist conventions when he made the *Virgin of the Annunciation* at Montughi in the shape of the grand duke's *Medici Venus*. So did Santi di Tito (1536–1603) when he abandoned the style of Francesco Salviati for that of Taddeo Zuccari (1529–1566) during his formative years in Rome – and when he thus laid 'the solid base of Florentine classicism' of which he became a leading proponent after his return to Florence.[104]

The most determined revolt against Mannerism was the one launched in Bologna in the 1580s by the brothers Agostino (1557–1602) and Annibale Carracci (1560–1609) and their cousin Lodovico (1555–1619). In the name of Vasari's principle of the primacy of drawing (*disegno*), which contradicted their occasional Vincian pronouncements about 'painters talking with their hands', in the name of 'the study of mathematics and all the more noble disciplines', in which they were proficient, and in the imitation of Correggio and Titian, whose works they discovered during study tours of Lombardy and the Veneto, the Carracci formally broke with their Bolognese masters, even at the cost of going for years without major commissions. With Annibale's *Crucifixion* of 1583 (Santa Maria della Carità, Bologna) and with their jointly executed mythological scenes in Palazzo Fava, they launched a completely new style.[105] This style was characterized by the exact conformity of the objects painted with what could be observed in reality, even in so exceptional a reality as *Francis of Assisi in Ecstasy* (Venice: Accademia), by unity of space and geometrically centred arrangement of the figures, by natural colours (even if one colour was allowed to dominate all the others), and by the direct relevance of all the parts to a single theme: none but a few bewildered apostles (and four cupids to assist with the take-off) around the tomb of the *Assumption* (Rome: Santa Maria del Popolo); nothing but scales, hooks, pieces of raw meat and a selection of uncultivated and uncouth workers in the *Butcher Shop* (Oxford: Christ Church).

The new style was firmly rooted in Bologna by the academy the Carracci founded to perpetuate it. It was advertised all over Italy by the latest engraving techniques that Agostino learned from the Dutch visitor in Venice, Cornelius Cort. It conquered Rome when Federico Zuccari's Accademia di S. Luca officially adopted it and when Agostino and Annibale projected it onto the walls of the most magnificent collective art project of the day, the great gallery in the Palazzo Farnese. It percolated down into the villages of the Romagna with the 'tender colours and compact geometric forms veiled with epidermic luminosity' of Francesco Brizio's (1574–1623) murals in the Oratorio della Trinità at Pieve di Cento. It was taken to Piacenza by Ercole (1596–1676) and Giulio Cesare Procaccini (d. 1625) of Milan, who put two exactly parallel scenes of Mary being married and presenting the baby Jesus, with the same number of cupids in each, in Pordenone's suburban church of the Madonna di Campagna. It was taken to Parma by Lionello Spada (1576–1622) and Bartolomeo Schidoni (d. 1615), who put a real roast lamb on the table of the Last Supper and a real – thin but not emaciated – thirty-three-year-old Jesus on the road to Calvary (Parma: Galleria Nazionale). It was taken to the Abruzzi coast by an assistant of Giacomo Della Porta when Charles v's twice-widowed daughter Margherita finally retired to her domains at Ortona in 1584. The new style was received with particular favour in Venice; for there it coincided with Paolo Veronese's (1528–1588) rejection of Tintoretto's 'dazzling fantasy' in favour of unified space, multiple yet perfectly coordinated action and 'Olympian serenity' – and with his independent anticipations of the architectural as well as pictorial aspects of the new style in the Villa Maser.[106]

The new style was much more than simply a restoration of the High Renaissance. It accepted some of the more courageous experiments of the

Mannerists – like the artifically foreshortened legs of Annibale's *Dead Christ* (Stuttgart: Staatsgalerie), like Veronese's 'subversion' of certain 'classic rules of perspective'[107] and like the hyper-realism of Giovanni Ambrogio Figino (1548–1608) of Milan, in which 'lips tremble, nostrils swell and retract, mouths open and the light of the eyes languishes'.[108] It permitted Barocci to watch Francis of Assisi receiving the stigmata from a point some six feet above his right shoulder. It permitted Poccetti to make 'form dissolve into a sort of atmospheric mist full of light, so that an exact definition of the contours of the figures no longer exists'.[109] It allowed the anonymous decorator of the ambulatory chapel at S. Francesco in Piacenza to eliminate all but three perfectly balanced stucco-white assistants and thus to maximize the impact of the very dead body of Christ. Above all, the new style encouraged a considerable broadening of the canonical range of subject matter – from Jacopo Ligozzi's (1547–1612) minutely reproduced botanical specimens to Cigoli's lascivious woman with her inviting smirk and protruding breasts in *Joseph and Potiphar's Wife* (Rome: Galleria Borghese) and even to the 'most obscene gestures', the 'decomposed representations' and the other 'monstrosities' that so shocked Agostino Carracci's biographer Filippo Baldinucci a half-century later.

The new style thus avoided just those characteristics that had first provoked the Mannerists' departures from High Renaissance standards: immobility, detachment, monotony; and it incorporated the one Mannerist innovation that could most easily be justified by High Renaissance standards: the emphasis upon rhetorical effect. Like Mannerism, it too was not given a name at the time, or even for a long time afterward. Today it can appropriately be referred to not as 'anti-Mannerism' – since the term bears the same negative or reactionary overtones that make the companion term 'Counter-Reformation' equally inappropriate – but as the 'Neo-Renaissance'. For its proponents looked forward to surpassing the High Renaissance models from which they drew their theoretical precepts, just as the creators of those models had once sought to surpass the ancient models they imitated.

THE PHILOSOPHIC ESTABLISHMENT

In still other realms of culture, the construction of theoretical systems during the last half of the sixteenth century progressed to the point of rendering unnecessary, or even of discouraging, any further reference to imitable models. That is what happened most notably in those realms for which Aristotle had written, or may have written, a textbook.

Aristotle was by no means a discovery of the late Renaissance. Several of his works had provided the philosophical foundation for most schools of theology ever since the thirteenth century, and they had served throughout the fifteenth century as the foundation for physics and metaphysics in the arts faculties of the Italian universities. But Aristotle became much more widely known after the 1530s as ever greater numbers of the disciples of humanist schools began attending the universities and as the former barriers between university and humanist culture gradually withered away. He also became better known. The inclusion of his principal works in the Aldine series of Greek texts, and the introduction of Greek courses into the normal university curriculum, permitted his modern disciples to read him in the original – or at least to consult the original when preparing their lectures. More important, the recovery of the ancient Greek commentators – Philoponus, Alexander of Aphrodisias, Ammonius and, above all, Simplicius, whom Giovanni Fasolo translated into readable Latin in 1543 – permitted them to eliminate the 'barbarous Britons' and the 'Parisian sophists' who had once justified Petrarch in banishing all the Aristotelians from the realm of humanist studies. New Latin translations, beginning with those of Leonardo Bruni that were included in the authoritative Giunti edition of 1550–52, made him at least less unpalatable to humanist tastes and somewhat more worthy of Cicero's puzzling epithet 'elegant'. Finally, several Volgare translations and commentaries made him accessible to monolingual readers as well. The humanist-philosopher Alessandro Piccolomini collected into fifteen large volumes everything Aristotle had ever said about economics and ethics; and that at last dispelled the common belief in the irrelevance of university Aristotelianism to the real problems of daily life.[110]

One of the principal advantages of having Aristotle as the founder of a philosophic system was his actual, or at least potential, universality. A few Aristotelians – like Girolamo Borro, who taught at four different Italian universities after 1553, and Cesare Cremonini, who settled permanently at Padua in 1591 – thought that the corpus of his extant works contained everything worth knowing. The task of modern philosophers consisted simply in 'understanding in what sense such philosophers' terms as *materia* and *subiectum* were in use among the Peripatetics'.[111] But most of them were sufficiently aware of the breadth of what was then considered knowledge to admit that the corpus was not complete. They were willing to let Galen take his place in medicine and Ptolemy in astronomy. They were also willing to let modern editors round out the corpus with discreetly disguised pages lifted from Theophrastus, Plotinus, Proclus and Leonardo Bruni, as well as from the anonymous *De mirabilibus auscultantibus*, which Girolamo Cardano used in correcting Aristotle's otherwise inexplicable miscalculation of the earth's circumference.[112]

Even greater proof of Aristotle's universality was provided in 1536, when Alessandro de' Pazzi published a Latin–Greek edition of two previously little-known or little-studied works – the *Rhetoric* and the *Poetics* – and when the already famous philosopher-rhetoricians Vincenzo Maggi (*c.* 1498–1540) and Francesco Robortello bolstered them with long commentaries. The two works were then translated into the Volgare – first by the Florentine humanist Bernardo Segni and then, on the basis of Pier Vettori's and Sigonio's emendations of the original Greek, by Alessandro Piccolomini. Aristotle thereupon replaced Horace, Virgil and Plato as the undisputed authority in the whole broad field of literary criticism.[113]

Another of Aristotle's advantages was the incomplete and sometimes unclear state in which his works had survived. The *Poetics* gave many, but by no means all, of the precepts that the sixteenth-century Aristotelians thought necessary for the guidance of epic poets. It was therefore up to the Venetian polygraph Orazio Toscanella (d. *c.* 1579), among others, to dig the rest of them out of Virgil. It was up to Sebastiano Regoli (1514–1569) to look for the rest of the 5,197 theses of his *De triplici hominum vita* in Plato, whom he learned to read in the original Greek. None of Aristotle's works said anything about such recently invented literary genres as the romance, the sonnet, the pastoral drama and the madrigal; and the Aristotelians tapped all their polemical ingenuity in trying to decide how or whether to include the protagonists of these new genres within their extensions of Aristotle's disciplinary compartments.[114]

Aristotelianism provided a unified system of interrelated explanations for the principal phenomena observable in many different disciplines. This system was not dependent upon Aristotle alone: it could easily do without even those pieces of the *Poetics* that Castelvetro discarded on the supposition that the surviving text was only 'a rough and unpolished . . . collection of material' of a never-completed work.[115] It was also immune to the challenge of empirically observed phenomena, since they by definition remained valueless until they had been assigned a place within it. Rather, the system rested upon a concatenation of propositions all held together by their common deduction through infallible syllogisms from the same self-evident axioms. If any of these propositions momentarily became detached, the prudent Aristotelian mason had only to plaster it over with a bit of 'metalanguage' – or even with some of the 'insipid and confused language' that 'puts to the test the most tenacious resistance' of twentieth-century readers of Lodovico Boccadiferro's 1571 commentary on the *De generatione*. Whatever defects may have become apparent in the structure itself were entrusted, one by one, to specially trained logicians: Marc'Antonio Zimara (1460–1532), Bernardino Tomitano (d. 1576) and the inventor of the 'regressive demonstration', Girolamo Balduino (fl. 1560–1570). The remaining defects were then corrected once and for all in the most complete and – as it turned out – the last great *summa* of sixteenth-century Aristotelian logic, the *Opera logica* of the most industrious, if not necessarily the most original, of the sixteenth-century logicians, Giacomo Zabarella (1533–1589).[116]

Whether derived from Aristotle or from the High Renaissance masters, this system – or these related systems – were not really as solidly founded as the system builders thought them to be. Occasionally, for instance, one of the bricks came dangerously loose. That is what happened in the still autonomous, if subaltern, discipline of anatomy, when the dissections performed at Padua by the immigrant Belgian Andreas Vesalius turned up a good number of bones and muscles that Galen had not mentioned – and when Vesalius hired one of Titian's pupils to broadcast his discoveries on copper plates. That is what happened also in the hierarchically superior discipline of medicine, when Andrea Cesalpino (1519–1603) tried to squeeze all the novelties of his pharmacological researches into his *Peripatetic Questions* (1588). He was forced to invent a wholly new system of genres, to move the centre of the veins from the liver to the heart and to describe the behaviour of blood with a metaphor about 'flowing streams' that pushed him to the brink of the discovery of circulation. The only way out of this dilemma was, for the moment, to follow the example of the eminent physicians whose names have been memorialized in the human body, Gabriele Falloppio (d. 1562) and Bartolomeo Eustachi (d. 1574). They described the concrete and the individual and let the abstract and the general take care of themselves.[117]

Sometimes, on the other hand, two disciplines that should have coexisted harmoniously suddenly became mutually antagonistic. Two such disciplines were physics and astronomy. Aristotle had made the superlunary spheres around the earth solid and contiguous in order to transmit motion from the farthest to the nearest. But Ptolemy permitted the planets to rotate upon rotating axes that in turn rotated upon centres not necessarily coterminous with the centre of the earth – as if in open space – in order to permit those beyond the sphere of the sun occasionally to go 'backwards'. Two other such disciplines were metaphysics and theology, long rivals for the top place in the hierarchy. According to one, the universe was eternal, and the human 'form', or soul, vanished at death along with the corresponding 'matter'. According to the other, the universe had been created and would end in time, and the soul was immortal. The only way out of these dilemmas was to forget about them. That is what the metaphysicians – and then the theologians – had done earlier in the century when the bishop of Padua complained about Averroes and when the Fifth Lateran Council complained about Pietro Pomponazzi. That is what they did again at the end of the century when the Jesuit historian and diplomat Antonio Possevino, annoyed at the opposition of the faculty to the founding of a Jesuit college on their doorstep, raised the age-old, but by now rather stale, spectre of atheism.[118]

A still more troublesome pair of disciplines was logic and mathematics. Like astronomy, mathematics had long been consigned to the subaltern spheres reserved for mere calculation devices or for wholly unreal abstractions. As the Jesuits' Benito Pereira (*c.* 1535–1610) put it in 1576:

The mathematical disciplines . . . are not properly sciences. . . . To have science is to understand something in terms of its causes. The mathematician, however, does not consider the essence of quantity. Neither does he explain [phenomena] in terms of the proper causes by which they are present in quantity, nor does he fashion his demonstrations from predicates proper and *per se*, but from common and accidental ones.[119]

However, the unexpected recovery, emendation, translation and publication of the works of the ancient Greek mathematicians – Euclid in ever more correct texts from 1509 to 1579, Apollodorus in 1537, Archimedes in 1543, Diophanus in 1575 and Pappas in 1588 – made such judgements ever less tenable. With the exception of Niccolò Tartaglia (1499–1557) of Brescia, all the mathematicians were bilingual, even trilingual humanists. They were assured of the enthusiastic support of such prominent patrons of humanist letters as Pietro Bembo, to whom the historian and Hellenist Francesco Maurolico dedicated his *Cosmographia* in 1543, and Cardinal Ranuccio Farnese, who put all the many mathematical manuscripts in his celebrated library at the disposal of Federico Commandino (1509–1575) of Urbino. Inspired by the humanist goal of surpassing their models, the mathematicians drew up ambitious plans for a general 'renaissance of mathematics'; and they set themselves to realizing the plans with such fervour that they soon accomplished major advances in algebra, which had been dormant for some three centuries, and in geometry and statics, which had been dormant for some fifteen centuries.

When the mathematicians then noticed that their mathematical formulas corresponded to what they actually observed in nature – as did Cosimo Bartoli in his *How to Measure Distances* of 1569 and Lodovico Ferrari (1522–1565) when Ferrante Gonzaga put him in charge of tax assessments in Milan – they began to assert boldly what the Greek mathematicians had never dared to claim: that nature operated according to mathematical, rather than syllogistic, logic. A bitter quarrel ensued over the relative certitude of the two kinds of logic, with the orthodox Aristotelians Alessandro Piccolomini and Pietro Catena (1501–1576) on one side and the translator of Proclus' commentary on Euclid, Francesco Barozzi (1537–1604), on the other. When the Archimedans Guidobaldo Del Monte (1545–1607) and Giovan Battista Benedetti (1530–1590), both of whom were also engineers, discovered that objects thrown upward returned along the path of a parabola and that floating bodies behaved as Archimedes, not Aristotle, said they did, they struck at the heart of what had long been spotted as the weakest link in Aristotelian physics: the theory of motion. A few of them went even so far as to put mathematics in the place reserved by Aristotle for the 'Queen of the Sciences'. One of them, indeed, Christopher Clavius of the prestigious Collegio Romano, demanded that 'those *quaestiones* which are of little help in understanding the things of nature' be replaced in the Jesuit school curriculum by mathematics, 'the ignorance of which', he added, 'has led many professors of philosophy to commit many errors in physics', and a knowledge of which is indispensable for correctly understanding the Fathers of the Church.[120]

A still greater challenge to the system-builders came not from the students of any one discipline, but from the ever greater number of individuals who succumbed to the current passion for amassing objects without regard to the concerns of any discipline. Some collectors preferred one kind of object rather than another. Marco Mantova Benavides was interested in books, albeit in every conceivable kind of book on scores of different subjects; and his 'rich collection of prints, vases and coins' remained peripheral with respect to his 'beautiful and copious library'.[121] Tommaso Tommasi was interested in the 'many marvellous secrets of nature' hidden in his garden that might be of use against the plague, just as Francesco Malocchi was interested in 'botany and all natural history'; and their interests led to the establishment of the first botanical gardens in Pisa, Padua and Ferrara. Others were interested in works of art: Vincenzo Gonzaga, for example, who dissipated his family's fortune through 'an unbridled and insatiable desire to get hold of every painting of some value that came onto the market', and Francesco Vendramin, who stuffed the 90 busts, 10 statues, 20 torsoes, 15 bas-reliefs, 6 paintings by Giorgione, etc., into his palace on the Grand Canal. Their interests led to the development of a new kind of institution, or a least a modification of established forms of architecture: the gallery – like the one with 'noble statues placed on pedestals on either side with paintings by the best masters' built by Niccolò Gaddi in Florence, or the one built by Buontalenti on the top floor of the Palazzo degli Uffizi, into which Grand Duke Francesco 'retired for incredibly long periods'.[122]

Above all, the collectors were interested in 'fantastic and bizarre things' – as was Antonio Giganti, for instance, when he set out to supplement the library he inherited from the Bolognese prelate Ludovico Beccadelli with 'ancient and modern works of art, musical instruments, archaeological items, armour, medals, cameos, tapestries . . .'. The institutions they developed were more often *Wunderkammern* – 'wonder chambers' with inlaid wood drawers inserted into false classical façades and all kinds of stuffed animals hanging from the ceiling.[123] Even the relatively circumscribed collection of the greatest of the sixteenth-century naturalists, Ulisse Aldrovandi, was appreciated largely for 'the matter so varied and so delightful and so abundant in many singular bits of information' it contained. Most collections were meant to serve the purpose not of advancing the sciences, but of entertaining or impressing the guests of the proprietor – and sometimes the general public as well. And the public was indeed entertained when such collections were published in the form of the ever more numerous 'encyclopaedias' of the age: it bought up the 90,000 copies of Tommaso Garzoni's *Universal Market of All the Professions of the World* that were printed in Venice alone during the decades after the first edition of 1585.[124]

These collections might indeed have had little more than entertainment value had it not been for the radical empiricism that was forced upon even those collectors most committed to preserving the theoretical systems. Even more upsetting were the frustrations felt by all collectors whenever they tried to organize their collections according to established theoretical criteria. For many of their items, they simply could not find a proper slot; and, like the art theorist Gian Paolo Lomazzo, they left them just as they had found them: 'a vast baggage of big and little bits of information, anxiously picked up as they happened by, even if they were logically and economically extraneous to [the collector's] concerns'.[125] But forcibly shoving other items into an apparently appropriate place often produced irreparable damage to the surrounding structure. Aldrovandi was willing to spare the ancients; they, after all, did not know about the art of engraving. But he would not spare the moderns. For they copied the descriptions written by the ancients without looking at the things that the ancients had described; and they thus filled their works with 'many doubtful statements and infinite errors'. After 'giving myself wholly to making observations' and 'travelling all over Italy, France and Spain looking for new things', Giovan Battista Della Porta also decided that 'our masters have mixed a little truth with much falsehood and have splendidly dirtied their pages with lies'. He therefore went ahead all on his own to put together lenses, which no ancient had ever heard of, in a manner that no modern could explain; and he gave the resulting 'wonder' the portentous name, 'telescope'.[126]

A few philosophers eventually came up with even more radical solutions. Diagnosing the anomalies as proof that the established systems were hopelessly flawed, they set about to find new ones in their stead. They looked first to the normative ages of classical antiquity; and there, happily, they found several alternatives: the sceptical epistemology of Sextus Empiricus reported in Cicero's *Academia*, the heliocentric cosmology of Aristarchos of Samos recently revived by Nicolaus Copernicus − and fully expounded at the court of Pope Clement VII − and the Platonism of the Neoplatonists canonized in the translations and commentaries of Marsilio Ficino. What they could not find in the ancients, they could sometimes find in an adventurous modern transalpine − for instance, in the anti-Aristotelian logic of Pierre de la Ramée (Ramus), who was offered a chair at Bologna in 1551, or in the proto-chemical speculations of Paracelsus. Not only 'high-level fakers', like Leonardo Fioravanti, but even serious anatomists like Gabriele Falloppio were thus induced to search for 'diverse miraculous secrets', which they expected would 'show an easy way to cure all the infirmities of the human body'.[127]

Unfortunately, all the new systems built upon these foundations turned out to have many of the same flaws as the old ones. Copernicus' finite solar system was still afflicted with Ptolemaic epicycles. It did not prove to be noticeably more efficient in predicting planetary movements. It offered no explanation for the 'new star' that suddenly appeared in the orb of the supposedly immutable 'fixed stars' in 1572. Giordano Bruno's synthesis of the Neoplatonists, Nicholas Cusanus and Copernicus made the universe infinite in space and consubstantial with God; but it took no account either of mathematics or of Tridentine theology. Bernardino Telesio's radical empiricism reduced Aristotle's four elements to two, replaced his immobility with innate motion and posited the existence of a corpuscular 'spirit'; but it could not verify any of these alterations empirically.

Similarly, Francesco Patrizi's ideas, emanations and poetic inspirations were inspired by the piety of a Ficinian Franciscan and commended in the name of Augustine to Cardinal Federico Borromeo. They justified the creation of the first chairs of specifically Platonic philosophy − and his appointment to the chairs − at Ferrara and at Rome. And they frightened the Aristotelians in the Holy Office to the point where they delayed the approval of his *Nova de universis philosophia* ('A New Philosophy of the Universe') until the author gave up trying to publish it. But in the end, Patrizi's *L'amorosa filosofia* failed to take account of the abundant post-Ficinian speculation on the nature of love. It reduced the Christian virtue of charity to mere *philautia* − love of self. And it contributed nothing at all to the solution of the other problems that interested the versatile author: how to increase the productivity of cotton on his estates in Cyprus and how to keep the river Reno from silting up the Po east of Ferrara.[128]

SALVAGING THE SYSTEMS

The systems were thus saved by the inherent weaknesses of their metaphysical rivals. At the same time, they were unexpectedly strengthened by the decline, and even demise, of those very realms of contemporary culture that were the least compatible with them. One of these realms was theology, which succumbed to two of its own most important institutions, the Inquisition and the Index. True, Venetian book dealers continued to smuggle prohibited books right past the noses of vigilant border guards. Music for the songs in Machiavelli's *Mandragola* continued to be composed for private performances long after Machiavelli's works were put on the Tridentine Index 'until corrected' (which, fortunately, they never were); Aretino's more salacious writings continued to be printed under disguised titles. And at least one important Jewish text emerged from the censors' hands with nothing removed but a few references to the non-Jewish doctrine of the eternity of the world.[129]

In sixteenth-century Italy, freedom of expression was invariably equated with license – as it was, for instance, by Botero, who blamed it for the rise of Protestantism in Germany. No one ever thought of it as a principle to be defended. Moral aberrations were commonly blamed – even by Machiavelli's nephew, who laboured tirelessly to get his uncle's books approved – on 'the many books that show princes how to be tyrants . . . lawyers how to plead false cases, merchants how to cheat and young men . . . how to steal and get drunk'. Even the self-confident Society of Jesus shielded its recruits from 'obscene books like those of Catullus, Propertius, Plautus, Horace and Martial' that the Tridentine Index had specifically exempted from censorship because of their elegance. No one, therefore, saw much point in exposing himself to charges of error, or worse, heresy, on behalf of questions that Trent, after all, was supposed to have settled. Except for a few obscure monks, Italians stopped writing about theology; and the great post-Tridentine debates over faith, justification and just what Jansenius actually said shifted to the more fertile fields of Louvain and Port Royal.

The other withering realms of culture were all those dedicated to the maintenance of Mannerist forms of expression. Some story and comedy writers, like Anton Francesco Grazzini, tried to insulate themselves from the critics by denigrating Aristotle. Others, like Antonio Riccoboni in his paraphrases of the *Poetics* of 1585, tried to forestall the critics by appropriating for comedy the totally inappropriate Aristotelian quality of catharsis. At least one of them, Raffaello Borghini, tried to return to Bemban orthodoxy with ever more abstract definitions of beauty and grace. But in practice none of them had any better remedy for the progressive rigidity of their art except to add still more complications to the already well-known Plautan and Boccaccian plots and to intersperse ever more salacious details with 'moralistic reflections and maxims'. None of this was at all relevant to an age in which, according to the writer Girolamo Parabosco (d. 1560), 'virtue is so well received and vice so abominated'. Audiences began to doze; and by the 1580s comedy no longer served any other purpose than that of providing intermissions between the acts of what really was interesting: the totally extraneous musical and often dramatic *intermedi*.[130]

Likewise, the last great collective project of Mannerist painting, the Studiolo in the Palazzo Vecchio of Florence, 'died almost at the moment of its birth' in 1574. For the gigantic thighs and protruding buttocks of Girolamo Macchietti's (1535–1592) Pozzuoli bathers were too much even for that most 'Mannerist' of prince-patrons, Francesco de' Medici; and the various pieces of what Vasari intended as an aesthetic whole were not finally put into place until 1910. Shortly afterwards, the magistrates of the Opera del Duomo turned over Vasari's uncompleted frescoes in the cupola not to Vasari's Mannerist disciple, Allori, but to the herald of the Neo-Renaissance in Rome, Taddeo Zuccari. The Accademia del Disegno lost interest in the 'Herculean anatomy' with which an earlier team of its members had decorated its own chapel in the Annunziata. Even the staunch Mannerist Antonio Campi finally threw aside all his 'turgid forms and spectacular effects' and turned instead to 'an intelligent meditation on the value of light'.[131]

What was left of Mannerism retreated to the provinces. It withdrew to Viadana on the Po, where as late as 1587 one Andrea Scutellari could still portray the Baby Jesus with a blue head bent back 180 degrees to look at a boy with a spike hammered into his head (Cremona: Museo Civico). It withdrew to Massa Carrara, where Prince Alberto Cybo hired outside professionals to direct local talent in putting on the now neglected comedies of Sforza degli Oddi (1540–1611) and Parabosco. What remained of Mannerism in the larger cities included such holdovers as the church of S. Paolo Converso in Milan, where the Campi brothers and Giovan Battista Crespi felt obliged to remain faithful to the original designs until they were finally completed in 1611.

Meanwhile, the very forces that are often blamed for ruining Italian culture in the late sixteenth century were actually injecting it with ever greater vitality – namely, the Tridentine Reform and the newly consolidated governments. The reforming bishops returned from Trent with little in hand but the vague injunctions adopted in the last hurried sessions of the Council: that music in churches should not impede the intelligibility of the sung texts, and that paintings in churches should present 'histories', personages and mysteries clearly, accurately and persuasively. Carlo Borromeo, it is true, set out to embellish these injunctions with his own. He rearranged Alessi's aesthetic and iconographical programme on the Holy Mountain. He sold off (but did not destroy) all the 'many statues and beautiful monuments of ancient art' that he found inappropriate in an episcopal palace. And he provoked one dissident painter into publishing – in Brescia, indeed, which lay within his metropolitan jurisdiction – all the letters of support he had solicited from artists throughout Italy.[132] Similarly, ecclesiastical censors occasionally stretched the definition of morality to the point where it encroached dangerously, and in one case ridiculously, upon the officially autonomous realm of literature. That is what happened when they made the philologists of the Accademia Fiorentina 'correct' Boccaccio's *Decameron* – and when, repentant philologists that they were, they then let them italicize 'student' every time it stood for 'priest' in the original and to signal with dots all the excised passages.

Even Borromeo's prescriptions constituted an agile and flexible structure within which diverse forms could move about freely without ever submitting to fixed models.[133] And most of Carlo's colleagues followed instead the example of Gabriele Paleotti, who consulted the experts of his diocese in drawing up his guidelines. Since Paleotti's diocese happened to be Bologna, they happened to be Sigonio and the Carracci; and his widely admired *Discourse on Sacred and Profane Images* of 1582 turned out to be one of the first important manifestoes of Neo-Renaissance art.[134]

The reformers of culture and the reformers of religion, albeit for different reasons, were in complete agreement – when, indeed, they were not the same persons, like Federico Borromeo, the first 'protector' of the Accademia di San Luca in Rome and the founder of the Biblioteca Ambrosiana in Milan. They insisted that works of art be displayed or performed with consideration for a particular time, place and audience; and all of them recognized one another's authority within their particular fields of competence. Barocci's *Visitation*, they admitted, had sent Filippo Neri into ecstasy. It therefore belonged at the Chiesa Nuova in Rome, where Barocci obtained a *carte-blanche* commission. His portrait of Giuliano Della Rovere could do no such thing. It therefore belonged somewhere else – and now resides in the Kunsthistorisches Museum of Vienna. Even where jurisdictions seemed to cross, the men of culture usually had their way. The Oratorians' favourite painter, Cristoforo Roncalli, called 'Il Pomarancio' (1552–1626), modelled his Christian heroes on statues of pagan gods. Palestrina put sacred texts to the music of current popular songs. Lodovico Carracci, after winning his argument with Silvio Antoniano over the dependability of tradition, painted the Apostles looking upward at the *Assumption*, even though the New Testament said nothing about it. Where the jurisdictions remained distinct, the men of culture did as they pleased – as a visitor from Turin discovered in 1577 on a visit to Rome, where, he reported, 'the works of heretics in which they do not write *ex professo* about religion circulate freely, . . . even those of [the Genevan book publisher] Henri Estienne'.[135] Civil censors were usually more arbitrary, then as previously. Whoever wrote, circulated or printed anything without prior permission in Palermo could be sentenced to life in the galleys. A German emissary passing through Venice in 1607 was kept in jail overnight while his bags were searched for anti-Venetian tracts. But ecclesiastical censors replaced the pre-Tridentine 'rigidity of Girolamo Savonarola' with the post-Tridentine rule of Pope Pius v: 'Let the ancient deities stay where they are', said this, the least humanist of the post-conciliar popes, 'even with all their "dishonesties"'. Just keep them out of the way of 'old maids, boys and [other] scrupulous persons'.[136]

Whatever negative effects culture may have suffered from censorship or from self-censorship were amply offset by the great increase in the demand for the products of culture. Someone had to build all the fountains that the viceroys of Naples considered to be necessary for maintaining the magnificence of their capital. Someone had to restructure, paint and stucco the apartments of the nephews of Pope Clement VIII – and thus prove that the new pontificate would equal the praise won by its predecessor, 'in which all the noble arts and talents (*virtù*) were so much appreciated'.[137] Someone had to compose, arrange and execute the masses, vespers, triumphal arches and musical floats with which the Venetian Senate sought to impress both resident subjects and foreign dignitaries; and competition soared whenever the duke of Bavaria or the duke of Parma dispatched another talent-raiding expedition. Someone had to build and decorate all the new confraternity chapels and private residences in provincial Pordenone; and so rapidly (or inefficiently) were commissions assigned that many square metres of fresco are still today waiting for their paternity. Someone had to fill the many positions opened up at Palermo when King Philip II endowed the cathedral choir and when the city council decreed the creation of a civic band. Someone had to construct façades worthy of those of Dosio and Buontalenti in the capital for all the new or restructured 'main streets' of Pescia, Pisa, Colle Valdelsa and San Miniato. Someone had to staff the new travelling theatre companies, whose actors and singers were constantly being drained off for the benefit of the new permanent companies – like the one established by the duke of Mantua in 1589.

Above all, someone had to satisfy the needs of an ever-growing number of literate and discriminating consumers. In 1587, 4,481 boys were enrolled in the humanistic and 'vernacular' schools of Venice, who, by the time they grew up, would constitute 30 percent of the adult male population.[138] By 1574, the 'nobility of Bologna' had realized all of Leon Battista Alberti's fondest hopes for a humanist citizen body. According to the French traveller Nicolas Audebert,

there is none of them who does not have some special virtue to which he dedicates himself entirely – some to good letters, or at least to learning the Latin language, which few of them do not know; others to philosophy, to histories written in their language . . . to playing the lute or singing music.[139]

By the 1580s, local notables even in distant Urbino could read much of ancient and modern literature in their own homes: Giovan Maria Alessandri, for instance, had Guicciardini, Cavalcanti and Panvinio as well as Virgil and Sallust among the 285 titles in his private library. Their sons could thus hope to rival the not uncommon accomplishments of Bernardino Baldi (1553–1617), who mastered mathematics, logic, mechanics and the Greek Church Fathers; who studied Petrarch, Homer, Pindar, Aeschylus and Theocritus in order to express himself properly after falling in love; who 'read

St Augustine's *The City of God* three times from beginning to end while seated at the supper table', who 'after supper, for recreation, took in hand Euclid translated into Arabic or some book in German or French', and who applied his copious learning to biographies of the mathematicians – including Copernicus.[140]

That this rise in demand for talent succeeded in provoking a corresponding rise in supply was due in large measure to the ever increasing openness of Italian society toward whoever possessed it. Birth, first of all, was no more a deterrent in the late sixteenth century than it had been since the time of Leonardo. The otherwise obligatory proofs of office-holding ancestors for admission to the Order of Santo Stefano were instantly waived to accommodate the learned printer Aldo Manuzio the younger. A Ferrarese shopkeeper named Figotto was given a court pension, an expense account for his family and 'all the extravagant costumes he wanted' after Duke Alfonso II heard him recite his 'jokes and witty stories'. Cardinal Cinzio Aldobrandini visited the ailing poet Tasso in a Roman hospital and provided him with a carriage and two servants. And the physicians Giovan Paolo Turri and Zanino Cigalino were rewarded for their 'singular eloquence' as well as for their 'exceptional knowledge of all the disciplines' with two of the largest funeral monuments in the cathedral of Como.[141]

Gender became much less a deterrent to the advancement of women than it had been in the days of Castiglione's courtier. Falloppio's dissections of female sex organs dealt a severe blow to both the Aristotelian thesis of the passive role of women in the act of generation and Alessandro Piccolomini's thesis of their 'natural' delicacy and frivolity. The Academy of Piacenza's reception of such 'learned' as well as 'beautiful and honest' members as Ippolita Borromeo and Camilla Valente challenged Platonic notions of women as silent abstractions.[142] A number of women had successful careers in the arts and letters. Lucrezia Bendidio (1547–c. 1583) won an important place in the court of Ferrara by playing a leading role in Tasso's *Aminta*. Laura Peverara's (c. 1547–1601) soprano voice won her the dedications of three madrigal anthologies, one of them by the Accademia dei Rinnovati. Laura Battiferri (1523–1589) of Urbino became not just the wife, but also the professional colleague of the architect Ammannati, and she published several volumes of her own poetry.[143] The painters Lavinia Fontana (1552–1614) and Sofonisba Anguissola (1527–1625) painted portraits of gentlemen (Cremona: Museo Civico) as well as much admired self-portraits – Lavinia on enamelled copper (Florence: Uffizi), Sofonisba playing a small harpsichord (Naples: Capodimonte). And Fede Galizia (1578–1630) managed to overcome her adolescent shyness by the age of eighteen to paint an impeccably Neo-Renaissance portrait of the leading scholar of Milan, Paolo Morigia, with pursed lips and slightly closed eyes holding a pair of eyeglasses with one hand and a pen with the other (Milan: Pinacoteca Ambrosiana).

Meanwhile, whatever barriers had previously separated men of culture in one city from those in another totally disappeared. Florentines in the mid-fifteenth century may have offered 'a chilling, if not inhospitable climate for visiting scholars', who complained about the 'feuding and intrigue' that left them 'no peace of mind at all'.[144] But Florentines in the late sixteenth century enrolled the Pugliese historian Scipione Ammirato and the Genoese poet Gabriello Chiabrera into their academies within moments of their arrival. Venetians had once been suspicious of Genoese. Now they persuaded the Genoese patrician Gabriele Salvago to stay with them for ten years. As Salvago wrote to his friends back home:

Outsiders, whether gentlemen or men of letters, are very well regarded, sought after and esteemed by these noblemen; they never give offence, and they converse with dignity and great pleasure.[145]

Local specializations remained, even in such new disciplines as dramatic music. But what happened in one city was immediately broadcast in all the others. Artists and writers moved willingly to wherever they were called by offers of commissions or honours – Veronese to Rome in the company of the Venetian ambassador, Federico Zuccari (1542/3–1609) to Venice in the company of Veronese, and the 'itinerant painters' of Ravenna between Macerata, Forlì, Rimini and Bologna – which is where they probably learned to paint like the Bolognesi.

The remaining barriers between Italians and non-Italians collapsed as well. The Florentines welcomed as one of their own Giambologna from Boulogne-sur-Mer and Pauwels Franik ('Paolo Fiammingo'), Tintoretto's assistant for *San Rocco nel Deserto*, from Flanders. The citizens of the small southern town of Muro Lucano invited the Fleming Cornelius Smet to work in their cathedral church. The citizens of Parma commissioned Jean Sons of Bar-le-Duc to complete Parmigianino's unfinished *David and St Cecilia*. The Romans, in what the Tridentine Reform had made the most 'international' city of all Europe, hired the musicians Firmin de Bel from France, Francisco Soto de Langa from Spain and Christian Ameyden from Belgium. Titian in Venice welcomed into his workshop Domenico Theotokopoulos of Crete; and, after studying Tintoretto and Taddeo Zuccari, working for Alessandro Farnese and then migrating to Toledo in Spain, Domenico became the most famous of all the migrant artists with the nickname of 'El Greco'.

Many foreigners came to Italy to learn from the Italians. Prince Ludwig of Anhalt-Kothen, for example, learned enough during his stay in Florence in 1600 to make his court the centre of *Italienisches Geschmack* in Germany; and he adopted the statutes of the Accademia della Crusca, of which he was a member, as the basis of the Fruchtbringende Gesellschaft he founded for the parallel purpose of encouraging German literature. At the same time Italians were often just as anxious to learn from foreigners. Alessandro Allori took his notions of anatomy not only from the immigrant Belgian Vesalius, but also from the Spaniard Juan de Valverde, whose *History of the Composition of the Human Body* was published in Rome, first in Spanish (1556) and then in Italian (1560). Chiabrera borrowed many of his themes and some of his lines from the Pléiade poet Ronsard's *Les Amours*, about which he subsequently wrote a commentary. The Italian compilers of the *Political*

Treasure of 1600 plagiarized René de Lucinge, whose *Birth, Duration and Fall of States* had appeared in Italian translation ten years earlier.

What most persuasively seemed to confirm the validity of the systems, however, was their effects, or at least the effects attributed to them, in the realm of the arts and letters. First of all, the systems were given credit for the several masterpieces of Aristotelian literary genres composed by the most prolific of the poet-critics of the Neo-Renaissance, Torquato Tasso. He was the son of the eminent Mannerist poet Bernardo and a disciple of the eminent Aristotelian philosopher-rhetoricians Sperone Speroni and Antonio Minturno. He was a close friend of the leading poets and scholars of all the several Italian cities in which from time to time he resided – Mantua, Venice, Padua, Ferrara, Rome, Naples, Turin; and he was thus one of the most prominent representatives of a national, rather than a regional or municipal, culture. He was imbued with all the literary classics of the High Renaissance and took inspiration even from the one of them to which his own work was most often critically contrasted, the *Orlando furioso*. He mastered all the poetic and philosophical literature of antiquity, from Virgil to Demetrius of Phaleron, whom he read with the help of Pier Vettori's commentary of 1562; and he put red-ink annotations in the margins of the works of all the leading critics, poets and scholars of his own day – including Giovanni Lorenzo d'Anania's vast *Cosmografia* (1573) of miscellaneous geographical, astronomical and botanical information.[146]

Tasso was better prepared than most of his learned and creative contemporaries to elaborate on the High Renaissance models – e.g., by 'hiding the rhetorical figure' and reducing the excessive ornamentation to make the rhetoric of contrast and the ethos of naturalness agree, in place of Bembo's profusion of measureless oppositions in his own sonnets[147] – and to block the theorists' objections to authorized epic devices, like 'marvels', by introducing a device that they had not yet thought of – in this case, allegory.[148] Being a theorist himself – notably in his discourses *On the Art of Poetry* and *On the Heroic Poem* – he fully concurred in recognizing the primacy of 'critical consciousness in the process of poetic creation' and in 'subordinating spontaneity . . . to the lucid control of the norms authorized by the tradition and justified by reason'.[149] Being a talented creator, he could add to and modify the culture he had inherited without ever 'doubting for a moment that the only truth lay precisely in [that] culture'.[150] In spite of bouts of temporary insanity, he produced a *Canzoniere* that was less static and therefore more emotionally forceful than all other sixteenth-century imitations of Petrarch, scores of dialogues on philosophical moral subjects that equalled in quality those of Cicero and Castiglione and a tragedy, based on a recent translation of the Scandinavian chronicle of Olaus Magnus, that avoided the stiff formalities of his chief High Renaissance model, Trissino's *Sofonisba*. More important still, he finally arrived at the goal toward which so many of his predecessors – including his close friend, Ariosto's great-nephew Orazio – had striven in vain. He gave the Italian Volgare an epic poem worthy of Homer in Greek, Virgil in Latin and, a half-century later, Milton in English: the *Gerusalemme liberata* ('Jerusalem Delivered') published in 1581. So well did he succeed, indeed, that he failed, in the subsequent *Gerusalemme conquistata*, to surpass his own masterpiece. Cardinal Scipione Gonzaga copied the entire text in his own hand. The Florentine linguistic purists retreated into silence. And the glory-seeking Rinaldo, the tormented lover Tancredi, the female warrior Clorinda, the sorceress Armida, the devils, the duels, the 'Fortunate Isles' and the enchanted garden soon became common reference points on all levels of Italian culture.

Even more important, the systems managed to accommodate themselves to the admission of a wholly new discipline to the ranks of those previously sanctioned by the humanists and the philosophers: music. Throughout the early Renaissance, the theory of music had remained locked in the metaphysical categories of the seven liberal arts, and the practice of music was condoned by the Ficinian Platonists mainly for its soothing, not for its stimulating or exciting, qualities. Church music was entrusted almost entirely to Flemings – like the composer-conductors Josquin des Prez, Adrian Willaert and Cipriano de Rore and like the singers in the papal chapel in Rome. Secular music too was imported, even when the performers themselves were natives, at least for such occasions as a performance of Machiavelli's *Mandragola*.[151]

This music was totally untouched by the Aristotelian notion of decorum, since each of the increasing number of autonomous and equally weighted voices in *a cappella* choirs sang different words at the same time. Occasional attempts to draw attention to certain words like 'flee', 'hell' or 'heaven' by making the melodic line go faster, down or up did little to satisfy the humanists' interest in the effect, rather than just the definition, of the word. Moreover, this music was increasingly out of step with what the ancients were found to have reported about music in antiquity – not only Augustine and Boethius, who had been known throughout the Middle Ages, but now Ptolemy, Plutarch and Quintilian, whose relevant texts were collected by Giorgio Valla and Carlo Valguglio, and Aristoxenes, whose *Three Books on the Elements of Harmony* were published in Latin translation in 1550.

The Italian musicians who were trained by the Flemings began to look for alternatives. They did not reject their masters just because they were 'foreigners', since no one had yet discovered that such a category had anything to do with anyone's qualifications as an artist or anything to do with art. Indeed, the canons of Ravenna continued to hire Flemish organists until 1595, and Giovanni Maria Artusi specifically commended one of the chief accomplishments of Flemish music in his *Art of Counterpoint* of 1586. But the disciples were searching for what the masters could not provide: a music that moved as well as pleased and that could be appropriately set to Petrarchan sonnets or to the Mass without either distracting the listener or making him laugh. They pushed the system of eight medieval modes almost to its breaking point. They replaced a 'horizontal' with a 'vertical' arrangement of the parts, as in Vincenzo Ruffo's five-part Mass of 1557, so that all the singers sang the same word at the same time.[152] They experimented with chromaticism, 'kaleidoscopic' chord changes, and 'tricky rhythm[s] abounding in syncopation, upbeats and unexpected accelerations, retards and sudden stops', like those of the Italian theorist-composer, Nicolò Vicentino (1511–1576).[153]

At the same time, Italian artisans elaborated upon the popular lute to the point where it would hardly fit onto the lap of Bernardino Campi's aged David in San Sigismondo at Cremona. They added more keyboards to the organ and thus justified the growing number of Italian organ makers in remaking all the organs of Italy. And they invented new instruments – for example, the violin, of which the first seems to have been made in Brescia in the 1510s or 1520s; the domestic positive organ, which was apparently so easy to play that Titian's young organist could keep his eyes fixed not on the keyboard, but on the reclining nude amusing herself with a little dog behind his back (*Venus and the Organ Player*, Madrid: Prado); Vicentino's *arcicembalo* of 1555, which was so difficult to play that no one but the inventor ever managed to play it; and the *lira da braccio* (a sort of fiddle), which they supposed to be a reincarnation of the ancient lyre. They improved upon the system of musical notation so that it could express fractions of tones, and they refined the art of printing to produce elegant volumes like that held up by a cupid while Domenichino's *St Cecilia* (Paris: Louvre) plays on one of the new six-stringed *viole da gamba*.

Some of these experiments were hazardous enough to provoke complaints. 'These modern dances', said the Florentine critic Anton Francesco Doni,

are a strange enigma. Jump up, jump down, run there, come back, skip around, and make a thousand motions capable of splitting a suit of armour, not to speak of your lungs.[154]

Some of them were so hazardous that they have led those modern musicologists with a limited knowledge of other aspects of sixteenth-century culture to denigrate them with loaded adjectives borrowed from anti-Mannerist art historians – and to ignore the impossibility of Mannerist music in the obvious absence of High Renaissance music.[155] But some of them were also successful in achieving the aims of humanist and Aristotelian rhetoric. When Psyche finished singing Alessandro Striggio's score to her *Lament* at the marriage of Prince Francesco de' Medici in 1565, the whole audience was in tears.[156]

What finally funnelled these experiments into what modern historians of music have called 'a veritable revolution' (Lowinsky) and the most important 'change in styles [*Stilwandel*] in Western music' in early modern times (Fellerer) was the fortuitous conjunction of four circumstances. First, the experimenters submitted to the guidance of the theoreticians: Vicentino, Cosimo Bartoli, and Gioseffo Zarlino's (1517–1590) ostentatiously rebellious disciple, Vincenzo Galilei (d. 1591), the lute-playing father of the philosopher Galileo. These theorists clearly defined the purpose of music as rhetorical, and they thus assured its promotion within the established philosophic and aesthetic systems as a qualitative equal of all the other arts and sciences. Second, the Council of Trent's call for intelligibility coincided exactly with what the experimentalists were striving for; and it spurred the Vatican's *maestro di capella*, Giovanni Pierluigi da Palestrina (d. 1594), into demonstrating that intelligibility could be achieved through his own specialty, polyphony. 'I', declared Palestrina,

who for so many years have concerned myself with this art, not wholly unsuccessfully, decided that, following the counsel of the most grave and religious men, I should henceforth dedicate myself wholly to the greatest and most divine affair of the Christian religion: that is, the most holy sacrifice of the Mass, and to put all my efforts into adorning it according to new modes.[157]

Third, several forms of popular vocal music required the coordination of the various voices in such a way as to assure the communicability of the words – the *villanella*, the *villota*, the *canzone alla napolitana*, the liturgical *falsobordone*, the *laude spirituale* – and similar aesthetic aims guided composers of the madrigal, 'the most forward looking and experimental genre of the sixteenth century'.[158] All that remained to be done by one of the greatest of the revolutionists, Claudio Monteverdi (1567–1643), was to restrict polyphony in his theatrical music and to make the lower voices accompany, rather than compete with, the highest voice; and thus a single melodic line could be followed without interference throughout the entire composition. Fourth, and last, the gentleman-philologist from Florence, Girolamo Mei (1519–1594), during one of his exploratory expeditions through the Vatican Library, happened upon several pieces of ancient musical notation. And even though neither he nor anyone since could be sure what they meant, he, and his Florentine correspondent Vincenzo Galilei, were certain that they furnished indisputable empirical evidence of what they had gathered from the testimony of the ancient observers: that ancient music was so effective precisely because it was monophonic, not polyphonic.

That is just the news that the increasing number of professional virtuoso singers wanted to hear. Rather than being lost in a choir, they could now use their musical skills to play on the emotions of their audience, just like poets and actors – for example, with such devices as the sixteen bars of 32d notes placed by Luzzasco Luzzaschi (d. 1607) over the penultimate syllable of a final *morire* in 1601. It was good news also to the associates of such learned music patrons as Giovanni de' Bardi in Florence and Mario Bevilacqua in Verona; and both Bardi's informal Camerata and Bevilacqua's well-organized music school, the Accademia Filarmonica, set out to explore in scores and performances all the possibilities of single melodies supported by a *basso continuo*. The instrumentalists were happy as well. Freed at last of their role as supplementary voices, they could develop an independent, and equally emotive, music for accompanied instrumental soloists; and early in the next century Biagio Marini (d. 1663) produced the first datable examples of what became one of the most important forms of concert music, the solo sonata.

Most important of all, the systems proved capable of facilitating, even of promoting, the generation of new forms of art through the conjunction of old ones. The art of engraving, for example, encountered the science of geography, which had recently been reconstructed upon ancient foundations by such latter-day Strabos as Leandro Alberti, in his *Description of Italy*, and Giovan Battista Ramusio, in his vast collection of accounts of overseas voyages. Engraving and geography were then introduced to the grandiose geometrical and sociological designs of the ideal city planners, like those in Vignola's Vitruvian Academy in Rome. The traditional bird's-eye thereupon took off. In Matteo Pagani's *Venice* of 1559 it reached a point well above the level of nearby hills or towers. In Stefano Bonsignori's *Florence* of 1584 and *Tuscany* of 1589 and in Antonio Tempesta's *Rome* of 1593 it arrived at a point directly over its object. And in Giacomo Castaldo's *Italiae novissima descriptio* of 1573 it floated up into the stratosphere – so far up, indeed, that the Po Delta seemed to be twice its real size, Tuscany and the Marche appeared to have lurched several degrees off their axis, and Neptune was caught making love to a nymph next to a double-bellied Corsica. The now autonomous art of cartography was then presented to the public; and the response was such that the Venetian cartographers alone were able to exhibit sixty-seven samples at the Frankfurt fair by as early as 1573.[159]

Similarly, architecture was introduced to sculpture through the good graces of botany, as in Sannazaro's *Arcadia* and Tasso's enchanted garden. It was immunized against the artificiality of those nervous Neapolitans who buried 'certain small things that are really marvellous' under an excessive number of 'fountains, cedars and loggias'.[160] It was protected against Titian's overcast forests and Girolamo Muziano's (1528–1592) craggy precipices – which marked the early steps in the direction of independent landscapes in painting.[161] It reached adolescence at Vignola's and Taddeo Zuccari's Villa Giulia outside the Porta del Popolo at Rome. And it finally matured in the series of cascades that the Neapolitan architect Pirro Ligorio (d. 1583) designed, after a study tour of the nearby ruins of Hadrian's Villa, for Ippolito II d'Este at Tivoli and in the straight paths, clipped shrubs and nymph-populated pools that Tribolo (1500–50), Buontalenti and Giambologna unfolded upward from the back of the Palazzo Pitti and downward from the terrace of the Villa di Castello at Florence.

Nature submitted to *virtù* at Pratolino, where water gushed forth, far from any known springs, for the benefit of Giambologna's colossal Appenine. Nature bowed to Aristotle himself in the park that the architect-engineer, Ascanio Vitozzi of Orvieto (*c*. 1539–1615), built for Duke Carlo Emanuele I outside of Turin: one *allée* was named for the senses, another for the liberal arts. And nature realigned itself according to Aristotelian categories at the ducal garden in Parma, which constituted

a compendium of all happy and delightful things . . . beds divided with remarkable order and artifice, long and spacious walkways, a labyrinth with intricate and twisted paths, some six thousand orange trees, pines, oaks, and plane trees where live various wild animals . . . ponds with a great quantity of fish . . .[162]

The 'Italian Garden' thereupon proceeded to conquer the whole of Europe, from the Luxembourg to the Tuileries; and its dominion was not challenged until the appearance of the 'English Garden' a century and a half later.

Meanwhile in Ferrara pastoral poetry had been combined with music, in Agostino de' Beccari's *Il sacrificio*, and in Giraldi's version of a satyr play, the *Egle*, performed in Ferrara in 1545, to produce pastoral drama – plays in which the action was removed from reality by entrusting it to nymphs, satyrs and equally unreal shepherds and in which dramatic climaxes were reinforced by having the actors sing, rather than recite, the corresponding lines. Pastoral poetry was then combined with painting and technology by the poet Tasso and the ducal engineer Pasi da Carpi in the *Aminta* of 1573; and this was done with 'a vivaciousness of inventive fantasy' that guaranteed 'original solutions' to current questions about the effectiveness of drama.[163]

In Florence, which some historians still persist in decrying as 'an artistic backwater',[164] music and painting were joined with dance. Fortunately, dance had just recently been established as an autonomous art form by the ballerino-choreographer Cesare Negri, first in the performances put on for Don Juan of Austria in Milan, then in the fifty-eight copper plate illustrations of his *Le gratie d'amore* and *Nuove inventioni di balli* of 1602. Cristiano Lambertini was therefore free to add twelve more to the conventional three couples in his *Ruota di fortuna* ('Fortune's Wheel') and *La battaglia* ('Battle') of 1589; and after the grand duke's guests had 'danced most of the night' in the Palazzo Pitti, dance, painting and poetry poured out into Piazza Santa Croce in the *Mascherata de' fiumi* ('Masquerade of the Rivers'), with one of the grand duke's cousins representing the Arno and another the Seine, a scene that made an enormous impression upon the papal nuncio.[165] All the world became a stage, or at least 'all Padua' became 'a theatre where Echo resounds'; and theatre metaphors soon became a popular way of describing everything from the planets to the Venetian Republic.[166]

Theatrical space, on the other hand, was separated from other kinds of space in the form of permanent theatres, first at the Teatro di Baldracci located in what is now a parking lot behind the Uffizi, and then inside the Uffizi itself. Rejecting the archaeological staticism of Palladio's Teatro Olimpico at Vicenza, Buontalenti extended the stage outward into the orchestra, made it slope so as to be fully visible from all U-shaped tiers of spectators' seats and equipped it with pulleys and trap doors. 'Pisa' could thus be transformed instantly into a 'garden'; a mountain could rise up and then break apart into grottoes; and gods could fly down from heaven without visible supports.

Similarly, the 'sumptuous *intermedi*' with 'excessively expensive scenery' that alone could lure audiences to 'ridiculous comedies' even in Ferrara finally swallowed up the last of the Florentine comedies, Francesco D'Ambra's (1499–1558) *La Cofanaria*. German visitors were not the least annoyed at not being able to understand the 'conceits of the comedy', for they were made perfectly 'happy by the beautiful variety of the *intermedi* and the excellent music'.[167] As for tragedy, the theorists of the Accademia degli Alterati joined the theorists of the Camerata in proposing a bold remedy for all its all-too-apparent defects: have the entire text, not just a few arias, put to music. What the theorists proposed, the partrician poet-librettist Ottavio Rinuccini (1562–1621) carried out, first in an expanded pastoral *intermedio*, the *Dafne*, and then in a full-length play, the *Euridice*, in which blank verse and rhymed verse were blended into a single recitative. When first Giulio Caccini (d. 1618) and then Jacopo Peri (1561–1633) set Rinuccini's second text to monodic lines, with an instrumental accompaniment strictly limited to the function of reinforcing the emotive quality of the words, Orfeo needed the help only of a few instruments 'to break the hard surface of every rock' (Scene 5). When he reminded Pluto of how he too once 'did weep . . . on the mountain of eternal ardor' (Scene 4), he succeeded in obtaining the first, and last, dispensation from Pluto's pragmatic rule of never allowing exceptions to the law. 'Tragedy' thus made sure that 'every gentle spirit that Apollo inspires/will tread in the tracks of my new path' (Prologue) for some four centuries thereafter – namely, in the path of what Peri called *dramma in musica* and what ever since has been called 'opera'.[168]

The vitality as well as the validity of the Aristotelian and High Renaissance theoretical systems was thus spectacularly confirmed. And the aesthetic and philosophic establishments gave every promise of being as solidly founded and as potentially immortal as peace, prosperity, the political order and the Tridentine Church.

NOTES AND REFERENCES

1. *Memorie di un terrazzano di Rivoli dal 1535 al 1586*, in *Miscellanea di storia italiana*, VI, Turin 1865.
2. Giovanni Pietro Contarini, *Historia delle cose successe dal principio della guerra mossa da Selim Ottomano a' Venetiani fino al dì della gran giornata vittoriosa contra Turchi*, Venice 1572.
3. Lodovico Paterno quoted from his *Della Mirtia* (Naples 1564) by Francisco Elias de Tejada in 'El primado napolitano', in *Le parole e le idee*, 1, 1959, p. 11.
4. Antonia Rumeu de Armas, *Alfonso de Ulloa, introductor de la cultura española en Italia*, Madrid 1973; Gian Luigi Beccaria, *Spagnolo e Spagnoli in Italia: Riflessi ispanici sulla lingua italiana del Cinque e del Seicento*, Turin 1968.
5. Franco Saba, 'Grano e diplomazia: Milano, Svizzera e Spagna in un trattato del tardo Cinquecento', *RSI*, 92, 1980; Giovanni Vigo, *Fisco e società nella Lombardia del Cinquecento*, Bologna 1979, part 1, ch. 11.
6. Quoted by Antonio Panella in 'Il principe nuovo in una lettera di Cosimo I', in *Pegaso*, 1, 1929.
7. Antonio Rotondò, 'Esuli italiani in Valtellina nel Cinquecento', *RSI*, 88, 1976, pp. 762 ff.
8. Anon., *Diario della ribellione d'Urbino nel 1572 d'ignoto autore* (here quoted), ed. Filippo Ugolini in *ASI*, n.s., 3, 1856.

9. Giovanni Forcheri, 'Il ritorno allo stato di polizia dopo la Costituzione del 1576', *Atti della Società ligure di Storia Patria*, 83, 1969.

10. Michelangelo Mendella, *Il moto napoletano del 1585 e il delitto Storace*, Naples 1967; but the most authoritative study is that of Rosario Villari, *La rivolta antispagnola di Napoli: Le origini (1585–1647)*, Bari 1967. The figures given here appear on p. 320 of the selection from this book published in English translation in my *The Late Italian Renaissance, 1525–1630*, New York 1970.

11. Quoted by Rosario Villari in *Ribelli e riformatori dal XVI al XVIII secolo*, Rome 1979, p. 47.

12. Onofrio Panvinio in the preface to his edition and continuation of Bartolomeo Platino, *Vite de' pontefici*, quoted from p. 597 of the edition of Venice 1730.

13. Massimo Livi Bacci, *La société italienne devant les crises de mortalité*, Florence 1978.

14. Lorenzo Del Panta, *Una traccia di storia demografica della Toscana nei secoli XVI–XVIII*, Florence 1974.

15. Claudio Povolo, 'Evoluzione demografica della valle nei secoli XVI–XVIII', in Paolo Preto (ed.), *La Valle del Chiampo: Vita civile ed economica in età moderna e contemporanea*, Vicenza 1981, I; Brian S. Pullan, *Rich and Poor in Renaissance Venice: The Social Institutions of a Catholic State to 1620*, Oxford 1971, p. 218 (on Verona). In general: Daniele Beltrami, *Storia della popolazione di Venezia dalla fine del secolo XVI alla caduta della Repubblica*, Padua 1954.

16. Mario Rotili, *L'arte del Cinquecento nel Regno di Napoli*, Naples 1972, p. 35.

17. Dante Zanetti, *Problemi alimentari di una economia preindustriale: Cereali a Pavia dal 1398 al 1700*, Turin 1964, pp. 27, 36.

18. Marzio Achille Romani, *Nella spirale di una crisi: Popolazione, mercato e prezzi a Parma tra Cinque e Seicento*, Milan 1975.

19. The recent bibliography on the economic history of this period is summarized by Renato Giusti, 'Problemi di storia economica tra Cinquecento e Seicento', *ASI*, 138, 1980, pp. 3–39. Referred to here are: Domenico Sella, 'The rise and fall of the Venetian wool industry' (from the original French version of 1957), in my *The Late Italian Renaissance, 1525–1630* (above, n. 10); Paolo Malanima, 'Industria e commercio in Toscana tra Cinque e Seicento', in *SS*, 21, 1980, and in *La decadenza di un'economia cittadina: L'industria di Firenze nei secoli XVI–XVII*, Bologna 1982 (on which note the debate between Malanima and Osvaldo Raggio in *QS*, 52, 1983); Roberta Morelli, *La seta fiorentina nel Cinquecento*, Milan 1976; Tito Broggi, *Storia del setificio comasco*, II. *La tecnica: Dalle origini alla fine del Settecento*, Como 1958; Giovanni Muto, 'La economia del Mezzogiorno continental de la segunda mitad del Cinquecento a la crisis de los años cuarenta del siglo XVII' in *Cuadernos de Investigación Historica*, 1, 1977; F. Ruiz Martin in the introduction to his edition of *Lettres marchandes échangées entre Florence et Medina del Campo*, Paris 1965, pp. lvii ff.; Carmelo Trasselli, 'I banchi delle città minori nel Cinquecento siciliano', in *Nuovi quaderni del meridionale*, 8, 1970; Luigi Fosco Girard, 'Toscana e Mezzogiorno' in *Napoli nel Cinquecento e la Toscana dei Medici*, Naples 1980 (on interest rates).

20. Giulio Mandich, *Le pacte de ricorsa et le marché italien des changes au XVIIe siècle*, Paris 1953; José Gentil Da Silva, *Banque et crédit en Italie au XVIIe siècle*, Paris 1969; Domenico Gioffrè, *Gênes et les foires de change de Lyon à Besançon*, Paris 1960.

21. Bernardo Segni, *Storie fiorentine di Messer Bernardo Segni, gentiluomo fiorentino, dall'anno MDXXVII al MDLV. Colla vita di Niccolò Capponi . . . descritta dal medesimo*

Segni suo nipote . . ., Milano, Società tipografica de' Classici italiani, 1805, vol. 3, p. 278.

22. Renzo Amedeo, 'Un viaggio da Garessio a Roma', in *Bollettino della Società per gli studi storici, archeologici ed artistici nella provincia di Cuneo*, 82, 1980.

23. Giuseppe Betussi, *Ragionamento sopra il Cathaio*, Padua 1573.

24. Giovan Battista Del Tufo, in Calogero Tagliareni (ed.), *Opera manoscritta del marchese Giov. Battista del Tufo, poeta napoletana del '500*, Naples 1954, p. 44.

25. Archivio di Stato, Florence, Mediceo del Principato 354.

26. Michele Cassandro, *Le fiere di Lione e gli uomini d'affari italiani nel Cinquecento*, Florence 1979, Ch. 3.

27. Quoted by Armando Frumento in *Imprese lombarde nella storia della siderurgia italiana*, vol. 2: *Il ferro milanese fra il 1450 e il 1796*, Milan 1963, p. 78.

28. Cipriano Piccolpasso, *I tre libri dell'arte del vasajo, nei quali si tratta non solo la pratica, ma brevemente tutti i secreti di essa cosa che persino al dì d'oggi è stata sempre tenuta nascosta*, ed. G. Vanzolini, Pesaro 1879.

29. Giovanni Botero, *Della ragion di Stato* (1589), ed. Luigi Firpo, Turin 1948, Book viii, Ch. 3, pp. 246, 249.

30. Cornaro quoted by Giuseppe Fiocco, *Alvise Cornaro: Il suo tempo e le sue opere*, Vicenza 1965, p. 102. Other information from Vincenzo Fontana, *Alvise Cornaro e il suo tempo*, Padua 1980, and from Angelo Ventura (here quoted), 'Le trasformazioni economiche nel Veneto tra Quattro e Ottocento' in *Bollettino del Centro Internazionale di Studi di Architettura Andrea Palladio*, 18, 1976, pp. 127–42.

31. Salvo Di Matteo and Francesco Pilliteri, *Storia dei monti di pietà in Sicilia*, Palermo 1973; Henri Lapeyre, 'Banque et crédit en Italie du xvie au xviiième siècle' in *Revue d'histoire moderne et contemporaine*, 8, 1961; Romolo Camaiti, 'L'attività bancaria a Siena nel Seicento . . . Monte dei Paschi . . .' in *Archivi storici delle aziende di credito*, 1, 1956.

32. Domenico Demarco, *La struttura economica-sociale del Mugello nei secoli xv–xvi*, Accademia Nazionale dei Lincei (Quaderno no. 129), Rome 1969; Elisa Luzzatti Gregori, 'Vicende del patrimonio Cavalcanti e organizzazione della "fatoria" tra xv e xvii secolo', in *Ricerche di storia moderna*, 2, 1979; Mauro Ambrosoli, *'L'Opus agriculturae di Palladio'*, in *QS*, 52, 1983; Marino Berengo, 'Un agronomo toscano del Cinquecento. Francesco Tommasi da Colle Val D'Elsa' in *Studi Sestan*, vol. 2 (above, Chapter 4, n. 36); Vettori to Baccio Valori, 4 September 1580, quoted by Francesco Niccolai in his *Pier Vettori (1499–1585)*, Florence 1912, p. 18, n. 61.

33. 12 December 1542, in her *Lettere*, ed. Isidore Del Lungo, Florence 1883, p. 29.

34. Quoted by Ennio Concina in 'Per la *conditione* contadina nel secondo cinquecento. Note al villano in Tommaso Garzoni', in *Archivio veneto*, 138, 1974, p. 76.

35. Ruggero Moscati, 'Documenti su Rocca Cilento', in *Clio*, 14, 1978; Giuseppe Galasso, *Economia e società nella Calabria del Cinquecento*, Naples 1967, Ch. 4, which contains many other relevant statistics.

36. Paolo Malanima, 'La proprietà fiorentina e la diffusione della mezzadria nel contado pisano nei secoli xv e xvi', in *Contadini e proprietari nella Toscana moderna: Atti del convegno di studi in onore di Giorgio Giorgetti*, Florence 1979, vol. 1, p. 367; Marzio Achille Romani, *Nella spirale di una crisi* (above, n. 18); Giovanni Masi, *Organizzazione ecclesiastica e ceti rurali in Puglia nella seconda metà*

del Cinquento, Bari 1957; Amelio Tagliaferri, *Struttura e politica sociale in una comunità veneta del '500 (Udine)*, Milan 1969.

37. Ruggiero Romano, 'La Marine marchande vénitienne au XVIe siècle' in *Les sources de l'histoire maritime en Europe du Moyen Age au XVIIIe siècle*, Paris 1962, pp. 33–68; *Guerra e commercio nell'evoluzione della marina genovese tra XV e XVII secolo*, Genoa and Florence 1970, especially the article by Manlio Calegari; Luciana Gatti, 'Costruzioni navali in Liguria fra XV e XVI secolo' in *Studi di storia navale*, Florence 1975 (with an abundance of figures and graphs).

38. Quoted by Cassandro in *Le fiere di Lione* (above, n. 26), p. 97.

39. Halil Inalcik, 'L'Empire Ottoman', in *Actes du premier congrès international des études Balkaniques et sud-est européennes*, Sofia 1969, III, pp. 75–103; Marian Malowist, 'Capitalismo commerciale e agricoltura', in *Einaudi Annali 1*. For bread statistics, see Dante Zanetti in his *Problemi alimentari* (above, n. 17), pp. 60 and 88; *Corriere della sera*, 25 April 1982.

40. *Bandi* of 2 March 1545 and 26 May 1576, Chicago, Newberry Library MS K 2553.302.

41. Quoted by Massimo Petrocchi, *Aspirazioni dei contadini nella Perugia dell'ultimo trentennio del Cinquecento ed altri scritti*, Rome 1962, pp. 51–52.

42. Bassano: Private collection, published in *Arte veneta*, 32, 1978, p. 179 (pl. 6).

43. Texts published by Emilio Faccioli in *Arte della cucina: Libri de ricette . . .*, Milan 1966, I.

44. Quoted by Lino Pertile, 'Un umanista francese in Italia: Il *Voyage d'Italie* (1574–1578) di Nicholas Audebert', *Studi mediolatini e volgari*, 21, 1973, p. 159.

45. Quoted by Giuseppe Giarrizzo in *Storia della Sicilia* (above, Chapter 4, n. 21), p. 46.

46. *Canons and Decrees of the Council of Trent*, tr. H. J. Schroeder (4th edn), St Louis and London 1960, p. 259 (Latin original on p. 523).

47. Angelo Turchini, *Clero e fedeli a Rimini in età post-tridentina*, Rome 1978, Ch. 1.

48. Cornaro quoted from his report on his own activities in *Gli atti della visita apostolica di S. Carlo Borromeo a Bergamo (1575)*, ed. Angelo Giuseppe Roncalli (= Pope John XXIII) and Pietro Forno, Florence 1936–, I, pp. 227–8.

49. Mario Scaduto, 'La vita religiosa in Sicilia secondo un memoriale inedito del 1563', *RSCI*, 28, 1974.

50. Garimberto, *Delle vite overo fatti memorabili d'alcuni papi e di tutti i cardinali passati*, Venice 1558, p. 371.

51. All this from Scaduto, 'La vita religiosa' (above, n. 49).

52. Letter of Beccadelli to Carlo Borromeo, 17 July 1563, in *Monumenti di varia letteratura, tratti dai manoscritti di monsignor Lodovico Beccadelli*, Bologna 1804, 1, II, p. 385.

53. Appendix no. 1 to Pasquale Lopez, *Riforma cattolica e vita religiosa e culturale a Napoli: Dalla fine del Cinquecento ai primi anni del Settecento*, Naples 1964.

54. Paul Grendler, 'The Tre Savii sopra Eresia, 1547–1605: A prosopographical study', *SV*, n.s. 3, 1979–80; Christopher Cairns, *Domenico Bollani, Bishop of Brescia: Devotion to Church and State in the Republic of Venice in the Sixteenth Century*, Nieuwkoop 1976, on which see Angelo Baiocchi in *SV*, n.s. 3, 1979–80, pp. 378 ff.; Pillinini in *DBI*, vol. 11, pp. 291–93. Paruta's text has most recently been edited by Gino Benzoni in *Storici e politici veneti. Del Cinquecento e del Seicento*, Milan and Naples 1982.

55. Specifically on the schools: John Patrick Donnelly, 'The Jesuit College at Padua. Growth, suppression, attempts at restoration: 1552–1606', *Archivum Historicum Societatis Iesu*, 51, 1982; Pio Paschini, 'Le origini del Seminario Romano', in his *Cinquecento romano e riforma cattolica*, Rome 1958; Philip Caraman, *University of the Nations: The Story of the Gregorian University . . . 1551–1962*, New York 1981; Aldo Scaglione, *The Liberal Arts and the Jesuit College System*, Amsterdam and Philadelphia 1986.

56. Vincenzo Paglia, 'Vita religiosa nella confraternita della Pietà dei Carcerati (secc. XVI–XVII)', *Ricerche per la storia religiosa di Roma*, 2, 1978; Luisa Proietti Pedetta, 'Alcune note sulla situazione delle confraternite ad Assisi nel periodo post-tridentino', in *Chiesa e società dal secolo IV ai nostri giorni: Studi storici in onore del p. Ilarino da Milano*, Rome 1979, vol. 2.

57. Manuzio quoted by Pio Paschini on p. 270 of his 'Guglielmo Sirleto prima del cardinalato', in his *Tre ricerche sulla storia della chiesa nel Cinquecento*, Rome 1945 (the source of much of the information in this paragraph). Other information from Georg Denzler, *Kardinal Guglielmo Sirleto (1514–1585)*, Munich 1964.

58. José L. de Orella y Unzue, *Respuestas católicas a las centurias de Magdeburgo*, Madrid 1976; Eric Cochrane, *Historians and Historiography in the Italian Renaissance*, Chicago 1981, pp. 457 ff.; Cyriac K. Pullapilly, *Caesar Baronius, Counter-Reformation Historian*, Notre Dame, Ind. 1975; and the several relevant essays published in Romeo De Maio, Luigi Gulia and Aldo Mazzacane (eds), *Baronio storico e la controriforma: Atti del convegno internazionale di studi, Sora, 6–10 Ottobre 1979*, Sora 1981, on which see my comments in *Cristianesimo nella storia*, 4, 1983, pp. 500–504.

59. Gustavo Galeota, *Bellarmino contro Baio a Lovanio: Studio e testo di un inedito Bellarmino*, Rome 1966, here quoted from p. 57. The most complete, although by .now somewhat old-fashioned, biography is still that of James Brodrick, *The Life and Work of Blessed Robert Francis Cardinal Bellarmine, S. J., 1542–1621*, London 1928. The particular question described here is in the text edited by Galeota, pp. 178–79 ('Utrum Primus Homo sit Creatus in Gratia').

60. Pio Paschini, 'Il Catechismo romano', in his *Cinquecento romano* (above, n. 55), and, much more extensively, Pedro Rodriguez and Raul Lanzetti, *El Catecismo romano: Fuentes e historia del texto y de la redacción*, Pamplona 1982. A new edition in Italian translation by Tito S. Centi has been published in Siena (1981).

61. Carlo Marcora, 'Un trattato sui doveri del vescovo del p. Achille Gagliardi', *MSDM*, 14, 1967, and 'Nicolò Ormaneto, vicario di S. Carlo', *MSDM*, 8, 1961, quoted from p. 210.

62. Serafino Razzi, *Hymnario dominicano, in cui si comprendono tutti gli hymni . . .*, Perugia 1583 (the date 1587 given on the dedication is undoubtedly a mistake. I am grateful to the Rev. John Fiore for having brought this text to my attention); Silvio Antoniano, *Tre libri dell'educatione cristiana dei figliuoli*, Verona 1584.

63. The most complete biography of Maria Maddelena is still that of M. M. Vaussard, *Sainte Marie Madeleine de Pazzi, 1566–1607*, 2nd edn, Paris 1925. On Caterina Vannini da Siena, see Agostino Saba, *Federico Borromeo e i mistici del suo tempo*, Florence 1933.

64. Quoted from the *Proemio* to the Florentine edition.

65. Anon., *Vita del venerabile Cardinale Roberto Bellarmino, arcivescovo di Capua e religioso della Compagnia di Gesù*, Rome 1743, here quoted from pp. 169–70.

66. Quoted by Luigi Cervaro in *Storia e cultura al Santo*, ed. Antonio Poppi, Vicenza 1976, p. 596.

67. Quoted by Pierre Blet in 'Pio v e la riforma tridentina', in *San Pio v e la problematica del suo tempo*, Alessandria 1972, pp. 35–36.

68. Marco Antonio Ciappi, *Compendio delle heroiche et gloriose attioni, et santa vita di papa Greg. XIII, distinto in tredici capi, in memoria delli XIII. anni ch'egli visse nel suo felice pontefcato*, Rome 1596.

69. S. L. Forte, 'Il libro dei frati professi del convento di S. Domenicani di Palermo 1416–1583', *Archivum Fratrum Praedicatorum*, 50, 1980.

70. Kristas Papagiotopoulos, Πατριαρχικὰ γράμματα καὶ ἄλλα ἔγγραφα (1571–1576) γιὰ τὸν Ἱέρωνα-Ἰωάννη Μποναπὲ θησαυρίσματα 12, 1975.

71. Casale's *Diario* is published by Carlo Manacorda, 'Il diario di Giambattista Casale (1554–1598)', *MSDM*, 12, 1965. Parts of it are translated by Eric Cochrane and published in *University of Chicago Readings in Western Civilization*, vol. 5: *The Renaissance*, ed. Eric Cochrane and Julius Kirshner, Chicago 1986. See also Giuseppe Alberigo, 'Studi e problemi relativi all'applicazione del Concilio di Trento in Italia (1945–1958)', *RSI*, 70, 1958; Mario Rosa, 'Le parrocchie italiane nell'età moderna e contemporanea', in his *Religione e società nel Mezzogiorno* (cited above, Chapter 7, n. 1), and his 'Per la storia della vita religiosa e della Chiesa in Italia tra il '500 e il '600', *QS*, 15, 1970.

72. Paolo Prodi, 'San Carlo Borromeo e il cardinale Gabriele Paleotti: Due vescovi della riforma cattolica', *CS*, 3, 1964; the most thorough study of any sixteenth-century diocese is still Prodi's *Il cardinale Gabriele Paleotti, 1522–1597*, Rome 1959–67. On Borromeo: M. Bendiscioli in the Treccani *Storia di Milano*, vol. 10; on Carafa: Romeo De Maio, *Alfonso Carafa, cardinale di Napoli*, Vatican City 1961.

73. Castelli here quoted from the appendix to Turchini, *Clero e fedeli* (above, n. 47), p. 175.

74. Pietro Usimbardi, bishop of Arezzo, *Costitutioni et ordini per lo buon governo, e osservanza de monasterii della sua città e diocesi*, Siena 1603, Article 30; Achille Erba in *La chiesa sabauda tra Cinque e Seicento: Ortodossia tridentina, gallicanesimo savoiardo e assolutismo ducale (1580–1630)*, Rome 1979, quoted from p. 379; Serafino Razzi quoted from the title and dedication of his edition of *Libro primo delle laudi spirituali da diversi autori*, Venice 1563 (I am grateful to Rev. John Fiore for lending me a Xerox copy of this work).

75. Francesco Pucci, *Lettere, documenti e testimonianze*, ed. Luigi Firpo and Renato Piattoli, vol. 2 (with biographical introduction), Florence 1959; Mario Rosa, 'Vita religiosa e pietà eucaristica nella Napoli del Cinquecento' *Riv SLR*, 4, 1968; Daniele Ponchiroli and Guido Davico Bonino (eds), *Lirici del Cinquecento*, Turin 1968, pp. 134–35 (where selections of Fiamma's poems are published); Adriano Prosperi, 'Echi italiani della condanna di Serveto: Girolamo Nègri', *RSI*, 90, 1978.

76. Giacomo Luccari, *Copioso ristretto de gli annali di Ravsa, libri quattro*, Venice 1605, p. 125.

77. Quoted by Lanfranco Franzoni in *Atti e memorie dell'Accademia d'Agricoltura, Scienza e Lettere di Verona*, 31, 1981, p. 146. Giorgio Spini traces to the Paduans, in 'Noterelle libertine,' *RSI*, 88, 1976, what Carlo Ginzburg attributes to a 'sostrato di credenze contadine, vecchio di secoli', in *Il formaggio e i vermi: Il cosmo di un mugnaio del '500*, Turin 1976 (available in an excellent

English translation by John and Ann Tedeschi, *The Cheese and the Worms: The Cosmos of a Sixteenth-century Miller*, Baltimore 1980).

78. Quoted by Davide M. da Portogruaro, *Storia dei Cappuccini veneti*, Venice and Mestre 1957.

79. William Monter and John Tedeschi, 'Toward a Statistical Profile of the Italian Inquisition', in Gustav Henningsen and John Tedeschi (eds), *The Inquisition in Early Modern Europe*, Decalb, Ill., 1986. I read an early manuscript version through the kindness of the authors.

80. Quotation from Gabriele De Rosa, in *Chiesa e religione popolare nel Mezzogiorno*, Rome and Bari 1978, p. 39.

81. The bull is quoted by Luigi Fiorani in 'Astrologi, superstiziosi e devoti nella società romana del Seicento', *Ricerche per la storia religiosa di Roma*, 2, 1978.

82. Letter of Silvestro Landini in *Monumenta historica Societatis Jesu, Epistolae Mixtae*, vol. 3, 1900, p. 115.

83. Archbishop Scipione Gesualdo quoted by Pasquale Lopez in *Riforma cattolica* (above, n. 53), p. 25. Many more such cases are described by Albano Biondi, 'Streghe ed eretici nei domini estensi all'epoca dell'Ariosto', in Paolo Rossi (ed.), *Il Rinascimento nelle corti padane*, Bari 1977, pp. 165–200.

84. Fulvio Salimbeni quoting Bisanti in his introduction to *Le lettere di Paolo Bisanti vicario generale del Patriarca di Aquileia (1577–1587)*, Rome and Vicenza 1977, p. xix. One of many cases of a 'dabene' priest with 'una donna' in residence: Lorenzo and Mary Madeline Tacchella, *Il cardinale Agostino Valier e la Riforma tridentina nella diocesi di Trieste*, Udine 1974, p. 23.

85. Giuliano de' Ricci, *Cronaca (1532–1606)*, ed. Giuliana Sapori, Milan 1972, pp. 53–54.

86. A. D. Wright, *Federico Borromeo and Baronius: A Turning Point in the Development of the Counter-Reformation Church*, Reading 1974.

87. This and many other such episodes in Maria Franca Mellano, *La Controriforma nella diocesi di Mondovì (1560–1602)*, Turin 1955.

88. Mosé Dammert Bellido, 'Le attività culturale di S. Pio v', in *Il Collegio Ghislieri, 1567–1967*, Milan 1967; Arnalda Dallaj, 'Le processioni a Milano nella Controriforma', *SS*, 23, 1982.

89. Luigi Donvito and Bruno Pellegrino, *L'organizzazione ecclesiastica degli Abruzzi e Molise e della Basilicata nell'età postridentina*, Florence 1973.

90. Angelo Turchini, 'Legislazione canonica e tradizioni locali nella Romagna del xvi secolo in fatto di celebrazione matrimoniale', *Aevum*, 50, 1976, pp. 411–35; Baronio quoted by Pullapilly in *Caesar Baronius* (above, n. 58).

91. Montaigne, *Journal de voyage en Italie par la Suisse et l'Allemagne en 1580 et 1581*, ed. Maurice Rat, Paris 1955, p. 68.

92. Eckhard Kessler, here quoted from 'Die Ausbildung der Theorie der Geschichtsschreibung im Humanismus und in der Renaissance unter dem Einfluss der wiederentdeckten Antike', in *Die Antike–Rezeption in den Wissenschaften während der Renaissance*, ed. August Buck and Klaus Heitman, Weinheim 1983, p. 49. The thesis here presented, which differs from Kessler's, is that of my *Historians and Historiography in the Italian Renaissance* (see above, n. 58), pp. 479ff.

93. Orsini to Pier Vettori, 5 July 1580, in Pierre de Nolhac, *La Bibliothèque de Fulvio Orsini*, Paris 1887, pp. 39–40; Anthony Grafton, *Joseph Scaliger: A Study in the History of Classical Scholarship*, Oxford 1983, Ch. 2.

94. 'Della istoria' = *Della ragion di Stato* (above, n. 29), II, p. 3.

95. Rita Baldi, *Giovan Battista Pigna: Uno scrittore politico nella Ferrara del Cinque-cento*, Genoa 1983; Rodolfo De Matteis, 'Un cinquecentista confutatore del Machiavelli: Antonio Ciccarelli', *ASI*, 125, 1967; Giuseppe De Gennaro, 'Il Machiavelli e l'Ammirato: Spunti economici e sociali', *Economia e storia*, 18, 1971. In general: Kenneth Schellhase, *Tacitus in Renaissance Political Thought*, Chicago 1976.

96. Paruta, *Discorsi politici*, ed. Giorgio Candeloro, Bologna 1943, pp. 237 and 241. This passage is quoted on p. 43 of Rodolfo Brändli, *Virgilio Malvezzi, politico e moralista*, Basel 1964.

97. The most important texts are edited by Carlo Curcio in *Utopisti e riformatori sociali del Cinquecento*, Bologna 1941; Ludovico Agostini's *La repubblica immaginaria* I read in the edition of Luigi Firpo, Turin 1975. The most convenient modern edition of Tommaso Campanella's *La città del sole* is that of Adriano Seroni, Milan 1962. An excellent translation has been published by Daniel J. Donno, *The City of the Sun*, Berkeley 1981. For the fifteenth-century origins of sixteenth-century Utopianism, see Stelio Cro, 'L'utopia rinascimentale: conformismo e riforma', in Vittore Branca, *et al.* (eds), *Il Rinascimento: Aspetti e problemi attuali: Atti del x Congresso de l'Associazione internazionale per gli studi di lingua e letteratura italiana, Belgrado, 17–21 aprile 1979*, Florence 1979, pp. 325 ff.; for the still broader context of the six centuries between Dante and Carlo Pisacane: Leandro Perini, 'Gli utopisti: Delusioni della realtà, sogni dell'avvenire', in *Einaudi Annali 4*.

98. All references in the following paragraph are to the texts published (and amply annotated) by Paola Barocchi in the Ricciardi edition of *Scritti d'arte del Cinquecento*, Milan and Naples 1971–73, reprinted in nine paperback volumes by Einaudi, Turin 1977–79. Page numbers for the quotations are given in parentheses in the text. See also Anthony Blunt, *Artistic Theory in Italy, 1450–1600*, Oxford 1956.

99. I read Borghini's *Riposo* in the 'Classici Italiani' edition (Milan 1807), which Barocchi says is still the standard critical edition. The first edition appeared in Florence in 1584.

100. Paul C. Hamilton in his introduction to the catalogue *Disegni di Bernardino Poccetti*, Florence 1980.

101. Giulio Bora, 'Un ciclo di affreschi, due artisti e una bottega a S. Maria di Campagna a Pallanza', *Arte lombarda*, n.s., 52, 1979.

102. Michelangelo Sermartelli *et al.*, 'Composizioni di diversi autori in lode del ritratto della Sabina . . .', in Paola Barocchi (ed.), *Scritti d'arte del Cinquecento*, vol. 2 of the original Ricciardi edition, pp. 1121–42.

103. Giovanna Gaeta Bertelà in her introduction to the catalogue *Disegni di Federico Barocci*, Florence 1975, p. 9.

104. For Cigoli, see the introduction to the catalogue *Disegni dei Toscani a Roma (1580–1620)*, ed. Miles L. Chappell *et al.*, Florence, 1979; Charles H. Carmen, 'Cigoli's *Annunciation* at Montughi: A new iconography', *Art Bulletin*, 58, 1976; Marco Collareta, 'Tre note su Santi di Tito', *Annali della Scuola Normale di Pisa*, 7, 1977 (here quoted). See also Carolyn Valone, 'Giovan Antonio Dosio: The Roman years', *Art Bulletin*, 58, 1976.

105. Charles Dempsey, *Annibale Carracci and the Beginnings of Baroque Style*, Glückstadt 1977, and his 'The Carracci reform of painting', in *The Age of Correggio and Carracci* (National Gallery of Art, Washington), Washington

1986; and Filippo Baldinucci, *Notizie dei professori del disegno*, which I cite hereafter in the SPES offset edition, Florence 1974–75, of the edition by V. Batelli, Florence 1845–47, here quoted respectively from p. 1 and vol. 3, p. 323. What follows is based on Donald Posner, *Annibale Carracci: A Study in the Reform of Italian Painting around 1590*, London 1971; Anton W. A. Boschloo, *Annibale Carracci in Bologna: Visible Reality in Art After the Council of Trent*, tr. R. R. Symonds, The Hague 1974; and Anna Ottani Cavina, *Gli affreschi dei Carracci in Palazzo Fava*, Bologna 1966, as well as, more generally, S. J. Freedberg, *Circa 1600: A Revolution of Style in Italian Painting*, Cambridge, Mass. 1983.

106. Franca Zava Boccazzi, *Veronese (I Maestri del Colore)*, Milan 1976, p. 4; Terisio Pignatti, *Veronese: La Villa di Maser*, Milan 1968.

107. Freedberg, *Circa 1600* (above, n. 105), p. 160; David Rosand, 'Theater and structure in the art of Paolo Veronese', in his *Painting in Cinquecento Venice: Titian, Veronese, Tintoretto*, New Haven 1982.

108. Roberto Paolo Ciardi, *Giovan Ambrogio Figino*, Florence 1968, p. 39, quoting Comanini.

109. *Disegni* (above, n. 100), p. 19.

110. Giulio Cesare Giacobbe, 'Il *Commentarium de certitudine mathematicarum disciplinarum* di Alessandro Piccolomini', *Physis*, 14, 1972, pp. 162–93; Cesare Vasoli, 'Su alcuni problemi e discussioni logiche del Cinquecento italiano', in his *Studi sulla cultura del Rinascimento*, Manduria 1968; Antonino Poppi, 'Il problema della filosofia morale nella Scuola Padovana del Rinascimento: Platonismo e Aristotelismo nella definizione del metodo dell'etica', in *Platon et Aristote à la Renaissance. XVIe Colloque international de Tours*, Paris 1976, pp. 105–46; Charles B. Schmitt, 'Renaissance Averroism', in *L'Averroismo in Italia* (Accademia Nazionale dei Lincei: Atti di Convegno, no. 40), Rome 1979, and 'L'Aristotelismo veneto e le origini della scienza moderna', in Luigi Oliveri (ed.), *Aristotelismo veneto e scienza moderna (Atti del 250 anno accademico del Centro per la storia della tradizione aristotelica nel Veneto)*, Padua 1983; and, for a general introduction, Charles B. Schmitt's *Aristotle and the Renaissance*, Cambridge, Mass. 1983; Bruno Nardi, 'La fine dell'Averroismo', in his *Saggi sull'aristotelismo padovano dal secolo XIV al XVI*, Florence 1958.

111. Simone Porzio quoted from Chapter 3 (no page numbers) of his *De rerum naturalium principiis*, Naples 1553.

112. Jean-Claude Margolin, 'Cardan, interprète d'Aristote', in *Platon et Aristote* (above, n. 110). On Cardano: Alfonso Ingegno, *Saggio sulla filosofia di Cardano*, Florence 1980, is indispensable.

113. Ettore Bonora, 'Dalla critica umanistica all'aristotelismo', in his *Critica e letteratura nel Cinquecento* (above, Chapter 5, n. 1); the most authoritative work in this field (and the one I most often refer to) is Weinberg, *A History of Literary Criticism in the Italian Renaissance* (above, Chapter 6, n. 1).

114. Brian Vickers, 'Epideictic and epic in the Renaissance', *New Literary History*, 14, 1982–83.

115. Lodovico Castelvetro, *Poetica d'Aristotele vulgarizzata e esposta*, ed. Werther Romani, Bari 1978, 1, p. 11. An abridged English translation by Andrew Bongiorno is now available as *Castelvetro on the Art of Poetry*, Binghamton, N. Y. 1984.

116. Giovanni Papuli, *Girolamo Balduino: Ricerche sulla logica della scuola di Padova nel Rinascimento*, Manduria 1967 (here quoted from p. 55); Antonia Poppi,

La dottrina della scienza in Giacomo Zabarella, Padua 1972; Cesare Vasoli, 'La Logica', in *Storia cult ven*, III and the articles by Wilhelm Risse and William Edwards in Oliveri (ed.), *Aristotelismo veneto e scienza moderna* (above, n. 110).

117. Paola Zambelli, 'Scienza, filosofia, religione nella Toscana di Cosimo I', in Bertelli, Rubinstein and Smyth (eds), *Florence and Venice*, 2 (above, Chapter 4, n. 19); Angelo Capecci, 'Finalismo e meccanismo nelle ricerche biologiche di Cesalpino ed Harvey', in Oliveri (ed.), *Aristotelismo veneto e scienza moderna* (above, n. 110).

118. Gregoria Piaia, 'Aristotelismo, "heresia" e giurisdizionalismo nella polemica del p. Antonio Possevino contro lo studio di Padova', *Quaderni per la storia dell'Università di Padova*, 6, 1973. See also Edward Mahoney, 'Trombetta and Agostino Nifo: A philosophical dispute', in Antonio Poppi (ed.), *Storia e cultura al Santo*, Vicenza 1976.

119. I have slightly altered the translation from p. 24 of *De communibus omnium rerum naturalium principiis et affectionibus* of 1576 given by Frederick Homann in *Archivum Historicum Societatis Iesu*, 52, 1983, p. 239 (in his important article, 'Christopher Clavius and the renaissance of Euclidean geometry'), to make it fit better with my own sentence structure.

120. Quoted by Giuseppe Cosentino in 'Le matematiche nella Ratio studiorum della Compagnia di Gesù', *Miscellanea storica ligure*, 2, 1970. Other information from Paolo Galluzzi, 'Il "platonismo" del tardo Cinquecento e la filosofia di Galileo', in Paola Zambelli (ed.), *Richerche sulla cultura dell'Italia moderna*, Rome and Bari 1973, pp. 37–79; and the articles by Adriano Carugo, Maria Daniele, Carlo Maccagni and, above all, the introduction of Eugenio Garin in Oliveri (ed.), *Aristotelismo veneto e scienza moderna* (above, n. 110). I also follow Maino Pedrazzi, 'Sul tentativo di Alessandro Picçolomini di ridurre a sillogismi . . .', *Cultura e Scuola*, 52, 1974, pp. 221–30; Judith Bryce, 'Cosimo Bartoli's *Del modo di misurare le distanze*', *Annuario ISIEMC*, 5, 1980; and P. Speziali, 'L'école algébriste italienne du XVIᵉ siècle et al résolution des équations des 3e et 4e degrés', in A. Buck *et al.*, *Sciences de la Renaissance*, Paris 1973, pp. 107–20. Paul Lawrence Rose's *The Italian Renaissance of Mathematics: Studies on Humanists and Mathematicians from Petrarch to Galileo*, Geneva 1975, is by far the most comprehensive and clearly written treatment currently available.

121. Irene Favaretto, 'Alessandro Vittoria e la collezione di Marco Mantova Benavides', *Atti dell'Istituto Veneto di Scienze, Lettere ed Arti*, 135, 1977. In general: Lanfranco Franzoni, 'Il collezionismo veneto del XVI secolo', in his *Verona: La Galleria Bevilacqua*, Milan 1970, and 'Antiquari e collezionisti nel Cinquecento', in *Storia cult ven*, III (1980–81), pp. 207–66; Carlo Maccagni, 'Le raccolte e i musei di storia naturale . . .', in Laetitia Boehm and Ezio Raimondi (eds), *Università, accademie e società scientifiche in Italia e in Germania dal Cinquecento al Settecento*, Bologna 1981; and Eric Cochrane, 'Science and humanism in the Italian Renaissance', *American Historical Review*, 81, 1976.

122. Donatella Mattioli, 'Vincenzo I Gonzaga e la Pietà di Gaudenzio Ferrari', *Arte lombarda*, 47/48, 1977, p. 139; Carolyn Valone, 'A Note on the Collection of Niccolò Gaddi', *Critica d'arte*, 42, 1977.

123. Gigliola Fragnito, 'Il museo di Antonio Giganti', in *Scienze, credenze occulte, livelli di cultura*, Florence 1982; Julius von Schlosser, *Raccolte d'arte e di meraviglie del tardo Rinascimento*, Leipzig 1908, Ital. trans., Florence 1974, Ch. 2.

124. Giuseppe Olmi, *Ulisse Aldrovandi: Scienza e natura nel secondo Cinquecento*, Trent

1976, p. 36, quoting Grand Duke Ferdinando de' Medici (much of this short essay is devoted to the insoluble puzzle of how a bright person like the hero could have lived in such an oppressive age as that of the 'Counter Reformation'); Paolo Cherchi, *Enciclopedismo e politica della riscrittura: Tommaso Garzoni*, Pisa 1981.

125. Barocchi, Introduction to her *Scritti d'arte* (above, n. 98).

126. Aldrovandi to Paleotti, 1581, in the Ricciardi *Scritti d'arte* (above, n. 98), 2, p. 513; Della Porta quoted by Giovanni Aquilecchia in *Schede di italianistica*, Turin 1976, p. 220, and from the *Proemium* to his *De telescopio*, ed. Vasco Ronchi and Maria Amalia Naldoni, Florence 1962, p. 29.

127. I translate the title of Falloppio's *Secreti diversi et miracolosi*, Venice 1563; on which: Marco Ferrari in his very learned 'Vie di diffusione in Italia di Paracelso', in *Scienze, credenze* (above, n. 123).

128. For Francesco Patrizi: the introductions to the edition of Patrizi's *Della poetica* and *Lettere ed opuscoli inediti* (the latter on pp. 45–51 contains the autobiographical letter to Baccio Valori to which I here refer) by Danilo Aguzzi Barbagli, and Patrizi's *L'amorosa filosofia*, ed. John Charles Nelson, all published by the Istituto Nazionale di Studi sul Rinascimento, Florence 1969, 1975 and 1963, respectively. On Patrizi (not 'Patrizzi', as some Anglophone historians spell his name) and the Holy Office: Luigi Firpo, 'The flowering and withering of speculative philosophy – Italian philosophy and the Counter Reformation: The condemnation of Francesco Patrizi', in my *The Late Italian Renaissance* (above, n. 10), pp. 266–86.

129. The first of these and several later examples come from the most objective study of the question currently available, Paul F. Grendler, *The Roman Inquisition and the Venetian Press, 1540–1605*, Princeton 1977. Other references are to: Wolfgang Osthoff, *Theatergesang und darstellende Musik in der italienischen Renaissance*, Tutzing 1969, vol. 2, p. 243; Mario Baratto, *Tre studi sul teatro: Ruzante, Aretino, Goldoni*, Venice 1964, p. 78.

130. Quoted from the introduction to *Novellieri minori del Cinquecento. G. Parabosco – S. Erizzo*, ed. Giuseppe Gigli and Fausto Nicolini, Bari 1912; Ettore Bonora on Riccoboni in 'La teoria del teatro negli scrittori del Cinquecento', in his *Retorica e invenzione: Studi sulla letteratura italiana del Rinascimento*, Milan 1970.

131. Maria Luisa Ferrari on Campi in Antonio Boschetto (ed.), *Studi di storia dell'arte*, Florence 1976, p. 346.

132. Anna Maria Brizio in the introduction to Galeazzo Alessi's *Libro dei misteri: Progetto di pianificazione urbanistica, architettonica e figurativa del sacro Monte di Varallo in Valsesia (1565–1569)*, ed. Stefania Stefani Perrone, Bologna 1974. The *Monte* is beautifully illustrated in *Il Sacro Monte sopra Varese*, Milan 1981. Carlo Bascapé here quoted from his *Vita e opere di Carlo, arcivescovo di Milano*, Milan 1965, p. 106. The dissident is Martino Bassi in his *Dispareri in materia d'architettura et perspettiva*, Brescia 1573.

133. Maria Luisa Gatti Perer, 'Cultura e socialità dell'altare barocco nel'antica Diocesi di Milano, *Arte lombarda*, 42/43, 1975, p. 15.

134. Paolo Prodi, *Ricerche sulla teorica delle arti figurative nella riforma cattolica*, Rome 1962, whose theses have been recently reinforced by Christopher Cairns in 'Venice and censorship', in *Altro Polo: A Volume of Italian Studies*, ed. Richard Bosworth and Gianfranco Cresciani, Sydney 1979.

135. Letter of Benedetto Vanguolo to Claude Dupuy, 7 June 1577, in Bibliothèque Nationale, Paris, MS Dupuy, 704, f. 135. I owe this reference to the kindness

of Anthony Grafton.

136. Giulio Mancini, in his *Considerazioni sulla pittura*, in *Scritti d'arte*, ed. Adriana Marucchi, Rome 1956, vol. 1, p. 41.

137. Andrea Gabrieli to Gregory XIII, quoted by Flavio Testi in *La musica italiana nel Medioevo e nel Rinascimento*, Milan 1969, vol. 2, p. 511.

138. Vittorio Baldo, *Alunni, maestri e scuole in Venezia alla fine del XVI secolo. Fonti editi*, Como 1976: this is the printed version of a Paduan *tesi di laurea*. Paul Grendler gives a slightly higher figure in the independently written and much more elegant and accessible 'What Zuanne read in school: Vernacular texts in sixteenth-century Italy', *The Sixteenth Century Journal*, 13, 1982.

139. Quoted by Lino Pertile in 'Un umanista francese in Italia' (above, n. 44), p. 133.

140. Maria and Luigi Moranti, 'Librerie private in Urbino nei secoli XVI–XVII', *Atti e memorie della Deputazione di Storia Patria per le Marche*, 83, 1978; Federico Zuccardi in the preface to his edition of Bernardino Baldi's *Vita e fatti di Federigo di Montefeltro*, Rome 1824 (here quoted). In general: Bronislaw Bilinski, *La vita di Copernico di Bernardino Baldi* . . . (Accademia Polacca, Rome; Conferenze, no. 61), Wroclaw 1973.

141. I quote here the inscriptions from the monuments in Como.

142. On Falloppio: Ian Maclean, *The Renaissance Notion of Woman. A Study in the Fortunes of Scholasticism and Medical Sciences in European Intellectual Life*, Cambridge 1980; on Piccolomini: Arnaldo di Benedetto (ed.), *Prose di Giovanni Della Casa e altri trattatisti cinquecenteschi del comportamento*, Turin 1970, p. 547; on the academy: Giuseppe Betussi in his *Raverta*, quoted by Riccardo Scrivano in his *La norma e lo scarto* (above, Chapter 6, n. 47), p. 108.

143. A selection of Battiferri's poems is published in Ponchiroli (ed.), *Lirici del Cinquecento* (above, Chapter 3, n. 2), pp. 400 ff.; Anthony Newcomb, 'The three anthologies for Laura Peverara', *Rivista italiana di musicologia*, 10, 1975. The opposite thesis is presented by Anne Jacobson Schutte in her review of Patricia Labalme (ed.), *Beyond Their Sex: Learned Women of the European Past* (1980), in *The Sixteenth Century Journal*, 13, 1982, pp. 135–36; but see also Alison Brown in *Journal of Modern History*, 54, 1982, pp. 537–40.

144. Diana Robin, 'A reassessment of the character of Francesco Filelfo (1398–1481)', *Renaissance Quarterly*, 36, 1983, p. 217.

145. Quoted by Antonio Ceruti in the introduction to Gabriele Salvago's 'Lettere', *Atti della Società ligure di Storia Patria*, 13, 1877–84, p. 711.

146. For what follows see the authoritative historical and philological commentary by Fredi Chiappelli (ed.), Torquato Tasso, *Gerusalemme liberata*, Milan 1982; and Ettore Mazzali's introduction to the *Opere*, Naples 1969.

147. Ezio Raimondi, *Poesia come retorica*, Florence 1980, p. 40.

148. Michael Murrin, *The Allegorical Epic: Essays in Its Rise and Decline*, Chicago 1980, Ch. 4.

149. Walter Moretti, *Torquato Tasso*, Bari 1973, p. 35.

150. Dante Della Terza, 'Tasso's experience of Petrarch', *Studies in the Renaissance*, 10, 1963.

151. In general: the information-packed and lucid Flavio Testi, *La musica italiana nel Medioevo e nel Rinascimento* (above, n. 137) and Howard M. Brown, *Music in the Renaissance*, Englewood Cliffs, N. J. 1976.

152. Everything that could possibly be found out about Ruffo is chronicled in Lewis Lockwood, *The Counter-Reformation and the Masses of Vincenzo Ruffo*,

Vienna–London–Milan 1970.

153. Edward E. Lowinsky here quoted from 'Humanism in the Music of the Renaissance', in Frank Tirro (ed.), *Medieval and Renaissance Studies*, Durham, North Carolina 1982, p. 122, and paraphrased from Lowinsky's *Tonality and Atonality in Sixteenth-Century Music*, Berkeley, 1961, pp. 52–53, with reference to his more general 'Music in Renaissance Culture', Paul Oskar Kristeller and Philip P. Wiener (eds), *Renaissance Essays. From The Journal of the History of Ideas*, New York 1968.

154. Antonio Francesco Doni, *Dialogo della musica*, ed. G. Francesco Malipiero, Vienna–London–Milan 1964, p. 7.

155. Luigi Ronga proposes the thesis I agree with in 'Premessa sul manierismo musicale', in *Critica e storia letteraria: Studi offerti a Mario Fubini*, Padua 1970; Maria Rika Maniates proposes the opposite, without, apparently, having read Ronga's article, in *Mannerism in Italian Music and Culture, 1530–1630*, Chapel Hill, N.C. 1979.

156. Howard M. Brown, 'Psyche's lament: Some music for the Medici wedding in 1565', in Laurence Berman (ed.), *Words and Music . . . in Honor of A. Tillman Merritt*, Cambridge, Mass. 1972.

157. Palestrina quoted by Karl Gustav Fellerer in his, as usual, eloquent and scholarly *Der Stilwandel in der abendländischen Musik um 1600*, Opladen 1972, p. 13.

158. Barbara Russano Hanning in her indispensable review of the whole question in *Renaissance Quarterly*, 37, 1983, here quoted from p. 13.

159. Bartolomeo Ammannati, *La città: Appunti per un trattato*, ed. Mazzino Fossi, Rome 1970, p. 9; Robert Klein, 'L'urbanisme utopique de Filarète à Valentin Andreae', in *Les Utopies à la Renaissance*, Bruxelles 1963; Juergen Schulz, 'The printed plans and panoramic views of Venice 1486–1797', *Saggi e memorie di storia dell'arte*, 7, 1970, and his 'Una raccolta di carte geografiche del secolo XVI', *Bergomum*, 73, 1979; Pietro Amato (ed.), *Le piante di Roma*, Rome 1962, 2, CIX.

160. Scipione Ammirato quoted from his *Opuscoli*, ed. Scipione Ammirato, Jr., Florence 1637, 1, p. 419.

161. A. Richard Turner, *The Vision of Landscape in Renaissance Italy*, Princeton 1966, Ch. 8.

162. Quoted by Bruno Adorni in his *L'architettura farnesiana a Parma, 1545–1630*, Parma 1974, p. 39.

163. Adriano Cavicchi, 'La scenografia dell'*Aminta* . . . ', in Maria Teresa Muraro (ed.), *Studi sul teatro veneto fra Rinascimento ed età barocca*, Florence 1971 (quoted from p. 62). In general: Ettore Bonora, 'Il dramma pastorale', in Emilio Cecchi and Natalino Sapegno (eds), *Storia della letteratura italiana*, vol. 4, Milan 1966; and the dense and informative Ch. 8 of Wolfgang Osthoff, *Theatergesang und darstellende Musik in der italienischen Renaissance* (above, n. 129).

164. H. G. Koenigsberger, 'Republics and courts in Italian and European culture in the sixteenth and seventeenth centuries', *Past and Present*, 83, 1979, p. 48.

165. Giorgio Lise, *La danza a Milano nelle stampe*, Milan 1978; Gino Corti, 'Cinque balli toscani del Cinquecento', *Rivista italiana di musicologia*, 12, 1977.

166. Mario Costanzo, *Il 'Gran theatro del mondo': Schede per lo studio dell'iconografia letteraria nell'età del manierismo*, Milan 1964.

167. Quoted by Osthoff in *Theatergesang* (above, n. 129), pp. 344–45.

168. I follow here Barbara Russano Hanning's *Of Poetry and Music's Power: Humanism and the Creation of Opera*, Ann Arbor 1980, while realizing that it has admit-

tedly not been revised since the first draft of 1969, and Nino Pirrotta, 'Temperaments and tendencies in the Florentine camerata' (now in his *Music and Culture in Italy from the Middle Ages to the Baroque*, [Cambridge, Mass. 1984]), even though Pirrotta's theses are not always in accord with my main authority, Howard Mayer Brown, 'How opera began', in my *Late Italian Renaissance* (above, n. 10). The passages here quoted are from Brown's translation, which was republished along with Rinuccini's original in the programme notes for the performances by the Harwood Early Music Ensemble, 8 and 9 June 1985.

CHAPTER NINE

Destabilization

CONSOLIDATION COMPLETE

In many ways, the accomplishments of the first decades of the seventeenth century represent the fulfilment or the further elaboration of the accomplishments of the last decades of the sixteenth century. At least two historians, Enrico Caterino Davila of Padua (1576–1631) and Guido Bentivoglio of Ferrara (1577–1644), succeeded in overcoming the 'crisis of content' that had afflicted the 'definitive historians' of the Italian states. They did so by following the example of the earlier Italian humanist historians of non-Italian countries – that is, by looking beyond the frontiers of peace-plagued Italy to such war-torn, and therefore event-filled, regions as France and the Netherlands. They learned about these regions by going there themselves – Davila as a page at the court of Queen Caterina de' Medici and a soldier in the army of King Henry IV, Bentivoglio as a papal nuncio. They learned to shape their narratives in accordance with humanist historiographical principles in the literary circles of Carlo Salice in Padova, of Bishop Alvise Lollini at Cadore and of Traiano Boccalini in Rome. Having thus become aware of 'the splendour and amenity of history' and 'the many and varied scenes from human life that it presents' (Bentivoglio), they were able fully to appreciate the value as a source of 'lessons about human behaviour' of what their subject offered them: more 'bloody battles, unheard-of sieges, horrible sackings, burnings, destruction and atrocities on land and sea' than those recorded of any previous wars (Davila). They were able to explain all these horrors as the consequences of 'their most intimate causes', which invariably turned out, in deference to the strictly observed separation of political and sacred history, to be political or personal rather than religious.[1] Better yet, they were able to make the foreign events they described relevant to their Italian readers by weaving them around the career of an Italian hero, Alessandro Farnese, the commander of the Spanish forces in the Low Countries.

Similarly, at least one poet, Gabriello Chiabrera, proved that the literary forms sanctioned by the sixteenth-century theorists were applicable to many more situations than the theorists had imagined.[2] They could be used to eulogize preachers, captains and princes, to make shepherds celebrate Florentine carnivals, to comfort widows and orphans, to praise painters and sculptors, to describe the 'fresh rose' colour of a lady's 'amorous cheek', to glorify the minutiae of this world and contrast them unfavourably with the glories of the next world. And Chiabrera could justify all his innovations in the name of Petrarch, Bembo, Sannazaro, Pindar, Horace, Anacreon and a score of other ancient, and therefore automatically imitable, poets.

Another poet, Federico Della Valle (1560–1607), who was Chiabrera's junior colleague for several years at the court of Turin, did the same for tragedy. In the name of Seneca, whose example justified his occasional dips into the macabre, Della Valle broke not with the theory, but with the half-century-old practice of removing tragic action to a remote place or age. In *La reina di Scozia* ('The Queen of Scotland'), he re-enacted an event that had taken place just three years before he began writing about it and that had the great merit of satisfying the quest of the Tridentine reformers for up-to-date martyrs. He increased the dramatic effect by assigning the prologue to the shade of Mary's husband, King Francis II, by revealing her inflexible doctrinal fidelity in the very first scene, when she is offered a less unpleasant alternative, and by insisting upon the contrast between her nostalgia for 'the sweet fields of Scotland and the beloved coasts of my country' and the reality of the gloomy jail cell where all the action takes place.

When political reality then proved to work against dramatic effect, as it did in his subsequent tragicomedy *Adelonda di Frigia*, Della Valle dropped it in accordance with the directions suggested by his mentor, Giovanni Botero; and in *Esther* and *Judith*, which he wrote after moving to Milan in 1606, the standard military hero was demoted to the rank of a drunken Holofernes:

> . . . The night and the bed will have
> more slumber than delight;
> instead of sweet words and
> desirous, amorous sighs,
> it will have wine-soaked pants
> and fetid breath.[3]

He abandoned the classical topos of a predetermined causality in order to present the outcome as the product solely of 'the struggle of passions within [the soul of] the weak and fragile' heroine. Finally, he corrected the theoretically false assumption made by his predecessor Giovan Francesco Alberti in an earlier version of the same plot in 1594 – that is, the assumption that tragedy is merely the opposite of comedy.[4]

What Chiabrera did for lyric poetry and Della Valle for tragedy was done by many of their lesser known contemporaries in other literary genres – by the Venetian Leonardo Quirini in the madrigal with his *Narciso* of 1612, by the Neapolitan Marcello Macedonio in the religious poems he began writing after his retirement to a Carmelite monastery. What all the poets did was reinforced by the launching of one of the first major teamwork undertakings of modern times. In 1591 the Florentine Accademia della Crusca decided to restrict the encyclopedic attivities sanctioned by its charter in order to direct all its efforts to completing the aborted projects of the solitary word gatherers of the previous half-century.[5] Half the patrician men of letters of Florence set forth to crawl through all the 'language texts' canonized by Bembo and the Accademia Fiorentina – as well as the *Divine Comedy* of Dante, which they revised on the basis of some thirty different manuscripts and published in corrected form in 1595. And in 1612, after two decades of hard work, the *Vocabolario*, the first full dictionary of a modern European language, at last appeared in print.

The *Vocabolario* in turn was buttressed by the efforts of the Florentine mathematician-turned-parish-priest, Benedetto Buonmattei (1581–1648). Buonmattei may have disfigured somewhat the peculiar character of the 'Tuscan' language by analysing it as if it were Latin – e.g., by stretching out into 'cases' what in Tuscan were obviously prepositional phrases: *mondo, di mondo, a mondo*, etc. But he fully succeeded in his main aim of demonstrating two theses: that Tuscan had a fixed grammar as well as a fixed vocabulary, and that it was as rigorously grammatical as its traditional competitor. He was triumphantly admitted into the academy upon his return to Florence in 1627; and the third, expanded edition of his *Della lingua toscana libri* II (1643) remained the standard grammar of the Italian language for over a century thereafter.

Meanwhile, the musical revolution that had first occurred in Florence rapidly spread to the rest of Italy. Jacopo Peri's invention of sung drama, or opera, was taken to Mantua under the auspices of Duke Vincenzo Gonzaga. There a closely coordinated team of artists – much like the team of lexicographers who were then preparing the Crusca's *Vocabolario* – collaborated on staging a series of dramas. The most famous, the *Orfeo* ('Orpheus'), on a libretto by Alessandro Striggio and with music by Claudio Monteverdi, was loosely patterned on Peri's and Rinuccini's *Euridice* but with 'ampler and more expansive choral parts' (according to Pirrotta) that revealed 'the greater richness of Monteverdi's experience with the madrigal'.[6] *Orfeo* was first performed in 1607. The next year, Rinuccini, who was brought up from Florence for the occasion, collaborated with Monteverdi, the librettist Alessandro Striggio, the poet Scipione Agnelli (1586–1653) of Mantua, the architect Antonio Maria Vanni, and a score of other experts in staging a series of dramas in celebration of the marriage of Vincenzo's son Francesco with Margherita di Savoia. Among other things, they produced one of the specialties of the Mantuan and Ferrarese courts, a dance drama – a genre adapted from the French *ballet de cour* – *Il Ballo delle Ingrate*. But the high point of the celebrations was the performance of Monteverdi's opera *L'Arianna*, on a libretto by Rinuccini, with its famous final lament (the only fragment of the work that survives) – an occasion made still more moving to the work's first hearers because they knew it had been written for Monteverdi's prematurely deceased pupil, the singer Caterina Martinelli.

The commitment to the musical drama was encouraged by a major innovation in theatre architecture – one which finally freed directors from dependence upon makeshift scenery in hastily converted ballrooms. The earlier form of the projecting proscenium still survived, to be sure. For it proved to be very amenable to such complicated staging as the one prescribed for the dancers and singers who descended from an elevated stage onto an 'island' surmounted by a large statue of Typhoeus in *La liberazione del Tirreno* at the Uffizi in 1616.[7] But more common now was the adaptation of Serlio's and Palladio's adaptations of ancient Greek theatres designed by the leading theatre architect of the day, Giovan Battista Aleotti (1546–1636). Aleotti made waves splash across the stage for the 1598 performance of Guarini's *Pastor fido* at Mantua. He figured out how to change a pastoral scene into a maritime scene (with boats floating in the background) and then into a temple in the theatre he built for the Accademia degli Intrepidi at Ferrara. And he surrounded the spectators with stage-like statues in the most famous, but, alas, least used of his structures, the Teatro Farnese in Parma.

So obvious were the advantages of permanent over temporary theatres that one was constructed, in rented quarters, the moment the Venetian government lifted its ban on theatrical performances in 1608. Companies previously accustomed to performing in public squares forthwith moved inside and invited in not only their pre-paying patrons, but also whoever could afford the price of admission. So profitable were these ventures that Venetian patricians began investing in them – first Alvise Vendramin, who built the theatre of San Salvador in 1622, and then the sponsors of the nine other theatres that were built during the next thirty years.

In Naples, meanwhile, which became the second theatre capital of Italy, the new theatre of San Giovanni de' Fiorentini finally succeeded where its two predecessors had failed in their competition for space with rapidly expanding Tridentine religious institutions. One of the latter, the Ospedale degli Incurabili, decided to use it as an income-producing endowment; and by 1618 its 22 boxes and 256 seats were ready for the first performances of Guarini's *Pastor fido* by the Ferrara company of Pier Cecchini. A still larger theatre was constructed at San Bernardino two years later with the two tiers of boxes surmounted by an open balcony running perpendicular to the stage on both sides of the rectangular main floor space. That, rather than Aleotti's Palladian semi-circle, was the form adopted by most Italian theatres until Ferdinando Bibbiena (1657–1743) of Bologna launched the next architectonic revolution in stage design early in the following century. Since it called for a stage as large as the auditorium itself, this form permitted rapid and frequent changes of scenery – 'from palaces to gardens, woods and Hell, with talking angels flying through the air . . . a large cloud falling down to reveal the glory of Paradise' and, in the case of a performance of a play called *L'inondazione del Tevere* ('Flood of the Tiber'), water flowing over the edge of the stage into open pipes.[8]

Such spectacles were sanctioned at the time in such impeccably Neo-Renaissance theoretical treatises as Cigoli's *Trattato di prospettiva pratica* (1629), Guidobaldo Bourbon Del Monte's *Perspectivae libri* vi (1600) and Scipione Chiaramonti's *Delle scene e teatri* (1610–14 – but first published in 1675). The theorists in turn were vindicated shortly afterward by the construction of such famous theatres as the private Teatro Barberini in Rome and the commercial Teatro della Pergola in Florence.[9]

The same fidelity to Neo-Renaissance aesthetic standards observable in music and musical drama was also characteristic of early seventeenth-century sculpture. Giambologna died in 1608, just as his last great bronze monument, the equestrian statue of Grand Duke Ferdinando I, was put in place in the middle of the Piazza Annunziata. But ready to succeed him as the leader of the populous school of sculptors in Florence was Pietro Tacca (1577–1640), who went on to surpass his master in technical virtuosity. He got the grand duke to capture a boar so that his *Porcellino* in the Mercato Nuovo would be true to life. He went down to Livorno in search of real African and Moorish slaves as models for the base figures in his statue of Ferdinando dominating the Mediterranean. He added curled tails to his bronze fish in the Piazza Annunziata so skilfully that they seem not to have been added. He combined coloured wax, crystal eyeballs and real hair so skilfully that the dowager grand duchess thought she was looking at the real head of her deceased husband. Finally, he made King Philip IV's horse rear up on its hind legs and stay there ever after, in an eternalized split-second, in front of the Royal Palace in Madrid, with nothing but space under its centre of gravity.[10]

Even more productive was the fidelity to Neo-Renaissance standards in the realm of painting. Annibale Carracci died in 1609; but the well-indoctrinated team of Emilians he had transplanted to Rome had been expanding on his heritage for almost a decade, and they did so with such fervour that they dominated the artistic worlds of both Rome and Bologna for the next two decades.[11]

These disciples were by no means passive imitators, and they did not hold themselves strictly bound by the prescriptions of the academies in which they had been nourished. Guido Reni was attracted by the early Christian archaeological interests of the Roman Oratorio, with which two of his first Roman sponsors were closely associated; and one of his first Roman works was dedicated to the current favourite of the Oratorians' proto-Christian heroes, St Cecilia, whose body had been discovered just two years before. Francesco Albani (1578–1660) still recalled the lessons of his first master, the pre-Carracci Fleming Denis Calvaert (1540–1619); and in 'the ingenuity of the profiles and the foreshortening and in the clinging garments of the angels' of his first independent commissions at San Giacomo degli Spagnoli and Palazzo Maffei, he followed not so much the example of Annibale as the sustaining tradition of Ludovico Carracci.[12] Giovanni Lanfranco (1582–1647) went beyond Annibale to Annibale's own source of inspiration, his fellow-countryman Correggio, whose work he studied during a vacation in his native Parma in preparation for one of his greatest masterpieces, the Buongiovanni chapel at Sant'Agostino in Rome (1616). He 'gave body to the supernatural'; and he thus 'demonstrated in a surprising manner his extraordinary ability to alter the poetic registers of his own vision, either toward the idyllic or toward the romantic as the occasion demanded' – and to surpass the lexical limits of the modern art historians who try to describe what he painted.[13]

The Carraccians felt just as free to differ among themselves – and even, at times, to quarrel openly. Domenichino (Domenico Zampieri, 1581–1641) developed a 'staid but elegant version' of Annibale's later classicism, one that emphasized 'the rigorous frontality and the frozen gestures of [his] idealized figures' and the 'static balance of [his] scenes', particularly in his *St Cecilia before the Judges* in San Luigi de' Francesi of 1613–14.[14] Lanfranco mastered the technique of making the unlit Baby Jesus light up the pitch dark night for the adoring shepherds (Collection of the Duke of Northumberland)[15] in a manner reminiscent of Barocci. He tempered Annibale's 'structural and expressive serenity' with 'a certain buoyant elasticity' (Posner). He thus achieved still greater masterpieces: the giant nudes holding up the painted cornice beneath the open sky on the ceiling of Villa Borghese (1624–25) and the swirling entourage of the Virgin in glory in the cupola of Sant'Andrea della Valle (1625–26). Reni dedicated himself to a search for a 'perfect idea'. He found it in the placidity of his protagonists and victims of violence – e.g., the St Sebastian with his hands tied over his head (Genoa: Palazzo Rosso) or behind his back (Madrid: Prado) who seems totally unaware of the arrows piercing his nude torso, and the Samson looking upward toward his raised hand with his left foot resting casually upon one of the many dead bodies sprawled on the field around him (Bologna: Pinacoteca). He also found it in stark simplicity: nothing but two inadequate blowing cloths and one small apple to distract attention from the spotlit bodies, aligned in impeccable geometric balance, of Hyppomenes and Atalanta (Naples: Capodimonte and Prado).[16]

Fidelity to Neo-Renaissance norms was encouraged by the further expansion of what, since the 1540s, had been the chief institutional base of all humanist culture: the academies. The example of the Carracci academy in Bologna and the Accademia di San Luca in Rome was imitated by the architect, engineer and stage designer Giulio Parigi (1571–1635) in Florence: he opened his house on the Via Maggio to budding military architects, some of whom went on to brilliant careers in Spain and Germany; to budding painters willing to read Euclid while learning 'a beautiful and new manner of painting marvellous landscapes'; and to 'the whole Florentine nobility'.[17] The same example was followed – specifically for the purpose of promoting religious art, but also for the purpose of studying in general the relation between theory and practice in all the arts – by Carlo Borromeo's cousin and his successor as archbishop of Milan, Cardinal Federico. Indeed, Federico had been one of the original sponsors of the San Luca. He followed Federico Zuccari's *Idea de' scultori, pittori et architetti* of 1607 in composing his own treatise *De pictura sacra* in 1624. And his ever-growing personal library, which still exists today at the Biblioteca Ambrosiana, became the meeting place for all the men of arts and letters of Milan.[18]

Another specialized academy was founded in Rome in 1603 (and then refounded in 1609) for the specific purpose of remedying what was thought to be the chief defect of university curricula: the application of mathematics and the experimental method to the study of nature. The Accademia dei Lincei, as it was called, followed the example of the Crusca in electing foreign members, whom it commissioned to keep it informed of the latest scientific discoveries in the rest of Europe. By 1625 it numbered thirty-two members and enjoyed the support of a sister academy of the same name in Naples, whose leader was the famous, although now elderly, inventor, playwright and 'natural magician', Giovan Battista Della Porta.

But most of these new academies adopted the encyclopedic model of their mid-sixteenth-century precursors – with the sole exception that they no longer had to worry about being forced into 'an extremely uncertain and precarious role' on the margins of the world of learning and could be as 'open' as they pleased 'to many varied and complex interests'.[19] The Accademia degli Addormentati ('Fallen Asleep') became the centre of cultural life in Genoa after its refoundation, in 1591, as the Addormentati Secondi under the sponsorship of the wealthy patron Anton Giulio Brignole Sale. The Accademia degli Umoristi became the centre of cultural life in Rome soon after its foundation in 1603. It drew talent from as far away as Pesaro, Lecce and Cosenza. It attracted the support of poets of the rank of Battista Guarini, who moved definitively to Rome shortly after the annexation of his native Ferrara. It also enjoyed the protection of no less potent a prelate than Cardinal Odoardo Farnese. The same services to the arts and letters were performed in Naples by the Accademia degli Oziosi, which was officially inaugurated in the cloister of Santa Maria delle Grazie in 1611. Its founder was Giovan Battista Manso, the author of a voluminous encyclopedia of academic Platonic 'questions'. Its literary model was the greatest of the Neo-Renaissance poetic monuments, Tasso's *Gerusalemme liberata*. And its official sponsor was none other than the viceroy, the Conde de Lemos, who, being a man of letters himself, formally abrogated the anti-intellectual policy of his predecessors that had shattered all previous attempts to endow the capital with a durable institution of humanist learning.

Most Italian observers of early seventeenth-century Italy were thus relatively satisfied with what they found. The Jubilee of 1600 had been an unheard-of success; and Pope Paul v completed what Pope Sixtus v had begun:

Time yields [its domination], and the peak of every mountain emerges covered with golden roofs. . . . The useless beast no longer covers the ample spaces; they are now adorned with fountains that waters flood, and above Rome there has been made a new Rome.[20]

'At present this city [of Genoa] is more flourishing than ever', noted Filippo Casoni in his (alas, still unpublished) *Short Description of Liguria and of the City of Genoa in 1613*, 'both for the multitude of its people, the variety of its arts and its immense wealth and for the magnificence of its sumptuous buildings'.[21] Admittedly, Andrea Doria's promise had not yet been fully realized: after all, a mere eighty years was certainly not enough time for the Genoese to master 'the arts of government' that the Venetians had taken 500 years to learn. But the republic was now 'more highly regarded by the king of Spain than ever before'. 'The nobles, who very recently were divided into two pernicious factions', were now, 'by the grace of God, completely united by will and', thanks to numerous intermarriages, 'by blood'. 'The magistracies once . . . scorned were now sought after by everyone'. The war fleet had grown from three to eight galleys, with fourteen others 'waiting in the arsenal'. And the once 'small and mechanical public palace was now being made grand and magnificent'. Or at least so thought one of the most powerful and most reflective of the patricians of Genoa, Andrea Spinola.[22]

The other states of Italy were even more successful in realizing the promises of their distant or recent founders. In Venice, the biggest problem posed to all traditional oligarchical republics in an age of state-building was met with apparent success: that is, the problem of reconciling government by a hereditary patriciate, upon which the republic's much-applauded stability was thought to depend, with government by trained specialists, upon which its efficiency was known to depend. This problem was solved in part in 1582 by effectively reserving all purely administrative offices for members of the subaltern, but still privileged and loyal, citizen class and by prescribing a series of competitive examinations for graduates of a special chancery school. It was further addressed in 1628 by forbidding the citizen-administrators from meeting together, thus avoiding the possibility of their creating a pre-Montesquieu intermediate body between prince and subjects. In Naples, the chronic problem of administrative corruption was once again exposed by a particularly conscientious royal visitor in 1607–10. But it was apparently solved once and for all by the energetic measures adopted by the new viceroy, the same Conde de Lemos of the Accademia degli Oziosi, the 'philosopher among princes and prince among philosophers, [in whom shone] much more eminently than in all [his] very illustrious predecessors all virtue and knowledge'. Lemos issued a long series of *prammatiche* regulating every organ of local and central administration. He then appealed to the Neapolitan men of letters to come forth with proposals not just for preventing old abuses, but also for obtaining previously unheard-of benefits – benefits like those promised by the economist Antonio Serra as a result of the development of native manufacturers in his *Brief Treatise* of 1613 on 'how to make kingdoms abound in gold and silver'.[23] And Naples, stimulated by the example of the reform literature then being generated in the court of their distant monarch, Philip III, succeeded Florence and Venice as one of the most innovative schools of political thought and political economy in Italy.

Meanwhile in Florence the problem of how to maintain 'concord among the princes of Italy' was solved by that conscious emulator of his ancestor Lorenzo, Grand Duke Ferdinando de' Medici, who gave up his cardinalate to succeed his brother Francesco in 1587. While protecting Italy both from the 'internal turbulence' of France and, through the marriage of his niece Maria to King Henry IV of France, from 'the formidable power of Spain', Ferdinando reversed Machiavelli's maxim and ruled 'by making himself loved rather than hated'. He appealed to his subjects' imaginations by sending his knights of Santo Stefano on several spectacularly successful pirating expeditions in the eastern Mediterranean:

From the Tyrrhenian shores,
And from where the Arno makes its banks fecund
With sublime valour, the Great Leader
Moves arms and warriors,
The terror of distant lands, the dread of the seas,
Hunter after glory, and beloved of Heaven,
Who one day in Byzantium itself
Will unfurl the ancient Sign. . . .[24]

He appealed to their sense of adventure by planning a colonizing expedition – fortunately never carried out – to Venezuela. So consistently did he act as if 'his own interest' consisted solely in promoting 'the increase of the wealth and honour of his subjects' that those of them who 'for such a great number of years had been accustomed to commanding and dominating [others] now easily and happily learned to obey'. Best of all, he caused 'all the sciences and arts [once again] to take up residence' in his capital, with the consequence that it soon surpassed even Athens and Rhodes in the quantity and quality of its marble and bronze statues.[25]

Meanwhile, whatever resentment the citizens of Ferrara might still have borne toward their conquerors of 1598 was swept away by the 'magnanimous' legate, Cardinal Cincio Passero of Monferrato – and by the prospects of finally settling the quarrel with Bologna over water-courses that for so long had threatened to ruin the Este's reclamation projects and fill up the Comacchio lagoons. Whatever resentment the Sicilians might still have nourished against the viceregal government vanished under the 'many good viceroys' subsequently appointed. 'The whole kingdom is peaceful and quiet in all its parts', proclaimed the elderly jurist Rocco Gambacorte. 'It works like a clock or a well-tuned organ. More than this, the divine Philosopher could not have wished for in his Republic'.[26] By 1600 the prophecy made in 1577 by the Genoese writer Lorenzo Cappelloni had at last come true. 'Italy', said Cappelloni,

is the most beautiful part of the world. It has the greatest number of villages, towns and cities with the greatest abundance of inhabitants; and its inhabitants are valorous and prudent in the letters and arts, excellent in architecture, sculpture and painting as well; trained and learned in the other liberal arts, diligent and expert in agriculture. There is no doubt that the princes who are born there are . . . the richest and the greatest and the most illustrious and celebrated that can be found anywhere.[27]

THE NATION DEFINED

The greatest accomplishment of the first decades of the seventeenth century was one of which none of the commentators of the age was fully aware: the definition of Italy as a nation in a form much more precise than any since Cato first proposed the term on the morrow of the second Punic War – and in a form that was to remain standard until the rise of nationalism in the early nineteenth century.

Before 1600, the term 'Italy' generally meant what it had meant to Petrarch and Machiavelli, even when accompanied by sentimental overtones or historical reminiscences: the geographical area that the Alps guarded and the Apennines parted and that was roughly coterminous with the ancient Roman 'province' of the same name. By 1600 the term had come to mean all those regions, wherever they might be, that fulfilled all of the following criteria: that they recognize the Bemban Tuscan codified in the Crusca *Vocabolario* as their official written, even if not yet spoken, language; that they recognize the works of Dante, Petrarch, Ariosto and Tasso as the classics of poetry and the works of Castiglione and Guicciardini as the classics of prose; that they recognize the works of Raphael, Michelangelo and the Carracci as normative in the realm of art; that they recognize Tridentine Catholicism as the only true, and therefore the only legitimate, religion, however imperfectly it might be observed in practice. The land borders of Italy as defined in this manner had no necessary connection with political borders: indeed, along the northern frontiers, they criss-crossed each other far more often than they coincided. They were seldom coterminous with traditional geographical designations. The Venetians declared the whole Adriatic Sea to be Venetian territory; and since the ships that sailed on it were almost all manned by Italian-speaking crews, it too was part of Italy. So were the settled parts of Corsica, which were administered by Ligurians. But Sardinia was not; for nothing remained there of the former Pisan domination except a few ruined churches.

This definition excluded from 'Italy' several small non-Italian enclaves on the Italian peninsula itself. One group of such enclaves was the one along the Adriatic coast in Calabria and eastern Sicily inhabited by immigrants from the Slavic and Albanian areas of the Balkans. Balkan immigrants had begun to arrive, in response to the Ottoman invasions, as early as the mid-fifteenth century: already by the 1480s there were enough of them in Camerano to warrant their establishing a parish all of their own, and there were enough of them in Trani to make possible the election of two of them to the fifteen-man city council. Immigrants became much more numerous after 1520 in response to an increasing demand for labour; to the myth of a 'felix Italia' spread about by itinerant Italian merchants; and to the prospects of better living and legal conditions. Some immigrants had difficulty relinquishing the more primitive customs of their homelands: 'Since the nation of the Albanians is prone to shedding blood', reads a statute of Ancona, 'a brake must be applied to their audacity and to their uncivilized style of life'. But most of them worked hard, as sailors, carpenters and stewards; and they were soon able to buy land, acquire citizenship rights, build whole villages, and thus contribute to the economic recovery of the war-devastated lands on which they were invited to settle. At the same time, most of them studiously maintained their ethnic identities — with their own churches, confraternities, guilds, priests and even a separate Collegium Ungaro-Illyricum at the University of Bologna. And apart from one or two exceptional, and unsuccessful, attempts to 'Latinize' them – like the one by the bishop of Anglona and Tursi in Basilicata in the early seventeenth century – they were generally allowed, and even encouraged, to do so.

The inhabitants of another set of such enclaves were actually obliged to maintain a separate identity: the Jews. Unlike the Slavs, the Jews always remained at least potentially mobile. Many had come recently to Italy as refugees from Germany or Spain; and many of them were obliged to become refugees once again as one or another Italian state alternately expelled and readmitted them. They were expelled from the city of Venice in the early sixteenth century and from the duchy of Milan at the end of the sixteenth century. They were expelled from the Kingdom of Naples in 1501 and then re-admitted, at the insistence of the Parlamento, in 1509. Pope Pius V confined them to Rome and Ancona; Pope Sixtus V removed the residence requirement and most commercial restrictions; Pope Clement VIII reinstated them.

A few Jews achieved a certain degree of integration. At Ancona they participated in commercial firms as the partners of Christians, and their services were particularly valued because of their contacts with other Jews in the Ottoman Empire. At Sorano they invested money even in their chief competitor, the Monte di Pietà. At Siena they founded one of the most important banks in the city and 'lived in dignity and tranquillity with their [Christian] neighbours'. At the University of Padua they were permitted to take degrees, like Protestants, without submitting to the Tridentine loyalty oath; and the number of Jewish students enrolled there doubled between the sixteenth and the seventeenth centuries. Some governments granted them special protection in the hope of converting them to Christianity – to which a few were attracted by such institutions as the Sodality of San Giuseppe dei Catecumeni financed by a tax on un-converted Jews.

More often, Jewish communities were protected because of the indispens-able banking and commercial services they alone could, or were willing to, provide. Jewish banks were licensed in Bagnoregio in 1546 and in Orvieto in 1553, and at Lugo in the Romagna, where Jews comprised a tenth of the total population, they assumed the entire burden of financing the local fairs. In 1539 Pope Paul III forbade Passion plays in the Colosseum to protect the Roman Jews against outbursts of Christian enthusiasm. In 1566 Cosimo de' Medici prescribed heavy penalties for anyone who 'molests Jews either by word or by deed on the streets' of Florence. Everywhere Jews were exempt from the jurisdiction of the Inquisition in religious matters; in Piedmont they could be summoned on other charges only if accompanied by a civil conser-vatore. Only once were they made the objects of officially sanctioned violence: in Ancona, in 1555, when Pope Paul IV suddenly abrogated the modus vivendi by which immigrant Spanish Marranos were quietly permitted to return to Judaism. The some twenty-four Marranos who did not manage to escape into the welcoming arms of Duke Guidobaldo II in Pesaro were burned or strangled as lapsed converts – without the older Jewish community, which resented their competition, lifting a finger to help them.

Nevertheless, most Jews, before as after the Tridentine Reformation (which, contrary to what is often thought, had little effect on their status), were forced to live in ghettos on the model of the one established in Venice in 1516. They could usually gain permission to operate shops outside the ghetto and sometimes even to engage in the lucrative grain trade, as they did in Pitigliano through the new statutes of 1622. Most ghettos were administered by the inhabitants themselves through something resembling the nine-man *collegio* officially recognized by the duke of Mantua in 1549. And internal autonomy permitted the Jewish communities to preserve unimpaired their own social, literary and theological traditions, even when they had to borrow from the surrounding culture whatever those traditions lacked, like the interior decoration of synagogues.[28]

By far the largest of the resident non-Italian communities, however, was the Greek, which was reinforced by waves of new immigrants every time still another of the Italian outposts in the former Byzantine Empire fell to the Turks. These Greek immigrants were occasionally the objects of harassment. Virtuous republicans that they were, the Venetian senators did all they could to prevent the projection of the polyethnic character of their empire onto its dominant city; and it took the special intervention of Popes Leo x, Clement vii and Paul iii at last to secure for resident Greeks the right to build their own church of San Giorgio (1539–73), to assert the independence of their clergy from the Latin-rite patriarch and eventually (1577) to secure the appointment of their own bishop. After Trent, moreover, a few bishops in southern Italy tried to resurrect the old Norman policy of imposing the Latin rite throughout their dioceses. One of them sharply decreased what he thought to be an excessive number of Greek priests (1:100 laymen, twice that of the Latin clergy) by making them live up to Tridentine standards of learning and piety or resign. Another seriously proposed 'throwing all of them out of the kingdom'.[29]

But generally Greeks in Italy continued to enjoy the prestige earned by their ancestors for having transmitted to Italians the literary heritage of Greek antiquity, Christian as well as pagan. They gained additional prestige through their adherence to a creed which, although possibly schismatic, was impervious to the most recent temptations to doctrinal aberration; and the much more cacophonous doctrinal questions raised by the sixteenth-century reformers soon banished the old quarrels about the *Filioque* and the Procession of the Holy Spirit to a back room in most theological mansions. The Greeks benefited from the special services of such important ecclesiastical institutions of the Tridentine Reformation as the Greek College and the Congregation of the Greeks in Rome and of such prestigious secular institutions as the University of Padua, where the Greek student population alone rose from 34 in 1500 to 1,746 in 1700. They also benefited from the special protection of such high-ranking Tridentine prelates as Cardinal Giulio Antonio Santoro, who happened also to be the bishop of Santa Severina in Calabria, where many of them lived. 'The rites may be Greek', Santoro reminded the Sicilian bishops in 1575, 'but they are Catholic and not repugnant to the holy faith'.[30]

Thus the Greek colonies prospered – particularly the largest and most active of them, the one in Venice, which counted some 4,000 members by the mid-sixteenth century. There the resident Greeks supported their own separate clergy. They alternatively corresponded with and denied the jurisdiction of the patriarch of Constantinople, notwithstanding the annoyance of the Venetian government over the bloated titles he claimed for himself. They introduced many new words and expressions – 278 of them at the latest count – into the Venetian dialect, which, not being protected, was receptive even to Slavic neologisms. They encouraged the importation, and thus the preservation, of modern and Byzantine Greek art – like the icons brought from Crete to Cephalonia in the mid-seventeenth century. And they made Italian classics available to their brethren back home – including Boccaccio's *Teseida*, which was published in modern Greek in 1529. Taking advantage of, and in part offsetting, the Ottoman prohibition against book printing, they sent most of some 100,000 volumes they printed in Venice in the last quarter of the sixteenth century back to Greece. And since they all lived in the expectation not of having to move, like the Jews, but of eventually being able to move back to the lands from which they had fled, they remained staunchly Greek even when they rose to positions of prominence as scholars, teachers, merchants and men of letters in their host country.

Outside the enclaves, the process of Italianization proceeded almost without resistance. The conversion of the isolated Apennine Val di Lima began in 1555, when the new Tridentine pastor persuaded the local confraternities to purchase their ecclesiastical ornaments in Florence, or at least in Pistoia. The conversion of Puglia began in 1542, when the men of Giovinazzo sent an order for some paintings through a merchant in Barletta to Venice; and it was completed during the half-century thereafter, when most local artists went to study in Naples or Rome. Meanwhile, 'the noble city of Cosenza', which 'raised its proud walls on the banks of the clear river Crati' in Calabria, became the 'nest and residence of rare minds', where 'Mars assembles his arms and Apollo is adorned with laurels' in one of the most active academies of all Italy.[31] Messina had hosted the great Greek scholar Janis Lascaris in the early sixteenth century and the first Jesuit college in the mid-sixteenth century. In 1599 it entered the orbit of pan-Italian university chair competitions, and it won one of Padua's most prominent professors of surgery and anatomy, Giovan Battista Cortesi, who paid tribute to his adopted *patria* by putting its name in the titles of his widely acclaimed textbooks – like the *Pharmacopoeia seu antidotarium Messanense*. Even Malta was annexed. The masters of the Knights of Malta were still elected without regard for nationality, but they hired Italians (specifically Francesco Laparelli of Cortona) to build their fortresses and design their cities; and they sent to Rome for Tridentine pastors qualified 'to give sermons, to supervise other spiritual activities and to instruct the youth'.[32]

The borders of Italy coalesced as well where they were marked by land rather than by sea. In Istria they retreated somewhat as the Venetian government, which was interested in crops, not culture, created a special magistracy to encourage the settlement of the countryside by immigrants from Croatia. Soon, according to the Italophone regional chronicler Gian Francesco Tommasini, the old Istrian dialect had all but vanished, and 'the inhabitants of many villages [could] not even pronounce Italian'. But in the towns, Slavic was spoken only by plebeians; all 'civil persons' spoke exclusively Italian, which remained the sole language of trade and of civil and ecclesiastical administration. With its new statutes of 1550, Trieste yielded some of the autonomy it had enjoyed since Charles v declared it to be a 'republic': the city council found it very convenient to be able to appeal to an emperor or an archduke, who tactfully appointed only Italians as their local representatives, whenever the council got into a quarrel with the bishop, the captain of the fortress or the Venetians. But the 'republic' still maintained its own consulates in Ancona and Puglia. It forbade the association of its own nobility with that of the neighbouring Austrian province of Kärnten. Its poets, chroniclers and administrators all wrote exclusively in Bemban Tuscan or Bemban Latin, the official languages of the government-supported schools, and no longer in the mixture of Venetian and Ladino that was generally spoken on the streets. Its Italian character was formally recognized by Pope Clement viii in 1597, when he refused the archduke's request for an exemption from the general requirement that all Italian bishops-elect be examined in Rome. 'No one has the slightest doubt', said the pope, 'that Trieste is in Italy'.[33]

No one had any doubts about the Italian character of Trent, either, even though the Cambrai Wars had left the temporal state of the prince-bishop hemmed in by pockets of land ruled directly from Innsbruck and severed from his other temporal domains around wholly Germanophone Brixen. The local dialect, which was easily understood by other Italians as early as the fourteenth century, gave way to standard Italian after 1547, when the local poet Jacopo Vargnano di Arco celebrated the emperor's victory at Mühlberg in his *Il trionfo tridentino*. The bishops continued to be chosen from the Tridentine-Roman family of the Madruzzo that had hosted the council; and they steadfastly defended the independence of their state against the pretensions both of the archdukes of Tyrol and the pro-Habsburg faction in the city council. Except for the Valtelline question, which remained to be settled in the first decades of the seventeenth century, no one had doubts about the Alpine frontiers of Italy. Canton Ticino remained Italian in language even after it was made a political dependency of the northern Swiss cantons in 1512; and the ensuing religious differences within the confederation enabled Carlo Borromeo to bring it back under Milanese influence, although not Milanese rule, when he supported a separate league among the Catholic cantons in 1586.

Meanwhile, whatever doubts remained about the borders of Italy in the domains of the House of Savoy were cleared up unequivocally by decree of Duke Emanuele Filiberto. The Alpine valleys of Piedmont remained French, even after the annexation of Pinerolo, because he had been forced to recognize the complete administrative autonomy of the league of Waldensian communes. The Valle d'Aosta also remained French because he had declared that to be its official language; and he appointed only Gallophone representatives to the otherwise autonomous local councils. But the rest of Piedmont, including the province of Saluzzo that was finally annexed in 1601, became wholly Italian by virtue of the same language decrees; and the continuing presence at the Italianized court of Turin of French or Alsatian princesses, choreographers and musicians constitutes no more 'irrefutable' evidence of a persisting Franco-Italian (rather than Piedmontese-Italian) bilingualism in Piedmont than does their well-known presence in most of the other courts of Italy.[34]

Only in the east did the borders remain hazy. Chios was lost in 1566 and Cyprus in 1570; and most of the native Greeks who might have been receptive to Italian culture, like the Cypriot Dimitris Laskaris Megadoukas, fled to the remaining Hellenic dominions of their former masters. In Crete, the resident Italians built the new fortress of Rethimno and redesigned the town, after its destruction by the Turks in 1570, according to an Italian plan. But they made no effort to Italianize their Greek-speaking subjects, who continued to write even the ceremonial verse eulogies customarily addressed to arriving and departing Venetian governors in their own language. Indeed, the Venetian government did all it could to discourage contact between the ruling and the subject population, in its Ionian as well as in its Cretan dominions. It prohibited intermarriage. It barred non-Italians from public office. It nominated Latin-rite bishops to all the sees and then, in recognition of their uselessness, permitted them to reside abroad. It forced the Orthodox clergy to seek ordination on the mainland; and that Orthodoxy continued to predominate in Kerkyra (Corfù) was the result largely of papal protests against Venetian attempts to impose religious conformity.

The one remaining border area in the east remained an anomaly by becoming completely bi-cultural: the independent republic of Ragusa (Dubrovnik). The upper classes all spoke Italian and read Latin, since many of them had travelled to or studied in Italy. But they also spoke Croatian, which was the native language of the entire population, noble and plebeian. Both native and imported artists adopted Italian Renaissance styles, although they occasionally took liberties in mixing Roman classical and Venetian Gothic styles in a manner that would never have been tolerated in the Italy of Sansovino. The chief playwright of Ragusa in the sixteenth century was Marino Darsa, who permitted his characters to speak one or another kind of Italian when it was appropriate, just as the Venetian comedy writers permitted theirs to enliven Venetian dialogues with Slavic expressions. The chief Ragusan poet of the early seventeenth century was known both as Divo Franov and as Giovanni Gondola. Franov wrote a Slavic version of the *Gerusalemme liberata*, in addition to publishing numerous translations. The forms, then, were Italian, but the language was Slavic; and Ragusa was consequently both inside and outside of Italy at the same time.[35]

Italy was, of course, not yet a nation in the sense that it would become one in the age of the Risorgimento. But it was more of a nation than Germany, where the mapmakers constantly oscillated between the two irreconcilable criteria of 'sprachlich-ethnische' similarities and 'reichsrechtliche Zugehorigkeit' and alternatively cut out and reincorporated such border areas as Schlesien, Luxemburg and Metz.[36] Italy was more of a nation than the Burgundian Low Countries, which by 1600 were hopelessly split not only politically and confessionally, but, with the emergence of Dutch both as a literary and as a commercial language, linguistically as well. It was more of a nation than the agglomeration of constitutionally divided Iberian kingdoms that belonged to the king of Naples and Sicily and the duke of Milan, notwithstanding the widespread custom of the time of referring to them collectively as 'Spain', for two of these kingdoms resisted the imposition of Castilian as a common 'national' language as vigorously as they resisted any infringement of their political autonomy. Italy was not much less of a nation than France. Most Italians still accepted as axiomatic Machiavelli's invidious comparison of Italy to a 'united' France, even though they now believed the papacy to be the chief pan-Italian institution. But neither the new Bourbon nor the former Valois kings of France paid the slightest attention to the ethnic or linguistic character of the provinces they added, or sought to add, to their royal domain; and many of such provinces, from Saluzzo to Brittany, from Roussillon to Navarre, were 'French' only by virtue of the famous decree of Francis I making the *langue d'oïl* obligatory in official administrative correspondence.

Unlike that of nineteenth-century nation-states, moreover, Italian national unity was achieved without the slightest sacrifice of the pan-Christendom universalism characteristic of both medieval and Renaissance Italian culture. This universalism was particularly notable in the realm of the fine arts. Italians were by no means uncritical of what they found abroad. But they were fully receptive to whatever appeared to be a technical improvement – like the 'velvets and other silk drapes' of the Flemish masters, who 'made them seem very natural and [thus] deceived everyone', and like 'the refined and abstract elegance' of Giambologna's fountains.[37] Since by 1600 Italian High- and Neo-Renaissance forms, styles and standards had spread to the whole of Europe, they now found much that pleased them; and they were encouraged in their acquisitions by the example of such 'eclectic and cosmopolitan' art collectors as Monteverdi's patron, Duke Vincenzo Gonzaga of Mantua, who was guided solely by considerations of quality, never of provenance.[38]

Non-Italian artists were thus welcomed in Italy on the same terms as natives: as actual or potential collaborators in a common enterprise. Most of them – like Paul Brill (1554–1626) and several of his fellow Antwerpers who worked under the direction of Girolamo Muziano at Palazzo Orsini in Monterotondo in the 1580s – came initially to learn; for Italy in general and Rome in particular had come to be recognized as the art school of Europe. But most of them were already well trained by the time they arrived. Jacques Callot had studied under Philippe Thomassin in Lorraine before coming to study in Rome and Florence with Antonio Tempesta (1555–1630) and Giulio Parigi; and in Rome he was still close to home, for a large colony of his compatriots had settled there as masters of his own master art-form, engraving. Some of the immigrant artists supported themselves in part by copying the works of others, for copying had become a lucrative profession at a time, more than three centuries before the perfection of colour photography, when it was nourished by a widespread demand for examples of the latest artistic innovations.

When they gave promise of excelling their Italian competitors, non-Italian artists invariably won the commissions – as Anton Van Dyck (1559–1641) did when he made a lady of the Durazzo family of Genoa into an incarnation of aristocratic refinement, looking off to her left in detached tranquillity while a large red drape sets off her chokingly high starched white collar (*Portrait of a Lady, Called the Marchessa Durazzo*, New York: Metropolitan). One of the most successful of them was Van Dyck's compatriot and master, Peter Paul Rubens. In spite of his tender age (he was in his early twenties when he arrived from Antwerp in 1600) Rubens quickly attracted the attention of some of Italy's most discerning patrons – the Oratorians in Rome, Duke Vincenzo in Mantua and Niccolò Pallavicino, the patron of the Genoa Jesuits. He then did for the Doria what his disciple was to do fifteen years later for the Durazzo: he memorialized Brigida in the same over-dressed aristocratic pose (*Marchesa Brigida Spinola Doria*, Washington: National Gallery), and he placed Gian Carlo in merry-go-round detachment astride an over-excited horse charging at the viewer over the back of a black spaniel (Uffizi: Depositario; but I saw it on loan at the Metropolitan in New York in April 1985). After eight packed years, Rubens returned home to make use of his vast collection of 'citations' of a hundred years of Italin art in becoming the most celebrated painter of his generation.[39]

The achievement of pre-nationalist national unity did not prevent Italians from welcoming non-Italians and importing non-Italian products. Nor did it prevent them from exporting products and talents of their own. Notwithstanding the Puritan-inspired wave of Italophobia, Ariosto's comedies had been translated and performed in England ever since 1566, and his poems had been plundered for themes and motives by Marlowe, Spenser, and Sidney. The whole *Orlando furioso* finally appeared in English translation in 1591, while his *Satires* were not fully translated until 1608:[40] Ariosto then went off to conquer Spain as well – and, in Canto 23, to provide Cervantes with the theme of Don Quixote's lament. Meanwhile, back in England, he was followed by many of his compatriots, thanks in part to John Wolfe, the publisher of the chief works of such productive resident exiles as the philosopher Giordano Bruno, the jurist Alberico Gentile (1552–1608) and the critic Jacopo Castelvetro. Aretino's comedies appeared in 1588, Tasso's *Gerusalemme* from 1594 to 1600, Guarini's *Pastor fido*, bound with Tasso's *Aminta*, in 1591, and Stefano Guazzo's *Civile conversazione*, the most important manner book since Della Casa's, in 1586.

At least after the completion of the Escorial, the successor to Fontainebleau as the greatest Italian project beyond the Alps, Italian artists generally preferred to remain at home – or at least to confine their incessant migrations to the cities of Italy. But now that war had ceased in Italy and the task of state building had been completed, all those Italian business, administrative and military technicians who still had a taste for adventure found in emigration an increasingly attractive, and remunerative, outlet for their skills. 'A veritable wave of Italian bankers, contractors and merchants' fell on Valladolid from the mid- to late sixteenth century; and they organized themselves into an autonomous community from which the host city drew many of its financial officers.[41] Genoese bankers had directed and financed many of the Spanish overseas ventures ever since the late fifteenth century. By the end of the sixteenth century they had become 'the absolute masters of the country', at least in financial matters; and by remaining a 'homogeneous group' in control of 'a tightly closed system', they managed to maintain their position for another century thereafter, in spite of outbursts of hostility on the part of their clients.[42]

Of military experts, to be sure, by far the most famous emigrant of the age was Alessandro Farnese. But his career was not atypical. Pietro Malvezzi was rewarded for his service as head of a 3,000-man Italian regiment in the armies of Philip II by being made the chief administrator of all the armies in Spain, where he was buried with great honours in 1605. Lodovico Gonzaga, the uncle of Duke Vincenzo, was rewarded for his service in the royal army during the civil wars in France by being made governor of Picardy and Champagne and duke of Nevers – and by being made the hero of his fellow Mantuan Antonio Possevino's handbook for Tridentine Catholic soldiers. Don Giovanni de' Medici, the illegitimate product of one of Grand Duke Cosimo's late romances, was rewarded for his service in the armies of Emperor Rudolph II during the wars in Hungary – and compensated for the loss of 120,000 *scudi* when he bet on the wrong candidate to succeed Pope Urban VII – by being made a grandee of Spain.

THE CRISES

Then, just as this least imperfect world seemed to have approached sufficient perfection that it might reasonably be considered exempt from the usual dangers of historical contingency, at least for the foreseeable future, it was unexpectedly visited by a series of increasingly sharp shocks.

The first shock occurred in July 1600, when Michelangelo Merisi, better known as Il Caravaggio from the place of his birth, unveiled his first large-scale religious *istorie*, the *Calling* and the *Martyrdom of St Matthew*, on the walls of the Contarelli Chapel at San Luigi de' Francesi in Rome.[43] Anyone who had noticed the dew-drops on the flowers and the bruises on the peaches carried by several of his boys shown in torso, the scream formed by the mouth of another of them as he is bitten by a lizard, the half-parted lips and drooping eyelids of his adolescent musicians as they eye one another's sensuously undressed bodies, the dirty fingers that barely sustain the broad-rimmed glass of his oval-faced young Bacchus – anyone who had seen these early expressions of the young Lombard's effrontery should have realized that he was something more than just a disciple and collaborator of the Cavalier d'Arpino, the semi-official painter of the family of the reigning pope. Anyone who had noticed the suggestive, barely veiled backside of the bisexual angel playing a violin from a score held for him by a tired and aging Joseph resting on the road to Egypt should have realized that what had so titillated the wealthy admirers of his unusual genre paintings could be easily transposed into *istorie*.

But no one was prepared for the tense passion on the face of Jesus, with his clipped black beard, as he thrusts his arm in the direction of a baffled Matthew sitting across the room at his counting-table, the violent contortions of the nude body of the executioner, and the terrified eyes of the boy, perhaps a self-portrait, running off to the right. That was more 'dramatic value' than the clerical commissioners had counted on; and they made him tone it down. Nor was anyone prepared for the *St Matthew* of the altarpiece who 'did not look like a saint' – no one, that is, except Vincenzo Giustiniani, Caravaggio's principal patron at the time, who happily added the artist's works to his own collection. For Giustiniani had just acquired as well the most scandalous of all of his protégé's genre works, the lewd and leering *Amor Victorius* (Berlin: Dahlem Gallery) exposing his distorted, underdeveloped genitals as he kicks aside the musical instruments at his feet; he kept it veiled in order better to scandalize the guests he frequently invited in for tours of his well-stocked gallery.

What disturbed many of Caravaggio's contemporaries was that all his innovations could be traced directly to impeccably Neo-Renaissance models and principles. Brilliant spotlights shattering almost total obscurity actually constituted a further exploration of the single light source used so effectively by Barocci. Putting biblical personages in modern dress was perfectly consonant with the ultimately rhetorical purpose of all art: it associated the viewer even more closely with what he viewed. Forty-five-year-old apostles with bald scalps and sunburned faces and old women with swollen thyroids were excellent examples of 'realism', particularly when Caravaggio dispensed with preliminary sketches and painted them directly onto his canvases. Catching the aged Virgin with a wrinkled brow at the moment of her death, not after her body had been prepared for burial, made the mourning of the bystanders even more intense. Catching the apostles at Emmaus at the very instant of recognition heightened the intensity of their surprise. Giustiniani was therefore justified, when he began writing his *Discorso sopra la pittura* in 1610, in presenting his protégé not as a rebel, but as the greatest of the Neo-Renaissance painters. Caravaggio, he said, had wiped out the last traces of painting 'from fantasy rather than from a model' by conscientiously painting always 'with natural objects before his eyes'.[44] But he had also demonstrated that the rhetorical potentialities of Neo-Renaissance painting were far greater than any of its previous proponents had ever imagined.

The Carraccians lost no time in launching a counterattack; and Caravaggio himself contributed to its eventual success by refusing to train disciples, by his bouts of violent, even homicidal, behaviour – and by dying prematurely, in very suspicious circumstances, just ten years after his entry into the world of great artists. But in the meantime he gained the support not only of Giustiniani, but also of such well-informed and powerful collectors as

Cardinal Scipione Borghese, the nephew of Pope Paul v; Ottaviano Costa, a wealthy Genoese banker; Cardinal Francesco Maria Del Monte, a practising experimental scientist; Grand Duke Ferdinando de' Medici (who acquired Caravaggio's *Medusa*, now in the Uffizi); and, of course, Duke Vincenzo Gonzaga. He also gained the respect of many of the artists then resident in Rome, Italian and non-Italian. 'Caravaggism' spread rapidly all over Europe in the innumerable copies that have so complicated the task of establishing correct attributions ever since. And it remained an indelible feature of painting in Italy for another half-century.

The second major blow fell on 17 June 1606, when Pope Paul v informed the Venetian Senate that it would incur sentences of personal excommunication and that all its dominions would fall under a papal interdict if it did not comply with several specific conditions set down in his bull within twenty-four days.

This crisis too had been brewing for some time. Well before he had become the sole surviving heir to the throne of France, the Venetians had given open support to the future King Henry IV, even though the pope still considered him to be a heretic. The pope had encouraged the bishop of the small town of Ceneda in the Veneto foothills, which the Venetians considered part of their domain, to forward criminal appeals to Rome rather than to the regular Venetian magistrates – as if the town were part of the Papal State. The Venetians had refused to recognize the excommunication of Cesare d'Este, whom the pope was trying to expel from Ferrara. The pope had then objected to their establishing diplomatic relations with England, the greatest of the Protestant powers – despite the ample precedent of the very Christian kings of France, who had never hesitated to negotiate directly with the sultan in Istanbul and with the Protestant states in Germany.

These controversies were usually smoothed over by carefully avoiding questions of principle, a policy whose undisputed master was the historian and political philosopher Paolo Paruta, who usually represented the Senate at the court of Clement VIII.[45] But between May 1605 and January 1606, the same Camillo Borghese whose taste for jurisdictional brawls had re-ignited the old quarrel over Ceneda was elected Pope Paul v, and Leonardo Donà, who had 'dedicated himself to public life as if it were a priestly vocation' while still, according to the papal nuncio, 'showing his great [religious] conscience by going frequently to confession and communion', was elected doge.[46] Roberto Bellarmino, whose *Controversies* had established him as the most authoritative theologian of the Tridentine Church, became the official theological counsellor to the new pope; and Paolo Sarpi (1562–1623), the austere reformer of the Order of Servites – a man who combined formidable rhetorical skills with an unrivalled ability to summon up authoritative quotations – became the official theologian of the Senate. The time was thus right for reasserting the rights of the pious to secure their salvation by making bequests to tax-exempt ecclesiastical institutions. The time was also right for renewing the pre-Tridentine bans aimed at blocking the obviously disastrous economic and fiscal consequences of this aspect of Tridentine piety and for assuring lay subjects of protection against the increasing menace of criminal violence on the part of persons supposedly exempt from civil laws. The pope demanded that the two recent laws making future bequests subject to state approval be repealed and that two clerics arrested on murder charges be turned over to ecclesiastical courts. The Senate in response declared the excommunication and the interdict contrary to Holy Scripture, the Fathers and the councils and prohibited their publication in its dominions. The Roman Inquisition summoned Sarpi to appear in person and excommunicated him when he put off the trip until a more opportune moment. The Senate gave the Jesuits – who, as it happened, were almost the only clerics to comply with the interdict by refusing to perform their usual ecclesiastical functions – three days to clear out of Venetian territory.[47]

The two major powers whose cooperation had long been considered the principal guarantor of the peace and 'liberty' of Italy were now locked in a contest that, at least for the moment, seemed to defy resolution. Worse yet, this contest threatened to split the world of the Tridentine Reformation into irreconcilable parts. However, negotiations began almost immediately, since neither the other powers of Italy nor the kings of France or Spain had any interest in seeing either of the two contestants emerge as the unqualified victor. Indebted to the success of the Tridentine Reformation, which assured them all but complete control of their dioceses, the Venetian bishops had little trouble in assuring the continuation of religious services; and the people themselves collaborated with the civil authorities in capturing fugitive priests and in tearing down pro-papal posters. But the senators found it increasingly embarrassing, as the self-proclaimed rulers of the most unequivocally Tridentine state in Europe, to be at odds with the see it just as unequivocally recognized as the spiritual head of the Tridentine Church; and they were particularly fearful of reviving their pre-1509 isolation from the other states of Italy, all of which, in this instance – although some less vigorously than others – decided to side with the pope. Hence just ten months later, on 21 April 1607, the interdict was 'lifted' in accordance with a formula worked out by Sarpi himself that made it appear as if it had never been imposed.

In the meantime, however, the controversy had sparked a pan-Christendom 'paper war' that ended by making all too explicit, and hence irreconcilable, theses that hitherto had been reconcilable precisely because they had been left undefined. These theses had nothing to do with doctrine. Both sides remained rigorously Tridentine; and to pretend that Sarpi or anyone else became a 'Protestant', a 'materialist' or even an 'atheist' just because his curial opponents hurled such epithets at him or because he corresponded with Protestant scholars and proposed a political alliance with Protestant powers simply cannot be maintained on the basis of the abundant surviving documents.[48] But the conflict had much to do with ecclesiology, which was the one branch of theology that the Fathers at Trent had done their best to avoid, and particularly with that branch of ecclesiology that concerned the relation between spiritual and temporal powers. Sarpi was forced to exaggerate the commonly held, if still ill-defined, principle that the temporal power too was responsible for the spiritual welfare of its subjects. Indeed, he did so almost to the point of making it solely responsible – at least in the case of the temporal power of which he was a subject. And by rummaging about in the writings of the most violent anti-papal polemicists of the fourteenth century, he almost ended by breaking up the Church universal into separate and autonomous regional churches dependent wholly on their respective civil governments.

Likewise, Bellarmino was forced to recast as theory the century-old practice by which some ecclesiastics were also invested with civil authority. In doing so, he was forced to go back to the late Middle Ages, to isolate from their polemical context the extravagant theses of the opponents of Sarpi's authorities, to forget about all the memos he had addressed to Pope Clement VIII about the theological limitations of the pope's authority even in ecclesiastical matters, and to proclaim as eternally orthodox the proposition that 'as temporal ends are subordinate to spiritual ends', so 'the pope has full power (*plenissimam potestatem*) over the whole earth in political as well as ecclesiastical affairs'.[49]

Once committed to paper these theses could be invoked to justify extending book censorship in Venice, at Sarpi's insistence, from religious to purely political matters. They could be invoked to reinforce the anti-clerical stance of such ardent secular jurisdictionalists as the Neapolitan lawyer Camillo de Curtis. They could be invoked to extend the use of the royal *exequatur*, or civil censorship of papal decrees, to the point of practically isolating local churches from Rome. Almost every time the Church invoked one of these principles during the course of the following century, it lost. Almost every time a state invoked them, it won. Their periodic invocation thus had precisely the effect predicted by the French ambassador at Venice in 1606: that of 'damaging papal authority more than a very serious war'[50] – and, he might have added, that of discrediting the Tridentine Church as a whole.

Except for immunizing native religious and educational institutions from further competition from the Society of Jesus, which they refused to readmit, the Venetians won very little from the Interdict controversy. Determined to avoid ever again having to pose as the diplomatic suppliants of the rest of Europe, they quietly returned to a policy of accommodation – albeit now in practice rather than in principle. They swiftly stamped out the least sign of backsliding among their subjects, particularly among those who were momentarily misled into attributing natural disasters to their not having been fully 'absolved'. And they carefully cultivated the new image of themselves – no longer as the guardians of the 'liberty' of Italy, but as models of stability and durability – that their Dutch and German admirers now bestowed upon them.[51]

Sarpi, the Venetians' chief ideologue, continued to perform his duties as an adviser on a vast range of foreign and domestic issues – how to prevent the nomination of a non-Venetian patriarch and how to respond to· proposals for defence alliances with foreign powers. But his own personal interests turned from politics and ecclesiology to history. He first wrote a polished humanist 'commentary' on the Interdict itself – one in which, in line with post-Interdict Venetian foreign policy, a pre-existing state of event-less harmony is restored without modification after being momentarily, and without permanent consequences, interrupted by the first cause of all the 'events', Pope Paul. He then returned to the project he had been contemplating ever since his youthful encounter with the great Tridentine reformers. He rearranged the mass of material he had collected from them at the time and about them after his admission into the Venetian archives into a form borrowed from Guicciardini. The result was an unprecedented fusion of the two previously separate disciplines of civil and ecclesiastical history and a remarkable anticipation of the scholarly historiography of the late seventeenth century: the *History of the Council of Trent*. Smuggled out of Venice and carefully patched up to make it look like a pro-Anglican attack on the Council, the *History* was published pseudonymously at London in 1619.[52]

The papacy won nothing and lost much – namely, its carefully promoted prestige as the leader and guarantor of the Tridentine Reformation. Its principal purpose now became that of promoting the interests of the papal family. The pope's brothers and nephews were loaded with offices, outright gifts, and even such monetarily profitable spiritual concessions as station-church indulgences for their private chapel. His sister's son Scipione, who adopted his mother's family name after receiving a cardinal's hat in 1605, was made governor of the Papal State, archbishop of Bologna and secretary of the *brevi* and provided with a sufficient income to buy estates all over Latium, an entire principality in the Kingdom of Naples, an entire collection of ancient statues and the works of half the current painters in Rome. The Council's injunctions about high-living cardinals were put aside. Nepotism returned with a virulence unheard of since the days of Paul III. And the pope celebrated the elevation of his family to the rank of the richest in Rome by carving his name in huge letters right across the new façade of St Peter's.[53]

Meanwhile, the papacy and its extra-Roman emissaries, the nuncios, became increasingly preoccupied with the very question that had precipitated the Interdict controversy. Theology yielded its queenship to law; and the papal lawyers, starting with the lawyer-pope himself, embarked on a campaign to 'defend to the limits the privileges and immunities' of ecclesiastical persons and institutions without regard for the possibly 'ruinous consequences', religious as well as economic and political, of constantly diminishing the area of civil authority.[54] The nuncios at Naples talked of nothing else. Soon, neither did the bishops. 'The subordination of juridical to pastoral concerns' and the 'confident [dedication to] implementing reforms' observable in the synodal decrees of the late sixteenth century gave way, in those of the early seventeenth century, to ever more vociferous 'demands for the observance of traditional' – and not so traditional – 'rights of fiscal and jurisdictional immunities'.[55]

These demands were frequently countered by protests lodged by the civil authorities – by the prince of Conca, for one, in a speech before the Neapolitan Parlamento of 1628 in which he identified the demands as the chief cause of 'the great ruin and calamity of this kingdom'. Even more often, they were thwarted by appeals from ecclesiastical to civil courts, where they dragged on for years and thus robbed excommunication, to which the bishops of the Terra di Lavoro resorted ever more frequently against delinquent rent-payers, of much of its sting. But they were tacitly seconded by those ever-greater numbers of laymen 'who take minor orders . . . for the sole purpose of escaping the jurisdiction of secular courts and the obligation to pay taxes' – and by all those other laymen who put the titles to their income-producing property under the name of an 'ecclesiastical' relative or institution for the same purpose.[56]

The collaboration of the bishops in this enterprise was in turn facilitated by the concerted efforts of the papacy to break down the sense of common purpose they had generated on a national level at the Council and on a regional level at the post-conciliar provincial synods. This was accomplished first by encouraging local patriots to demand the secession of their churches from the corresponding metropolitan provinces – Rimini from Ravenna, Pavia from Milan – and second by transforming the model metropolitan bishop, Carlo Borromeo, into a model of asceticism in all iconographical representations: that is the way he was depicted, fasting, with nothing before him on a bare table but a book, a loaf of bread and a jug of water, even in his own diocese of Milan (Daniele Crespi, *The Fast of Saint Charles*, in S. Maria della Passione). It was accomplished also by the papacy arrogating to itself appointments to benefices within bishops' jurisdictions, entertaining lawsuits against bishops in ecclesiastical tribunals and regularly siding with regulars in their inevitable disputes with the seculars to whom the Council had made them responsible. Thus when the monks of San Lorenzo tried to take possession of a confraternity church at Bobbio in 1607, the city council, happy at last to have a resident Tridentine bishop, threw them out of town. When the bishop then excommunicated them for forcibly invading the church when he himself was saying Mass there, they appealed to Rome; and the Roman authorities awarded them title to the church on the sole condition that the bishop be permitted to visit it from time to time.

In one case, the pursuit of such policies drove the victim to the brink of apostasy. So annoyed was Marc'Antonio De Dominis (1556–1624), archbishop of Spalato (Split) in Dalmatia, at being forced to pay a pension from his own income to a well-connected prelate in another diocese that he left for England. In a 2,200 folio treatise *De republica ecclesiastica* (1617–20) and then later in his preface to Sarpi's *History of the Council of Trent*, he drew to their logical conclusions certain episcopalian theses implicit in the Tridentine disciplinary decrees; and the offended curial anti-episcopalians had to wait until the death of his protector, the non-lawyer pope Gregory xv, before taking their revenge – i.e., letting him die in jail and then having his body burned as if he had been a heretic. But most bishops reacted by lapsing into passivity, as the chief posts in their own churches fell once again into the hands of the local patriciate to which they too invariably belonged. But then there was also 'very little new' to be done on the diocesan level anyway except to remind everyone of 'what has been decreed by our predecessors' in the face of mounting evidence that those decrees were being ignored in practice. And diocesan synods became correspondingly less frequent and more monotonous.[57]

The laity, meanwhile, objected neither to the dissolution of the episcopacy nor to the emasculation of the bishops. For they were now provided with much more immediate means of sanctification. The Capuchins and the Franciscans paid the best artists to rid them of the burdens of Tridentine Christology with a plethora of 'absolutely personal and introspective' representations of a much more tractable Francis of Assisi.[58] The Dominican Arcangelo Caraccia spared them the effort of following Serafino Razzi in 'Tridentinizing' the rosary with biblical and poetic meditations. The 'ignorant and unlettered who cannot read' need only recite a string of Ave's and Pater's, said Caraccia; and if they choose not to do even that, they need only hold onto a 'crown' of indulgence-packed beads at the moment of death and their salvation was assured.[59] The canonization commissions saved them the bother of looking for guidance to the mystics: Maria Maddelena dei Pazzi became nothing more than a post-mortem miracle worker capable of doing nothing more inspiring than changing bad wine into good; and having avoided 'not only accusations but even suspicions' concerning his virginity became the greatest accomplishment of Filippo Neri.[60] The Tuscan Observant friar Bartolomeo Cambi (1558–1617) freed them of all obligation to understand what they had only to love; after all, the fear of death was a much more effective check on immorality than 'the intellect', against which he urged his penitents to 'arm themselves'; and he went on to to make death as fearsome as possible:

Your beauty, poor soul, will vanish. Your flesh will rot. It will become like excrement and the idol you make of yourself will stink. You'll die, you'll collapse, and you will leave, perhaps damned, that dirty, smelly body of yours. . . .[61]

The Tridentine New Jerusalem may have still been standing, but its walls, having suffered a series of daunting blows, were beginning to crumble.

The third shock took place on the night of 7 January 1610. It was not wholly unexpected, at least not by its perpetrator, the son of the Florentine musical theorist and since 1591 a professor at the University of Padua, Galileo Galilei. For Galileo combined four of what had always before been observed as separate, if not mutually exclusive, professions. He was first of all a technician. He had devised more efficient ways of increasing the velocity of ships and of pumping water out of flooded fields. Most recently, with the help of friends in the budding Venetian glass industry, he had devised ways of increasing the magnifying power of the telescope, which shortly before had been invented by the Neapolitan philosopher Giovan Battista Della Porta and then manufactured by some skilled artisans in Holland; and he eventually managed to produce an image some thousand times greater than the apparent size of a distant object – to the delight of his employers, the Venetian Senate, who could now spot enemy ships far into the Adriatic. Galileo was also a mathematician. He had studied mathematics in Florence with Niccolò Tartaglia; and by reading the newly edited texts of one of the great ancient mathematicians, Archimedes, he had come to appreciate the relevance to physics (from which Aristotle had banished it) of what, except in the art academies, was still thought of as little more than an intellectual exercise. He was a philosopher, too – in the contemporary meaning of the term, which included physics and cosmology as well as metaphysics. He had mastered the latest repairs in the shaky structure of Aristotelian logic wrought by the Jesuit professors at the Collegio Romano; and he had studied all the current astronomical systems thoroughly enough to be able to furnish solid reasons for preferring that of Copernicus to those of Ptolemy or Tycho Brahe. At the same time, he was a man of letters. He wrote good imitations of his favourite poet, Berni. He took an active part in the current debates about the relative merits of Ariosto and Tasso. He corresponded about painting with Cigoli. And he could express himself very effectively in witty, pungent expository prose.[62]

Still, even Galileo was not wholly prepared for what he beheld that night: not just mountains on the moon, the height of which he had calculated with amazing accuracy on previous nights, not just the thousands more stars than anyone had ever dreamed existed, but several small spots of light near Jupiter that changed their position in a manner that, when plotted geometrically, could only be explained as the Jovian equivalents of the earth's moon. Jupiter, then, was a body much like the earth, not a disk or a sphere stuck in a solid orb or forced to gyrate in inexplicable epicycles; or, rather, and still more revolutionary, the earth was a planet much like Jupiter, and not the immobile centre of the universe, generically different from everything that revolved around it. During the following days and nights, Galileo focussed his 'eye-cane' on the sun, which, with its moveable sunspots, turned out to be no more exempt from 'corruption' than the earth. He then focussed it on Venus and Mercury, whose apparently constant magnitudes, an apparently unbeatable argument for assigning them orbits around the earth, turned out to be the effect of moon-like phases.

For the first time, the Copernican hypothesis was provided with seemingly irrefutable empirical confirmation. So was Copernicus' thesis that the heliocentric solar system was a description of reality, not, like the Ptolomaic earth-centred solar system, merely a calculating device. The entire venerable, if shaky, Aristotelian cosmos was thus swept away. So too were all the alternatives to the Aristotelian cosmos conjured up by the anti-Aristotelian cosmographers of the late sixteenth century – including that of the Platonist Patrizi, who, like Galileo himself, had denounced all his rivals for having isolated astronomy from cosmography.[63]

Galileo hurriedly described these spectacular discoveries in a short, concise and carefully illustrated book entitled *Sidereus nuncius* – the 'Starry Messenger' – which became a best-seller throughout Europe from the moment it appeared in print a few months later in 1610. He then put his telescope aside and set out to propagate the new cosmos and the new science from which it had emerged. Turning down almost irresistible offers from his current employers, he returned in triumph to his native Florence. His former student and now grand duke Cosimo II rewarded him for returning with the highest academic salary in Italy, guaranteed by ecclesiastical tithes, and the post of professor in his former University of Pisa without obligation either to teach or to reside. He went on an equally triumphant trip to Rome, where he was received by his professional colleagues at the Collegio Romano, by his new academic colleagues in the Accademia dei Lincei, and by Pope Paul himself. He won the support of several eminent representatives of religious orders – from the Servites' Sarpi and Fulgenzio Micanzio to the Benedictines' Girolamo Spinelli, prior of Santa Giustina of Padua, and Benedetto Castelli, soon to become one of his most productive disciples. Above all, he won the acclamation of educated, non-specialist laymen – those who had been the chief bearers of humanism and who had been acquiring a competence in scientific matters ever since Benedetto Varchi first moved philosophy out of the universities and into the academies. It was for the benefit of the latter that he chose to write not in the Latin of the philosophical faculties but in the Tuscan Italian of the Accademia Fiorentina, of which he had been a member since the 1580s.

Emboldened by such strong support, Galileo embarked upon a campaign to provide the Tridentine Church with the last bulwark it needed to become completely impregnable. Aristotle's science had long been an embarrassment to true religion because of its tendency to spill over into the realms of theology and sacred history. By transforming their master from a man into an abstraction, the Aristotelians were forced to maintain as absolute truth opinions which Aristotle himself – or so Galileo believed – 'would without doubt have changed if the novelties of our times had been seen in his'. They denied 'that the Lord God Almighty can at his pleasure produce new stars and extinguish old ones' in Aristotle's immutable and impenetrable crystalline spheres.[64] In vain did the Aristotelian philosopher and Galileo's friend and colleague at Padua, Cesare Cremonini, try to persuade the Holy Office that criticism of Thomas Aquinas' interpretation of Aristotle had nothing to do with theology. Galileo and Thomas agreed that Aristotle was the final word in physics, and Aristotle said clearly that in physics the heavens were eternal, the soul was material and God was only the final cause – and those were universally held to be theological propositions.

On the contrary, the new science discovered by Galileo held none of these dangers. It was mathematical and empirical, not logical or historical in method, and consequently free of theological overtones. It fitted exactly into the place reserved for it by the Fathers of the Church; and any noisy Florentine preacher who still nurtured doubts had only to consult the long catalogue of Tridentine authorities Galileo assembled in his open *Letter to the Grand Duchess Christine*. By giving official sanction to the new science, the Church would assure itself of the same benefits from science that it had already gained from history, fully assured that whatever new knowledge was gained by the scientists would support, or at least not undermine, its dogmas. Galileo thus accepted a position as the Carlo Borromeo of the diocese of philosophy, and he armed himself with all the weapons of humanist rhetoric and a warehouse of quotations from all the ancient philosophers in order to carry out his version of the Tridentine Reformation. The parallel was not missed by those of his converts who were equally enthusiastic members of both dioceses – particularly not by the Florentine Giovanni Battista Ciampoli (1590–1643), for whom 'the vibrant seminary of virtue' in Milan furnished, among other hyperboles, 'an inexhaustible mine of jubilation and joy', as he wrote Archbishop Federico Borromeo himself.[65]

Admittedly, just as Borromeo's intentions occasionally collided with the special interests of merchants, monks and cathedral canons, so Galileo's new science aroused the fury of those preachers and professors who were loathe to discard their favourite analogies and their yellowed lecture notes. They fell back on the only defence left them: not public opinion, not the protection of the mighty, but that of the Holy Office; and, caught in the cross-fire, the Holy Office suddenly asked Galileo, somewhat to his surprise, to submit to the same rules it had lately imposed on the contenders in the fight over the doctrine of Grace: to lay low for a while.

Galileo was aware that he could not count on his good friend and admirer Bellarmino, now the leading member of the Holy Office, who had submitted to the same request after the appearance of his controversial *Controversies*. He also knew that Bellarmino was much too busy at the moment trying to plug up the holes he had found in the Plantin edition of the 'official' Vulgate Bible to give this new question the attention it deserved. Reluctantly, in 1616, he submitted to the Holy Office's request and was immediately granted another eulogistic audience with the pope. At the same time, Galileo realized that the new science contained many more mansions than just those occupied by the motion of the planets; and he set out to explore them. In 1619, when the appearance of a comet started to melt away what little crystal was still left in the heavens, he was ready to report on his findings; and soon all Rome and then all Italy was busy amusing itself with his brilliant and pungent satire, *Il Saggiatore* ('The Assayer') of 1623. Heat and cold were not 'elements', wrote Galileo, but merely the effects of motion. Colour and sound were purely subjective responses to purely physical stimuli. Matter was not continuous, and did not 'abhor a vacuum'; rather, it was composed of minute particles separated by nothing. Such was the force of the argument that even the most nature-loving poets were obliged to yield. 'I have read that the celestial spheres, revolving, make a sweet harmony', confessed Niccolò Barbieri in his *La supplica*, 'but experience cannot demonstrate anything of the sort'.[66]

The next shock recurred sporadically over the thirteen-year interval between the publication of Alessandro Tassoni's *Considerazioni sopra le rime del Petrarca* of 1609 and the publication of Giambattista Marino's *Adone* in 1622. Tassoni had been born in Modena, Marino in Naples. But both of them toured the courts of Italy as secretaries or protégés of high-ranking princes and prelates. Both of them were rebels, or at least 'rebels with the permission of the authorities'[67]; they also displayed the personal qualities that one modern critic has summed up in a string of roaring epithets: 'quick-witted, foul-mouthed . . . peevish, hypocritical, fatuous, egocentric'. [68] For their acts of rebellion were motivated not so much by the principles they professed as by their desire to attract attention; and neither of them hesitated to embrace current notions of propriety whenever that too produced the same effect – as Marino did so spectacularly when he moved in with the Theatines after his return to Naples and 'sought to purge his soul' by 'throwing into the fire [copies of] all his humorous (*giocose*) and other indifferent compositions'. [69]

Both Tassoni and Marino were dedicated above all to the promotion of their own careers; and they were equally willing to pick fights with anyone who got in their way – as soon became apparent to the court poet at Turin, Gaspare Murtola (1560–*c*. 1624), when Marino provoked him into an attempted assassination with his biting satire, *Fischiate* ('Jeers'), and then, as a supreme gesture of disdain, persuaded the duke to pardon him. Both were remarkably successful in this endeavour – particularly Marino. He was almost the only Italian then resident at the court of the queen dowager of France, Maria de' Medici, who managed to survive the disgrace of her hated Italian favourite, Concino Concini; he was elected 'prince' of the Accademia degli Oziosi upon his return to Rome; and he was granted a canonry for his young nephew by the viceroy himself upon his retirement at Posillipo shortly before his death. Their careers are noteworthy precisely for an indifference to the ethical aspects of the well-established humanist goal of personal glory.

Still, Tassoni to some extent and Marino in exemplary fashion were very well versed in all the ancient and modern literary classics. Indeed, most of their innovations could be traced back to some canonical predecessor, as their opponents took delight in pointing out. Such, indeed, was Tassoni's mastery of humanist philosophical and critical literary forms that he wrote another work about the much debated contest between heroes and tyrants in a manner identical with that used by the first contributor to the genre, Leonardo Bruni. He merely shifted the argument from what Dante said about Brutus to what he said about Alexander; and, realizing that the argument was totally outmoded in the age of *ragion di stato*, he quickly forgot about it. Such was Marino's youthful admiration for Tasso, whom he had met at the court of their common patron, Giovan Battista Manso, that he finished three cantos of what he seems to have intended as a 'modern' parallel to the 'medieval' *Gerusalemme liberata*: the *Anversa* ('Antwerp') *liberata*. He then scrapped it for being equally out-of-date; and no one heard of it again until it was discovered at the turn of the twentieth century. [70]

When they chose to declare their independence of all the classics and of the Aristotelian poetics in which the classics had been enshrined, Tassoni and Marino were as well informed of what they were rejecting as Galileo had been when he cast aside the Aristotelian cosmos. Tassoni transformed Modena into the frog capital of Lombardy, founded, according to 'an ancient author', by an old woman tavern keeper, with 'smoke-filled houses' and 'a tower that looks like an upside-down pole'. No one had ever before dared to say such things about his own *patria*; and four centuries of patriotic, or 'campanilistic' ('flag-waving'), panegyrics, legends and histories and what was left of a lingering nostalgia for the medieval commune forthwith drowned in a 'marsh' of 'mud and mire'.[71] He 'transformed Helen into a bucket' and the heroic Trojan War into a bloated, bloody and absolutely pointless version of a minor skirmish between the fourteenth-century survivors of the Guelph–Ghibelline feuds that he had read about in Sigonio. He made 'the gods of Homer' rumble out of 'the stalls of heaven' drawn by 'pack mules' and accompanied by 'more than a hundred servants in costume'. He put 'the Golden Fleece of the king of Spain . . . around the neck' of Apollo. He dressed up 'a somewhat annoyed Pallas' in 'a half-Greek, half-Spanish outfit' like the ones worn by the current mistress of Roman salons, Diana Vettori; he then let her put off obeying Jove's summons in order 'to do her laundry in a spring in the Tuscan Maremma'. Three centuries of mind-exhausting effort – from Dante's often puzzling *Divine Comedy* to Tommaso Stigliani's hopelessly boring saga of Columbus' discovery of the *Mondo nuovo* – were swept away in a gale of laughter; and desk-fulls of verse-stained paper drawn forth by the proposition that the epic was the highest form of poetry vanished amid the lines of what is still, at least for those who read it with some knowledge of what it is parodying, one of the funniest poems ever written: the *Secchia rapita*.[72]

Similarly, Marino turned love into war and thus enabled no less refined a pair of newlyweds than Francesco Gonzaga and Margherita di Savoia to fight it out in bed until he, not she, was finally exhausted:

> Here I lie, a useless weight, at the side
> Of my beloved nymph.

He then revealed kissing to be no more than a way of stimulating, and of procuring the satisfaction of, purely corporeal passions:

> From kiss to kiss taking me to that pleasure
> Which ties souls together and blends bodies into one.[73]

He let his shepherdess repeat three times the usual, and by now empty, Platonic platitudes,

> What are you doing, cruel man,
> Do you wish to impoverish me
> Of my greatest treasure?

that were meant only to increase the joy of the moment when

> I at last arrived at my sweet goal,
> And, giving free course to impetuous desire,
> Seized her flower and the fruit of my sighs.

Finally, in the culminating scenes of the *Adone*, he let Venus use the conventions solely for the purpose of arousing her earthly lover:

Bashfully drawing herself to the side,
Cautiously her beauties now hiding, now showing.[74]

That put an end to the whole hallowed tradition of pastoral poetry, from
Virgil to Guarini – and of the epic romance as well, Ariosto's included. Love
was no longer an invitation to contemplation, heroism, beauty, or self-
sacrifice. It was nothing but a cover-up for sex.

So extensive, and so untactfully virulent, was this rebellion against the
whole Petrarchan-Platonic-Aristotelian literary cosmos, that it provoked an
equally virulent counterattack. Ferrante Carli roused the academies of Bologna
and Perugia. Tommaso Stigliani (1573–1651) roused that of Parma, of which
he was then 'prince'. Their supporters in Rome then persuaded the authorities
to put the *Adone* (but not the equally scabrous *Lira* and *Sampogna*) on the
Index until its more pornographic passages were toned down.

But the 'Marinists' were as well-armed for combat as their nymphomaniac
creations. While aligning himself with his old friend and fellow revolutionary,
Caravaggio, Marino took care also to cultivate the still undaunted protagonists
of orthodoxy in the realm of the visual arts – from the 'fabbro gentil', Guido
Reni, to Domenichino, who painted his Adonis dying. In the realm of
philosophy, where orthodoxy seemed to be totally doomed, he unequivocally
sided with his other fellow revolutionary, Galileo: he paraphrased the *Sidereus
nuncius* in describing Diana's moon, and he locked up the 'vices and virtues',
which Galileo had banished from nature, in a grotto on the 'Island of
Dreams'.[75] Meanwhile, he enlisted the support of well-placed connoisseurs of
literature. At the urging of the Galileian law professor and poet Claudio
Achillini (1574–1640), the well-beneficed co-founder of the Oziosi, Girolamo
Aleandro, wrote an 'intransigent defense' of his *Adone* on the eve of his death
in 1629. Secondo Lancillotto joined him in consigning Virgil, Castiglione,
Sannazaro and all the rest to an 'age of iron' that had now given way to an
'age of gold'.[76] Marino also enlisted the support of those poets who had long
complained of the restraints placed on them by models and rules. At last,
observed Monteverdi's librettist Gianfrancesco Busenello (1598–1659), 'the
style of the immortal Petrarch . . . has fallen into disuse; it is studied by few,
condemned by many and abandoned by all'. 'Poor Aristotle', declared Giulio
Cesare Capaccio of Eboli (1552–1634), is no longer 'touted' by anyone but
those 'worthless poets' who need to 'build up their reputations'. As soon
as they are seated in a tavern, they 'start making an uproar: one backs himself
up with [the principle of] imitation; the other defends himself with the unity
of subject matter'.[77] Real poets need neither Petrarch nor Aristotle, neither
Horace nor Tasso. Away with them all!

More important still, the Marinists were ready with a literary version of
the Copernican cosmos to replace the Petrarchan-Aristotelian cosmos they
were destroying. This 'cosmos' was based in part on Boccalini's reproach to
Aristotle for having abridged 'the absolute liberty' that by right belonged
to all 'brilliant minds, free from the bounds of rules and precepts, to continuously enrich the schools and libraries with beautiful compositions woven

from new and curious inventions'. It was also based on Tassoni's defence of the 'pluralism' of the 'literary vagabond or adventurer' who, in an eternal struggle with the 'Hercules' of literary orthodoxy, takes on one form after another until he exhausts all realms of knowledge.[78]

The first principle of the new poetic cosmos was that subject matter was relatively unimportant. The provisional summary of the plot of the *Adone* that Marino sketched out for a friend as early as 1605 is devoid of any trace of what eventually would be identified as its qualities as a great poem[79]; and the lugubrious description of Death in the final version (Canto 13) is aesthetically effective precisely because it was not meant to be taken seriously. The second principle was that the ultimate measure of aesthetic quality was the size and the enthusiasm of the audience. 'This', Marino told Stigliani,

is the kind of poetry that pleases these days, in this century; and I'll admit that it corresponds to my natural genius and that it pleases me as much as it displeases you. You need not praise it as good; but you should at least tolerate . . . what corresponds to the universal desire of a world that is now sick to tears of dry little songs. . . . Nature erred greatly in having you born in our days, rather than in the good old days when you would have had Dante, Petrarch and fra Guittone on your side. Whoever wants to please the dead, who can't hear, let him do so. For myself, I intend to please the living, who can hear.[80]

The third principle followed from the first two. Modern audiences, stated Marino, want not sentiment, catharsis, or spiritual uplift, but the 'marvellous'. Therefore,

> The poet's aim is to create marvels;
> He who cannot amaze and shock,
> Let him be howled down.[81]

And it is just this principle that has provoked all those critics, from the time of Stigliani to the time of Benedetto Croce, who think that poetry should contain at least some elements of 'the sublime, the ideal and the beautiful'.[82] The last principle prescribed as the best way to achieve this end was the abundant use of iteration ('amasti amato amante'), pleonasm ('aspro e sassoso'), opposition ('piaga dolce d'amore'), alliteration ('vago vaso di vermiglie rose') and, above all, unexpected juxtapositions of what no one had ever before dreamed of juxtaposing.

After a half-century of overexposure to Aristotelian rules, that is just what Italian – and French – audiences wanted to hear. And that is what a small army of Marinist warriors set out to give them – Girolamo Preti with his 'beautiful woman on horseback', Gianfrancesco Maria Materdona with the mosquito he commissioned to bite his lady-love, Pier Francesco Paoli with his young lady in love with a snow-headed man, Giuseppe Salamone with a lady whose 'serene forehead' had been 'furrowed by the cold plough of old age'. Thanks to their efforts, 'Marinism' became a major force in Italian – and French – poetic literature until the end of the seventeenth century.

The next shock occurred on 22 May 1618, when the Protestant defenders of Bohemia 'defenestrated' two envoys of their king-emperor in the royal palace at Prague and thus set off what, when it was finally over, came to be called the Thirty Years War, by far the most widespread and destructive pan-European conflagration during the three centuries between the Hundred Years War and the wars of the French Revolution.

None of the Italian powers had anything to do with what went on in Bohemia. But at least one of them, Venice, was particularly prone to being dragged into (and another, the duke of Savoy, was anxious to take advantage of) any alteration in the relations among the powers of transalpine Europe. Moreover, when the new emperor, Ferdinand II, chose to respond to his 'deposition' in Bohemia with a final crusade against Protestantism in his domains, he all but obliged the king of Spain, and hence the king's delegates in Naples and Milan, to come to his assistance.

The gradual erosion of Italy's half-century peace had actually begun in the 1590s, when the Venetians were at last compelled – by the threat that otherwise the Turks would act – to take strong measures against the Uskoks (Uscocchi). The Uskoks were a polyethnic collection of refugees from the Ottoman conquest of the Balkans who had settled in the more remote corners of the Croatian coastline, particularly at Segna (Senj). Unfortunately, too many of them had settled there to enable them to follow the example of their productive brethren in Italy. Being 'a wild and uncivilized people', as Sarpi noted in his history of their depredations, and living 'in a sterile and inaccessible country', they had no way to live except by hiring themselves out as mercenaries or by robbing whomever they could. Unfortunately, they failed to persuade one prospective employer, the grand duke of Tuscany, that 'they could in a moment turn themselves from long-standing criminals into good men',[83] and they undermined their application to another, the Venetians, by capturing a well-stocked frigate and sinking all the fishing boats in the Venetian port of Torcola while negotiations were in progress. That left them with piracy. Notwithstanding a certain amount of unbelievable propaganda about their being a 'protective wall against the infidels', keeping them in business as pirates appeared to be in the interests of the legal overlords of the ports they occupied, Emperor Rudolph II and then Archduke, later Emperor, Ferdinand, who were looking for ways to break the Venetian monopoly of Adriatic commerce. In their pursuit of the Uskoks, the Venetians thus became involved in constant quarrels with their eastern neighbours. When the quarrels at last broke out – or bogged down – into a two-year war of attrition (1615–17), they suddenly came to realize that Italy's eastern frontier was more fragile than they had imagined, that the 'military academies' in their *terraferma* cities were producing dancers, not officers, and that their field commissioners could no longer count on the loyalty of their mismanaged and mutinous mercenary soldiers.

At the same time, the western frontier established by the Peace of Lyon in 1603 was being eroded not by external enemies, but by the expansionist appetites of Duke Carlo Emanuele of Savoy. Since Carlo Emanuele could not expand unaided, he tried to conjure up an anti-Spanish alliance among the non-dependent states of northern Italy. But that produced little more than Boccalini's nostalgic *Filippiche* about the good old days of Philip II and Tassoni's strings of anachronistic insults:

> When I hear it said: 'He's a Spaniard',
> I conclude: *'Id est*, he's a wicked
> Sodomite, a clever crook,
> A Lutheran who doesn't believe in Christ,
> An enemy of Italy,. an assassin,
> A cousin, a brother, of the Antichrist.[84]

He therefore tried to conjure up an alliance to be manipulated by himself for the purpose of replacing the 'sleeping ogre', as Tassoni called Spain ('orco che dorme'), with France as the hegemon of Italy. When that scheme collapsed upon the assassination of King Henry IV, he tried to force what diplomacy would not yield by invading Monferrato (1612).

The first Monferrato War finally succeeded in creating Carlo Emanuele's 'Italian alliance'. But it was one aimed at him, not at Spain; and it had the disastrous consequence of drawing war, for the first time since 1559, from the frontiers into the interior of Italy. It also provoked the first serious challenges to the internal harmony of several of the newly consolidated Italian states, as supposed allies sought to tap whatever unrest they could find – or generate – among potential enemies. In 1617 the Spanish ambassador in Venice was caught meddling with certain Hispanophile patricians – including one former proponent of one of Carlo Emanuele's anti-Spanish alliances – in order to get Venetian deserters to assist the viceroy of Naples in seizing Chioggia. The same year, the majority of the Genoese oligarchy decided to respond to increasing expressions of dissatisfaction with the 1576 constitutional settlement by permitting judges to expel anyone of whatever rank in whom they suspected 'a mind different from what is required for public tranquillity and civil life'.[85] That legitimized *ex post facto* the exile of one patrician in 1600 and the prohibition of the writings of two others in 1611. It authorized the imprisonment, two years later, of the eminent patrician and political writer Andrea Spinola – 'Andrea the philosopher', as his admirer Galileo called him – for the 'crime' of having referred to certain 'ills of the republic' in a number of political tracts. But it did not discourage Carlo Emanuele, after a raid into Genoese territory had backfired in 1614, from arranging for two successive *coups d'état*, which were blocked only at the last minute with the capture and execution of the Genoese ringleaders, Claudio De Marini and Giulio Cesare Vachero.

The most serious case of internal destabilization occurred in the Kingdom of Naples. In 1616, the cultivated and tactful viceroy Lemos was succeeded by 'the terrible persecutor of criminals and the capital enemy of all liars', Girón Pedro Téllez, duque de Osuna – or Ossuna, as the Italians called him.[86] Safeguarded against sabotage in Madrid by the promotion of his predecessor to the Council of Italy, assured of backing from the Spanish propagandist-playwright Francisco de Quevedo, armed with the maxims of the Neapolitan jurist Giulio Genoino and hailed by his old friends in the intellectual circles of Sant'Agostino and the Accademia degli Oziosi, Ossuna embarked on a mission to remedy once and for all what the Neapolitans themselves recognized as their last major sore spots: bureaucratic corruption at home and piracy on the Mediterranean. Assuming the responsibilities formerly reserved to royal visitors, he personally toured the magistracies of the capital, threw all the delinquents he caught *in flagrante* into jail and substituted his own appointees for the elected officers. He blocked the payment of ransom for Christian hostages and he sent some twenty new galleys, equipped with Galileo's telescopes, to apprehend the abductors.[87]

These measures should have put the finishing touches on the process of reconstruction and consolidation begun almost a century earlier by Pedro de Toledo. Instead, they came near to undoing it altogether. When the Venetians protested, Ossuna sent his fleet right into their private preserve, the Adriatic. When the powerful Consiglio Collaterale protested, he shipped its members off to different prisons in the extremities of the kingdom and murdered the emissary they had tried to send to the king behind his back. When the nobility of the *Seggi* protested, he redirected his favours toward the plebeians, who applauded his abolition of fruit and flour taxes, and he encouraged the middle-class *popolo* to resurrect the old spectre of equal representation in the *Seggi*. 'I far prefer division among us and royal authority over us to your damnable union', retorted one of them to a noble who accused him of breaking rank.[88]

These measures thus shattered in one blow the delicate alliance between nobles and viceroy that had been worked out on the morrow of the uprising of 1585. They violated the principle practised by Philip II and restated in 1599 by Philip III:

From now on they may freely write me what they want without the viceroys or other ministers being able to stop them. I want, and it is my will, that the said city [of Naples] freely write to me about their troubles.[89]

They threatened to drag Spain into a war with an Italian power just at the moment when it was being dragged into much bigger wars in Germany and the Netherlands. They tore up half the articles of what the Neapolitan jurists agreed was the inviolable constitution of their strictly limited monarchy. And they lent some credence to the otherwise absurd rumour spread about by disgruntled nobles that the viceroy was trying to make himself a king.

Ossuna was thereupon recalled to Spain and permanently dismissed from royal service. His adviser Genoino was thrown into prison, and the most obviously guilty of the barons he had arrested was set free. Within a year the capital was once again shaken by popular riots – for the first time in forty-five years. Five years later a royal visitor discovered so many instances of the kind of financial chaos and administrative disorder that Ossuna had tried to get rid of that he decided to hide what he discovered behind vague generalities and to put the blame on Ossuna's own supposedly 'dissolute character'.

Ossuna's appointees were thrown out of the magistracies and the magistrates proceeded to collaborate with his successor in bleeding Naples for the benefit of their distant ruler's foreign adventures. Instead of looking for ways to improve the current regime, the still-active political writers of Naples – from Francesco Imperato in his *Discorsi intorno all'origine . . . della gran' Casa della Santissima Annunziata* of 1628 to Giovanni Domenico Tassone in his *Observationes iurisdictionales* of 1632 – turned to imagining a completely different kind of regime, one which, like those of Holland and Venice, would be free of the kind of brisk changes in policy they had just experienced in their own.

While it threatened both the internal and external security of the Italian states, the expansion of local into pan-European warfare also exacerbated the effects of a contemporary pan-European economic recession. Occasional setbacks had not been uncommon even in the best years of post-Cateau-Cambrésis prosperity. But occasional setbacks even in such traditionally key sectors of the economy as banking and wool manufacturing had generally been offset by the expansion of other sectors – like silk, in which the *nouveau-riche* Riccardi family of Florence increased its investments from 10 percent to 34 percent between 1590 and 1610. They had also been offset by the opening of new sectors – like Venetian glass, which Grand Duke Ferdinando tried to establish in Pisa as well, and like Piedmontese pottery, which Carlo Emanuele permitted a woman entrepreneur from Lodi 'to manufacture wherever she pleases in all our states' with the help of whatever workmen she could lure away from her native city.[90]

But during the 1610s, Italian industry was suddenly faced with a precipitous collapse of the demand for its products in all its traditional markets – in the Levant, where the arrival of cheaper English cloth transported in smaller and less expensive ships made Italian cloth uncompetitive; in the heartlands of the Ottoman Empire, where repeated currency devaluations and uncontrollable inflation reduced the buying power even of military personnel; in Spain, where the expulsion of the Moriscos was followed by a sudden contraction of the overseas commerce of Seville; in France, which Henry IV surrounded with tariff barriers for the benefit of his manufacturers in Lyon; in England, in the Baltic, in Poland and, of course, as a result of the defenestration affair, in Germany.[91] Since the recession was world-wide, and since Italy was still economically the most developed part of Europe, there was little Italians could do to avoid it; and since the science of economics was still in its infancy, what little they tried to do simply made it worse. They ignored the warnings of those few writers who unwittingly proposed anticipations of the policies of the eighteenth-century Physiocrats. Instead they followed the recommendations of their fact-finding commissions in tightening regulations, privileges and monopolies in accordance with traditional guild practices that were soon to be codified as 'mercantilism'.

Meanwhile, the long-depressed shipbuilding industry in Venice came to a halt, and the ever-jealous Senate at last agreed to grant docking privileges in their own home port to foreign as well as domestic carriers. In Milan, the number of silk looms fell from 3,000 in 1606 to 600 in 1635, while the price of finished wool cloth dropped by 36 percent and admissions to the gold and silk guild dropped from 136 (1611–20) to 61 (1631–40). In Vigevano, tax receipts for exported silk thread fell from £1,500 (1616) to £800 (1623). In Pavia, the price of construction materials fell by 36 percent. In Puglia, the number of estates suddenly put up for sale rose so precipitously that frustrated sellers were forced to divide them up into small plots and let them out. Around Pisa, the flight of peasants from the land had become so severe already by 1616 that the grand duke appointed an investigating commission; and when its recommendations failed to halt the flight, he appointed another to figure out simply how to produce more with fewer workers.[92]

The immediate consequence of the depression was massive unemployment. It was so massive in Siena that a special commission was elected 'to make sure that in these depressed times great numbers of vagabonds do not sneak into the city' and further augment the 50 percent of the 'mouths' in one parish that had to be fed by charity. It was so massive even in less industrialized, and hence less vulnerable, Saluzzo that by 1624 some 66 percent of the total urban population was no longer able to provide for itself. Civil governments joined the ever-present Tridentine confraternities to prevent massive unemployment from becoming massive starvation. But neither of them could reverse the psychological effects – those, for example, expressed by a member of the crowd gathered to witness one of those typical pre-industrial revolution rites of reestablishing the 'just' price. 'What good', he shouted,

does lowering the price do me? I still don't have enough money to feed myself and my three children. I'm a weaver by trade. Give me work, and I'll pay even the higher price![93]

And he was only one of millions of helpless victims of what was rapidly becoming the most severe, widespread, and long-lasting economic depression since the 1340s.

Economic historians have identified some of the causes that were generally hidden from the baffled observers of the age. Italian industry had become excessively dependent upon export markets, which absorbed two-thirds of the production of Tuscany alone; and it could not fall back, when distant markets dried up, upon a sustained domestic consumption. It had become so bound up in guild regulations, which fixed salaries, prescribed size and quality of goods and confined production to urban areas, that it could not, like English and Dutch industry, take advantage of cheaper rural labour and changes in taste. Resorting to contraband alone, for example, may have saved the silk manufacturers of Vicenza in 1610, when the government doubled the tax on imported silk cloth and prohibited the exportation of raw silk.

War was, if not a cause, certainly one of the most important aggravants of the depression. For war, or the threat of war, forced the government of Venice to funnel large amounts of capital into 'one of the most grandiose public building operations in its history': a wall five miles in circumference around Vicenza and the usual 'overrun' in accompanying consulting fees.[94] It forced the government of Milan to build a new wall around Lodi and ten new bastions at Novara and to spend an extra £3,100,000 annually to pay, feed, and lodge extra contingents of German and Swiss mercenaries. It forced the government of the Papal State, which was expected to finance the emperor's Catholic crusade in Germany, to let its deficit rise from 12 to 35 million *scudi* between 1620 and 1640. It forced the government of Naples to increase its subsidies to the government of Spain by a figure roughly proportional to the rise in Spain's annual shortfall – from 835,000 ducats in 1616 to 6,502,000 ducats in 1626 – and to compromise future income by selling several of the larger cities in the royal domain. It forced the government of Spain to try once again stabbing its traditional golden goose, the Genoese who were the king's chief creditors. This time, alas, they were unable to fight back. 'The entire nobility, all the well-to-do citizens of the inferior orders, the widows, orphans and charitable institutions of the city were all struck by this lightning bolt' as the king suspended the interest payments and ran the 'Spanish sponge' over a century's accumulation of Genoese capital.[95] And Genoa lost forever its century-old status as the banking capital of Europe.

Some Italians were ready to rekindle a European war on Italian soil the moment pressure from abroad abated – as it did, for example, after the great Catholic victory at the 'White Mountain'. On 19 July 1620 the Catholic majority in the Valtellina rose up against its Protestant rulers and dispatched them in three days in what came to be called the *Sacro Macello* ('Holy Butchery'). They then invited in the army of the governor of Milan, who was as happy to be able at last to open up a direct (if treacherously high) land route to the Habsburg lands in Germany as the Venetians were distressed at the prospect of being encircled by Habsburg territory; and the first Valtelline war ended only after Grissons, needless to say with backing from France, rewon its sovereignty and papal replaced Spanish troops in the fortresses. Since the king of France was busy crushing Huguenots, Carlo Emanuele changed sides and joined the governor of Milan in dividing up the Monferrato. In 1628 Cardinal Richelieu, the new and much more enterprising first minister of France, finally crushed the Huguenots. Carlo Emanuele thereupon changed sides once again and invited the king's army across the Alps.

Thus opened the War of the Mantuan Succession. Olivares, the equally enterprising power in front of the throne of King Philip IV of Spain, responded by sending his troops across the Alps from Germany. The Venetian army fled on the heels of its pusillanimous general the moment the Spanish–Imperial army appeared on its northern border. And the history of the Spanish–Imperial army of 1525 repeated itself in the sack of Mantua – or of what was left of Mantua after several months of siege. The Treaty of Cherasco in 1631 at last tossed to Carlo Emanuele's successor a bit of what his father had so long fought for – not Lombardy, not a royal title, but a slice of Monferrato. But it did so at the cost of handing Pinerolo over to the French and of recognizing the succession of a Gallicized lateral branch of the Gonzaga, now the Gonzaga-Nevers family, in Mantua. That put the French back in Italy more than a half-century after, to the relief of all peace-loving

Italians, they had been thrown out. When, later that same year, a Swedish army led by King Gustavus Adolphus and subsidized by Richelieu set forth to plunder and butcher its way from the Baltic to Bavaria, Italy found itself on the verge of becoming once again what it had been between 1494 and 1530: the battlegound, and the paymaster, of the transalpine superpowers.

Severe economic dislocations and the desolations of warfare were exacerbated by plague. Unlike the localized plagues of the late sixteenth century, the plague of 1630-33 was all but universal in scope. Parma fell from 30,000 inhabitants in 1627 to 14,000, Verona from 56,000 in 1620 to 30,000, Como from 11,364 reported in 1592 to 8,032, Pieve di Dongo and Coloniola in upper Lombardy respectively from 5,416 to 3,927 and from 500 to 133, Gravina and Polignano in Puglia respectively from 16,000 to 5,145 and from 6,000 to 2,500. Florence lost 12,000 of its more than 72,032 inhabitants in 1630 and 1,700 more in 1633. Milan lost 46 percent of its inhabitants, Venice 32 percent, Prato 25 percent, Turin 27 percent, Villafranca in Piedmont 80 percent. The psychological effects of the accompanying horrors were then recorded systematically in the piles of contemporary documents upon which the nineteenth-century historian-novelist Alessandro Manzoni later built his literary masterpiece, *I promessi sposi*.[96]

Although no one yet suspected fleas, scores of empirically-based treatises had identified the phenomenon of contagion and had prescribed cleanliness as an effective antidote. Health commissions were appointed in all cities and villages and authorized to impose strict quarantines, to confiscate suburban villas for use as hospitals, to scrub out the homes and burn the bedding of the dead, to wash down streets, and to distribute food. Outside communications were cut off entirely, and no one was permitted to step outside, often for months at a time. At least Italians were spared the desolate scenes pictured a century earlier by Jacopo Bassano in his *San Rocco and the Plague Victims* (Milan: Brera), with half-naked, boil-covered bodies spread out in every direction.[97] Some of them even profited from the plague: the notaries of Bologna, for instance, who wrote – often taking dictation from a window to avoid contact with their customers – 625 wills in 1629-30 as opposed to 260 in 1625-26, even though by then most of the wealthier citizens had fled the city.[98]

Nevertheless, the economic consequences of the plague were even worse than those of the wars. All productive labour was halted, while most of the savings from previous productive labour were syphoned off to prevent the forced idle from starving; and much of what managed to survive the systematic draining of the treasuries of charitable organizations went into expensive votive monuments in the following years – not only in Venice, but even in tiny Montrigone near Novara, where the heads of families taxed themselves to build a sanctuary on top of a nearby hill. The demographic consequences were equally catastrophic, despite an almost immediate increase in the number of marriages among the survivors. In three years the plague wiped out most of the population gain of the previous century; and, as it became more or less endemic, it prevented the population from recovering its pre-plague numbers until late in the following century. Indeed, it seemed to be appropriately symbolized, just as it was beginning to lose its virulence, by the greatest natural catastrophe of the age, the eruption of long dormant Mt Vesuvius on 16 December 1631, which Domenichino immortalized on the walls of the cathedral of Naples.

The final shock occurred on 22 June 1633 at the Dominican church of the Minerva in Rome. Now seventy years of age, spiritually and physically exhausted after some two months of almost uninterrupted interrogations and memo-drafting, and perhaps under the threat of torture, Galileo Galilei, the most famous scientist-philosopher of his generation, finally signed the 'confession' prepared by the confessor-judges of the Congregation of the Holy Office. The 'confession' removed any doubt about Galileo's full membership in the Church Visible. But it also branded as 'contrary to the Holy Scriptures' and therefore 'vehemently suspect of heresy' the 'false opinion' 'that the sun is the centre of the world and does not move and that the earth is not the centre of the world and does move'.[99] Seven of the ten judges then signed another document. This one declared their 'penitent' guilty of having disobeyed a previously unheard-of 'injunction' by Bellarmino that someone had, at the last minute, surreptitiously slipped into their dossier. It sentenced him to imprisonment at the discretion of the judges. And it imposed upon him the penance of reciting the seven penitential psalms once a week for three years.

That such an event could ever have taken place remained inexplicable to some theologians 350 years later, who proposed 'rehabilitating' the innocent victim, even though he had been legally and sacramentally 'reconciled', never condemned. That such an event would ever have taken place was equally puzzling to contemporaries, and most particularly to the protagonists themselves. Indeed, the majority of theological experts consulted by the Inquisitors agreed in declaring Galileo's theses about the relation between cosmology and the Bible to be in harmony with those of Augustine, Aquinas and Melchior Cano. The Church, they declared, had never accepted either Aristotelian physics or Ptolemaic astronomy as anything but a means of saving the phenomena. It had accepted Copernican astronomy for the same reason when it embarked upon Pope Gregory's calendar reform. And it did not betray Lactantius or Dante by acknowledging that neither the Mountain of Purgatory nor the Antipodes had been discovered on the other side of the globe.[100]

Even more telling, Galileo's campaign to win the support of high-ranking prelates was crowned with success when, in 1623, the most cultivated, broad-minded of the cardinals, the Tuscan poet Maffeo Barberini, became Pope Urban VIII. Galileo promptly dedicated to the new pope the printed version of Il Saggiatore he had delighted in reading in manuscript. The pope, in turn, after assuring his control of the Curia by packing it with his relatives and fellow Tuscans, proceeded to promote orthodox Galileans to important posts in the world of learning. He had Campanella smuggled out of his Neapolitan prison and set free to receive the homage of all the resident and transient men of letters in Rome. He made Giovanni Ciampoli a papal secretary. He made

Niccolò Ridolfi, or 'il Padre Mostro' as he was called because of his large stature, the master of the Sacred Palace and gave him final authority for granting publishing permits. He gave Benedetto Castelli a chair in the university. 'This election', reported Ciampoli, 'will be the cause of universal satisfaction and joy, especially for us who are the particular servants of His Holiness and who have been enriched by his love and benevolence'.[101]

Galileo could not but conclude that Bellarmino's request of 1616 had now lapsed. Padre Mostro, the Inquisitor, the episcopal vicar and the civil censor of Florence all granted an *imprimatur* to his *Dialogo* ('Dialogue on the Two Chief World Systems'); and in February of 1632, after two more years of careful negotiations aimed at blocking all possible obstacles to a favourable reception, one of the greatest of the philosophical dialogues of the Renaissance was finally published – one in which two well-informed and intelligent Venetian patricians disputed seriously and even amicably with an academic philosopher about the relative merits of an earth-centred and a sun-centred universe.[102]

Then, suddenly, as copies of the *Dialogo* began circulating in Rome, something went wrong. Three theologians with connections in the Curia correctly realized that Galileo's triumph would be the undoing of all the analogies with the Aristotelian cosmos upon which they, and many of their colleagues in their respective religious orders, had built their theological systems. The two of them who were Jesuits also realized that this might be their last chance to avenge themselves for the biting satire that the author of *Il Saggiatore* had directed toward one of their colleagues – and by association toward the greatest of their institutions of learning, the Collegio Romano.

The theologians unearthed the depositions of the obscure Florentine Dominicans who had provoked the timorous reaction of the Inquisition in 1616. They persuaded the pope that the pseudonym 'Simplicio' in the *Dialogo* referred not to the ancient Aristotelian by the same name but to the pope's own 'simple-mindedness'; and that, in the opinion of a pope who believed popes to be the wisest of all men and himself to be the wisest of all popes, was an intolerable sin. Urban now became an implacable foe of the man of whom until then he had been an unqualified, if not always very understanding, admirer. The three theologians and their supporters also persuaded the pope that the *Dialogo* would stir up a theological dispute quite as noisy as the one over grace that had made miserable the last years of his predecessor, Clement VIII. Determined at all costs to forestall the impending controversy, the pope ordered the Inquisitors to do whatever was necessary to suppress the *Dialogo* and to silence its author. He terrorized all the unwanted troublemaker's supporters into passivity – from his book-collecting nephew, the Cardinal-Inquisitor Francesco, who dared only to forward Galileo's protests to his colleagues and to withhold his signature from the 'penance' they eventually imposed upon him, to the still immature and politically vulnerable young Grand Duke Ferdinando II, who, as Galileo's 'natural sovereign', might have intervened in his favour. After that, even the most reluctant of the

Inquisitors had no choice but to follow their own procedural rules to their logical conclusion.

For all that, the wounds inflicted on Galileo and his supporters appear, at first glance, to be superficial. None of the Galileans in papal service was actually fired. Galileo's 'prison' in Rome was, after a few days, commuted to the Tuscan embassy, then to the palace of his friend, the archbishop of Siena, and within a year to his own house at Arcetri, just outside the walls of Florence. And all the protagonists set forth studiously to pretend that the unfortunate 'event' had never occurred. But owing to the pope's megalomania, and to his feeling of gratitude toward the Jesuits for having almost alone had the temerity to compare his poems with those of Petrarch and Chiabrera, the three theologians succeeded beyond anything they had anticipated. For the first time since Pius v, responsible officers had been made the tools of an irresponsible bureaucracy. For the first time since Nicholas v, a wedge had been lodged between the world of human learning and at least one official institution of the Church. For the first time since the death of Paul ii, the then very sparse but subsequently increasingly numerous crowd of persons who chose to congregate on one side or the other of the wedge were encouraged to drive it ever deeper. And the many but thereafter increasingly fewer men of science and the faith who wished instead to remain on both sides were left precariously straddling a crevasse that they despaired of ever being able to bridge.

NOTES AND REFERENCES

1. Quoted from the edition of *La historia della guerra di Fiandra* in the *Opere del cardinal Bentivoglio*, Paris 1649, p. 2, and Bentivoglio, *Memorie e lettere*, ed. Costantino Panigada, Bari 1934, p. 6.
2. I follow Marcello Turchi in 'Gabriello Chiabrera e la lirica del classicismo barocco', in *Studi in memoria di Luigi Russo*, Pisa 1974, and in the introduction to his edition of Chiabrera, *Opere di Gabriello Chiabrera, e lirici non marinisti del Seicento* (2nd edn), Turin 1973.
3. Quoted, from 'perhaps the most famous and admired scene', by my chief authority, Franco Croce, in *Federico Della Valle*, Florence 1965, p. 167.
4. Andrea Gareffi in the preface to his edition of Della Valle's *Iudit*, Rome 1978, pp. 11 and 23.
5. Severina Parodi in *Gli atti del primo Vocabolario*, Florence 1974, and *Quattro secoli di Crusca*, Accademia della Crusca, Florence 1983, p. 25. For the predecessors: Maria Corti, 'Un grammatico e il sistema classificatorio nel Cinquecento', in *Metodi e fantasmi*, Milan 1969.
6. 'Monteverdi and the problems of opera', in Nino Pirrotta (ed.), *Music and Culture in Italy from the Middle Ages to the Baroque: A Collection of Essays*, Cambridge, Mass. 1984, p. 238; Leo Schrade, *Monteverdi, Creator of Modern Music*, New York 1969; Gary Tomlinson, 'Madrigal, monody and Monteverdi's "Via naturale alla imitazione"', *Journal of the American Musicological Society*, 34,

1981, and 'Music and the claims of the text: Monteverdi, Rinuccini, and Marino', *Critical Inquiry*, 8, 1982.

7. Preserved in Callot's engraving, of which I saw the copy in the St Louis Art Museum.

8. Franco Mancini, *Scenografia napoletana dell'età barocca*, Naples 1964, quoting from a contemporary diarist on p. 44. Many more examples of this art in Janos Scholz (ed.), *Baroque and Romantic Stage Design*, with introduction by A. Hyatt Mayor, New York 1949.

9. Ferruccio Marotti, *Lo spazio scenico: Teorie e tecniche scenografiche in Italia dall'età barocca al Settecento*, Rome 1974.

10. All these details, and many others concerning the artists mentioned below, are from the lives by Filippo Baldinucci in *Notizie dei professori del disegno* . . . , Florence 1845–47, 5 vols.

11. My basic text hereafter is Rudolf Wittkower, *Art and Architecture in Italy, 1600–1750* ('The Pelican History of Art', 1958), which I read in the 3rd rev. edition of 1980. Carlo Cesare Malvasia's *Life of Guido Reni* has been translated into English by Catherine and Robert Enggass, University Park, Penn. 1980.

12. From Antonio Boschetto's biographical profile of Francesco Albani in *DBI*, vol. 1, pp. 601–4.

13. Evelina Borea in *Pittori bolognesi del Seicento nelle gallerie di Firenze*, Florence 1975, p. 174.

14. Donald Posner, 'Domenichino and Lanfranco: The Early Development of Baroque Painting in Rome', in Walter Cahn *et al.*, *Essays in Honor of Walter Friedlaender*, New York 1965, p. 138.

15. But I saw it at the exhibit of Caravaggio at the Metropolitan Museum of New York in the Spring of 1985.

16. D. Stephen Pepper, *Guido Reni: A Complete Catalog*, Oxford 1984, p. 34.

17. Baldinucci in *Vite*, 4, pp. 122 ff. (above, n. 10).

18. For the context: my own 'The Renaissance academies in their Italian and European setting', in *The Fairest Flower: The Emergence of Linguistic National Consciousness in Renaissance Europe*, Florence 1985.

19. Cesare Vasoli, 'Le accademie fra Cinquecento e Seicento e il loro ruolo nella storia della tradizione enciclopedica', in *Università, accademie e società scientifiche in Italia e in Germania dal Cinquecento al Settecento, Annali-Jahrbuch dell'Istituto Storico Italo-Germanico in Trento*, 9, 1981 (quoted from p. 83).

20. Francesco Della Valle, 'Le nuove fabbriche di Roma', in Carlo Muscetta and Pier Paolo Ferrante (eds), *Poesia del Seicento*, Turin 1964, p. 834.

21. Quoted from *Breve descrittione della Liguria e della città di Genova* by Renato Martinoni in *Gian Vincenzo Imperiale politico, letterato e collezionista genovese del Seicento*, 1983, pp. 163–64.

22. Andrea Spinola, *Scritti scelti*, ed. Carlo Bitossi, Genoa 1981, pp. 81–82.

23. Vittor Ivo Comparato, *Uffici e società à Napoli (1600–1647)*, Florence 1974. Serra's *Breve trattato delle cause che possono far abbondare li regni d'oro et argento* was edited by Raffaele Colapietra in *Problemi monetari negli scrittori napoletani del Seicento*, Rome 1973, quoted from p. 164.

24. From Prospero Bonarelli's tragedy *Il Solimano*, IV, which I cite in the *Teatro italiano* edition of Verona 1725, vol. 3.

25. Bentivoglio, *Memorie* (above, n. 1), pp. 30–31; Scipione Ammirato, Jr., in the preface to his edition of his father's *Delle famiglie nobili fiorentine*, Florence 1615.

26. Quoted from Gambacorta's *Foro christiano* (1594) by Vittorio Sciuti Russi in *Astrea in Sicilia*, Naples 1983, p. 191.

27. Capelloni in the dedication to Duke Emanuele Filiberto of the first edition of his *Ragionamenti varii*, Genoa 1576.

28. On all the foregoing: Giangiacomo Musso, 'Per la storia degli Ebrei nella Repubblica di Genova tra il Quattro e il Cinquecento', *Miscellanea storica ligure*, 3, 1963; Simonetta Ferretti, 'Attività finanziarie degli Ebrei in Ancona nel secolo XVII', *Atti e memorie della Deputazione di Storia Patria per le Marche*, 83, 1978; Emilia Veronese Ceseracciu, 'Ebrei laureati a Padova nel Cinquecento', *Annali dell'Università di Padova*, 13, 1980; Adriano Franceschini, 'Privilegi dottorali concessi ad ebrei nel secolo XVI, *Atti e Memorie della Deputazione Ferrarese di Storia Patria*, 19, 1975; Viviana Bonazzoli, 'Gli Ebrei del Regno di Napoli all'epoca della loro espulsione', *ASI*, 138, 1980 and 139, 1981; Aldo Luzzatto and Amedeo Tagliacozzo, 'Una comunità ebraica a Bagnoregio nei secoli XV e XVI', *Rassegna mensile d'Israel*, 44, 1978; Ariel Toaff, 'Nuova luce sui Marrani di Ancona', in Elio Toaff (ed.), *Studi sull'ebraismo italiano*, Rome 1974; Gemma Volli, 'Rapporti fra la comunità ebraica di Lugo e la cittadinanza lughese', *Studi Romagnoli*, 21, 1970; Maria Grazia Sandri and Paolo Alazraki, *Arte e vita ebraica a Venezia, 1516–1797*, Florence 1971; Pier Cesare Ioly Zorattini, 'Nota sul S. Uffizio e gli Ebrei a Venezia nel Cinquecento', *RSCI*, 33, 1979; Maria Giuseppina Muzzarelli, *Ebrei e città d'Italia in età di transizione: Il caso di Cesena dal XIV al XVI secolo*, Bologna 1984; Giuseppe Celata, 'Gli Ebrei in una società rurale e feudale: Pitigliano nella seconda metà del Cinquecento', *ASI* 138, 1980. Cosimo's edict is quoted by Pietro Battara in *La popolazione di Firenze alla metà del '500*, Florence 1935, pp. 5–6.

29. Manussos Manusakas, 'Gli arcivescovi di Filadelfia a Venezia', Vittorio Peri (who quotes Antonio Minturno), 'Chiesa latina e Chiesa greca', and Domenico Minuto, '*Il Trattato contra Greci* di Antonio Castronovo', all in *La Chiesa greca in Italia dall'VIII al XVI secolo* (Atti Convegno 1969, 'Italia Sacra', nos 20–22), Padua 1973; Giorgio Fedalto, *Ricerche storiche sulla posizione giuridica ed ecclesiastica dei Greci a Venezia nei secoli XV e XVI*, Florence 1967.

30. Santoro quoted by Minuto, '*Il Trattato contra Greci . . .*' (above, n. 29).

31. Francesco Della Valle, 'Alla città di Cosenza', in Muscetta and Ferrante (eds), *Poesia del Seicento* (above, n. 20), 1, p. 835.

32. Alessandro Parronchi, 'La "camera oscura" del Caravaggio', *Michelangelo*, 5, 1976, p. 46.

33. Franco Crevatin, 'Per una storia della venetizzazione linguistica dell'Istria', *Studi mediolatini e volgari*, 23, 1975; Attilio Tamaro, *Storia di Trieste*, Trieste 1976, vol. 2.

34. Here quoted: Marie-Thérèse Bouquet-Boyer, 'Les relations musicales franco-piémontaise', *XVIIe siècle*, 35, 1983.

35. Francis Carter, *Dubrovnic (Ragusa), A Classic City-State*, London and New York 1972.

36. Heinrich Lutz, 'Die deutsche Nation zu Beginn der Neuzeit . . . ', *Historische Zeitschrift*, 234, 1982.

37. Caterina Limentani Virdis, 'La fortuna dei fiamminghi a Venezia nel Cinquecento', *Atti dell'Istituto Veneto di scienze, lettere ed arti*, 135, 1977; Eugenio Battisti quoted from his 'Fontainebleau in Italia', in *Studi di storia dell'arte in onore di Vittorio Viale*, Turin 1967.

38. Susanna Muliari Moro here quoted from 'Mantova e la corte gonzaghera alla fine del secolo XVI', in *Rubens a Mantova*, Milan 1977, p. 24.

39. Mario Labo, *I palazzi di Genova di Pietro Paolo Rubens e altri scritti d'architettura*, Genoa 1970.

40. So states Joseph Gibaldi in 'The fortunes of Ariosto in England and America', in Aldo Scaglione (ed.), *Ariosto 1974 in America: Atti del congresso ariostesco, dicembre 1974*, Ravenna 1976.

41. Bartolomé Bennassar, 'Marchands flamands et italiens à Valladolid au XVIe siècle', in Hermann Kellenbenz (ed.), *Fremde Kaufleute auf der iberischen Halbinsel*, Cologne 1970.

42. Ruth Pike, *Enterprise and Adventure: The Genoese in Seville and the Opening of the New World*, Ithaca 1966; Felipe Ruiz Martin, 'Los hombres de negocios genoveses de España durante el siglo XVI', in Kellenbenz (ed.), *Fremde Kaufleute* (above, n. 41), here quoted.

43. I follow the chronology of Mina Gregori in *The Age of Caravaggio* (the large illustrated catalogue of the exhibit of Spring 1985, which I saw at the Metropolitan in New York), New York 1985.

44. I read the *Discorso* in the reprint of the eighteenth-century edition of Giustiniani's *Discorsi sulle arti e sui mestieri*, published in Florence in 1981. On what follows: Alessandro Parronchi, 'La "camera oscura" del Caravaggio', *Michelangelo*, 5, 1976; R. Ward Bissell, *Orazio Gentileschi and the Poetic Tradition in Caravaggesque Painting*, College Park, Penn. 1981, and the review by John Spike in *Art Bulletin*, 66, 1984, pp. 696–98: Mina Gregori, *70 pitture e sculture del '600 e '700 fiorentino*, Florence 1965; Alfred Moir, *Caravaggio and His Copyists*, New York 1976; Benedict Nicolson, *The International Caravaggesque Movement*, Oxford, 1979; and, above all, the very scholarly *Caravaggio and His Followers* by Richard Spear (the catalogue for the exhibit at the Cleveland Museum of Art, 1971).

45. Gaetano Cozzi, 'Paolo Paruta, Paolo Sarpi e la questione della sovranità su Ceneda', *SV*, 4, 1962.

46. Gaetano Cozzi, *Il doge Nicolò Contarini: Ricerche sul patriziato veneziano agli inizi del Seicento*, Venice 1958, p. 32 (the nuncio quoted in the note).

47. Pietro Pirri, *L'interdetto di Venezia del 1606 e i Gesuiti*, Rome 1959.

48. As I have pointed out in my review of David Wootton, *Paolo Sarpi: Between Renaissance and Enlightenment*, Cambridge 1983, in *Journal of Modern History* 57, 1985, pp. 151–53, and as Elizabeth Gleason and Edward A. Gosselin have pointed out in their reviews, respectively in *Renaissance Quarterly*, 37, 1984, pp. 622–24, and in *The Sixteenth Century Journal*, 16, 1985, pp. 139–40. The last word on Sarpi's alleged 'Protestantism' is that of Boris Ulianich in 'Il principe Christian von Anhalt e Paolo Sarpi: Dalla missione veneziana del Dohna alla relazione Diodati (1608)', *Annuarium Historiae Conciliorum*, 8, 1976, pp. 429–506.

49. The documents here quoted are in his *Scritti politici*, ed. Carlo Giacon, Bologna 1950, and *Auctarium Bellarminium*, Paris 1913; on which: Vittorio Frajese, 'Una teoria della censura: Bellarmino e il potere indiretto dei papi', *SS*, 25, 1984.

50. Philippe Canaye de Fresnes, quoted by Gaetano Cozzi in his splendid introduction (upon which I rely heavily in these pages) to the Einaudi 1976 reprint of the 1969 Ricciardi edition, edited by him and Luisa Cozzi, of Sarpi's *Pensieri*, p. xlix.

51. Eco O. G. Haitsma Mulier, *The Myth of Venice and Dutch Republican Thought in the Seventeenth Century*, Assen 1980.

52. I give all the relevant bibliographical references in my 'Paolo Sarpi storiografo', to be published in the proceedings of the meeting on Sarpi in Venice in 1983. Sarpi's *consulti* appear in the 1969 edition published by Ricciardi cited above at n. 50.

53. All the details in Wolfgang Reinhard, *Papstfinanz und Nepotismus unter Paul v* ('Papste und Papsttum', ed. Georg Denzler), Stuttgart 1974.

54. Agostino Lauro, *Il giurisdizionalismo pregiannoniano nel Regno di Napoli*, Rome 1974, p. 35.

55. Abundant documentation in Pasquale Villani (ed.), *Nunziatura di Napoli*, Rome 1962. Here quoted is Salvatore Palese in *RSCI*, 38, 1984, p. 554.

56. Quoted from proceedings of the Parlamento on p. 43 of Francesco Caracciolo, *Sud, debiti e gabelle: Gravami, potere e società nel Mezzogiorno*, Naples 1983, where the phenomenon is described in detail.

57. I quote here from the bishop's preface to the published decrees of the Synods of 1623 and 1629.

58. All thoroughly enumerated by Raoul Manselli in 'Continuità e ripresa del Francescanesimo nella controriforma' in *L'immagine di San Francesco nella Controriforma*, Rome 1982, pp. 17–19.

59. Mario Rosa, 'Pietà mariana e devozione al rosario nell'Italia del Cinque e Seicento', in his *Religione e società nel Mezzogiorno*, Bari 1976.

60. *Summarium Actionum, virtutum et miraculorum servae Dei Mariae Magdalenae de Pazzis Ordinis Carmelitarum ex processu remissoriali desumptorum*, ed. Ludovico Saggi, *Archivum historicum Carmelitanum*, 2, Rome 1965, pp. 120 ff. Borromeo quoted from 'Dicta et facta Sancti Philippi Neri' in Agostino Saba, *Federico Borromeo e i mistici del suo tempo, con la vita e la corrispondenza inedita di Caterina Vannini da Siena*, Florence 1933, pp. 261–77.

61. This, along with many other such gems, is in Alberto Vecchi, *Correnti religiose nel Sei-Settecento Veneto*, Venice 1962 (this one on p. 28).

62. I refer here specifically to Dante Della Terza, 'Galileo, man of letters', in Carlo L. Golino (ed.), *Galileo Reappraised*, Berkeley 1966; William Shea, *Galileo's Intellectual Revolution*, New York 1972; William A. Wallace, *Galileo and His Sources: The Heritage of the Collegio Romano in Galileo's Science*, Princeton 1984. For Galileo in relation to his age, among others: Alistair Crombie, 'Galileo in Renaissance Europe', in *Firenze e la Toscana dei Medici nel Europa del '500*, vol. 3, Florence 1983, which was apparently written independently both of my 'The Florentine background of Galileo's work', in Ernan McMullin (ed.), *Galileo: Man of Science*, New York 1967, and of Book III of my *Florence in the Forgotten Centuries*, Chicago 1973, since it mentions neither. I also take account of several other contributions to the McMullin volume, particularly those by the editor himself, by Thomas Settle, and by Willy Hartner. For biographical details: Stillman Drake, *Galileo at Work: His Scientific Biography*, Chicago 1978.

63. Paolo Rossi, 'La negazione delle sfere e l'Astrobiologia di Francesco Patrizi', in Rossi (ed.), *Il Rinascimento nelle corti padane*, Bari 1977; Paolo Galluzzi, 'Il Platonismo del tardo Cinquecento e la filosofia del Galileo', in Paola Zambelli (ed.), *Ricerche sulla cultura dell'Italia moderna*, Bari 1973. Della Porta's *De telescopio* is available in the modern edition edited by Vasco Ronchi and Maria Amalia Naldoni, Florence 1962, and Galileo's *Sidereus nuncius* in a photostatic reprint of the original 1610 edition by the Domus Galileiana in Pisa, 1964.

64. Quoted by Marialaura Soppelsa, *Genesi del metodo galileiano e tramonto dell'Aristotelismo nella scuola di Padova*, Padua 1974, p. 30.

65. Letter of 7 April 1613, edited by Marziano Guglielminetti and Mariarosa Masoero in 'Lettere e prose inedite (o parzialmente edite) di Giovanni Ciampoli', *Studi seicenteschi*, 19, 1979, p. 159.

66. Barbieri, *La supplica, discorso famigliare a quelli che trattano de' comici*, ed. Ferdinando Taviani, Milan 1971, p. 39. *Il Saggiatore* has been translated by Brendan Dooley, in *University of Chicago Readings in Western Civilization*, vol. 6: *Early Modern Europe. The Crisis of Authority*, ed. John Boyer and Julius Kirshner, Chicago 1987.

67. The phrase appears in the introduction to the selections from Tassoni in Muscetta and Ferrante (eds), *Poesia del Seicento* (above, n. 20), p. 1004.

68. Alberto Asor Rosa in the introduction to his edition of Marino, *Opere*, Milan 1967. I have also consulted the edition of *Tutte le opere* by Giovanni Pozzi, Milan 1976, and of the *Adone* by Marzio Pieri, Bari 1975. For biographical and analytical details, I rely on Marziano Guglielminetti, *Tecnica e invenzione nell'opera di Giambattista Marino*, Messina 1964, and James V. Mirollo, *The Poet of the Marvelous: Giambattista Marino*, New York 1963.

69. Francesco Ferrari, 'Vita del Cav. Marino', in the appendix to Marino's *Lettere*, ed. Marziano Guglielminetti, Turin 1966, here quoted from p. 637.

70. Tassoni, *Difesa di Alessandro Macedone*, ed. Giorgio Rossi, Livorno 1904; Marino, *Anversa liberata*, ed. Fernando Salsano, Bologna 1956.

71. Tassoni, 'Sopra Modena', in Muscetta and Ferrante (eds), *Poesia del Seicento* (above, n. 20), p. 1055.

72. See Dino Provenzal's edition of *La secchia rapita*, Milan 1950, here quoted from I, p. 2; II, pp. 29 ff.

73. In this instance, I quote Mirollo's translation in his *The Poet of the Marvelous* (above, n. 68), p. 285.

74. In all other instances, I follow the versions in Muscetta and Ferrante (eds), *Poesia del Seicento* (above, n. 20), pp. 422, 486, 505–6.

75. Quoted by Guglielminetti and Masoero in 'Lettere e prose inedite . . .' (above, n. 65), pp. 110 and 114.

76. From the text in *Trattatisti e narratori del Seicento*, ed. Ezio Raimondi, Milan 1960, p. 271.

77. Bruno Brizi, 'Teoria e prassi melodrammatica di G. F. Busenello e *L'incoronazione di Poppea*', in Maria Teresa Murano (ed.), *Venezia e il melodramma nel Seicento* (1976); Capaccio quoted by Amedeo Quondam in *La parola nel labirinto . . .*, Bari 1975, pp. 196–97.

78. Traiano Boccalini, *I ragguagli di Parnaso*, ed. Giuseppe Rua, Bari 1910–48, vol. 1, p. 221; Pietro Puliatti, 'Le letture e i postillati del Tassoni', *Studi seicenteschi*, 18, 1977, here quoted from p. 4. On Traiano Boccalini, see Luigi Firpo in *DBI*, vol. 11, pp. 10–19, and '*I ragguagli di Parnaso* di Traiano Boccalini', *Bibliografia delle edizioni italiane*, Florence 1955.

79. In Marino, *Lettere* (above, n. 69), p. 53.

80. *Ibid.*, p. 618.

81. Quoted by Renato Delle Piane in *Cultura e letteratura del barocco*, Turin 1973, p. 11.

82. Benedetto Croce, *Storia della età barocca in Italia* (2nd edn), Bari 1946, p. 252.

83. Sarpi quoted from p. 133 of his 'Supplimento' and p. 29 of his 'Aggionta all'istoria degli Uscocchi', both edited by Gaetano and Luisa Cozzi in his *La*

Repubblica di Venezia, la casa d'Austria e gli Uscocchi, Bari 1965. Much relevant information also in Alberto Tenenti, *Venezia e i corsari, 1580–1615*, Bari 1961, translated by Janet and Brian Pullan as *Piracy and the Decline of Venice*, Berkeley 1967; and in Kálmán Benda, 'Les Uscoques entre Venise, la Porte Ottomane et la Hongrie', in Vittore Branca (ed.), *Venezia e Ungheria nel contesto del barocco europea*, Florence 1979.

84. Boccalini 'Su, fatevi spagnuoli', in Muscetta and Ferrante (eds), *Poesia del Seicento* (above, n. 20), p. 1058; Tassoni's *Filippiche contra gli Spagnuoli* are edited, with a critical introduction, by Giorgio Rossi in *Prose politiche e morali*, Bari 1930.

85. Quoted by Roberto Savelli in 'Repressione penale, controllo sociale e privilegio nobiliare: La legge dell' "ostracismo" a Genova agli inizi del Seicento', in *Materiale per una storia della cultura giuridica*, 14, 1984.

86. Giulio Cesare Capaccio, *Descrizione della città di Napoli ne' principi del secolo* XVII, ed. B. Capasso, Naples 1882.

87. For this and for what follows: Vittor Ivo Comparato, *Uffici e società*, Ch. 7 (above, n. 23); Rosario Villari, 'Appunti sul Seicento', *SS*, 23, 1982; Américo Castro, 'El grande duque de Osuna', republished in his *Teresa la santa. Gracián y los separatismos con otros ensayos* (2nd edn), Madrid 1972; Giovanni Muto, 'Le "università" del Mezzogiorno tra '500 e '600', *Quaderni sardi di storia*, 1, 1980.

88. Genoino quoted by Comparato in 'Società civile e società letteraria nel primo Seicento: L'Accademia degli Oziosi', *QS*, 23, 1973, p. 388.

89. Quoted by Rosario Villari in 'Note sulla rifeudalizzazione del Regno di Napoli alla viglia della rivoluzione di Masaniello', *SS*, 6, 1965, p. 304.

90. Gino Corti, 'L'industria del vetro di Murano alla fine del secolo XVI in una relazione al Granduca di Toscana', *SV*, 13, 1971. Carlo Emanuele's privilege to Tadea di Dus of 3 August 1613.

91. The universality of the recession is made clear by Ruggiero Romano, 'Tra XVI e XVII secolo. Una crisi economica, 1619–1622', *RSI*, 74, 1962; by Paolo Malanima in 'Industrie cittadine e industrie rurali nell'età moderna', *RSI*, 94, 1982 (on England: p. 269); and by Carlo M. Cipolla in *Before the Industrial Revolution: European Society and Economy, 1000–1700* (2nd edn), New York 1980.

92. These figures come from Paolo Malanima, *La decadenza di un'economia cittadina: L'industria di Firenze nei secoli XVI–XVIII*, Bologna 1982; Giovanni Vigo, 'Manovre monetarie e crisi economica nello Stato di Milano 1619–1622', *SS*, 17, 1976; Andrea Menzioni, 'L'estimo pisano del 1622', in *Ricerche di storia moderna*, 1, 1976; Luigi Masella, 'Appunti per una storia dei contratti agrari in Terra di Bari', in Pasquale Villani (ed.), *Economia e classi sociali in Puglia nell'età moderna*, Naples 1976; Domenico Sella, *Crisis and Continuity: The Economy of Spanish Lombardy in the Seventeenth Century*, Cambridge, Mass. 1979.

93. Quoted by Dante Zanetti in his *Problemi alimentari di una economia preindustriale: Cereali a Pavia dal 1398 al 1700*, Turin 1964, p. 87. Other references: Irene Polverini Fusi, 'Lo Stato e i poveri: Siena fra '600 e '700', *Ricerche storiche*, 10, 1980; Lidia Lero, 'Grano e pane a Saluzzo nel secolo XVII', *Bolletino della Società per gli Studi Storici di Cuneo*, 85, 1981.

94. J. R. Hale, 'Francesco Tensini and the fortifications of Vicenza', in his *Renaissance War Studies*, London 1983.

95. Raffaele Della Torre quoted by Costantini in *Miscellanea storica ligure*, 7, 1977, p. 43.

96. From Marzio Achille Romani, *Nella spirale di una crisi: Popolazione mercato e prezzi a Parma tra Cinque e Seicento*, Milan 1975, p. 51; Giorgio Borelli in Amelio Tagliaferri (ed.), *Scritti storici in memoria di Paolo Zovatto*, Milan 1972, p. 282; Raul Merzario, *Il paese stretto: Strategie matrimoniali nella diocesi di Como, secoli XVI–XVIII*, Turin 1981, pp. 14–15; Luigi Masella, 'Mercato fondiario e prezzi della terra nella Puglia barese', in *Mél EFR*, 88, 1976, p. 274. For Florence, see Marisa Brogli Ciofi, 'La peste del 1630 a Firenze con particolare riferimento ai provvedimenti igienico-sanitari e sociali', *ASI*, 142, 1984, pp. 47–75; Daniela Lombardi, '1629–1631: Crisi e peste a Firenze', *ASI*, 137, 1979, pp. 3–50.

97. Carla Maria Caimi, 'Problemi politici di pubblica sanità ad Ancona', *Atti e memorie della Deputazione di storia patria per le Marche*, 83, 1978; and, for its literary value, Carlo M. Cipolla, *Chi ruppe i rastelli a Monte Lupo?*, Bologna 1977, now in Muriel Kittel's translation as *Faith, Reason and the Plague in Seventeenth-Century Tuscany*, Ithaca 1979.

98. Alessandro Pastore, 'Testamenti a Bologna in tempo di peste', *Società e storia*, 16, 1982.

99. The original of this as well as of many other pertinent documents is published by Enrico Genovesi in *Processi contro Galileo*, Milan 1966. This one and several others appear in English translation in Chapter 15 of Giorgio de Santillana, *The Crime of Galileo*, Chicago 1955 – a work that is largely unsurpassed both for its theses and for its literary qualities. Paolo Galluzzi (ed.), *Novità celesti e crisi del sapere* (Atti del Convegno Internazionale di Studi Galileiani, 1983) Florence 1984, contains a number of interesting contributions. On Pietro Redondi's controversial *Galileo eretico*, Turin 1983 (translated as *Galileo: Heretic*, by Raymond Rosenthal, Princeton 1987), see the criticisms of Vincenzo Ferrone and Massimo Firpo in 'Galileo tra inquisitori e microstorici', *RSI*, XCVII, 1985. For the English version of their piece, see 'From inquisitors to microhistorians: A critique of Pietro Redondi's *Galileo eretico*', *Journal of Modern History*, 58, 1986. Redondi's reply and Ferrone and Firpo's ferocious rejoinder have been published in *RSI*, XCVII, 1985.

100. All this and much more in Mario D'Addio, 'Considerazioni sul processo di Galileo', *RSCI*, 37, 1983, and 38, 1984. Zdenko Solle, *Neue Geschichtspunkte zum Galilei-Prozess*, Vienna 1980, and Sergio M. Pagano, *I documenti del processo di G. G.*, Vatican City 1984, contain little that is not already known.

101. Ciampoli to Galileo, 18 August 1623, in 'Lettere e prose . . . di Giovanni Ciampoli', ed. Marziano Guglielminetti and Mariarosa Masoero (above, n. 65), p. 144.

102. *Dialogo dove ne i congressi di quattro giornate si discorre sopra i due massimi sistemi del mondo*, available in Stillman Drake's English translation as *Dialogue Concerning the Two Chief World Systems – Ptolemaic & Copernican*, Berkeley 1962.

Appendix: Tables of Succession

1. POPES

Sixtus IV	1471–1484	Pius IV	1559–1566
Innocent VIII	1484–1492	Pius V	1566–1572
Alexander VI	1492–1503	Gregory XIII	1572–1585
Pius III	1503	Sixtus V	1585–1590
Julius II	1503–1513	Urban VII	1590
Leo X	1513–1522	Gregory XIV	1590–1591
Adrian VI	1522–1523	Innocent IX	1591–1592
Clement VII	1523–1534	Clement VIII	1592–1605
Paul III	1534–1550	Leo XI	1605
Julius III	1550–1555	Paul V	1605–1621
Marcellus II	1555	Gregory XV	1621–1623
Paul IV	1555–1559	Urban VIII	1623–1644

2. EMPERORS

Charles V of Habsburg (abdicated)	1519–1556	Maximilian II of Habsburg	1564–1576
Ferdinand I of Habsburg	1556–1564	Rudolph II of Habsburg	1576–1612

3. FERRARA, THE ESTE (DUKES FROM 1471)

Ercole I	1471–1505	Alfonso II	1559–1597
Alfonso I	1505–1534	Cesare	1597–1598
Ercole II	1534–1559		

(Ferrara henceforth under direct papal rule)

4. FLORENCE, THE MEDICI (DUKES FROM 1532, GRAND DUKES FROM 1569)

Alessandro	1531–1537	Ferdinando I	1587–1609
Cosimo I	1537–1574	Cosimo II	1609–1621
Francesco I	1574–1587		

5. GENOA (DOGES)

Giano Fregoso	1512–1513	Giannotto Lomellini	1571–1573
Antoniotto Adorno	1513	Giacomo Durazzo	
Ottaviano Fregoso	1513–1515	Grimaldi	1573–1575
Under French rule	1515–1522	Prospero Fatinanti	1575–1577
Antoniotto Adorno	1522–1527	Giovanni Battista	
Oberto Cattaneo		Gentile	1577–1579
Lazzaro	1528–1531	Nicolò Doria	1579–1581
Battista Spinola	1531–1533	Geronimo de Franchi	1581–1583
Battista Lomellini	1533–1535	Geronimo Chiavari	1583–1585
Cristoforo Grimaldi		Ambrogio di Negro	1585–1587
Rosso	1535–1537	Davide Vaccà	1587–1589
Giovanni Battista Doria	1537–1539	Giovanni Battista	
Andrea Giustiniani	1539–1541	Negrone	1589–1591
Leonardo Cattaneo	1541–1543	Giovanni Agostino	
Andrea Centurione	1543–1545	Giustiniani	1591–1593
Giovanni Battista		Antonio Grimaldi Cebà	1593–1595
Fornari	1545–1547	Matteo Senarega	1595–1597
Benedetto Gentile	1547–1549	Lazzaro Grimaldi Cebà	1597–1599
Gaspare Grimaldi		Lorenzo Sauli	1599–1601
Bracelli	1549–1551	Agostino Doria	1601–1603
Luca Spinola	1551–1553	Pietro de Franchi	1603–1605
Giacomo Promontorio	1553–1555	Luca Grimaldi de	
Agostino Pinelli	1555–1557	Castro	1605–1607
Pietro Giovanni		Silvestro Invrea	1607
Ciarega Cybo	1557–1559	Gerolamo Assereto	1607–1609
Geronimo Vivaldi	1559–1561	Agostino Pinelli	1609–1611
Paolo Battista Calvo	1561	Alessandro Giustiniani	1611–1613
Battista Cicala Zoagli	1561–1563	Tommaso Spinola	1613–1615
Giovanni Battista		Bernardo Clavarezza	1615–1617
Lercaro	1563–1565	Giovanni Giacomo	
Ottaviano Gentile		Imperiale	1617–1619
Oderico	1565–1567	Pietro Durazzo	1619–1621
Simone Spinola	1567–1569	Ambrogio Doria	1621–1623
Paolo Moneglia		Giorgio Centurione	1623
Giustiniani	1569–1571	Federigo de' Franchi	1623–1625

Giacomo Lomellini	1625–1627	Andrea Spinola	1629–1631
Gianluca Chiavari	1627–1629	Leonardo Torre	1631–1633

6. MANTUA (MARQUISES UNTIL 1530, THEN DUKES)

Francesco II Gonzaga	1484–1519	Guglielmo Gonzaga	1550–1587
Federico II Gonzaga	1519–1540	Vincenzo I Gonzaga	1587–1612
Francesco III Gonzaga	1540–1550		

7. PARMA (DUKES)

Pier Luigi Farnese	1545–1547	Ottavio Farnese	1550–1586
Ottavio Farnese	1547–1549	Alessandro Farnese	1586–1592
Papal rule	1549–1550	Ranuccio Farnese	1592–1622

8. SAVOY (DUKES)

Filiberto II	1497–1504	Emanuele Filiberto	1533–1580
Carlo III	1504–1533	Carlo Emanuele I	1580–1630

9. URBINO (DUKES)

Guidobaldo I di Montefeltro	1482–1508	Papal rule	1519–1520
Cesare Borgia	1502–1503	Francesco Maria I Della Rovere	1521–1538
Francesco Maria I Della Rovere	1508–1516	Guidobaldo II Della Rovere	1538–1574
Lorenzo de' Medici	1516–1519	Francesco Maria II Della Rovere	1574–1621

10. VENICE (DOGES)

Leonardo Loredano	1501–1521	Pietro Lando	1539–1545
Antonio Grimani	1521–1523	Francesco Donà	1545–1553
Andrea Gritti	1523–1538	Marcantonio Trevisan	1553–1554

Francesco Venier	1554–1556	Leonardo Donà	1606–1612
Lorenzo Priuli	1556–1559	Marcantonio Memmo	1612–1615
Girolamo Priuli	1559–1567	Giovanni Bembo	1615–1618
Pietro Loredano	1567–1570	Nicolò Donà	1618
Alvise Mocenigo I	1570–1577	Antonio Priuli	1618–1623
Sebastiano Venier	1577–1578	Francesso Contarini	1623–1624
Nicolò da Ponte	1578–1585	Giovanni Cornaro	1625–1629
Pasquale Cicogna	1585–1595	Niccolò Contarini	1630–1631
Marino Grimani	1595–1605	Francesco Erizzo	1631–1646

Index

academies: organization of, 63–4, 128–9;
  Platonic, 63, 72–3, 128 (*see also*
  Ficino, Marsilio; Platonism);
  specialization and expansion of, 247–8;
  see also under specific cities and states
Achillini, Claudio, 272
Adrian VI, Pope, 29
Adriani, Giovan Battista, 61
Agnelli, Scipione, 244
Agostini, Lodovico, 204–5
agriculture: entrepreneurship in, 179–81;
  failure of, 15, 182, 278; humanist
  idealization of, 179–80; resiliency of, 5
Alamanni, Lodovico, 42
Alamanni, Luigi, 79
Alba, Ferdinando Alvarez de Toledo, Duke
  of, 40
Albani, Francesco, 246
Alberti, Giovan Francesco, 243
Alberti, Leandro, 59, 226
Alberti, Leon Battista, 26, 28, 43, 76,
  91, 94, 118, 124, 180, 205, 206,
  219
Albertini, Francesco, 191
Alciato, Andrea, 78
Aldobrandini, Cinzio, 220
Aldobrandini, Piero, 168
Aldrovandi, Ulisse, 214
Aleandro, Girolamo, 149, 272
Aleotti, Giovan Battista, 245
Alessandri, Giovan Maria, 219
Alessi, Galeazzo, 97–8, 190, 217
Alexander VI, Pope, 11, 16, 108, 111,
  120, 143
Alfonso della Bastelica, 169

Allori, Alessandro, 71, 205, 207, 221
Altoviti, Antonio, 185
Alvarez, Juan, 39
Amaseo, Gregorio, 64
Amaseo, Romolo, 64
Ambruos, Margherita d', 199
Ameyden, Christian, 221
Ammannati, Bartolomeo, 29, 96, 99,
  187, 206, 220
Ammirato, Scipione, 203, 205, 221
Amphiareo, Vespasiano, 94
Anania, Giovanni Lorenzo d', 222
Andrea del Sarto, 77, 82, 207
Andreasi, Osanna, 107, 108
Angelico, fra, 120
Angelo of Jerusalem, 109
Angiò (Anjou), Carlo and Roberto d', 33
Anguissola, Sofonisba, 220
Annio da Viterbo, 109
Anselmi, Michelangelo, 78
Antoniano, Silvio, 192, 218
Antonino, Archbishop of Florence, 113,
  123
Antonio da Crema, 108
Antonucci, Giovan Battista, 192
Aquila: architecture and urban planning,
  93, 98; constitution, 46, 47
Aquinas, Thomas, 73, 138, 191, 268,
  281
Aragona: Alfonso II d', 10–11, 57; Don
  Carlos d', 99; Ferdinando, d', 11;
  Ferdinando (Ferrante) I d', 11;
  Ferdinando (Ferrante) II d', 16, 45,
  48, 57, 170; *see also* Naples, Kingdom
  of; Sicily

Ardoino, Andrea, 45
Aretino, Pietro, 62, 79, 122, 136, 138:
  censorship of, 216; letters of, 90;
  Mannerist variations on, 80, 83; and
  Scripture, 118–19; translation of, 258;
  and Volgare, 25
Aretusi, Cesare, 72
Arezzo: architecture, 61; painting, 82;
  urban planning, 92
Ariosto, Ludovico, 3, 14, 62, 95, 251,
  272: debunking of, by Marinism,
  269–73; Mannerist variations on, 80;
  as model for Mannerists, 71; as model
  in Neo-Renaissance, 222, 251;
  translation of, 258; and Volgare,
  24–5
Aristotelianism
  challenges to universality of, in conflict
    between sciences: logic and
    mathematics, 212–13, 267;
    metaphysics and theology, 212;
    physics and astronomy, 212, 213
  challenges to universality of, in
    empiricism, 214–15: anatomy and
    medicine, 211–12; astronomy, 4–5,
    267–9, 281–3; collecting, 213–14;
    mathematics, 213
  and music, 223–5
  poetics, 5, 69, 79, 210–11, 216,
    222–23: debunking of, by
    Marinism, 269–73
  revival of, 209–10
  survival of: due to decline and
    censorship of competing culture,
    216–17; due to lacunae in
    Aristotle's works, 211; due to
    weaknesses in rival systems, 215–16;
    in providing new theoretical
    underpinning for arts and letters, 5,
    222–8
  see also Neo-Renaissance
Armenini, Giovan Battista, 205
Arnolfini, Beatrice, 111
Artusi, Giovanni Maria, 223
astrology, 17, 109, 138, 199
astronomy, 4–5, 189, 212, 215, 267–9,
  281–3
Atanagi, Dionigi, 202
Audebert, Nicholas, 183, 219
auditori, 45–6

Augustinians, 123, 142: reform of, 112;
  see also religious orders

Baldi, Bernardino, 219
Baldinucci, Filippo, 209
Balduino, Girolamo, 211
Banco di San Giorgio, 40, 44, 113, 169
Bandello, Matteo, 81, 82, 113, 142
Bandello, Vincenzo, 113
Bandinelli, Baccio, 206
banking and finance: Banco di San
  Giorgio, 40, 44, 113, 169; crises in,
  174, 178, 181–2, 279; as dependent
  on Spanish debt, 174, 181–2, 279;
  entrepreneurialism in, 178–9; growth
  in, 173–4, 178–9, 259; Jews in, 252;
  Monte della Fede, 8; monti di pietà, 113,
  179, 252; see also under individual states
  and cities, and trade and manufacture
Barbaro, Daniele, 55
Barberini, Francesco, 282
Barberini, Maffeo, 281
Barbieri, Niccolò, 269
Bardi, Giovanni de', 225
Barnabites, 130, 131, see also
  congregations of priests
Barocci, Federico, 207, 209, 218, 247
Baronio, Cesare, 190–1, 202
Baroque, 4–5
Barozzi, Francesco, 213
Barozzi, Giacomo, 177, 207
Barozzi, Pietro, 131
Bartoli, Cosimo, 78, 213, 224
Bartolomeo, fra, 75, 110
Bascapè, Carlo, 193
Basilians, 194, see also religious orders
Bassano, Jacopo da Ponte, 97, 280
Bassano, Leandro da Ponte, 183
Bassi, Martino, 190
Bàthory, Stephan, 175
Battiferri, Laura, 220
Beccadelli, Ludovico, 88, 120, 186, 214
Beccari, Agostino de', 227
Beccuti, Francesco, 75
Bedoli, Girolamo Mazzola, 62, 72, 169
Bel, Firmin de, 221
Bellarmino, Roberto: and Galileo
  controversy, 269, 281–3; and Interdict
  controversy, 261, 263; theology of,
  191–2, 193

Bellentani, Mattia, 193
Bembo, Gian Francesco, 75, 96
Bembo, Pietro, 120, 122, 126, 134, 213
  and language questions, 19–26:
    acceptance of, 23–6, 66; opposition
    to, 20–3, 83–4; *see also* philology
  as model for Mannerists, 72–4, 87
  variations on: Mannerist, 75, 83, 84,
    90; Neo-Renaissance, 222, 243
  see also Petrarch
Benavides, Marco Mantova, 213
Benci, Tommaso, 72
Bendidio, Lucrezia, 220
Benedetti, Giovan Battista, 213
Benedictines: humanism of, 119, 122;
  reform of, 112, 194–5, 201; *see also*
  religious orders
Benenato, Cesare, 69
Benigno, Giorgio, 109
Bentivoglio, Guido, 242
Beolco, Angelo, *see* Ruzante
Bernardini, Paolo, 141
Bernardino da Feltre, 113
Bernardino da Siena, 113, 197, 245
Berni, Francesco, 24, 267
Bernini, Gian Lorenzo, 4
Bertini, Giovan Battista, 59
Betussi, Giuseppe, 72, 73, 175
Bevilacqua, Mario, 225
Beza, Theodore, 140
Bibbiena, Ferdinando, 245
Biondo, Flavio, 202
Biondo, Michelangelo, 66, 205
Boccaccino, Camillo, 75, 83
Boccaccio, Giovanni: Mannerist variations
  on, 81–2, 84; as model for
  Mannerists, 72–3, 85–6; Tridentine
  "correction" of, 218; and Volgare, 20
Boccadiferro, Lodovico, 211
Boccalini, Traiano, 242, 275
Bocchi, Achille, 129, 135
Boffoli and Vecchietti, firm of, 173
Boiardo, Matteo, 24
Bollani, Domenico, 186
Bologna: academies, 208, 247, 272;
  architecture, 91; church of, 195;
  confraternities, 117; hospitals, 198;
  humanism, 129, 219; painting, 208,
  246; theatre, 245; trade regulation,
  183; university, 4–5, 60, 215, 251

Bolzoni, Alessandro, 59
Bonanimo, Lazzaro, 23
Bonaré, Giovanni, 195
Bonarelli, Prospero, 250
Bonfadio, Jacopo, 75, 97, 136
Bonifacio, Curione, Giovan Bernardino,
  and Vergerio, 153
Bonsignori, Stefano, 226
Bonucci, Agostino, 112
Borghese, Camillo, *see* Paul V
Borghese, Scipione, 261, 264
Borghini, Raffaello, 206, 207, 216
Borghini, Vincenzo, 55–6, 87–8, 90, 95
Borgia: Cesare, 12, 16, 143; Lucrezia,
  108, 168
Borra, Luigi, 62
Borro, Girolamo, 210
Borromeo, Carlo, 3, 129, 184–5, 193,
  195, 197, 200, 201, 217–18, 255,
  265
Borromeo, Federico, 193, 215, 218, 247,
  269
Borromeo, Ippolita, 220
Borromini, Francesco, 4
Boscoli, Giovanni, 57
Bossi, Egidio, 45
Bosso, Matteo, 131
Botero, Giovanni, 177, 203–4, 216, 243
Botticelli, Sandro (Alessandro Filipepi), 30
Bozio, Tommaso, 204
Bramante, Donato, 28, 71, 75
Brigid of Sweden, 108
Brignole Sale, Anton Giulio, 248
Brill, Paul, 257
Brizio, Francesco, 208
Brizziano, Giovan Battista, 94
Brocadelli, Lucia, da Narni, 108
Brocardo, Antonio, 23
Bronzino, Angelo, 57, 61, 77, 81, 82–3,
  85, 88, 95
Brucioli, Antonio, 42, 121, 142, 152
Brunelleschi, Filippo, 28, 91
Bruni, Leonardo, 43, 120, 210, 270
Bruni, Vincenzo, 193
Bruno, Giordano, 198, 215, 258
Brusasorci, Domenico, 83
Bruto, Giovan Michele, 198, 202
Bucer, Martin, 142
Bugni, Chiara, 107
Buonmattei, Benedetto, 244

Buontalenti, Bernardo, 180–1, 214, 219, 226, 227
Burlamacchi, Francesco, 38
Busenello, Gianfrancesco, 272

Cacciaguida, Bonsignore, 198
Caccini, Giulio, 228
Caimi, Bernardino, 113
Cajetan (Tommaso de Vio), 138
Calabria: academy, 254; agriculture, 180; banking, 182; revolt in, 170–1; Slavs in, 251–2; trade and manufacture, 173; see also Naples, Kingdom of
Calcagnini, Celio, 141
Callot, Jacques, 257
Calmo, Andrea, 62, 70, 80
Calvaert, Denis, 246
Calvin, John, 140, 152
Camaldoli, 112
Cambi, Bartolomeo, 266
Cambi, Piero di Niccolò, 174–5
Campana, Francesco, 45, 59
Campanella, Tommaso, 171, 205, 281
Campeggi: Lorenzo, 127, 138; Tommaso, 127, 148
Campi: Antonio, 96, 119, 217; Bernardino, 60, 86–7, 96, 119, 217, 224; Giulio, 96, 97, 119, 217
Cano, Melchior, 281
Capaccio, Giulio Cesare, 272
Capodiferro, Girolamo, 127
Cappelloni, Lorenzo, 43, 250
Capponi, Piero di Niccolò, 174
Capuchins, 114, 123, 137, 187, 266, see also religious orders
Caraccia, Arcangelo, 266
Caracciolo, Giulio Cesare, 43
Carafa, Alfonso, 195
Carafa, Gian Pietro, see Paul IV
Carafa, Oliviero, 126
Caraglio, Jacopo, 94
Cardano, Girolamo, 91, 210
Carioni, Battista, da Crema, 109, 135
Carli, Ferrante, 272
Carmelites, 112, see also religious orders
Carnesecchi, Pietro, 153
Carnesecchi, Zanobio, 173
Caro, Annibal, 62, 71, 80, 82, 83–4, 90, 95
Carpi, Ugo da, 94

Carracci: Agostino, 207–8, 218, 251; Annibale, 207–8, 209, 218, 246, 247, 251; Lodovico, 193, 207–8, 218, 246, 251
Carrara, 49: theatre, 217; trade, 177
Caravaggio (Michelangelo Merisi), 4, 259–61, 272
cartography, 226
Casale: academy in, 63; painting, 98
Casale, Giambattista, 195
Casoni, Filippo, 248
Cassiano del Pozzo, 45
Castaldo, Giacomo, 226
Castelli, Benedetto, 268, 282
Castelli, Giovan Battista, 196
Castello, Giovan Battista, 58
Castelvetro, Lodovico, 65, 83, 143, 211, 258
Castiglione, Baldassare, 3, 22, 26, 47, 118, 272; Mannerist variations on, 78–9; as model for Mannerists, 70; Neo-Renaissance variations on, 222, 251; see also manners
Cataneo, Pietro, 93
Catena, Pietro, 213
Caterina of Sicily, 199
Caterina of Siena, 108
Cattaneo, Giovan Battista, 113
Cattaneo, Girolamo, 41
Cattaneo, Silvano, 81
Cavalcanti, Bartolomeo, 42, 69, 181
Cavalcanti, Giovan Battista, 61
Cavalier d'Arpino (Giuseppi Cesari), 259
Cavalli, Alberto, 83
Cavalli, Ambrogio, 137
Cavallini, Taddeo, 176
Cecchi, Giovan Maria, 81
Cecchini, Pier, 245
Cellini, Benvenuto, 56, 60, 88, 91
Celsi, Mino, 153
Ceneda, papal and Venetian competition for, 261
Cerda, Juan de la, duke of Medinaceli, 186
Cervantes, Miguel de, 258
Cervini, Marcello, see Marcello II
Cesalpino, Andrea, 212
charitable institutions: Company of St Ursula, 108; in economic depression and plague, 278, 280; hospitals, 15,

109, 117, 119, 128, 197–98, 245; *luoghi pii*, 200; *monti di pietà*, 113, 179, 252; *scuole grandi*, as art patrons, 61, 97, 119; *see also* confraternities

Charles V, Emperor, 30, 81, 170, 255: abdication and death of, 166–7; as architect of Imperial alliance, 3, 33–5; methods of government by, 34–6, 38; *see also* Imperial Alliance; Rome, Sack of

Charles VIII, king of France, 9, 11, 110

Cherubino da Spoleto, 115

Chiabrera, Gabriello, 221, 242–3

Chiaramonti, Scipione, 245

Chiari, Isidoro, 139, 144

Church and state: conflict of, in Interdict affair, 261–6; and ecclesiastical reform, 147–8, 186–7, 200, 202, 204; and heresy, 142–3, 186, 218

Ciampoli, Giovanni Battista, 269, 281, 282

Ciccarelli, Antonio, 204

Cigalino, Zanino, 220

Cigoli, Lodovico, 207, 209, 245, 267

Clavius, Christopher, 189, 213

Clement VII, Pope, 8–9, 12, 19, 29, 34, 35, 110, 114, 115, 125, 128, 138, 253

Clement VIII, Pope, 111, 168, 194, 219, 252, 255, 261, 263, 282

Clichtove, Josse, 151

Clovio, Giorgio Giulio, 95

Colomba da Rieti, 108

Colonna, Ascanio, 39

Colonna, Pompeo, 125

Colonna, Vittoria: sacred writings and activities, 119, 122, 123, 129; secular writings, 74

Comanini, Gregorio, 205

Commandino, Federico, 213

Como: heresy punished in, 142; hospitals, 117; population, 280; trade and manufacture, 173

Concini, Concino, 270

confraternities: as crossing class boundaries, 114, 115, 188; described, 114; growth of, post-Tridentine, 187–8, 195; national dimensions of, 116–17; as patrons of art, 61, 96, 119, 207, 219; purposes of, 115–16;

revival of, 114–18; and social activism, 116–18; women in, 115, 116, 188; *see also under individual cities and states, and* charitable institutions

congregations of priests: constitutions of, 130–1; creation of, 129; Tridentine reform of, 146, 187; *see also* Barnabites; Jesuits; Oratorians; Somaschi; Theatines

Contarini, Gasparo, 42, 127, 132, 136, 141, 143, 149

Conte, Jacopino del, 96

convents, 196, 200

Cordores, Antonio, 193

Cornaro, Alvise, 76, 178

Cornaro, Federico, 185

Correggio, Antonio, 72, 77, 95, 206, 208, 246

Corsica, 40, 169

Cort, Cornelius, 208

Cortesi, Giovan Battista, 254

Cortesi, Paolo, 135

Cosenza, academy in, 254

Costa, Ottaviano, 261

Council of Trent
  Bible, 3, 150, 188–9
  calendar, 189
  confession manuals, 3, 123, 192
  confraternities, 187–8
  cultural reform, 217–19
  doctrinal consolidation in, 150–1, 198: as arresting theological debate, 216; dissemination of, by publication, 188–9; elaboration of, by historians, 190–1; elaboration of, by patristic scholars, 189; elaboration of, by theologians, 191–2; resistance to, 152–3; *see also* theology
  heresy, 152–3, 198, 216, *see also* heresy
  indexes, 188: *see also* indexes; Inquisition
  institutional reforms of, 3: in cardinalate, 193; in clergy, 151; in congregations of priests, 187; in dioceses, 151–2, 185, 195–6; in papacy, 193, 194; in religious orders, 194–5; state cooperation in, 186–7; *see also* Church and state; ecclesiastical institutions; religious orders

institutional reforms of, resistance to: by
  bishops, 185–6, 201; in conflict
  among ecclesiastical authorities,
  200–1; in conflict between Church
  and state, 200, 202, 261–6; by
  monasteries and convents, 200–1; by
  papacy, 264; by religious orders,
  201–2, 266; on local level,
  199–200; see also Church and state;
  ecclesiastical institutions; religious
  orders
lay reform, 4, 147, 195, 196, 201, 202
liturgy, 3, 130, 189, 196
manuals of piety, 122, 140, 192–3
pan-Italian culture, as contributing to,
  151–2, 251
participants in, 148–9, 184–5
preaching, 197, see also preaching
restoration of ancient churches, 190
superstition, 198–9, 201
works, emphasis on, 197–8
Cremona: congregations of priests, 130;
  painting, 75, 83, 96
Cremonini, Cesare, 210, 268
Cresci, Giovan Francesco, 94
Crespi, Daniele, 265
Crespi, Giovan Battista, 193, 198, 217
Crispoldi, Tullio, 133, 136
Cristoforo da Monza, 113
Croce, Benedetto, 1–2, 273
Curione, Celio Secundo, 153
Curtis, Camillo de, 263
Cybo, Alberto, 93, 217
Cybo, Innocenzo, 125
Cybo Malaspina, Alberto, 177

Dalla Vedova, Gaspare, 83
D'Ambra, Francesco, 227
dance, 227, 244
Daniele da Volterra (Daniele Ricciarelli), 96
Daniello, Bernardino, 72, 87
Danti, Vincenzo, 205–6
Darsa, Marino, 256
Dattaro, Francesco, 96
Davanzati, Francesco, 189
Davila, Enrico Caterino, 242
De Dominis, Marc'Antonio, 265
Delfinone, Scipione, 95
Della Casa, Giovanni, 78–9, 87, 88, 124,
  126, 127

Della Porta, Giacomo, 93, 190, 208
Della Porta, Giovan Battista, 215, 248,
  266
Della Rovere: Francesco Maria, 35, 39;
  Giuliano, 218; Guidobaldo II, 170,
  252; see also Urbino
Della Valle, Federico, 243
Del Migliore, Filippo, 59
Del Monte, Antonio Maria, 125
Del Monte, Francesco Maria, 261
Del Monte, Guidobaldo, 213, 245
Del Tasso, Giovanni Battista, 57, 92, 96
Del Vasto, Marchese Alfonso d'Avalos, 36
De Marini, Claudio, 275
De Sanctis, Francesco, 1–2
De Zan, Giovan, 97
Dionisi, Paolo, 23
Diplovatazio, Tommaso, 42
Dolce, Lodovico, 56, 62, 70, 73, 75–6
Domenéch, Giovanni, 186
Domenichi, Lodovico, 66, 95
Domenichino (Domenico Zampieri), 224,
  247, 272, 281
Dominicans: and confraternities, 115; as
  political advisors, 113; reform of,
  112–14, 194, 201–2, 266; see also
  religious orders
Donà, Leonardo, 261
Donatello (Donato di Niccolò Bardi), 28
Doni, Agostino, 198
Doni, Anton Francesco, 61–2, 65, 70–1,
  86, 224
Doria, Andrea, 13, 37, 39–40, 41, 57,
  58, 97, 116, 139, 248
Doria, Gian Carlo, 258
Dosio, Giovan Antonio, 186, 219
Duns Scotus, John, 73, 119, 135, 191
Dürer, Albrecht, 84–5

ecclesiastical institutions
  experimentation in, 128
  as "pan-Italian," 151–2
  as personal benefices, 124–5, 184, 264:
    advantages of, 126–8; criticism of,
    125, 146–7
  as pluralistic confederation, 124, 128
  pre-Tridentine reform of: by
    congregationalism, 147; in dioceses,
    131–4; by state, 147–8; failure of,
    146–7

Tridentine reform of: *see* Council of
Trent, institutional reforms of
vicars, 126
see also congregations of priests;
Inquisition; religious orders
Eleonora di Toledo, duchess of Florence, 88,
111
Emiliani, Girolamo, 131
encyclopaedias, 214, 222, 248
Epicuro, Marcantonio, 80
Erasmus, Desiderius, 20–1, 43, 121,
122–3, 125, 135
Erizzo, Sebastiano, 73
Este, 10, 14: Alfonso II d', 37, 168, 220;
Cesare d', 168–9, 261; Ercole I d',
108; Ercole II d', 37, 60, 168;
Ippolito I d', 39, 125; Ippolito II d',
39, 60, 226; reconciliation of, with
Medici, 168; *see also* Ferrara
Estienne, Henri, 218
Eustachi, Bartolomeo, 212

Faenza, 179
Faerno, Gabriele, 203
Faggio, Angelo de, 112
Falconetto, Giovan Maria, 62, 92
Falloppio, Gabriele, 212, 215, 220
Farnese, 14: Alessandro, 62, 169, 242,
259; Alessandro, Cardinal, 121, 221;
Odoardo, 248; Ottavio, 40, 57, 88;
Pier Luigi, 39–40; Ranuccio, 213; *see
also* Parma
Fasolo, Giovanni, 210
Fausto da Longiano, 70
Ferramolino, Antonio, 41
Ferrara, Duchy of: constitution, 44; papal
jurisdiction in, 168–9, 250; Protestant
theology in, 139; schools, 64;
sculpture, 62; theatre, 60, 62, 71, 79,
227, 245; trade and manufacture, 179;
university, 60, 215; *see also* Este
Ferrari, Gaudenzio, 72, 98, 119
Ferrari, Giolito de', 85
Ferrari, Lodovico, 213
Fiamma, Gabriele, 198
Ficino, Marsilio, 63: as model for
Mannerists, 72–3; as theologian, 118,
215; *see also* academies: Platonic;
Platonism
Fieno, Ludovico, 176

Fieschi, Caterina, 3, 108–9, 116
Fieschi, Gian Luigi, 39
Figino, Giovanni Ambrogio, 193, 209
Filarete (Antonio Averlino), 91
Filonardi, Ennio, 125
Fini, Daniele, 21
Fioravanti, Leonardo, 215
Flaminio, Marcantonio, 121, 140
Florence: academies, 63, 65, 91, 218,
221, 244, 247, 268; architecture, 29,
57, 58, 61, 87, 92; banking, 173,
174; confraternities, 115, 117;
constitution, 43, 44; dance, 227;
decorative arts, 95, 96; diocese, 196;
Grand Duchy of, 2; language, 20, 22,
24, 25, 70–1, 244; opera, 227–8;
painting, 56, 61, 71, 83, 87, 88,
217; Pazzi faction in, 11; political
stability in, 249–50; population, 280;
Protestant theology in, 140, 142;
Republic of, 8; Savonarolans in, 11,
13, 16, 110–11, 185, 188, 196;
sculpture, 3, 29, 60, 88, 207, 221,
246; state regulation of church in,
147–8; theatre, 79, 227, 246; trade
and manufacture, 173, 175–6, 182,
277; university, 134; urban planning,
58, 59, 91–2; *see also* Machiavelli,
Niccolò; Medici; Tuscany
Florimonte, Galeazzo, 127, 133, 139, 190
Florio, Michelangelo, 153
Foglietta, Uberto, 202
Folengo, Teofilo, 23
Fontana, Carlo, 117
Fontana, Lavinia, 220
Fontanini, Benedetto, 140
Foppa, Lucio, 193
Fornari, Giovan Battista, 88
Fornovo, Giovan Battista, 75
Foscarari, Egidio, 143
Fracastoro, Girolamo, 76
Francesco da Montepulciano, 109–10
Francis I, king of France, 9, 11–12, 34,
39, 110, 257
Franciscans, 138, 191: and confraternities,
115; as political advisors, 113; reform
of, 112–14, 201–2, 266; *see also*
religious orders
Franco, Gianbattista, 71
Franco, Niccolò, 83

Franov, Divo, 256
Frederick II, Emperor, 33
Fregoso, Antonio, 122
Fumi, Bartolomeo, 192
Fusco, Paolo, 196

Gaddi, Niccolò, 214
Gaetano da Thiene, 126, 131
Gagliardi, Achille, 192
Galeazzo di Tàrsia, 48, 73
Galesini, Pietro, 189
Galilei, Galileo, 272: astronomical
  discoveries of, 4–5, 267–8; conflict of,
  with Church, 4, 268–9, 281–3;
  professions of, 266–7
Galilei, Vincenzo, 224, 225
Galizia, Fede, 220
Galliani, Giuseppe Leggiardo, 168
Gambacorte, Rocco, 250
Gambara, Giovan Francesco, 184
Gambara, Laura and Paola, 107
Gambara, Lucrezia, 108
gardens, 226–7
Garimberti, Girolamo, 186
Garzoni, Tommaso, 180, 214
Gatti, Bernardino, 96
Gattinara, Mercurino di, 34
Gelli, Giambattista, 81, 86
Genga, Girolamo, 57
Genoa, Republic of: academies, 64, 248;
  architecture, 57, 97; banking, 173–4,
  259, 279; Carlo Emanuele's
  interference in, 275; confraternities,
  115, 116; constitution, 43, 44;
  constitution, crises of, 170, 275; and
  Corsica, 40, 44, 169; Jesuits, 187;
  political stability, 248–9; Sforza
  dominion in, 10, 13; trade and
  manufacture, 176; urban planning,
  58–9; see also Doria, Andrea; states,
  Italian
Genoino, Giulio, 276
Gentile, Alberico, 258
Gesualdo, Filippo, 191
Gheri, Cosimo, 133
Giambologna, 207, 221, 226, 246, 257
Giannotti, Donato, 42, 81
Giberti, Gian Matteo, 3, 132–3, 151
Giganti, Antonio, 214

Gioacchino da Fiore, 109
Giovanni da Capistrano, 113
Giovanni da Fano, 123
Giovanni da Torano, 136
Giovio, Paolo, 127: benefice of, 61, 124;
  dialogues of, 78; Erasmianism of, 122;
  as historian and biographer, 16, 88, 90
Giraldi, Giambattista (Cinthio), 62, 79,
  82, 227
Giraldi, Lelio Gregorio, 64
Giulio, fra, 94
Giulio Romano (Giulio Pippi), 55, 56,
  59, 83, 89–90, 91, 94, 207
Giunta, Bernardo di, 22
Giunti, Agostino, 62
Giunti, Domenico, 93
Giussano, Giovan Pietro, 193
Giustiniani, Agostino, 121
Giustiniani, Paolo Tommaso, 112, 126
Giustiniani, Vincenzo, 260–1
Gondi, Bernardo di Antonio, 179
Gondola, Giovanni, 256
Gonzaga, 14, 108: Eleonora, 39; Ercole,
  39, 177; Federico, 37, 38, 47, 59;
  Ferrante, 36, 40, 41, 56, 93, 107,
  108, 213; Francesco, 244, 271;
  Francesco III, 253; Giulia, 129;
  Ippolita, 60; Lodovico, 259; Scipione,
  223; Vespasiano, 56, 93; Vincenzo I,
  214, 244, 257, 261; see also Mantua
Gonzalo del Cordoba, 16
Gozzoli, Benozzo, 30
Grassi, Giampietro, 127
Grazzini, Anton Francesco, 70, 82, 216
Greco, El (Domenico Theotokopoulos),
  221
Greeks, 253–4
Gregorian calendar, 189, 281
Gregory XIII, Pope, 117, 170, 183, 189,
  190, 198, 201, 281
Gregory XV, Pope, 265
Grimani, Giovanni, 185
Gritti, Andrea, 48, 92
Gropper, Johann, 151
Guarini, Alfonso, 46, 71
Guarini, Battista, 64, 71, 165, 245, 248,
  258, 272
Guazzo, Stefano, 258
Guercino, Giovanni, 193

Guicciardini, Francesco, 8, 15–16, 17, 28, 30, 42, 90, 95, 251, 264, *see also* historiography
Guicciardini, Isabella, 180
Guidiccioni, Giovanni, 127
Gustavus Adolphus, king of Sweden, 280

Henry II, king of France, 40, 41, 165
Henry IV, king of France, 242, 249, 261, 275, 277
heresy: as arising from theological confusion, 137, 139, 145; after conciliar settlement, 152–3, 198–9, 216; Protestant, 137–41; response to, by Inquisition, 142–5, 152, 268–9, 281–3; response to, by state, 142–3, 186; superstition as, 198–9; *see also* Council of Trent; Galilei, Galileo; indexes; Inquisition; Protestants; religious humanism; theology
historiography, 85, 90, 97, 190–1, 202–3, 242, 264
Hordognez, Alfonso, 80

Ibn Habib, Moses, 121
Ignatius of Loyola, 3, 128, 130, 187, *see also* Jesuits
Imperato, Francesco, 277
Imperial alliance: crises in, 39–42; as dependent on emperor's authority, 34–5, *see also* Charles V; as dependent on voluntary alliance of Italian states, 36–9; and the language question, 20–1; as permitting political stability within Italian states, 3, 42; as shifting from Imperial to Spanish hegemony, 166–8, *see also* Philip II; states, Italian
Imperiale, Vincenzo, 58
indexes, 142–3, 145, 188, 216, 218–19, 272
Inquisition, 143–5, 152, 198, 201, 216, 252, 262, 268–9, 281–3: *see also* heresy; indexes
Italic League, 10–11
Italy, nation of: contribution of Mannerism to, 93–9; contribution of Tridentine reform to, 151–3; definition of, cultural, 16, 250–1, 254–7;

exclusions from cultural definition of, 251–4; and pan-Christian universalism, 257; *see also* states, Italian

Jacopone da Todi, 109
Jesuits, 3, 128, 130, 131, 136, 143, 146, 190: colleges, 4–5, 187, 189, 191, 212, 213, 254, 267, 268, 282; in Galileo affair, 282; in Interdict affair, 262, 263; *see also* congregations of priests
Jews, 121, 216, 252–3
Josquin des Prez, 223
Julius II, Pope, 11, 12, 120, 168, 194
Julius III, Pope, 40, 48, 133, 150, 185

Laínez, Diego, 149
Laínez, Jacob, 136
Lama, Giovan Battista, 98
Lambertini, Cristiano, 227
Lancerio, Sante, 183
Lancillotto, Secondo, 272
Landi, Claudio, 48
Lando, Ortensio, 84, 85–6, 122
Lanfranco, Giovanni, 246, 247
language questions, 19–26: *see also* Bembo, Pietro; philology; Tuscan language
Laparelli, Francesco, 254
Lascaris, Janis, 254
Lasso, Orlando di, 60
Lateran Council: Fifth, 12, 146, 184, 212; Fourth, 130
Latini, Bruno, 203
Latini, Latino, 189
Lauro, Pietro, 123
League of Cognac, 12
Lecce: diocese, 133, 195; Mannerist culture in, 98; population, 172
Lefèvre, d'Etaples, Jacques, 151
LeJay, Claude, 150
Lemos, Conde de (Pedro Fernan de Castro), 248, 249
Leo X, Pope, 12, 19, 26, 120, 138, 194, 253
Leonardo da Vinci, 72, 206, 208, 220
Leonceno, Niccolò, 83
Leoni, Leone, 56, 61, 89, 97
Lepanto, Battle of, 166

libraries, 120–1, 189, 218, 219–20, 247
Licheto, Francesco, 113
Ligorio, Pirro, 96, 226
Ligozzi, Jacopo, 209
Lippomano, Luigi, 126–7, 132, 192
literary criticism, 69, 72, 79, *see also*
  Aristotelianism: poetics; Bembo, Pietro:
  and language questions; Neo-
  Renaissance: poetry; Petrarch;
  Platonism
Livorno, 178
Lollini, Alvise, 242
Lomazzo, Giovan Paolo, 205–6, 214
Lorenza da Firenze, 111
Lorenzo da Brindisi, 187, 197
Lotto, Lorenzo, 88
Louis XII, king of France, 11, 12, 110
Lucca, Republic of: constitution, 43, 44;
  Protestant theology in, 139; rulers, 37
Lucinge, René de, 222
Ludwig, prince of Anhalt-Kothen, 221
Luini, Aurelio, Bernardino and Giovan
  Pietro, 72, 207
Luther, Martin, 8, 137–9, 140, 141,
  142, 150, 152
Luzzaschi, Luzzasco, 225
Luzzi, Luzio, 87

Macchietti, Girolamo, 217
Macedonio, Marcello, 243
Machiavelli, Niccolò, 22, 118
  comedies: Mannerist variations on, 80,
    81; as model for Mannerists, 70–1
  political theory of, 16–17, 26–8, 70,
    122: censorship of, 216; Tridentine
    revision of, 204
  and Volgare, 25
Madruzzo, Cristoforo, 43, 48
Maggi, Alessandro, 56
Maggi, Vincenzo, 210
magic and superstition, 198–9, *see also*
  astrology
Maglio, Ferdinando, 57
Magno, Celio, 87
Malaterra, Goffredo, 186
Malocchi, Francesco, 213
Malta, 254
Manare, Baldassare, 179
Mannerism
  aesthetics of, 75–6, 216–17, *see also*

Vasari, Giorgio
  decline of, 4, 216–17, *see also* Neo-
    Renaissance
  decorative and minor arts in, 93–6
  and High Renaissance models, imitation
    of: ancient models, 69–70; modern
    models, 19, 29, 70–4, 205–9
  and High Renaissance models, variation
    on, 74–91: variation as experiment,
    not revolution, 3, 75, 82, 84–6,
    87, 209; variation as parody and
    confrontation, 83–4; variation on
    High Renaissance imitators, 82–4;
    variation on High Renaissance
    masters' "mannerism," 86–91
  humour in, 86
  individuality in, 89–91
  joint projects in, 95–6, 217
  as national culture, 96–9
  realism in, 78–82, 87–9
  urban planning in, 91–3
  *see also under individual artists, writers,
    states and cities*
manners
  in comedy and the novella, 23, 25, 71,
    80–2
  court language and conversation, 22,
    26, 132–3, 258: debunking of, by
    Marinism, 269–73; revision of,
    78–9; disappearance of "culture" of,
    60, 84
  post-Tridentine cosmopolitanism of,
    220–2, 257–8
  in tragedy, 79
  see also Castiglione, Baldassare; Della
    Casa, Giovanni; Guazzo, Stefano;
    patronage; women
Mansano, Domenico, 194
Manso, Giovan Battista, 248, 270
Mantegna, Andrea, 87
Mantua, Duchy of: architecture, 56,
  89–90; decorative arts, 94; language,
  25; opera, 244; sack of, and succession
  of Gonzaga-Nevers, 279–80; sculpture,
  56; theatre, 219; trade and
  manufacture, 177; *see also* Gonzaga;
  Sabbioneta; states, Italian
Manuzio, Aldo, 64, 220
Manuzio, Paolo, 189
Manzoni, Alessandro, 280

Marcellino, Evangelista, 197

Marcello II, Pope, 121, 123, 136, 148, 150, 183, 189, 191

Marco da Faenza (Marco Marchetti), 87

Marenzio, Luca, 74–5

Margherita of Parma, 39, 208

Mariani, Gian Pietro, 95

Marini, Biagio, 225

Marino, Giambattista, 4, 269–70, 271–3

Marino, Tommaso, 97

Marliani, Fabrizio, 125

Marlowe, Christopher, 258

Martelli, Braccio, 98, 133, 195

Martelli, Carlo, Cosimo and Giovan Battista, 175, 182

Martelli, Ludovico, 79

Martinelli, Caterina, 244

Martirana, Bernardino, 61

Mary Stuart, 243

Mary Tudor, 145, 165

Masaccio (Tommaso di Giovanni di Simone Guidi), 28

Masi, fra Modesto, 110

Massimi, Massimo, 137

Materdona, Gianfrancesco Maria, 273

mathematics: and aesthetics, 205, 208; and astronomy, 189, 267; humanist elevation of, 212–13, 247–8, 267; and logic, 212, 213

Matteo da Bascio, 110, 114

Maurolico, Francesco, 213

Maximilian I, Emperor, 11

Mazzanti, Battista, 179

Mazzolini, Silvestro (Prierias), 138

Meder, Lorenz, 174

Medici, 8, 11, 14: Alessandro de', Cardinal, 39, 111, 195–6; Alessandro de', Duke, 37; Caterina de', 242; Cosimo I de', 36, 37–8, 39, 40, 47, 48, 49, 55–6, 57, 58, 59, 60, 84, 88, 94, 110, 117, 147–8, 168, 175, 252; Cosimo II de', 88, 268; Ferdinando I de', Cardinal, 39, 150, 169, 178, 180, 182, 246, 249–50, 261, 277, 279, 282; Ferdinando II de', 282; Francesco I de', 214, 217, 224, 249; Giovanni de', 259; Giovanni dalle Bande Nere, 16; Giuliano de', 29; Giulio de', see Clement VII; Lorenzo de', 29, 39, 60, 84, 109;

Lucrezia de', 168; Maria de', 270; Piero de', 11; reconciliation of, with Este, 168; Virginia, 168; see also Florence; Leo X, Pope; Tuscany

medicine and anatomy, 83, 211–12, 215, 221, 254

Megadoukas, Dimitris Laskaris, 256

Mei, Girolamo, 225

Melanchthon, Philip, 138, 139, 143, 144

Melchiori, Girolamo, 185

Melone, Altobello, 96

Memmo, Giovan Maria, 70

Mercati, Michele, 203

Merici, Angela, 108

Messina: congregationalism in, 147; university, 254

Messisbugo, Cristoforo di, 183

Mezzabarba, Fabrizio, 187

Micanzio, Fulgenzio, 268

Michelangelo (Michelangelo Buonarroti), 3, 28, 30, 59, 61, 93, 95, 129, 136: as model for Mannerists, 71, 87; as model for Neo-Renaissance, 205–6, 251

Michele da Milano, 113

Mignanelli, Fabio, 143

Milan, city of: academies, 63, 247; architecture, 61, 89, 97–8, 190, 217; banking, 178; confraternities, 117, 195; congregations of priests, 130–1; constitution, 43, 44; decorative arts, 88, 95; diocese, 200; music, 60; painting, 60, 72, 89, 206, 207, 209; population, 280; see also Milan, Duchy of

Milan, Duchy of: agriculture, 182–3; church of, 195; heresy punished in, 142; language, 21; and Swiss cantons, 11–12, 167, 255; trade and manufacture, 277–8; Tridentine reform in, 192; Visconti in, 10; see also Milan, city of; Sforza; states, Italian

military architecture, 41, 56, 93

Minturno, Antonio, 70, 72, 184, 222

Minucci, Minuccio, 201

Modena: congregationalism in, 147; population, 172; Protestant theology in, 140, 143

Molza, Francesco Maria, 82, 88

Monferrato, Savoyan expansion in, 4, 275, 279

Montaigne, Michel de, 202
Monteverdi, Claudio, 225, 244
monti sacri, 113, 119, 197, 217
Montoro, Pietro Francesco, 201
More, Thomas, 84, 121, 204
Morigia, Jacopo Antonio, 130
Morigia, Paolo, 220
Morone, Giovanni, 136, 143
Moroni, Giovan Battista, 89
Muret, Marc Antoine, 203
Murtola, Gaspare, 270
music: humanist and theoretical elevation
    of, 223–5; instrument building, 224;
    madrigal, 225, 243; opera, pastoral
    drama, and *intermedi*, development of,
    217, 227–8, 244; and Tridentine
    reform, 196, 216, 217, 218
Musso, Cornelio, 119–20, 193
Muziano, Girolamo, 226, 257
Muzio, Girolamo, 24, 119, 190
mysticism, 107–9, 111, 137, 138: and
    lay/clerical boundaries, 107, 123,
    192–3; prevalent among women, 107;
    as social/political activism, 108–9

Nadal, Gerónimo, 130
Naldini, Battista, 96
Naples, city of: academies, 248;
    architecture, 219; confraternities, 115,
    116, 117; decorative arts, 95; diocese,
    195; hospitals, 197–8; humanism,
    128–9; Jesuits in, 187; Mannerist
    school of, 98; painting, 85, 89;
    sculpture, 87; theatre, 245; trade and
    manufacture, 173, 183; university, 60;
    urban planning, 57, 58; *see also*
    Naples, Kingdom of
Naples, Kingdom of: administrative
    corruption, 249, 276–7; agriculture,
    180; Angevins in, 10–11; Aragonese
    in, 10–11, 13, 14; clergy, 200;
    constitution, 43–4; language, 21–2,
    24; piracy, 276–7; Spanish domination
    in, 167; Tridentine reform in, 186;
    uprising of 1585, 170; *see also*
    Aragona; Naples, city of; Ossuna;
    states, Italian; Toledo, Pedro Alvarez de
Nasi, Francesco, 175
natural science, 213–14

Negri, Cesare, 227
Negri, Francesco, 139
Negri, Girolamo, 198
Negri, Mariola de', 115
Negri, Paola Antonia, 108
Negroni, Veronica, da Binasco, 108
Neo-Renaissance
    architecture and sculpture, 219, 221,
        246
    joint projects, 208, 227, 243–4
    music, *see* music
    new art forms in, 226–8, 242–5
    painting, 218–21, 246–7: aesthetics of,
        205–6; Caravaggism and, 260–1;
        landscape, 226; style of, 207–9, 251
    and pan-Italian culture, 219–22
    patronage in, expansion of, 219–22
    poetry, 222–3, 242–3, *see also*
        Aristotelianism: poetics
    tragedy, 243
    and Tridentine reform, 217–19
    see also Aristotelianism, *and individual
        artists, writers, and musicians*
Neri, Filippo, 129–30, 187, 190, 193,
    202, 266: *see also* Oratorians
Nerli, Filippo de', 42
Netherlands, wars in the, 39, 167, 169,
    173–4, 198
Nicholas V, Pope, 120, 185, 194, 283
Nifo, Agostino, 17
Nizoli, Mario, 23, 69
Nola, Giovanni da, 87, 89

Observants, *see* Franciscans
Ochino, Bernardino, 140, 141, 142, 187
Odasi, Tifo, 23
Oddi, Sforza degli, 217
Olivares, Gaspar de Guzmán, 279
Olivieri, Maffeo, 94
Oratorians, 116–17, 129–30, 131, 187,
    190, 218, 246, 258, *see also*
    congregations of priests
Orlandini, Niccolò, 190
Ormaneto, Niccolò, 126, 194
Orme, Philibert de l', 91
Orosio, Jeronimo, 122
Orsini, Fulvio, 203
Ossuna (Girón Pedro Téllez, duque de
    Osuna), 275–7

Ottoman Empire: checking of, 41; at Lepanto, 166; trade with, 37, 42, 174, 252

Padua: academies, 63, 70; architecture, 56, 92; confraternities, 115; diocese, 131; Jesuits, 187; language, 21, 23, 80; theatre, 62; university, 4–5, 60, 134, 252, 253, 266
Pagani, Matteo, 226
Pagliarini, fra, 137
Paleario, Aonio, 144
Paleotti, Gabriele, 192, 195, 218
Palestrina, Giovanni Pierluigi da, 218, 225
Palladio, Andrea, 71, 227, 245
Pallavicino, Marcello, 187
Pallavicino, Niccolò, 258
Palmieri, Matteo, 26
Palmio, Benedetto, 187
Palmio, Francesco, 187
Panciatichi, Bartolomeo, 140
Panigarola, Francesco, 192, 197
Panvinio, Onofrio, 189
Paoli, Pier Francesco, 273
Paolo Fiammingo (Pauwels Franik), 221
Papal State: dominions of, 37; *Monte della Fede*, 8; state-building of, 12, 40; and Venice, Interdict controversy, 4, 261–6; *see also* Rome; states, Italian; *and individual popes*
Parabosco, Girolamo, 81, 135, 217
Parigi, Giulio, 247, 257
Parisani, Giulio, 184
Parisio, Pietro Paolo, 127
Parma: academy, 272; architecture, 57, 75; painting, 72, 77–8, 208, 221; patronage, 219; population, 280; theatre, 245; university, 60; *see also* Farnese; states, Italian
Parmigianino (Girolamo Francesco Maria Mazzola), 77–8, 85, 94, 96
Paruta, Paolo, 187, 203–4, 261
Pasi da Carpi, 227
Passero, Cincio, 250
Pateri, Pompeo, 187
Paterno, Lodovico, 166
Patrizi, Francesco, 204, 215–16, 267
patronage: as affording social mobility for beneficiaries, 61–3; by charitable institutions, 61, 96, 97, 119, 207, 219, 245; by Church institutions, 61, 119, 120, 127–8, 187, 218, 219, 246, 248; cosmopolitanism of, 220–2, 223, 257; galleries, 214; by government, 55–60; post-Tridentine growth in, 219–22; princes' scouts and commissars for, 59, 219; by private individuals, 61, 62, 119, 260–1; *see also* academies
Paul II, Pope, 120, 147, 283
Paul III, Pope, 35, 39, 57–8, 60, 72, 77, 94, 120, 125, 126, 127, 148–9, 168, 252, 253
Paul IV, Pope, 40, 126, 131, 144–5, 150, 167, 188, 198, 252
Paul V, Pope, 4, 248, 261–6, 268
Pavesi, Giulio, 133
Pavia: hospitals, 197; population, 15, 172; trade and manufacture, 278; university, 60
Pazzi, Alessandro de', 79, 210
Pazzi, Maria Maddalena de', 193, 266
Pellegrini, Domenico, 193
Pellegrini, Pellegrino, 201
Pellini, Pompeo, 203
Peranda, Sante, 193
Peranzone, Niccolò, 17
Pereira, Benito, 212
Peri, Jacopo, 228, 244
Perin del Vaga, 57, 60, 77, 96, 97
Perna, Francesco, 153
Perugia: academy, 272; architecture, 98; confraternities, 116; decorative arts, 94; language, 21, 24; and salt tax, 39; university, 60
Peruzzi, Baldassare, 28, 71, 76, 119
Petrarch: debunking of, by Marinism, 269–73; as model for Mannerists, 72–4, 83, 86, 91; as model for Neo-Renaissance, 222, 243, 251; and Volgare, 20; *see also* Bembo, Pietro: and language question; Trissino, Gian Giorgio
Peverara, Laura, 220
Philip II, king of Spain, 40, 44, 145, 170, 243: accession of, 166; methods of government by, 166, 167, 168, 276; and Spanish debt, 174

Philip III, king of Spain, 168, 200, 249, 276
Philip IV, king of Spain, 246, 279
philology: Latin and rhetoric, 19–21, 69, 202–3; and patristic study, 120–21, 132, 135, 136, 138, 189, 192; and Scripture study, 121, 134, 135, 142, 188–9, 191; textual criticism, 70, 120–1, 189, 203, 210; translation, 65, 70, 72, 85, 121, 123, 135, 142, 153, 167, 179, 190, 210, 254; Tuscan grammar and *Vocabolario*, 244; Volgare, 20, 21–6, 65–6, 69, 72, 83–4, 86, 97, 121, 147, 189–90, 192, 210, 222–3; *see also* academies; Bembo, Pietro: and language questions; literary criticism; Tuscan language
philosophy: *see* Aristotelianism; Platonism; religious humanism
Piacenza: academy, 63, 220; benefice, 125; painting, 208, 209; urban planning, 59
Piccolomini, Alessandro, 80, 81, 88, 210, 213, 220
Piccolomini, Francesco, 143
Piccolpasso, Cipriano, 177
Pico, Giovan Francesco, 125
Pico, Giovanni, della Mirandola, 121
Piedmont: Italian and French character of, 255–6; population, 280; trade and manufacture, 277; after Treaty of Cateau-Cambrésis, 165; Waldensians, 141, 169; *see also* Savoy, Duchy of; Turin
Pietro Antonio da Cervia, 140
Pietro da Cortona (Pietro Berrettini), 4
Pigna, Giovan Battista, 59, 203, 204
Pinelli, Luca, 193
Pino, Marco, 98
Pino, Paolo, 76
Pio, Alberto, 135
Pisa: agriculture, 278; architecture, 92; university, 4–5, 60, 134, 268
Pius II, Pope, 125, 133, 138
Pius IV, Pope, 129, 150, 185, 187, 189, 193
Pius V, Pope, 41, 49, 117, 166, 177, 191, 193–4, 201, 218–19, 252, 283
Placido da Parma, 149
plague, 15: of 1630–3, 280–1

Platina, Bartolomeo, 133
Platonism, 93, 121, 205, 215, 223, 248, 267: academies, 63, 72–3, 128; *see also* Bruno, Giordano; Ficino, Marsilio; Patrizi, Francesco
Ploti, Bernardino, 45
Poccetti, Bernardino, 207, 209
Podiani, Mario, 21
Poggiano, Giulio, 189
Pole, Reginald, 129, 136, 143, 145, 150
Politi, Ambrogio Catarino, 122, 129
political theory, 4, 42–3, 203–5, 221–2: *see also* historiography; Machiavelli, Niccolò; utopians
Poliziano, Angelo, 70, 86
Pomarancio (Cristoforo Roncalli), 218
Pomponazzi, Pietro, 118, 135, 212
Pomponio Leto, Giulio, 120
Pontano, Giovanni, 26
Pontormo, Jacopo, 62, 76–7, 84, 85
population, 3, 15–16, 171–2, 280–1
Pordenone, architecture, 219
Pordenone (Giovanni de' Sacchis), 75, 96, 97, 208
Pornassio, Raffaello de, 113
Possevino, Antonio, 212, 259
Possevino, Giovan Battista, 193
Prado, Pietro, 93
Prato: architecture, 93; confraternities, 187–8; population, 280; religious orders, 111
preaching, 119–20, 133, 134, 142, 187, 197, *see also* prophecy
Preti, Girolamo, 273
Prierias (Silvestro Mazzolini), 138
Primaticcio, Francesco, 83
printing, 61–2, 64–6, 95, 97, 108, 109, 153, 167, 179, 189, 254
Priscianese, Francesco, 64
Priuli, Girolamo, 21
Procaccini, Giulio Cesare, 208
prophecy, 125: as crossing class boundaries, 109–10; decline of, 110–11; as political activism, 110, 170–1; *see also* Savonarola, Girolamo; Florence: Savonarolans in; utopians
Protestants, 8, 137–45, 150, 152–3, 169, 190, 198, 216, 261, 274, 279, *see also* heresy; theology; Valtellina
Puglia, 98, 254, 278, 280

Pusterla, Cesare, 95
Puteo, Antonio, 185

Quevedo, Francisco de, 276
Quinzani, Stefana, 107
Quirini, Leonardo, 243
Quistelli, Ambrogio, 122

Rabelais, François, 23
Ragazzoni, Girolamo, 184, 196
Ragusa, 80: as bi-cultural, 256; shipping,
    174, 181; Tridentine reform in, 186
Rambaldo, Antonio, 88
Ramus (Pierre de la Ramée), 215
Ramusio, Giovan Battista, 90, 226
Raphael (Raffaello Sanzio), 3, 28, 29,
    134: Mannerist variations on, 71, 77,
    82, 83, 86, 89, 96, 207; Neo-
    Renaissance variations on, 251
Razzi, Serafino, 111, 192, 196, 266
Regio, Paolo, 190
Regoli, Sebastiano, 211
religious humanism: and new piety,
    121–3, 133, 136, 192–3; response of,
    to heresy and Protestantism, 138, 141;
    and secularism, 27, 118–19, 136,
    184–5, 204; and study of Church
    Fathers, 120–21, 132, 135, 136, 138,
    189, 192; and study of Scripture, 121,
    134, 135, 142, 188–9, 191; supported
    by Papacy, 120
religious orders: as patrons of art, 61,
    266; reform of, pre-Tridentine,
    111–14; reform of, Tridentine, 194–5;
    resistance to reform, 146, 201–2, 266;
    see also Augustinians; Basilians;
    Benedictines; Capuchins; Carmelites;
    Dominicans; Franciscans; Servites
religious reform: see Church and state;
    Council of Trent; ecclesiastical
    institutions; Florence: Savonarolans in;
    heresy; indexes; Inquisition; Neo-
    Renaissance; prophecy; Protestants;
    religious orders; Savonarola, Girolamo;
    theology; utopians
religious revival: causes of, 106–7; see also
    confraternities; congregations of priests;
    mysticism; prophecy; religious
    humanism; religious orders
Remigio Fiorentino, 76

Renato, Camillo, 140
Renée of France, duchess of Ferrara, 139
Reni, Guido, 193, 246–7, 272
Riario, Raffaello, 186
Riccardi, family, 181, 277
Riccardi, Gabriele, 98
Ricci, Caterina de', 111
Riccoboni, Antonio, 216
Richelieu (Armand-Jean du Plessis),
    Cardinal, 279, 280
Ridolfi, Niccolò (Padre Mostro), 39, 282
Rinuccini, Ottavio, 228, 244
Robortello, Francesco, 202, 210
Rojas, Fernando de, 80
Rome: academies, 4, 208, 218, 226,
    247–8, 268, 270; architecture, 28–9,
    72, 83, 91, 93, 96, 190; banking,
    179; confraternities, 115, 116, 117,
    188; congregations of priests, 129–30,
    187; engravers, 257–8; humanism,
    120, 121, 129, 189, 203; language,
    22, 23, 25; music, 221; painting, 3,
    28–9, 60, 77, 87, 96, 120, 208, 218,
    219, 246; printing, 64, 189;
    sculpture, 3, 28–9, 71, 96; theatre,
    80, 245; tourism, 8, 175; trade and
    manufacture, 177; university, 60, 134,
    215; urban planning, 57–8, 93; see also
    Papal State; Rome, Sack of; and
    individual popes
Rome, Sack of, 7–17: disintegration
    following, 12–17; precedents for,
    8–10; significance of, 10, 13
Ronsard, Pierre de, 221
Rore, Cipriano de, 223
Rosa, Persiano, 129
Roseo, Mambrino, da Fabriano, 34
Rossi, Ippolito de', 126
Rosso Fiorentino (Giovanni Battista di
    Jacopo), 75, 82
Rota, Bernardino, 98
Rubens, Peter Paul, 258
Rubiales, Pedro de (Roviale Spagnuolo),
    85
Rucarelli, Silvestro, 17
Rucellai, Giovanni, 25, 179
Rudolph II, Emperor, 259, 274
Ruffo, Vincenzo, 224
Ruzante (Angelo Beolco), 21, 24, 55, 80,
    81, 178

Sabbioneta, 56, 71, 83, 93, 94
Sabellico (Marc'Antonio Coccio), 64
Sacchini, Francesco, 190
Sadoleto, Jacopo, 23, 121, 132, 136, 149, 150
Salamone, Giuseppe, 273
Salerno: diocese, 133; Protestant theology in, 139
Salice, Carlo, 242
Salvago, Gabriele, 221
Salviati, Francesco, Cardinal, 39
Salviati, Francesco (Francesco de' Rossi), 56, 82, 85, 89, 95, 96, 97, 206, 207
Salviati, Leonardo, 197
Salvio, Ambrogio, da Bagnoli, 115
Sampiero della Bastelica, 40, 169
Sangallo, Antonio da, the Elder, 58
Sangallo, Antonio da, the Younger, 41, 71–2, 83, 91, 97, 119, 207
Sangallo, Francesco, 88
Sanmicheli, Michele, 56, 75
Sannazaro, Jacopo, 24, 69, 226, 243, 272
Sansovino, Andrea, 72
Sansovino, Francesco, 82, 95, 179
Sansovino, Jacopo, 59, 62, 92, 97
Santacroce, Girolamo, 89
Santi di Tito, 207
Santoro, Giulio Antonio, 253
Sanudo, Marino, 21
Saracino, Annibale, 200
Sarpi, Paolo, 261–4, 265, 268, 274
Sauli, Alessandro, 185
Sauli, Filippo, 133
Sauli, Stefano, 127
Savelli, Giacomo, 194
Savonarola, Girolamo, 11, 110–11, 113, 124, 188, 218; see also Florence, Savonarolans in
Savoy, Duchy of: constitution, 44; dominions of, 49; expansionism of, 274–5, 279–80; French occupation of, 39, 41; state regulation of church in, 147; see also Piedmont; Savoy, dukes of; states, Italian
Savoy, dukes of: Carlo II, 35, 37, 39; Carlo Emanuele, 226, 274–5, 277, 279–80; Emanuele Filiberto, 49, 62, 93, 169, 255; Margherita, 244, 271
Scamozzi, Vincenzo, 97
Schidoni, Bartolomeo, 208

schools, preparatory, 64
Sciarra, Marco, 171
Scopulo, Girolamo, 45
Scrivà, Pedro Luis, 57
Scrofa, Camillo, 23, 86
Scrupoli, Lorenzo, 193
Scutellari, Andrea, 217
Sebastiano del Piombo (Sebastiano Luciani), 86, 88
Sega, Filippo, 201
Segni, Bernardo, 174, 210
Sepùlveda, Juan Ginés de, 122, 167
Sereno, Bartolomeo, 193
Seripando, Girolamo, 112, 133, 149, 195
Serlio, Sebastiano, 63, 76, 91, 245
Serra, Antonio, 249
Servites, 123: reform of, 112, 261; see also religious orders
Severus of Ravenna, 108
Sforza, 14, 108: Francesco II, 35, 36, 39, 56, 108; Giangaleazzo, 11, 39; Ludovico 'Il Moro', 11, 16, 60; Massimiliano, 12
Sforza di Marcantonio, 179
Sicily, Kingdom of: banking, 173; constitution, 44–5; Mannerist culture in, 98–9; prosperity, 183, 250; Slavs in, 251–2; Tridentine reform in, 186; see also Aragona; states, Italian
Siculo, Giorgio, 135, 144
Sidney, Sir Philip, 258
Siena, Republic of: expulsion of Imperial garrison, 40; Protestant theology in, 140, 142, 143; rulers, 37; theatre, 62, 80; trade, finance and manufacture, 179, 183, 252, 278; university, 60; see also states, Italian
Sigonio, Carlo, 61, 78, 86, 90, 195, 202–3, 210, 218, 271
Simoni, Simone, 198
Sirleto, Guglielmo, 189, 190
Sixtus IV, Pope, 10, 60, 109, 147
Sixtus V, Pope, 171, 177, 192, 194, 199, 203, 248, 252
Slavs, 251–2, 254–5
Smet, Cornelius, 221
Society of Jesus, see Jesuits
Somaschi, 131, see also congregations of priests
Sons, Jean, 221

Soto, Francisco, de Langa, 221
Soto, Pedro de, 151
Sozzini, Lelio, 140
Spada, Lionello, 208
Spenser, Edmund, 258
Spernazzati, Agostino, 177
Speroni, Sperone, 63, 78, 79, 222
Spinelli, Girolamo, 268
Spinola, Andrea, 249, 275
Spinola, Lodovico, 43
Spinola, Luca, 58
states, Italian
   alliances among: through marriage, 15,
      38, 39, 168; see also Imperial
      alliance; Italic League; League of
      Cognac; Savoy, dukes of: Carlo
      Emanuele
   borders of, political, 14–15, 48–9
   constitutions of, 42–5, 46–7
   destabilization of, before Imperial
      hegemony: due to collapse of Italic
      League, 10–13; due to economic
      disaster, 15; due to opportunism of
      powerful families, 13–15; due to
      plague, 15–16; see also Rome, Sack
      of
   destabilization of, following Tridentine
      peace, 4: by Carlo Emanuele's
      expansionism, 274–5, 279–80; by
      European economic recession, 4,
      277–9; by Interdict affair, 261–6;
      by internal strife in Naples, 275–7;
      by plague, 280–1; by Uskoks on
      eastern frontier, 274; by Valtellina
      war, 279; by War of Mantuan
      Succession, 279–80
   emigration from: artists, 258; military
      experts, 258–9; religious dissenters,
      140–1, 143, 153, 198
   exchange of culture among, 220–1
   immigration to: artists, 85, 221–2,
      257–8; Greeks, 253–4; Jews,
      252–3; Slavs, 251–2, 254–5
   law and administration of, 45–6, 48
   as nation, see Italy, nation of
   peace in: control of banditry, 14, 171;
      through diplomatic and legal
      solutions, 38–9, 168–71; under
      Spanish hegemony, 3, 34–9, 166,
      167–8, 248–50

   prosperity of, see banking and finance;
      patronage; trade and manufacture
   territories of, policy toward, 13, 46–9
   vernaculars in, 21–4
   see also individual states
Stella, Tommaso, 115
Steuco, Agostino, 73, 121
Stigliani, Tommaso, 271, 272, 273
Straparola, Gian Francesco, 81
Striggio, Alessandro, 224, 244
Strozzi, Alessandro, 173
Strozzi, Francesco di Soldo, 137
Strozzi, Giovan Battista, 73
Summonte, Gianantonio, 203

Tacca, Pietro, 178, 246
Taddeo da Fiesole, 110
Tansillo, Luigi, 61, 73, 74
Tarcagnota, Giovanni, 59
Tartaglia, Niccolò, 212, 267
Tasso, Bernardo, 73–4, 76, 222
Tasso, Fausto, 190
Tasso, Torquato, 220, 222–3, 226, 227,
   248, 251, 258, 270
Tassone, Giovanni Domenico, 277
Tassoni, Alessandro, 4, 269–71, 275
Tedeschi, Tommaso Radini, 138
Telesio, Bernardino, 215
Teller, Giovanni, 188
Téllez, Girón Pedro, duque de Osuna, see
   Ossuna
Tempesta, Antonio, 226, 257
Teofilo, Massimo, 121, 123
Teresa of Avila, 112
Theatines, 131, 136, see also congregations
   of priests
theatre design, 62–3, 71, 227, 244–5
theology: patristic, 120–21, 135, 136,
   138, 189; pre-Tridentine confusion in,
   134–7, 139, 145; Protestant, dismissal
   of, 137–9; Protestant, spread of,
   139–41; scholasticism, 191; and
   superstition, 198–9; Tridentine
   consolidation of, 150–53, 191–2, 216;
   Tridentine, as "pan-Italian," 151–2; see
   also Council of Trent; heresy; religious
   humanism
Thirty Years War, 274
Thomassin, Philippe, 257

Tintoretto (Jacopo Robusti), 88, 97, 119, 208, 221
Titian (Tiziano Vecellio), 30, 88–89, 97, 166–7, 205, 208, 221, 224, 226
Toffanino, Lodovico, 181
Toledo, Pedro Alvarez de, 36, 39, 40, 41, 48, 57, 87, 98, 129, 276
Tolomei, Claudio, 22
Tomitano, Bernardino, 69, 211
Tommasi, Francesco, 179–80
Tommasi, Tommaso, 213
Tommasini, Gian Francesco, 255
Torelli, Lodovica, 107, 130
Toscanella, Orazio, 211
trade and manufacture
  communications, improvement in, 175
  decline of: during calamities, 15; during European recession, 4, 5, 277–9
  dependent on Spanish debt, 174, 181–2, 279
  entrepreneurialism, 175–81: in agriculture, 179–81; support of, by state, 177–8; versatility of, 178–9
  growth of: after calamities, 172–81, 183; after European recession, 5
  pan-European scope of, 174–5, 277, 278
  regulation of, 182–3, 277
  shipbuilding, decline of, 181, 277
  technology, 176–7, 266
  tourism, 8, 175
  wool and silk: growth, 172–3, 277; decline, 181–2, 277–8
  see also banking and finance
Tramezzino, Michele, 65
Treaty of Cateau-Cambrésis, 3, 41, 165
Treaty of Cavour, 169
Treaty of Cherasco, 279
Trent, 149: constitution, 43; Italian character of, 255; urban planning, 58
Tribolo, Niccolò, 226
Trieste, 255
Trissino, Gian Giorgio, 34, 70, 76; Mannerist variations on, 79; Neo-Renaissance variations on, 222; and Volgare, 22, 25–6
Turin: court of, 256; population, 280; Tridentine reform in, 200–1; see also Piedmont; Savoy, Duchy of
Turri, Giovan Paolo, 220

Tuscan language, 22, 134, 244, 251, see also philology
Tuscany, Duchy of: academies, 2; formation of, 41; state entrepreneurship in, 178; see also Florence; Medici; states, Italian
Tyrol, 139

Ulloa, Alfonso de, 85, 167
universities, 59–60, 66, 134, 210, see also under specific cities
Urban VII, Pope, 259
Urban VIII, Pope, 281–3
urban planning, 57–9, 91–3
Urbino: architecture, 56–7, 220; humanism, 219–20; language, 22; rulers, 13; trade and manufacture, 179; uprising of 1572, 169–70; see also Della Rovere
Urbino, Carlo, 95
Uskoks, 274
Usodimare di Rovereto, 176
utopians, 26–7, 42–3, 84, 170–1, 184, 204–5, 277, see also prophecy

Vachero, Giulio Cesare, 275
Valdés, Alonso de, 34
Valdés, Juan de, 128–9, 135–6
Valente, Camilla, 220
Valguglio, Carlo, 223
Valier, Agostino, 192, 193
Valier, Francesco, 26
Valier, Giovan Battista, 187
Valla, Giorgio, 223
Valla, Lorenzo, 70, 86, 118
Valtellina: Italianization of, 254; religious wars in, 255, 279
Valvassori, Giovan Andrea, 95
Valverde, Juan de, 221
Van Dyck, Anton, 258
Vanni, Antonio Maria, 244
Vannini, Caterina, 193
Varchi, Benedetto, 66, 76, 90, 126, 268
Vargnano, Jacopo, di Arco, 255
Vasari, Giorgio: aesthetics of, 29, 60, 75–6, 94, 136, 205, 206, 208; as biographer, 91; as painter and architect, 57, 58, 61, 69–70, 83, 85, 87, 92, 96, 97, 98, 119, 120, 217
Vecchietti, Bernardo, 207

Vega, Juan de, 45, 186
Vegio, Maffeo, 118
Vendramin, Alvise, 245
Vendramin, Francesco, 214
Venice, city of: architecture, 97; banking, 182; confraternities, 116; congregations of priests, 128, 131; music, 219; painting, 30, 55, 71, 87, 97, 208; population, 172, 280; printing, 64, 97, 167, 179, 189–90, 254; schools, 219; sculpture, 62, 97; theatre, 62, 63, 80, 245; trade and manufacture, 172, 174, 179, 277; urban planning, 92; see also Venice, Republic of
Venice, Republic of: church in, state regulation of, 147; constitution, 43, 44, 46–7; dominions of, 37, 38, 46–7, 48, 251; dominions of, Ionian and Cretan, 256; government, corruption in, 170; government, reconciliation of patriciate with specialists in, 249; immigrants to, 253, 254–5; Interdict controversy, 4, 261–6; land reclamation in, 178; language, 21, 83, 254; Protestant theology in, 139, 142; Protestant states, diplomacy with, 261; and Turks, 41–2, 166; and Uskoks, 274; see also states, Italian; Venice, city of
Vergerio, Pier Paolo, 141, 142, 143
Vermigli, Pietro Martire, 140
Vernazza, Ettore, 116
Verona: academies, 225; architecture, 75; confraternities, 116, 117; diocese, 131, 132–3, 146, 202; population, 15, 172, 280; Scaligeri in, 10
Veronese, Paolo (Paolo Caliari), 95, 208, 209, 221
Vesalius, Andreas, 83, 211, 221
Vettori, Diana, 271
Vettori, Francesco, 42
Vettori, Pier, 61, 70, 86, 180, 203, 210, 222
Vicentino, Nicola, 224

Vicenza: academies, 63, 71; architecture, 71; confraternities, 117; constitution, 46; painting, 83; population, 172; trade and manufacture, 179
Vico, Enea, 203
Vida, Marco Girolamo, 69, 119
Vielmi, Girolamo, 195
Vigevano, 278
Vignola, Giacomo Barozzi da, 91, 226
Vigri, Caterina de', 107, 108
Vio, Tommaso de, see Cajetan
Violi, Lorenzo, 110
Virginio, Gian Francesco, 135
Visconti, Bartolomeo, 131
Visconti, Giangaleazzo, 33
Viterbo, Egidio, 112
Vitozzi, Ascanio, 226
Vittori, Mariano, 189
Vittoria, Alessandro, 97
Volgare, see philology
Volterrano (Raffaele Maffei), 138

Waldensians, 141, 169, 198
Willaert, Adrian, 223
Winckelmann, Johann Joachim, 75
Wolfe, John, 258
women: advancement of, 220, see also Colonna, Vittoria; in charitable institutions, 108, 115, 116, 188, 192, 197; convents, 196, 200; as mystics, 107–9

Zabarella, Giacomo, 211
Zaccaria, Anton Maria, 130
Zambelli, Damiano and Stefano, 94
Zarlino, Gioseffo, 224
Zeffi, Giovan Francesco, 121
Zerbi, Giovan Antonio, 178
Zimara, Marc'Antonio, 211
Zini, Pier Francesco, 121
Zorzi, Francesco, da Venezia, 123
Zuccari, Federico, 193, 206, 208, 221
Zuccari, Taddeo, 207, 217, 221, 226
Zwingli, Huldrych, 139, 152